Tormented Master

Tormented Master

A Life of Rabbi Nahman of Bratslav

Arthur Green

THE UNIVERSITY OF ALABAMA PRESS
University, Alabama

Library of Congress Cataloging in Publication Data

Green, Arthur, 1941–
Tormented master.

(Judaic studies series ; 9)
1. Nahman ben Simhah, of Bratzlav, 1770?–1810? 2. Rabbis—Poland—Biography. 3. Hasidim—Poland—Biography. I. Title. II. Series: Judaic studies ; 9.
BM755.N25G73 296.6′1′0924 [B] 78–16674
ISBN 0–8173–6907–4

Manufactured in the United States of America

Contents

Acknowledgments

As this work reaches completion, I am overcome by a sense of gratitude to the many whose teaching, counsel, criticism, and patience have helped to make it possible. While work on this book from the outset was a completely individual and highly personal endeavor, and responsibility for its contents is thus entirely my own, there are a great many influences to be traced here. A few inadequate words of thanks are in order.

An earlier version of the present study, here much revised, was a doctoral dissertation under the direction of Professor Alexander Altmann. Dr. Altmann has been my teacher for many years, and I am grateful to him for much more than his careful reading of this manuscript and his many suggestions. Another important teacher whose influence is, I hope, to be felt in this work, though he died just as the writing of it was beginning, is the late Abraham Joshua Heschel. In his death as in his life he remains a source of inspiration to me.

My serious study of Nahman began in connection with a course on Bratslav which I taught at the Havurat Shalom Community Seminary in 1971/72. The students in that course taught me a great deal about how to read the Bratslav texts, indeed about how to read a text altogether. Each of them contributed his or her unique understanding, and all are deserving of thanks: Jonathan Chipman, Larry Fine, Janet Wolfe, Gershon Hundert, Joel Rosenberg, and David Roskies. Various other students, including Danny Matt, Jeffery Dekro, and the participants in a seminar on Nahman's *Tales* which I taught with Zalman Schachter in the spring of 1977, have further contributed to my understanding.

Having turned to both teachers and students, there remain colleagues and friends. Zalman Schachter is one with whom I have had many a fruitful argument over the meaning of a passage in Nahman's writings; I cherish the sharing of those arguments. Everett Gendler has been friend, teacher, and source of encouragement for many years now. His help in the publication of this volume is deeply appreciated. Van Harvey, though far removed from the subject matter of this work, was a colleague from whom I learned much at the time I was writing on Nahman; his ever-questioning presence is also to be felt here. I am grateful to Rivka Horwitz, Max Ticktin, and Joseph and Gail Reimer for having read parts of the manuscript and for their many helpful suggestions. For a very different sort of learning I am indebted to Tom Gruner, Mark Goldenthal, and several others. Wherever they are, my thanks reach out to them.

Though I know he would be uncomfortable to see his name in this context, I cannot help but express my appreciation to Rabbi Gedaliah Koenig, one of the leaders of the Bratslav community in Jerusalem, for the kindness and warmth he showed me on a visit there. I can only pray that he somehow understand that I, too, in a way so different from his, stand in close relation to his master.

My wife, Kathy, has been a constant source of support and understanding throughout the years in which this book was written. Without her help and patience its accomplishment would have been unthinkable. In love and gratitude I dedicate this study to her.

PHILADELPHIA
2 Ḥol ha-Moʿed Sukkot, 5738
September 30, 1977

Tormented Master

Before I became close to our master, of blessed memory, I could not picture in my mind how it was that Moses our Teacher was a human being like others. But once I had become close to our master and had seen how human he remained despite his greatness, I was able to understand how it was that Moses, too, was still a human being.

RABBI NATHAN of Nemirov

In the case of great young men . . . rods which measure consistency, inner balance, or proficiency simply do not fit the relevant dimensions. On the contrary, a case could be made for the necessity of extraordinary conflicts, at times both felt and judged to be desperate. For if some youths did not feel estranged from the compromise patterns into which their societies have settled down, if some did not force themselves almost against their own wills to insist, at the price of isolation, on finding an original way of meeting our existential problems, societies would lose an essential avenue to rejuvenation and to that rebellious expansion of human consciousness which alone can keep pace with the technological and social change. To retrace, as we are doing here, such a step of expansion involves taking account of the near downfall of the man who took it, partially in order to understand better the origins of greatness, and partially in order to acknowledge the fact that the trauma of near-defeat follows a great man through life.

ERIK ERIKSON
Young Man Luther

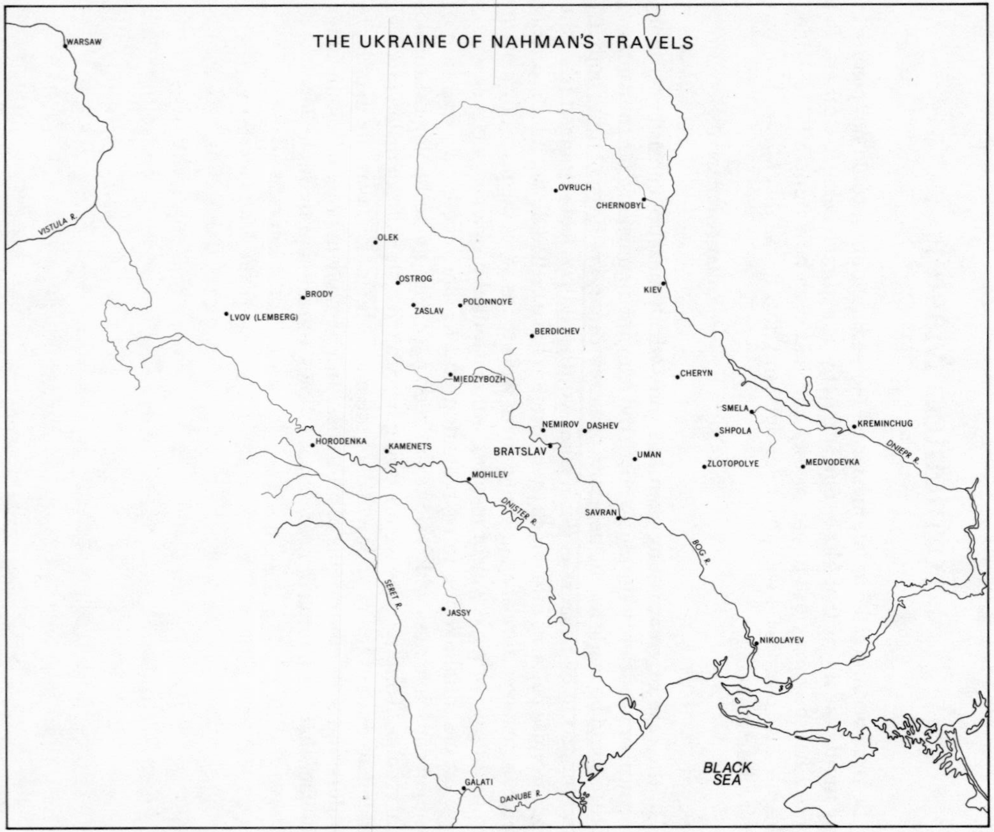
THE UKRAINE OF NAHMAN'S TRAVELS
WARSAW
VISTULA R.
OVRUCH
CHERNOBYL
OLEK
OSTROG
BRODY
ZASLAV
POLONNOYE
LVOV (LEMBERG)
KIEV
BERDICHEV
CHERYN
MIEDZYBOZH
SMELA
SHPOLA
KREMINCHUG
NEMIROV
DASHEV
HORODENKA
KAMENETS
BRATSLAV
UMAN
ZLOTOPOLYE
MEDVODEVKA
DNIEPR R.
MOHILEV
DNISTER R.
SAVRAN
BOG R.
SERET R.
JASSY
NIKOLAYEV
BLACK SEA
GALATI
DANUBE R.

Introduction

The role of biography in the history of religion is a changing and problematic one. From time immemorial, pious devotees of various masters and saints have sought to compose memoirs of their teachers' lives that were to serve as sources of moral and spiritual edification for those who came after them. The example of the master's own life always took a place of prime importance within the educational ideals of religious communities. Much of what we know about the great religious teachers of the pre-modern world has come to us thanks to the activity of such pious hagiographers. The founders of the great religions, as well as those who established new sects, orders, or movements within their respective traditions, have had their lives told and retold in each generation, the subject of the biography strangely changing and growing with the changing tastes and mores of those for whom the tales were told. The writers of such works, of course, were not usually concerned with separating fact from edifying legend. As the fame of a particular figure grew, apocryphal tales inevitably sprang up about him; such tales were happily included if they served the moralistic purposes which the writer had in mind.

As modern biographers first began to turn their attention toward the religious past, it was generally out of a longing for the greater wholeness and simplicity of earlier times that they were attracted to the lives of the masters. While such writers, beginning with the nineteenth century, did make some attempt to distinguish fact from fancy, their own romantic predilections often carried them far along the path of 'reconstructing' the lives of figures from the past in the image of their own times. Such values as the love of nature, the love of fellow man, and the simplicity of devotion, though indeed present in the sources, were emphasized out of all proportion; such 'negative' factors as harsh asceticism, conflict, jealousy, and the like were either ignored or explained away into insignificance.

The shift from this sort of modern romantic hagiography to an attempt at critical biography is often slow and subtle. The faithful, both of the traditional and romantic varieties, have good reason to regard attempts at 'scientific' biographies of their saints with a suspicious eye. Such a biography must first and foremost see its subject within his or her own historical context. This in itself may threaten those who insist upon the utterly unique and unprecedented character of their heroes' lives and teachings. Might not such a critical view rob the master of his eternal message, one which is supposed to remain valid for readers of all times, despite any changes in historical circumstance? Placing such a figure against the background of the intellectual and spiritual world in which he lived, and particularly tracing those currents of thought that may have influenced his own development, indeed diminishes something of that unique stature which he bore in the eyes of the naive believer. Further, the biographer who treats his subject with some critical distance may be forced to probe certain sensitive psychological areas, dealing in profane terms with matters that the faithful have chosen to accept as sacred mystery. There is a worry that the master will be degraded as he is humanized, and often a lingering fear that the biographer may raise issues that will prove a source of embarrassment to the faithful.

The critical biographer does not seek to destroy or to debunk, but merely to understand. In order to achieve an understanding of his subject, however, he will indeed have to brush aside the web of pious fancies that so encumbers the sources in order to see whether, first of all, there remains sufficient authenticable material out of which to fashion a life of the one who interests him. If such sources do exist, it is a wide-ranging series of skills and sensitivities he must bring to them in order to bring his work to completion. When the subject is the founder of a sect or order which still flourishes in his day, or when he writes of a figure who is still widely venerated for some other reason, his task is doubly sensitive. He can only seek to reassure the faithful that the true greatness of their master may in fact stand out in clearer relief once the circumstances of his life are as fully elucidated as possible.

All of the above has a special relevance to the task of critical biography within Hasidism, and most particularly to the present undertaking: a critical life of Rabbi Nahman of Bratslav. Hasidism, that pietistic and mystical revival movement which conquered the hearts of East European Jewry in the eighteenth and nineteenth centuries, continues to flourish, albeit much diminished, in the new homes that the remnants of Polish and Russian Jewry have found for themselves since the Nazi holocaust. The pious continue to embellish the tales of the earlier masters' lives, now coupling these with tales of the masters' descendants who lived through the darkest years of Jewish history. Cast into the maelstrom of twentieth-century living mostly against their will, they are often astonished to find anyone outside their own communities who has a real interest in their masters' lives and teachings. Alongside the Hasidic community itself, the image of a romanticized neo-Hasidism continues to exert significant influence. Ever since the turn of the current century, marking the end of the long, and often bitter, battle fought between Hasidism and the representatives of *haskalah* or Western "enlightenment" among the Jews, modern writers and thinkers have increasingly turned to the early days of Hasidism as a source of personal enrichment and literary-intellectual inspiration. Such writers of fiction as Y. L. Peretz and S. Y. Agnon, theologians led by Martin Buber, and historians or memoirists on the order of S. A. Horodezky and Hillel Zeitlin are all leaders in the twentieth-century rereading of early Hasidism. This trend continues into our own day in the works of Eliezer Steinman, Elie Wiesel, and a great many others. Through their works the tales of the Hasidic masters have reached a wide audience, and something of the masters' lives, however legendary the form, has entered into the spiritual legacy of modern Jewry.

There is a particular appropriateness to the use of biography as a way to approach the world of Hasidism. This is a movement which, as Gershom Scholem has noted, was willing to subordinate whatever doctrinal teachings it offered to the personalities of its leaders. Many a Hasidic tale emphasizes the fact that it was not so much what the master taught as the way he lived his life or the simple forcefulness of his personality that caused disciples to flock to him. In contrast to the earlier esoteric traditions of Judaism, in which the mystic often sought both the merit and safety of anonymity, here the teacher as person took on a central role. The differences between the various masters, and the reasons for a particular *ḥasid's* choice of one over another as his spiritual guide, was as often a matter of personality as it was of differences in teachings. The religion the masters taught reflected this as well: there is in Hasidism an appreciation of the uniqueness of each individual and his spiritual task rare in the earlier sources of Judaism, rare indeed in the literature of religion as a whole. The religious life of the individual, long subordinated in Judaism to the sense of collective fate and singular mission, was here treated with a new seriousness. The *ḥasid* sought out that *rebbe* who could lead him to the root of his own soul and the sparks of light he alone could raise up: in such an encounter the legitimacy of his individual and even idiosyncratic relationship to God is confirmed.

The life and teachings of Nahman of Bratslav (1772–1810) take all this as their point of departure, going on to portray inner life and inward struggle to a degree otherwise unknown in Jewish sources. Here it is made utterly clear that the true core of religion is that struggle for faith which goes on within the heart of the individual believer, that the essence of prayer is *hitbodedut,* or lone outpouring of the soul before God, and that the single most important model for the religious life is the tortured young master himself, one who spent all his years engaged in a life-and-death battle over the issues of faith and doubt, truly an idiosyncratic and problematic religious personality if ever there was one. In order to understand a religious phenomenon of this sort, biography must clearly be our starting-point.

The figure of Nahman has long played a major role in the attempts of moderns to approach the world of Hasidism. Beginning with Buber's German translation of Nahman's *Tales* in 1906 and the first of Zeitlin's many writings on Nahman in 1910, the *ẓaddiq* of Bratslav has been recognized as a major figure in the history of the Hasidic movement. This has been so despite, or perhaps in part because of, the relative smallness of the Bratslav community and the suspicion it frequently engenders in other Hasidic circles. Even to the casual observer, Bratslav presents itself as a unique and challenging phenomenon. The curious fact that the Bratslavers, uniquely among Hasidic communities, never appointed a successor to their original master, is perhaps a starting-point of their special mystique. Designated by others as the "dead *ḥasidim*" because they have no living master, they were known until the beginning of this century for their long and somber processions to Nahman's grave-site in Uman. Even now, the Uman graveyard having been destroyed and turned into a housing project, many a Bratslav tract will provide directions—in both legal and extralegal versions—for the furtive traveler to the Soviet Union who wishes to offer prayers at that most holy of shrines. Originally perhaps the most elitist of Hasidic groups, the fact that they have not been subject to a dynastic progression of *ẓaddiqim* may in fact have saved them from certain experiences of disappointment and decline that inevitably occur as one confronts some latter-day descendants of such dynasties.

The literature of Bratslav confirms the impression of special mystery surrounding the memory of Nahman and the lives of his followers. Nahman's teachings as well as his tales, published and commented upon many times by his disciples and their descendants, are filled with half-hidden references to meanings that cannot be told outright. One major student of Bratslav literature has referred to the entire *oeuvre* of Nahman's writings as a "mythological autobiography," in which the author uses both traditional rabbinic homiletics and wild imaginative fantasies to ever explore, reveal, and hide some further aspect of his own inner secrets. To express it differently, one might say that here the entirety of Jewish tradition is being used in a wholly personal way, to a degree unknown previously. The psychological complexities of the individual and the theological mysteries of the universe are intertwined to an extent that makes any attempt at separating them seem foolhardy. For those who take theologizing as a personal enterprise, and are not embarrassed at the presence of their own selves in the theological work which they produce, there is much to be learned from Nahman.[1]

The sources for a study of Nahman's life are threefold: his own writings, the works of his leading disciple and *de facto* successor as leader of the community, Nathan of Nemirov (1780–1845), and the writings of later Bratslav *ḥasidim*. References to Nahman outside Bratslav literature are scant and often highly polemical; while they are considered where appropriate in our study, they hardly constitute a major source of understanding.

The two major works by Nahman are his collected homilies, *Liqquṭey MoHaRaN* (henceforth: *Liqquṭim)* and his volume of tales, *Sippurey Maʿasiyot.*[2] The former is in turn divided into two parts, the first of which was published during Nahman's lifetime; the latter portion was published by Nathan in the year following his master's death. Like most of the theoretical works of Hasidism, these were abbreviated transcriptions of informal talks, originally delivered to the assembled *ḥasidim* around the Sabbath or festival table. While such talks were always delivered in Yiddish, it seemed fitting that the master's words be preserved in Hebrew, the proper tongue for sacred writings if not for oral use. Nahman's teachings in their written form were often the combined product of the master's thought and homiletical genius and the disciple's fine sense of Hebrew literary style, a rare virtue among Hasidic authors. The tales were first published by Nathan in 1816. These, designated to appeal to women and simple folk as well as the more educated readers of Hebrew, appeared in a bilingual format, a practice which has been followed by the *ḥasidim* in nearly all later editions of that work.

In addition to these two major sources by Nahman, there are two lesser works that may also be treated as primary sources for Nahman's thought. *Sefer ha-Middot* ("The Book of Moral Qualities") is an alphabetical listing of brief prescriptions for the life of moral virtue, begun by Nahman in his youth and completed just a few years before he died. Much more important is another short volume, *Siḥot ha-RaN* ("Conversations of Rabbi Nahman"), parts of which were first published as an appendix to the *Tales* in 1816. Here Nathan records, generally verbatim, various short teachings and brief comments by his master. The comments were often uttered in connection with some larger tale or teaching, and the *Siḥot* thus serves as an important companion volume to the larger collections.

Nathan of Nemirov was one of the most prolific writers and publicists in the history of Hasidism. He outlived his master by thirty-five years, and throughout that period he seemingly never ceased working on commentaries, memoirs, letters, and new editions, which would serve to further spread the fame of his master. His major work, *Liqquṭey Halakhot ("Selected Laws"),* is a multi-volume application of Nahman's teachings to the *Shulḥan ʿArukh,* Joseph Caro's universally accepted codification of Jewish law and practice. Less a commentary on Caro's work than an explication and expansion of Nahman's, this often profound and insightful discussion of the commandments has yet to be studied in its own right by a modern scholar.

Of greater interest to us here, however, are Nathan's biographical and autobiographical writings. In the years immediately following his master's death, Nathan took it upon himself to gather together all that was known of Nahman's early years, and particularly the details of his journey to the Holy Land in 1798–99. As Nathan himself had not appeared on the scene in Bratslav until 1802, none of this knowledge was firsthand; it was rather a combination of what the master had told regarding himself and the recollections of disciples of longer standing and members of Nahman's family. The result of this first collection was *Shivḥey ha-RaN ("The Praises of Rabbi Nahman")*, published in 1816.[3] Here Nathan first turns his attention to the inner life of the young Nahman, sparing no detail as to the torments and conflicts of his master's stormy adolescence. He then offers a highly elaborate account of Nahman's journey to Erez Israel, an account which, though generally accurate in crucial details, is put in the format of an adventurous novella. In later years, Nathan collected a great deal more material on the life of his master, but he did not succeed in publishing a further biographical work. This latter material, consisting of crucially important memoirs, statements by Nahman, tales, parables, etc., was later published by Nathan's followers as *Ḥayyey MoHaRan*,[4] and forms the single most important source for the life of Nahman after 1799, including the central period of his public career. Though published nearly thirty years after Nathan's death, the writing is almost completely his own. Only a few carefully delineated parenthetical remarks are added by Nahman of Cheryn, Nathan's disciple, who prepared the material for publication. The same is true of Nathan's autobiography, *Yemey MaHaRNaT*, written toward the end of his life (Nathan died in 1845) and published in Lemberg, 1876.

The passing of Nathan and the others who had been present in Nahman's lifetime did not mean that all unpublished sources on the early days in Bratslav had ceased to exist. Both carefully guarded manuscripts and well-preserved oral traditions continued to exist in the Bratslav community well into the twentieth century, and undoubtedly persist in our own day as well.[5] One late nineteenth-century leader of the Bratslav community in particular, Abraham Hazan, continued the tradition of publishing new materials by and about his master. He in turn was followed by Samuel Horowitz, who was active in the nineteen-thirties. While such works as *Kokhvey 'Or ("Stars of Light")*and *Sippurim Nifla'im ("Wondrous Tales")*, first published by Horowitz in the thirties, must be treated with certain reserve, they do contain a surprising measure of old and authentic source material. Even more recent books and pamphlets, published at a greatly accelerated rate by Bratslav *ḥasidim* since 1960, occasionally contain some previously unknown account of the master, which bears the stamp of authenticity.[6]

This of course is the major critical question in writing a biography of such as figure as Nahman: how far are the sources to be trusted? We have not a single line of what may be considered primary source material that even claims to be written from an objective point of view. As is the case in all such writings, involvement rather than detachment was seen as the writer's greatest virtue. We are dealing throughout with works written or edited by loving and admiring disciples, utterly convinced that their master was the greatest of all time. Such hardly seem to be the type we would trust as sources. What is unique about the biographer's position with regard to Nahman is that despite this fact—and in part because of it—the authenticable material is very considerable indeed.

Insofar as the first category of source materials is concerned, our problem is rather minimal. Nahman's own writings, published within his lifetime and immediately after his death, bear no sign of falsification. Nathan as editor is quite careful, particularly in the *Liqquṭim,* to remain in the background. He tells us which of the teachings were recorded in the master's own words and which he received only secondhand through the notes of others; he is a reporter who is not afraid to say on occasion that he has failed to recall or comprehend a teaching in its entirety, and will present the reader only with that of which he is sure. While this reticence is less clearly obvious in the tales than in the teachings, everything we see of Nathan's conduct as editor tends toward an acceptance of Nahman's works as presented by him.[7]

There is nothing directly autobiographical about any of Nahman's writings. Nowhere in the *Liqquṭim* does he lapse into the first person, to speak unequivocally about himself. On the other hand, the constant involvement with self, which peers through on every page of these teachings, the half-open references to "a certain *ẓaddiq*" being only the most obvious of a great many, make it clear that Nahman's own writings, teachings as well as tales, are absolutely vital as sources for biography, particularly for the inner life of their author. As the most nearly uncontestable of all writings we have surrounding Nahman, these become the cornerstone upon which the edifice of biography must be constructed.

In dealing with Nathan's biographical writings and memoirs, we are also in a surprisingly felicitous position. Nathan is no mere teller of pious legends; the task he sets for himself is to collect, as fully and accurately as possible, the sources on his master's life. In contrast to all other Hasidic chroniclers of his day, he explicitly excludes all miracle tales from his writings, with the exception of certain tales of supernatural rescue on the seas in his account of Nahman's journey to the Holy Land. It is certain that such tales already abounded in Nathan's lifetime; many of them were later collected and published by subsequent disciples. Nathan, however, would have no truck with such fantasies. Throughout his works, particularly in the notes that comprise *Ḥayyey MoHaRaN,* the reader is struck by the concern for precision and detail that characterizes Nathan. Insofar as was possible, he dated the major teachings in the *Liqquṭim,* and provided whatever recollections he had of the circumstances under which each was offered. One could hardly imagine that Nathan would trouble himself to provide fictitious dating for his master's teachings. At times he faithfully records conversations between his master and himself, even allowing some of the differences between them to come through in his report.[8]

Within the works properly attributed to Nathan, and again especially in *Ḥayyey MoHaRaN,* a great deal of material is quoted verbatim from the master, including a wealth of reflections on himself and his teachings. Also included among the fragments of Nahman's life his disciple recorded are a number of dreams, a particularly rare and valuable source for any reconstruction of Nahman's inner life. Throughout the presentation of these materials, Nathan maintains the same care he had exercised in the *Liqquṭim,* distinguishing that which he had heard with his own ears from that which came to him through others, admitting lapses in his own information, and the like. His own exclamations of exaggerated veneration for Nahman, with which these works are frequently punctuated, are quite readily distinguishable from his accounts of events and conversations. All in all, the basic veracity of Nathan as a reporter seems to be largely unimpeachable. The same is true of his disciple Nahman of Cheryn, who served as final editor of Nathan's posthumous publications. Here notes by the editor are clearly distinguished from Nathan's writing, which had already achieved a certain degree of sacred status. The assumption of the basic veracity of these sources has been a cornerstone of all modern scholarship on Nahman, and it is also the general presupposition of the present work.[9]

We should also note here that all the printed editions of Nathan's biographical works have endured a heavy hand of censorship, partially Nathan's own. Whenever the account comes too close to revealing something of the master's character that might be better left unsaid, or whenever Nahman's own statements border too closely on what might be considered heretical in certain Hasidic circles, the narrative is interrupted by an "etc." and takes up again at some later point. The veil of censorship on certain of these passages was lifted in 1933, when a little volume entitled *Yemey ha-Tela'ot* ("Days of Woe") was published in Jerusalem, containing an appendix of "Deletions from *Ḥayyey MoHaRaN.*" Various later works by Bratslav authors reveal further small bits of that which was deleted earlier, and there is still hope that a fully uncensored version of *Ḥayyey MoHaRaN* may someday be available.

When we come to the third group of sources, those composed in the period after Nathan, and particularly those published in the nineteen-thirties, the situation is quite different. Here the embellishments are tremendous, and one has to searech out the kernel of history to be found amid the abundant fantasies. Our general criterion for the use of such materials has been their relationship to the more obviously authentic sources. Where an account in *Kokhvey'Or* seems to conflict, either in detail or in spirit, with that of Nathan, we prefer Nathan as an authority. Where the later writings serve to supply details lacking in the earlier sources, but are neither fantastic in content nor seemingly serving the convenience of the later movement, we are more prone to accept them as authentic bits of oral tradition. Certain short tales ascribed to Nahman, though not printed prior to the *Sippurim Nifla'im,* also seem to bear the unmistakable stamp of authenticity. It is hard to imagine, for example, a later disciple composing anything so daring as a tale in which the true *ẓaddiq* is revealed to be a madman in disguise or a healer disguised as a madman. Only the master himself would have been capable of such audacity.

Our willingness to accept Nathan's memoirs as a historical source, however, requires further explanation. If rabbinic and pre-modern Jews generally are thought to have shown little interest in contemporary history (as distinct from the sacred events of Biblical times, which were constantly the object of new commentary and investigation), Hasidism should represent an extreme form of this tendency. A world where pious enthusiasm is the supreme value, and where wonder-tales are the basic stock-in-trade of any conversation between disciples, hardly seems a likely one to spawn a recorder of history. If we examine such a classic work of Hasidic hagiography as *Shivḥey ha-BeSHT,*[10] for example, all our expectations are confirmed. Composed some fifty years after the death of the Ba'al Shem Tov, it thoroughly interweaves the strands of historical memory and pious fabrication. Tales of the master's lifetime are told in the form of classical folk-narrative, wonder-tales abound, including some which in other generations had been ascribed to earlier heroes, and the use of the work for historical/biographical purposes is doubtful at best. While Nahman was the great-grandson of the BeSHT, and a figure closer to modernity in a number of ways, the fact is that Nathan's first attempts at composing a life of his master were published only a year later than *Shivḥey ha-BeSHT,* and in a not-dissimilar format. How is it, then, that we insist on his works' being treated as an entirely different literary *genre* from earlier tales of the Hasidic masters?

In order to resolve this question to our satisfaction, we shall have to examine the unique place of Nahman and his life within the literary canons of Bratslav Hasidism. The fact is that proper attention to biographical detail is essential to the *religious* task which Nathan of Nemirov has set for himself. Not only is Nathan more than a mere teller of tales; he is also not simply a chronicler of events. Nathan is a self-conscious creator of a *new sacred history,* one in which the life of his master stands as the unique and all-important center of events in recent times.

For the *ḥasidim* of Bratslav, Nahman is not one *ẓaddiq* among many. He is an utterly unique figure, one whose "fire will burn until Messiah comes." The days of his earthly life are a unique period in the history of the human race. Nahman is described as the last in a series of five great holy men who have appeared in the history of Israel; his predecessors are no less than Moses, Rabbi Simeon ben Yohai, Isaac Luria, and Nahman's own great-grandfather, Israel Ba'al Shem Tov.[11] These figures, as seen in Bratslav, were the only universally acclaimed *ẓaddiqey ha-dor*, spiritual leaders of their respective generations, in Jewish history. The ministry of Nahman is greater than that of his predecessors, however, in that it will last until the end of time. As we shall see, such formulations serve to rather thinly veil a messianic claim for Nahman himself. Nathan constantly thanks God for having allowed him to live in these epoch-making times, and for the merit of being present at the world-shaking events that he records. His accounts of even the most minor details of Nahman's life are replete with such statements of thanksgiving. Of those disciples who remained faithful to Nahman, despite the great controversies which surrounded him, Nathan says:

> Blessed are those who remained and struggled with great perseverance, breaking through all barriers, to cleave to our master, of blessed memory. Fortunate are they and all their descendants and all of Israel, forever and unto eternity.[12]

He compares his master's travels through the Ukrainian countryside to the wanderings of Israel in the desert, and never tires of such formulae as: "Blessed is he who merits to know even a bit of what happened to our master at any time; all of his activities were filled with tremendously awesome and wondrous secrets."[13]

Such statements of the eternal validity and ever-enduring significance of the life and teachings of a single master are *not* to be found elsewhere in Hasidic literature. They are not part of the tradition of tales of the *ẓaddiqim* which was the common property of all Hasidic groups. The repeated emphasis on the belief that all generations until the end of time will be nourished by the life and teachings of one particular *ẓaddiq* goes far beyond the claims of any other Hasidic school. It is no accident that only in Bratslav was no one allowed to act as *rebbe* after the original master's death: Nahman is *the ẓaddiq* for all time; it is inconceivable that anyone should attempt to stand in his shoes. The recording of Nahman's life, then, not completely unlike the recording of the Christian gospels, is a holy act, which will provide all the generations to come with their most basic spiritual sustenance.

The Bratslav community, socially as well as literarily, represents the promulgation of a new sectarian consciousness, built around the life of a unique and vitally important master. Nathan's world, as reflected in all of his writings, is clearly divided between *anshey shelomenu*, the disciples of our master, and all others. The fact that Nahman and his disciples suffered severe persecution at the hands of other Hasidic masters (referred to in the Bratslav sources as *mitnaggedim!)* added to this feeling of sectarian isolation. Even into the twentieth century, other Hasidic groups were not quite sure of the Bratslavers' legitimacy, and the latter-day disciples of Nahman tended to see themselves as a much-misunderstood elite whose ultimate vindication would one day clearly shine forth.

Though Jewry has certainly given rise to any number of sects in its long history, several of them attached to claims for messianic figures, the birth of a new movement of this sort among nineteenth century *ḥasidim* is somewhat surprising. The memories Jews carried with them of sectarian behavior were generally negative ones; in the mind of the educated *ḥasid* such groups as Sadducees, early Jewish Christians, Karaites, and Sabbatians were all to be seen as sinful sects, spiritual descendants of Korah, denying the authority of rabbinic law, which of course reached back to Moses himself. What positive model might Nathan and his followers have had in mind which would have allowed them to legitimize such a vision of themselves as they had? In a search for parallels to the situation of Bratslav in the early years of the nineteenth century, one is immediately drawn to the examples of Christianity and Sabbatianism, both of them sectarian movements built around the charismatic attraction of a spiritual leader/messiah and persecuted by the larger Jewish community. Neither of these two earlier parallels, however, could possibly have served as a positive model for Nahman and Nathan; the names of both Jesus and Sabbatai Sevi were anathema in the pious Jewish circles from which they were nourished. The larger Hasidic movement itself, while defined as a "sect" by its detractors, both rabbinic *(mitnaggedim)* and "enlightened" *(maskilim)*, does not have within itself the same degree of intentional sectarian separatism. The author of *Shivḥey ha-BeSHT*, while he is primarily interested in the tales of one central figure, lives in a world that abounds with *ẓaddiqim*, any and all of whom are to be venerated by the reader. Hasidism is concerned above all with the promulgation of a new religious *ethic*, the embodiment of which is to be found in the lives of the great masters, both of the Ba'al Shem Tov's day and of the past. Faith in the BeSHT over and above any other religious teacher certainly does not have the place in Hasidism that faith in the single saving figure had in those two earlier movements, and has, as we shall see, in the consciousness of Bratslav.

Viewing the events of past history from our perspective, we can indeed find no figure or group that might have served as a model for Nahman and his disciples. We must recall, however, that our history is not necessarily that which was recalled as history in the past. If we place ourselves within the pseudo-historic framework of the nineteenth-century *ḥasid*, and look at the past experiences of Jewry from that perspective, we can quite readily see the model upon which the self-image of the Bratslav community was most directly based: the life of Rabbi Simeon ben Yohai and his disciples as "recorded" in the *Zohar*.

The *Zohar*, composed in late thirteenth-century Christian Spain, takes the literary form of a series of mystical conversations between the second-century Rabbi Simeon ben Yohai, his son Eleazar, and various disciples. No matter for our purposes that such modern scholars as Scholem and Baer have pointed out the utterly fictional character of these narrations, the anachronisms of language, geography, etc., and even the influence on these narratives of the Spiritual Franciscans who flourished in Spain during the days of Moses De Leon, the *Zohar's* now-established author.[14] For Nahman and his generation the authenticity, including historic accuracy, of the *Zohar* was unchallenged, and no book was more highly venerated in the mystic circles in which he lived.

The *Zohar's* accounts of Rabbi Simeon's life, and even more that of his death, are replete with statements as to the cosmic significance of the events of his lifetime. If the *Zohar's* Rabbi Simeon is not fully a mythic hero,[15] he certainly is a Moses, a central figure around whom a new *Heilsgeschichte* has been created, and his disciples are a unique group in all of human history.

> He who sees Rabbi Simeon ben Yohai sees the entire world; he is the joy of those above and below.

> Rabbi Judah taught: The generation in which Rabbi Simeon ben Yohai lives is filled with righteous and pious men (*ḥasidim*), all of them fearing sin. The *Shekhinah also dwells among them, in a way which is not true of other generations.*

Even more significantly as a source for the type of veneration offered to Nahman in the literature of Bratslav:

> Blessed is the generation in which Rabbi Simeon ben Yohai is present. Blessed is its lot above and below. Of it scripture says: "Blessed are you, land whose king is free" (Eccles. 10:17). What is the meaning of "free"? He lifts up his head to reveal [secret] things, and is not afraid. What is the meaning of "your king"? This refers to Rabbi Simeon ben Yohai, master of Torah, master of wisdom. When Rabbi Abba and the companions would see Rabbi Simeon, they would run after him, saying: "They walk behind the Lord; He roars like a lion" (Hos. 11:10).[16]

There is an aura felt throughout the *Zohar* that the lifetime of Rabbi Simeon is sacred time; not since the generation of the Exodus and Sinai has the *shekhinah* been so fully present or the world so abounded in wonders.[17]

The figure of Rabbi Simeon ben Yohai takes a central place in the world of Bratslav Hasidism, more so than in any other Hasidic group. Nahman and Nathan were both avid students of the *Zohar*, and Rabbi Simeon, the great revealer of secrets, was often on their minds. A number of the most important teachings in the *Liqquṭim* are based on passages in the *Zohar*, and Rabbi Simeon himself is mentioned with some frequency in that work. Nathan's account of his master's visit to the Holy Land places special emphasis upon his visit to the cave of Rabbi Simeon. Once, perhaps in a moment of exasperation with his own disciples, Nahman said longingly to Nathan: "Where can you get a group like that which R. Simeon had!".[18]

Up to this point there is nothing particularly surprising about Nahman's relationship to Rabbi Simeon ben Yohai. A close examination of the Bratslav sources has shown, however, that the nature of this relationship is in fact far more than is seen on the surface. When Nathan published the second part of *Liqquṭey MoHaRaN*, only a year after his master's death, he prefaced it with a paragraph entitled: "*Go Forth and See the Works of God! A Wondrous Revelation of the Secret of the Holy Teacher Simeon ben Yohai, of Blessed Memory.*" There follows a short recapitulation of certain passages from the Talmud and the *Zohar* in which Rabbi Simeon promises that the Torah will never be completely forgotten by Israel, and that "by means of this book [i.e., the Zohar] Israel will go forth from exile."[19] From the placement of such a quotation at the front of *his* master's book, and knowing the great value that both Nahman and Nathan placed upon the publication of the *Liqquṭim*, we can readily see the transference from Rabbi Simeon to Nahman that has taken place in the disciple's mind. This and various other hints in sources which originate within Nahman's own lifetime point to an assertion growing already then, which was to be proclaimed quite clearly by Bratslav disciples in later times: Simeon ben Yohai and Nahman of Bratslav are in fact one and the same. Nahman's soul is none other than that of Rabbi Simeon, reincarnate in a later generation.[20]

We are now in a position to appreciate properly the overwhelming sense of sacred history which permeates the writings of Nathan of Nemirov, and encourages him to be such a careful biographer. He is privy to the secret knowledge that his master is none other than Rabbi Simeon, the greatest teacher in all the history of Jewish spirituality. His days upon the earth, limited as were the days of *Zohar's* hero, are a great age when hidden things are to be revealed. The author of the *Zohar* felt an urgency about such revelations; surely they will cease with the master's death, and thus the world must hurry to derive as much benefit as it can from his presence while he is yet alive.

> This generation in which R. Simeon lives is one beloved by God for his sake; through him secret things are revealed. It is astonishing that the sages of his time could depart even for a moment from studying Torah in his presence, though in this time none of Torah will be forgotten. But woe to that generation when he dies: sages will be few and wisdom will be forgotten in the world . . .[21]

Nathan has that same sense of urgency and self-importance with regard to his own task. The secrets of Nahman's lifetime are to sustain the future world much as the great revelations of the earlier master, some seventeen hundred years previously, by his reckoning, had helped to sustain the world through the entire history of Israel's suffering and exile. No wonder then that every word Nahman spoke and every moment of his life are to be recorded so carefully. Who knows what seemingly insignificant detail may be the source of sustenance to some unknown future generation? Who is to know whether the fragments of a teaching that seems incomprehensibly garbled may not in fact prove to be prophetic utterances in some other time or place? With regard to the life of such a figure, the careful recording of detail is a task for which all the world will be grateful.

The model of Rabbi Simeon helps us to understand how it is that Nathan becomes such a careful biographer. It does not fully explain, however, his aversion to tales of the miraculous and the supernatural in connection with his master. On the contrary, one might well expect that the greatest of masters would perform the greatest of wonders. Other Hasidic praises of the *ẓaddiqim* are filled with tales of miraculous healings, divination, exorcisms, and various other demonstrations of supernatural powers. If Nathan's master bears the great soul of Rabbi Simeon himself, should not this soul manifest itself by some demonstration of such powers?[22]

Here we come face to face with the first of the paradoxes that will confront us in our study of the highly complex Bratslav literature. Nahman was indeed a unique soul; surely he must have possessed powers greater than those of ordinary mortals. At the same time, however, Nathan takes pains to emphasize the fact that his master's great spiritual attainments were not to be attributed to any inborn powers which were not also the property of everyone.

> He [Nahman] was very cross with those who thought that the main reason for the *ẓaddiq's* ability to attain such a high level of understanding was the nature of his soul. He said that this was not the case, but that everything depended first and foremost upon good deeds, struggle, and worship. He said explicitly that everyone in the world could reach even the highest rung, that everything depended upon human choice.[23]

This is a new and unique contribution to the understanding of the *ẓaddiq* in Hasidism, one which sets Bratslav apart from all other schools of thought within the movement. Nahman and Nathan were concerned that the *ẓaddiq* be an *accessible* model to his disciples; his path must be one that others may follow. If the *ẓaddiq's* achievements come about through the uniqueness of his soul, of what use is he as a model for imitation?

Until Nahman, and in all other Hasidic communities contemporaneous with his, the *ẓaddiq* was seen as a clearly superior figure, who chose to bind his lot with that of others by a willful act of generosity. The *Toledot Ya'aqov Yosef*, the classic model for Hasidic literature, sees the *ẓaddiq* as one who is himself virtually untainted by sin or conflict. He belongs to the small spiritual elite of mankind who make it their task to lead and uplift the masses. The great problem for the *Toledot* is the bridging of the seemingly great gap between the two; in order to be in a position to uplift the sin-burdened masses, the *ẓaddiq* must first create some bond between himself and his charges. Often this is described as the allowing of a sinful thought: in order to go down among the *qelipot* where the masses dwell, the *ẓaddiq* allows himself to entertain a thought (though not an act!) of sin, thus creating that bond of common sinfulness between himself and others which enables him to engage in his work of uplifting. True, there are times when the nature of this bond is described as the 'fall' of the *ẓaddiq* rather than as an act of willful descent, but in such passages it is generally the masses themselves who are blamed for having dragged their leader down with them. If the *ẓaddiq* is to be blamed at all, it is only for not having exerted proper care in the dangerous work of redeeming souls, but not for any sinfulness of his own.[24]

In direct contrast to this earlier model, Nahman functions so well as a *ẓaddiq* not because he has always remained above the reaches of sin, but rather precisely because he himself has undergone all the conflicts and torments that even the most beleaguered of his followers could ever imagine—and has emerged triumphant. A basic reversal has here taken place in the rationale of the *rebbe:* Nahman is capable of lifting you out of despair and transforming your spiritual life not because of his great compassion from above, but rather because he has been through all of your torments, and worse, in his own life. This is the meaning of such oft-repeated statements by Nathan as: "He underwent great and awesome sufferings, the like of which have never existed in the world."[25] As we shall see, the young Nahman in particular is described as a person filled with doubts and inner torment.

This new approach to the figure of the *ẓaddiq* completes our explanation of why Nathan is such a faithful biographer, and particularly why he eschews tales of the miraculous. Accounts of his master's supernatural powers would defeat the religious purpose of his writing. In contrast to all other Hasidic chroniclers, Nathan has no desire to minimize the humanity and the personal struggles of his master and model. If anything, it may be that Nahman's conflicts are disproportionately magnified by the repeated way in which Nathan makes reference to them, particularly in *Shivḥey ha-RaN*. The reader must be given the full story of Nahman's life and struggles, with no omission of the very human conflicts which many a saint's biographer would prefer to pass over in silence. Of course there is some idealization in Nathan's description of the total victory his master won over various areas of personal conflict. The total inner victories Nathan depicts are often belied by the master himself, as the motifs of struggle continue to appear in tales and sermons that date from the final months of his life.

Nathan recalls that he had visited various other Hasidic courts before he settled upon a master who suited him.[26] That which most impressed him about Nahman was his humanity, including his willingness to talk about his own failings and the struggles of his life. Nathan did not forget this impression as he took on the roles of faithful disciple and biographer; it is to this awareness of the master's humanity that we are indebted for the rich and balanced portrayal of Nahman that emerges from his disciple's writings.

Critical and historical study of Hasidism, inspired jointly by the interwar flourishing of historical writing among Polish Jews and by the researches in Jewish mysticism undertaken by the Jerusalem school of Gershom Scholem and his students, is still in its early stages. While a great many monographs and articles in this area have been published since the second World War, chiefly in Jerusalem, an up-to-date history of the Hasidic movement is still lacking, and biographical studies of a critical nature, in this movement where the personalities of the various masters played so great a role, are relatively few. In this country, where a great deal of popular interest in Hasidism has been shown in the last few decades, historical research on the movement has been slow to start. The present work is much indebted to the work of the Israeli scholars in this field, and would have been unthinkable without constant reference to the previous studies in Hasidism by Scholem, Isaiah Tishby, Joseph Weiss, Rivka Schatz, and others.

The first outsider to the Bratslav community to engage in a major study of Nahman was Hillel Zeitlin, himself a key figure in the religious and literary world of interwar Polish Jewry. Beginning in 1932, Zeitlin published a long series of articles on Nahman in the Warsaw daily *Der Moment;* after the elder Zeitlin's death at the hands of the Nazis in 1942, his son, Aaron Zeitlin (well-known as a Yiddish and Hebrew poet in his own right), collected his father's writings and reprinted them, publishing the only full-length biography of Nahman to exist until this time.[27] Hillel Zeitlin was a product of the Hasidic milieu and was deeply rooted in its emotional setting. Attracted in his youth to the study of Western philosophy (he published a study of Spinoza in 1900), he remained deeply attached to his Hasidic heritage, and in his later years he sought to recover the beauties of the traditional Hasidic world for his secularized contemporaries in Warsaw. His work on Nahman is at once deeply perceptive and highly romanticized. Writing in the style of popular scholarship which was typical of Yiddish journalism in his day, he traced the course of Nahman's life and offered selected Yiddish translations of certain key teachings of Nahman which the *ḥasidim* had published only in Hebrew. His work is published without notes, and it is clear that he undertook no critical examination of the sources which he employed. The major contributions of his work lie in the collating, for the first time, of the various fragmented accounts of Nahman's life in the traditional sources, and in his particularly perceptive analysis of messianism as a key motif in Nahman's writings.

The volumes on Nahman edited by Samuel Abba Horodezky and Eliezer Steinman[28] are in fact nothing more than anthologies of the Bratslav source material, selected with an eye to whatever would prove attractive to the modern reader. Horodezky's treatment of Nahman in his more general work on Hasidism[29] consists of a brief biography, which falls short of that by Zeitlin in terms of both critical awareness and personal perceptivity. A brief monograph by Jacob Becker, promisingly entitled *Rabbi Nahman of Bratslav: A Psychoanalytic Study*, is equally disappointing, containing nothing more than a hodgepodge of Bratslav sources interspersed with a few quotations from Freud. The greatest of the pre-war historians of East European Jewry, Simon Dubnov, is perhaps at his weakest in his comments on Nahman. The strength of Dubnov's *History of Hasidism* lies in his examination of Russian archival materials, and the setting of Hasidism in its general sociopolitical context. When it came to an understanding of the profundities of mystical theology, however, Dubnov's genius failed him. Completely unable to find any meaning in Nahman's tales, Dubnov was forced to dismiss them as the feverish rantings of Nahman's illness; the centrality of the *ẓaddiq* in Nahman's thinking led the historian to consign him to the period of Hasidism's decline, in which the cult of personality and the intentional manipulation of a believing public was said to have replaced the pristine and noble sentiments of the movement's earliest days.

The most serious scholarly work on Nahman undertaken to date is that of the late Joseph Weiss, in a series of articles published between 1952 and 1969 and recently republished in a single volume.[30] Weiss, a student of Gershom Scholem, undertook a thorough critical examination of Nahman's life and thought. In studies ranging from the most detailed bibliographical research to a sweeping analysis of major themes in Nahman's thought, Weiss established the key guidelines for all further research in the study of Bratslav Hasidism. In his major articles he employed a method that combined the tools of intellectual history with the insights of psychoanalysis, demonstrating that in the case of so fully self-preoccupied a person as Nahman was, there can be no separation between biography and an understanding of his thought. Throughout both Nahman's teachings and his stories, Weiss has shown, the central figure of concern is none other than Nahman himself. Whether he is offering a homily on the role of the true *ẓaddiq* in the world or spinning a fantastic yarn about kings and princesses, it is the clarification and justification of his own life-task that is constantly at the center of Nahman's attention. This most basic insight of Weiss, though it has been somewhat criticized by Mendel Peikarz, has not been refuted, and is also a cornerstone of our present study.

In the wake of Weiss' research, other scholars have continued to explore various aspects of Nahman's life and thought. Mendel Piekarz' book, *Ḥasidut Braslav,* is a major contribution particularly in the realm of biobibliographical detail; his work serves to clarify a number of issues crucial to a full understanding of Bratslav literature. Piekarz has an eye for the fine points of language and nuance of meaning much to be admired. He has also paid attention for the first time to Nathan's own work, *Liqquṭey Halakhot,* as a source of information, and in general to the career of Nathan and the later history of the movement. It is only a compliment to the seminal strengths of his work to note that much more remains to be done in these latter areas. Another scholar who has written in a similar vein is Ada Rapoport Albert, a student of Weiss, who has contributed two highly illuminating studies on particular aspects of Nahman's career.

The present work, the first attempt at a full-scale biography of Nahman since that of Zeitlin, necessarily synthesizes and is reliant upon the more detailed researches of scholars in the intervening years. At the same time, the writer has in all cases gone back to reexamine the primary sources, and in not a few cases takes issue with previous readers. In most cases such discussions among scholars have here been relegated to the notes. As to the general framework for an understanding of Nahman suggested in this volume, though it is influenced by all these scholars and not a few others, particularly in the fields of psychology and history of religions, ultimately it is my own, the child of that unique form of human intimacy which can exist only between the biographer and his subject.

Any biography written in our day, and particularly one of a figure who, as we have already hinted, is so interesting from a psychological standpoint, must take the questions of "psychohistory" into consideration. To what extent is it possible or legitimate for us to seek to explain Nahman from a psychological point of view? How nearly adequate, on the other hand, in our post-Freudian and now post-Eriksonian age, is any account of Nahman's life which does *not* penetrate into the psychological concerns which were clearly so formative for him?

The writer is neither a trained psychoanalyst nor a complete innocent in the area of psychohistorical research. My lay status in this field has allowed me to feel justified in following my own instincts in avoiding nearly all use of technical psychoanalytic terminology. A number of such terms suggested themselves in the course of this study: manic-depression, obsessive guilt, megalomania (a term which actually did creep into the text), and sublimated homosexuality are a non-exhaustive list. Fearing both the reductionism which often accompanies the labeling of such phenomena and the imprecision with which they might be used in such a work as this, I have limited myself to an extensive use of the layman's psychological vocabulary in our ever so psychologically conscious age. Talk here of guilt, inner struggle, insecurity, and doubt may be translated (with caution, it is to be hoped) by the reader who prefers his understanding in more clinical terms.

In connection with psychohistory, however, one further note of some significance must be added. The classic work in that field, Erik Erikson's *Young Man Luther*, is claimed to be of particular significance because it was the study of a personality who, perhaps more than any other, embodied within himself the struggles and crises of his age. Luther's battle with the father-figure and the problem of authority, while seen by Erikson as the reformer's own psychological difficulties, were also depicted as representing Western Christian man's emergence from the Middle Ages and his struggle with God the Father and the authority of His church. It is fully the intention of this work to claim that with regard to the post-medieval Jew of Eastern Europe, Nahman is precisely such a figure. The central issue of his religious life, his constant awareness of the absence of God from the ordinary universe of human experience, still unique for a Hasidic master, was to become dominant in the lives of generations of Jews who came after him, most fully so for those who lived through the years of the Holocaust. His struggle, at some points with guilt and thus with his own unworthiness to evoke the presence of God, at other times with doubt, or the absence of God from those lives and moments that did seemingly merit His attention, remains a *single* struggle. No matter where the blame is to be fixed, the issue remains constant. There may be places in this work where it seems merely psychological, the pain of a young man in coming to terms with his own guilt burden. There are other places where the concern perhaps seems detached and theoretical, the speculation of the philosopher about the absence of divine providence. It is hoped that this statement of intention will serve to underline the oneness of that struggle. Nahman not only *was* a figure who personified the crisis of his age and who fought internally with issues that his contemporaries had not yet learned to articulate, but also, unlike Luther, *was conscious* of his role as such a figure and sought the words to assert such a claim for himself. In seeking to restore the old Kabbalistic traditions of *ẓaddiq ha-dor*, the notion of a single leader who stood at the center of his generation, and combine them with the model of the suffering *ẓaddiq*, the one who could lead his followers beyond anxiety because he himself had already suffered all their woes, Nahman had found a way, through the use of traditional religious language, of protraying himself as a pivotal figure in a crucial age for the spiritual history of the Jewish people. It is more with a sense of resignation than of triumph that this work serves to witness history's vindication of his claim.

NOTES

1. Scholem, *Major Trends*, p.304. "Mythological autobiography" is a comment by Weiss, *Meḥqarim*, p.108. For insight into the role of personality in Hasidism and the movement's legitimization of idiosyncratic relationship to God I am indebted to a conversation with my friend Dr. Barbara Harman.

2. There exist two bibliographies of Bratslav literature: Gershom Scholem, *'Eleh Shemot*, Jerusalem, 1928, with supplements in *Qiryat Sefer* 6 (1931) 565 *ff.*, and Nathan Zevi Koenig, *Neweh Ẓaddiqim*, Beney Beraq, 1969. The latter work, while not critical, is an extremely valuable source of bibliographical and historical information, especially concerning the various leaders and writers of the Bratslav community after Nathan's death in 1845.

3. The work was published as an appendix to the first edition of the *Sippurey Ma'asiyot*, Ostrog, 1816. The two parts of *Shivḥey ha-RaN* are henceforth designated as *Shivḥey* and *Shivḥey II*. The second part of this work, dealing with Nahman's journey to the Land of Israel, has at times been published separately under the title *Masa'ot ha-Yam*. It may be that these are the first two chapters in a projected complete biography of Nahman, which was never finished. Large portions of *Shivḥey ha-RaN* are also preserved in a manuscript at the YIVO library in New York (Dubnov Archive #36), virtually identical with the printed version.

4. *Ḥayyey MoHaRaN*, Lemberg, 1874. This work is also divided into two parts, henceforth designated as *Ḥayyey* and *Ḥayyey II*. Some editions of *Ḥayyey II* are subtitled *Shivḥey MoHaRan*, but this should not be confused with *Shivḥey ha-RaN*, discussed in the preceding note. *Ḥayyey* opens with a number of observations concerning the teachings in *Liqquṭey MoHaRaN* and the tales in *Sippurey Ma'aṣiyot*. This section is crucial for the dating of a great many of Nahman's teachings. After recounting a number of short stories and dreams or visions of Nahman, the book turns to a sequential biography, following the course of Nahman's travels to Erez Israel and to various cities in the Ukraine. It would be fair to characterize this section as a collection of Nathan's memoirs of his master's career. *Ḥayyey II* deals with the spiritual life of Nahman and the Bratslav community. Its biographical importance lies mainly in the many conversations between Nahman and the disciples which it records, often providing a life-setting within which the teachings of the *Liqquṭim* can be better understood. The chapters in this work are titled but not numbered; references to it are traditionally to chapter title and paragraph number, e.g., *Ḥayyey, meqom yeshivato* 25 or *Ḥayyey II, 'avodat ha-shem* 6. The present writer has found it convenient to number these chapters for the sake of brevity in footnote references. A key to these chapter numbers accompanies the list of abbreviations at the head of the bibliography to this work.

5. This writer was told by a Bratslav *ḥasid* in about 1970 that the community is still in possession of an uncensored version of *Ḥayyey MoHaRaN*. A most important work of Nahman, *Megillat Setarim*, which was long thought to have been destroyed, is quoted by N. Z. Koenig, *Neweh Ẓaddiqim*, pp. 87*ff.*, and apparently still exists. Cf. the remarks by Joseph Weiss in *Qiryat Sefer* 44 (1969) 279*ff.* and discussion below.

6. The most valuable among these later works are Abraham Hazan's *Kokhvey 'Or*, Jerusalem, 1896 and 1933, Samuel Horowitz' *Sippurim Nifla'im*, Jerusalem, 1935, and *'Avaneha Barzel*, Jerusalem, 1935. All of these were reprinted in a single volume, Jerusalem, 1961. Also of great value is Abraham Sternharz' (Kokhav Lev) *Ṭovot Zikhronot*, Jerusalem, 1951. Sternharz was a great-grandson of Nathan, and was leader of the Jerusalem Bratslav community in the nineteen-forties and fifties. Nathan Zevi Koenig, in addition to his above-mentioned bibliographical work, has also provided two reference tools which are of great value to the student of Bratslav literature. The Jerusalem, 1969 edition of the *Liqquṭim* contains an excellent subject index, *Sefer ha-Mafteaḥ*, which he compiled; his *Pittuḥey Ḥotam*, Beney Beraq, 1968, is an index to the later Bratslav commentaries on Nahman's works.

7. The edition of the *Liqquṭim* mentioned in the preceding note also contains alternate versions of several teachings, allegedly from an autograph manuscript of Nahman's, first discovered by Nathan in 1824. When compared to the versions printed in the *Liqquṭim*, they show a comparative lack of literary skill, but no serious changes in content. These may, of course, be notes of Nahman's oral discourses recorded by another disciple. Nathan's care in delineating exactly which teachings were written by Nahman and which by himself is noted by Piekarz, *Ḥasidut Bratslav*, p.64.

8. See, for example, *Ḥayyey* 8:20.

9. The one area where Nathan is not generally taken to be trustworthy as a reporter involves his own place in the Bratslav community during his master's lifetime. Cf. Piekarz, p.203*ff.* and the discussion, below, in chapter four.

10. The laudatory biography of Israel Ba'al Shem Tov (1700–1760), published in simultaneous editions in Kapust and Berdichev, 1815. An English translation by Dan Ben Amos and Jerome R. Mintz has appeared under the title *In Praise of the Ba'al Shem Tov*, Bloomington, 1970.

11. *Ḥayyey II* 3:66; 2:39.

12. *Yemey MaHaRNaT*, p. 37*f.*

13. *Ḥayyey* 4:18, 25; *Yemey MaHaRNaT*, p.46*f.*

14. *See* Scholem, *Major Trends*, fifth lecture, and the further references noted there; Baer, *A History of the Jews in Christian Spain*, p.266*ff.*

15. I am not completely persuaded of this by the argument of Y. Dan, *Ha-Sippur ha-Ḥasidi*, p.13.

16. *Zohar* 1:156a; 3:79a–b. In 2:15a Rabbi Simeon is compared to a lion.

17. *Zohar* 3:262a and see further *Sefer ha-Gilgulim* 7b, quoting *Zohar ha-Raqi'a*.

18. *Siḥot* 128; *Shivḥey II* 19; *Ḥayyey II* 2:45.

19. Piekarz, p.13*ff.* has undertaken this examination. The *Zohar* quotation is from 3:124b.

20. Cf. *Sippurim Nifla'im* p. 110.*f.* and especially p.166. The latter text is part of a document attributed to Nahman of Cheryn. It should be noted that similar claims were made elsewhere in Hasidism. The BeSHT was said to be a reincarnation of Saadya Gaon *(Shivḥey ha-BeSHT*, p.67) and Levi Yizhak of Berdichev was claimed as a reborn Rabbi Akiba (A. Walden, *Shem ha-Gedolim he-Ḥadash*, p.78). Elsewhere in this same collection *(Sippurim Nifla'im*, p.120*f)* Nahman is associated with his namesake, the Talmudic Rav Nahman. On the belief in reincarnation among Kabbalists *cf.* Scholem, *Pirqey Yesod* p.308*ff.*

21. *Zohar* 2:149a.

22. The miracle tales ignored by Nathan are collected in *Kokhvey 'Or*, p.41*ff.*

23. *Shivḥey* 26; *cf.* also *Siḥot* 165–166. In his introduction to *Shivḥey*, Nathan makes it clear that he is intentionally deleting miracle tales, since they would be of no didactic value.

24. The *ẓaddiq*-idea in the *Toledot* has been studied by J. Weiss in a most important essay, which appeared in *Zion* 16 (1951) 46*ff.* and by S. Dresner, in *The Zaddik.* See the many passages cited by both authors, as well as the opening chapters of the *Tanya* by Shne'ur Zalman of Liadi, Nahman's contemporary, in which the essential superiority of the *ẓaddiq* to all other mortals is emphasized.

25. *Shivḥey* 24.

26. *Yemey MaHaRNaT*, p.11*f.*

27. Hillel Zeitlin, *R. Nakhman Braslaver*, New York, 1952. Zeitlin had published a much shorter biography of Nahman many years earlier: *Rabbi Nahman mi-Braslav—Ḥayyaw we-Torato*, Warsaw, 1910. This Hebrew version is reprinted, though with many changes, in the second volume of Zeitlin's essays, *'Al Gevul Sheney 'Olamot*. Piekarz, pp. 56*ff.*, has noted the differences between the two recensions of the Hebrew text. Zeitlin's major work on Nahman, however, is the Yiddish volume.

28. *Rabbi Nahman mi-Bratslav*, Berlin, 1923; *Be'er ha-Ḥasidut: Kitvey Rabbi Nahman mi-Braslav*, Tel Aviv, n.d. (1958?).

29. *Ha-Ḥasidut weha-Ḥasidim*, v.3, p.18*ff.*

30. *Meḥqarim be-Ḥasidut Braslav. See* the present writer's review in *Conservative Judaism* 29 (1975) 97*ff.* References to Weiss' articles in the notes to this volume have only partially been transposed to the new pagination of *Meḥqarim*.

1

Childhood and Early Years 1772–1798

The latter half of the eighteenth century was a time of great and radical transformations in the history of European Jewry. At the very same time that Western cultural 'enlightenment' and political emancipation were effecting a revolution in the lives of Jews in Germany and the West, the much larger Jewish communities of Eastern Europe, centered in Poland and the Ukraine, were being swept by a religious movement perhaps no less radical in its transforming character, but one that called for an 'enlightenment' of an entirely different sort. That movement, which came to share the name Hasidism with several other pietistic revivals in the history of Judaism, had emerged from small circles of contemplatives and enthusiasts who made their appearance in the Ukrainian backwater of Podolia in the seventeen-forties and fifties to become a dominant force in the lives of large sections of East European Jewry by the turn of the nineteenth century. At once mystical and popularizing, Hasidism sought, by means of a daring simplification of the long and often abstruse Kabbalistic tradition, to place the goals of contemplative religion within the reach of every Jew. While specific formulations of Hasidic teaching could vary greatly from one master to another, it may be said that the early movement was characterized by a sense of the presence of God in all places and in every moment, a belief that all of human life is a way to His service, and an emphasis on enthusiastic prayer (as opposed to study) as the central act of the religious life.

Though hardly the creation of a single individual, the forces that made for Hasidism crystalized around mid-century in the figure of Israel ben Eliezer, the Ba'al Shem Tov (1700–1760). The BeSHT, as he is also called, was the first widely recognized leader of the nascent movement, and all later Hasidic teachings claim to be authentic continuations of the path he had first proclaimed. Early Hasidism was characterized by a unique series of charismatic leaders, many of them disciples of the BeSHT or his successor, who were known as *rebbes* ("teachers" or "masters"), *ẓaddiqim* ("righteous ones"), or, especially among the folk, simply as *gute yidn* ("good Jews"). By the third or fourth generation of the movement, Hasidic leadership had tended to become dynastic, the son or leading disciple of the *ẓaddiq* automatically expected to serve as leader of an already established Hasidic community.

The year 1772 was for several reasons a crucial turning point in the history of Hasidism. It was early in that year that the first bans against the *ḥasidim* were proclaimed by the communal leaders of Vilna and Brody, marking the outbreak of a controversy that was to have a deep and lasting effect upon the inner life of the movement. It was the year of the first partition of Poland, by means of which the major Hasidic centers were to be divided between the Russian and Austrian realms. That year also saw the death of Dov Baer, the Maggid of Miedzyrzec, the successor to the BeSHT, and the last single figure whose authority was acknowledged by most of the Hasidic world. After 1772, each of the disciples of Dov Baer was free to teach and practice Hasidism as he saw fit, thus giving rise to the varied and often contradictory styles of Hasidic life as lived in such centers as Berdichev and Chernobyl in the Ukraine, Lezajsk in Galicia, and Vitebsk and Karlin in White Russia. The group that had seen its center as Miedzyrzec was never again to organize under the leadership of any one man or to lend universal credence to any single religious path; each of the disciples was now on his own.[1]

It was also in 1772, on the Sabbath, the first day of Nisan (April 4), that Nahman the son of Simhah, later to be known to the world as Nahman of Bratslav, was born.[2]

The world Nahman first saw around him was little affected by the great events of that year. He was born in Medzhibozh, the home of the Ba'al Shem Tov and the original capital of the Hasidic world, and into the family of the Ba'al Shem Tov himself, a family still trying to maintain its place as the first family of the Hasidic community. Nahman's mother, Feige, was the granddaughter of the BeSHT, the daughter of his daughter Odel. Feige's two brothers, Moshe Hayyim Ephraim of Sudilkov (*ca.* 1737–1800)[3] and Barukh of Medzhibozh (*ca.* 1750–1812), were among the important leaders of Ukrainian Hasidism in the latter decades of the eighteenth century.

Podolia, the original central Ukrainian heartland of Hasidism, was already too deeply under Hasidic influence by 1772 for the bans to have had much effect. Even in Volhynia, to the north and west of Podolia, such large towns as Ostrog and Korets, not far from Brody itself, had become important Hasidic centers.[4] This area was not dominated primarily by disciples of Dov Baer, who had chosen rather to conquer new territories for Hasidism. The spiritual leadership of Podolia and adjacent eastern Volhynia was left largely to the family of the BeSHT and to the disciples of such more-independent figures as Pinhas of Korets (1728–1791) and Yehiel Mikhel of Zloczow (1721–1784). The elder of Nahman's illustrious uncles served as rabbi[5] in Sudilkov and was well known as a preacher. His collected homilies, published under the title *Degel Mahaneh Ephraim* (Korets, 1810), are generally considered, along with the writings of Rabbi Jacob Joseph of Polonnoye, to provide the most nearly authentic source for the teachings of the BeSHT, free from the influences of the Miedzyrzec school. Apparently a scholarly and retiring figure, he was highly critical of those he considered to be false *ẓaddiqim,* a criticism that may have affected his impressionable young nephew.[6] He left the personal and political leadership in the hands of his more charismatic younger brother, Barukh.

Barukh of Medzhibozh was neither an original thinker nor a particularly skillful preacher. Those of his teachings that have come down to us[7] preserve the terse, epigrammatic quality of the sayings of the BeSHT and are unaffected either by the greater theological profundity of Miedzyrzec or the homiletical skill of the *Toledot* and the *Degel.* Their power lies in the new and often radical twist given to a Biblical verse or a rabbinic saying; one has the impression that their true power could only be appreciated in the setting in which they were offered, and that they do not well survive the transition into written record. Barukh was, from all reports, a towering figure in terms of emotional impact; he could arouse great love or strike terror in the hearts of those who drew near to him. Zevi Hirsch of Zhidachov *(d.* 1831) recalled once nearly going out of his mind when he was witness to the burning intensity with which Barukh recited the Song of Songs on the Sabbath eve.[8] His style of Hasidic leadership emphasized those aspects of his grandfather's teachings that had been most important to the simple village Jews of the Ukraine among whom the BeSHT had achieved his first success: healing, for which he could use both amulet and blessing, an emphasis on the virtues of simple piety, ecstatic prayer, and a certain healthy acceptance of the foibles of ordinary humans. To these, Barukh added the establishment of an impressive princely court, complete to the point of hiring a well-known jester, Hershele Ostropolier, who perhaps served to offset the overbearing presence of the master himself.[9] It was in this setting that Nahman had his first exposure to the Hasidic world.

Nahman's father's family was hardly less distinguished than that of his mother. His paternal grandfather Nahman of Horodenka (Gorodenka) *(d.*1772)[10], was a member of the original circle around the Ba'al Shem Tov. The fact that he is quoted by both Jacob Joseph of Polonnoye and Moshe Hayyim Ephraim of Sudilkov[11] shows that he was held in high esteem in the Hasidic world. In 1764 he settled in Erez Israel, leading the first Hasidic settlement in Tiberias along with Menahem Mendel of Peremyshlyany.[12] The family of Nahman of Horodenka traced its ancestry to the MaHaRaL of Prague (*d.*1609), and through him claimed descent from the House of David, a claim that may have had some effect on the mind of his grandson.[13] Nahman of Bratslav's own father, Simhah, who stayed behind when the elder Nahman went to the Holy Land, is described in late Bratslav sources as a saintly but retiring figure.[14] Unfortunately, we know nothing more of Nahman's father.

Much of the information we have concerning Nahman's childhood falls within the domain of legendary account. Before retelling the legends of Nahman's early years, a few words are in order concerning the nature of this material and its value for the purposes of critical biography. We have already sought to explain why Nathan is so concerned with the fine details of his master's life, and have generally evaluated him as a highly reliable chronicler. In the case of these childhood tales, however, it is appropriate to recall that Nathan did not meet Nahman until 1802, when the master was in his thirtieth year. Anything he records from before that date is at best second-hand, told him by Nahman, by members of the family, or by long-term acquaintances. Nathan must thus in this case be seen as collector and editor, rather than actual recorder of the materials with which we are dealing, and his reliability is of a different sort than it is with regard to the later period in Nahman's life.

Legends surrounding the childhood of a future great rabbi or Hasidic master are by no means lacking in the folk-literature of East European Jews. Generally these followed rather standardized form, emphasizing precociousness in studies, a certain aloofness from the playful concerns of ordinary children, and the seeking out of the company of elders and scholars. Of Nahman's older contemporary we are told, for example:

> The boy Shne'ur Zalman [of Liadi] was a wonder in his studies, outshining all his contemporaries, the wisest person of his generation . . . when he was sixteen years old he had been through the entire Talmud with all its commentaries, as well as the earlier and later legal codes . . .[15]

Such was the ideal male child of Polish-Jewish society: a miniature of the ideal man. The great revolution in consciousness wrought by the Hasidic movement is nowhere more clearly seen than in the portrayal of the Baʿal Shem Tov's childhood in the *Shivḥey ha-BeSHT*.[16] The young Israel ben Eliezer is there depicted as one who had little use for formal education. He had to be forcibly kept in school, and when the teacher's back was turned he would flee the schoolroom, only to be found later wandering in the woods. Thus is the anti-intellectual strain of early Hasidism lent respectability: even in his childhood the master was one who knew that God was not first to be sought in the world of books.

Had the tales of Nahman's childhood followed either of these established patterns, we would tend to dismiss them as merely imitative fabrications. The fact is, however, that neither of these strains is dominant in the Bratslav legends, and the young Nahman here portrayed emerges as a quite distinctive and rather troubled person, neither the little scholar nor the romantic wanderer in the forest. The childhood depicted here is that of a pained young ascetic, one who at an early age knew the difficulties of the religious life and struggled with all his strength to overcome them. This image, standing in direct contrast to the counsel offered by many other teachers of early Hasidism, is as much a pronouncement of the new path of Bratslav as is the *Shivḥey ha-BeSHT* depiction an announcement of the Ba'al Shem's teachings. Here it is suffering that is to serve as the mark of the *ẓaddiq;* only a childhood filled with pain and inner torment could create the man around whom Bratslav was to be fashioned. To state it differently, one might say that this is a childhood which totally fit the very particular adult Nahman of whom the tales were told; to what extent they actually record the events that led to the formation of that adult and to what extent they are backward projections, reconstructing the child on the basis of the man, is something we will never fully know.

Externally, we are told, Nahman was a happy and even playful child. To all eyes he seemed to enjoy the games of his companions. This, however, was but a cover intended for public view; within himself he was concerned only with a constant search for the nearness of God.[17] The true focus of his life was to be found neither in childish play nor in the books of the schoolroom; his energies were all centered around a life of intense and pain-filled prayer. The young Nahman was not satisfied with the prescribed prayers of the liturgy; he would compose his own prayers, in the Yiddish that he spoke, and through them he would plead to God to draw him near to His service. Alone in the attic of his parents' house, he poured out his heart in insatiable longing, a longing filled with an overwhelming awareness of his distance from his Creator. This longing was always to remain with him and was to become a cornerstone of his unique religious path.[18] Of these childhood years in Medzhibozh Nathan writes:

> He would often speak to God in heartfelt supplications and pleas . . . but nevertheless he felt he wasn't being noticed or heard at all. On the contrary, it seemed to him that he was being pushed away from the service of God in all kinds of ways, as though he were utterly unwanted. Days and years passed by, and still he was far from Him; he had not attained any sense of nearness at all . . . Despite all this, he would fortify himself and refuse to leave his place. At times he would become depressed, when he saw that despite all his begging and pleading to draw near to God's service, no attention was being paid him at all. At such times he would cease his private prayers for a number of days. Then he would catch himself and be overcome with shame for having called the goodness of God into question . . . and he would begin again to plead before the Lord as before. All this happened to him any number of times.[19]

Not surprisingly, the young Nahman's prayer life seemed to center particularly around the Psalms. He would go through the Psalter and seek out all those passages that reflect a sense of crying out to God. He trained himself to recite all the outcries of the Psalms in one sitting, leaving aside all the rest. The very terms which are so frequently used to characterize Nahman's devotions, *hitqarevut* and *hitraḥaqut* ("nearness" and "distance"), and so fill the literature of Bratslav Hasidism, are hardly to be found in the writings of other Hasidic masters in the eighteenth century. They are rooted directly in the Psalter, and in those very passages the child Nahman chose for his private prayers.[20]

The life of prayer was supplemented by various ascetic practices, acts at which the founder of Hasidism might have looked askance. When he was six years old (if we are to believe the reports), Nahman would go out in the midst of cold winter nights to visit the grave of the Ba'al Shem Tov "to ask of him that he might help him draw near to God." He would then go and immerse himself in the outdoor *miqweh* in order to chastize himself.[21] In this same period of early childhood, we are told, he sought to overcome the pleasure he took in eating. Realizing that he could not do without eating altogether, he began to eliminate chewing, swallowing his food in large pieces so that he should not enjoy the taste. He was forced to abandon this practice when his throat became swollen and presumably the matter caught the attention of his mother's watchful eye.[22]

What is it in a child's heart that can so fill him with such an oppressive sense of longing, that stirs in him a constant need to cry out to a seemingly distant God? In the world of the Ba'al Shem Tov's court, where the service of God through joy and wholeness was an essential part of the message, and where ascetic practices, though not forbidden, were held in rather low regard, why should a child become attracted to a religious life marked by an overwhelming feeling of rejection by God and a repeated need through mortification to reject his bodily self?

Of course we are not in a position to answer these questions. One utterly fruitless claim has been made for a "psychoanalytic study" of Nahman along classic Freudian lines;[23] we shall not repeat its efforts here. When it comes to Nahman the young adult, or even the adolescent, we do have a good deal of material that is psychologically interesting: dreams, stories, first-person confessions, and much more. Without contravening the psychoanalyst's assumption that the personality reflected in such documents is in fact formed in childhood, we must confess that we simply do not know enough about Nahman's childhood years to say anything authoritative about the origin of his deep and lasting inner conflicts. As we have said, we have absolutely no reliable information whatever with regard to Nahman's father. We know from a casual reference that he was still alive as late as 1807, and it may well be that he outlived his famous son. The adult Nahman did visit his parents in

Medzhibozh on occasion, and there is no reason to suspect that relations between them were in any way strained. Nahman's mother, the BeSHT's granddaughter Feige, was still alive in 1803, when Nahman's conflicts with her brother Barukh first became serious,[24] but we do not hear of her later. Feige was reputed to have inherited some of the 'supersensory' powers of her own mother, Odel, but no details are given.

By the time of Nahman's childhood this was a family of considerable prominence and, one would imagine, some wealth. Material want was hardly Nahman's problem; we are specifically told that his was a comfortable, perhaps even spoiled, childhood.[25] Two of his siblings, a brother named Yehiel and a sister whose name is lost, are known to us from later in his life,[26] but we have no idea of the size of the original family or of Nahman's relationship with his siblings. Since he alone became a *rebbe,* it is likely that he was the eldest son. We should also mention that Uncle Barukh, who was certainly a major figure in Nahman's childhood, had no sons of his own who might have taken center stage in the Medzhibozh court, and it thus seems likely that the young Nahman was the focus of a good deal of family and community attention.

In the absence of documentation, a certain degree of conjecture as to Nahman's childhood situation is inevitable. It should be emphasized that the following is just that: conjecture where evidence is lacking. A picture may be constructed of a child who is the object of high expectations, the offspring of two great families, and the heir-apparent to the Medzhibozh dynasty. Nahman was probably constantly watched for signs of incipient greatness. For a child who took his own religious life seriously, of course, this brought about grave conflicts with the values of humility and pure devotion taught by his ethical tracts. A conflict developed between the grand public display of religious enthusiasm (or even occult powers) and expectations of himself in this regard, and the values of inwardness in which he was coming to believe. How does the favorite child of a great rabbinic court, ever crowded about by hundreds of admiring *ḥasidim,* dare to disappoint their expectations? At the same time, how does one who allows himself to participate in the public display of virtuoso piety live with himself when the crowds are gone? This conflict came to manifest itself in Nahman as an increasing shyness about any show of piety or learning, a shyness that forced him to learn that he must hold a great deal within himself, sharing it with no one. *Inwardness* and *loneliness* go hand in hand in the descriptions of Nahman's early years; it seems that he dared not share his religious strivings with those around him, lest they only be used as further public confirmation of the image that would-be admirers sought in him, one which he felt a deepening need to avoid. The more such a child felt that the secrets of his inner life might be betrayed by those he trusted, including those proud and well-intentioned adults to whom he felt closest, the more deeply within himself he might feel a need to hide, and the thicker the wall of loneliness he might construct.

For such a child, the Psalmist's "Place not your trust in princes" might have had a particularly true ring; in an atmosphere already saturated with the language of piety it would be natural that he turn to God as the only other with whom he could share his lonely burden. When the response of reassurance the child needed was not forthcoming, a religion of longing and a constant sense of alienation began to well up in him. Surely *doubts* or lack of faith were unthinkable in the court of the Ba'al Shem Tov's family; if God did not respond to the outpourings of the heart, the fault could lie in no one but oneself. This burden too had to be borne in silence.

We would not be surprised to learn that Nahman's father was to a certain degree shunted into the background of the child's early family life, and that it was Feige and her brother Barukh who were posed as the significant models for him. Certainly the bitterness with which Nahman was later to denounce "false" *ẓaddiqim* and the disdain in which he held Barukh's style of popular Hasidism have about them a ring of adolescent rebellion. Might the young Nahman not have been aware of a sharp contrast between his own rather quiet and perhaps relatively 'unsuccessful' father and the dominant Uncle Barukh, whose example he was supposed to follow? It may also be said that Nahman's search for a new revival within Hasidism, a return to the pristine days of his great-grandfather the BeSHT, in contrast to the compromised Hasidic style he must have perceived in the adults around him, represents a psychological pattern which is well-documented in other times and places. Thus far conjecture.

His course of studies as a child was more or less typical of the curriculum for the Hasidic elite of his time. In addition to Talmud and codes, the mainstays of any traditional Jewish education, emphasis was placed upon mystical and ethical literature: he studied the *Zohar* and the *Tiqquney Zohar*, the entire corpus of the Lurianic writings (with particular emphasis on the *Peri 'Eẓ Ḥayyim*), *Reshit Hokhmah*, and various other ethical tracts. It is also noteworthy and somewhat surprising that the Bible *(TeNaKH)* is listed as an item of his curriculum; Nahman had a thorough knowledge, unusual for his day, of even the more obscure parts of the Hebrew Bible, a knowledge which greatly aided his skill as a preacher. In addition to the regular diet of Talmudic subjects, special mention is also made of the study of *'Eyn Ya'aqov*, a popular selection of the Aggadic passages in the Talmud. The legends of the *'Eyn Ya'aqov* and the *Zohar* must have provided rich sustenance for Nahman's fertile imagination, an imagination already weaving together the strands of fantasy that were to emerge later with startling originality in his *Sippurey Ma'asiyot*.[27]

Nahman's efforts at study were also marked by the surging emotionalism we have seen in his prayer life. We are told that when he had difficulty in understanding a particular passage encountered in a text, he would cry out to God for help in understanding. Though it seems surprising for one who was such a master at juggling and reinterpretation of rabbinic sources later in life, we are told that learning did not come easily to Nahman as a child: he would seek to break through the blocks in his mind by means of countless tears. While the accounts tell us that he had a love of learning, and that he would even use his own spending money to bribe the teacher to tutor him in a few extra pages of text beyond his regular allotment (though this sounds rather like a standard future-rabbi legend), we are also told that at times his teacher would become angry with him for not concentrating hard enough on his studies. Somewhere the child had picked up the mystical practice of constant concentration on the four-letter name of God, a practice associated in early Hasidism with the BeSHT's contemporary, Nahman of Kosov. While concentrating on the name of God rather than on the text before him might have won approval in some Hasidic circles of the time, it apparently did not impress the teacher who was charged with Nahman's education.[28]

As we have noted, these childhood tales are significant at least as backward projections, if they are not fully accurate in historical detail. Perhaps the most revealing of them is the one with which we began: the account that says that, while to all appearances Nahman was a 'normal' and playful child, his true concerns were kept deeply hidden within himself. As an adolescent, we know, he tried to keep his piety hidden from his elders, pretending on one occasion that he had even forgotten how to read Hebrew, while in fact he was deeply engrossed in a secret life of prayer and study.[29] In this he may have been imitating the BeSHT, who was said to have hidden his esoteric knowledge behind the veneer of an ignorant peasant-like Jew. This sense of dual personhood, of the need to separate the 'true' self from the self he dared to show to others, was characteristic of Nahman throughout his life. We have speculated on its origins in childhood, but its later presence is not in doubt. He seemed to live in fear of revealing his inner self. "If I were to reveal myself," the adult Nahman once confided to a relative, "the whole world would run after me. But I don't want that." On another occasion he said that he intentionally hid his fear of God, for if he were to reveal it fully, no person would be able to stand in his presence. Whether that awesome inner power would prove overwhelmingly attractive or repulsive to others (indeed, he seems to have thought that both were the case), Nahman tried to keep it in check. "I can hold in a great deal; I don't speak until the waters overflow their banks and break through the dam."[30]

This need to hide what was going on within himself continued to contribute to his great loneliness, which was only increased by the crowds that surrounded him when he, as an adult, again became a public figure. "When am I alone?" he once rhetorically asked a disciple, referring to *hitbodedut,* the aloneness required for private conversation with God. "When everyone is standing around me and I am seated in their midst—that is when I practice *hitbodedut.*" And on that same occasion he spoke of a still, small voice he possessed, with which he could cry out in such a way that it would ring from one end of the earth to the other—but those around him would hear nothing. He was capable of a dance, he said, that was so delicate that no one who saw him could detect even the slightest movement of his body.[31] The picture emerges of a hidden and lonely figure, surrounded by admirers who occasionally merit to be told how little they understand of who he really is. The child who seeks a lone path to God, apparently not pleased by the attention or companionship of others, grows into the adult who knows that he is deeply alone, even in the midst of the admiring crowd.

One further aspect of Nahman's inner life as a child (though it is hard to know which of these traditions belongs properly to childhood and which to adolescence) remains for us to detail here. The young Nahman was plagued, so Nathan tells us, by an inordinate fear of death.

> He had previously recounted that in his youth he had a very very great fear of death. Death frightened him terribly; he would plead with God that he die as a martyr, for the sanctification of His name. This lasted for quite some time, but he did not recall just how long . . . for perhaps a year he would constantly make this request. Not a single conversation [with God] or prayer would go by in which he did not ask for martyrdom. His fear of death was so great that this very request was tantamount to an act of surrender unto death itself . . .
>
> He said that several times he had pictured [his own] death; it was so vivid that it was as though he were really dead, tasting the very taste of death. I have heard that he told how in his youth he would picture his death to himself, [seeing] how people would weep for him, etc.[32]

It is interesting that no fear of punishment or hell enters into these accounts, fears that would not be surprising for a child so steeped in the study of *Zohar* or *mussar* literature as was the young Nahman. It is rather death itself, and particularly the meaninglessness of death, that is the source of terror. Nahman's significant and complex relationship to death—which seems to have included fascination/attraction as well as terror—pursued him through his adult life.[33] The great personal tragedies of his life—the death of his infant son, his wife's death the following year, and the onset of his own fatal three-year bout with tuberculosis when he was only thirty-five—were all seen by him through the uniquely well-developed eyes of one who knows from childhood what the struggle with death is all about. He identified strongly with Rabbi Akiva, the Talmudic sage whose longing for martyrdom as the ultimate token of his love for God was finally awarded him by the Romans.

> It is possible to concentrate your thoughts so fully on martyrdom that you could really die from the suffering, just as though you had actually died in that very way. There is no difference between real death and the pain you can feel in such thinking about death. For that reason, you have to avoid remaining there when you feel that your soul is about to leave you—so that you not, God forbid, die before your time.[34]

It is worthy of note that the Ba'al Shem, too, had spoken of the possibility of dying during prayer, but his remarks on the subject reflect an entirely different concern. The BeSHT spoke of the total expending of energy which takes place in the moment of ecstasy. If prayer is truly as it should be, he said, it is only by dint of miracle that people have the strength to go on living afterwards.[35] In Nahman's case, rather than a concern for ecstasy, it is morbid fascination and an intentional confrontation with death that has become the focus of his fears.

An acute awareness of his own mortality, a sense of aloneness and isolation both from man and from God, a rich imagination fired by early study of the mythic imagery of the Kabbalah, and a deep well of inner pain and longing—these were the legacies of childhood that Nahman was to carry with him into his adult life. Throughout his later years, and despite the constant growth he made his sacred goal, they never seemed to recede very far from the surface of his consciousness. Nahman was one of those thinkers whose internalized childhood always abides with them. His ability as an adult to create a world of fantasy that seems to parallel with such richness the most archaic mythic memories of mankind was not unrelated to this continued presence of his "inner child." That this child within the adult also provided a constant confrontation with ancient pain need hardly be added.

Shortly after Nahman's Bar Mitzvah, at which his uncle the rabbi of Sudilkov addressed him in a way that he took very seriously, perhaps charging him with the responsibility of carrying on the family name, a marriage was arranged between Nahman and Sosia, the daughter of one Ephraim, a respected and somewhat wealthy tax-farmer who lived in the small village of Usyatin, near the town of Smela, on the western shores of the Dnieper some two hundred miles to the east of Medzhibozh.[36] Following the custom of the times, the couple went to live at the home of the bride's father. Thus it was that sometime in early adolescence Nahman left Medzhibozh and the court of his uncle, moving from the deeply Jewish milieu of that town[37] to the isolated life of a village, at some distance from even the smallest organized Jewish community.

In later years, Nahman was wont to look back with fondness upon his days in Usyatin.

> Rabbi Simeon said that once, after our master had become a public figure, the two of them traveled together through the village of Usyatin . . . As they passed through the fields, our master was filled with longing and said:

"How good it was for me here; with every step I felt the taste of Eden . . . At another time he said in my presence that when he had been alone somewhere in the woods or the fields, he would find on his return that he had come back to a completely new world. The world that he saw now, so he imagined, was completely different, not at all like that world which he had known before.[38]

Despite all the harsh spiritual struggles of his adolescence, which we shall presently describe, the affinity for the outdoors he discovered in himself in those years was very precious to him. His private prayers were no longer confined to an attic; when weather permitted he would go out to the fields and forests to be alone with God. The love he had for trees and meadows, often lending bright color and a unique quality of pastoral poetry to his later teachings, undoubtedly stems from the time he spent in the woods around Usyatin. On some days he would take a horse from his father-in-law's yard and ride to the edge of the forest, leaving the horse tied to a tree while he wandered through the woods alone, lost in thought. At other times he would take a small boat out into the nearby river, one of the tributaries of the great Dnieper, to be alone with God in the midst of the water.[39]

Little is recorded of the personality of Nahman's wife, and the nature of their relationship is virtually unknown to us. His marriage was apparently not an object of concern for Nahman; at least such concern is not given expression in his otherwise often highly romantic writings. The religious life of Hasidic men was by and large conducted in an all-male world of community, prayer, and study; marriage among such men was universal, but hardly seemed worthy of discussion within the sacred sphere. Still, it is noteworthy that the sort of sexual and marital imagery the BeSHT often employed to describe the relationship between God and man is mostly absent from Nahman's writings.

Stemming from the same time as his marriage, however, was the first great friendship of Nahman's life, a relationship that did play a major role in his public affairs. Simeon ben Baer, who was perhaps a few years older than Nahman,[40] was present at Nahman and Sosia's wedding, which took place in the town of Medvedevka, near Usyatin. From that time forth he came to see himself as Nahman's friend and disciple.[41] It was this Simeon who accompanied Nahman on his journey to Erez Israel and who was to remain the closest of his confidants, at least until the arrival of Nathan on the scene some seventeen years later. Simeon's account of the conversation he and Nahman had on the latter's wedding day gives us a rather good indication of who Nahman was at the age of about fourteen:

Right after our master had veiled the bride [this traditionally takes place a short while before the wedding ceremony] on the day of the wedding, he went and called some of the youngsters, speaking to each of them individually. He was wisely testing them to see where they stood. Then he called

> R. Simeon and began to speak cleverly with him, pretending that he was concerned with this-worldly vanities. Simeon stood there astonished and did not answer, for he wanted no part of such things. Our master said to him: 'Aren't you human? Don't you want worldly things?' Simeon answered him: 'I am a simple man and I seek simplicity.' Then our master replied: 'It seems that you and I will be getting to know each other.' He then told him how he had tested the other youngsters and found that they were far from God; some were even sinners, God save us. He took Simeon directly out into the field, and they conversed about the service of God with great longing. Our master said rousing things to Simeon about how the only meaning in life was to be found by turning aside from worldly desires and serving God. 'Especially for me,' he added, 'for this is my wedding day, on which all my sins are forgiven. Surely I have to search my deeds.' He said much more in this vein, and they continued this conversation until the ceremony began.[42]

Part of this conversation is probably not particularly unusual for the shy adolescent bridegroom of East European rabbinic society. Supplied with no sexual information other than that which came in the course of Talmudic studies, his head full of the evils of concupiscence derived from the ethical tracts that were so widely read, the prospect of marital expectations was in all likelihood rather terrifying to many a young man. In Nahman's case, the discovery of a friend with whom he could share holy talk on the evils of 'worldly desires' must have been quite a comfort. One also has a sense that those passionate energies, aroused by the moment but which could find no outlet in the very proper behavior expected of the bridegroom at his wedding-feast, were here given an expression that could be considered quite proper: conversation filled "with great longing" about the pure and ascetic service of God. It may well be that the conversations these two friends had in their early years were to provide Nahman with his model for the importance he laid upon honest talk among friends about spiritual problems.[43] This recognition of the need for deep friendship and honest communication was to become a cornerstone of the *qibbuẓ ha-qadosh*, the community of Bratslav *ḥasidim*.

The daily routine of Nahman's religious life continued despite the great changes effected by his move from Medzhibozh to Usyatin. He continued to devote himself fully to his studies, the institution of board at his father-in-law's house intended for exactly that purpose. If anything, Nahman's studies seem to become more serious as he became both adolescent and husband. The ascetic tendencies that had been present in earlier years now grew in intensity and demand. Fasting from Sabbath to Sabbath became part of his ordinary routine, as he sought to transcend any human pleasure he might still take in the act of eating. He would mortify his body by rolling in the snow in winter, and, in the warmer months, by allowing insects to bite at his flesh unmolested. During occasional visits with his family in Medzhibozh, on which his wife accompanied him, he would resume his midnight vigils at the grave of the BeSHT. When he was not able to go to Medzhibozh, he would go to the cemetery at Smela, there to send messages to the Ba'al Shem Tov through the *ẓaddiq* Isaiah of Yanov, who lay buried in the Smela graveyard.[44] He sought, and at times felt he found, various miraculous signs proving to him that God was present in his life and showed some special concern for him.

The choices of two of these signs are rather revealing in psychological terms, each of them showing a different face of Nahman's ongoing fascination and struggle with the idea of death. We have already mentioned that the young Nahman would row a small boat out into the middle of the nearby river in order there to be alone with God. Not knowing very well how to handle the boat, Nahman would sometimes stop rowing when he was at the place farthest from shore and nearly allow the boat to capsize. At that moment he would call out to God to save him from drowning.

Another account of Nahman's search for such 'signs' tells us that

> he wanted to see a dead man. He pressed for this until it happened: once, while he was sitting in the attic room of his father-in-law's house, a dead person came to him. Our master became very frightened, for this was the first time he had seen a dead man with his own eyes; this was in his early youth. Afterwards our master said that this dead man had been a particularly wicked one, and that was why he had become so overwhelmed by terrible boundless fear in his presence. He began to cry out in a most awful way, and everyone in the house came running and tried to get into his room. They were unable to do so, however, since he had already locked the door from the inside. They had to resort to some trick in order to get into the room; I don't remember if they broke through a wall or climbed over the partition. After they got to him his fears were eased.[45]

These must be seen as tests of personal worthiness. In the former, Nahman wants to know both that his faith is strong enough to risk death for the sake of God and that he is not yet so sinful that God's providence would allow him to die. In the second, the young would-be *ẓaddiq* is testing out his supersensory powers, seeing whether God is yet ready to grace him with a vision of the dead, but also wanting to know whether he can stand such an experience. It was well known, surely within Nahman's family, that much of the BeSHT's concern as a holy man was with the redemption of the souls of those who had already died. One legend, preserved in the *Shivḥey ha-BeSHT*, tells of the thousands of such souls that would attack the master in his Friday afternoon prayers (for even the souls in hell rise up to celebrate the Sabbath), and of the tremendous fear that overcame R. Gershon Kitover, the BeSHT's skeptical brother-in-law, when he tried to imitate the other's behavior. Here Nahman seems closer to R. Gershon than he does to the BeSHT; the test showed that he indeed had the power to call forth the dead, but was not sufficiently strong to handle them once they did make their appearance.[46] No wonder Nathan tells us that a major portion of Nahman's self-designated spiritual task over the years was the struggle to overcome his fear of death.[47]

In other ways, too, Nahman's spiritual life as an adolescent was turbulent. It was during these years that his soul acquired the scars of one who sees his inner self as a great battlefield of powerful warring forces. While the earlier themes of his struggle did not disappear, such concerns as eating, fear of death, concentration on studies, and the nearness of God all came to be pushed aside by that greatest source of conflict in the life of many an early adolescent: his own sexuality.

It is likely that this sexual awareness did not fall upon Nahman only at the time of his early marriage. While the documentary evidence does not allow for clear dating, it seems more likely that by the time he was twelve or thirteen, while still as Medzhibozh, the new consciousness of puberty was welling up inside him. The intensity of the torments and temptations ascribed to him do not seem to be those of one who has already found the normal outlets of marriage, but rather bears the marks of the overwhelming need to repress that which could not find any form of legitimate expression.

> The great power of the holy level he achieved in breaking down the most basic of all desires, sexual lust, which includes all other base passions within it, cannot possibly be fully told. He said that he had undergone countless trials . . . great and awesome trials with regard to this desire which cannot be discussed in detail. When he was still very young, at the time when a person's blood boils, he suffered countless trials in this regard. It was within his power to satisfy his lusts, and he was thus in very grave danger. Being a powerful warrior, however, he succeeded in overcoming his passions. This happened to him a great many times. Nevertheless, he would not seek to avoid being tested further in this matter. On the contrary, he longed to be tested, and would pray to God that He try him once again. He did this out of a confidence that he would not rebel against God. How could he possibly sin and transgress His will unless, God forbid, he were to go mad right then and there?[48]

The specific focus of Nahman's youthful sexual torments is not known to us. While the dangers of which he was so afraid may have involved a sexual act with another person, it should be noted that the Kabbalistic ethical literature he read was filled with dire warnings about the evils of masturbation or even of involuntary nocturnal emissions.[49] In any case, the great emphasis in Nahman's later teachings on the conquest of sexual desire, an emphasis far beyond that of other Hasidic writings, is clearly a direct result of his own youthful trials in this area. It was due to his realization that this was the most difficult of all the passions to conquer that he came to see the only true test of the *ẓaddiq* to be that of sexual purity. "All other desires are easy to break down," he said, "but the true rung attained by a *ẓaddiq* is only according to his holiness with regard to this desire—when he breaks it down completely."[50]

That was just what the young Nahman sought to do with sexual desire—to break it down completely. For a certain time, every other goal in his spiritual life was set aside; all his energies were focused upon the conquest of sexual feelings.

> He said that the evil one wanted to give him everything, if he would just give in on this one matter. But he said just the opposite: he would set aside everything else, but he would in no way relax his efforts to break this particular thing . . . This was the way he conducted himself at first: all of his struggle was directed toward the single goal of breaking through that most basic of desires. He would pay no attention to his desire for food, but would eat a great deal more than other people, saying that he was drawing all his lusts into the desire to eat. He suffered various kinds of struggles and battles, countless wars, before he succeeded in breaking the most basic of desires. He would pray and pour out his heart to God in the most tearful supplications and pleas, begging of God to help him in overcoming this desire . . .[51]

At some point in early adulthood, Nahman deemed himself victor in this long struggle. He came to see sexuality as the most ridiculous of man's weaknesses. "I cannot understand" he once confided to Nathan, "what the rabbis mean when they say one should engage in sex 'as though forced by a demon.' Who forces you? If a man wants to conquer his desire completely, no one forces him." He claimed to have reached the point where the presence or thoughts of women caused no greater sexual arousal in him than did men. "To me there is no difference between male and female [with regard to sexual desire]."[52] One way he had of conquering desire within himself was to make the human body repulsive through a study of anatomy. If the body was nothing but a mess of organs and unpleasant organic functions, it could no longer be terribly attractive or the object of desire.

> "Whoever knows the science of anatomy, and is aware of the human organs as seen by the surgeon, is prepared to find this desire utterly repulsive." And he went to great lengths to tell of the repulsiveness of this desire.[53]

Conquest of sexual passion did not lead Nahman to a life of total celibacy. He fathered at least seven children, the youngest of whom was born in the fall of 1806, only half a year before the onset of his final illness.[54] One gets the sense, however, that it was only the *halakhic* obligations to father children and to fulfill the needs of his wife that kept him from a celibacy he might himself have found more attractive. So repulsive was the sex act to him that he came to describe it in terms of physical pain.

> Copulation is difficult for the true *ẓaddiq*. Not only does he have no desire for it at all, but he experiences real suffering in the act, suffering which is like that which the infant undergoes when he is circumcised. This very same suffering, to an even greater degree, is felt by the *ẓaddiq* during intercourse. The infant has no awareness; thus his suffering is not so great. But the *ẓaddiq*, because he is aware of the pain, suffers more greatly than does the infant.[55]

The fact is, despite all claims to the contrary, that Nahman's complex attitude toward his own sexual drives was not something that could simply be dismissed once a 'victory' had been achieved. True, he may have been master of himself insofar as sexual *activity* was concerned. But throughout his adult life, as we shall see, the theme of sexual guilt and the sense of the overpowering evils and dangers of sex colored much of his thinking. If there was a victory here, it was at an awful price. Perhaps the later Bratslav tradition points to something significant when it says that "he wanted to destroy this thing completely . . . but nature cannot be changed."[56]

Nahman's struggle to overcome the forces of nature within himself continued to focus on the act of eating and the desire for food as well as on sex. We have seen that the tales of his early childhood describe fasting as the first manifestation of his incipient asceticism. These accounts also say that the child Nahman placed great emphasis on the need to pray in connection with food. In addition to the required blessings before and after meals, he would compose spontaneous prayers in Yiddish, thanking God individually for each item of food on his plate. We do know that after the battle against sexual desire had been deemed won, Nahman turned the focus of his energies back to the matter of eating. His fasts became more frequent, and he sought to train himself, even when not abstaining totally, to eat as little as was necessary for bare survival. He had previously had a rather hearty appetite, which increased still further, as we have seen, in the course of his struggle with sexuality. Now he sought to destroy appetite altogether. According to one account, he had a dream or vision in which the Ba'al Shem Tov came to him in his father-in-law's house and told him to work on this matter. Nahman had sought a vision of the patriarchs; the BeSHT came instead and rebukingly told him that such visions were accessible only to those who were in full control of their animal nature.[57]

Knowing as we do that Nahman left his father-in-law's house when he was approximately eighteen years of age,[58] and that his marriage and the accompanying move to Usyatin had taken place a short time after his Bar Mitzvah, we can place the struggles of which we are speaking primarily within the years 1785–1790, or between Nahman's thirteenth and eighteenth years. It was in this crucial period that the basic character of

Nahman's spiritual life was determined, and it was this period in Nahman's life that was to provide the most significant model for his disciples. This life was one of constant struggle, or constant rise and fall in relationship to God, a life alternating between periods of bleak depression leading him to the brink of utter despair, and redoubled efforts to try once more to come close to God. The sense of alienation from God that he had felt as a child was undoubtedly exacerbated by the guilt and conflicts normal to adolescence; there seemed to be hardly a day in his life when he did not touch the borders of both heaven and hell.

> No act in the service of God came easily to him; everything came only as a result of great and oft-repeated struggle. He rose and fell thousands and thousands of times, really beyond all counting. It was terribly difficult for him even to enter into the service of God, to accept the yoke of His service. He would enter into worship for a certain number of days, then he would experience a fall. He would go back, start over, and then fall again. Finally after many such cycles, he would gain strength and decide that he would remain committed to God's service forever, allowing nothing in the world to lead him astray. From that time forth his heart was strongly with God—but even afterwards he would constantly undergo countless rises and falls . . .
>
> It was his way to start anew each time. When he fell from his rung, he would not allow himself to despair, but would rather set himself to beginning again, as though he had never yet entered the service of God . . . At times he had several such new starts within one day, for even within a single day he could fall several times and have to begin all over again.[59]

The most essential religious reality for Nahman was always the realm of his own inner struggle. Neither the difficult times in which he lived nor the external personal conflicts that were to rage about him ever dislodged this inner reality from its place of prime, virtually singular importance. The outer events of his life were rather seen through the filter of their effect upon the inner man; everything which caused him pain and conflict was given him by God in order to fashion him into a more perfect vessel: that which comes easily is not to be taken seriously; the only authentic religious life is produced by the most desperate struggle within the self.

In the midst of this adolescent struggle, however, Nahman's mind began to effect a transformation, a new view of his own suffering, which may be considered the starting point—even before there were any disciples—of Bratslav Hasidism. The descriptions make it clear that Nahman was more than once at the very brink of despair, a state from which he was able to save himself only with the greatest of efforts. At the same time, those around Nahman continued to see him as a soon-to-be-revealed *ẓaddiq*, and constantly sought evidence of the greatness they longed to find in him. Neither his in-laws nor his family back in Medzhibozh seem to have had any idea of the torments within Nahman's soul.

Their expectations undoubtedly increased his conflict, but perhaps also helped bring it to a crucial point of development. For in contemplating why it was that he, of all people, should be marked by God for such uniquely bitter sufferings, the young Nahman began to develop the notion (perhaps a crucial one for his emotional survival) *that his very pain was the mark of greatness and the proof that he was to be a true ẓaddiq after all*. His torments were to be seen as 'sufferings of love';[60] *the pain felt by Nahman the individual was transformed into that of the suffering servant, the ẓaddiq chosen by God for some great purpose.* The greater the torments in such a case, the greater the *ẓaddiq* who would emerge from them. If Bratslav Hasidism means belief both in the man Nahman as a guide and in the teachings he proclaimed, the most difficult step in its emergence was surely the first—Nahman's incredible struggle to believe in himself.

While he was still living in his father-in-law's home, Jews from around Usyatin who had heard that a descendant of the Ba'al Shem Tov was in their midst began to come to him and treat him as their *rebbe.*[61] Nahman apparently allowed this to happen, initially keeping whatever ambivalence he may have felt about it to himself. At the same time, he in no way sought disciples. While he may have been making his way from personal struggle toward self-definition as a suffering *ẓaddiq*, this hardly meant that he was ready to emerge as a public figure.

From the earliest years of Nahman's adulthood, his self-definition as a *ẓaddiq* was an ambiguous one. Hasidic lore knew two types called by that name: the *nistar* and the *mefursam.*[62] The former, a hidden saint, was said to retain a spiritual purity that could only be the envy of the latter, a publicly known and accessible spiritual leader. The figure of the *nistar* has deep and ancient roots in Jewish folklore;[63] his humility, which is seen in the anonymous way in which he acts, is central to his character. The *Zohar* is replete with tales of such hidden *ẓaddiqim*, who often reveal the most profound mysteries in their encounters with the disciples of Rabbi Simeon.[64] The early traditions of Hasidism also abounded with tales of these hidden ones. It was not uncommon in Hasidism for the scion of a great family to emulate such figures, and to seek to live a life of quiet piety. Such a person, for example, was Abraham 'the Angel' (1740–1777), the son of Dov Baer of Miedzyrzec.

A young man who took his religious life as seriously as did Nahman must have been greatly tempted to follow such a path. On the other hand, Hasidic literature places great value on the willingness of the *mefursam* to make himself available to those who need him. At times the reclusive *ẓaddiq* is seen as selfish or insecure; the greater figure is the one who can serve as a beacon to others, while still maintaining the intensity of his own religious life.[65] The institutionalization of the *ẓaddiq* as the central figure in the communal life of Hasidism made it essential that a high value be placed upon the *mefursam's* acceptance of the mantle of leadership. The dual values thus expressed built into the role of public *ẓaddiq* a certain ambiguity, which could add a needed measure of humility to those figures who tended toward self-assurance in this role, but which could also exacerbate terribly the conflicts of those who approached it with hesitation.

In looking back upon his early years, Nahman was later to claim that he had fought against becoming a *mefursan*, that this was a role cast upon him against his will.[66] Personally, he said, he would have preferred to remain a 'hidden one.' Whether these statements reflect the wisdom of hindsight and the regrets of an adult at the spiritual opportunities missed in youth or whether they indeed do reflect Nahman's feelings as he emerged from adolescence is beyond our power to discern. We do know, however, that throughout his adult life Nahman showed a certain ambivalence toward his vocation. He once referred to his earliest and most faithful disciples as 'murderers' who pursued him, presumably for having burdened him with the public role. Even after he had come to see himself as the greatest of all the *ẓaddiqim* and the unique leader of his generation, he continued to regret not having remained hidden from public view. He acted out the fantasy of being a *nistar* on his mysterious journey to Navritch in 1807, when he traveled about in disguise. At various times within his life he toyed with the idea of fleeing his disciples and going off to live in hiding. The tale of the *Master of Prayer*, which Nahman told in the winter before his death, contains an idealized view of the *ẓaddiq* and his community as a ragged band of ascetics living in the woods. Even while in the throes of his final illness, the dying Nahman was to speak of feeling trapped by his communal responsibilities and of his longing to run away.[67]

While we have seen that some local Jews had sought him out earlier, Nahman's real career as a public figure began with his move to Medvedevka in 1790. That move was prompted by the remarriage of his father-in-law, an event which was to have a double significance in Nahman's life, launching him on his way toward his public career. R. Ephraim, who had been widowed, sought to take a second wife. Nahman himself, perhaps using his family's connections, arranged a marriage for his wife's father. The wedding took place in Mogilev-Podolski, a major city in the southwestern Ukraine. The young son-in-law of the groom was asked to speak at the wedding-feast, and having his tongue somewhat loosened by drink, he was less reticent than usual about his thoughts. His words made a great impression on those who attended, and reports reached the ear of Rabbi Dov Baer of Zaslav (Izyaslav), presumably through the relatives of Ephraim, who came from that city. The rabbi of Zaslav, who had been a disciple of the BeSHT and of Pinhas of Korets, thus became the first of the *ẓaddiqim* to publicly attest to Nahman's greatness.[68]

When the newly wed couple returned home to Usyatin it became clear that the house was too small for the two families to share. Ephraim's new wife could not understand why a room had to be set aside in the house for Nahman's solitude. The attic room, which for several years had been Nahman's place of prayer, now became this woman's bedroom. Nahman felt that he could not live in a place where he had no room to be alone; it also seems plausible that he and his wife may have felt less than comfortable with a new stepmother in the house, and that the prayer-room was a symbolic issue between them. In any case, Nahman and Sosia (along with two or three children)[69] left Ephraim's house, and the eighteen-year-old *ẓaddiq* and his family settled in the nearby town of Medvedevka. At first they were supported by the rather large dowry of three hundred red rubles which had been promised them before their marriage. When this money ran out, however, they faced a period of real poverty. It was at this point that Nahman first allowed himself to be supported as a *rebbe,* accepting a fixed stipend from a group of local admirers.[70]

Whether it was economic necessity that forced Nahman to accept this stipend or whether acceptance of the money was but a by-product of a decision finally to accept the public role, Nahman now began to speak and act as one who was ready to take on the greatest of responsibilities. In his rejection of the popular Hasidism of his uncle and the 'miracles' offered by the various wonder-workers to be found throughout the Ukraine, Nahman sought to present a renewed Hasidism, which would truly concern itself with spiritual search and the creation of a new ideal type of Jew. His task was that of leading a revival within a waning Hasidism;[71] the goal of such a revival would have to be to fashion each of his disciples into a *ẓaddiq*. No lesser definition of the master's task would do.[72]

The nature of Nahman's religious life and emerging style of leadership did not permit him to become the temporal successor of Barukh of Medzhibozh any more than he was his spiritual heir. Barukh's place was inherited rather by such figures as Abraham Joshua Heschel of Opatow (1755–1825), who settled in Medzhibozh after Barukh's death, Mordecai of Chernobyl (1770–1837), and later by Israel of Ruzhin (1796–1850). Nahman rather openly contrasted his attitude toward money with that of his Uncle Barukh, claiming that he preferred the devoted gift of the poor man over certain large sums his uncle was said to have received. His intense dislike of certain traits of popular Hasidism is also seen in the following:

> The day on which our late and sainted master arrived in Bratslav was a Tuesday, which was the market day. People spoke about him, telling how

> he despised the ways of the famous ones who proclaimed the center of worship to be gatherings where people eat and drink. (Once our master said: 'I can no longer stand their festivities!') Our master would only speak of Torah and prayer and order people to confess to him . . .[73]

In the utter seriousness of the Bratslav revival there was no room for the often light-hearted gatherings common to other Hasidic courts. In this matter there is a direct parallel between the attitudes of Nahman and those of Mendel of Kotzk, who led a revival of Hasidism in central Poland some forty years later. Nahman's path, based on the model of the suffering *ẓaddiq* rather than on the regal model, and seeking out deep religious conflict as the sign of spiritual growth, could never achieve broad-based popular support. The privilege of following Nahman was reserved for a spiritual elite.

He did not allow himself to be treated as one would treat another *rebbe*. When people came to him in search of help in worldly matters, he would at times dismiss them brusquely. "I don't know how you find it in yourself," he once said to such a visitor

> to confound me with the vanities of this world! I am like a man who digs in the desert, day and night, trying to build a settlement. Each of you has a heart like a desert, with no dwelling-place in it for the Presence of God. I am constantly digging in your hearts, working to fashion that dwelling. Do you know how hard a person has to work, starting with an oak tree, in order to fashion from it vessels fit for use? First you have to chop the tree down, then saw the boards, make them smooth, and all the rest. I am doing all that for each of you. And you bother me with such trifles?[74]

The first disciples to come to Nahman from beyond the immediate area were three men from the town of Dashev.[75] A young man named Dov, referred to in Bratslav literature as Dov of Cheryn (where he was later to settle), left his father-in-law's home in Dashev to return to his own parents' home near Medvedevka. While at his father-in-law's, he and his friend Samuel Isaac had been students of R. Yudil of Dashev, who was in turn a disciple of Pinhas of Korets, a major teacher of early Hasidism.[76] Word of Nahman's activities in Medvedevka had already reached the ears of R. Yudil, who warned his student Dov not to have any contact with the young *rebbe*. A time came, however, when Dov was filled with melancholy and depression, and needed the solace of a teacher.[77] Nahman's own experiences with such emotional states apparently made him a successful counselor on this and countless later occasions. Convinced that he had found in Nahman a true *ẓaddiq*, Dov returned to Dashev to fetch his friend Samuel Isaac and his earlier teacher, Yudil. On their way to Medvedevka, the three of them passed through the townlet of Tirhavits, the home of one Yekutiel the Maggid, who had once been a disciple in Miedzyrzec. It may have been their enthusiasm on that first journey that made Tirhavits, like Dashev, an early center of Bratslav Hasidism, and persuaded the maggid there later to himself become a disciple of the much younger Nahman.

The account given of the first meeting between Nahman and Yudil of Dashev is highly revealing of the intense personal style in which Nahman conducted himself in his early years as *rebbe.* Yudil, who was surely the elder of the two by quite a few years, was a highly respected man in his own community. In addition to having studied with Pinhas of Korets, he was the son-in-law of the *ẓaddiq* Leib of Strestinits, and was reputed to be something of an authority on Kabbalah. He thus entered Nahman's room rather self-confidently and said: "Let our master show us a path in the service of God." Nahman, feeling a touch of arrogance in the other's tone, replied by quoting in a questioning voice: "To know Thy ways in the earth?" (PS. 67:3), as though to say: Can one so filled with earthly concerns as you indeed be seeking a way to God? At this R. Yudil became so filled with awe and terror that he stepped back to the doorway and was afraid to come any closer to Nahman than that. Nahman then began to smile, lessening the tension in the room, and said: "Why should you be afraid of me? I'm only a human being, just like you—except that I am more clever than you." He continued to appease the visitor until R. Yudil drew near and stood right next to him. Then once again he let out with a word that shook the poor man to the core, and he again fled to the threshold. Again Nahman began to smile and draw him near. This happened a number of times, until R. Yudil's spirit was so broken that Nahman could order him to confess to him all that had transpired in his life.[78] This moment of *widui* or confession to the *ẓaddiq* was apparently the moment of initiation into the circle of Nahman's *ḥasidim.* So central was this confession to Bratslav and so well-known did it become that other *ḥasidim* referred to the disciples of Nahman as *widuiniks* (confessors).

This rite of confession before the *ẓaddiq,* seemingly so alien to Jewish religious practice, is not completely unique to Bratslav. The practice of unburdening one's conscience before a wise man and receiving his counsel in matters of penance was already known and encouraged among German-Jewish pietists in the middle ages, and occasional evidence of it continues to crop up in the literature of East European Jews. It should be noted, however, that in none of these pre-Hasidic examples did the rabbi claim the power to grant absolution. Within Hasidism itself there is evidence that confession was not unique to Bratslav, and the question of absolution is a moot one. In a broad sense one may of course say that no master/disciple relationship is possible if the disciple is not fully open about his spiritual problems, including whatever guilt it is that burdens him. A formal rite of confession, however, existed only in small circles of the most intense enthusiasts: it is evidenced in the group around Hayyim Haykl of Amdur, in the circle of Abraham Kalisker in Tiberias, and here in the early followers of Nahman. This initiatory rite made it quite clear to the would-be joiner of the community that a bond of unusual intensity was being forged here, and therefore that becoming a part of this particular community was a matter not to be taken lightly. (It seems that even Nahman abandoned the insistence on confession in his later years—or at least the sources are silent about it.)[79]

The groups from Dashev and Tirhavits joined Nahman's old friend Simeon and perhaps a few others to form the inner circle of the young master's followers. While he did accept their discipleship, his continuing ambivalence toward his role in their lives is witnessed by the fact that he did not permit the Dashev group to move their homes to Medvedevka so that they could always be near him. To be constantly surrounded by disciples was more than he could bear. Later in life, too, he restricted the visits of *ḥasidim* from other towns to three times a year: Rosh Hashanah, the Sabbath of Hanukkah, and Shavu'ot. Other visits, unless justified by some special circumstance, were frowned upon.[80]

When the disciples did come to Medvedevka to spend a Sabbath or festival with their master, they would encounter alternating experiences of overwhelming love and chilling awe. We are told of one Sabbath evening when

> as soon as he had eaten the first morsel of bread, his mind ascended to a certain place, and he cleaved to God in a great and awesome way. He sat there, eyes open, in a wondrous state of religious intensity, all night long. No food was placed upon the table, for all were struck with awe of him and were afraid lest they confound his thoughts. When day dawned and the sun began to shine, they recited the blessing after meals and left the table.

Even when the table conversation ostensibly was more casual, each word seemed to the disciples to be filled with meaning. Nahman's own brother Yehiel became his disciple after Nahman revealed to him the secret meanings contained in a seemingly ordinary conversation that had taken place around his table. At the same time, the love which Nahman and his disciples felt for one another was legendary; Nahman himself said that until the end of time men would be learning from the love that had existed among them, and that the love of master and disciple was like that of David and Jonathan, greater than that of man and woman. Nevertheless, this love was not something to be taken for granted; even the closest and most beloved disciples continued to approach Nahman in fear and trembling.[81]

The great demands Nahman made upon himself in the 'fashioning' of his disciples placed a tremendous strain on the young master who, as we have seen, was already plagued with great burdens of self-doubt and guilt. How can one who is at times so unsure of his own relationship to God place himself in the role of guide to others? What price is exacted of a man who, while still doing daily battle with his own temptations, speaks to others about the need to overcome their base desires? Nahman felt this tension constantly; the more he railed against false *ẓaddiqim*, the greater the pressure he felt to be the perfect master. The leader of the new Hasidic revival that he was proposing would have to be a man of absolute purity and integrity, one whose depths of learning, piety, and personal magnetism could challenge all the others. Many were the moments in which Nahman felt inadequate to the rôle he had created. At times he sought to justify his situation:

> Once there was a very rich man who had some tens of thousands [of rubles]. He let it be publicly known that he was willing to lend this money, and that whoever wanted to borrow should come to him. Of course there are always lots of takers for such an offer; many people came and borrowed from this man. He kept a record-book of all his accounts.
>
> Once the rich man took his record-book in his hands and began to look through it. He realized that he had invested a great deal of money in these loans, and that not a single one of the borrowers had come of his own accord to pay him back. He became deeply troubled about this.
>
> Now among those who had borrowed from this rich man there was a certain fellow who had lost all his money in a business venture and could in no way pay back the loan. He felt terribly distressed that he could not pay off his debt. Finally he decided that he would have to go see the rich man face to face, to tell him what was in his heart, that he was unable to do anything about it, and all the rest. He came before the rich man and told him [the entire story] . . . His creditor answered him: 'What do I care about the petty sum you owe me; it makes no difference to me whether you pay it off or not. What I am owed altogether goes into the tens of thousands! What I want of you rather is this: Go around to all my debtors, reminding them of what they owe and asking them to pay. Ask them why they haven't paid; even if you can collect a small percentage on each of those debts, it will come to several thousand times more than that which you owe . . .'[82]

Here the personal meaning of the parable is quite transparent. How can one who is himself a sinner assume the mantle of God's representative to others? Being a *rebbe* is nothing more than the way this poor sinner pays off his own debt to God, atoning for his own sins by bringing others to repentance.

Nahman's sense of fitness for his role as *rebbe* fluctuated with the ups and downs of his own personal and religious life. There were moments when he did seem fully convinced that he was fit to wear the mantle he had chosen. At such times he saw himself as a figure of impenetrable mystery, as one who could never be fully understood or appreciated until the end of time. With an audacity typical of such periods of elation, the young Nahman once said to his disciple Aaron, whom he later had designated as town rabbi of Bratslav, "I love you so much that I wish you be granted in the world to come the power to understand my ordinary conversations."[83] At such times he spoke of himself as one who had overcome all self-doubt, as one who was fully prepared to handle the task that lay before him. He once confided: "I used to think it was my evil urge that said to me: 'No one can lead the young people as well as you.' But now I know clearly that I really am the single leader of this generation in the world, and that there is no other leader like me."

He records a dream or vision in which he sees himself standing at the "royal table" and swimming in the "sea of wisdom," as all the kings of earth come and stand before him, hoping that some bit of his mystery will be revealed to them. When they reach the world of truth, all the *ẓaddiqim* will long to hear Nahman's teachings.[84]

These moments of extreme and seemingly arrogant self-confidence continued to alternate, in adulthood as in adolescence, with moments of the most bleak and overwhelming depression. The two states would sometimes come and go within minutes of one another. In one moment, recalls the faithful Nathan, his master would reveal teachings the like of which the world had never heard, while in the next moment he would be overcome by unbearable sadness, proclaiming that he knew nothing at all, that he did not even know how to begin to be a Jew. At such times he spoke of himself as a "lost sheep," struggling to return to the fold. Even daily prayers remained a struggle for Nahman in his adult life. Once, when unable to pray, he called out to Nathan: "Why do I have to struggle so hard in everything I do—as though I were giving my life for it?"[85] At times like this the hiddenness of his true self was not a matter of sublime mystery, but rather one of his own inner darkness. "You see in me a great, beautiful tree with wonderful branches," he exclaimed to his awestruck disciples, "but the roots of that tree are lying in Hell!"[86] Despite Nathan's claims to the contrary, such passages make it quite clear that the youthful conflicts which he so willingly and vividly describes as such were not ended as Nahman grew into adulthood.

Of Nahman's thoughts and teachings in this early period there survive only a slim volume of aphorisms and a very few teachings in his *Liqquṭim*.[87] After his return from Erez Israel in 1799 Nahman proclaimed that any of his teachings that dated from before that journey were relatively worthless and thus should not be studied or preserved.[88] As a result, there is almost no evidence in the *Liqquṭim* of Nahman's concerns as a young man. What we do know of his early teachings comes mainly through the aphorisms, entitled *Sefer ha-Middot* and first published in Mogilev in 1811.[89]

This alphabetical list of moral qualities, though it purports to be Nahman's selection of teachings he had learned from other authors, is a more nearly original work than is admitted; its originality emerges in the careful selection of materials as well as from not-infrequent reworkings of earlier sources. The work is ascribed by Nathan to the period of Nahman's "childhood."[90] While such a ledger-book of moral teachings may have been started while Nahman was at Usyatin, or still at Medzhibozh for that matter, a good deal of the material seems to reflect the experience of a young adult who has already begun to give serious thought to his role as a public figure. The ledger was probably kept open and added to over a good many years. Despite the claim that the maxims of this volume are based on earlier writings, one may gain from a careful reading of it a rather clear sense of certain emerging concerns in Nahman's thought. Because this document is so revealing of the early stages of Nahman's development, we shall quote from it at some length, setting it off against his later works, which are to be treated more fully below.

There are passages in *Sefer ha-Middot* where the reader has the impression that he is reading a collection of *hanhagot*, or rules for personal conduct, by some Hasidic leader other than Nahman. Here one does feel that the young master is paraphrasing the teachings of the BeSHT or the Maggid; the attitudes of early Hasidism are presented in ways that one seldom finds them in Nahman's later works.

> He who loves God in His eating, drinking, and other pleasures will merit to sustain many peoples.

> When you perform true deeds of lovingkindness with the *ẓaddiqim* you will come to know that all paths—prayer, eating, other pleasures—all are the way of God.[91]

Here we have the Hasidic motif of *'avodah ba-gashmiyut*, the service of God through corporeal things. "God needs to be served in all ways," taught the earlier masters, and all human acts, including the fulfillment of bodily needs, can become acts of worship. The grouping together of "prayer, eating, and other pleasures" is particularly reminiscent of passages in the *Me'or 'Eynayim* by Menahem Nahum of Chernobyl.[92] The attitudes of that work are a far cry from Nahman's preoccupation with the evils of excessive attachment to material pleasure, especially as reflected in eating:

> Overeating leads to a fall from faith.
> Coarse eating leads a man to adultery.[93]

It seems that these two attitudes co-existed in Nahman's mind: one *can* serve God through eating and drinking, but one must be constantly wary of excess. The latter concern has clearly come to dominate, as we shall see, in Nahman's later writings.

Early Hasidic views of prayer are also found in *Sefer ha-Middot* in formulations that are absent from Nahman's later works. The emphasis upon *devequt* and on prayer for the sake of the *shekhinah*, well-known particularly in the Miedzyrzec school, are seen in the early Nahman:

> Before prayer one must bind *(dabbeq)* his spirit to the Creator; this attachment will cause the words to flow of their own accord.

> He who prays only for the sake of the *shekhinah* will not be subject to distracting thoughts.[94]

The focus of prayer in Nahman's later writings is considerably more personal and petitionary; in the *hitbodedut* of the later Nahman it is clearly the self rather than the *shekhinah* which is the most immediate concern of prayer. Mystical prayer as described here has little place in Nathan's *Liqquṭey Tefillot* or in later Bratslav literature.

Simple Hasidic pronouncements on the importance of joy and the dangers of melancholy are also to be found scattered throughout the collection. The tortuous complexity of the struggle for joy, central to all Nahman's later reflections on the subject, is here not yet developed. Such statements as

> Joy opens the heart

or

> God is not with a person who is sad

seem to reflect the Ba'al Shem Tov more than they do Nahman. The idea that

> Prayer which is offered in joy is pleasant and sweet to God

is also typical of early Hasidic thinking.[95]

It would seem that what we have here are the reflections of a young man who seeks to immerse himself deeply in the world of the first Hasidic masters, particularly in the teachings of the BeSHT himself. That Nahman's inner conflicts are to lead him along a very different path has not yet been recognized. Indeed, *the attempt by the young Nahman to follow in the footsteps of his predecessors, while the complexities of his own life gave evidence that his religious needs were quite different from those prescribed, created the intense inner conflict out of which Nahman's later thought was to emerge.*

There are some areas where the particular concerns of the young Nahman as we have portrayed him are clearly seen in *Sefer ha-Middot*. The tremendous preoccupation with sexual sin and sinful thoughts is very frequently reflected in this little volume. The motifs of sexual desire for a non-Jewess, homosexual desires, and onanism are all to be found—with both their causes and dangers detailed. The reader is told, for example, that pride leads to homosexual lust, that the desire for a Gentile woman will cause one's children to convert, and all the rest.[96] Given the intensity of Nahman's own struggles in this area, one cannot help but feel the pain he must have experienced in recording some of these dour pronouncements.

Perhaps the most interesting section of *Sefer ha-Middot* as a reflection of Nahman's thought is the section on faith *('emunah)*. Nahman goes far beyond any of the Jewish sources he may have read in emphasizing the centrality of faith to the religious life. While Maimonides lists belief in God as the first of the commandments and there is much discussion in works of Jewish philosophy and theology as to the proper *content* of that belief, the tremendous emphasis Nahman places upon faith alone as the way to God and upon the need for absolute purity of faith is quite unique. Thus we find such statements as

> One must believe in God in the way of faith and not in the way of proof.
>
> Through faith, the Holy one, blessed be He, will forgive all your sins.
>
> By means of faith a man can come to understand God.
>
> He who has faith will afterwards merit to serve God with great understanding *(da'at)*.
>
> Faith will increase your livelihood.
>
> Picture the letters of the word *'emunah* before you and you will never be disgraced.[97]

The longest single statement in the book, which takes the form of a direction given man by God, also deals with faith, and should be quoted in its entirety:

> When a person begins to serve God, the Holy One, blessed be He, says to him: 'I know that your [present] desire is to serve Me, but what assurance am I given? Suppose you leave Me tomorrow? In that case, how can I draw you near to Me, knowing only of your good will, and reveal secret things to you? Rather do this—at first love Me this way; do my commandments even though you do not know the reasons for them. Serve Me simply and without cleverness, but serve Me constantly. Then I will have faith in you and will reveal to you the meaning of each thing and the reason for it. I will draw you near to Me in all kinds of ways, for the time in which you have already served Me will be My assurance.'[98]

A most revealing statement. We shall see later that Nahman does not hesitate to draw parallels between man's relationship to God and that of the disciple to his master. Is it really God here who needs to be assured of the constancy of love before He can draw the other near and reveal secrets—or might it not be the insecure young master speaking through these lines? Or might we do better to find in them another early attempt at self-justification? Years spent in seemingly unrewarded spiritual struggle cry out for explanation. The claim here that devotion which seems to have no meaning ultimately will find both its explanation and its reward is one which Nahman could hardly afford not to assert.

A far less surprising preoccupation of this collection is the motif of the *ẓaddiq*. False *ẓaddiqim* and unscrupulous communal leaders are denounced in several passages,[99] while a great deal of attention is focused upon the powers and role of the true *ẓaddiq*. Quite a few of the statements in this, the longest single section of the book, are repetitions of what is to be found elsewhere in Hasidic literature, but a number of them are peculiarly reflective of the direction of Nahman's thinking. "It is better to be close to a *ẓaddiq* who is merciful" may intend a negative comment on Barukh of Medzhibozh, who was known for his angry mien.[100] "A person can be a *ẓaddiq* even if he has not studied much" is an unusually frank admission of what was accepted practice in certain early Hasidic circles. However, "a person can be a *ẓaddiq* even if he doesn't have complete trust (in God)" is a more original thought, and one that grows out of Nahman's own situation. Similarly, such statements as "Sometimes suffering comes upon the *ẓaddiq* in order to lessen the sorrows of Israel" and "sufferings by the *ẓaddiq* are atonement for all of Israel," introducing the notions of vicarious suffering and atonement to the figure of the *ẓaddiq*, must be seen as personal attempts at self-explanation. While *Sefer ha-Middot* does mention that "the *ẓaddiq* can raise the dead to a high rung,"[101] we are specifically told elsewhere that the major theme of *ẓaddiq* as redeemer, engaged in the restoration of the souls of both the living and the dead, a theme which plays so great a role in Nahman's later thought, was first developed by him after his return from Erez Israel.

With this survey of the major themes in *Sefer ha-Middot* we conclude our tale of Nahman's early years. The picture we have drawn is that of a young man possessing deep and painfully-acquired religious insight, of one both driven by dreams of greatness and tormented by self-doubt and guilt. The young *ẓaddiq* was already beginning to acquire a name for himself in the Hasidic circles of the Ukraine, by virtue of both his family background and his unique and exacting style of leadership. The full fruits of Nahman's labors were not to be felt, however, until he had passed through what is perhaps the most fascinating and often misunderstood event of his life: his mysterious journey to Erez Israel. It is to the preparations for this journey that we must now turn our attention.

NOTES

1. The centralization of Hasidism under the leadership of Dov Baer should not be overstated. By no means all of the Ba'al Shem Tov's followers had accepted the Maggid as their master's successor. Both Jacob Joseph of Polonnoye and Pinhas of Korets, to name two of the people closest to the BeSHT, refused to accept the

authority of Dov Baer. Nevertheless, not counting the rather small circle around Medzhibozh in the BeSHT's last years, Miedzyrzec was the closest Hasidism ever came to having a single center.

2. *Ḥayyey* 4:1. Aaron David Twerski, in his frequently useful *Sefer ha-Yaḥas mi-Chernobyl we-Ruzhin,* gives the date of Nahman's birth as the eighteenth of Tishrey, 1769 (p.100). This date is not verified by any other source.

3. There is some confusion as to the year of the elder brother's birth. See the discussion by Heschel in HUCA 23, pt.2 (1950–51), Hebrew Section, 17, *n*.63.

4. The rabbi of Ostrog from 1777–1790 was Meir Margulies, who as a young man had considered himself to be a follower of the BeSHT, and continued to support the Hasidic effort. His *Sod Yakhin u-Vo'az* was published in Ostrog, 1794, with approbations by such leading Hasidic figures as Levi Yizhak of Berdichev and Zusya of Anipol. (Biber, *Mazkeret le-Gedoley Ostrog,* p.198*ff.)* As chief rabbi of the Ukraine *(ibid.,* p.200) during those crucial years of the spread of Hasidism, Meir Margulies probably had a great deal to do with the success of the movement. The religious life of the Jews in Korets was under the influence of Pinhas Shapira, known as Pinhas of Korets, where he served as preacher until sometime in the 1780s. As a result of his conflict with the disciples of Dov Baer, led by Shelomo of Lutsk, Pinhas was forced to move to Ostrog, where he died in 1791 *(ibid.,* p.211*ff.).* Pinhas has been studied by M.Y. Guttmann *(Rabbi Pinhas mi-Korets)* and A.J. Heschel ("Le-Toledot R. Pinhas mi-Korets"). Of his four sons, three became rabbis in the important communities of Zaslav, Slavuta, and Shepetovka, contributing greatly to the dominance of Hasidism in Volhynia. Moshe, the rabbi of Slavuta, also founded a printing press in that city, which issued Kabbalistic and Hasidic works. *See* H. Lieberman, "Le-Toledot ha-Defus ha-'Ivri be-Slavuta", *Qiryat Sefer* 27 (1958) 358*ff.*

5. He is referred to as *'av bet din* in the *haskamot* to *Degel Maḥaneh Ephraim.*

6. *Degel Maḥaneh Ephraim,* 11b and 48b.

7. Barukh's teachings are recorded in *Buẓina di-Nehora,* Lemberg, 1880, and at the end of *Ḥesed le-Avraham,* Chernovtsy, 1851.

8. This story is told in *Buẓina di-Nehora* p. 63*f.*, and is quoted by Dubnov, *op. cit.*, p.209. Dubnov's dislike for Barukh of Medzhibozh carries him beyond the bounds of objective scholarship. Thus when the rabbi of Sudilkov denounces the false *ẓaddiqim,* Dubnov assumes it is because "he wants to return Hasidism to its simplicity of the days of the BeSHT" (p.207). The same denunciations in the mouth of Barukh are taken to be the presumptuousness of an arrogant "businessman" staving off competition (p.211). While Barukh indeed was more in the center of the political fray than was his brother, Dubnov's judgments are far too extreme. See chapter three for further discussion of Barukh and the conflicts surrounding him. Perhaps Dubnov's views on Barukh are still overly influenced by the ugly caricature of him in A. B. Gottlober's memoirs, *Zikhronot u-Masa'ot*, v.1, p.167*ff.*

9. Dubnov, *op. cit.*, p.212. Witness to the harsh and often frightening character of Barukh are the story of how Hayyim of Chernovtsy, a leading Kabbalistic author of his time, stood in awe of him *(Buẓina di-Nehora,* p.62*f.)* and Barukh's own confession to Menahem Nahum of Chernobyl, to whom he once supposedly said: "People think of me as an angry master *(a bayzen guter yid),* while you are thought of as a good master." (Twerski, *op. cit.*, p.3)

10. For a discussion of the date of the elder Nahman's death, see I. Halpern,

Ha-'Aliyot ha-Rishonot shel ha-Ḥasidim le-'Ereẓ Yisra'el, p.19. Sometime before the death of the Ba'al Shem Tov in 1760 Nahman of Horodenka took up residence in Medzhibozh, where his brother Aryeh Leib served as town rabbi during the BeSHT's lifetime. *Cf.* Heschel in *YIVO Bleter* 36 (1952) 117.

11. The quotations in Jacob Joseph's works are listed in S. Dresner's *The Zaddik*, p.311*f.*, *n.*52. The Jerusalem, 1963, edition of the *Degel* has a list of quotations on the last page.

12. Their journey and settlement is described by Simhah ben Joshua of Zalozhtsy in his *Sippurey 'Ereẓ ha-Galil*, first published in his *Ahavat Ẓiyyon*, Grodno, 1790, and reprinted in A. Yaari's *Masa'ot 'Ereẓ Yisra'el*.

13. Koenig, *Neweh Ẓaddiqim*, p.9. The family of the Ba'al Shem Tov also claimed Davidic lineage, via the descendants of R. Moses Isserles. *Cf.* Twerski, *op. cit.*, p.101.

14. *Naḥal Nove'a*, p.8*ff.*

15. *Shivḥey ha-Rav*, p.3.

16. *Shivḥey ha-BeSHT*, p.13.

17. *Shivḥey* 13.

18. Nathan's follower, Nahman of Cheryn, composed a topically arranged anthology of Hasidic sources, *Derekh Ḥasidim*. He chose not to include in it any quotations from Bratslav sources, in order to make it acceptable to anti-Bratslav Hasidic groups. It is interesting to note that the section *raẓon we-kissufim* ("desire and longing") in that volume, which it was perfectly natural for a Bratslav *ḥasid* to include as a major theme, contains almost nothing! When he set the Bratslav works aside, the editor was hard-pressed to find any emphasis on this in Hasidic writings.

19. *Shivḥey* 11–12.

20. *Shivḥey* 10. For the motif of nearness and distance from God in Bratslav *cf.* *Shivḥey* 10 and 12; *Liqquṭim* 63, 261, and the third and fourth episodes in the *Seven Beggars*. The terms are also used constantly in Nathan's volume of prayers, *Liqquṭey Tefillot*. The Bratslav usage is most reminiscent of such passages as Ps. 22:12, 20; 35:22; 73:28, etc.

21. *Shivḥey* 19.

22. *Ibid.* 1. On his mother's concern for Nahman's health during later periods of fasting, *cf.* *Ḥayyey II* 1:9.

23. J. Becker, *R. Nahman mi-Bratslav, Meḥqar Psikho'analiti.*

24. Cf. the reference to his father in the letter published at the end of *Ḥayyey* 6, the reference to a visit with his parents in *Shivḥey II* 15, and the further reference in *Ṭovot Zikhronot* 5.

25. The Hebrew *meguddal be-tafnuq* could have either meaning.

26. *Yemey MaHaRNaT*, p.84; *'Avaneha Barzel*, p.18.

27. *Shivḥey* 7. The *sifrey mussar* ("ethical tracts") would include the early works of Hasidism, which were published beginning in 1780 and a number of which were thus available to Nahman as an adolescent. Nahman does not quote other Hasidic authors at all and it is difficult to determine just which works he had read. Minimally it is certain that the works of Jacob Joseph and some writings from the school of the Maggid were part of his library. *Peri 'Eẓ Ḥayyim* is a compendium that applies the Lurianic system to the liturgical calendar and was very popular in Hasidic circles. *Reshit Ḥokhmah* is a work of Kabbalistic ethics by Elijah de Vidas

(1550–1587); *'Eyn Ya'aqov* is a compendium of the non-legal sections of the Talmud, edited and supplied with a commentary by Jacob Ibn Habib *(ca.*1459–1516). Both these works were frequently printed and very widely read in Eastern Europe, and were accessible to those with even only the rudiments of a Talmudic education. It is noteworthy that the earliest teachings in Nahman's *Liqquṭim* take the form of extended commentaries on the fantastic tales of Rabbah bar bar Hana (Baba Batra 73–74), showing an attraction to fantasy that long predated his turn to original storytelling. On the importance of the Bible to Nahman, see the quote attributed to him in *Sippurim Nifla'im,* p.113: "My 'ethical tract' is the Bible."

28. *Shivḥey* 8; *Shivḥey II* 4. The practice of constant meditation on the name YHWH is first mentioned by Isaiah Horowitz in *Sheney Luḥot ha-Berit,* ed. Fürth, 1764, 329b, in the name of an elder from Safed. As for the practice of Nahman of Kosov, *cf. Shivḥey ha-BeSHT,* p.55, and Heschel in *H. A. Wolfson Jubilee Volume,* Hebrew Section, p. 113*ff.*, and especially *n.*4, p. 117. On study in early Hasidism *cf.* J. Weiss in *Essays Presented to Chief Rabbi Israel Brodie, p. 151ff.* and the remarks by R. Schatz in *Ha-Ḥasidut ke-Mistiqah,* p.157*ff.*

29. The powerful tale told to illustrate this point in *'Avaneha Barzel,* p.22*f.*, does however seem to be of late origin.

30. *Ḥayyey II* 2:6, 54; 4:29.

31. *Ḥayyey II* 2:1, *Cf.* also *Siḥot* 158: "He said that . . . when he was a young man . . . and had not yet reached the point where he could remain attached to God and involved with Torah even while talking to people . . . 'it was difficult for me to be among people,' for all he wanted was to be involved in the service of God . . ." The ability to retain this dual consciousness was essential to the very existence of the Hasidic *ẓaddiq*. On its roots in earlier Judaism *cf.* Scholem, *Messianic Idea* p.203*ff.* and J. Weiss in JJS 8 (1959) 199 *n.*3. The BeSHT also had to struggle to maintain the simultaneous holding of these two levels of consciousness. *Cf. Shivḥey ha-BeSHT,* p.110.

32. *Siḥot* 57, 190. On a parallel concern in Nathan's life *cf. 'Avaneha Barzel,* p.3. This seems to indicate an affinity of personality between master and disciple essential to any attempt to study Nathan or to sort out the part of each of them in the editing of Nahman's writings.

33. On Nahman's relationship to death *cf.* J. Weiss, *Meḥqarim,* p. 172*ff.*

34. *Liqquṭim* 193. The original is written in the third person. On Akiva *cf. Berakhot* 61.

35. *Ẓawa'at RIVaSH* 4b-5a, 6b-7a; *Liqquṭim Yeqarim* la; *Siftey Ẓaddiqim* 29c.

36. *Shivḥey* 3; *Ḥayyey* 4:2. *Neweh Ẓaddiqim* is the source for Nahman's wife's name, which is not mentioned by Nathan. Nahman's father-in-law came from a well-known family in Zaslav.

37. Medzhibozh is one of the oldest Jewish communities in the Ukraine. Jews are mentioned as having lived there as early as 1518. Joel Sirkes (1561–1640), author of the *Bayit Ḥadash,* served as rabbi there for a time. As late as 1897, after migration patterns had decreased the percentage of Jews in many Russian towns, the Jews still comprised 73.9 percent of the Medzhibozh population. *Cf. Encyclopedia Judaica* s.v. Medzhibozh.

38. *Ḥayyey* 4:4; *Siḥot* 162.

39. *Ḥayyey II 1:1: Siḥot* 117; *Liqquṭim* 65:1–2; *II* 11. Nahman's love for the outdoors is also reflected in several of his tales.

40. When Nahman and Simeon were together in Istanbul on their way to the Holy Land, Simeon spoke to others as though he were Nahman's older chaperone: "I am accompanying this young man *(rakh be-shanim)* to the Holy Land" *(Shivḥey II* 9). This could only be said by one who appeared significantly older.

41. *Ḥayyey* 4:2–3; *Neweh Ẓaddiqim* p.16.

42. *Ḥayyey* 4:3.

43. *Ḥayyey II* 11:8.

44. *Shivḥey* 9,19,20,24. Isaiah of Yanov was a contemporary of the BeSHT. *Cf.* A. Walden, *Shem ha-Gedolim he-Ḥadash,* p.73, #286. Heschel has shown him to be none other than Isaiah of Dinovits, the editor of *Ẓawa'at RIVaSH. YIVO Bleter* 36 (1954) 122.

45. *Ḥayyey* 4:7; *Siḥot* 117.

46. An important difference is to be noted between this tale and that of the BeSHT: the BeSHT calls forth the dead by performing *yiḥudim,* while Nahman does so by insistent appeal to God. The quasi-magical elements of the BeSHT's religious life have disappeared in Nahman.

47. *Siḥot* 57.

48. *Shivḥey* 16. The closing phrase is based upon the Talmudic dictum (Soṭah 3a) that a man does not sin unless the spirit of folly enters him. Here this "folly" is taken to be madness. Is it possible to learn from here that the intensity of Nahman's youthful struggles aroused in him a fear that he would go mad?

49. For a few among many examples, *cf. Reshit Ḥokhmah, sha'ar ha-qedushah* 17; *Sheney Luḥot ha-Berit, sha'ar ha-'otiyot* s.v. *qedushah; Ṭaharat ha-Qodesh* II 24b–25b. This last-named work, typical of the non-Hasidic *mussar* literature of eighteenth-century Poland, refers to this as "one of the worst sins of the Torah" and prescribes penance for it which includes "great mortifications, practically unto death." Kabbalistic literature, beginning with the *Zohar,* was much concerned with sexual sin, and particularly with onanism. This is an area in which mystical preaching greatly affected later halakhic stringencies. According to the *Zohar,* 1:62a and especialy 1:219b, repentance is not possible for this sin, which brings about irreparable damage in the upper spheres. The authors of *Reshit Ḥokhmah* and *Sheney Luḥot ha-Berit* are deeply troubled by this notion of an unforgivable sin and offer various attempts to resolve the *Zohar's* seeming intransigence. *Cf.* also the halakhic sources quoted by R. Margulies in *Niẓoẓey Zohar* to 1:219b. The great value Nahman placed upon his *Tiqqun ha-Kelali,* a group of ten psalms to be recited for the expiation of sexual sin, is to be found here. The new Simeon ben Yohai now reveals that which he had kept hidden in the *Zohar:* a way to relieve oneself of the burden of this greatest and most basic of sins. *Cf. Liqquṭim* 29 and *Siḥot* 71. Further Hasidic sources on *ṭume'at qeri* are listed by Heschel in the *Wolfson Jubilee Volume,* p.139*f.*, *n*.32 and by R. Schatz in *op. cit.*, p.48.*f.*

It should also be noted that the *mussar* sources often applied the Talmudic adage "Sinful thoughts are worse than sin" (Yoma 29a) to this area. *Cf.* the interesting explanation in *Galey Razaya* p.9, to the effect that deeds bear heavily on one's conscience and therefore call forth immediate repentance, while thoughts alone, sinful as they are, often go unrepented and are thus more likely to continue to eat away at man's moral fibre. It seems likely that this was the case with Nahman: it was thoughts and desires that ever continued to torment him and that no act of penance sufficed to dismiss.

50. *Ḥayyey II* 11:149; *Liqquṭim II* 79.
51. *Shivḥey* 16.
52. *Ḥayyey II* 1:4–5; 11:84; *Shivḥey* 18. The Talmudic source is Nedarim 20b.
53. *Shivḥey* 16. M. Piekarz has shown (p.193*ff.*) that Nahman was familiar with *Sefer ha-Berit* by Pinhas Elijah Horowitz, first published in Brünn, 1797, when Nahman was twenty-five years old. That work contains (v.1, sections 16–17) a treatise on anatomy, which may have been the basis of Nahman's knowledge in that area. Horowitz, an early *maskil* of the traditionalist sort, makes extensive use of Kabbalistic sources as well as eighteenth-century science, medicine, and philosophy. It is interesting to note that he, too, involves himself in the above-mentioned (*n.*49) discussion as to whether there is possible penance for onanism. *Cf. Sefer ha-Berit* 17:3, ed. Brünn, 124b.
54. His son Jacob, whose birth is mentioned in *Yemey MaHaRNaT*, p.27.
55. *Shivḥey* 17. Scholem records a childhood dream of Sabbatai Ṣevi (p.113, 226) in which he saw his sexual organ consumed in fire. This, too, was later taken as a sign of special purity.
56. Abraham Ḥazan, quoted in *Neweh Ẓaddiqim*, p.79.
57. *Ḥayyey II* 1:8, *Shivḥey* 21; *Ḥayyey* 3:12. For descriptions of the extremity of Nahman's fasting *cf. Siḥot* 160–161. On this dream, see the further discussion in chapter two.
58. *Ḥayyey* 4:5.
59. *Shivḥey* 5–6. While definite dating is impossible, it is my assumption that this passage refers to Nahman's adolescence, rather than to early childhood.
60. On traditional Jewish attitudes toward suffering and on the history of term *yissurim shel 'ahavah cf.* Heschel, *Torah min ha-Shamayim*, v.1, p.93*ff.* and Urbach, *ḤaZaL*, p.392*ff.*
61. *Ḥayyey* 4:5 *Kokhvey 'Or*, p.66, tells a story of how Nahman first came to the attention of the local folk, through his unusual teaching of a Mishnah passage at the synagogue of nearby Aleksandrovka.
62. This is the term commonly used in the Bratslav literature (lit. "a famous one"), perhaps chosen because of its neutrality. Elsewhere in Hasidic writings he may be referred to as *ẓaddiq le-'aẓmo ule-aḥerim*, as opposed to the *nistar*, who is only *ẓaddiq le-'aẓmo*.
63. *See* Scholem on "Zaddik, der Gerechte" in *Von der mystischen Gestalt der Gottheit* and on "The Tradition of the Thirty-Six Hidden Just Men" in *Messianic Idea*.
64. The famous *Saba de-Mishpaṭim* who makes his appearance in *Zohar* 2:94b is such a figure, as is the mule driver (1:5a) who turns out to be R. Himnuna the Elder. A special type of hidden *ẓaddiq* is the *yenoqa* (Wunderkind) who appears in 3:186a and elsewhere.
65. Typical of such passages are *'Or Torah* 119b, *No'am Elimelekh*, p.75, *parashat shelaḥ*. The Maggid himself once confided that he saw his fame as a punishment for his sins! *'Eser 'Orot*, p.25.
66. *Ḥayyey* 4:4 and 8; 8:12–13; *Liqquṭim* 18:2. According to the last of these sources, leadership is of necessity thrust upon the *ẓaddiq*, who never feels himself adequate to it. It is only his compassion for the folk that keeps him from fleeing the role altogether and ultimately leads him to an acceptance of his duty. This teaching is dated winter, 1804. *See also Ḥayyey* 1:59, which is the major source for dating

the teachings in the *Liqquṭim*.

The following parable, told in *Shivḥey II* 36, sheds much light on Nahman's attitude toward his having become a public figure:

> A king once sent three men to a certain country with a secret message for another king. They had to pass through various provinces which were peopled by the king's enemies. The first man conducted himself very cleverly, and passed through these lands without anybody having any idea that he bore a secret message. But when the second man came through, the people realized what was happening, and they captured him, hoping to force him to reveal the secret to them. By means of cleverness or bravery, he managed to escape his captors. The third messenger was also captured, but this one was tortured terribly in many different ways. He managed to withstand all the tortures until finally they decided that he must know nothing, and so they let him free. He then returned to the king.
>
> It was then debated which of the messengers should receive the greatest reward. Some said that the first should be rewarded most handsomely, for he had kept the secret best. Others preferred the second, for even though they had understood what was happening, he was clever enough to get away. But the king decided that it was the third who should be most highly rewarded, for he had been caught in their trap . . . and had been so tormented. Ḥad he revealed but one of the secrets, everyone would have run after him [with honors]. But despite this, he withstood the test, and thus he deserved the greatest reward.

That this statement is about Nahman himself is seen by the parallel statement in the first person, quoted earlier in this chapter (*n.*30). The view of the masses of *ḥasidim* as dangerous forces, "enemies of the king" who catch the *ẓaddiq* in their trap is clearly a radicalized outgrowth of the relationship between *ẓaddiq* and community as portrayed in the *Toledot*, and prefigures the despair of the Kotzker with the role some forty years later. It is of course typical of Nahman to assert that he who has suffered most—even though this third messenger hardly seems to have succeeded better in his mission than the others—is deserving of the greatest reward.

67. *Ḥayyey* 6:4; *Ḥayyey II* 2:23. See *Ḥayyey II* 2:19: "He thought that he would take his wife and go live in some far-off place, hidden from the public. Sometimes he would go out to the market to have a look at the world—and to laugh at it." See also the letters appended to *Ḥayyey* 6. From the first of these letters, written during his Navritch journey, it does not appear that he planned to return to Bratslav at all. *The Master of Prayer* dates from early in 1810. See also *Ḥayyey* 8:12–13, discussed by Piekarz, p.41.

68. *Ḥayyey* 4:5; *Neweh Ẓaddiqim* p.20. There is occasional mention of Dov Baer of Zaslav (Izyaslav) in Hasidic sources. He is mentioned in *Shivḥey ha-BeSHT*, p.46, in connection with Pinhas of Korets, one of whose sons married his daughter. He later settled in Erez Israel. Y. Alfasi (*Sefer ha-'ADMORim*, p.18, #8) speaks of him as a disciple of the BeSHT, one of the first *ḥasidim* to be chosen as rabbi of a major town. His son-in-law, Ya'aqov Shime'on, the son of Pinhas of Korets, succeeded him in the Zaslav rabbinate. *Ibid*, p.15, #B4.

69. The years in which Nahman's daughters were born are nowhere mentioned. It is recorded that his daughter Odel was married in Elul, 5560 (summer, 1800); *cf. Ḥayyey* 4:11. The earliest possible age for marriage ordinarily being twelve years, she was born by 1788, when Nahman was sixteen years old and living at Usyatin. The next recorded marriage among Nahman's daughters was that of Sarah, which took place on her father's thirty-first birthday in 1803 *(Yemey MaHaRNaT* p.13). According to *Shivḥey II* 6 he had three daughters in 1798, when he set out for the Holy Land. It seems that the middle daughter in age was betrothed, while her older sister was not. Assuming this middle child to be Odel, whose marriage was then performed on her father's return, there would be a child born before 1788—perhaps when Nahman himself was fourteen or fifteen years old.

70. *Ḥayyey* 4:4–5, 7–9. Nahman is quoted here as saying that he would even prefer begging to accepting such a stipend for support. The fact is, however, that he did accept it.

71. Bratslav is clearly described as a revival movement in *Ḥayyey* 2:19. This is also reflected in the conversation between Nahman and Gedaliah of Linits recorded in *'Avaneha Barzel* p.16*f*. These passages will be further discussed below, in chapter four.

72. *Ḥayyey II* 3:80; 11:5. *Cf.* also *Liqquṭim* 123.

73. *Ḥayyey II* 3:87; *'Avaneha Barzel* p.8.

74. *Ḥayyey II* 1:11. *Cf.* the interesting parallels—in Freud and Luther—cited by Erikson, *Young Man Luther*, p.9. Nahman was by no means the only *ẓaddiq* to complain of being bothered by the petty needs of his followers. *Cf.* for example the similar complaints of R. Abraham Kalisker in his letters in *Peri ha-Areẓ*, 45b–46a. The influence of Bratslav on Kotsk is yet to be studied.

75. Dashev is a smaller town near Bratslav. The fact that Dashev had become a major center of his disciples may have been a contributing factor to Nahman's choice of Bratslav as a location for himself when he moved there in 1802.

76. It is not simply coincidence that it was *ḥasidim* from the school of Pinhas of Korets who first found Nahman's teachings so attractive. The two have much in common, as distinct from the more abstract metaphysical school of Miedzyrzec. Heschel (*'Aley 'Ayin* p.223*ff*.) has characterized Pinhas' teaching as one that emphasized the need to struggle for moral improvement before seeking initiation into the Kabbalistic mysteries. The description of Pinhas in Heilman's *Bet Rabbi*, p. 89, is most instructive:

> From Rabbi Pinhas of Korets our teacher [Shne'ur Zalman of Liadi] received humility and truth. This holy rabbi was a very humble and honest man, who struggled for twenty-one years to find the truth. Seven years he spent on determining what is true, seven years on uprooting falsehood from within himself, and seven more years on implanting that truth in its place. This was because he sought to utterly banish the darkness before bringing in the light.

All this is contrasted by Heilman and Heschel with the approach of the Maggid, who believed that light itself would dispel the darkness, i.e. that the study of Kabbalah and intense mystical devotion *(devequt)* would themselves bring about a change in the personality and the moral conduct of the disciple. In such a dichotomization, Nahman seems somewhat closer to the view of R. Pinhas. For Pinhas' attitude toward questions of faith and doubt, which is also not far from that of Nahman, *cf.* the interesting story published by Heschel in *YIVO Bleter* 36 (1954) 132*f.* It should be clear that we do not claim that Pinhas and Nahman were less interested in Kabbalah than was the Miedzyrzec school; the argument concerns proper preparation for such studies, not the essential value of the Kabbalistic tradition. The views of Pinhas will be discussed further in chapter three in connection with Barukh of Medzhibozh.

77. It is possible that this depression had something to do with his children. *Cf. Kokhvey Or* p.24, *n.*5. The reference in that note, however, is inaccurate. In any case, it is noteworthy that the truth of Nahman's path became known to Dov in response to his personal despair; this is entirely appropriate to all we know of Nahman's teachings.

78. This story is told in *Siḥot* 292, *Kokhvey Or* pp.24–30, and *Neweh Ẓaddiqim* pp.20–24. A rather different version of it, in which the confession is not initiatory, is preserved in *Ṭovot Zikhronot* 4. *Cf.* the discussion by Albert in the article quoted in the following note, p.70*f.*

79. On the matter of confession in Bratslav see the very important article by Ada Rapoport Albert, "Confession in the Circle of R. Nahman of Braslav," *Bulletin of the Institute of Jewish Studies* 1 (1973) 65*ff.* That very thorough treatment quotes all the major sources on confession to Nahman, particularly during his stay in Zlotopolye (1800–1802). Albert claims that the institution of confession was discontinued by Nahman, probably just as he moved to Bratslav in 1802, for reasons unknown to us. It is indeed significant that we have no evidence of such practices from later in Nahman's lifetime. I am generally in agreement with Albert's conclusions, though I would add the few following notes. I am not fully convinced that confession to the *ẓaddiq* ceased as early as 1802. It is hard to imagine that the term *widuiniks,* later a popular designation for Bratslav *ḥasidim,* actually has as its reference-point only this brief two-year period when Nahman lived in relative obscurity. Nahman of Cheryn, in his *Parpera'ot le-Hokhmah,* New York, 1955, 5b, to *Liqquṭim* 4 speaks of the virtues of confession at the pilgrimage to Nahman's grave, which has such a place of importance in Bratslav Hasidism. Though such confession is addressed to God Himself, it is the deceased *ẓaddiq* who "brings the confession up before Him." I must also add some reservation concerning Albert's claim that confession *fully* atoned for sin, and that *tiqqunim* (penances) were directed toward the correction of future behavior, not toward atonement. The term *tiqqun* itself makes such a reading problematical: it is an ellipsis for *tiqqun ha-pegam,* the repair of that cosmic damage wrought by sin. The statement that *tiqqunim* "had nothing to do with atonement for the sin confessed" seems to me to be going much too far. Albert is driven into this position by applying too rigorous a logic to Nahman's highly unsystematic way of thinking, feeling forced to choose between the view that confession either does or does not atone. It seems better to say that confession is an essential but in itself not completely adequate part of penance; *tiqqunim* prescribed by the confessor complete the atonement. The same is true, by the way, of the sacrament of penance in the Catholic Church: absolution granted by the priest is contingent upon the performance of the deeds of penance which he prescribes.

As regards the content of confessions, there is a most interesting reference in Eliezer Zweifel's *Shalom 'al Yisra'el.* Zweifel, the first of the *maskilim* to see beyond the struggle with Hasidism and to appreciate the movement's importance, notes (v.3, p.30*f.)* that the subject of confession in Hasidism is almost always sexual sin, and cannot understand why this is emphasized "more than the most serious sins according to the Torah, to the point where all those coming before the *ẓaddiq* mention . . . only the damaging of the covenant [i.e., sexual sins], which they consider to be the most serious of offenses. They do so despite the fact that some authorities hold onanism to be only a rabbinic prohibition . . ." This record of the content of most confessions fits perfectly with Nahman's own obsession with sexual guilt and the need for *tiqqun* in this area of life. From p.37 of that section of *Shalom 'al Yisra'el* it is clear that Zweifel was reading Bratslav sources as he composed that part of his book. The *maskil,* having a much more liberal outlook on *halakhah* in this area, feigns a naive shock at the extent of sexual preoccupation in the confessions. He seems to have had some source, now lost to us, that told him what Bratslav confessions were largely about.

80. *Ḥayyey II* 3:51; *Sippurim Nifla'im* 168.

81. Quotation from *Ḥayyey II* 1:11. Other sources are *Liqquṭim* 135; *Ḥayyey II* 3:52, 78; 11:26.

82. *Ḥayyey II* 11:4.

83. *Ḥayyey II* 11:63. It is there stated that this conversation took place before Nahman's journey to Erez Israel.

84. *Ḥayyey II* 2:18; *Ḥayyey* 3:1; 5:19–20. This last remark is also dated as preceding the journey to the Holy Land.

85. *Liqquṭim* 206; *Ḥayyey* 1:10,24,59; 8:31; *Ḥayyey II* 4:2. Nathan's fullest description of his master's depressed states is found in his *Liqquṭey Halakhot, tefillin* 5:5 and is discussed by Piekarz, p.42.

86. *Ḥayyey II* 2:5. The preserved Hebrew version of the statement, which concludes with *"ule-maṭah 'ani munaḥ ba-'areẓ mamash,"* has lost the punch of what was clearly the oral Yiddish original: *"ober fun unten lig ikh take in dr'erd"!* At the same time, however, this passage is a reflex of Daniel 4:11–12, immediately following on Daniel 4:10 *('ir we-qadish min shemaya neḥit)*, which is taken in Bratslav literature as an acronym for Simeon and an esoteric way of referring to Nahman. *Cf.* Nathan's introduction to the *Liqquṭim*. What we have here, then, is a complicated double pun, in which Nahman both bemoans his lowly state and hints at his exalted origins.

87. *Liqquṭim* 1 *(cf. Ṭovot Zikhronot* 1–2) and 96 belong to his days in Medvedevka.

88. *Ḥayyey* 1:55; *Ḥayyey II* 4:18, 43; 11:33.

89. In fact *Sefer ha-Middot* contains two separate alphabetical lists of moral qualities, but it is only the first list that is ascribed to "the time of his youth." All the following quotations are from the first alphabet.

90. The writing and publication of *Sefer ha-Middot* is discussed at length by Koenig in *Neweh Ẓaddiqim* p.47*ff.*

91. *Mammon* 39; *Da'at* 31. The term *ḥesed shel emet,* used in the second passage, usually refers to honoring the dead and participation in burial rites. It is not clear whether it has that connotation here.

92. First published in Slavuta, 1798. The author was a disciple of the BeSHT who did accept the Maggid as his master after the BeSHT's death. His work, however, generally reflects rather little of the Miedzyrzec influence, and seems quite close to what we know of the BeSHT's teachings. On the religious meaning of eating and drinking *cf.* pp. 23 *(lekh lekha)*, 147 *('emor)*, and 169 *(maṭṭot)*. Accord-

ing to *Neweh Ẓaddiqim* p.14, the *ẓaddiq* of Chernobyl, who died in 1797, met the young Nahman and spoke highly of him. Other Hasidic masters, aware of the potential for vulgarization in *'avodah ba-gashmiyut*, limited the 'sacred' qualities of eating and drinking to the *ẓaddiq* himself, *Cf. No'am Elimelekh, qoraḥ*.

93. *'Emunah* 13; *Ni'uf* 50.

94. *Tefillah* 76; *Hirhurim* 37. For parallels, *cf.* Schatz, *op. cit.*, chapters 3, 8–9. The theme of *maḥashavah zarah*, the distracting thought that keeps one from concentration in prayer, is very widely discussed in early Hasidism. *Liqquṭim* 96, dating from before 1798, is also concerned with this subject. It is seldom mentioned in Nahman's later writings. Where the essential prayer activity is Bratslav-style *hitbodedut*, broken-hearted conversation with God, free association within the mind is desirable and *maḥashavah zarah* ceases to be a problem. For a discussion of the uplifting of distracting thoughts in early Hasidism *cf.* Weiss in *Zion* 16 (1951) 88*ff.* and Jacobs, *Hasidic Prayer*, chapter 9.

95. *Simḥah* 2; *cf.* also 8, 14. *'Aẓvut* 14; also *Hamtaqat ha-Din* 99. *Tefillah* 81; the classic expression of such a thought in Hasidism is found in *Ẓawa'at RIVaSH*, 13a.

96. *Ga'awah* 2; *Hirhurim* 39. *Cf.* also *Hirhurim* 50–51, 58; *Ni'uf* 1, 4, 26, 33, 39, 41; *Banim* 41; *Pidyon* 6, 11.

97. *'Emunah* 1, 33, 31; *Da'at* 17; *Mammon* 28; *Bushah* 9. The last of these statements involves a transference from contemplation of the name of God (*cf. n.*28 above) to a contemplation of the word 'faith,' a very strange transference indeed. One is tempted to wonder whether faith itself may not displace God as the central object of that struggle which is so central to Bratslav religion. The place of faith in Nahman's later writings will be fully discussed in excursus I.

98. *Teshuvah* 76.

99. *Banim* 95; *Bushah* 2, 28; *Ẓaddiq* 18.

100. *Ẓaddiq* 39. *Cf. n.* 9, above, and *Liqquṭim* 100, which explains the impatience of certain *ẓaddiqim* as a result of their own religious frustrations!

101. *Ẓaddiq* 81, 103, 167, 169, 26; *Ḥayyey* 6:2.

2

Nahman's Journey to the Land of Israel

Nahman's journey to the land of Israel in 1798–99 has long been seen as a major turning-point in his life. No wonder: Nahman himself, both in direct statements and through various half-hidden references, first revealed the centrality of this event to any understanding of him. Though he had already overcome his great reluctance and taken on a small band of followers before this journey, it was only upon his return from Erez Israel that the twenty-seven-year-old Nahman really allowed himself to become a public figure. As we have seen, he ordered that any teachings of his that dated from before the journey be deleted from his collected works, claiming that they were now of little value. In later periods of spiritual dryness Nahman was to proclaim that it was only the fact and memory of his journey to the Holy Land that kept him "alive" and allowed him to continue in his role as *ẓaddiq*.[1]

The account of Nahman's journey has survived in two versions, both of them recorded by Nathan of Nemirov. One of these versions, that which comprises the second part of Nathan's *Shivḥey ha-RaN* (also published separately under the title *Masa'ot ha-Yam)*, was written with considerable literary flourish, and indeed with just a touch of the mythic imagination that characterizes Nahman's own later *Tales*. The second version, forming a chapter of the fuller biographical memoir *Ḥayyey MoHaRaN*, is highly fragmentary and unpolished, but contains a wealth of material, particularly with regard to explanation of the journey.[2]

While Nathan pursues his usual concern for carefully recording every small detail of his master's life and adventures, this high regard for precision does not keep the chronicler in *Shivḥey ha-RaN* from adorning his account with an exciting aura of mysterious moments of seemingly-great but hidden significance: Nahman's nocturnal visit to Kamenets-Podolsk, the childish games he played in Istanbul, his readiness to leave the land almost as soon as he had set foot on its soil, his strange encounter with a young Arab in Haifa, his visits with the Hasidic community of Tiberias and at the graves of the saints—all of these lend to the account a sense of some secret and divine mission, the precise nature of which remains as hidden as the mysterious nature of Nahman himself. One cannot help but feel, in reading this account, that here Nahman in life has appeared as a character out of one of his own later stories.[3]

The fact that Nahman should choose to embark upon a journey to the land of Israel is on the face of it no cause for surprise. The eighteenth century had seen a great increase in travel and emigration of Eastern European Jews to the Holy Land. At first these journeys took place in circles closely connected to the Sabbatian movement,[4] but the voyagers later came to include key figures of early Hasidism. The meaning and possible messianic implications of these journeys have been much discussed by modern historians of the Hasidic movement.[5]

The first major figure within circles close to Hasidism to settle in the Holy Land was Gershon of Kutow (Kitov), the brother-in-law of the Ba'al Shem Tov and a member of the Klaus in Brody, who arrived in Erez Israel in 1747.[6] R. Gershon first settled in Hebron and later in Jerusalem, where he joined the already established Kabbalistic community of Beth-El. Nahman's own paternal grandfather, Nahman of Horodenka, who was also a member of the Ba'al Shem Tov's circle, settled in the Galilee in 1764, along with Menahem Mendel of Premyshlyany.[7] The Ba'al Shem Tov himself had set out on such a journey, as did his disciple Jacob Joseph of Polonnoye. The BeSHT interrupted his journey at Istanbul and returned to Podolia, a fact that has led to much speculation by historians.[8] It would seem that in some way he felt it would not be right for him to proceed further. Whether this had to do with a sense that his leadership was needed at home or with a feeling of some other spiritual "obstacle" cannot be determined from the available sources, shrouded as they are in legendary embellishments. In his famous letter to Gershon of Kutow, written around 1750, the BeSHT admitted that he had given up his plans to visit the Holy Land. In the case of Jacob Joseph, who was to serve as courier for that letter, it was apparently the BeSHT himself who advised him to stay at home. Years later, Pinhas of Korets also attempted a journey to the Holy Land, but he died shortly after he had set out on his way, in 1791. Of the Miedzyrzec circle, Menahem Mendel of Vitebsk and Abraham of Kalisk arrived in Erez Israel in 1777, settling first in Safed and later in Tiberias. They became the effective leaders of the Hasidic community in the Holy Land.[9]

Among Nahman's stated purposes in journeying to the land of Israel was his desire to commune with his grandfather, who lay buried in the graveyard of Tiberias. Given the young Nahman's penchant for visiting the grave of the Ba'al Shem Tov, it is hardly surprising that he should have wanted to be at the burial place of his paternal grandfather as well, "so that he always have access to that which he is to know through him."[10] A visit to the grave of his saintly forebear was not merely a matter of respect, but might be a source of some revealed "knowledge" from the upper world.[11] He sought the same sort of instruction at the graveside of the elder Nahman that he felt himself to have received at the grave of the BeSHT. In a larger sense, in seeking to undertake the dangerous but sacred journey to the Holy Land, Nahman was following the example of his two revered ancestral heroes. We must hasten to add, however, that communion with the spirit of his late grandfather was perhaps the least of the highly complicated purposes that moved Nahman toward this voyage. As we shall see, he nearly missed visiting Tiberias altogether, and it seems to have required both the pleas of the living and the attraction of the gravesite to get him there.

Before seeking to understand Nahman's complex motives for visiting the Holy Land in 1798, it is appropriate that we recount the details of the journey itself. It should again be emphasized that none of Nathan's account here is first-hand; Nathan arrived on the scene only several years after his master's return from Erez Israel. The account must thus be seen as based entirely on recollections shared with Nathan by Nahman's friend and earliest disciple, Simeon, who accompanied him on the journey, and to a lesser extent by Nahman himself. As Nathan retold the tale, he embellished it lavishly with remarks on the great trials and dangers his master had undergone, frequent proclamations of Nahman's heroism, and praises to God for having saved him from the dangers that threatened constantly to overwhelm him. He was careful in the midst of all this, however, not to tamper with the basic account as it had been given to him; names, dates, and places appearing in this most fantastic-seeming tale, whenever they can be traced, always turn out to be accurate records. Since our concern here is with the journey itself rather than with Nathan's literary effort, we shall retell the tale in a simple form, as it may be culled from Nathan's writings.

Nahman's announcement of his decision to travel to Erez Israel was preceded by another mysterious journey, a visit to Kamenets-Podolsk, which he undertook in the early spring of 1798.[12] This journey set the pattern for a number of such visits to various locales in the Ukraine, which Nahman would visit incognito and where he was reputed to have performed the unfathomable acts of a hidden *ẓaddiq*. On his journey to Kamenets he was accompanied by his friend Simeon and by another disciple, whose name is not given. When they set out from Medvedevka their destination was not yet known to them; it was only after a stop at Medzhibozh and a visit with his parents[13] that Nahman was "informed by heaven" as to the destination of this journey.

The city of Kamenets-Podolsk is well-known in Jewish history and in

Hasidic lore for one reason: it was here that the famous debate with the followers of Jacob Frank had taken place in 1757, and the city—which had no Jews—was thus seen as a locus of the much-hated Frankist movement. According to Hasidic legend, both the Ba'al Shem Tov and Nahman of Horodenka had debated the Frankists (though some sources connect this legend with the Lvov debate);[14] it is no wonder that Kamenets should have held some fascination for the later Nahman.

This fact has led Hillel Zeitlin to the highly interesting conclusion[15] that Nahman visited with Frankists in Kamenets, perhaps trying to win back their souls for Judaism. This theory, however, misses the mark in one crucial way: we know of no community of Frankists surviving in Kamenets as late as 1798, and it seems highly unlikely that there was one. The Frankists were driven out of that and other cities of Podolia following the death of their protector, Bishop Dembowski, a few months after that first debate. After the Lvov debate and the conversions of 1759/60 we do not hear of Frankists' settling in Kamenets, where as Jews they would not formerly have been permitted to dwell. By the end of the eighteenth century the center of Frankism had moved westward to Moravia and Germany, and those Polish Frankists who had converted were centered in Warsaw. While there may have been isolated crypto-Sabbatians in the Ukraine as late as the turn of the nineteenth century, it is clear that forty years after the debates the association of Kamenets-Podolsk with Frankism was a matter of memory, not of living fact.

Nevertheless, it is quite clear that Nahman's visit to Kamenets had something to do with the *former* presence of Frankists in that city. After violating the local ordinance forbidding any Jew from spending a night within the city limits, Nahman and his anonymous disciple (Simeon had remained behind at Medzhibozh) went calling at certain houses in the city. Once inside a house, Nahman would recite the proper blessing and have a drink of liquor. It would seem that during the night Nahman had inquired, or by some means divined, which had been the houses occupied by Frankists during the Kamenets debate. He then gained entry to those houses, and by means of his blessing and the glass of schnapps sought to perform some mysterious rite of purification. The custom of having a drink for the *tiqqun* of a soul is well-known in Hasidism; here it seems to be the dwellings, rather than the souls, which Nahman had in mind. These houses had to be purified of the Frankist stain so that Jews might dwell in them again. Indeed, Nathan tells us, shortly after Nahman's visit the residence ban on Jews in Kamenets was lifted.[16]

That the visit to Kamenets had something to do with the heretical past of that city is confirmed by Nahman's own words concerning the meaning of his visit there: "Our master said that he who understands why the Land of Israel was first ruled by Canaanites and only afterwards by Israel will understand why he was first in Kamenets and only afterwards in Erez Israel."[17]

The analogy clearly points to a version of the "descent of the *ẓaddiq*" into the realm of impurity before he could attain to a higher rung of perfection. This idea, itself deeply rooted in Sabbatian thinking, generally referred in Hasidism to the work of the *ẓaddiq* in redeeming the souls of others. It plays a major role, as we shall see, in Nahman's own later thinking.[18] To reach the great heights Nahman sought on his journey to the Holy Land, he would have to stoop to the greatest depths. He who seeks to rise to that most sacred of places must first descend and seek to purify the most defiled of human space.

Shortly afterwards, on the eve of Passover in 1798, Nahman announced his plans to depart for Erez Israel. At the gathering of *ḥasidim* on that holiday he offered an interpretation of the verse: "When your way led through the sea, your path through mighty water, and no one saw your footprints . . ." (Psalm 77:20), making reference, we should note, to a journey across the seas rather than to a visit to Erez Israel.[19] He evinced no regard for family or property in the planning of his journey. When his daughter asked what would become of the family while he was away, he replied:

> You will go to your in-laws. Someone will take your older sister as a household servant. Your younger sister will be taken into someone's home out of pity. Your mother can find work as a cook, and I shall sell everything in the house to cover expenses for the journey.[20]

Nahman saw the expected opposition of his family to the journey as a *meni'ah*, an obstacle in the path which had to be overcome. This accounts for the harshness of his retort. In much the same way did Nathan view the violent anti-Hasidic feelings of his own family when he first set out to become Nahman's disciple.[21]

It was about a month after Passover, on the eighteenth of Iyyar—May 4, 1798—that Nahman and Simeon[22] set out on their way. From Medvedevka they traveled overland to Nikolayev, where they found a barge carrying wheat down the Dnieper to Odessa. Departure from Odessa was not the usual route of Jewish travelers, who generally preferred to embark on the Black Sea voyage from Galati (Galatz), at the mouth of the Danube. Nahman of course saved time by choosing Odessa; it may also be that he had gotten word of the particularly severe pogrom that had nearly wiped out the Galati Jewish community in 1797.[23]

From Odessa they found a ship that took them, after a dangerous and stormy four-day journey, to Istanbul. Nahman spent his time on board writing down his teachings, but even his friend Simeon was not permitted to see what it was that he had written. This is the earliest reference we have to Nahman's habit of composing "secret" writings, which paralleled his exoteric literary production until his final illness set in; most of these writings were destroyed, on Nahman's orders, by his closest disciples.[24]

On his arrival at Istanbul, where he was forced to stay for some time awaiting a ship bound for Erez Israel, Nahman began to behave in a strange manner.

> He acted in all sorts of childish[25] ways, going about barefoot, without a belt, or without a top hat. He would go about [in the street] in his indoor clothing, running around the market like a child. There he would play war games, as children do. They would call one side 'France' and the other something else, and they would war with one another, using real battle tactics. He did very many childish[25] things in Istanbul.[26]

While in the Turkish capital, Nahman and Simeon came across a Hasidic emissary from the Holy Land who was on his way to Russia to collect funds for the Hasidic community of Tiberias, which was then headed by Abraham Kalisker. Nahman refused to reveal his true identity to the emissary, who, beset by the troubles of his own community, assumed that Nahman was an enemy of the Tiberias *ḥasidim* who was being sent to the Holy Land to create some mischief. Nahman compounded the difficulty by practicing his "childish" behavior on this man and his companions as well. Each time they would ask him his name he would offer a different reply. Once he said that he was a *kohen*, then he denied it; he pretended for a while that he was the son of the Komarno *ẓaddiq*, but once the other was convinced of this he turned around and heaped curses upon his alleged father. They became frustrated and angry and began to insult him. Nahman seemed to enjoy their degradations and insults, and once awakened them for no reason in the middle of the night, just to annoy them further. Although one of the emissary's companions was a ritual slaughterer and they thus had kosher meat available to them (pious Ashkenazim would not rely upon the somewhat different rules of kosher slaughter practiced by the Sephardic Jews of Istanbul), they would not share their food with the pestering young man, who was in this matter separated from his more docile, if tight-lipped, companion.[27]

What was the meaning of all this strange behavior? Nahman himself later explained it as having been an essential part of his journey to the Holy Land:

> The fact is that he did all this intentionally. He allowed himself to be reviled in all sorts of ways. He told the one who accompanied him that this degradation would be of great help, both on the forward journey and on their return. For the power of the great obstacles *(meni'ot)* which he had to overcome in going to Erez Israel cannot be imagined, measured, or told. As he later explicitly said, it would have been impossible for him to get to Erez Israel without these degradations and this *qatnut* . . . He saw that he would be forced to remain in Istanbul and to die there. The *qatnut* and degradations saved him . . .[28]

The point is again that of the dialectic of spiritual ascent and descent in the life of the *ẓaddiq*, though here in a somewhat less dramatic sense. Just as one who reaches for greater purification must do so by means of prior descent into the realm of defilement, so must one who reaches for *gadlut*, a state of higher spiritual consciousness, begin from an exaggerated position of *qatnut*. Here, as frequently in Hasidism, the Sabbatian sting has been removed from this dialectic, and it is portrayed in almost moralisitc terms. The issue has now become one of humility, in an effort to avoid the accusations of the *meqatregim*, negative or "accusing" forces, who would claim that one is seeking to rise beyond that place which is proper for a human being. Such accusations may be avoided by beginning the ascent in the guise of self-humiliation.[29]

It is clear that Nahman's choice of Istanbul as the scene for this *qatnut* was in part a reaction to the Ba'al Shem Tov's unsuccessful journey to Erez Israel some fifty years earlier. Hasidic legend recounts, we will recall, that the BeSHT had terminated his journey in Istanbul. It was in Istanbul that he saw that "Heaven was not allowing him to go on to the Holy Land." Another version of the legend has it that the BeSHT saw the fiery sword of Eden warning him of danger unless he returned home without completing his mission.[30] Given this association with Istanbul, Nahman must have considered this to be the crucial point in his journey. If only he could pass through this city in safety, he would be able to reach the Land of Israel.

Once the emissary and his men had left Istanbul, Nahman began to return to his adult self. He admitted his true identity to a Jewish ship-agent, who set out to arrange his passage. Meanwhile, a group of *ḥasidim* from the Ukraine arrived in Istanbul on their way to Erez Israel. The group included Rabbi Ze'ev Wolf of Charny-Ostrog, a disciple of the Maggid of Miedzyrzec who was later to become a leader of the Hasidic community in the Galilee. The elder *ẓaddiq*, informed of Nahman's identity, treated him with the respect due to a descendant of the BeSHT, despite some degree of continued erratic behavior on Nahman's part.[31]

As Nahman and Simeon made their plans to sail from Istanbul, another obstacle threatened to hold them back. By the beginning of 1798, the Napoleonic navy was fighting in the Eastern Mediterranean; Napoleon had by then begun the invasion of Egypt. Due to the dangers of battle, the Jewish community of Istanbul announced a ban on any further Jewish pilgrimages to the Holy Land. Having traditionally assumed primary responsibility for the victims of maritime disasters and piracy in the area, the community did not want to take on unnecessary risks. Nahman's reaction to this ban is highly instructive, and lends credence to the interpretation of the journey we will propose:

> Our master did not pay any attention to this [ban] and *wanted to risk his life.*[32] He said to the one who accompanied him: 'Know that *I want to place myself in danger, even great and terrible danger.* But I do not want to risk your life. Therefore, if you want, take money for expenses and go home in peace. I

> shall travel on alone, unbeknown to the people of Istanbul. *For I risk my life, come what may'* and so forth. His companion declined, saying 'where my master is, whether for life or death, there will your servant be. Whither Thou goest, I shall go'.[33]

As it turned out, Nahman's refusal to change his plans was shared by an elderly and respected Sephardic sage from Jerusalem, who, as one already close to death, did not mind the risk. Under pressure from this *ḥakham*, the community allowed one last ship to sail for Jaffa, and Nahman and Simeon were given passage. Interestingly, Nahman asked the *ḥakham* to take him directly to Jerusalem, "for he said that he did not want to be in either Safed or Tiberias."[34] Since almost the entire Hasidic community of the Holy Land lived in those two towns of the Galilee, it might seem that Nahman wanted to avoid contact with them. It would also seem from here that a visit to his grandfather's grave in Tiberias was less than essential to his journey. It may be suspected, however, from the fact that Nahman never did go to Jerusalem, that this was but another ruse to fool those demonic powers who might hold him back if he were to reveal his true destination.

The voyage was not an easy one. The ship encountered a terrible storm, and the rising waves threatened to engulf them all. Again, Nahman's attitude is instructive as to the meaning this journey had for him:

> Nobody thought that they would be saved from death. Everyone cried out to God, and there was a night which was just like Yom Kippur, with everyone crying, confessing his sins, and seeking atonement for his soul. They recited *seliḥot* as well as other prayers and supplications. But our master sat in silence. When asked why he was silent in such a time of woe, he refused to reply. But then the wife of the rabbi of Khotin, herself a learned woman, who had been crying and screaming all night, asked him the same. It would seem that he cursed her and said 'If only you too would be quiet, it would be good. *By this you will be tested.* If you are still, the waters of the sea will become still as well.'[35]

The group, we are told, then followed Nahman's counsel, and soon the seas were still again. Having weathered the storm, however, the passengers were confronted with the new danger of a shortage in the supply of drinking water. When these and other tribulations were finally overcome, a fortuitous wind blew them into the port of Jaffa, the point of disembarkment for Jerusalem. Nahman sought to accompany the elder *ḥakham* to Jerusalem, but the port officials, especially cautious in times of war, were suspicious of his foreign dress and his ignorance of the local languages. They feared he might be a French spy in some outlandish disguise (!) and refused to allow him off the ship. He thus remained on board, proceeding northward along the coast to Haifa, and disembarked on Monday, September 10—the eve of Rosh Hashanah.

Nahman's feeling as he first set foot in the Holy Land was one of great elation. He promptly informed his faithful companion that he should consider himself especially blessed to have been witness to such a momentous event. On his arrival in the Holy Land, Nahman conducted himself as a *rebbe,* accepting petitions for prayer and conducting a public festive meal on the eve of Rosh Hashanah. Here he showed none of the reluctance that had characterized his earlier forays into the public arena. By the end of prayers on the following morning, however, he had become depressed. "Tremendous worry and brokenheartedness were aroused in him, and he did not speak to anyone at all."[36] Immediately after the holiday, he announced that he wanted to depart at once, without traveling to Tiberias or visiting any of the other holy places. It was only the pleas of Simeon and of the *ḥasidim* in Safed and Tiberias, who had meanwhile heard of his arrival, that persuaded him to remain awhile in the Holy Land.

While Nahman was in Haifa, another strange thing to which he attributed great significance occurred. It seems that a young Arab "discovered" Nahman and began to visit his quarters regularly. The young man took a great liking to Nahman, but in vain did he seek to transcend the language barrier which existed between them. Failing to make his affection for Nahman understood, he at one point became angry and challenged the *ẓaddiq* to a duel. Frightened by the prospect, Nahman hid himself in the home of his friend the rabbi of Charny-Ostrog, who had arrived in Haifa with him. The "Ishmaelite," however, was soon appeased, and again showed great affection for Nahman. This, too, Nahman found disquieting, and said that he "suffered more from the love of this Ishmaelite than from his hate or anger." He felt that some great danger might await him in this person, and he may have claimed that the young man was none other than Samael himself.[37]

Exactly what it was about this man that the already depressed Nahman found so alarming is impossible to reconstruct from the single account of their encounter. The fact that a *ẓaddiq* should find himself the object of affection on the part of a non-Jew was not in itself any cause for wonder; in Eastern Europe it was very common for non-Jews, peasants and nobles alike, to pay homage to certain of the *ẓaddiqim.* The relationship here, however, gives no indication of such veneration. The Arab seems to have seen himself as a peer, rather than as a would-be disciple, of Nahman. Perhaps this thought in itself was upsetting to the *ẓaddiq,* who was unaccustomed to anyone's relating to him outside the traditional canons of his role. His own inability to respond to this offer of friendship may be the reason the other's offer of love caused Nahman more pain than his hate. We should further note that the word *ahavah* when used in these sources may refer to almost any degree of affection, love, or friendly feeling; it is also within the realm of possibility that Nahman feared sexual advances on the part of the young man. Nahman, ever tormented by his own conflicts with regard to sexuality, would have been particularly terrified by such an advance, a much more common and accepted happening in the Near East than in Eastern Europe. This would account for Nahman's sharp designation of this Arab as the demonic power incarnate.

The depression that had begun to set in on Rosh Hashanah remained with Nahman through the holiday season. Even on Simḥat Torah, when a great spirit of celebration engulfed the newly-arrived *ḥasidim* in Haifa, Nahman refused to join in the festivities. At the conclusion of the holidays, a month after his arrival, Nahman once again sought to embark on the journey homeward, and it was again only Simeon's insistence that moved him to travel to Tiberias. While the sources offer no particular explanation of this depression, it seems understandable as a kind of post-climactic letdown after the conclusion of what had become to Nahman's mind (as we shall see) the great and transforming journey. Realizing as he did, a day after his arrival, that the burdens which had always weighed down upon his soul had not been lifted from him as he set foot on the holy soil, and that his initial elation had in fact been transitory, he fell into a depression that troubled him until he left Haifa.

At Tiberias the two were greeted with warm affection by Abraham Kalisker and his *ḥasidim*. Nahman showed great respect for the leader of the Tiberias Hasidic community, and refused to 'say Torah' in the presence of one he deemed greater than himself. Though Abraham's teachings were presented in such a manner that "not a word could be heard amid all the ecstasy and shouting," Nahman praised them lavishly. He was later to confide to Nathan that of all his contemporaries in the Hasidic world, he would attribute the quality of wholeness only to this *ẓaddiq*. Indeed, the small and elite community of the Tiberias *ḥasidim* seems to have served as an important model for Nahman, both in the creation of the Bratslav community and in his fantasy of an ideal Hasidic brotherhood with which he opened his tale of *The Master of Prayer*. His respect for Abraham Kalisker went so far that when he became ill for a few days while in Tiberias he treated the other as his master, sending him a gift *(pidyon)* accompanied by a petition for prayerful intercession. The local master in turn showed great deference for Nahman (in part, no doubt, because of his lineage), and when the latter on one occasion bowed his head to receive a blessing, Kalisker deferred as a sign of their equality.[38]

Cheered by the warm welcome they received, and perhaps attracted by the pleasant climate of Tiberias in the winter months, Nahman and Simeon remained there until February or March of 1799. From Tiberias they journeyed to several of the holy places in the Galilee. Of particular interest is the account of Nahman's visit to the cave of Simeon ben Yohai:

> When they arrived at the cave of Rabbi Simeon, the young people recited prayers and studied the *Zohar*, as he had instructed them to do. They did not see him do anything, however. He was very elated, and would constantly go back to the one who accompanied him and say: "Blessed are you," *etc.* At night he went from chamber to chamber, encouraging them to keep reciting passages from the *Zohar*, *etc.* He himself said nothing, but went about singing to himself, in great happiness, until the light of dawn. When day broke, he donned his *tallit* and *tefillin* and prayed for several hours.[39]

This passage, like so many others in the Bratslav corpus, has undergone the heavy hand of censorship. Nahman, at least later in life having seen himself as R. Simeon reincarnate, clearly was depicted in an original version as viewing this "return" as a highlight of his journey. The words which are blocked by the "et ceteras" of this passage most likely gave some clear indication, later considered too dangerous for publication, of his identification with the hero of the *Zohar*.

Sometime during that winter Nahman made yet another attempt to leave for home. He sent Simeon ahead to Haifa to book passage for them. In Haifa, however, Simeon met Jacob Samson of Shepetovka,[40] who had just returned from a mission abroad to collect funds for the *ḥasidim* of the Holy Land. At that time, however, a certain Jewish informer had told the local Turkish pasha in Tiberias that large sums of money were about to arrive from abroad, and there was a danger that the entire amount would be confiscated by the authorities. Jacob Samson, who was well-known as an emissary, was therefore afraid to deliver the funds in person, and Simeon offered his services as an intermediary. He thus returned to Tiberias safely bearing the funds, but without having arranged a return journey.[41] Seeing that his plans to leave had been thwarted once again, Nahman finally decided that it was indeed meant that he remain in the Holy Land for a longer period of time. He actually made plans for a journey to Jerusalem, but was discouraged by Abraham Kalisker, apparently because of dangers thought to await Jerusalem from the invading Napoleonic army.

Whatever was his resolve at that point, it was the Napoleonic conquest of the Palestinean coastline, and specifically the threat to the port of Acre, that forced Nahman's hand and finally persuaded him to set out for home at once. When he heard that Acre was about to be laid under siege (Haifa having already fallen), he set out for the port immediately, hoping to find a ship still flying the flag of neutral Ragusa.[42] They arrived on Acre on Friday, March 15, and were straightaway caught up in the great rush of civilians to leave the city. The siege actually began on March 19,[43] but the Turks had already warned all civilians to leave the city by Sunday, on pain of death. Passage on a neutral ship became an impossibility and on the last possible day (March 17) the two passengers were fortunate even to find passage on a Turkish merchant vessel.

In the tumult of the evacuation, however, things went from bad to worse. Not speaking the local tongues and not knowing one ship from another, Nahman and Simeon wound up on a Turkish warship which, as soon as it had left the harbor, became entangled in battle with the French. The two begged to be put ashore but were unable to make themselves understood, and so they soon found themselves in the midst of a raging battle at sea. The Turkish captain and sailors, as can be imagined, were none too happy to discover their two "accidental" passengers, and Nahman and Simeon hid in a small cabin, fearing to show themselves on deck lest they be killed by the sailors. They were kept alive only by the ship's cook, who took pity on them and brought them a bit of coffee twice a day.[44]

The dangers of battle gave way, after a while, to the even greater dangers of storm. Blown back and forth between one coastline and another, the ship, perhaps already damaged in battle, began to take on water. All cargo was thrown overboard to lighten the vessel, but still the ship seemed certain to sink. The two passengers feared to leave their cabin, yet it was so filled with water that they had to climb to the top of some tall piece of furniture to escape drowning. They thought little of their chances for survival, and even if they should survive they were quite convinced that the sailors would sell them as slaves. At this point Nahman reached a most interesting resolve: even should he be enslaved and thus prevented from living the ritual life of a Jew, he announced, he would still be able to fulfill the *miẓwot* in spirit.

> He had reached the understanding of how to serve God even if he were, God forbid, not able to observe the commandments. He had attained the service of the patriarchs who had served God before the Torah was given, fulfilling all the *miẓwot* even though they did not observe them in their ordinary form *(ki-feshutan)*. Just as Jacob fulfilled the commandment of *tefillin* by stripping the sticks and so forth—until he understood how he would fulfill all the *miẓwot* in this way if forced to do so in the place where he might be sold, God forbid.[45]

As the ship's pumps were reported to fail, the men's fear worsened. Here the bravado Nahman had borne on his journey to the land seems to have fled him. Simeon was so paralyzed by terror that he could not even open his mouth in prayer. Nahman too, now faced with a truly desperate situation, found that his personal fears were coming between himself and God. Finally he called out in the name of his ancestors, depending on the collective merits of the BeSHT, his daughter Odel, and Nahman of Horodenka to save him. While the seas did not grow calmer, somehow the sailors managed to repair the leaks in the vessel and they survived the storm.

After a month of terror, the ship sailed into the harbor of Rhodes on the eve of Passover. Nahman and Simeon, having nearly despaired of life itself, now found themselves within near reach of a Jewish community that would save them from the sailors, and would even enable them to celebrate the festival of deliverance. Negotiations ensued between the ship's captain and Jewish communal leaders, and for an adequate price the two captives were released to the Rhodes Jewish community on the third day of Passover. As it turned out, the captain of this ship was well known to the local Jews, and the dangers of murder or enslavement had in fact been quite real.[46] The rabbis of Rhodes, knowing the writings of Jacob Joseph of Polonnoye, were honored to have a descendant of the Ba'al Shem Tov among them. After much rejoicing through the remainder of the holiday, they were put on a safe and fast vessel which got them to Istanbul after only three days' journey. In Istanbul their adventures resumed when they were told that their passports were out of order, and it was only through the helpful hand of bribery that they were permitted to depart for Galati. This ship, too, was caught in a storm and most of the passengers drowned. After various other encounters with ransom, storm, and plague, they arrived home, having traveled overland from Galati via Jassy, sometime in early summer of 1799.[47]

In Nathan's first account of his master's journey, from which most of the above rendition has been culled, little attention was paid to the reasons for the voyage or the meaning it had in his master's life. Only when he returned to this aspect of his biographical writings, after an interval of at least a decade, did he begin to set forth the traditions with regard to the journey's meaning. Though this second of Nathan's accounts is, as we have said, more fragmentary, it may also be said to reflect the concerns of a more mature biographer. The relevant chapter in *Ḥayyey MoHaRaN* suggests four explanations of the journey, all of them offered in Nahman's own name. This multiplicity of explanations provides no problem for Nathan, we should note, a biographer who will never be found guilty of underestimating the complexity of his subject's mind:

> It was thus heard that there were several reasons for his voyage to the Land of Israel, in addition to those hidden reasons which he never revealed at all. Indeed, for all the things he did he never had only a single reason, but rather thousands and tens of thousands of deep and elevated motivations—most especially so for this great journey to Erez Israel, for which he risked his life so very greatly.[48]

One of Nahman's stated motives for the journey has been discussed above: the hope of receiving some revealed knowledge at the grave of his grandfather. The three other reasons given for the journey also have to do with some higher form of religious knowledge or illumination accessible only through a journey to the Holy Land. Our task is now to examine each of these in some detail, hoping to see whether they can be integrated into any overarching interpretation of the journey that will avoid over-simplification while at the same time not veer too closely toward Nathan's recourse to esotericism in explaining his master's actions. We shall quote each of the three explanations directly from Nathan's account.

> 1) I heard in his name that he said before his journey to Erez Israel that he wanted to go in order to attain *ḥokhmah 'ila'ah* [supernal wisdom]. There exist higher and lower forms of *ḥokhmah;* the lower he had already acquired, but he was yet to attain the higher. For this he had to go to the Land of Israel.[49]

The motif of the two aspects of *ḥokhmah* has a long history in Kabbalistic literature. While the terms have been employed by Kabbalists in varying ways, it may generally be said that *ḥokhmah 'ila'ah* is associated with the second of the ten *sefirot* (or the first, according to some reckonings), and *ḥokhmah tata'ah* is associated with *malkhut*, the lowest of the ten sefirotic rungs within divinity.[50] In Nahman's own later writings, the lower *ḥokhmah* is taken to be the immediate source of all worldly wisdom, while the higher *ḥokhmah* is the source of the primordial Torah, the "holy of holies" in the sefirotic world, the primal root of all existence.[51] More significantly, *ḥokhmah 'ila'ah* is identified with the esoteric aspect of each of the *miẓwot*, always higher than the 'revealed' aspect which is embodied in the performance of the act. In Nahman's dialectic of spiritual ascent, the upper *ḥokhmah* is to be pursued to the point of complete self-transcendence and absorption in the divine *nihil.*[52] Thus our passage would mean that Nahman had already mastered all that could be attained by one who still held on to this-worldly existence and wisdom; only by journeying to the Holy Land could he achieve that total transcendence of self which was the goal of much of early Hasidic piety.

> 2) It was heard from his holy mouth during the Passover season that preceded his journey from Medvedevka to the Land of Israel that he wanted to go to Erez Israel in order there to fulfill all of the six hundred and thirteen commandments, including those which are dependent upon the land together with those which may be fulfilled outside it, fulfilling them all spiritually so that afterward he would be able to fulfill them all physically.[53]

Once again, now more clearly, the notion of an esoteric aspect of the *miẓwot* makes its appearance. Even the most pious of Jews, living after the destruction of the Temple and outside the Land of Israel, observes far fewer than the originally prescribed six hundred and thirteen commandments of the Torah. Many of the *miẓwot* are completely in abeyance since the Temple's destruction and the suspension of the sacrificial cult; others, particularly those relating to the agricultural cycle, apply only to Jews living in or eating the produce of the Land of Israel. Based upon older mystical speculations propounding the view of Torah as an organism, according to which each of the commandments was seen as a particular 'limb' of the Torah's 'body,' in turn both reflecting the 'limbs' of the divine 'body' of *Adam Qadmon* and corresponding to the limbs of the human body, these unobservable *miẓwot* became a problem in Hasidic thought. If the Torah is a single whole, and if its 613 commandments bespeak the fulfillment of the 613 limbs of man's spiritual body that is the image of God in him, how can one possibly achieve that fulfillment if not all the commandments may be followed?[54] Even he who does all he can to live in accordance with the Torah would of necessity leave whole areas untouched, thus not allowing for the completion of the system of correspondences that leads to fulfillment. In response to this and similar problems, Hasidic teachers propounded the rather dangerous doctrine of purely spiritual fulfillment of these divine commandments. While certain of the Torah's precepts still required a bodily act, others could be fulfilled by means of *kawwanah* alone, thus allowing the worshiper not to feel that these were 'dead letters' in his spiritual life. Combined with ancient and well-known speculations concerning the abrogation of certain or all of the *miẓwot* in messianic times, Hasidism here approaches the border of antinomian thinking. The distinction between the Hasidic view mentioned here and the antinomian view that the true fulfillment of *all* the commandments is purely spiritual is a fine one.[55]

Examining the passage at hand more closely, we will note that the text as it stands does not quite make sense. In order to *spiritually* fulfill the *miẓwot ha-teluyot ba-areẓ* one would not have to travel to the Holy Land. The order of the final line should probably be reversed to read: "fulfilling all of them physically so that afterward he should be able to fulfill them all spiritually." One who had never experienced the actual observance of a particular *miẓwah* would not know how properly to spiritualize it. Thus Nahman's journey is seen as an attempt to gain access to those areas of the Torah that apply in the land alone, so that afterwards he might include them in his 'spiritual observance' of the *miẓwot*.

This reading of the passage is confirmed by that most curious and rather shocking statement Nahman made during the return voyage, to the effect that he could now continue to observe all the *miẓwot* in spirit even if he were to be impressed into slavery and thus unable to keep them in the flesh. It now seems that this statement was not merely a rationalization born of his dire situation on the sea; the realization of the spiritual Torah was in fact an essential and planned part of his journey from the outset. Such an intent, of course, in no way indicates that Nahman sought to abandon the *miẓwot* in their ordinary sense.

In that statement on the seas Nahman claimed that he had attained to the rung of the patriarchs and their spiritual fulfillment of the commandments. The idea that the patriarchs had fulfilled the divine will before Sinai by means of acts other than the accepted *mizwot*, or even by *kawwanah* alone, is well known in early Hasidic writings. Scholars have seen in this theme the projection of a certain ambivalence the Hasidic authors felt about the need for the actual corporeal fulfillment of the *mizwot*, given a world-view in which pure spirituality was the ultimate religious value. Here we see that Nahman as a young man was also strongly attracted to such thinking, and that while such antinomian tendencies were not acted out in his life they did occupy a significant place in his speculations.[56] From this perspective, the journey to Erez Israel may be seen as an attempt to reach new heights of spiritualization with regard to the *mizwot* by including the commandments relating to the land in his repertoire of contemplation.[57]

> 3) He then told R. Yudil that he wanted to go to the Land of Israel. R. Yudil offered him his blessing and said to him: 'Our master! Surely you want to perform some great thing there. May it be God's will to help you do that which you intend.' Our master nodded in response to his blessing and afterwards said: 'I could fulfill that which I seek and desire to do in Erez Israel right here by means of prayer and supplication alone. Then I would not have to travel to Erez Israel. The difference is that if I merit to be in Erez Israel I will receive my understanding in "garments," whereas if I stay here I will receive it without the "garments." This is also the difference between the holiness of the Sabbath and that of the festival.' He opened the prayerbook of the ARI of blessed memory for R. Yudil and showed him in the *kawwanot* that this was the difference between Sabbath and festival: that on Sabbath the light is clothed in garments, while on festivals it does not have this garb, as is known.[58]

Here once again Nahman's journey is depicted as an attempt to achieve some higher degree of spiritual attainment, speaking here in somewhat different and more paradoxical Kabbalistic language. Before Nahman was in the Holy Land, according to this source, he had received his spiritual understanding *(hassagah)* directly, without the 'garb' in which such understanding should be clothed. Contrary to what one might expect, 'garbed' understanding is here presented as a higher rung of attainment than that which comes to man without such 'garb'; the need for covering the understanding indicates that it is derived from a higher source, one which could not be attained by man without such a protective *levush*.

While Nahman did not explain this rather cryptic reference to his disciples, he did make reference to *Siddur ha-ARI*, the prayerbook edition of Isaac Luria, as the source of his thoughts. While the phrase *Siddur ha-ARI* in the mouth of a late eighteenth-century Eastern European Jew could well have been applied to any one of several Kabbalistic compendia on the liturgy,[59] all of them based on the Lurianic system, we are here in the fortunate position of being able to identify the precise text Nahman had been reading. This turns out to be none other than the famous *Siddur Qol Ya'aqov* by Jacob Koppel Lipschütz of Miedzyrzec, whom Tishby has shown to have been a secret Sabbatian, but whose *Siddur* was highly prized by the Ba'al Shem Tov and others.[60] In his introduction to the *kawwanot* of the festivals, which immediately precedes his discussion of Passover, Jacob Koppel discusses the difference in holiness between Sabbath and festival. Because the Sabbath day is possessed of an inherent holiness, he says, deriving from the blessing of Genesis 2:3, its spiritual status is higher than that of the festivals, the sanctity of which is derivative from the holiness of Israel.[61] For this reason, he continues, the light of *ḥokhmah* shines more brightly on the Sabbath than it does on other holy days of the sacred calendar. The Sabbath light is so bright that *binah,* the next lower divine emanation, could not receive it unless it were veiled in some *levush* in order that it be partially hidden. If the much dimmer festival light, on the other hand, were to be transmitted in the same *levush,* it would be totally imperceptible.[62] On the following page the author connects all of this with the difference between the Holy Land and the rest of Creation. That higher 'garbed' consciousness, available outside the land only on the Sabbath, is present also on weekdays in the Land of Israel. Here he may be basing himself on older sources, which relate the Land of Israel to another sort of garb: the garment of the soul, which the righteous are to wear in the world to come.[63]

It was on the eve of Passover in 1798 that Nahman first announced to those around him his plans for a journey to the Holy Land. In preparing for the holiday, he had been reading the appropriate passages in the Kabbalistic liturgy which was revered by his esteemed great-grandfather and had been passed on to him. In it he found confirmation of an idea that had already taken hold of him: in order to achieve a higher rung of enlightenment he would have to journey to Erez Israel. The image of a veiled revelation emanating from a higher divine rung than an unveiled truth, so typical of the paradoxical dialectic of the Kabbalah, would have been precisely the sort of formula to have had greatest appeal to Nahman's ever-paradoxical turn of mind.

These explanations, all of them recorded in succession in Nathan's memoir, all generally point in the same direction. The purpose of the journey was a search for some higher form of spiritual illumination than that which was accessible to Nahman outside the land. Though the young ascetic had, through his countless earlier struggles, attained a very high rung of personal development and religious understanding, he now stood at an impasse: further growth now required a major breakthrough, one which was possible only by means of such a journey. In the Holy Land he could receive the garbed or "higher" wisdom, apprehend the secret of the commandments, and commune with the spirit of his grandfather in pursuit of direct knowledge from above. It seems here, in contrast to a certain tendency toward spiritual glorification of life in the diaspora to be found elsewhere in early Hasidism, that Nahman is in his own way echoing the well-known rabbinic dicta to the effect that prophecy or the holy spirit could not ordinarily be attained outside the Land of Israel.[64]

Our thorough biographer Nathan could not, however, resist passing on to us one further account of Nahman's announcement of his journey, one that throws all of the above into new relief. Included in a later section of his second account of the voyage, the passage has about it a ring of almost startling authenticity, conveyed not least by the broken bits of language it records.

> Shortly before he departed for the Land of Israel, someone asked him why he did not draw them [the disciples] near and speak with them. He said that he now had no words, but he said that 'by means of the verse "When you pass through water I shall be with you" (Isaiah 43:2) it has become known to me *how one may see the patriarchs Abraham, Isaac, and Jacob whenever one wants.* I wondered why it should be through that particular verse, but now I think it is because I have to cross the sea. But why [should I tell] you this? What need have you for it? Even were I to dress it in some moral teaching that would be appropriate to everyone—but I have no words now.' Afterwards he walked to and fro in the house saying: 'I am poorer and more destitute than any of the great ones. One has money, another has towns [dominated by his *ḥasidim*]—and I have nothing. My only comfort comes when I recall that in the world of truth they will all need me and will long to hear my teachings *(ḥiddushim)* which I create in every moment. What is this "I"? Rather "which my soul creates." '[65]

In this fragment, reported to Nathan by one of Nahman's early disciples, we are given a rare glimpse of the young master in a terrible state of agitation. Before he decided on his trip to Erez Israel, he was undergoing one of his famous 'dry' periods, which continued to evidence themselves throughout his later life and which, as we shall see, had so great an effect upon his teachings. He had distanced himself from his students, saying that he 'had no words,' that he was not able to teach them anything. His problem was a purely personal one, knowledge of which would not be of any help to others. True, he retained a faith in his ultimate vindication, but his present crisis could only be resolved by a journey over the seas. Here we have an explanation of the journey of a most dramatic and immediate sort: it was not in order only to *increase* his knowledge or illumination that Nahman set out, but rather in response to a deep personal *crisis*. Here it is no longer an ordered pattern of ascent but rather a precipitous fall that stands behind Nahman's decision for the journey. The depths to which he was shaken by this crisis are poignantly reflected by his pacing through the house and by the confusion recorded in his closing lines. Nahman hastens to correct the impression that it is his 'I' which constantly speaks *ḥiddushey Torah;* it is rather his soul that continues to create, even in those times when his 'I' is afflicted by spiritual dryness and cannot speak. I *as a person,* he is saying to his disciples, have nothing to offer you at this time. If *my soul* continues to create, do not assume this to mean that *I* have anything to give you.[66] We should also note that in this text, as well as in the brief reference to this moment in *Shivḥey ha-RaN,* quoted earlier, where a different scriptural verse is adduced, the reference is to a voyage across the seas, rather than to Erez Israel.

What was the nature of this crisis in Nahman's life? And how was it that a sea journey was seen as its proper resolution? A careful examination of this text will yield some interesting results. The most direct goal of his voyage, and the resolution of his personal crisis, seems to be sought in a vision of the patriarchs. This same motif of a vision of the patriarchs is reported from an earlier period in Nahman's life, in a dream we have mentioned briefly in discussing Nahman's adolescence. Here it would be fitting to quote that highly-revealing text in full:

> He was once sitting at his father-in-law's table during the third Sabbath meal. He was seated in a corner and it began to grow dark in the house. He as usual went his own way, and he began to ask God *to show him the patriarchs Abraham, Isaac,* and *Jacob.* He promised God that 'when You show me this, I will cast aside this desire [eating] as well.' He did what he did in this matter, entering into the thoughts very deeply, until he fell asleep. His forebearer the BeSHT came to him in a dream and recited to him the verse 'I shall put grass in the field for your animals' (Deut. 11:14). He awoke wondering what possible connection there could be between this verse and that which he had sought. He then recalled a passage in the *Tiqquney Zohar* which interprets the word *'esev* ['grass', consonantally *'sb*] as referring to the pupil of the eye [abbreviation for *bat 'ayin,* the locus of vision] and the patriarchs, the three of them alluded to by the three-pronged *shin.* This is its meaning: it is impossible to see the patriarchs unless you have first destroyed your animal nature, namely the desire for food. Then he overcame this desire.[67]

The relationship between these two texts has not heretofore been recognized. The desire to obtain a vision of the patriarchs was not new to Nahman in 1798. On the contrary, it had been with him at least since adolescence, the period of his hardest struggles against the desires of the flesh. That this early dream remained crucial to him is witnessed by its being one of those few events in his life he specifically instructed his disciples to retell among themselves. The vision of the patriarchs was to be his reward for ultimate victory in the battle against his own animal nature, symbolized here by his desire for food, but elsewhere by his sexual struggles. It appears that now, at the age of twenty-six, he had still not achieved that final victory, for the vision of the patriarchs, or at least constant access to that vision, was still something to be sought. Given the violent ups and downs in Nahman's self-esteem, we may well assume that there were points in his life when he felt this goal to be well within his reach—but that these were only to be followed by further falls, during which times the patriarchs once again seemed to distance themselves from him. *The patriarchs, who fulfilled the miẓwot in purely spiritual ways, are, in Nahman's imagination, symbols of complete transcendence of the bodily self.*

It is now clear that Nahman's announcement of his journey has to do with his ongoing struggle and its promised rewards. In his earlier days he had suffered periods of emptiness and awareness of God's distance from him, which he had come to attribute to his failure to achieve mastery over his 'animal' self and its base desires. As he accepted the role of *ẓaddiq*, these periods manifested themselves as times when he 'had no words,' when he felt himself unworthy to address his disciples. In a world where the teaching of Torah was seen as a pneumatic act rather than as an intellectual exercise, this transition is perfectly clear. If the teaching of Torah is an event in which "the *shekhinah* speaks through his mouth,"[68] the *ẓaddiq* who feels himself to be far from God can only be embarrassed by the demands of his disciples.

But what has all this to do with a journey to the Holy Land? The fact is that there is no intrinsic connection between Nahman's struggle to overcome his desires and a visit to the Land of Israel. Our passage speaks only of a sea voyage, and it is the voyage itself that is crucial in this connection. Erez Israel itself was of great importance for Nahman; he *did* believe that there were higher forms of religious knowing accessible only there. But in this passage and in much of the discussion of the journey *it is the voyage rather than the destination that seems to occupy Nahman's thoughts.*

This view of the journey is sustained by a number of other interesting references in the writings of both Nahman and Nathan. Only two months before his death in 1810, Nahman underwent the best-known of his depressed periods. During that time he spoke to his disciples about the *ẓaddiq* (the reference is clearly to himself) as one who at times is like the most simple of men. At such moments he knows nothing and has no access to Torah. His only sustenance at such times is through *derekh ereẓ*, here taken to refer to *derekh ereẓ yisra'el*, the way to the Land of Israel. "He sustained himself in times of simplicity only by the way to Erez Israel."[69] In other words, the fact that he had made the journey to the Holy Land, and the memory of that journey, were sufficient to sustain him through even the most bitter periods of dryness and self-doubt.

In order to further understand why the journey itself, as distinct from the destination, should play so central a role in Nahman's thinking, we must touch upon another central motif of his thought, to which we have made occasional reference above. This is the motif of 'obstacles' *(meni'ot)* which the man of faith has to overcome in his search for a path to God. These *meni'ot* are best described in Nahman's tale of *The Rabbi and His Son,*[70] where the obstacles are at once the result of the doubts the rabbi entertains about the true *ẓaddiq* and the work of the demonic forces themselves. This dual understanding of the *meni'ah,* as psychological block to faith and as the work of demonic powers, is crucial to Nahman's self-understanding. Man's task is ever to do battle with the *meni'ot,* whether they take the form of mental or physical barriers; the search for God requires the strength of a Samson.[71] And the great example in Bratslav literature of the battle to overcome *meni'ot* is none other than the journey of Nahman to the Land of Israel!

> He said that he was very happy to have merited to be in Erez Israel. For on the way to Erez Israel he had undergone many obstacles, confusing thoughts, delays, and struggles, including financial obstacles. But he had overcome them all and had brought the matter to completion by reaching Erez Israel. He further said this: I believe, and indeed I know well, that of all the movements, thoughts, and deeds that one undertakes in order to perform some holy act, not a single one is ever lost. For after all the obstacles have been broken through and the act has been completed, all those confusing thoughts and movements which had taken place while one was still weighing the act . . . are elevated to the highest state of holiness. Everything is recorded above for good, including every move one had to make along the way. Blessed are those who manage to overcome all the obstacles and to complete some good deed.[72]

The lesson to be learned from Nahman's journey to the Holy Land is not that "the atmosphere of Erez Israel makes one wise" or gives one access to visions, indeed it is not that one should follow in the master's footsteps by making such a pilgrimage, but rather that one should struggle constantly to overcome *meni'ot!* Given this use of the journey, it is no wonder that the voyage itself rather than the destination takes a central place here.

The journey from the Ukraine to the Holy Land was in fact a dangerous one. As we have seen, the frail ships upon which Nahman and his disciple finally did sail were subject to all sorts of natural disasters, and shipwrecks were fairly common. Added to these were the dangers of shipboard disease, piracy, and the battles of the Napoleonic wars in which Nahman was to become embroiled. The journey was an act of *mesirut nefesh,* of willingness to endanger one's life in order to achieve some sacred purpose. As we look back over the account of the journey, we see that Nahman repeatedly sought to stand in the face of the greatest dangers. What greater act of overcoming *meni'ah* and of transcending the bodily self than the willingness to risk one's very life for God? Despite the rabbinic injunctions against testing the Lord, it apparently became clear to Nahman in the twenty-sixth year of his life that only by such a radical act of self-sacrifice could he overcome those 'base' desires that continued to torment him, and thus prove his faith in God. When he later spoke of the relationship between purity in the act of eating and the sanctity of Erez Israel,[73] he clearly had his own journey in mind, a journey undertaken for the purpose of self-purification by ordeal, the ordeal of "when you pass through water." Indeed, this is not the first trial by water that we hear of in Nahman's life. Of the adolescent Nahman we will recall that: "He would take a boat out into the river, even though he did not know how to operate it, and when the boat was in the midst of the river, far from land . . . and he was about to drown, he would call out to God."[74] Is it any wonder that this same person, now a young adult, should test his faith by a dangerous voyage across the seas? The journey to Erez Israel is a repetition on a much grander scale of a 'trial by water' Nahman had already undertaken—repeatedly, it would seem—as an adolescent!

It is now clear that Nahman's journey to the Holy Land may best be defined as a *rite de passage* or a 'voyage of initiation,' the likes of which have been studied in various other religious cultures, both pre-literate and classical, but which are not generally considered to be a part of latter-day Judaism. The would-be initiate (whether in primitive tribal culture or here re-created in the rich myth-making imagination of a religious figure at the edge of modernity) seeks to undertake the death-defying voyage to the center of the world in order to receive that knowledge only the initiate may possess. Nahman, in confronting the real possibility of death and disappearance in a watery grave, tests his trust in God and his transcendence of his lower self once and for all. If he survives the great ordeal he will reach the Holy Land, at once the source of renewed life through Creation (for it was here that Creation had begun) and the locus of prophetic inspiration. Indeed his voyage corresponds to classic descriptions of the initiatory journey:

> The road is arduous, fraught with perils, because it is, in fact, a rite of the passage from the profane to the sacred, from the ephemeral and illusory to reality and eternity, from death to life, from man to the divinity. Attaining the center is equivalent to a consecration, an initiation; yesterday's profane and illusory existence gives place to a new, to a life that is real, enduring, and effective.[75]

There are in primitive societies particular forms of initiation that must be undertaken by one who seeks to assert himself as a shaman,[76] a type of religious figure who in several ways may be seen as parallel to the Hasidic *ẓaddiq*. Nahman now feels a call he can no longer seek to escape: he is to become the leader of a Hasidic community. Later, indeed, he is to see himself as the single leader of his entire generation. The dialectic of descent and ascent, of death and rebirth, must assert itself. If ambivalence and hesitation are ever to be overcome, it can only be by means of the ultimate journey.

Our explanation of Nahman's journey as a death-defying *rite de passage* does not necessarily contradict any of the interpretations offered by Nahman himself, and mentioned above. On the contrary, it provides them with a clarity of focus they had previously been lacking. The granting of higher wisdom, *ḥokhmah 'ila'ah* or 'garbed' wisdom, as a result of such initiation corresponds directly to that which is claimed for rites of initiation in the most varied religious cultures. That account in which Nahman claims that his goal was attainment of the spiritualized commandments is equally made transparent through this explanation. Whatever ambiguity may be found elsewhere in Hasidism with regard to the enjoyment or transcendence of this-worldly goods is lacking in Nahman. For him it was quite clear that only he who achieves *hitpashtut ha-gashmiyut,* total transcendence of the bodily self,[77] can reach the spiritual Torah. Yes, it was the higher Torah of Erez Israel that he sought—but that Torah could only be obtained by the *ordeal* of *derekh ereẓ yisra'el*—the transforming journey. It would seem that Nahman chose varying ways in which to account for his imminent journey, varying according to whom he was addressing or the degree of self-revelation he felt prepared to offer in a particular moment. All of them, however, point to the same basic meaning: the journey as an attempt to transcend his own lower self.[78]

This understanding of the voyage also helps us to explain the most curious fact of all in Nahman's visit to the Holy Land: as soon as he set foot on the soil of Erez Israel, on the eve of Rosh Hashanah in 1798, he announced that "when he had walked four ells in the Land of Israel he had already achieved all that he had sought"[79] and he was ready to return home immediately after the festival. Had his goal in fact been a pilgrimage to the Holy Land, including prayers at the holy places, a visit to the grave of his grandfather, or contact with the local Hasidic community, such a readiness to depart after only two days in the port of Haifa makes no sense whatever. If, however, his real goal was the adventurous journey itself, and *arrival* in Erez Israel signified the *attainment* of his goal and the completion of the ordeal, his willingness to return home at once is rendered completely understandable.

It was indeed through the strength gained on his journey to Erez Israel that Nahman returned to establish his place as a major figure in the Ukrainian Hasidic community. This strength was not, however, a matter of external 'authorization' or prestige; it was rather a sense that he had, in some way that seemed absolute, achieved mastery over his own inner self. He had 'passed through water' for the sake of God, and had seen his faith withstand the threat of imminent death. He was now one who could deserve the vision of the patriarchs, having followed their example by the utter denial of his corporeal self. Having survived his awesome encounters with danger on the seas, he had arrived at the great center and thus had felt his life renewed. He was now ready, reborn from amid the waters of his great trial, to return to his people and to assert himself as a major figure among the leaders of Hasidism in the Ukraine.

NOTES

1. *Siḥot* 153.

2. The dating of these two accounts and the relationship between them has been the subject of a thoroughgoing study by Ada Rapoport (Albert) in *Qiryat Sefer* 46(1971) 147–153. Rapoport has shown that the version of *Shivḥey ha-RaN* is the earlier of the two accounts. This version, first published in 1816, as an addendum to the first edition of Nahman's *Sippurey Ma'asiyot*, was probably composed sometime shortly after Nahman's death in 1810. The account in *Ḥayyey MoHaRaN* must have been composed sometime after Nathan's own visit to the Holy Land in 1822, to which he makes reference there in paragraph 10. Rapoport's conclusions, which are thoroughly convincing to this reader, are disputed by Yosef Dan (*Ha-Sippur ha-Ḥasidi*, p. 185) insofar as he claims that an early recension of the *Shivḥey* version was written by someone other than Nathan. Nahman's sayings with regard to the Holy Land and its sanctity (as distinct from his own journey there) have been collected by Nahman of Cheryn and published under the title *Zimrat ha-Areẓ*.

3. There have been many treatments of Nahman's journey in the modern literature on Hasidism. The chief sources are to be found in S.A. Horodezky's *Ha-Ḥasidut weha-Ḥasidim*, v.3, p.23*ff.*, *idem.*, *'Oley Ẓiyyon*, p.160*ff.*; H. Zeitlin, *Reb Nakhman Braslaver*, p.82*ff.*; S.M. Dubnov, *Toledot ha-Ḥasidut*, p.292*ff.*; M. Buber, *The Tales of Rabbi Nachman*, p.179*ff.*; J.K. Miklishansky in *Ha-Ḥasidut we-Ẓiyyon*, p.246*ff.*; N. Rose in *Journal of Hebraic Studies* 1(1970)63ff. There seems to be no basis in the sources either for Horodezky's claim that Nahman's intention was to settle permanently in the Holy Land or for Dubnov's reading of the journey as resulting from Nahman's quarrel with his Uncle Barukh, who could not tolerate Nahman's competition for power among Ukrainian *ḥasidim*. Since Nahman could muster no major support in this battle, according to Dubnov, "a new idea arose in his mind: To journey to the Land of Israel and to receive a sort of authorization from the holiness of the land and the group of *ẓaddiqim* there." *(op. cit.*, p.292) The fact is that while Nahman did, as we shall see below, have a major falling-out with his uncle, this did not occur until several years after his return from Erez Israel. In the winter of 1802/03 "there was still peace between them" *(Yemey MaHaRNaT*, p.12*f.)*; Nahman returned from his journey in summer of 1799. Further, Nahman was on good terms with any number of *ẓaddiqim* in the Ukraine during this early period. His struggles with the Zeide and others all began after his return; surely Levi Yizhak of Berdichev, who stood by Nahman through all his later difficulties, would gladly have supported him had he been in trouble in 1798. Along with the view of Dubnov we must dismiss the shockingly vituperative attact on Nahman by S. Zeitlin in *Jewish Quarterly Review*, n.s. 27(1937) 251, as having no basis in fact. The most interesting reading of the journey is that of Rose, who first proposed the term *rite de passage* to describe this event and who suggested the applicability of

Mircea Eliade's studies in the history of religions. The present chapter is in substantial agreement with Rose, but with some serious shifts of focus. The fact is that despite these many treatments of the subject, there has not yet been a thorough and dispassionate analysis examining all the sources in Nathan's writings, including several very important statements by Nahman himself, in order to understand the true motivation for the journey and its meaning in Nahman's life. Buber's truly beautiful essay on Nahman's journey bases itself largely on Nahman's later statements—some dating from more than ten years after his return—about the land, an approach with which I can not methodologically agree. His basic point, however, that Hasidism marks a new beginning of a realistic relationship with Erez Israel, in contrast to earlier over-spiritualization and romanticization, is worthy of further consideration.

4. Best known of these is the pilgrimage led by Judah Hasid and Hayyim Mal'akh in 1700. For a full discussion of that journey *cf.* M. Benayahu, "The Holy Brotherhood of R. Judah Hasid" in *Shne'ur Zalman Shazar Jubilee Volume*, p.131*ff.*

5. *Cf.* I. Halpern, *Ha-'Aliyot ha-Rishonot shel ha-Ḥasidim le-'Ereẓ Yisra'el.* These journeys have been discussed within the context of the place of messianism in the Hasidic movement. Those who tend to place a greater emphasis on the role of messianism within Hasidism (Dinur, Tishby) will seek to find significance in the journeys of early Hasidic figures to the Holy Land (especially Dinur in his *Be-Mifneh ha-Dorot*, p.192*ff.*), while their opponents in this larger controversy (Buber, Scholem, Schatz) would tend to see such pilgrimages as lacking in larger significance.

6. *Cf.* A. J. Heschel, "R. Gershon Kutover," HUCA 23 (1950–51), part I, Hebrew section p.46*ff.* This article contains a wealth of valuable information on the earliest Hasidic journeys to Erez Israel.

7. Their journey and settlement was described by Simhah ben Joshua of Zalozhtsy in *Sippurey 'Ereẓ ha-Galil*, published as a section of his *Ahavat Ẓiyyon*, Grodno, 1790, and reprinted by A. Ya'ari in *Masa'ot 'Ereẓ Yisra'el*, Tel Aviv, 1946.

8. The BeSHT's aborted journey is briefly mentioned in *Shivḥey ha-BeSHT*, ed. Horodezky p.48 and p.111*f.* A. Ya'ari has pointed out that the Yiddish version of *Shivḥey ha-BeSHT* treats the journey more explicitly than does the better-known Hebrew version. *Cf.* his remarks in *Qiryat Sefer* 39(1964) 559*ff.* Dinur, *loc. cit.*, makes much of this journey, seeing its failure as the crucial turning point in the early history of the Hasidic movement.

9. The BeSHT wrote to R. Gershon: "If God wills it, I shall be with you—but this is not the proper time for it." The letter was published by Jacob Joseph of Polonnoye at the end of his *Ben Porat Yosef*, Korets, 1781, and has been frequently reprinted. On Jacob Joseph's intended voyage *cf. Shivḥey ha-BeSHT*, p.50, and on Pinhas of Korets M. Biber, *Mazkeret li-Gedoley Ostrog*, p.212 and Horodezky, *Ha-Ḥasidut weha-Ḥasidim*, v.1, p.152*f.* On the settlement by the Vitebsker and the Kalisker *cf.* Halpern, *op. cit.*, and further details in Gershon Hundert, "Toward a Biography of R. Abraham Kalisker" (unpublished master's thesis, Ohio State University).

10. *Ḥayyey* 5:5. This account contains a typical example of the self-censorship found in many Bratslav sources. When Nahman was living in Medvedevka and was unable to make the journey to Medzhibozh, where the BeSHT was buried, he would send messages to the BeSHT through the *ẓaddiq* Isaiah of Yanov, who lay

buried in the nearby Smela graveyard. For a while he communed with Nahman of Horodenka in the same way, but at some point he was prevented from doing so. Nathan's account ends: "He also said that he was going to Erez Israel for this reason. Previously, when he had needed something from his grandfather R. Nahman, who lay buried in Erez Israel, he would send the *ẓaddiq* R. Isaiah, who lay in Smela. But now, etc., and he could not send him." It would be interesting to know what lies behind that *'etc.'* of censorship.

11. Communion with the spirits of the saintly dead as a means toward mystical enlightenment was well known among the Safed Kabbalists of the sixteenth century. The best example of such mystical visits to gravesites is to be found in Moses Cordovero's mystical diary *Sefer Gerushin*. The phenomenon has been discussed by R.J.Z. Werblowsky in his *Joseph Karo*, p.51*ff*. See especially in the passage by Hayyim Vital quoted on p.76.

12. *Shivḥey II* 15–16. Parallel in *Ḥayyey* 5:1.

13. Was this a visit of leavetaking for an already-anticipated long journey?

14. A.D. Twerski, *Sefer ha-Yaḥas mi-Chernobyl we-Ruzhin*, p.100. M. Balaban *(Toledot ha-Tenu'ah ha-Frankit*, p.295*ff*. and especially p. 316) denies the historicity of these traditions.

15. Zeitlin, *op. cit.*, p.84*f*.

16. Balaban, *op. cit.*, p.192*ff*. There were frequent expulsions of the Jews from Kamenets in the 17th and 18th centuries. The most effective of these bans seems to have been that of 1750, which may have in fact kept Jews out of Kamenets for as long as fifty years. These expulsions are discussed by R. Mahler in *Di Yidn in Poiln*, p.234. The ban was lifted, according to Mahler *(A History of Modern Jewry*, p.381) in 1797, a year before Nahman's visit. There was, however, a meeting of Podolian notables held at Kamenets in June of 1798 *(ibid.* p.383) which may have ratified this edict.

17. *Shivḥey II* 2. *Shivḥey II* 3 contains a censored reference to the fact that the journey to Kamenets caused a good deal of controversy: "Everyone offered some explanation of it, some praising it while others *etc.*"

18. *Cf.* for example *Liqquṭim* 64:3 which describes the *necessary* descent of the true *ẓaddiq* into the abyss in order to redeem those souls that are lost there. On the Sabbatian origins of *yeridat ha-ẓaddiq cf.* Weiss in *Zion* 16 (1951).

19. *Shivḥey II* 5. For the parallel in *Ḥayyey* 5:19, see below.

20. *Shivḥey II* 6.

21. *Yemey MaHaRNaT*, p.12 and passim.

22. While in the earlier account Nathan took care not to mention the name of the single *ḥasid* who accompanied Nahman on his journey, it does slip out in *Ḥayyey* 5:8. A. Rapoport *(op. cit*, p.147*ff)* claims that most of Nathan's information on the journey came from Simeon rather than from Nahman himself. Simeon returned to the Holy Land to settle there permanently in 1820. It is for this reason, Rapoport claims, that in the account written after 1822 Nathan is more willing to mention him by name. As Piekarz has shown, (p.203*ff)*, there was a struggle for leadership in the community in the early years following Nahman's death, and Simeon at that point may have been a threat to Nathan's position. Mentioning a rival as the one who accompanied the master on his sacred journey, and thus reminding the reader of his own latecomer status within the community, would not have served Nathan's ends at the time of the earlier version: hence the silence.

23. *Shivḥey II* 8. On the pogrom in Galati *cf. Jewish Encyclopedia*, v.10, p.513*f.*

24. *Shivḥey II* 8–9. Nahman's secret writings are discussed by Weiss in *Meḥqarim*, p.181*ff.*

25. Heb.: *'oseh kol miney qatnut.* The Hebrew has the double entendre of "childishness" and "lower spiritual state."

26. *Ḥayyey* 5:11–12.

27. *Shivḥey II* 10 and *Ḥayyey* 5:11. It is not clear whether they took him to be a *mitnagged* or a *ḥasid* of Shne'ur Zalman of Liadi, whose controversy with Abraham Kalisker of Tiberias had broken out a year earlier. I do not know to whom precisely the "Komarner" refers. He is said here to have had a son named Isaiah and to have been involved in some sort of controversy.

28. *Shivḥey II* 9.

29. In *Ḥayyey* 5:12 the matter is explained specifically with regard to the sanctity of the Holy Land. Because Erez Israel is *gadlut de-gadlut* one may only reach it through *qatnut de-qatnut.*

30. In the passage referred to in the preceding note, Nahman is quoted as saying that the BeSHT's journey had failed because he was not able to sufficiently descend into *qatnut.* On the BeSHT's journey *cf.* the passage in Dinur, *op. cit.*, p.192, quoted from *'Adat Ẓaddiqim* 4a, and *Shivḥey ha-BeSHT*, p.48.

31. *Shivḥey II* 12–13

32. Heb.: *le-hafqir et 'aẓmo.*

33. *Shivḥey II* 14. Emphasis mine.

34. *Shivḥey II* 14.

35. *Shivḥey II* 14. Emphasis mine.

36. *Shivḥey II* 15.

37. *Shivḥey II* 17. Heb.: *ki-medumeh she-nishma' mi-piw.* In a report published in 1842 (*Die Juden unserer Zeit*, p.8), the German historian B. Mayer includes a single very fascinating line concerning Nahman: ". . .dieser Mann, dessen Namen Nachmann ist, war aus seiner Verwandtschaft gebannt, ja sie hielten ihn für einen vom Teufel geleiteten Menschen; denn er hat, als er in Syrien war, den Götzendienst Merkulis getrieben." Mayer doubtless got this report from sympathizers of the rabbi of Savran, who had been most ferociously persecuting Nathan and his followers since 1835. But why this strange accusation that Nahman had been guilty of idolatry while in the Holy Land? Might it somehow be a distortion of this meeting with the young Arab?

38. *Shivḥey II* 18.

39. *Shivḥey II* 19.

40. Jacob Samson was a disciple of Jacob Joseph of Polonnoye and of Pinhas of Korets. He had settled in the Holy Land in 1794. *Cf.* Ya'ari, *Sheluḥey Ereẓ Yisra'el*, p.623.

41. *Shivḥey II* 19.

42. The city-state of Ragusa on the Adriatic coast remained neutral in the Napoleonic wars until 1805. *Cf.* F.W. Carter, *Dubrovnik (Ragusa): A Classic City-State*, p.524*f.*

43. M. Gihon, "Napoleon's Siege of Accho" in *Western Galilee and the Coast of Galilee*, p.165*ff.*

44. *Shivḥey II* 20–21.

45. *Shivḥey II* 22. The meaning of this rather startling passage will be discussed

below. The reference to Jacob is from Gen.30:37. We find the interpretation of this mysterious act of the patriarch as a kind of proto-observance of the *miẓwot* already in the writings of Dov Baer of Miedzyrzec. *Cf.* the sources quoted by R. Schatz in *Ha-Ḥasidut ke-Mistiqah,* p.56.

46. Piracy was indeed a major danger in the Eastern Mediteranean at that time. *Cf.* the comments by the Crimean Karaite traveller Benjamin Yerushalmi who sailed for Erez Israel in 1785, in J. D. Eisenstein's *'Oẓar Masa'ot,* p.214. For an account of Jews captured for ransom in the Aegean Sea as late as 1880, *cf. Jewish Encyclopedia,* v.10, p.40.

47. *Shivḥey II* 24–26

48. *Ḥayyey* 5:5.

49. *Ḥayyey* 5:6.

50. The two aspects of *ḥokhmah* are often mentioned in the *Zohar.* The upper *ḥokhmah* is the *sefirah ḥokhmah,* a hidden entity which cannot be known by man (1:141b). The lower *ḥokhmah,* sometimes known as the lesser *(ze'ira),* is more accessible and is identified with the wisdom of Solomon (2:223a R.M.), an appellative of the *shekhinah. Ḥokhmah* as a name for the tenth *sefirah* is already found in *Sefer ha-Bahir.* Thus it may be said that the earliest Kabbalistic sources contain, at least by implication, a notion of upper and lower *ḥokhmah. Cf.* G. Scholem, *Ursprung und Anfänge der Kabbala,* index s.v. *ḥokhma.* The parallels between this series of symbols and the world of ancient (particularly Valentinean) Gnosticism are known and have been discussed by Scholem there and in his *Von der mystischen Gestalt der Gottheit,* p.138*ff.*

Following the breakdown of each of the ten *sefirot* into a further ten, a move first popularized through the works of Moses Cordovero, Kabbalists variously assigned the term *ḥokhmah tata'ah* or *ḥokhmah ze'ira* either to the element of *malkhut* within the upper *ḥokhmah* or alternatively to *ḥokhmah* within *malkhut.* The former view is espoused by Hayyim Vital in his (pre-Lurianic) notes to the *Zohar* included in A. Azulai's *'Or ha-Ḥamah* to *Zohar* 1:141b. For the latter view, *cf.* the commentary to the liturgy by Nahman's contemporary Shne'ur Zalman of Liadi, p.112c. In devotional terms, Shne'ur Zalman identifies the lower *ḥokhmah* with *biṭṭul ha-yesh,* a semi-intellectual awareness that the world has no existence independent of God, while the higher *ḥokhmah* is identified with *biṭṭul be-'eẓem,* an experience of envelopment in the all-pervasive oneness of God. (p.108d) These terms seem roughly equivalent to the use of the terms *qatnut* and *gadlut* elswhere in the school of Miedzyrzec, and are quite parallel also to Nahman's later usage of these terms.

51. *Liqquṭim* 69:6 and II 91.

52. *Liqquṭim* 22.

53. *Ḥayyey* 5:5.

54. On the view of Torah as an organism *cf.* Scholem, *On the Kabbalah and Its Symbolism,* p.44*ff.* On the problem of the *miẓwot* in Hasidism see R. Schatz, *op. cit.,* chapter five. This notion of Torah as an organism also comes to be related to the image of *ḥaluqa de-rabbanan,* the mystical garment the soul is to wear in the afterlife, woven of the *miẓwot* one has fulfilled in this world. According to N. Shapira's *Megalleh 'Amuqot* 113 Moses wanted to enter Erez Israel so that he could perform the *miẓwot ha-teluyot ba-areẓ,* without which his garment would be incomplete. *Cf.* also *Qedushat Levi* by Levi Yizhak of Berdichev, p.247.

55. In addition to the Hasidic sources quoted by Schatz, *loc. cit.,* see the views

of Cordovero, A. Azulai, and Nathan of Gaza in Scholem's *Sabbatai Ṣevi*, p.319*ff*. The progression from the radical insights of the two 'orthodox' Kabbalists to the open antinomianism of the Sabbatian prophet leaves one somewhat in doubt as to where the actual cut-off point of heresy is to be found. Schatz demonstrates that the same is true with regard to much of early Hasidic thought on the *miẓwot*.

56. Schatz, *loc. cit.*, and Scholem, *Messianic Idea*, p.203*ff*. In this connection notice should be taken of another startling statement made by Nahman during his return voyage. He and Simeon were studying Mishnah to occupy themselves during their travels. When they reached *Soṭah* 5:2 and read "A generation will arise that will proclaim the purity of the third degree [of ritual impurity, those taboos not based upon Scriptural injunction]" Nahman became ecstatic, clapped his hands, and proclaimed: "Who sees as I do!" *Shivḥey II* 13. The implication seems to be that his is the generation that will find a way to purify this category of the defiled. This in itself cannot be called 'antinomian,' as it follows the law's own prediction, but it again is clearly reminiscent of well-known motifs in Sabbatian thought.

57. Levi Yizhak of Berdichev, in a most daring homily *(Qedushat Levi, lekh lekha*, p.15*f*.*)* employs a motif similar to that used here. In noting that Abraham came to know the commandments only after he entered Erez Israel, he says that until entering the land Abraham served by means of *mesirut nefesh* alone. He could not enter into the world of *miẓwot* until he was in that land where he could observe them in their totality, else he would have remained unwhole. Only after Sinai do *any* of the commandments become binding outside the land.

58. *Ḥayyey* 5:7.

59. Two versions of the Lurianic liturgy which were available in print in Nahman's day were those of Sabbatai of Raszkow (Korzec, 1794) and Asher Margulies of Brody (Lvov, 1788). Other versions are discussed by Scholem in his *Kitvey Yad ba-Kabbalah*, p.129*ff*.

60. Tishby, *Netivey 'Emunah u-Minut*, p.204*ff*. This *siddur* was first published in Slavuta, 1804. Tishby denies the existence of a Korzec, 1794 edition. Nevertheless, as Tishby notes, the work was widely circulated in manuscript, and exercised an influence on those works mentioned in *n*.59, even though they preceded it in print. *Qol Ya'aqov* is quoted by Simhah of Zalozhtsy as early as 1757.

61. *Cf. Beẓah* 17a and RaSHI *ad loc.*

62. *Qol Ya'aqov* 170b, 171b.

63. *Cf.* N. Shapira, *Megalleh 'Amuqot* 62 (10b).

64. *Cf. No'am Elimelekh, wa-yeshev* and the sources listed by Dinur, *op. cit.*, p.192, *n*.4. For the rabbinic sources *cf.* Mekhilta, *bo* (ed. Horovitz, p.2); *Mo'ed Qatan* 25a; *Zohar* 1:141a.

65. *Ḥayyey* 5:19. The concluding line reads as follows in the Hebrew: *mahu 'ani? raq mah sheha-neshamah sheli mehaddesh* (!). Emphasis here and in the following source mine. The context of the Isaiah passage refers to the return of the exiles to Zion.

66. The distinction Nahman is making here between 'self' and 'soul' is quite surprising. Jewish literature generally does not recognize a distinction. Note however the unusual formulation *ha-neshamah amerah leha-rav*, "the master's soul said to him" in *Ẓawa'at RIVaSH*, 4b. Nahman's *novellae* are seen by him as a sort of inner revelation, rather than as a creation of his own mind. See *n*. 68 below.

67. *Ḥayyey* 3:12. The pun cannot be fully translated. One reaches the vision *(bat 'ayin)* of the patriarchs (the three-pronged letter *shin)* by upsetting *(shaded,* here related to *sadekha)* one's animal nature. I have not been able to find such a statement in the *Tiqquney Zohar*. The references suggested in the editions of *Liqquṭim* 47 to *Tiqquna* 51 and *Zohar* 1:25b lead one to what is in fact an entirely different interpretation of the word *'esev,* containing no exegesis of Deut. 11:15.

68. Thus the act of preaching was described in the circle of Miedzyrzec. See *'Or ha-Me'ir* by Ze'ev Wolf of Zhitomir, 95c, and the discussion by J. Weiss in *JJS* 11(1960) 150. This phrase and similar ones were first employed to describe the prophetic experience of Moses. *Cf.* the sources quoted by A. J. Heschel in his *Torah min ha-Shamayim,* v.2, p.215*f* and 335*f*. Beginning in the sixteenth century, such phrases appear in the description of personal mystical experiences: revelations of *maggidim,* automatic speech, *etc. Cf.* Werblowsky, *op. cit.*, p.169 and *passim.* In Hasidism these phrases describe not only the act of preaching by the *ẓaddiq* but the act of prayer as well. For one of many examples see Dov Baer of Miedzyrzec, *'Or ha-Emet,* 1b, and the discussions by Weiss and by Schatz, *op. cit.*, p.95*ff*. This is one of the most striking examples of the popularization of mystical phenomena (or mystical terminology?) in Hasidism. For the use of the phrase within a Hasidic context to describe actual prophetic experiences, *cf.* Kalonymous Kalman of Cracow, *Ma'or wa-Shemesh,* 51b. A full account of *shekhinah medabberet mi-tokh piw (gerono)* would prove most rewarding. The dependence of the Jewish development upon those Islamic sources discussed by A. Altmann in his *Studies in Religious Philosophy and Mysticism,* p.150 might be a proper starting point for such an account.

69. *Siḥot* 153. Here Nahman is playing on the well-known rabbinic dictum *derekh ereẓ qademah la-torah. Leviticus Rabbah* 9:3.

70. *Sippurey Ma'asiyot* #8, 18b*ff*.

71. *Liqquṭim* 74, 115 249; *II* 43, 46; *Siḥot* 146.

72. *Siḥot* 11. *See* also *Shivḥey II* 28.

73. *Liqquṭim* 47. There clearly seems to be an unspoken personal meaning behind the otherwise rather bizarre chain of associations that makes up this teaching.

74. *Siḥot* 117.

75. M. Eliade, *The Myth of the Eternal Return (Cosmos and History),* p.18

76. M. Eliade, *Rites and Symbols of Initiation,* p.81*ff*.

77. The "stripping off" of corporeality is a central term for self-transcendence in Hasidic sources. This medieval term was popularized, if not created, by its inclusion in both the *Ṭur* and the *Shulḥan 'Arukh ('Oraḥ Ḥayyim* 98:1) as part of the prescription for proper prayer. *Cf.* the discussion by Werblowsky, *op. cit.*, p.61*f*. Scholem *(Von der mystischen Gestalt der Gottheit,* p.288, n.84) claims that the term originates in the *Ṭur*. It has not been traced to earlier philosophical or Kabbalistic literature. It would seem, however, that various parallel phrases were first employed to describe the prophetic state. *Cf.* for example the use of *shelilat ha-ḥomriyut* in Bahya ben Asher's commentary to Exodus 3:5, or the somewhat later *nitpasheṭ gufo mi-malbush ha-ḥomri* in Yehiel of Pisa's *Minḥat Qena'ot.* (ed. Kaufmann, p.25). In both of these cases the reference is to Moses. Here too, it would seem that we have a description of the prophetic state that later became prescriptive for every man in the life of prayer. A parallel development in medieval

Islam, where a description first applied to Mohammed's prophecy is taken over to describe mystical experience in general is traced by Alexander Altmann in "The Ladder of Ascension" in *op. cit.*, p.41*ff.*

78. Another curious passage (*Shivḥey* 31) reveals how secretive Nahman himself was with regard to the true meaning of his Erez Israel journey. When a certain scholar in the Holy Land pleaded with him to reveal the nature of his visit there, Nahman explained that he was sworn to secrecy on this matter. When pressed, he began to discourse on it indirectly. "But as he began to speak, blood came forth from his throat, and he said to the scholar: 'Now you see that God does not agree that I should reveal this to you.' "

79. *Shivḥey II* 15.

3

Conflict and Growth

The opening decade of the nineteenth century was a period of tremendous inner growth and outward expansion for the Hasidic movement. Large numbers of *ẓaddiqim* flourished in the Ukraine, Byelorussia, and Galicia, now largely unchallenged by rabbinic and communal authority. The turn of the nineteenth century had marked the end of open anti-Hasidic agitation on the part of the *mitnaggedim*. The second arrest of Shne'ur Zalman of Liadi in 1800 may be seen as the final act in an ongoing drama of conflict that had begun with the first bans against the *ḥasidim* in 1772. While personal enmities between *ḥasidim* and anti-*ḥasidim* of course continued to exist, and the Hasidic conquest of new territory, particularly in central Poland, met with some opposition, the rabbinic leadership of Eastern Europe had, by and large, made its peace with the movement. This lessening of conflict may be generally traced to two factors: the following of the *ẓaddiqim* had become so widespread and the influence of Hasidic practice so overwhelming, that the opposing forces simply did not have the strength to continue in the battle; at the same time the conservative tendencies within Hasidism had clearly demonstrated that the worst fears of the early *mitnaggedim* were not being realized. Hasidism had shown that it was no new Sabbatianism; despite a strong propensity for the most radical and startling homiletical formulations, infractions of the *halakhah* had not gone beyond those original changes in custom that had been the objects of the earlier bans.[1]

It is against this background of inner growth and lack of external conflict in Hasidism that the events of Nahman's first few years after the Erez Israel journey must be seen. While Nahman was to become the object of a series of particularly bitter controversies in his own right, the fact is that much of the Hasidic world was torn by inner conflict during the first years of the nineteenth century. *Ẓaddiqim* who had shown great outward affection for one another during the years of external pressure now began to enter into open conflict for control of the movement from within. In order for us to understand the nature of this conflict, it will be necessary first to turn our attention to certain of the major figures among the *ẓaddiqim* at the turn of the nineteenth century.

The two leading Hasidic figures in the Ukraine during this period were Barukh of Medzhibozh and Levi Yizhak of Berdichev. Barukh, as we have mentioned above, was not a great original thinker or spiritual teacher, but saw himself rather as custodian of the path that had been laid out by his grandfather, the Baʿal Shem Tov, and as heir to his authority. When later Hasidic tradition claimed that Barukh's soul contained a spark of the soul of King Solomon, it was probably more the opulence of Solomon's court than the king's great wisdom which came to mind. His strength seems to have lain in charismatic communal leadership and in a noble, if somewhat frightening, bearing. Levi Yizhak, one of the leading disciples of the Maggid of Miedzyrzec, had a large following and was to become a favorite of Hasidic folklore.[2] He had been in Berdichev since 1785, serving as both communal *rav* and *ẓaddiq*, and had succeeded in making that city a major center of Hasidism. While his teachings tend to some extent to de-emphasize the Kabbalistic component in the writings of the Maggid, he clearly saw himself as belonging to the circle which had been formed at Miedzyrzec, and perhaps for this reason he was never very close to Barukh, who was neither a great admirer of Dov Baer nor a follower of his rather intellectualized mystical path. Perhaps third in importance among the Ukrainian courts was that of Chernobyl, under the leadership of Mordecai, son of Menahem Nahum, author of *Me'or ʿEynayim*. His father, a wandering preacher who had been a disciple of both the BeSHT and the Maggid, had just died, in 1797. Mordecai was now imitating the grand manner of Medzhibozh, establishing an elaborate court modelled on that of Barukh.[3]

In addition to these central figures and others like them, there were in the Ukraine a number of popular wonder-working *ẓaddiqim*, known neither for original teachings nor for nobility of birth, but rather for their ability to effect miraculous cures, for the intensity and efficacy of their prayers, and for their concern with the lives of simple Jews. Such figures were clearly within the tradition of the Baʿal Shem Tov, who, it should be remembered, was concerned with providing material as well as spiritual help to ordinary, unlettered Jews. Among the "folk-*ẓaddiqim*" of this period, mention must be made of Aryeh Leib of Shpola (1725–1812), called the *zeide* ('grandfather' or 'old man'), whose major claim to authority stemmed from the fact that he was old enough to have met the BeSHT personally; by the beginning of the nineteenth century, forty years after the BeSHT's death, this was a unique claim among the *ẓaddiqim*. Other popular figures were the sons and disciples of Yehiel Mikhal of Zloczow (1721–1786), some of whom had spread westward from the

Ukraine into Galicia. The disciples of the Zloczower included such well-known figures as Mordecai of Neskhiz (1752–1800) and Zevi Aryeh of Olek *(d.*1811), both of whom typified this image of the Ukrainian Hasidic folk-leader, and whose descendants continued the traditions of popular Hasidism down to the final destruction of Ukrainian Jewry.

Also growing in importance during this period were several *ẓaddiqim* whose homes were outside the original Ukrainian heartland of Hasidism. Shne'ur Zalman of Liadi (1743–1814), the founder of the *ḤaBaD* school, was now undisputed leader of the *ḥasidim* of Northern Byelorussia and the border areas of anti-Hasidic Lithuania.[4] The fact that he had suffered imprisonment for the sake of his Hasidism added greatly to his popularity; in singling him out as the victim of persecution, the *mitnaggedim* and the Russian government had served to confirm his status as a leading figure of the movement. As the direct heir of Menaḥem Mendel of Vitebsk, he became a leader of the highly prestigious effort to collect funds for the Hasidic community in the Holy Land. His popular introduction to the tenets of Hasidism, *Liqquṭey 'Amarim (Tanya),* had been published late in 1796, and was achieving wide acclaim.

At the western end of the Hasidic "empire" there was also a leading figure who in some ways outshone many of his Ukrainian contemporaries. While Elimelekh of Lezajsk, who had first brought the Maggid's teachings to Galicia, had died in 1786, his leading disciple, Jacob Isaac the "Seer" *(d.*1815), had moved to Lublin and had thus established the first Hasidic center in a major city of Poland. Jacob Isaac was able to attract many important disciples. As his title indicates, he was reputed to have particular powers of clairvoyance. Out of his school were to emerge the leaders of Przysucha, Kotzk, and Ger, who were to set new paths in Hasidic life in nineteenth-century Poland. Mention should finally also be made of Israel Hofstein of Kozienice (1736–1813) who, along with Shne'ur Zalman, represented a type of scholarly Kabbalist within the Hasidic camp. The Maggid of Kozienice brought to the Jews of southern Poland a rare type of Hasidism, that managed to combine a great love of learning with the wonder-working qualities of the popular *ẓaddiqim.*

The central figure of the inner controversies that engulfed Hasidism at the turn of the century was Barukh of Medzhibozh. Between 1800 and the time of his death twelve years later, he had become embroiled in serious controversies with Shne'ur Zalman, Levi Yizhak the Seer, and his own nephew, Nahman.[5] There have been two schools of thought among historians of Hasidism as to the nature of these controversies. While Simon Dubnov has chosen to view them largely as political/economic power struggles, A.J. Heschel has tried to show that they were, in fact, ideological struggles as to the nature of Hasidic piety, struggles which had begun to take root as early as the conflict over succession to the BeSHT in 1760. Each of these interpretations, as we shall see, tells part of the story.[6]

That political/economic issues are involved when one speaks of a stuggle for authority over the lives of tens of thousands seems to need little justification. The gifts *(pidyonot)* which *ḥasidim* brought to the *ẓaddiq* were a very considerable source of revenue, if we are to judge from the life styles of Barukh, Mordecai of Chernobyl, and certain other figures. On the other hand, we must again recall the particular disdain with which Dubnov regarded Barukh of Medzhibozh; his attempt to make Barukh out as a selfish, money-hungry, power-grabbing charlatan seems quite overdone. Heschel tempers this one-sided view by pointing to the ideological dimensions of the controversies. Barukh of Medzhibozh, he reminds us, had been raised in the home of Pinhas of Korets, while both Levi Yizhak and Shne'ur Zalman were leading disciples of Dov Baer of Miedzyrzec. Pinhas had opposed Dov Baer from the outset, and had, toward the end of his life (he died in 1791), suffered persecution at the hands of the Maggid's disciple Gedaliah of Linits.[7] Heschel claims that the original difference between Dov Baer and Pinhas was in fact ideological, and not merely a matter of political power and the rights of succession. Pinhas saw in Hasidism a message of ethical self-perfection and simple faith; he was displeased with the Maggid's reintroduction of Kabbalistic concepts and his single-minded striving for *devequt*. The BeSHT's essential teaching, as Pinhas understood it, held that man had to work hard at the uplifting of the material world. True, sparks of divine light were to be found in all things, but it was only by means of disciplined struggle that man could discover them and bring them back to God. Any attempt at mystical flight before the lower self was thoroughly purified could only end in disaster. "Turn from evil and do good," Pinhas quoted from the Psalmist; before you seek to do good make sure that you have turned from evil. The Maggid, who brought to Hasidism a level of Kabbalistic learning and of general intellectual sophistication which it had hardly known in the times of the BeSHT, read his master's teachings differently. The lower world is only illusion, he taught in his more radically mystical moments, and to strive for perfection within it is to miss the point. For him, the BeSHT's central message was one of transcendence: when you realize that God is in all things, you will see through the veils of separation that keep you from Him, and discover that in truth there is nought but God. When you have reached that place of inner *devequt*, taught the Maggid, such lesser matters as the struggle for moral perfection will be rectified of their own accord; the light that shines forth from such a vision will also serve to illumine the "lower" aspects of a person's life.[8]

The fact that these issues were still alive at the end of the eighteenth century is witnessed by the conflict of Shne'ur Zalman and Abraham Kalisker over the publication of the *Tanya*. Although the arguments between them take a somewhat different form, the same underlying issues seem to be called forth. Kalisker himself had been a disciple of the

Maggid, but he had a preference for the simple faith of the Ukrainian *ḥasidim*. He wrote from Tiberias denouncing Shne'ur Zalman for "garbing the teachings of the BeSHT in the teachings of Luria" and thus confusing the minds of ordinary *ḥasidim.*[9]

One wonders what Kalisker would have thought of the teachings his friend Nahman was to publish about a decade later. In fact, these two figures cross paths in a way that sheds interesting light on both schools of thought and their problems. Kalisker, close to Mendel of Vitebsk and Shnu'er Zalman of Liadi, perhaps two of the most intellectual figures among the Maggid's disciples, rebelled against the uncontrolled growth of mental speculations he saw emerging as *ḤaBaD,* and idealized the Ukrainian simplicity, perhaps finding it at one point in the young Nahman. Nahman, having seen how the path of simplicity can degenerate into a dull and stylized pietism, was forging from the path of the BeSHT a new and highly complex synthesis of "simple" Hasidism and abstruse Kabbalah.

Despite the apparent abuses, Heschel claims, Barukh saw himself as defending the difficult path of the BeSHT and Pinhas of Korets against the followers of the Maggid who threatened to displace all other teachings with those of their master. Ultimately we have no way of deciding between Heschel and Dubnov in their readings of these controversies. It would seem, of course, that ideological and political/economic motives can hardly be separated in the struggle for control of a religious sect. No doubt Barukh did see himself as the legitimate heir of the Ba'al Shem Tov and viewed those who opposed him as usurpers.[10] It is clear that these usurpers were competing with him for political and economic power. The fact that these competitors were, however, disciples of the man whom his teacher Pinhas had opposed, and the fact that their approach to the religious life differed considerably from his own, were also real elements in the conflict, and not simply justifications for a struggle for authority. Perhaps it would be best to put the matter this way: the great success of Hasidism in the Ukraine and the relative stability it had achieved now called forth serious and complex rivalries among the *ẓaddiqim,* rivalries in which both politics and attitudes toward piety had their place.

Immediately upon his return from Erez Israel—perhaps even at the close of the journey itself—Nahman travelled to Liadi in an attempt to make peace between Shne'ur Zalman and Abraham Kalisker. The conflict between these two was now certainly both economic and ideological; it appears that in response to Kalisker's objections to the *Tanya* Shne'ur Zalman had cut the lifeline of charitable funds *(ḥalluqah)* to the Tiberias community.[11] The controversy had reached such dimensions that Shne'ur Zalman had come to blame Kalisker for all the troubles which *ḥasidim* had encountered since the beginning of the movement. Had the *ḥasidim* of Kalisker not been guilty of certain odd public displays of piety in 1770, said Shne'ur Zalman, the *mitnaggedim* never would have set out to destroy Hasidism.[12] While the truth behind this angry claim cannot be fully ascertained, it is, at very least, an oversimplification; the early opposition to Hasidism was due to much more than just the demonstrative enthusiasm of Hasidic prayer.

We do not know what transpired between Nahman and Shne'ur Zalman during this visit. It is certain, however, that Nahman did not succeed in solving Kalisker's problem. We are in possession of a letter written by Kalisker to Nahman, showing his great concern for the success of this mission. While the document is undated, internal evidence seems to indicate that it was written at least half a year after Nahman's return to Europe.[13] Kalisker writes:

> After the compromise we had worked out with the people in Volhynia, we still have not collected from them even once. We don't know what will be the end of the matter. We are 'confounded in the land' (Ex. 14:3) because of our many troubles and worries. We hope at all times for the salvation of the Lord, but to date we have not been saved by anybody. We also have no news from the province of Reisin [Byelorussia] as to what happened there after your visit, when you told them all the woe that has befallen us. We are anxious for you to tell us all the details of what transpired there. Know that we remain in debt to the governor, and must pay with whatever we have. The constant and fearful pressure applied to us is difficult to bear. . . .[14]

Later letters of Kalisker (not to Nahman) continue to testify that the privations of the Tiberias community did not come to a sudden end, and that the controversy between Shne'ur Zalman and the Tiberias *ḥasidim* continued unabated for some time.[15]

In contrast to the brief mention of this encounter, Nathan records at some length the warm reception Nahman found at the courts of Neskhiz and Olek, which he also visited upon his return. Mordecai of Neskhiz and Zevi Aryeh of Olek were two of the major figures in popular Ukrainian Hasidism at the turn of the nineteenth century. They were both quite close to Nahman's Uncle Barukh, with whom Nahman was still on good terms at this point. Both of the *ẓaddiqim* received Nahman with great honor, and the Neskhizer, who was very ill (he died in 1800), made a special effort to get up from his sickbed in order to play host to the young visitor. While Nahman gives the impression of having intended no open disrespect to these elder *ẓaddiqim,* and in fact parted (at least from Neskhiz) on good terms, the visits to these courts were not simply matters of courtesy. Nahman entered into rather serious controversy with both of these popular figures as to the nature of visionary experience. The *ẓaddiq* of Neskhiz in particular was known for his claims of angelic visions, and it was to these claims that Nahman took exception:

> I have heard from our people that his concern with them had to do with visionary experiences. Our master did not agree to the visions which they had. He had a great argument with the holy rabbi of Neskhiz, who was

> famous in this regard. I have no knowledge of the content of these arguments, but our master said that theirs was not the proper way of attaining visions. The rabbi of Neskhiz sent a message to our master saying: 'Before you came into town, I saw a vision of the angel Meṭaṭron, and his appearance was thus-and-thus.' And I believe that I heard that this holy rabbi claimed that he had seen him with his very eyes. Our master responded that this was not the way to see him. It seems that once again the holy rabbi argued with our master in person, and said: 'I saw him thus-and-thus,' but our master would not agree. He said to them: 'This is not the way to see Meṭaṭron. I saw him in such-and-such a way, and that is the true vision of Meṭaṭron.[16]

The *ẓaddiq* of Olek also claimed to have visions like those of the Neskhizer, and Nahman, here apparently skeptical from the outset, tried to respond with silence. When his host persisted, however, in pressing the legitimacy of his visions upon him, Nahman replied with a rather sharp use of a Talmudic quotation: "Many spoke of the *merkavah* without ever having seen it."[17]

Nahman also made a point of visiting the Shpoler Zeide on his return from Erez Israel. There, too, he was received with great affection, and the Zeide, soon to become Nahman's bitter enemy, was beside himself with joy at a visit from the Ba'al Shem's great-grandson.[18]

From the choice of these three *ẓaddiqim* as the objects of his visits, one gets the impression that Nahman wanted to have a firsthand look at popular Hasidism as it was practiced in the Ukraine. It may be that he sought direct confirmation of the negative feelings about this sort of Hasidism which had already been developing in him before his journey. In this case the conversation about vision may be seen as a test of spiritual knowledge Nahman was administering to the *ẓaddiqim;* before speaking out against them he wanted to know what sort and degree of real inner experience lay behind their popular appeal. Alternatively, we may surmise that after his visit to Erez Israel Nahman was getting ready to leave the relative obscurity of Medvedevka. Knowing that such a move might involve him in a territorial dispute with one *ẓaddiq* or another, he was mapping out a strategy for himself, while at the same time trying to impress his elders with the maturity of his own vision. It was probably as a result of these visits that Nahman decided upon Zlotopolye as his future residence.

Aside from these visits to various Hasidic courts, we know little of Nahman's activities during the first year after his return. He was concerned with the betrothal and marriage of his daughters,[19] and one may surmise also that it was a time in which he worked to consolidate the loyalty of his own *ḥasidim* after a year of absence.

When Nahman finally did make the move from Medvedevka to Zlotopolye, he did so quite suddenly and without any prior announcement.

He apparently did not even consult the local elders, a move which certainly would have been expected of a *rebbe* before he came to establish himself as a public figure in a new place. His daughter Odel was married in Chmelnik on August 22, 1800, and rather than returning home to Medvedevka after the wedding, he went directly to Zlotopolye, where he proclaimed his intent to settle. While he attributed this choice to the dictates of a vision, it would seem that this vision fitted well with some rather carefully-laid plans. There was nothing in particular to recommend the town of Zlotopolye over Medvekevka. He was still remaining at the far eastern edge of the Ukrainian Jewish area of settlement, far to the east of Medzhibozh and other major centers. Nor was he moving to a significantly larger or wealthier location; he did not, for example, choose the much larger nearby town of Smela, which would have borne greater prestige and perhaps greater wealth. Nahman does not seem to have had any *ḥasidim* or particular supporters in Zlotopolye before he moved there. In fact, it is clear that there was nothing special about this town except for one factor: moving there was a clear violation of the Shpoler Zeide's territory, and thus a challenge to the authority of the local *ẓaddiq*. Not only was Zlotopolye a mere two miles from Shpola; the Zeide himself, before moving to Shpola, had been beadle of the synagogue in Zlotopolye, and thus had particularly close links with that town.[20]

The elderly Aryeh Leib of Shpola does not give the impression of having been the cantankerous old fool described in the Bratslav sources. On the contrary, the tales surrounding him[21] describe a warm and kindly grandfather-like *ẓaddiq*, one who under other circumstances could have become a hero in one of Nahman's later tales. No collection of teachings has been preserved in his name; he was one of those among the *ẓaddiqim* who taught by deed and personal example rather than by the word. There is little reason to think that his rabbinic education was particularly strong, but the virtues of simplicity were well exemplified in him.

Nevertheless, it was the Zeide whom Nahman chose as the butt of his attack on popular Hasidism, and who was thus to become—with good reason—Nahman's bitterest enemy for the rest of the young *ẓaddiq's* days. Whether it was his old age (he was seventy-five when Nahman moved to Zlotopolye), his lack of an heir, or some other factor that caused Nahman to choose him as the personification of that within Hasidism which he wanted to fight—or perhaps all of these—is beyond our power to know.

When it came, the challenge was a clear and direct one, and it did not take long for the message to reach the Zeide's ears. For the holidays, which began only a month after Nahman's arrival in town, more than a hundred guests came to Zlotopolye to be with the young *rebbe*. Initially delighted at the honor (and perhaps at the potential economic boon) that had come to their community, the townsfolk suggested that Nahman take over the local synagogue for the holidays, rather than forming a separate quorum for prayer. This suggestion was in fact a handing over of authority; Nahman was to decide who would lead the services, blow the *shofar*, etc. In effect, the synagogue of Zlotopolye, where the Zeide had once served, now became the focal point for Nahman's activities.[22] When, on the Day of Atonement, Nahman accused the local prayer-leader of chanting the service beautifully more in order to impress his wife than to appeal to God, the aggrieved *ḥazzan* went to Shpola to seek justice at the hands of the Zeide.

Thus, according to the Bratslav sources, began the bitter feud between the two *ẓaddiqim*. Two weeks after the initial incident the Zeide himself came to Zlotopolye and publicly denounced Nahman. Most of the townspeople, either out of respect for the elder *ẓaddiq* or out of fear for his reputed powers, took sides against the newcomer. But Nahman refused to leave the town. For two years he continued to live in Zlotopolye, despite ever-increasing conflict and persecution. He said that it was the will of heaven that he live in this town; he aggravated matters by announcing that he had come to Zlotopolye to redeem it from the sin of the Biblical Jeroboam. As in his visit to Kamenets, he was on a heaven-appointed mission, and nothing could swerve him from his task. While we shall see later that the reference to Jeroboam had a particular meaning in Nahman's own life, the townspeople of Zlotopolye probably heard this as an accusation of idolatry—the veneration of one whom Nahman considered to be a 'false' *ẓaddiq*. It may also be, as has been suggested, that he was referring specifically to the sin of Jeroboam in erecting the golden calves at Bethel (I Kings 12:28); the name Zlotopolye in Ukrainian means "city of gold"—was it to denounce the worship of wealth that he felt the need to seek out a place with that symbolic name?[23]

Surprisingly little is known to us about the actual content of the controversy between Nahman and the Zeide. Did Aryeh Leib originally accuse Nahman of anything more than *hassagat gevul*, the violation of his territorial rights? One later Bratslav source[24] mentions an accusation (supposedly voiced by the Zeide in 1806) that Nahman had permitted the consumption of liquor before morning prayers in order to stimulate ecstasy in worship. This seems to be a rather unlikely charge to have been taken very seriously among *ḥasidim*, who had themselves long been accused by the *mitnaggedim* of excessive attachment to alcohol. We may suspect this tradition of having created a "straw man" version of the Zeide's claims. A further accusation supposedly made by one or another of Nahman's detractors was the highly unlikely claim that Nahman's teachings were not original. The accuser asserted that Nahman had a secret collection of teachings by his grandfather, Nahman of Horodenka, and that he simply copied them into his own teaching.[25] Aside from these two somewhat far-fetched matters, no explanation of these disputes is found in the highly censored printed sources of Bratslav literature.

Various modern scholars have tried to claim that the Zeide accused Nahman of Sabbatianism or Frankism. Indeed, this would account for the ferocity of the battle. The memory of Sabbatianism was vividly alive in the Hasidic world, and Sabbatai Sevi's name continued to serve as an anathema. In fact, however, hard evidence to support the claim that Nahman was accused of Sabbatianism is lacking. The document around which this assertion was largely built has been discredited, and without it there is insufficient evidence to defend this view.[26] The Bratslav sources, as is to be expected, tell us almost nothing of the Zeide's actual complaints against Nahman, and no other trustworthy sources exist.

The arguments placed in the Zeide's mouth by Yudl Rosenberg, an early twentieth-century "collector" of tales concerning him, are tempting at first glance, but Rosenberg's work has been shown to be nothing but fiction, and indeed his arguments, even as speculation, are without historical merit. Rosenberg surmised, undoubtedly on the basis of his experience with latter-day Hasidism, that the issue between the two was one of modernity, particularly one of the admissibility of secular learning. Nahman, said Rosenberg's version of the Zeide, was beyond his time in this regard, and had to be fought in the name of the traditional ways. Thus he tells the following tale:

> A certain merchant once praised the Bratslaver highly before the Zeide, saying that he was a wise man who knew many languages and also had a knowledge of . . . geography, understanding the map of any country. The merchant recounted how this knowledge had helped him greatly in some major commercial undertaking. The Zeide answered: 'I don't consider this to be any sort of praise for a *ẓaddiq*. I too was taught other languages and geography in my youth. But I have no need at all of such knowledge, or to consult maps. When I hold the *etrog* on the holiday of *Sukkot* I see on the *etrog* all the places on the globe.'[27]

Rosenberg has felt something of the difference between the simple wonder-working Zeide and Nahman the intellectual; Nahman indeed was more of a student than was the elder *ẓaddiq*. But with regard to *secular* studies Rosenberg was far off the mark, projecting inaccurately from the situation (perhaps in Kotzk or Ger) in his own day. Nahman was among the most conservative of all Hasidic teachers in this matter. His response to the Zeide's *etrog* would more likely have been a complicated play on words or *gematria* from somewhere in the *Zohar*, showing that the true *ẓaddiq* should think only of the highest worlds when holding the *etrog*, and not concern himself with such worldly matters as the reading of it as a map. Needless to add, the image of the Zeide studying geography and languages in his youth (in mid-eighteenth century Ukraine!) is also a rather ludicrous anachronism.

Lacking authentic historical sources on the nature of the Zeide's complaints against Nahman, we may attempt some surmises of our own.[28]

Ours, however, will be of a somewhat different and more theoretical nature. The conflict between them has to do with a struggle over leadership, and particularly a struggle between the old and the young. Though such conflicts take place in any society, young leaders showing their restlessness and their anxiousness to have their elders retire, such a conflict is exacerbated in the generations following a major upheaval in social and spiritual values. The young justify their desire to lead by their perception—never totally inaccurate—that their elders have sold out the "revolution."

From a certain point of view the elder leader here (interestingly he is always called *ha-zaqen*—'the old man'—in Bratslav writings) was justified in his attacks on Nahman, in the way that the old frequently see themselves as justified in hurling accusations at the young when they feel their leadership being seriously threatened. And Nahman's challenge was very clearly a threat to the Zeide and his generation.

Hasidism in its original heyday had been a movement characterized by a certain degree of religious rebellion, an attitude for which it had been severely persecuted. Persecution had, by the turn of the nineteenth century, taken a major role in the reshaping of the movement. By Nahman's time Hasidism was well on the road toward becoming that conservative force which it was to prove itself to be by the latter part of the nineteenth century. Nahman was perceptive enough to see this process and to seek to arrest it. In calling for a rededication of Hasidism to the Ba'al Shem's spirit, or for a new enflaming of souls grown cold, he was of necessity saying that Hasidism would need restored to it some of the brashness which had characterized it fifty years earlier and had gotten it into so much trouble. In the nature of things, this brashness would now have to be turned against the complacency of the older generation of Hasidism's own leaders. Some of the same furor which the *Toledot* had once unleashed upon the arrogant power of learned rabbis would now have to be turned upon grandfatherly wonder-working *ẓaddiqim*.

Nahman and his followers were so persecuted within the Hasidic community because it was the Hasidic community—or what it had become—that Nahman himself saw as the primary object of struggle. The turn to Hasidism had meant a revolution in religious consciousness for many East European Jews. The Zeide was one—undoubtedly one of many—who felt that the essential revolution had been successfully completed. The ways of intense piety and enthusiastic prayer as taught by the Hasidic masters had deeply influenced the lives of thousands of Jews. The *ẓaddiqim* were widely revered, and countless young men were flocking to their courts to seek (ideally, at least) a personal path to God. The powerful forces of opposition had been defeated, and the sometimes unbridled energies of sacred enthusiasm had been kept carefully within the bounds of law, thus avoiding schism in the community. From the point of view of a member of the Zeide's generation, what more was there to seek? The rapid growth of Hasidism must have seemed its greatest and most miraculous vindication. Nahman, as youthful (not excluding some degree of immaturity) in attitude as the Zeide was elderly, saw the matter rather differently. A movement which had sought great spiritual transformations had settled for changes in external style. The dedication of a persecuted few had quickly given way to the luxury-loving lifestyles of complacent *ẓaddiqim,* who would more than likely seek the role of comforter rather than that of challenger in their disciples' lives in order to insure the regular flow of *pidyonot*. Hasidism, from the point of view of a brash young man, had grown soft and overly accepting of its own inner abuses. The popularization of the movement had cost it its intensity; compromise had become the order of the day. If Nahman was going to allow himself to become a leader at all—and we have seen the great ambivalence with which he set out toward that role—it would of necessity have to be at the expense of such figures as the Zeide and his Uncle Barukh. The renewed charismatic intensity of the BeSHT's day could only be preached by contrast with the flabbiness of those in whose hands the leadership of the community presently lay.

One wonders also whether there may not have been another side to the Zeide's opposition to Nahman. Might he not have seen in the young man who so obviously and brashly challenged him something worrisome in what we would call a psychological sense? An established leader who is met by a serious challenge, especially when he is as concerned for the challenger as he is threatened by his barbs, will naturally seek some understanding of the challenge that involves an inward view of the one who issues it. We can imagine that the Zeide would have been pained by a challenge from the BeSHT's own family, and not only because of the chances of its success. In speaking of Nahman in such a way as to indicate that he was an unfit guide, we wonder whether the Zeide (surely, if anything, a perceptive observer of human nature) did not perceive that which we would think of as a neurotic component in Nahman's need to rise up against him. And, we might wonder, as in the case of many an elder's critique of more modern revolutionaries, whether the Zeide might not have had a temptation to dismiss the challenge as nothing more than the sign of a personal aberration.

Of course the Zeide would have been 'right' in finding such a component in Nahman's attitude toward him. There was indeed an element of anxiety-filled youthful rebellion in the stance Nahman took with regard to his elders. It seems likely that it was this very element in the struggle between them which in turn made Nahman so painfully vulnerable to the Zeide's counter-accusations as they were hurled against him, a vulnerability which the adult Nahman never escaped. He was not sufficiently confident in his self-proclaimed role to ignore the shouts of those figures his entire upbringing and education had taught him to revere. Aware that he was setting out on a new path, he bore all of that conflict and insecurity which is the lot of so many youthful challengers to accepted spiritual and social norms.

A large part of the social power of Nahman's challenge was deflected into personal or psychological consideration by the Zeide's response. For Nahman's opponents, he himself became the issue. "Is Nahman a fit guide?" is a question which pursued him through his life and has followed his disciples over the generations insofar as they sought some place within the larger Hasidic community. Nahman himself was plagued by a terrible sense of persecution. The Zeide's denunciations, whatever their specific content may have been, played into Nahman's own sense of guilt and inadequacy to his role.[29] We find in Nahman a radically polarized attitude toward his battle with the Zeide. Publicly he claimed that he was absolutely the victim of unjustified attacks; it was only the Zeide's wickedness that had led him to speak ill of a true *ẓaddiq*. Privately, however, the challenge which he himself had created turned in on him and caused him deep suffering. He who had set out to denounce the false leadership of the popular *ẓaddiqim* now found himself accused of false leadership, a charge he could not help but take to heart. This private suffering is also reflected in many of Nahman's writings: because his path was one of constant self-examination, and his writings are a mirror to the varied states of his soul, the most private of his thoughts are often known to us. We thus find in Nahman's utterances alternating statements of self-vindication and self-accusation with regard to the public controversy which grew around him. In a radical formulation typical of Nahman's style we are told:

> On several occasions he himself repeated the words of those who say that here there is no middle path. Either he is, God forbid, just as those who oppose him say he is . . . or, if not, he is a true *ẓaddiq*. In that case he is uniquely awesome and wondrous, to an extent which cannot be encompassed by the human mind.[30]

In fact such "either/or" statements serve to mask the deep ambivalence Nahman felt toward his own fitness for the mantle of *ẓaddiq*, and hence toward his opponents' claims. In some way he undoubtedly felt that *both* poles were true; the greatest and most wondrous of all the *ẓaddiqim had* to be seen by others as the greatest fraud. And that view of him was not simply a distortion, but rather a necessary part of his role in life. The highly complex inner dialectic of Nahman's mind tried to resolve the tension between his alternating states of self-confidence and self-doubt by formulating a paradoxical image of a *ẓaddiq* who would *inevitably* be the object of conflict and controversy. In challenging the authority of the Shpoler Zeide, Nahman had embarked upon a public career aimed at the promulgation of a new Hasidic revival. He knew that this would have to lead him through a world of bitter conflict. Personally vulnerable to all claims against him, and yet committed to his mission, Nahman's only way of psychologically surviving the attacks of his enemies was to build a constantly escalating claim of unique leadership and to elaborate an ever more tortuously paradoxical vision of himself.

What we are proposing here (following the insights of the late Joseph Weiss) is that Nahman's vision of the paradoxical *ẓaddiq* is a dialectical resolution of Nahman's own alternating states of elation and depression, now aggravated by the accusations against him. We have seen that these severe alternations of mood characterized Nahman in adolescence; they undoubtedly were exacerbated by the attacks of his enemies. But the *ẓaddiq* who was to restore Hasidism to the glory of the Ba'al Shem Tov's day could not allow himself to be held back by his own self-doubt; he who was to challenge the authority of his powerful elders needed to have the inner strength to follow that challenge through to its conclusion. Yet how could Nahman deny to himself those rises and falls which were so central a part of his personal and spiritual life? Nothing was more real to him, as we have seen, than the inner flux with which he lived so constantly. Even the journey to Erez Israel, an attempt at radical self-transcendence, had not succeeded in liberating him from cycles of presence and absence of God, of personal fulness and utter emptiness. The more highly inflated his claims for himself were to become, the more vigorously was he pursued by inner doubt. Finally—perhaps in an only partially conscious way—he came to realize that *only the paradoxical elevation of his own doubts to the level of sublime mysteries could save him from their crippling grasp.*

The BeSHT had spoken of the 'uplifting' of 'alien' or distracting thoughts as essential to the technique of mystical prayer. While the original doctrine had referred primarily to temptations and thoughts of sin, Nahman now turned this idea to fit his own needs. His worst 'alien' thoughts consisted of doubts, both in matters of faith and with regard to his own person and his right to lead a Hasidic community. He thus attempted to 'uplift' and transform these doubts, paradoxically seeking in them the ultimate confirmation of his mission.

This dialectical resolution of self-confidence and self-doubt into paradoxical self-assertion was by no means a conscious creation of a particular moment in Nahman's life, after which time it stood as a psychological *fait accompli,* never to be challenged. On the contrary, though the resolution began to take shape in Zlotopolye, in reaction to the conflict with the Zeide, it had a touch-and-go existence throughout the remaining years of Nahman's life; through all of those years we continue to see repeated manifestations of all three stages in this dialectical dynamic: elation, depression, and paradoxical resolution.

We have already seen how Nahman, plagued by his own sense of sinfulness, tried to justify the sinner's serving as spiritual guide to others. The formulations which took hold during his adult years are even more paradoxical than that rather self-effacing justification. The most audacious statements of self-definition that can be imagined were now justified as *'azut di-qedushah,* 'holy audacity.' To counter the boundless audacity of the evil forces (at times personified by the Zeide) which speak ill of the *ẓaddiq,* one needs to employ this holy audacity, answering them in kind. Thus Nahman could find it within his power to compare the true *ẓaddiq* to God Himself in the matter of transcendent incomprehensibility:

> It is *necessary* that objections be raised with regard to the *ẓaddiqim,* for the *ẓaddiqim* are imitating God, as is known. Just as there are objections to God, so there must be objections to the *ẓaddiq* who imitates Him.

> With regard to these objections to God he liked to say: Of course there have to be questions about Him; this is only fitting to His exalted state. For it is of *the very nature of His greatness* that He be beyond our minds' grasp. It is impossible that we understand His conduct with our intellect. There must be objections raised to Him . . . for if He conducted Himself as our minds dictate, our minds would indeed be equal to His own![31]

The true vindication of God's transcendence lies in the very fact that there are objections to the belief in Him! We shall have occasion later to dwell at length on the implications of this unique theological position.

Our interest here lies in the *ẓaddiq* and the fact that faith in him is included in this ultimate demand for paradoxical belief. Whatever objections are raised to such a *ẓaddiq,* whatever calumnies may be spread about him, will only raise higher the spiraling claims of such a dialectic. Even the external trappings of authority displayed by such a *ẓaddiq* are justified as parallel to the material displays of divine power: as God had to perform great miracles in Egypt so that Israel would believe in Him, so the *ẓaddiq* has need of fine clothing and noble bearing in order to attract a following.[32] Referring to himself more directly, he was once heard to say:

> How would it be possible that they not oppose me? I have taken an entirely new path, one which no man has walked before. In fact mine is a very old path—but at the same time it is also completely new.[33]

Nahman, the one who follows the old/new path, is also the hero of the opening tale in his *Seven Beggars,* where the youngest of the company turns out to be the foremost in wisdom.[34] Such claims of wisdom beyond that of any other *ẓaddiq* at once caused and justified further attacks on him. He understood that even an authentic elder *ẓaddiq* would have good reason to resent him:

> This is a matter of great envy. Here is a great *ẓaddiq,* who has struggled for years with body and soul to worship God. He allows himself no rest, suffering a great deal for the sake of His service. Then along comes a young man, and in a short period of time attains everything that this *ẓaddiq* had sought for so many years. . . .[35]

The aura of mystery surrounding Nahman's person played a major role in the Bratslav community's understanding of why he was so persecuted. Nahman frequently proclaimed to them what a great wonder he was and how little even the closest among them understood him. Surely if his own most faithful followers could not fathom the mystery of his inner self, it would be difficult to expect more of distant, self-proclaimed *ẓaddiqim* who approached him with hostility; Nahman lived in a world that accepted empathy as an essential component of understanding. Misunderstanding is thus a major theme in the explanations of why Nahman was the object of such bitter opposition: Nathan's writings abound in statements of "Had they only known . . ." It is not at all surprising to see that this motif of the misunderstood wonder-man, one which had been used by the previous generation of Hasidic authors to explain the mitnaggedic opposition to Hasidism altogether,[36] was now turned upon some of those same Hasidic leaders by the Bratslav disciples seeking to fathom why their particular master was to be singled out for such derision from within the Hasidic camp. The master himself, of course, could never be fully convinced by such an argument.

Statements of would-be generous understanding of his opponents alternated with statements of forthright denunciation. Nahman's struggle with the Zeide is often portrayed as a mythic battle between holy and demonic forces. The Zeide has been appointed by Satan himself to wage war on the innocent Nahman. The evil forces have their own *rav,* whose task it is to give them the power to do their evil deeds. The ferocity of Nahman's attacks on 'false leaders' in general was undoubtedly sufficient to make many a *ẓaddiq* nervous. "Lying hypocrites" he called them, "who imitate the true *ẓaddiq* like monkeys." He compares them to the false prophets who plagued Israel in the days of Jeremiah, and finds their hypocrisy only heightened by the fact that they "sit all day wrapped up in *tallit* and *tefillin.*"[37] Or elsewhere

> with regard to false leaders *(mefursamin)* he said that the devil himself finds it too difficult to lead the entire world astray from the proper path, so he appoints one leader in one place, another somewhere else . . .[38]

Later in Nahman's life, as he began to see the incipient *Haskalah* as the great enemy of Judaism, it too was attributed to the Zeide; the heretics must have access to some source of divine power that nourishes their existence, and that power could only come from the false *ẓaddiq,* the snakelike sorcerer who lends strength even to heresy itself in order to defeat the true master.[39] Here we begin to see in Nahman the growth of a highly developed personal mythology, allowing, like any good myth, for the projection of personal demons onto the external world. This mythic view Nahman had of his own situation and role in life was to lie at the core of the rich fantasy-production of his *Sippurey Ma'asiyot*, and was to form the basis of the particular religious outlook of Bratslav Hasidism after his death.

The controversy with the Zeide reached its first great heights in the summer of 1802, when the Zeide sought to obtain letters of denunciation against Nahman from the leading *ẓaddiqim* of the day. Whether he had more than denunciation, perhaps an actual ban *(ḥerem)* in mind, is unclear. If we are to believe the Bratslav sources, the attempt was an utter failure. Instead of letters denouncing Nahman, the Zeide received letters in defense of his enemy. Such letters in praise of Nahman arrived, Nathan records, from Levi Yizhak, Barukh, Gedaliah of Linits, Ze'ev Wolf of Charney Ostrog (with whom Nahman had traveled to Erez Israel), Abraham Kalisker, and the fathers-in-law of Nahman's two married daughters.[40]

From the absence of certain prominent names from this list, we may guess that the Zeide did in fact find some support for his cause, perhaps from such figures as Yizhak of Neskhiz or Zevi Aryeh of Olek. It is of particular interest to note that Barukh of Medzhibozh still appears here as a supporter of Nahman, a situation which was to change radically within a year. Nahman was so highly incensed by the Zeide's attempt against him that he took the strongest possible countermeasure: while on a visit to Berdichev later that summer he sought public support for a *ḥerem* against the Zeide, for the crime of having publicly shamed a scholar. Nahman was able to muster some support for this effort, though not among the greatest leaders.

Levi Yizhak, perhaps seeking to make peace between the warring factions, refused to permit the issuing of a ban in his city. A late Bratslav source has it that Levi Yizhak's wife, who used to receive large sums from the Zeide for the support of the poor in Berdichev, used her influence to stay the *ḥerem*.[41] (The source does not bother to tell us why the 'snake' of Shpola should have been so concerned with caring for the poor!) Faced with the opposition of Levi Yizhak, those *rebbes* who had supported Nahman also thought better of the matter, and the plans for a *ḥerem* against the Zeide were dropped. Barukh also sought to achieve further compromise, and it was probably at his urging that Nahman left Zlotopolye in late summer of 1802, to settle in the larger and more prestigious town of Bratslav, well to the west of the Zeide's immediate sphere of influence. By that time, however, the enmity between the two was so deep that the removal of the controversy's original cause in no way meant that either party considered the matter closed.[42]

It was in the following year that the quarrel broke out between Nahman and his uncle Barukh. Here we are told that evil talebearers brought to Barukh untrue stories which caused him to lose faith in his young and increasingly popular nephew. But the motif of the evil talebearers is too common in Hasidic legend for us to give credence to it each time it appears; it serves rather as a literary device for saying, "a controversy broke out."[43] It seems more likely to be the case that now, having Nahman close at hand, Barukh began to appreciate the Zeide's point of view. Bratslav was nearly as close to Tulchin, Barukh's current residence, as Zlotopolye had been to Shpola. It may even be that Barukh, who had no sons, had brought Nahman closer to examine him as a possible successor. In any case, Nahman had little regard for the Hasidism of Tulchin. He had no compunctions about taking *ḥasidim* away from 'false' *ẓaddiqim*, nor about contrasting his own greatness with the low state of other leaders. Any *ẓaddiq* could grow uncomfortable very quickly in the presence of such a neighbor.

Later Bratslav literature records two tales of the split between Barukh and Nahman, tales which conform enough to what we know of Barukh's self-image that we may well assume them to contain some kernel of truth. According to one of these, Nahman proclaimed himself, in Barukh's presence, greater than the Ba'al Shem Tov. He said that he had reached the BeSHT's level of holiness when he was only thirteen years old, and had since then progressed far further. The other version of the split says that the BeSHT, who had frequently appeared to Barukh in dreams, suddenly stopped these nocturnal "visits" to his grandson. When he asked why this had happened, he was told that the BeSHT had now abandoned him for the sake of Nahman.[44] It seemed clear from these stories that some claim was made concerning the legacy of the BeSHT. Barukh, who saw himself as the heir and protector of the patrimony, must have been made to feel at some point that Nahman was proclaiming himself the only legitimate heir, thus challenging Barukh as he had challenged the Zeide. This conflict, too, was extended and bitter. Despite the efforts of Nahman's sister to restore family peace,[45] the rivalry with Barukh continued until Nahman's death. The fact that Barukh and the Zeide in turn had their own falling out during that same year did not lead either to rethink his position with regard to Nahman.

It would seem that Barukh's denunciation led to a reversal of the trend in the attitudes of other *ẓaddiqim* toward Nahman. From the constant praise heaped upon Levi Yizhak in the Bratslav writings, one gets the distinct impression that he alone among the powerful *ẓaddiqim* supported Nahman in his later years, perhaps as much out of disdain for Barukh as out of love for Nahman.[46] The conflicts only worsened as the years went on. In the summer of 1806, Nathan and Naftali (another of Nahman's prominent disciples) were able to keep the Zeide from another attempt to poison the relationship between Levi Yizhak and Nahman only by the coincidence of their presence in Berdichev on the day when he came to tell his tales.[47] During the following winter the controversy grew still more harsh, and Nahman spoke of the winter of 1807 as the period of his greatest suffering.[48] As we shall see later, the accusations against Nahman increased in sharpness as his own claims for himself grew stronger and more open. After the summer of 1806, the height of Nahman's messianic activity, he suffered the worst of these recriminations. It is probably in denial of this messianic attempt that Nathan speaks when he says, rather frequently, that Nahman's enemies attributed thoughts and words to him "which never entered his mind . . ."[49]

There were times when even the faithful Levi Yizhak, despite his own secure and unchallenged position among the *ẓaddiqim* of his day, felt that he dared not lend his full and public support to Nahman:

> Said the copyist [Nahman of Cheryn]: I have heard that once the holy *ẓaddiq* of Berdichev was in Tirhavits. While seated at the table, surrounded by members of that community [Tirhavits was a stronghold of Nahman's followers], he spoke most highly of our master's holiness, praising him for his own merit as well as for that of his holy ancestors. Afterwards he also spoke most highly of our master's disciples, saying they were all great scholars, perfect God-fearers, and people of good deeds, etc. He then referred to R. Nathan as a *ẓaddiq*. Afterwards, when he had left there, R. Samuel Isaac was sitting with him in the carriage, and the rabbi said to him: 'Believe me, if I only knew that people would listen to me, I'd shout out loud from one end of the world to the other that whoever wants to truly serve God or to be a *ẓaddiq* should rush right to the holy Rabbi Nahman of Bratslav. But I know for certain that not only won't they listen to me, but that controversy against me would be raised by this as well. There may be a person somewhere who is considering becoming a penitent through me, and I would [because of the controversy] lose even him. For that reason I am forced to remain silent.'[50]

While the Bratslav source may exaggerate the praise offered to Nathan on that occasion, the portrayal of Levi Yizhak's hesitancy as realistic in regard to something that was already beyond his control seems to be authentic. Here we are witness to the depth of negative feeling Nahman had managed to arouse. Not only were he and his followers considered suspect; even a recognized Hasidic leader, by lending public words of support to him, would need worry about the dangers of being tainted by association. It would appear that this account, too, belongs to the period of Nahman's messianic activity.

The conflicts that surrounded Nahman gave him no rest. His teachings are filled with reference to the controversy. His attitudes toward his enemies and the troubles they caused him seem to have fluctuated constantly; on one occasion he denounces them for the terrible harm they have done him, ruining all his dreams, and shortly thereafter he is again grateful to them for having unwittingly done him some great favor. There were even moments when he showed a sense of humor about his troubles. Our rabbis tell us, he once joked to his disciples, that it is better to cast yourself into a lion's den than to be placed in the hands of your enemy. "What do you do," he asked, "When the enemy himself is a lion?

(Aryeh Leib = lion)" Or, on another occasion, he punned untranslatably on a scriptural verse (Prov. 19:21): "many are the thoughts of Leibush (= *lev 'ish)*, but the counsel of the Lord will stand!"[51]

The greatest evil controversy brought upon him, Nahman said, was that it forced him to become a public figure before his time. We know how ambivalent Nahman was toward the public role; we have also seen that by his challenge to the Zeide he may be said to have brought notoriety upon himself. Still, in the tortuous workings of his mind, he was able to blame his enemies for having forced him to enter the public arena, and he vents the very considerable power of his symbolic imagination upon them for it:

> Because of controversy, people become famous before their time. For when one enters into the service of God, he has to wait a while before he may become known to the world. But through the damaging power of controversy, he comes to be known before his time. In this way harm is done to that one who has become famous too soon, and perhaps the spiritual path which he had wanted to reveal to the world is also damaged. This brings death to those involved in the controversy, or, when the damage is of a lesser order, it brings on poverty. This secret is thus explained in the Torah: 'When two men quarrel and strike a pregnant woman, and her foetus is aborted' (Ex. 21:22). He who sets out upon a new path is like a pregnant woman; he has to remain hidden, just as the foetus is hidden until birth. This path which has not yet been known to the world is in a state of gestation, as Scripture says: 'I have taught you the path of Wisdom' (Prov. 4:11).[52] Such a person has to warm himself, like the foetus in the womb, before the time comes for him to expose his path to daylight. If he emerges [into the public eye] before his time, controversy may be said to have brought on a miscarriage.[53]

He had hoped, he once told his disciples toward the end of his life, to forge them all into great *ẓaddiqim*, the likes of which the world had not seen for many generations. But so much of his energy had gone into the battle with his enemies that he had not much left to give to them.[54] Controversy implants evil thoughts in the *ẓaddiq's* mind; try as he may, one who is involved in conflict with others cannot find the words to pray. Nahman feels his own religious life has been neglected as he has diverted his attention to warding off the attacks of his foes.[55] It seems that he at first tried to save himself from such distraction by ignoring the uproar and answering his detractors with silence.[56] But this very Hasidic response did not always work for him, and he sought various forms of public self-justification.

There are good reasons that the true *ẓaddiq* should be grateful for the storm of controversy that rages about him. Controversy saves him from pride, the most common sin of public leaders. As he flees his human enemies, he is forced to confront and examine himself; this self-scrutiny brings him closer to God. When the *ẓaddiq* begins to become too "successful" in achieving a following, accusations are brought against him in heaven. Denunciations in this world, however, cause his piety to go into hiding. Thus he is elevated to the higher rung of *nistar,* and saved from his more fearsome heavenly accuser. Indeed, there are times when one *ẓaddiq* will denounce his fellow as a favor to him, in order to effect *hamtaqat ha-dinim,* saving him from the greater evil.[57]

At times he seems to be actually overjoyed at the ill spoken of him. As we have seen, he saw in it a vindication, of his claim to be a true *ẓaddiq.* Beyond external vindication, however, he felt that his own spiritual life was enriched by severe conflict. Commenting on the well-known motif of the Psalter, in which the righteous one *(ẓaddiq)* is compared to a fruitful tree, he once said:

> "All the *ẓaddiqim* reach whatever rung it is that they are to attain, and they just remain there. But I, praise God, in every single moment become another person." Thus he provided an explanation for the fact that others opposed him. The *ẓaddiq* is likened to a tree, having roots, branches, and so forth. Every *ẓaddiq* is controversial before he reaches his particular rung. Thus the sages have said: "Controversy is like a burst of water." Controversy is the water that makes the *ẓaddiq* grow tall. [Other *ẓaddiqim,* when they are fullgrown, no longer require this flow of water.] But concerning me there *must be constant controversy,* for I keep moving, in every moment, from rung to rung. If I were to realize that I stand now at the same place where I stood an hour ago, I would be completely dissatisfied with myself.[58]

On another occasion he formulated the matter somewhat differently:

> Our *ḥasidim* were complaining to him how hard it was for them to withstand the controversy, with its accompanying persecutions. He responded: "Believe me, I have the power to make peace with the entire world, so that no one would quarrel with me. But what can I do when there are certain heavenly rungs which can be attained only by means of conflict . . . the more water you pour around the tree, the more it grows."[59]

Nahman's religious life demands of him that he be in a state of constant ascent and growth; this growth is spurred on by controversy and would be stunted by peace. Nahman is consistent in making the same demand upon himself that his call for a renewed Hasidism made upon the movement as a whole. Just as the complacency of relative peace had endangered the intensity of Hasidic religious and communal life as a whole, Nahman in these passages would seem to shun any real desire for personal acceptance by the community of *ẓaddiqim,* lest his drive for constant growth be smothered in their affectionate embrace. Elsewhere we shall have a chance to examine the elaborate metaphysical apparatus constructed in order to build a theology on this awareness of an inner need for constant growth. Here suffice it to say that Nahman's prescription of the need for ever-renewed challenges as a goad to constant growth applies equally to the *ẓaddiq*, his disciples, and the Hasidic community as a whole.

Perhaps here we may see yet another reason Nahman, by issuing his challenge to the Zeide, entered the fray in the first place: he felt even then that he needed the fight in order to grow. Controversy alone could bring out in him the strength he needed to realize his dream of the great Hasidic revival under his banner. And perhaps we will not be wrong in adding that Nahman, so long torn by conflict within his own soul, sought to make peace within himself by uniting the inner warring factions in a battle against an external foe. This indeed may lie behind the 'vision' which sent him to Zlotopolye in the first place. Nahman practically says this in a highly revealing passage in his writings:

> The whole world is full of controversy, between countries, towns, neighbors, and even within a household, between husband and wife, or with servants and children. No one pays attention to the ultimate fact that each and every day we come closer to death. Know that all these controversies are one: the conflict between a man and his wife is the same conflict as that which exists between kings and nations. For each one in the household represents a particular nation; their challenges to one another are like the wars between the nations . . . even one who has no desire to quarrel, but prefers to dwell in peace, is drawn into controversies and battles. Just as one sometimes finds among the kings and nations a country that wants to live in peace, and is forced to enter the war on one side or another (despite its willingness to be a subject nation), so it is with household 'wars.' For man is a microcosm, and he contains the whole world within him. Surely this is true of a man and his household, who contain all the warring nations.
>
> *That is why a person who sits alone in the forest can sometimes go mad.* This happens because he is alone, but nonetheless he contains within himself all the nations which are at war with one another, and he keeps having to switch back and forth, taking the role of whichever 'nation' has the upper hand. This turmoil of the mind can drive him completely mad. But when he is in a settled place, among people, this war can spread out among his household or his neighbors. The controversies that go on in the *ẓaddiq's* house also contain the wars of the nations . . .[60]

One gets the impression that Nahman, having discovered the dialectical mode of thinking for the resolution of both personal and intellectual conflicts, is trying to build a theology on the principle of conflict. He sees conflict as an underlying force in the universe, and the particular conflicts of *ẓaddiqim* at any given period as reflections of that force. In quarreling with one another, the *ẓaddiqim* are creating a space between themselves, repeating the primordial *ẓimẓum* (withdrawal) of God which allowed the non-divine some space in which to exist. The present controversies of the *ẓaddiqim* are repetitions of the most ancient conflicts,[61] which themselves but point to the ultimate dialectical nature of reality. The problem with the current conflicts is not that they exist, but that they exist in a fallen state; *maḥloqet* (controversy) itself is in a state of *galut* (exile). As earlier Hasidic masters had projected the historical situation of Israel onto the inner universe of man and spoken of *galut ha-daʿat* or *galut ha-dibbur* (the "exile" of thought or speech), Nahman saw that controversy, too, had undergone a fall. True *maḥloqet* exists only for the sake of heaven, and it in fact is the highest form of existence, higher than peace itself, as only through controversy can truth be apprehended. Thus the name of Moses (consonantally *MŠH)* is taken as an acronym for *Maḥloqet Shammai-Hillel,* the classic rabbinic controversy.[62] True *maḥloqet,* of course, contains no acrimony, but exists purely for the purpose of the dialectical revelation of truth. The task of the *ẓaddiq* is not to flee controversy, but to uplift it, returning it to its pristine state. Conflict thus serves the *ẓaddiq* both as a goad to personal growth and as the means to reveal that truth toward which he is ever striving.

This elevation of conflict to the level of cosmic principle served to further reinforce Nahman's paradoxical self-assertion as *ẓaddiq.* If the universe is apprehended only by conflict, and the *ẓaddiq* is the one who most deeply seeks to fathom the mysteries of existence, then surely conflict surrounding that *ẓaddiq* may be taken as a sign that he is coming near the truth. Here we begin to perceive just how complex is that web of inner paradox that forms the core of the adult Nahman's spiritual life: he believes in a God whose greatness is shown by the fact that He is doubted, in a *ẓaddiq* (himself) whose greatness is vindicated by the fact of his persecution, and in a world where truth may be attained only by constant struggle within the self and by spiritual conflict with others.[63]

But Nahman's attempts at self-vindication did not stop here. The elevation of his conflict with those whom he called 'false' leaders and the sometime view of himself as their innocent victim were only a part of his claim. For already in Zlotopolye, at the very outset of his challenge to the so-called false *ẓaddiqim,* Nahman had begun to promulgate a far more radical claim, one which must have greatly exacerbated his conflicts with others and one which was to remain constantly problematic even to himself. Nahman proclaimed himself to be not only the persecuted innocent *ẓaddiq,* and not only the embattled warrior for truth, but indeed the *single* true *ẓaddiq* of his time. Nahman asserted that he was in fact *ẓaddiq ha-dor,* the leader of the entire generation, and all other claimants to the title of *ẓaddiq* were, if not false leaders for opposing him, no better than lesser lights in a world where Nahman was the true king, the single authentic ruler of his generation.

This idea of *ẓaddiq ha-dor,* the belief that each generation has a single spiritual head, was by no means a creation of Nahman. While the specific term seems to be of late origin,[64] the idea behind it is deeply rooted in rabbinic tradition and was especially popular among Kabbalists, as we shall see presently. It seems that the Baʿal Shem Tov was taken to be *ẓaddiq ha-dor*, and may have even made such a claim in his own name. Some disciples made a similar claim for the Maggid of Miedzyrzec.[65] Since the death of the Maggid, some thirty years earlier, no one in the Hasidic world had attempted such a claim, with the possible exception of Barukh of Medzhibozh. Central authority within the Hasidic camp, such as it was, had died with the Maggid in 1772. Now the young Nahman, with an audacity that clearly shocked those around him, began to speak more or less openly of *himself* as such a figure, in a way that had never been done quite so directly. Given this, it is no wonder that people would be divided between those who believed in him utterly and those who considered him a total fraud. He was no longer claiming to be *a ẓaddiq;* he was claiming to be *the ẓaddiq*. Once a man makes a claim as extravagant as this, he has eliminated the possibility of any middle ground. But in order to fully understand both the radical nature of Nahman's claim and the traditional associations with which it reverberated, we shall here have to make a brief digression into the earlier sources of this notion.[66]

Despite the fact that the early Pharisaic and Rabbinic communities traditionally attributed their leadership to "pairs" of teachers rather than to individuals, the sense that true *charismatic* leadership is to be found in but a single figure in each generation is already echoed in old rabbinic sources. In an assembly of rabbis at which Hillel the Elder was present, we are told, a heavenly voice was heard to say: "One of you is deserving to have the *shekhinah* rest upon him, but the generation is not worthy." The fact that this event was said to have repeated itself in the generation of Yavneh may indicate that something more than the praise of Hillel himself was intended.[67]

Talmudic sources have it that in rabbinic as well as Biblical times no *ẓaddiq* is allowed to die until another of equal stature is born into the world.[68] From the examples given *(e.g.,* Moses and Joshua, Eli and Samuel, Rabbi Akiba and Judah ha-Nasi), it is clear that the reference here is to a single figure in each generation. In a similar vein, R. Yohanan said, "The world exists for the sake of a single *ẓaddiq*, as it is written: 'The *ẓaddiq* is the foundation of the world' (Prov. 10:25)."[69] It is of special interest to note that R. Simeon ben Yohai, who, as we have seen, was particularly significant in Nahman's consciousness, is the only one among the early rabbis to have proclaimed himself to be that single figure. Though he believed that there were supposed to be thirty great *ẓaddiqim* in any generation, he stated quite flatly that even if there were only one, "I am he."[70] It is also of interest to us that the terms *gedol ha-dor* and *ẓaddiq* at times appear to be interchangeable,[71] even though the term *ẓaddiq ha-dor* itself does not appear in the old rabbinic sources.

The Talmudic sages viewed themselves as heirs to the spiritual and political leadership of the great Biblical heroes. Biblical figures, including even such unlikely types as the patriarch Shem and the warrior David, were transformed in the rabbinic image and portrayed as students of the law. When God called upon the Biblical heroes Abraham, Jacob, Moses, and Samuel, He called each of their names twice, to show that "there is no generation which does not contain an Abraham, a Jacob, a Moses, or a Samuel."[72] It was Moses "our Rabbi" in particular who was seen as the great paradigm of rabbinic leadership, both in the Talmudic writings and throughout later homiletical literature. Moses is at times called a *ẓaddiq*, and is already in Rabbinic literature seen as a prototype of future *ẓaddiqim:*

> 'Unique is she, my dove, my perfect one' (Cant. 6:9). This refers to Moses, who is equal to all the others . . . [Rabbi Judah ha-Nasi was asked by a disciple] 'Who is greater, the world or the *ẓaddiq?*' He replied: 'The *ẓaddiq*.' Why? When Jochebed gave birth to Moses, he was equal [in importance] to the entire world.[73]

The Kabbalistic authors, building upon these rabbinic speculations, went much further in elaborating the figure of Moses as the prototypical unique leader of a generation. According to the rabbis, all souls ever to be born into the world were already present in the soul of Adam.[74] This notion, shared by the Aggadic authors and the early church, became central to Christianity in connection with the idea of original sin. Although little emphasis was placed upon it in early Judaism, the idea was rediscovered by the Kabbalists, who gave it a place of preëminence. Particularly in the Lurianic system, where the myth of the Fall is so central, the rootedness of all souls in Adam is strongly emphasized.[75] But equally crucial to the Kabbalistic myth is the belief that all the souls of Israel were to be found in the soul of *Moses*. Just as Adam, through the Fall, wrought damage to all human souls, so Moses, the lawgiver, brought potential redemption to all the souls of Israel. Moses not only reveals the law; he in fact *embodies* it. While the soul of each individual Jew is rooted in one of the six hundred thousand mystical letters of the Torah, the soul of Moses contains the entire Torah, the soul-root of the entire House of Israel. The Talmud had already seen the revelation at Sinai as the "antidote" to the poison of original sin; here however it is Moses, the bearer of that revelation, who is able to redeem all the souls by virtue of the fact that his soul contains them all.[76] The revelation to Moses is here presented in terms that are so reminiscent of some incarnational formulae of Christianity that a purely structural distinction between the two faiths would here perhaps be put to its severest test. No wonder that penitent Marranos, with their Catholic upbringing, were attracted to the Sabbatian version of Kabbalah, and no wonder that Christian occultists in the Renaissance, and later, found Kabbalistic symbols to be so attractive! The further step, claiming that Moses' soul was not only all-inclusive but in fact was different in origin from that of any other human, was also taken by some Kabbalists. According to the fourteenth-century author of *Sefer ha-Qaneh* (often known for his strikingly radical formulations), Moses at first refused to go into Egypt to redeem Israel because his soul was derived from the cosmic cycle of grace *(shemitat ha-ḥesed)*, while Israel were already living under the cycle of harshness *(shemitat ha-gevurah)*.[77] It was even claimed that Moses' soul was uniquely pre-existent: it was in fact the primordial light of which scripture says: "And God saw the light, and it was good" (Gen. 1:4).[78]

This soul of Moses, standing at the center of its generation, and indeed of the cosmos altogether, is associated both with the souls of later *ẓaddiqim* and with the soul of the messiah. Along with the soul of Moses, Kabbalistic literature is particularly concerned with the soul of Rabbi Simeon ben Yohai, the chief speaker in the mystical dialogues of the *Zohar* and the prototype of the post-Biblical *ẓaddiq*. We have seen how important was this figure of the Kabbalistic Rabbi Simeon to Nahman's understanding of his own self. Like Moses, Rabbi Simeon is the single leader not only of his own generation, but of many that are to follow in the afterflow of his lifetime. The "holy lamp," as he is commonly called in the *Zohar*, is the new Moses and the new Solomon; a pillar of cloud hovers over him as it did over the desert tabernacle when God spoke to Moses. By Lurianic times, it was a commonplace in Kabbalistic circles that the soul of Rabbi Simeon ben Yohai had been that of Moses reincarnate. That the soul of the first redeemer should also be embodied in the final redeemer, embodied meanwhile in certain of the greatest *ẓaddiqim*, should come as no surprise.[79] There was extensive and venerable precedent for the notion that messiah was to be anticipated as the new Moses.

It was upon this entire tradition of singular leadership that Nahman was drawing when he spoke of himself as *ẓaddiq ha-dor*. It should be understood, of course, that even he could not make the claim in a fully open way. His references to *ẓaddiq ha-dor* remain in the third person, or are couched in such phrases as "there is a *ẓaddiq* . . ." or "there is a certain soul . . ." But it is not only modern scholars who understand the transparency of these constant references; surely his *ḥasidim* and most likely his enemies were quite perceptive enough to realize that it was the figure of Nahman himself, in countless verbal guises, who filled both his homilies and his tales. On at least one occasion he is said to have spoken quite openly of five great *ẓaddiqey ha-dor* in the course of history: Moses, Simeon ben Yohai, Isaac Luria, the Ba'al Shem Tov, and himself.[80] He referred to himself—or to the great *ẓaddiq*—as the *'even shetiyah*, the mythical rock at the center of the world, which was the first object of Creation and upon which the Temple was built.[81] (Again the parallel to Christianity is rather shocking.) He is the true source of insight, necessary for all proper interpretation of the Torah:

> Know that there is a soul in the world through whom the meaning and interpretation of the Torah is revealed. This is a suffering soul, eating bread and salt and drinking measured bits of water, for such is the way of Torah. All interpreters of Torah receive from this soul. The words of this soul are as hot as flaming coals, as Scripture says: 'Are not my words like fire?' (Jer. 23:29)[82]

His is the all-inclusive soul of his generation, the soul Moses bore in the past and which messiah is to bear in the future. All other souls are but specifications or subdivisions of that 'general' soul; merely being in the presence of such a figure may thus be an experience of enlightenment, as communication flows between the general and the particular. Elsewhere this *ẓaddiq* is described as having a gravitational pull that attracts to him all the souls in the world, including those of all other *ẓaddiqim*. In this sense he is Moses, building the *mishkan* (tabernacle), which is here in a word play derived not from *ŠKN* ("dwell") but rather from *MŠK* ("attract"). All are drawn to the single *ẓaddiq*; he fashions a tabernacle out of the myriad human prayers that are channeled through him.[83]

Surely there is a touch of megalomania revealed here in Nahman; the more intense the spiraling need for self-vindication, the less room remained for the testing of his self-image against the touchstone of reality. His claims eventually went beyond those of any other *ẓaddiq* and came to be bound up, as we shall see further, with a messianic claim as well. At the same time, the availability within the tradition of the rich symbols he employed for this claim makes Nahman's use of *ẓaddiq ha-dor* interesting in more than a purely biographical sense. To some extent he was clearly making use of some ancient building blocks in the structures of Jewish piety which others had not quite had the audacity to put together in this way before him. The fact that parallel notions of singular generational leadership exist in the most widely varied and scattered religious traditions—from the *avatar* of India to the *qutb* in Islam and the "Christs" of the Russian dissenters—also seems to indicate that a certain inner logic of the Jewish esoteric tradition was here manifesting itself in Nahman, as could only be accomplished in one whose personal needs were strong enough to call it forth.

Given a world view in which all the contemporary souls of Israel are rooted in a single figure, the veneration of any other *ẓaddiq* would seem to be a rather vain activity, if not one of open sedition against the only true authority. The single earthly *ẓaddiq*, parallel to the *ẓaddiq*-figure within God,[84] is depicted as the one and only channel through whom heaven's blessings flow to man, and through whom all prayer should be directed if one wants assurance that it will reach its goal.[85] Such a figure may generously lend some respect to those other *ẓaddiqim* who happen to live in *his* generation, but one could hardly think of them as being anything near his equals. As early as the beginning of 1802, while still living in

Zlotopolye, Nahman spoke of a single *ẓaddiq* who, even in his fallen state, was certainly higher than any other *ẓaddiq* of his day.[86] While Nahman here was commenting on a Talmudic passage, and was thus ostensibly speaking of an earlier period, there can be little doubt that both his disciples and his adversaries well understood that he was in fact talking about himself. No wonder that even Levi Yizhak should feel that a full defense of Nahman was more than he could manage!

Once the *ẓaddiq ha-dor* (he is sometimes also called *ẓaddiq ha-emet* or *ḥakham ha-dor* in Nahman's writings) has revealed himself, the only real problem left to deal with is that of *meniʿot,* those "obstacles" that keep one from recognizing and approaching the true leader of the generation. Prominent among these obstacles is the negative influence of the false *ẓaddiqim,* who are all too ready to achieve personal gain by doing the work of the evil forces, keeping others from discovering the truth.[87] Even without their activities, however, the true *ẓaddiq* is not always as easy to recognize as were such figures as Luria and the BeSHT. Nahman realized the paradoxical fact that claim as he might to be the greatest and indeed the unique leader of his generation, an observer of the Hasidic scene would see quite clearly that he was, in fact, a rather obscure figure, leading a small band of the faithful, but greatly outshone in fame by those major *ẓaddiqim* we have mentioned above. How is it that the *ẓaddiq ha-dor* should have so little power, even within the Hasidic community? The hiddenness of the true *ẓaddiq* is discussed by Nahman in another of his characteristically paradoxical formulations:

> Every Jew has within him some degree of kingship, each according to his own qualities. Some rule over their homes, while others have wider authority, and others rule over the entire world, each according to the degree of kingship which he possesses. Thus there are 'rulers of thousands, rulers of hundreds, rulers of fifty, and rulers of ten' (Ex. 18:21).
>
> Now the degree of kingship which each person has exists in both revealed and hidden ways. The revealed kingship is the [obvious] authority which each individual has over certain others . . . but each man also has hidden kingship. Even though he may have no apparent power over certain people, in a deeply hidden way he does rule over them. Their souls are beneath him and humble themselves before him. This hidden kingship also exists in each person to varying degrees. . . .
>
> *And there is one who had no revealed kingship at all, but nonetheless, in a deeply hidden way, rules over the entire generation, even over the ẓaddiqim of the generation.* For all their souls are under his dominion and are bowed before him. This fact, however, is completely hidden, as scripture says: 'Everywhere fragrant sacrifices and gifts are offered to My name' (Mal. 1:11)—even though they are worshipping idols, in a hidden manner they are really humbling themselves before Him and worshipping Him, blessed be

> He. . . . The same is true of this hidden kingship with which he rules over them; they are all humbled before him, even though he has no apparent power.[88]

Again we see the close parallel between God and the *ẓaddiq*. Speaking of the true hidden leader, whose rule over all the *ẓaddiqim* of his generation is invisible, he uses the Kingdom of God itself as an example of hidden authority. Nahman's assertion of this true and unique authority over others and his increasing need to realize this claim at the expense of other *ẓaddiqim* are what, finally, lay at the heart of the controversy which engulfed him.

It is difficult to determine to what extent this extreme sense of his unique importance preceded and was thus an initial cause of Nahman's conflicts with others, and how much of it began to take root only after he was persecuted and as a response to the controversy around him.

We do not have sufficient documentary evidence from before the move to Zlotopolye on which to base such a judgment.[89] From what we have seen of Nahman's character, however, it would seem likely to surmise that such thoughts began to develop within his own inner struggles, only to be reinforced by external conflict. It may have been in reaction to the extreme senses of depression and worthlessness which so frequently overcame him that Nahman developed a compensatory sense of unique greatness and value to the world. As his inner tensions were exacerbated by the denunciations of others, his need for such radical self-justification continued to grow, thus creating a spiraling escalation of conflict and self-assertion. Increasingly tormented by the controversy which raged on about him, Nahman developed a need to see his detractors as demonic foes, at once enemies of God Himself and of the true *ẓaddiq*. Turning for solace to the inner world of his faith and to the adulating support of his own *ḥasidim*, it is no wonder that the man who saw himself as the true persecuted suffering servant would eventually come to the conclusion that he and he alone was the pillar of truth, the unique leader of his generation. Could this be what Nahman meant by describing controversy as the water which makes the *ẓaddiq* grow? If so, he surely was somehow right. His growth in self-assertion proceeded from the roots of inner torment and was pushed forward by the need for paradoxical self-vindication. In such a case, is it not the wrath of others which either breaks the man or urges him on to greatness?

It was out of a very particular and highly charged personal situation that Nahman came to learn about the relationship between conflict and growth. Like so many other lessons he had learned in this way, however, that which was *descriptive* of Nahman's own inner life was taken as *prescriptive* for the lives of his disciples, and was thus abstracted from its psychological context. As such, the motif of constant struggle, growth, and challenge became central to the Bratslav understanding of the religious life, and was discussed in theological rather than psychological terms. But before leaving this chapter, it seems appropriate to say a word about the meaning of Nahman's insight in the language in which such matters are more generally discussed today. When Nahman announced that controversy (the sort of controversy which in the lives of most *ẓaddiqim*—or most people—ceases at the point when they become established) in his case will go on forever, he was not merely offering an apology. He seems to be announcing here that he will not accept an end to the stage of life that we, in our time, generally label (and sometimes dismiss) as "adolescence." Nahman paraphrases and intentionally distorts the meaning of the Talmudic passage that says: "All my days have I grown up among the sages" to mean that it was only the conflicts between the sages that allowed him room to grow.[90] The young tree is watered by conflict; the young sage grows in that space where others have left him room. There is something thoroughly adolescent, from the point of view of our psychology, about this perception of the universe. Adolescence is indeed the great time of conflict in human life as well as the time of growth. Who is the adolescent if not one who gets into repeated conflict by rubbing up against the already-formed personalities of adults and having to take a stand against them? For Nahman—and for those who follow him—this process is not allowed to end as one moves on into adulthood. For all the inner torment and outer conflict which characterized his life (or perhaps because of them?) Nahman stands as one of those disturbing and challenging individuals who taught that the essence of the human and religious enterprise is the constant need to grow. To say that such a teaching represents a personality arrested at the stage of adolescent conflict—though not inaccurate as a psychological description—would be very much to miss the point.

NOTES

1. The texts of the various *ḥaramin* and other documents of this struggle have now been published by Mordecai Wilensky in his *Ḥasidim u-Mitnaggedim*. Discussion of the specific accusations contained in the bans is to be found in the introduction and notes to that work. A full bibliography on the anti-Hasidic controversy is given in v.2, p.363ff.

In the final round of the conflict, the Russian government took the part of the *ḥasidim*. Shne'ur Zalman was finally released from prison by order of Czar Alexander I on March 12, 1801 (old calendar). Relevant documents are printed in Russian and Hebrew in Heilman's *Bet Rabbi*, p.76. The constitution of 1804 denied the *kahal* the right to prevent separatist (i.e. Hasidic) groups from establishing their own places of prayer. This governmental position brought an end to active mitnaggedic opposition—at least on the legal front. Cf. Wilensky, v.1, p.15f.

2. A full critical study of the career and thought of Levi Yizhak would be a most important contribution to Jewish scholarship. His biography, first undertaken by M.Y. Guttmann in his *Tif'eret Bet Levi* in 1909—little more than a collection of the

traditional tales—has been redone in every work on Hasidism, but not yet in critical fashion. The recent work by Samuel Dresner weaves together some careful scholarly research with a retelling of the tales in popular fashion. A 1973 doctoral dissertation on Levi Yizhak (M. Luckens, Temple University) leaves room for further work. There is a vast amount of information available on Levi Yizhak, including works by his son and several of his disciples, a good deal of contemporary mention in various documents, and of course the great wealth of later tales and anecdotal materials. The controversy between Buber and Scholem as to the historical worthiness of the Hasidic tales could best be tested out around the figure of Levi Yizhak.

3. There is some possibility that it was Menahem Nahum himself who in his later days initiated some of the grand style which was to characterize the later Chernobyl (Twersky) dynasty and its many offshoots. Cf. Twerski, *Sefer ha-Yaḥas mi-Chernobyl we-Ruzhin*, p.2, n.5.

4. Although he had been designated as leader by Menahem Mendel of Vitebsk when the latter departed for Erez Israel in 1777, there was considerable opposition to him among the older *ḥasidim* who had remained in Byelorussia. Extensive material concerning Shne'ur Zalman and his struggle for control over the Byelorussian Hasidic community is to be found in *Bet Rabbi*, as well as in the letters of Menaḥem Mendel and Abraham Kalisker, published as an appendix to Kalisker's *Ḥesed le-Avraham*.

5. Barukh's conflicts with various *ẓaddiqim* are frequently mentioned in the collections of Hasidic tales. *Cf.* for example *'Eser 'Orot*, p.50; *Divrey Shalom*, p.56; *Seder ha-Dorot he-Ḥadash*, p.25; *Zikhron Tov*, p.6 (Barukh *vs.* Levi Yizhak); *'Or ha-Nifla'ot* #13 (in collection *'Ohel ha-Rabbi*); *Zikhron Tov*, p.13 (Barukh vs. Jacob Isaac of Lublin); *Bet Rabbi*, pp.86, 89 (Barukh vs. Shne'ur Zalman). A number of references to these controversies are found in the memoirs of Abraham Baer Gottlober (1810–1899), recently reprinted as *Zikhronot u-Masa'ot*. Gottlober, a well-known scholar, poet, and publicist of the Haskalah, was hardly an objective reporter. He had, in his youth, suffered greatly at the hands of *ḥasidim*. Thus his account of the meeting between Barukh and Shne'ur Zalman becomes an opportunity for him to create a purely fictitious dialogue and to place his anti-Hasidic witty barbs in the mouth of Shne'ur Zalman. Fact and fantasy must be sorted at least as carefully in using this work as in using later collections of tales by the *ḥasidim* themselves.

6. Dubnov, *Toledot ha-Ḥasidut*, p.309*ff.*; Heschel, "Le-Toledot R. Pinhas mi-Korets" in *'Aley 'Ayin*, p.226 and n.136–138.

7. M. Biber, *Mazkeret li-Gedoley Ostrog*, p.211.

8. Heschel, *op. cit.*, p.223*ff.* and the many sources quoted in the notes to that article. On the unique place of *devequt* in the Maggid's system, see Scholem, *The Messianic Idea*, p.216*ff.* and Schatz, *Ha-Ḥasidut ke-Mistiqah*, *passim*. The Maggid's reading of the Ba'al Shem Tov's message may well have been related to his own status as a *former* ascetic Kabbalist.

9. *'Iggerot ha-Qodesh*, appended to Kalisker's *Ḥesed le-Avraham*, #37. It may be to the conflict between Shne'ur Zalman and Abraham Kalisker that Nahman speaks in mentioning controversies that take place between two *ẓaddiqim* who are "of the same root." Conflict breaks out when one chooses to reveal his Torah, while the other keeps it hidden within himself. *Liqquṭim* 283. On the attitude of simple faith-centered Ukrainian Hasidism toward the abstruse theology of Shne'ur Zal-

man *cf.* the rather cutting remark attributed to Yizhak of Neskhiz in *Zikhron Tov,* p.6, #10. When asked his opinion of Shne'ur Zalman's writings, he replied circumspectly that his treatise on the *birkhot ha-nehenin* was indeed useful!

10. Barukh's second marriage was to his cousin, the daughter of R. Aaron of Titov, son of the BeSHT's son Herschel. A marriage with the granddaughter of the BeSHT's only son seems like a move calculated to strengthen his authority, and perhaps to assure that male heirs from that line not serve as competitors to his own descendants. In fact Barukh had no male issue, and after his time the family lost its prominence in the Hasidic world.

11. Gershon Hundert, op. cit., p.72*ff.*

12. Ibid., p.22*ff.*, p.80. Shne'ur Zalman's letters and Heilman's *Bet Rabbi* (also written from the viewpoint of a loyal *ḤaBaD ḥasid)* are the only sources that associate Kalisker with the excesses of 1770, referred to in the literature as *Ḥasidey TaLQ* (תלק = 1770). There is no way of determining the truth of these accusations. In any case, they are at least quite exaggerated, as the *ḥaramin* themselves give several reasons for their issuance other than the devotional extremes of certain *ḥasidim.*

13. Mention is made in it of a messenger who had arrived in Shevat (January/February), who told of Nahman's safe return from Erez Israel and of his visit to Liadi. Since Nahman arrived home in the summer of 1799, the earliest date for this letter could be February, 1800.

14. *Ḥayyey* 5, end. The first part of the letter seems to refer to the conflict between Barukh, who would have much to say about the collection of funds in Volhynia, and Jacob Samson of Shepetovka, the emissary from the Hasidic community of Tiberias who traveled to Europe in order to receive such monies as were collected. We are in possession of a letter of apology written by Jacob Samson to Barukh, asking forgiveness for some grievous sin against him. The letter was written in 1801. A. Yaari has claimed that Barukh's real enmity was toward Abraham Kalisker, and not toward Jacob Samson, who was just a messenger of the Tiberias *ẓaddiq. See* Yaari's *Sheluḥey 'Ereẓ Yisra'el,* Jerusalem, 1951, p. 623.

15. Cf. *'Iggerot ha-Qodesh* #38–45. Nahman's concern for the Hasidic community of Erez Israel continued throughout his life. *Liqquṭim II* 71, preached in January, 1810, reflects this continuing sentiment. Cf. also *Liqquṭim* 37 and *Ḥayyey* 1:47.

16. *Ḥayyey* 4:10. The teachings of Mordecai of Neskhiz are collected in *Rishpey 'Esh.* Tales concerning him are appended to the Bilgoray, 1932 edition of that work, entitled *Rishpey 'Esh ha-Shalem,* and are also found in *Zikhron Ṭov,* a collection mainly concerned with his son Yizhak.

17. *Megillah* 24b.

18. *Ḥayyey* 4:11 and 5:18.

19. Nahman had five daughters whose names are known to us: Odel, Sarah, Miriam, Feige, and Hayyah. There was apparently also a sixth daughter, who died shortly before his trip to Erez Israel. Odel was married, during the summer of 1800, to Abraham Dov, son of the Rabbi of Chmelnik (*Ḥayyey* 4:10). Sarah was married in the spring of 1803 to one Yizhak Eisik; the marriage took place at Medvedevka (*Yemey MaHaRNaT,* p.13). Nahman's daughter Feige died in 1803; her sister Miriam was married in the fall of 1804 to the son of Leib of Walichisk (*Yemey MaHaRNaT,* p.14). This family settled in Safed and formed a part of the

Hasidic community there. The date given by Alfasi (*Ha-Ḥozeh mi-Lublin*, p.195, n.19) for their *'aliyah* (1802) seems impossible, since Nathan claims to have been present at their wedding in 1804. This wedding is discussed by Piekarz, *op. cit.*, p.59. In 1805 Hayyah was living in Medvedevka, presumably married (*Ḥayyey* 1:26). A later Bratslav source (*'Avaneha Barzel*, p.22) mentions Yoske as the name of Odel's husband; it is not unlikely that she was widowed and remarried. Other sources on Nahman's daughters are to be found in *Ḥayyey* 1:16, 59; 4:11, 13–14; *Ḥayyey II* 11:129–131.

20. *Ḥayyey* 4:11.

21. Tales concerning the Zeide are scattered through various Hasidic collections. *See* Horodezky, *Ha-Ḥasidut weha-Ḥasidim*, v.3, p.155*ff*. The collection *Tif'eret MaHaRAL*, first published in Piotrkow, 1912, and reprinted in Israel in 1969, has been shown by Y. Dan (*Ha-Sippur ha-Ḥasidi*, p.220*ff*.) to be nothing more than a work of fiction. Its author, Yudl Rosenberg, claimed to have worked with old manuscripts handed down in the family of the Zeide's beadle, but apparently there is no substance at all to these claims. More on Rosenberg's book below.

22. *Ḥayyey* 4:11. Nahman of Cheryn, editor of *Ḥayyey MoHaRaN*, is most insistent on the point that the controversy began only with this incident, and stood in contrast to the warm welcome the Zeide had given him on his earlier visit to Shpola. Why this was seemingly still so urgent in the 1870's is puzzling, unless an earlier date for the conflict would point up its ideological rather than its competitive origins. The tale of the Zeide and his innovations as beadle of the Zlotopolye synagogue is found reworked by Rosenberg in *Tif'eret MaHaRAL*, p.91.

23. *Ḥayyey* 4:11. Cf. Weiss, *Meḥqarim*, p.24. The play on the Slavic word for gold would in itself not account for the reference to Jeroboam; why not refer to the much more obvious and powerful sin of the Golden Calf at Sinai? Further discussion of Jeroboam will be found in chapter five.

24. *Yemet ha-Tela'ot*, p.174f.; Piekarz, *op. cit.*, p.72f.

25. *Siḥot* 211.

26. The document is thoroughly analyzed and discredited in Weiss, *Meḥqarim*, p.26ff. For its earlier acceptance cf. Weiss in *Zion* 16(1951) 89, n.14; Tishby, *Netivey 'Emunah u-Minut*, p.343, n.178; Piekarz, *op. cit.*, p.75. The document was first published by M.N. Litinsky in his history of the Jews in Podolia in 1895. The text itself, entitled *Megillat Ḥasidey Bratslav*, is about a page in length, but purports to be a fragment of a much longer document, allegedly written by Nathan himself, and given to Litinsky in his home town of Vinnitsa in 1878 by none less than a brother of Nathan, one Judah Leib Mushkis, a leader of the Jewish community there. Found on p.62f of Litinsky's work, the passage reads in part:

> . . .as is known from history, Sabbatai Sevi claimed to be redeemer of Israel in 1648, the year in which Chmielnitsky slaughtered so many Jews in Podolia. It was in 1649 that Sabbatai Sevi made his messianic claim in the open. . . . In 1752 a letter arrived in Bratslav from the rabbis of Poland which sought to lead the hearts of Israel in Bratslav away from the teachings of the BeSHT and to destroy the Hasidic sect which had spread there, following the liberation which the BeSHT had wrought by means of his Hasidic path. In 1757, Frank married a Jewish girl from our city (the opponents of the Bratslav *hasidim* said that she was of the family of MaHaRaN of Bratslav, and that his disciple, who is writing this letter, was a descendant of Liebl Prossnitz, the well-known false prophet) . . . there were many [Frankists] there [Bratslav] who held onto the ways of Sabbatai Sevi. . . . When the path of my teacher and master spread

> forth . . . other *ḥasidim*, led by the old one [the reference is to the Shpoler Zeide] accused him of being a follower of that sect and a Sabbatian, though our master was innocent of the sin of which they accused him, as am I, his disciple.

The stylistic problems alone reveal the text as an obvious forgery, as any reader of Nathan's writings will notice immediately. It is only surprising that scholars did not come to this conclusion much sooner.

Even assuming that the parenthetical remarks are Litinsky's own "explanatory" additions, the text itself does not sound a bit like Nathan's writing. The opening phrase *qore' ha-dorot* ("history") clearly has the ring of Haskalah, not Hasidic, Hebrew prose. The direct reference to Sabbatai Sevi (and followed by no malediction at that!) is inconceivable for Nathan, who was such a master of circumspection on controversial matters. The term *'irenu* ('our city') referring to Bratslav is alien to Nathan's style, as is the spelling of the town's name (בראצלאב instead of ברסלב). In fact there is no way in which the document, on internal grounds, could be said to be the work of Nathan. Whether Litinsky himself was the forger or whether he himself was fooled by his "discovery" of what in fact was an older anti-Hasidic parody remains an open question but one which is of no particular concern to us here. On Litinsky's general unreliability in documentary matters, *cf.* Israel Halpern's *Yehudim we-Yahadut be-Mizraḥ 'Eropah*, Jerusalem, 1968, pp. 316*ff*.

Other "evidence" adduced in support of the alleged Sabbatian accusation against Nahman is as follows:

A. Weiss quotes *Siḥot* 211, where the accusation that Nahman copied from the works of his grandfather Nahman of Horodenka is mentioned. Coupling this with a reference to the vague accusation of Sabbatianism against the elder Nahman, Weiss suggests that this claim against the grandson is also a veiled reference to Sabbatian leanings. An unbiased reading of *Siḥot* 211, however, makes it quite clear that the issue there is one of plagiarism, not heresy: only the originality, not the content, of Nahman's writings, is called into question. Weiss' claim that originality was not considered a virtue in the culture of East European Jews and that therefore a charge of plagiarism would make no sense is highly contrived. *Ḥiddushim*, so often spoken of by Nahman, are *original* and creative readings of the traditional sources. The idea that his *novellae* were not his at all would indeed have been a somewhat scandalous matter. On the value of originality in Bratslav, *cf.* the note on the tales appended to the first introduction to the *Sippurey Ma'asiyot*.

B. Piekarz quotes from a later Bratslav source *(Yemey ha-Tela'ot*, pp.174*f*.) an account of a meeting between the Zeide and Levi Yizhak of Berdichev, at which Nathan and Naftali of Nemirov happen to have been present. Because of the presence of these disciples of Nahman in Berdichev, the Zeide was unable to denounce his enemy, which had been his intention in visiting Levi Yizhak. Upon his return to Shpola,

> he was visited by one who was from Nemirov. When he asked the man where he was from, and received the response: "From Nemirov," the Zeide said: 'In your town of Nemirov there are *meginey 'ereẓ*.' He was referring to R. Nathan and R. Naftali. And this was told to our master. Rabbi Abraham [Hazan] said that this justified the tradition among our people to the effect that the reference to *meginey 'ereẓ* in the teaching *Tiq'u 'Emunah (Liqquṭim II* 5) refers to R. Nathan, who in his books strengthens and refreshes fallen and weakened spirits. . . .

The phrase *meginey 'ereẓ* in the mouth of the Zeide is entirely obscure. Literally it means "defenders of the land"; to a traditional Jewish ear it also calls to mind, however, a code of law: *Meginey 'Ereẓ* is the title given to the printed editions of Joseph Caro's *Shulḥan 'Arukh*, section *'Oraḥ Ḥayyim*, with commentaries. This title was used beginning with the Dyhernfürth, 1692 edition. Piekarz is right in rejecting Abraham Ḥazan's harmonistic reading of the term; surely the Zeide had no intention of *complimenting* Nathan. What then is the meaning of *meginey 'ereẓ?* Unable to find any explanation for this strange phrase, Piekarz recalls that the Frankist debate in 1759 had opened with a question that read: "In the book *Meginey 'Ereẓ* . . ." Citing no evidence other than the 1759 debate itself, Piekarz is willing to assume that this leading phrase of the Frankists' question was well-known, and the phrase *meginey 'ereẓ* had thus become a term for Frankists, a term still in use, despite the lack of any documentary evidence, some fifty years later! Such a hypothesis can only be proposed if one is convinced in advance as to what the proper conclusions should be, and then looks for "evidence" to support his predetermined conclusion. In fact the phrase *meginey 'ereẓ* is not at all difficult to explain: the Zeide refers to Nathan and Naftali as those who defend *'arẓiyut* ("corporeality" or "materialism"): they are defenders of a *rebbe* who is not sufficiently spiritual to deserve their respect. If he was being very sharp, perhaps he meant that they were defending one whose proper place was in hell (Hebrew *'ereẓ*—Yiddish *erd*, meaning either "earth" or "hell"). In any case, one is certainly not *forced* by the term to wander so far as Piekarz would claim. Moreover, the phrase *meginey 'ereẓ* is used by Nahman to describe the *ẓaddiqim* in *Liqquṭim* II 5:7–9. If it were a known term of opprobrium for Frankists, Nahman would hardly use it in such a way. Indeed, Piekarz, who is generally so expert in stylistic questions, accepts the Litinsky document without question: this seems to be the real basis of his conclusions, to which these arguments are but secondary supports.

C. Piekarz, *op. cit.*, p. 211, also makes note of the fact that Nathan's son, in a letter written in 1835, mentions an accusation by Moses Zevi of Savran, a latter-day enemy of Bratslav, to the effect that the Bratslav *ḥasidim* "do not believe in the oral law." As the Frankists in their day had been designated as anti-Talmudists, here, too, Piekarz finds allusion to a Sabbatian or Frankist accusation against Bratslav. Particularly on the basis of Nathan's *Liqquṭey Halakhot, Yoreh De'ah, simmaney 'of ṭahor* 4, however, it is with the *philosophers i.e. maskilim* that such an accusation associates one, not with the Sabbatians. There is no particular reason to believe that in 1835, when Hasidism was doing serious battle with Haskalah, the issue of Frankism should have been revived, unless we have *clear* evidence to that effect. And even if such evidence were to be found, a deduction from the Savraner's 1835 accusations to the Zeide's views some thirty years earlier, with which Piekarz (p. 76) finds no problem, is a rather dubious scholarly procedure.

27. *Tif'eret MaHaRAL*, p.93*f*. The reader is reminded of the questionable age and reliability of these accounts.

28. The Zeide's habit of constantly checking into Nahman's behavior is referred to in *Liqquṭim* 38, said in Zlotopolye in the winter of 1802. It is claimed that Raphael of Bershad, the closest disciple of Pinhas of Korets, had similar objections to Nahman. *See* H. Zeitlin, *R. Nakhman Braslaver*, pp. 170*f*.

29. This is the main point of J. Weiss' article *"R. Nahman mi-Bratslav 'al ha-maḥloqet 'alaw"*, now in his *Meḥqarim*, p.42*ff*.

30. *Ḥayyey II* 2:22. *Cf.* also Nahman's reaction to the accusations in *Siḥot* 182.

31. *Liqquṭim II* 52, emphases mine. Faith in God and in the *ẓaddiq* are often connected in Nahman's thought. Like God, the *ẓaddiq* must be accepted with no mental reservations; "as long as any of [the *ḥasid's*] own intellect remains, he is not whole and is not bound to the *ẓaddiq*." *Liqquṭim* 123. *See* also *Ḥayyey, sippurim ḥadashim* 21 and *Siḥot* 32. In *Siḥot* 38 Nahman claims that those who raise objections to the *ẓaddiq* really would like to speak out against God. Lacking the courage to do so, they turn upon the *ẓaddiq*. This matter is discussed by Weiss in *Tarbiz* 27 (1958) 235*f.*, n.3. I would not go as far as he does in suggesting that this passage points to an unspoken *identification* of God and *ẓaddiq*. On the use of the term *qushiya* (here translated "objection" and "question") in Bratslav literature, *cf.* Weiss in *'Aley 'Ayin*, pp. 245*ff.*, and especially pp. 248*f.*, *Meḥqarim*, p.109*ff.* and the sources quoted there, and Excursus I, herein. The assertion of paradoxical faith in both God and the *ẓaddiq* is also found in *Liqquṭey Halakhot, Yoreh De'ah, shiluaḥ ha-qen* 5.

32. *Hayyey* 8:17. This passage is in surprising contrast to his idealized image of a Hasidic community at the beginning of *The Master of Prayer*, where it is specifically stated that they care nothing about fine clothing. *Cf.* M. Piekarz, *op. cit.*, p.118 and n.79 for a discussion of Nahman's complex and ambivalent attitude toward money and economic security.

33. *Ḥayyey II* 5:1.

34. This is explicitly stated in *Ḥayyey II* 2:32. *See* also *Liqquṭey Halakhot, 'Oraḥ Ḥayyim, tefillin* 5:4–5, as well as the most enlightening discussion by Piekarz on Nathan's understanding of the tales in *op. cit.*, p.140*ff.*

35. *Ḥayyey II* 11:23.

36. *Me'or 'Eynayim, naso*, p.154. "The *ẓaddiq* is a wonder and people cannot understand his actions; that is why there is opposition to all of the *ẓaddiqim*."

37. *Ḥayyey* 4:20–21; *Ḥayyey II* 11:90; *Liqquṭim* 8:1–4; *Liqquṭim II* 15.

38. *Ḥayyey II* 11:90

39. *Liqquṭim* 63; *Liqquṭim II*:4. Piekarz, op, cit., pp. 48f. Piekarz has also demonstrated (p. 61) that there are references to the Zeide in certain of Nahman's tales. *Cf.* also *Liqquṭey Halakhot, Yoreh De'ah, simmaney 'of ṭahor* 4. Here Nathan seems to be reminding his reader that controversy within the Hasidic community lends strength to the common enemy of all *ḥasidim*.

40. *Cf.* above, n.19. Here the record on Nahman's daughters' marriages becomes somewhat confused. The sources quoted above would have only Odel married at this time. From *Ḥayyey, meqom yeshivato* 11, however, it becomes clear that Miriam was already betrothed to the son of Leib of Walichisk in 1800. R. Leib is mentioned by A. Walden, *Shem ha-Gedolim he-Hadash*, p. 79, as a disciple of the Maggid of Miedzyrzec.

41. *'Avaneha Barzel* #28, as quoted by J. Weiss in *Meḥqarim*, p.36. I do not necessarily agree with the value Weiss places on this source. His manner of argument in its favor is again rather contrived.

42. *Ḥayyey* 4:19. It was Hillel Zeitlin who first suggested *(op.cit.*, p.196) that Barukh arranged Nahman's move to Bratslav.

43. Thus the motif of 'evil talebearers' is used to explain such varied and complex problems as the Vilna Gaon's opposition to Hasidism *(Bet Rabbi*, p.34), and the break between Elimelekh of Lezajsk and the Seer of Lublin *('Ohel Elimelekh,*

p.131). On the conflict between Nahman and Barukh *cf.* also Weiss, *op. cit.*, p.16f., n.20.

44. *'Avaneha Barzel*, p.17*f.*: *Naḥal Nove'a*, p.19. But see also *Siḥot* 166, where he denied that his descent from the Ba'al Shem Tov is the source of his greatness.

45. *'Avahena Barzel*, p.19. There is another late tradition (or another version of this one) recorded in *Ṭovot Zikhronot*, p.5, claiming that Barukh told Nahman's mother that the conflict was but a ruse on his part to hide his nephew's great holiness, for which the world was not prepared. It seems highly unlikely that Barukh would have said this—unless he did so after Nahman's death.

46. *Ḥayyey II*, 11:105. That passage contains a highly interesting list of *ẓaddiqim* whom Nahman respected, most of whom were long dead by 1800. It is particularly noteworthy that he praises the Maggid and his disciples. Might this reflect his siding with Levi Yizhak against his uncle Barukh? Shne'ur Zalman is noticed by his absence from this list; this may reflect later editing. Witness to the fact that Nahman supported Shne'ur Zalman in his battle with Barukh is the story that when the controversy broke out Nahman met with Shne'ur Zalman, and said to him (in an untranslatable play on words), "*Peterburg/Feter-Burekh*," meaning "Do you who have already suffered one controversy and landed in a Petersburg prison, now want to take on my uncle *(feter)* Barukh?" Dubnov, *op. cit.*, pp. 312*f.*

47. *Yemey ha-Tela'ot*, p.174*f*; Piekarz, *op. cit.*, p.71*ff*. This is the incident to which we have referred above in n.26.

48. *Yemey MaHaRNaT*, p.28. As for the worsening of the conflict in 1806–07, see chapter five. The controversy around Bratslav continued long after Nahman's death; its echoes could still be felt in the early twentieth century. In the 1830s, Moshe Zevi of Savran took on the role of the Zeide, and Nathan and his followers were bitterly persecuted, apparently to the point of *ḥerem*. See above, chapter two, n.37. This period in Bratslav history is recorded in *Yemey ha-Tela'ot*. Important references to these persecutions are also found in Nathan's collected letters, *'Alim li-Terufah*. Piekarz, *op. cit.*, p.209, has discussed these persecutions rather briefly, but a full treatment of them is still lacking. The two basic Hasidic bibliographies, A. Walden's *Shem ha-Gedolim he-Ḥadash* and M. Bodek's *Seder ha-Dorot he-Ḥadash* (both published in 1865) reflect some hesitancy in their listings of Nahman's work, hinting that his teachings were somehow distorted, perhaps by his own disciples. These views were widely held by later *ḥasidim* of other schools. Nahman's works are almost never quoted in Hasidic circles outside of Bratslav. The late A.J. Heschel told me that his uncle, the Novominsker rebbe of Warsaw, who had a large and well-known Hasidic library, would not keep any Bratslav books in his possession. When the young Heschel wanted to read Nahman, it was a Kotzker *hasid*—irreverent by tradition—who obtained a copy for him. Writing as late as 1912, Yudl Rosenberg found it necessary, while telling tales of the Zeide *(op. cit.*, p.94), to chide certain of his readers for mocking the Bratslav *ḥasidim*.

49. *Cf. Ḥayyey* 4:11 and the first introduction to the *Sippurey Ma'asiyot*. Discussed by Weiss, *op. cit.*, p.21. I would want to distinguish carefully between an accusation of Sabbatianism and an awareness that Nahman saw himself as a crucial figure in the messianic drama.

50. *Ḥayyey II* 3:93, and the full discussion by Weiss, *op. cit.*, p.36*ff*. Weiss has not entered into the much more complicated question of what *intellectual* affinity there may have been between Nahman and Levi Yizhak. Horodezky seems to

have felt some such affinity *(Ha-Ḥasidut weha-Ḥasidim*, v.3, p.30), but does not define it. An examination of the *Qedushat Levi* with this question in mind might be fruitful. As an example, *cf.* Levi Yizhak on *shemot*, p.92b, as compared with Nahman's notion of *maqqifin* to be discussed below in Excursus I.

51. *Ḥayyey* 4:21.

52. Based on a play on words associating the words for 'teach' *(horah*, from radical YRH), with the word for 'pregnancy' *(herayon*, from HRH).

53. *Liqquṭim II* 20.

54. *Ḥayyey*, 8:44. *Cf.* also *Siḥot* 163, said at Zlotopolye.

55. *Liqquṭim* 179, 238, 251, 258. A number of passages in Nahman's writings speak of controversy in images of clouds, which cover the eyes and block one's vision, or as the thunder which accompanies a storm. *Cf. Liqquṭim* 62:8; 283. Much has been made of these images by J. Weiss in *Studies in Mysticism and Religion:* Hebrew Section, pp. 109ff.

56. *Liqquṭim* 6:6 and 14:12, both dating from fall/winter of 1802, shortly after the move to Bratslav, reflect this. *Cf.* also *Liqquṭim* 207 on the importance of not judging one's enemies too harshly.

57. *Liqquṭim* 88, 95, 114, 181, 208, 241, 277; *Liqquṭim II* 13; *Siḥot* 96; *Ḥayyey II* 2:48.

58. *Ḥayyey II* 5:10. Emphasis mine. *Cf.* Sanhedrin 7a. Some other sources on the growth-producing or beneficial qualities of controversy are to be found in *Ḥayyey II* 11:57 and *Liqquṭim* 161. A letter by Elimelekh of Lezajsk explains the spiritual benefits derived by the *ẓaddiq* from the fact of his struggle against enemies *(mitnaggedim)* in very similar ways. Wilensky, *Ḥasidim u-Mitnaggedim*, p.170. Notice should also be taken of the very strange parable ascribed to Nahman in *Ḥayyey II* 2:41:

> It once happened that a controversy broke out concerning a certain person. He built for himself a tall tower and stayed within it. They fought against him, shooting at the tower with arrows and gunfire, but to no avail.
>
> Now there are precious stones which grow in the air, formed by mists. There was a certain precious stone growing there in the air, which had not yet reached perfection. They shot it down with their arrows, and it landed on the tower. This stone contained such grace that as soon as it fell upon the tower they all bowed down to him, saying: "Long live the king! Long live the king!"

What we see again here is Nahman's rare power—exemplified frequently in his tales—to lend a classic ring to his own personal mythology.

59. Or another version of this same incident? *Cf.* also *Ḥayyey II* 11:57.

60. *Siḥot* 77, emphasis mine. *Cf.* Weiss in *'Aley 'Ayin*, p.272.

61. *Liqquṭim* 62:2, 64:4, *Siḥot* 77 and 94. The idea that ancient controversies are repeated in later times is also found in *Shivḥey ha-BeSHT*, p.55*f.*, where the conflict between the BeSHT and Nahman of Kosov is said to be that of Saul and David. It is a common motif in later tales in explaining why *ḥasidim* are not to follow the lead of their *rebbes* in the denunciation of others.

62. *Liqquṭim* 56:8, based on N. Shapira's *Megalleh 'Amuqot, 'ofan* 74. *Cf.* also *Degel Maḥaneh Ephraim, Koraḥ*, p.199a.

63. *Liqquṭim* 36:1 and 65 make it clear that any new perception of truth is necessarily preceded by a period of particularly severe inner conflict.

64. The term *gedol ha-dor* is common in Rabbinic literature. While it is often used

in the plural *(Baba Batra* 36b, 91a) and thus does not necessarily refer to a single leader, such a figure as Abraham *(Qiddushin* 32b) or Amram *(Soṭah* 12b) is designated as the single *gadol* of his generation. A parallel term is *ḥasid she-ba-dor (Ta'anit* 8a), which does seem to indicate a single figure. The particular phrase *ẓaddiq ha-dor* is not found in early rabbinic sources; its origins may lie in the exegesis of Genesis 6:9, where Noah is seen as a "*ẓaddiq* in his generation." On the term *gedol ha-dor cf.* Weiss, *Zion* 16 (1951) 84, n. 6.

65. On the Ba'al Shem Tov *cf.* the sources quoted by Weiss in *Zion* 16 (1951) 85*f.* To these should be added the passage in *Degel, ẓaw,* 156b, beginning "The king is the heart of all Israel." It should also be noted, however, that the author of the *Degel* does not himself defend the idea of singular leadership. *Cf.* his words *loc. cit.* and *'emor,* 181b. It would seem that the *Degel's* brother Barukh was closer to their grandfather in this matter, and considered the role of *ẓaddiq ha-dor* to be a more or less hereditary matter. This, too, was a factor in his many conflicts with others. The editor of *Shivḥey ha-BeSHT* claims that the Ba'al Shem Tov's soul was that of Moses and Simeon ben Yohai, and that such a soul would not appear again until the advent of Messiah. *Shivḥey ha-BeSHT, haqdamat ha-kotev;* ed. Horodezky, p. 8. As for the Maggid, *cf.* the claim made by his descendant, Israel of Ruzhin, recorded in *'Eser 'Orot,* pp. 24*f.* It seems unlikely that this claim was made during the Maggid's lifetime. Even Elimelekh of Lezajsk, in whose work the theory of the *ẓaddiq* is so highly developed, does not advocate the notion of *ẓaddiq ha-dor.*

66. Weiss *(op. cit.,* p.84) has noted the need for a full treatment of the *ẓaddiq ha-dor* idea in the history of Judaism. See the present author's "The *Ẓaddiq* as *Axis Mundi* in Later Judaism" *JAAR* 45:3(1977) 327–347.

67. *Yerushalmi Soṭah* 9 (24b).

68. *Qiddushin* 72b; *Yoma* 38b; *Genesis Rabbah* 58:2.

69. *Yoma* 38b.

70. *Genesis Rabbah* 35:2.

71. *Gen. Rabbah* 35:2; See Theodor *ad loc.* In view of these rabbinic sources, one may question Scholem's thesis *(Von der mystischen Gestalt der Gottheit,* pp. 83*ff.* and *"Three Types of Jewish Piety"* in *Eranos Jahrbuch* 38, 1969) to the effect that the term *ẓaddiq* is used to designate normative piety in rabbinic literature (as in such phrases as *ẓaddiqim u-resha'im),* while *ḥasid* is the term for more extreme types. Scholem claims that eighteenth-century Hasidism represents a complete reversal in the usages of these two terms, for the first time using *ẓaddiq* to designate an intensity of religious life beyond that of the *ḥasid ("eine vollständige Umkehrung des Sprachgebrauchs stattgefunden zu haben scheint . . .", Von der mystischen Gestalt der Gottheit,* p. 114). The sources here quoted seem to indicate, however, that the term *ẓaddiq* is also used in the supranormative sense in early rabbinic sources. When God consults *"the souls of the ẓaddiqim"* before Creation *(Genesis Rabbah* 8:7) it hardly seems likely that he is taking counsel with all those who are more righteous than they are wicked; he is rather taking counsel with those unique figures whose special righteousness will be needed to protect the world from destruction. More strikingly, the "single pillar" upon whom the earth is founded *(Ḥagigah* 12b) is more than the ordinary Jew who avoids wickedness and fulfills the law; he is a unique charismatic figure who takes on the role of human *axis mundi.* Scholem's assertion thus seems to be somewhat one-sided. While he is of course right in noting that Jewish ethical literature, including such works of Kabbalistic ethics as

Hayyim Vital's *Sha'arey Qedushah,* place the *ḥasid* above the *ẓaddiq* in rank, we might reformulate his thesis to say that BeSHTian Hasidism rediscovers a certain old rabbinic usage of the term *ẓaddiq* and gives it new life. This interpretation of Scholem's has already been questioned by I. Tishby, *Mishnat ha-Zohar* II, p. 667, where he comes to the most interesting conclusion that once the term *ḥasid* had become a commonplace in the eighteenth century, the term *ẓaddiq,* with its supernaturalist overtones, was resurrected to designate the Hasidic leader.

72. *Genesis Rabbah* 56:7.

73. *Mekhilta, Shirta* 9. This passage and several others are discussed by E. Urbach, *ḤaZal; Pirqey Emunot we-De'ot,* Jerusalem, 1969, pp. 430*f.* On Moses as the paradigmatic *ẓaddiq,* see also *Yoma* 38b, where Moses and the *ẓaddiq* are linked by motifs of goodness and light.

74. *Tanḥuma, Ki Tissa* 12; *Exodus Rabbah* 40:3. See Ginzberg, *Legends of the Jews,* v. 5, p. 75, and Scholem, *Ursprung und Anfänge der Kabbalah,* Berlin, 1962, p. 139.

75. Scholem, *Major Trends,* pp. 278*ff.*, and in much greater detail in *Von der mystischen Gestalt der Gottheit,* pp. 226*ff.*

76. *Sefer ha-Qaneh (Peli'ah)* 12a–b; *Megalleh 'Amuqot, 'ofan* 113. *Cf.* Shabbat 146a. Note also Vital's *Sha'ar ha-Pesuqim,* 98a, where all those who lived in the generation of the wilderness are seen as branches of the soul of Moses. Further explanation *ibid.*, 56a. *Cf.* also *Sha'ar ha-Gilgulim,* beginning.

77. *Qaneh,* 12b. For an explanation of these terms, *cf.* Scholem, *On the Kabbalah and Its Symbolism,* New York, 1965, pp. 77*ff.* and *Major Trends,* pp. 178*ff.* It is likely that the passage Scholem quotes from Mordecai Yaffee's *Levush 'Or Yeqarot (On the Kabbalah,* pp. 82*f.*), is based on this passage in the *Qaneh.*

78. *Megalleh 'Amuqot, 'ofan* 113.

79. *Zohar* 2:148b–149a; *'Emeq ha-Melekh* 4b; *Sefer ha-Gilgulim,* chapter 19. *Cf.* Scholem, *Sabbatai Ṣevi,* p.57. Also *'Emeq ha-Melekh* 33b: "In every generation God creates one *ẓaddiq* who is worthy to have the *Shekhinah* shine upon him as it did upon Moses; if his generation is worthy, he may redeem Israel. . . ."

80. *Ḥayyey II* 2:39.

81. *Liqquṭim* 61:7. The same source refers to the *ẓaddiq* as the "holy of holies," another image of the center of the universe. The rabbinic background of this term is discussed by R. Patai in *Man and Temple,* London, 1947. On its Gnostic associations *cf.* A. Altmann, "Gnostic Themes in Rabbinic Cosmology."

82. *Liqquṭim* 20:1, *Cf. Avot* 6:4.

83. *Liqquṭim* 2, 70, II 72. From *Liqquṭim* 4:5 one might get the impression that every *ẓaddiq* has such a soul; this is clarified in 9:4 (said in 1803), where the reference is clearly to a single *ẓaddiq ha-dor.* The idea that simply being in his presence can have a great effect is already found in 4:8, dating from Nahman's Zlotopolye period.

84. The relationship between the earthly *ẓaddiq* and *yesod,* the ninth *sefirah,* which is also called *ẓaddiq,* will be discussed elsewhere. For a history of this symbol *cf.* Scholem's essay on the *ẓaddiq,* now to be found in his Hebrew collection *Pirqey Yesod,* p.213*ff.*

85. This is still part of the practice of Bratslav *ḥasidim* today. In the synagogues of the Bratslav *ḥasidim* in Jerusalem there is a sign that encourages the worshiper to bind his soul, while praying, with the souls of the great *ẓaddiqim,* and especially with the soul of Nahman. Only the *ẓaddiq ha-dor* knows all the proper gates

through which prayer must enter in order to ascend, and can thus direct the worshiper's prayer to the proper place. *Liqquṭim* 9.4. Again, in *Liqquṭim* 2:6, the *ẓaddiq* is depicted as Moses building the *mishkan*, assembled from the collected prayers of all Israel. *Cf.* also *Liqquṭim* 215. In *Ḥayyey II*, 2:59, it is made most clear that any attempts to live a religious life without the help of the *ẓaddiq ha-dor* are quite vain.

86. *Liqquṭim* 38:7.

87. *Liqquṭim* 70.

88. *Liqquṭim* 56:1. Emphasis mine. *Cf.* the continuation of that teaching as well as *Liqquṭim* 20:5 on Nahman's awareness of the dangers in asserting such power.

89. We do have one source *(Siḥot* 176) that tells us that before [his journey to] Erez Israel he said: "I am unable to sleep. Before I fall asleep all of the six hundred thousand letters of the Torah come and stand before me." This might reflect an early claim, still couched in very hesitant terms, that his is the soul which contains within it all the letters of the Torah, *i.e.*, which contains all the souls of Israel. *Ḥayyey* 4:9 tells us that Nahman was engaged in some sort of controversy already in Medvedevka, but details are completely lacking.

90. *Liqquṭim* 64:4.

4

Bratslav: Disciples and Master

Nahman's first attempt to have himself recognized as the greatest of all the *ẓaddiqim* had ended in utter failure. Two years after having settled in Zlotopolye and having issued his challenge to the popular Hasidism of the Zeide, he departed in humiliation. He was heard to say that he had suffered twice the torments of hell in that place: while the punishment of the wicked lasts for only twelve months, he had endured the torments of Zlotopolye for a full twenty-four! After two years of residence in that town he seems to have acquired no significant local following there, and at the end he finally felt himself to have been more or less chased out of town.

The choice of Bratslav as a new setting for Nahman's community seems to have been motivated by two factors. One, as we have mentioned, was the proximity of his uncle Barukh, with whom he had not yet had his falling out. Barukh himself, living in nearby Tulchin, had once thought of moving his court to Bratslav, and undoubtedly exercised considerable influence there. A second factor in the move was that of location itself. While not a large community (figures for 1797 indicate about a thousand Jewish families in the Bratslav district), it had the distinct advantage of lying near the center of Jewish population in the Ukraine, unlike Medvedevka or Zlotopolye, which lay at the far eastern edge of the Pale. Given Nahman's desire to influence the Hasidic community as a whole, this change of place was particularly desirable. In contrast to his rash conduct on moving into Zlotopolye, Nahman met, this time, under Barukh's aegis, with leaders of the Bratslav community, and they agreed in advance to his settling in their town.[1]

Nahman saw the move to Bratslav as a great turning point in his life. Rather than acting the part of the defeated renegade, he entered into Bratslav with a triumphal air. Arriving in late summer of 1802, he said of himself, "Until now I have dwelt alone, outside the camp. But now I begin. . . ." He depicted his "discovery" of Bratslav as an event of great spiritual dimensions. When, on a Sabbath shortly after his arrival, the wine cup for *kiddush* accidentally spilled onto the ground, he announced: "Today we have planted Bratslaver *ḥasidim!*" The name of the town was also given special significance: Nahman's disciples to this day always refer to the town as *Breslav,* which, by a play of letters, was associated with the 'heart of flesh' which is to accompany the promised redemption.[2] When speaking about his arrival in Bratslav, Nahman pictured himself as the mystical Abraham, making reference to the passage in the *Zohar* that describes the patriarch's move from Haran to the Land of Israel:

> Get thee forth (Gen. 12:1). That is, it is not fitting for thee to remain here among these sinners. The real truth of the matter is this. God inspired Abram with a spirit of wisdom so that he was able to discover by means of certain tests the character of all the inhabited countries of the world. He surveyed them and weighed them in the balance, discovering the [heavenly] powers to which each is entrusted. When he came to the central point of the inhabited world [the Holy Land] he tried to weigh it, but obtained no response. He tried to find the power to which it was entrusted, but could not grasp it, though he weighed it again and again. He noted that from that point the whole world was planted out, and he once more tested and weighed and found that the upper power in charge of it was one which could not be gauged, that it was recondite and hidden, and not like the [powers in charge of the] outlying parts of the inhabited world. He once more reflected, and came to the conclusion that as the whole world had been planted out in all directions from that point in the centre, so the power in charge of it was the one from which issued all the powers in charge of the other quarters of the world and to which they were all attached: hence: 'they went forth with them from Ur of the Chaldees to go to the Land of Canaan' (Gen. 11:31).[3]

This Nahman says of *his* discovery of Bratslav!

Bratslav is depicted in Nahman's teachings from this period as a new Holy Land, or a new Jerusalem. He has come to that place which he is prepared to claim as the new capital of the Hasidic universe, and thus, by extension, the new center of the world. No wonder, then, that he should employ the image of Abraham, who finds the place of God. At the same time, there is an important difference here. While in the *Zohar* Abraham was *finding* the place where God had dwelt since Creation, Nahman was himself *creating* the holy place by virtue of his own move there. If the *ẓaddiq* is the *'even shetiyah,* the central rock upon which the world is built, then the place where he chooses to dwell will inevitably be a spiritual Jerusalem.[4]

On the Sabbath preceding Rosh Hashanah of the year 5563 (September, 1802), some two weeks after his arrival, Nahman presented a teaching shot through with images of the Holy Land, to the point of being quite open about the image of Bratslav as sacred territory. The elated spirit of those first few weeks in Bratslav is well conveyed in the text of that teaching:

> Why is it that we clap our hands in prayer? Our sages, in explaining why it is that the Torah opens with 'In the beginning' [and not with the first direct commandment to Israel in Exodus 12], anticipate that the nations of the world will call us thieves for having usurped the land of the seven Canaanite peoples. For this reason, "He showed His people the power of His deeds, giving them the lands of [other] nations" (Ps. 111:6), saying that since all the worlds are His Creation, He may assign [lands] to whomever He wishes. . . . All things are called the power of His deeds, the word power [*ko'ah*, numerically twenty-eight] corresponding to the twenty-eight letters [in the first verse] of Creation and to the twenty-eight joints on a person's hands.
>
> As is known, the atmosphere of the pagans' lands is polluted, while the air of the Land of Israel is holy and pure, since God has taken it away from the other nations and given it to us. Outside the Holy Land, however, the air remains impure. When we clap our hands together in prayer [using the twenty-eight joints] we arouse the power of the twenty-eight letters of Creation, the 'power of His deeds,' showing that He has the power to give us the inheritance of the nations, since everything belongs to God. Thus we are able to purify the air of other peoples' lands, as these lands are brought back under the rule of God, and He can (re)distribute them as He wishes. Therefore Scripture says: 'giving them the lands of other nations.' Thus a Jew may purify the atmosphere of a place by praying there, and may then breathe holy air, just as he does in Erez Israel . . . for we see that air is pushed aside when a person claps his hands. . . .
>
> Thus our sages say: 'Whoever establishes a fixed place for prayer, the God of Abraham helps him.' For by his hand a new world is built, and this new building is through Abraham, as Scripture says: 'The world is built by *ḥesed*' (Ps. 89:3) . . . Abraham was the first to attain Erez Israel, as the *Zohar* says. . . .[5]

This piece, which may have served as a dedicatory sermon for a new Hasidic house of prayer in Bratslav, gives us great insight into Nahman's feelings about the move. If one reads between the lines and appreciates the *Sitz im Leben* of this teaching, it is clear that Nahman is here the new Abraham, or perhaps the new Joshua, spiritually "conquering" and purifying a new territory in the name of God and Israel. By a mere clap of the hands, he can drive out the corrupt Ukrainian atmosphere and convert Bratslav into a Holy Land. That which is to be created here in Bratslav, he tells his disciples, is to bear witness to the first Creation and to the ever-present power of God to reward the faithful. Part of this reward, apparently, is the sanctification and redistribution of the earth's territory.[6] We also see, here as in the story of the spilled wine cup, how closely Nahman remains within the tradition of the wonder-working Hasidic *ẓaddiq*, bringing about some great change in the cosmos by a small, even inadvertent, gesture here on earth.

The elation attendant on Nahman's arrival in Bratslav seems to have remained with him for a period of several months. In the latter part of 1802 and in early 1803 he remained rather free for a while from the violent depressions that had plagued him earlier and would return to haunt him throughout most of his later years. The teachings that date from these months make rather more frequent mention than usual of music, handclapping, and dance. In fact we are explicitly told that Nahman danced more in that year than in any other: on Simhat Torah, Hanukkah, Purim, at a wedding—whenever an appropriate occasion could be found—Nahman was out dancing among his *ḥasidim*. As we shall see shortly, this dancing was not simply an expression of unmitigated joy, but taken as a whole this period does seem to have been one of great relief to him. At times like these, the intensity of Nahman's self-directed inner vision, rather than turning to depression or thoughts of conflict, focused on the great beauty of his own spirit:

> The world has not yet tasted of me at all. If they were to hear but a single one of my teachings with the melody and dance that belong to it, they would simply pass out: their souls would just leave them in this great and wondrous joy. Even the animals and the blades of grass would be affected: everything in the world would simply pass out of itself.[7]

This image of himself as master of dance and music, flowing from a great sense of his own inner beauty, at times allowed Nahman to preach and write with a lyrical power that makes him unique among Hasidic authors. Turning sometimes to the pastoral memories of his adolescent years and at others to the joy felt by Jews at a wedding or festival celebration, Nahman was able to strive toward lyrical heights within the usually dry framework of Hasidic homilies. The rich power of literary imagination, which was to find its fullest expression only later in the *Sippurey Ma'aśiyot*, is by no means lacking in Nahman's teachings. An example of that literary richness of which he was capable in times of fullness and exultation is here in order:

> When our father Jacob sent his ten sons to Joseph, he sent with them the melody of Erez Israel. This is the meaning of 'take some of the land's produce' (Gen. 43:11). [Produce—*zimrat*—can also be translated 'melody'.] This refers to the melody which he sent to Joseph, as RaSHI has explained.

> Every shepherd has a particular melody, according to the grasses in the place where he tends his flock. Each and every animal has its own special

> grass which it needs to eat; since the shepherd does not always take his flock to the same spot, his melody varies according to the places where he leads them. As we know from *Pereq Shirah*, each blade of grass has its own song. The melody of the shepherd is made up of all these songs.
>
> This is why Yaval, the 'father of all who dwell in tents and keep cattle' was the brother of Yuval, 'the father of all who play the harp and lyre' (Gen. 4:20). For as soon as there were herdsmen in the world, there were musicians as well. This is why King David, the musician, was also a shepherd.
>
> Thus Scripture says: 'From the corners of the earth we have heard singing!' (Is. 24:16). These are the songs and melodies that come out of the ground. The music is formed through the grasses that grow there. By knowing that melody, the shepherd can put into the grasses the proper powers, so that the herds will have what they need to eat.
>
> This is also the meaning of 'The blossoms appear in the earth: the time of singing is come' (Cant. 2:12)—each blossom appears in the earth by means of that melody which belongs to it. . . .[8]

Such a teaching as this one on the shepherd and his music reflects the presence in Nahman of an element one rarely finds in the history of Jewish mysticism (the *Zohar* and the BeSHT are the other significant exceptions): a mystical appreciation of nature. A teaching like this one, reflecting upon the intimate bond between shepherd, flock, and land, is quite uncharacteristic of the religious life of the highly urbanized Jewish community. Nahman's writings contain a strong romantic element, which at times reminds one that he is as much a contemporary of Wordsworth as he is a latter-day student of Luria and Cordovero, mystics whose works are utterly lacking in such appreciation of the beauties of this world. At the same time, we should bear in mind that this remains a *mystical* teaching: its ultimate theme is the unity of all things, toward which an appreciation of their particularity is but a step. There are passages in which Nahman depicts the task of the religious person as that of seeking out the particular and unique bits of holiness in each aspect of creation, in each tree or blade of grass, in each person. Such a one becomes a channel for these individualized sparks to return to God; he is also depicted as a weaver, drawing the various strands of holiness together into a proper whole. In this way Nahman combines an appreciation for the particular and even the idiosyncratic with a mysticism which by its very nature sees all as one and seeks to transcend the separate and limiting identities of object, time, and space. At times the motif of underlying oneness overwhelms all individual identity, as is the case in the writings of more traditional Kabbalists. Then the theme is approached with a much heavier tread, and Nahman employs the older images of a return to primal nothingness or the endless longing of the mystical Community of Israel for redemption. Mysticism and romanticism are thus combined in Nahman, and the romantic in him could well appreciate the beauty of the shepherd's melody—or the preacher's metaphor, for that matter. It was only Nahman's constant attempt to explain and account for the enormous complexity of his own inner life that caused the tormented and anguished side of the romantic in him to be emphasized in so disproportionate a manner.

An example of the simple sense of joy and beauty and the way it combined with Nahman's complex attitude toward himself is to be found in the accounts of Nahman's dancing, centered in the year 1803. While on one level it undoubtedly was an expression of joy at finding a new and peaceful home, it contained other elements as well. A closer examination of this dancing will in fact afford us a significant glimpse into Nahman's areas of concern and his reactions to the world around him. For in addition to expressing joy, Nahman's dancing was a highly charged theurgic act, aimed at nothing less than changing the will of the Czar in distant St. Petersburg. He thus hoped to affect the fate of the entire Jewish community in Russia.

With the ascendance of Alexander I to the Russian throne in 1801, a new era had begun in the history of Russian Jewry. The liberal regime of Alexander's early years began to issue the first of many proposals for the "betterment" of the Jews within Russian society. While in part well-intended, neither these proposals nor those that followed them took any account of the Jews' desire to preserve their traditional way of life and were thus seen, particularly by Hasidic leaders, as *gezerot*, governmental threats to Jewish existence. In November of 1802, the Czar convened a "Committee for the Amelioration of the Jews" to investigate possible courses of action in this matter. Within a month or two, Jewish communities throughout the Pale were deeply alarmed by rumors of new "decrees", which, it was thought, would curtail both their economic position and their religious life. Despite their efforts, including a conference of *ẓaddiqim* at Berdichev in 1804 (which Nahman probably did not attend) and the sending of delegations from various provinces to St. Petersburg, the Jewish Constitution issued in final form in December of 1804 came as a terrible blow. Jews were to be expelled from rural areas and were to be forbidden to work as lease-holders or to sell liquor. More dangerously, however, as far as the *ẓaddiqim* were concerned, Russian schools and universities were to be opened to Jews, and the Jews themselves were to be encouraged to open schools where Russian language and secular subjects would be taught.[9]

This series of threatened measures, known in Bratslav literature as *gezerat ha-punktin (punktin* here probably means "clauses," of which there were many in the Constitution), was a matter of tremendous concern to Nahman. Several of his teachings from late in 1802 through 1804 contain references to the need for negating the evil decree. His most basic reaction to the *gezerah,* however, was expressed in dance.

> He himself said: I have danced a lot this year. This was because in that year the decree called *punktin* had been announced. It was because of this that he danced so much, for by means of dance one can transform the evil forces and nullify decrees.[10]

Nahman's dancing in the year 1803 is thus much more serious than might be assumed at first glance. Quite different from any other descriptions of the place of dance we find in Hasidism, this dancing is not simply an expression of joy, nor even a means to achieve *hitlahavut* ("ecstasy"); it is rather a theurgic act, aimed at doing battle with the forces of evil, by nullifying the acts of their earthly representatives, the Czar and his advisers, including the earliest Russian *maskilim.*

How did Nahman come upon this notion of the magical effects of dance, one well-known in far-flung "primitive" cultures, but hardly the stock-in-trade of later Judaism? While Jews did, of course, believe that their *ritual* actions could affect the upper forces and thus avert the evil decrees of both God and the nations, such beliefs were limited to the *prescribed* rituals, the *miẓwot.* Here Nahman is operating outside the framework of the commandments, instituting a purely *private* ritual act, for which he nevertheless claims the same cosmic dimensions. Nowhere in classical Judaism, surely not in the atrophied dance traditions preserved in such rituals as *hosha'not,* could Nahman have gotten the idea that dance in particular would have such power. How then was it that he was taken by this notion?

The answer to this question, as to so many others, seems to lie in the peculiar relationship between Nahman's own psyche and the Hasidic doctrine he had inherited from the BeSHT. Dance did, of course, have an important place in early Hasidism, as an expression of joy and ecstasy. Nahman's uncle, the rabbi of Sudilkov, quotes this parable in the name of the Ba'al Shem Tov:

> There was once a certain musician who played his instrument so beautifully that those who heard him could not contain themselves, and danced [jumping] almost to the ceiling, because of their great joy. The closer one came to the musician, the greater was one's joy, and the dancing only grew greater. Meanwhile, a deaf man came along, who could not hear the music at all. He saw all the people dancing about, and thought them to be madmen.[11]

The deaf man in the parable is of course the *mitnagged,* who does not "hear" the ecstatic music that makes the *ḥasid* dance. It should be noted that the ecstatic body motions the *ḥasidim* employed during prayer were mentioned in the bans against them, and were at times actually described as acts of "madness." What is of interest to us here is that an elaboration of this parable (or a close parallel to it) is to be found in Nahman's writings, but with its significance transformed. The change in this parable is highly instructive as to Nahman's character and relation to Hasidism; in it is also to be found the origin of his theurgic use of dance.

The religious world view of the BeSHT is marked by a clear attitude of ecstatic optimism. There is no place devoid of God; all things and all moments are filled with His presence, for those whose eyes and ears are open. Evil thoughts are in fact rooted in the holy; the goal of the religious life is to see through the illusion of evil, returning all to its source in the divine. Hasidism represents a definite loosening of the Gnostic tension that had characterized Lurianic Kabbalah. As such, it gave little serious attention to the problem of evil.[12] Nahman, plagued as he was by inner tensions, could not accept the rather facile advocacy of joy that was his Hasidic heritage. Nahman, it may be said, plays the role of Job in relation to BeSHTian Hasidism, seeing in his own personal suffering the ultimate denial of the attitude of religious optimism that had preceded him. Yes, Nahman agreed, the goal of life is sacred joy. But how is one to come to this joy, given the suffering that seems to be man's lot on earth? The only authentic joy for Nahman is that which is born of struggle, confronting fully the painful side of life and reaching out to bring it, too, into joy. The attainment of *simḥah* in Nahman's thought is thus a dialectical process: simple joy confronts sadness and brings it to itself, thus creating a new and more complex sort of joy. It is this dialectic Nahman expresses in his version of the Ba'al Shem Tov's parable of the dancers:

> With regard to joy, a parable:
>
> Sometimes when people are joyous and dancing, they grab a man from outside their dancing circle, one who is sad and melancholy, and force him to join with them in their dance. Thus it is with joy: when a person is happy, his own sadness and suffering stand off on the side. But it is a higher achievement to struggle and pursue that sadness, bringing it too into the joy, until it is transformed . . . you grab hold of this suffering, and force it to join with you in the rejoicing, just as in the parable.[13]

Here the outsider to the circle of dancers is no longer the *mitnagged,* but rather the *mitnagged* within the self, the depressed side of man, which refuses to join in the merry-making and maintains a sense of critical detachment. Nahman overcomes this negative influence by forcing it into the dance, sweeping it off its feet as it is brought into the circle. Here the symbol of dance has been transformed to speak to Nahman's inner self. No longer a mere *expression* of ecstatic joy, dance has become a *weapon* to be used in the battle against one's own inner forces of evil, manifested in feelings of melancholy and depression.

From this we can see how Nahman came to conceive of dance as a means by which to combat the evil decrees of the Czar in St. Petersburg. The external and internal evil forces are not clearly distinguished from one another in his thought; that which works within the self will also have power in the cosmos. The evil forces that lie behind *gezerat ha-punktin* must also be "forced into" the dance, transformed and uplifted as they confront the ecstatic energy of the true *ẓaddiq* who contends with them.

Nahman undoubtedly also had another motive in mind in "taking on" the Czar in this way. Having little political power even within the Hasidic world, he was probably not even consulted when the Ukrainian Jews chose representatives to plead their case. Barukh and Levi Yizhak, Mordecai of Chernobyl and the Zeide would have been the ones to make such decisions. And yet Nahman, powerless as he was, had already asserted his claim to being the only true *ẓaddiq* of his generation! Who should do battle with the Russian emperor, at once oppressor of the Jews and titular head of Russian Christendom, if not his direct counterpart on the side of the holy, the true *ẓaddiq ha-dor?* By employing esoteric and theurgic means to defeat the Czar, Nahman was indeed claiming his place as the one who "has no revealed kingship at all, but nonetheless, in a deeply hidden way, rules over the entire generation . . . for all their souls are under his dominion and are bowed before him."[14]

These actions contained a clear message to the surrounding Hasidic world: Nahman was a force to be reckoned with, and Bratslav was claiming its place as a major center, if not as capital, of the entire Hasidic "realm." Here and here alone lay true power; the acts of other *ẓaddiqim* merely served to hide the fact that Bratslav was now the true center of the world.

What was the nature of that center in its heyday? What sort of people formed the group around Nahman, and what kind of religious teaching did he offer them? The followers of Nahman at no time formed one of the larger of the Hasidic communities; it has been estimated that he had no more than a few hundred *ḥasidim* at the time of his death.[15] Despite Nahman's desire to assert his authority as *ẓaddiq ha-dor,* in fact the demands he placed upon his *ḥasidim* could appeal to but a small and intense spiritual elite and could never attract the masses. A *ẓaddiq* who was not to be bothered with worldly matters and who showed disdain for all but the most total devotion could not hope to gain the broad-based support that had naturally gravitated toward a man like Barukh of Medzhibozh. On the contrary, Nahman's closest positive models for Hasidic community were models of smallness and intimacy: the original circle around the Ba'al Shem Tov and the Tiberias community of Abraham Kalisker. Both of these, each for its own reason, stood in strong contrast to the great Hasidic courts of Nahman's time. The BeSHT had not been so well known in his early years as to attract a large following. At least as romanticized by legends abounding in Nahman's day, those original "sons of the palace" of the first Hasidic community were of a quality never later to be equaled. In Kalisker's case it was the physical isolation of Tiberias and the difficulties of life there that made it necessary for his community to be one of great intimacy. Only the most intensely devoted of Hasidic followers would have been willing to leave behind both family and livelihood to follow the master to the Holy Land.

In seeking to restore Hasidism to the fiery days of the BeSHT, Nahman had to oppose those tendencies within the movement that might have lent him greater popular support. His goal, clearly stated, was a revival within Hasidism: only by making the most serious of demands upon his followers could he hope to achieve this goal. Once again Nahman interprets the clapping of hands in prayer:

> Around the time when he first came to Bratslav, he spoke a great deal about clapping one's hands during prayer. He told me that when he first came here he had once stood at the entrance to the study of his house and had castigated people for not praying properly. He said: 'I don't hear anyone clapping his hands together as he prays!' From this we understand at once that his intention was to restore the crown to its former glory, to arouse people to pray with great ecstatic devotion, as the first *ḥasidim* had done in the days of the BeSHT and his holy disciples. For by the beginning of our master's time, the *ḥasidim* had started to cool off, etc. And he struggled to restore it all, to bring back the former glory.[16]

There were certain aspects of the new enthusiasm flourishing in Bratslav that are reminiscent of the Ba'al Shem Tov's day or of the Hasidic "outbursts" of 1770. Thus on Simhat Torah night of 1802, Nahman's disciples ran through the market place of the town singing, "Exult and rejoice, you who dwell in Bratslav!"—a play on Isaiah 12:6, in which Bratslav replaces "Zion" in the original verse. When Gedaliah of Linits protested to Nahman that the Bratslav *ḥasidim* prayed too loudly, Nahman answered, "I prefer those old-time *ḥasidim* who used to jump right into the King's palace with the grease still on their sleeves!"[17]—a response of which his great-grandfather would have been proud. But combined with this enthusiasm there was also a deep level of personal demand, and it was that which lent Bratslav its particular coloring.

Nahman believed that the core of the religious life lay in the inner world of the individual and in the intense struggle going on within each person's soul. Having attained all that he had in his own life as a result of the most bitter battle against temptations and depressions constantly threatening to overwhelm him, he came to demand that a similar battle be fought by each of his serious disciples. Nahman's own inner life and struggles became paradigmatic for *ḥasid*, both within Nahman's lifetime and later in the history of Bratslav.[18] While other Hasidic communities were often distinguishable from one another (particularly within the Ukraine) only by particular matters of style, dress, or customs in fulfilling one or another of the *mizwot*, Nahman's *ḥasidim* were set off in their early days as those who had performed the initiatory rite of confessing all their sins before the master, and later by the demand he made that each of them conduct daily heartrending personal "conversations" with God, pouring out all their burdens before Him as they gave utterance to their most private prayers.

The most essential religious practice of Bratslav, and that which Nahman constantly taught was to be placed above all else in his disciples' hierarchy of values, was this act of *hitbodedut*, lone daily conversation with God. The *ḥasid* was to set aside a certain period of time each day, preferably out of doors, if possible, and always alone, when he was to pour out before God his most intimate longings, needs, desires and frustrations. Nahman emphasized the need to do all this aloud, to bring those usually unspoken inner drives to the point of verbalization. He also insisted that one do so in one's native language (in his case Yiddish) rather than in Hebrew

> for we are not used to speaking in the holy language. In the Yiddish which we use for ordinary conversation it is easier to break one's heart. The heart is more readily drawn forth by Yiddish, being more used to it. In Yiddish it is possible to pour out your words, speaking everything that is in your heart before the Lord.[19]

Here Nahman has been struck by that same insight known to the Reformers in the history of Christianity: the vernacular has a power of direct access to the heart that no liturgical language, however beloved, can attain; this power must be harnessed for the purpose of a more intimate life with God. While he of course had no intention of abolishing the Hebrew liturgy, Nahman did go so far as to tell his disciples that this spontaneous heart-rending was the original form of human prayer, quoting Maimonides to the effect that liturgy was but a later innovation.[20]

Despite all the emphasis placed on master-disciple relationship and the intimacy of community among the disciples themselves in Bratslav, this lone act of *hitbodedut* was depicted as the single most important activity of both *ẓaddiq* and *ḥasid*. There is simply no other way to be close to God, Nahman taught, and nearness to God was the single ultimate goal that a Bratslav *ḥasid* was to allow himself.

> I have been told he said that no person, whether great or small, could do what he truly must except by means of *hitbodedut*. He mentioned various true and well-known *ẓaddiqim*, saying that each of them had attained to his rung only in this way. He also made mention of a certain simple man from among the BeSHT's descendants, saying that he, too, regularly poured out his words amid great tears. The family of the BeSHT, he said, were espe-

> cially accustomed to this, since they were of the Davidic house, and David's only concern was that he break his heart before the Lord always. This too is the origin of David's Psalms.[21]

There are times, Nahman said, when you will set out to hold such converse with God and will not be able to do any more than call out to him: "Lord of the World!" On other occasions you may go for days just repeating a single word over and over again, until finally speech is freed up. Regularity, patience, and faithfulness are the chief virtues of the life of *hitbodedut*. Though it may appear to you at first that no change is taking place in your life, a person who has a regular life with God in this way is over time so transformed that a skilled observer may recognize it in his face and distinguish him from others: only patience and constancy will bring one to such reward. The effects of *hitbodedut* are compared by Nahman to drops of water falling upon a stone—his own adaptation of what a Jewish teacher long before him had said about words to Torah—eventually the stone will be worn away. The 'heart of stone' for Nahman is to be worn away by constant supplication. Indeed, it is only a compromise with reality that permits him to insist only upon a certain period of *hitbodedut* in each day. Really, he claims, the entire day should be spent in such a manner. The longing and intensity with which *hitbodedut* is performed should bring the person at times to the very edge of death; he who practices it regularly will live always in a state near to broken-heartedness, and will be ready to respond even to the slightest knock on the door of his heart.[22]

This claim that the core of religion lay in the inner life of the individual and in the impassioned outpourings of his innermost thoughts before God is quite unique in the history of Judaism. Intensity of prayer, to be sure, had always been known, and the tradition of adding spontaneous devotions to the liturgy goes back to the Talmudic rabbis, some of whom even did so in their native Aramaic. The term *hitbodedut*, first popularized through the influence of Bahya's *Duties of the Hearts* in the eleventh century, has a long history in Jewish philosophy and mysticism. In both Lurianic Kabbalah and BeSHTian Hasidism, prayer is at the very center of the religious life. And yet despite all this precedent, the tone in Bratslav is quite new; without rebellion against either law or liturgy, there is something dramatically new and daring about it, something almost "Protestant" and almost modern. For Judaism, not having had an Augustinian tradition, the notion that the struggle to be near to God, and the need to break one's heart in order to do so, are the very essence of religion, is not readily to be taken for granted. Religion as inner aloneness with God and the purely personal pouring out of the heart before Him does not easily sit well with the deeply communitarian and activist elements of the Jewish tradition. In a religious world where study of Torah and action through the *mizwot* are the essential categories of life with God, all this emphasis on personal prayer and individual needs might, at best, seem irrelevant, at worst solipsistic and perverse. The religious path of Bratslav combines an absolute and uncompromised devotion to Jewish orthodoxy with a knowledge—often unspoken, particularly to other pious Jews—that this life of inner openness and spontaneous discourse with God is on some level all that really matters.

Hitbodedut as the *speaking* of one's heart before the Lord has further significance as a new stage in the history of the *word* and its centrality in Judaism. The Jewish myth is one in which the verbal has a unique and almost all-powerful position: it is through the word that God creates and God reveals. Kabbalists had set the mysteries of words and letters at the very center of their speculative universe, exhibiting a tireless fascination with the building-blocks of human speech. In Hasidism, too, the word had been revered as an object of mystery. Here it was the world of prayer, now uttered by man himself, which returned to God those creative energies His word had first released into the world. The teachings of both the BeSHT and the Maggid often revolved around the divine power that lay hidden in the word. Until Nahman it was mostly clear that the word spoken of in such context was the *prescribed holy* word of liturgical devotion. True, it was given its power by the fullness with which the worshiper spoke it, but it still had about it the character of a sacramental vessel. Now Nahman transfers this redeeming power from the liturgical word in the sacred tongue to the spontaneous prayer, in Yiddish, which comes from the heart alone. This notion of redemption through the spoken word, or of the healing of the broken heart through the outpouring to God, in words, of all one's innermost torments must also be seen as an unrecognized precursor of that most basic therapeutic technique—also quintessentially Jewish—of Freudian psychoanalysis.

The reader will also immediately notice the close parallels between the type of religious life depicted in the calls for *hitbodedut* and the religious and personal struggles of Nahman's own youth as portrayed by the sources. The "therapeutic" or redemptive technique Nahman taught was one born of his own experience in constant outcry to God from the midst of his struggles. Nahman was daring enough to assume that those struggles characterizing his own attempts at life with God would reappear in one form or another in every person of serious religious strivings, and that therefore his own mode of broken-hearted outpouring of the soul before God should now become a general practice to be followed by all those who considered themselves his disciples. It is in this most profound sense that the Bratslav *ḥasid* was to follow the path of his master: he was to adopt for his own life the discipline of perseverance created by Nahman out of his own tearful longings to feel himself in the presence of God. Such a course would make most sense, needless to say, if the disciple, like the master, was one who felt beset by sufferings and in need of such release. If in the early days it was, perhaps, the matter of confession that kept large numbers of *ḥasidim* from joining Nahman's group, in later times it was probably the emphasis on broken-heartedness and outcry that put them off. Here was a doctrine for a very particular sort of spiritual elite: an elite of sufferers and strugglers who knew *with* Nahman as well as *through* him that "There is nothing so whole as a broken heart."

In the later memoir literature of the Bratslav *ḥasidim*, many tales are told of the early disciples in that group. Despite the relative peace in which Nahman lived during his years at Bratslav, it seems that his relationship to most of the townspeople there was not one of intimate spiritual guide. In descriptions of the inner circle around Nahman, the names that come up again and again are of those who remained his loyal followers from his earliest days. He first friend Simeon, the members of the Dashev circle, Aaron, now to become *rav* of Bratslav, Yekutiel the Maggid of Tirhavits and a group around him, a few others—these seem to have continued to be the group closest to Nahman throughout his life. While there were many in and near Bratslav who respected him and may even have considered themselves his *ḥasidim* to one degree or another—for a while there were enough of them in Nemirov to sustain their own *minyan* there—most were not admitted to close discipleship.[23] The two great exceptions to this are Nathan Sternharz and his friend Naftali, both the sons of well-to-do families in Nemirov, who joined the group almost immediately after Nahman settled in Bratslav.

It is not within our province here to write a biography of Rabbi Nathan, though such a project would be a most worthwhile undertaking. We cannot refrain, however, from offering just a brief outline of the life of the one who was to become Nahman's most well-known and important disciple, a life not atypical of the young *ḥasid* at the start of the nineteenth century. Nathan was born in 1780, the son of a wealthy merchant family in Nemirov, just a few miles from Bratslav. At the age of thirteen he was married to the daughter of an important rabbi in Shargorod, a great scholar and a bitter opponent of Hasidism. Nathan as a young bridegroom shared his father-in-law's sympathies, he tells us, and it was only when he left the rabbi's home and returned to Nemirov in 1796 that he first came under the influence of old childhood friends who were themselves now close to the teachings of the new masters. For the following six years he traveled about from one Hasidic court to another in search of a path that suited him: late Bratslav tradition claims he had contact in those years with R. Zusya of Anipol, Mordecai of Kremnitz, and Levi Yizhak of Berdichev. Convinced now of the rightness of the Hasidic path in general (he once said: "The difference between a *ḥasid* and a *mitnagged* is like that between a cold *knish* and a hot one; the ingredients are all the same, but the warmth makes all the difference!"), he had still not yet found a master who was suited to his own temperament. It was only in the summer of 1802, shortly after Nahman arrived at nearby Bratslav, that Nathan found what was to become his spiritual home.

The fact is that Nathan had a good deal more in common with Nahman than the mere coincidence of geography. If the later accounts are to be believed, the young Nathan had experienced rises and falls in his own spiritual life not unlike those of his future master. He had also suffered from childhood fears of death, and the bitter enmity his Hasidism aroused in his wife's family and his own led him to share the feelings of persecution that so plagued Nahman as a young adult. At the very least we may say that this disciple, the only one about whom extensive information is available, brought with him to Bratslav the sort of experiential baggage that would allow him to identify strongly with the life of struggle uniquely being preached there. From the time of their first meeting he became increasingly attached to Nahman, and throughout the thirty-five years by which he outlived his master, he devoted himself to the dissemination and publication of his teachings.[24]

After Nahman's death, it is quite clear, Nathan became the central figure among the Bratslav *ḥasidim* and de facto leader of the community. His place within the group during master's lifetime is something of a question, however, and deserving of further comment. The problem is that virtually all the information we have concerning the early days in Bratslav comes to us as filtered through Nathan and his own later disciples. As editor of Nahman's works and as leader of the Bratslav community from 1810 until his death in 1845, it was Nathan who determined what would be the "official" history of the sect. While we have generally placed great trust in him as a chronicler, one area where his word is not completely to be taken for granted is that of his own importance in the Bratslav community during Nahman's lifetime. From reading the sources he and his school produced, one gets the clear impression that he was by far the most important figure in his master's life, from the very first day of his arrival on the scene. All of the other disciples, including those who had previously been Nahman's most trusted intimates, somehow begin to recede into the background. While there is no prima facie reason to reject this view of the story, modern students of Bratslav have begun to find it highly suspect.

There is evidence, as Weiss and Piekarz have pointed out,[25] that a struggle for leadership in the community took place after Nahman's death, a struggle in which Nathan's rivals were the original group of followers from Medvedevka and Dashev, led by Yudel and Shmu'el Isaac. Partly for this reason, it is claimed, Nathan had an important vested interest in portraying himself as the master's closest follower, and in downgrading the importance of his rivals. Surely it is striking that in

Nathan's early account of his master's journey to the Land of Israel, the name of Simeon is not mentioned once, and he is merely referred to anonymously as "the one who accompanied him." A threat to Nathan's own leadership claim is a likely explanation for such behavior.

Still, Weiss goes too far in saying that Nathan "apparently was not a member of Nahman's most intimate circle." Nathan's accounts certainly do contain a degree of exaggeration in the matter of his own unique relationship to the master (a typical example: "He said that had he come to Bratslav only to find me, it would have been sufficient."[26]). Despite this, there is surely no denying that Nahman did hold him in extremely high regard. As the master's literary secretary, Nathan worked very closely with Nahman, clarifying points in the teachings, reading to him the written versions as he had edited them, and the like. It is hard to imagine that Nahman would have assigned such a task to one who was not among his most trusted disciples. No outsider to the community of intimates was even allowed to *see* the written teachings before 1806; how then could the very one who recorded them not have been a member of the innermost circle? The closeness that existed between Nahman and Nathan is also apparent from even a cursory examination of Nathan's own life, particularly as reflected in his letters. Writing twenty or thirty years after Nahman's death, we still find Nathan constantly awed by the presence of his master. It hardly seems likely that one who had not been allowed into the intimate circle of a man's followers in his lifetime would remain so close to him many years after his death.

Because of these considerations, the position proposed by Weiss and Piekarz should be amended in the following way: Nahman and Nathan were probably indeed very close to one another during the master's later years, and it would have been this very closeness that the older disciples came to resent. The attention Nahman showered upon this relative latecomer, at times undoubtedly at the expense of long-time followers and trusted intimates, created a good deal of tension between Nathan and the others. While there was no lack of closeness between *Nahman* and Nathan, it was among the disciples that Nathan was never fully accepted. As long as the master was alive, this tension did not generally come to the fore—at least we have no clear evidence that it did[27]—but after Nahman's death these long-standing tensions broke out in the form of a struggle for leadership.

Neither Nathan nor most of the other close disciples came to live in Bratslav for any extended period of time. Unlike some other *ẓaddiqim*, Nahman did not want to establish a full-time "court" for which he would have constant responsibility. He seems to have valued his privacy and thus, in Bratslav as in Medvedevka, did not encourage his disciples to come live near him. There were three occasions during the year when the group gathered at Bratslav: Rosh Hashanah, Hanukkah, and Shavu'ot.

On certain other occasions, particularly such special Sabbaths during the year as *Shabbat Shirah* and *Shabbat Naḥamu*, Nahman would visit one of the other towns where he had a group of disciples.[28] By far the most important gathering of the year was that on Rosh Hashanah; presence in Bratslav for that annual occasion was virtually required of anyone who counted himself among Nahman's disciples. Many of Nahman's longer and more important teachings were delivered on one or another of these three ceremonial occasions, and thus they contain references to one of the three holidays.[29]

The climax of these visits was in fact the teaching itself. Eagerly anticipated by the disciples, and augmented by Nahman's own awe before the tremendous responsibility involved in expounding on the Torah, the presentation of the teaching was a moment of high drama. Particularly on Rosh Hashanah, when Nahman chose to speak in relative darkness as the first day of the festival was drawing to a close, the dramatic tension was at its highest. The opening words of the teaching, a Biblical or rabbinic passage on which he was to comment, were spoken in fear and trembling, and the disciples saw beads of sweat pouring down the master's face.[30] While Nahman did believe in carefully preparing his teachings beforehand, and there is evidence that he had some brief notes before him as he spoke, the gathered disciples experienced the moment as one of revelation. They were convinced that they were witness to a supernatural event: the voice of God, as it were, speaking through their master's lips.[31] Nahman himself has left us a description of what he meant by the act of teaching, a description that makes it clear that he, too, despite his preparations, felt his teaching to be a revelatory event:

> He who wants to interpret the Torah has to begin by drawing unto himself words as hot as burning coals. Speech comes out of the upper heart, which Scripture calls 'the rock of my heart' (Ps. 73:26). The interpreter [first] has to pour out his words to God in prayer, seeking to arouse His mercies, so that this heart will open. Speech then flows from the heart, and the interpretation of Torah comes from that speech. . . . As the heart's compassion is awakened, it gives forth blazing words, as it is written: 'My heart blazes within me; the fire of my words burns on my tongue' (Ps. 39:3). On this heart are inscribed all the interpretations of the Torah, as it says: 'Write them upon the tablet of your heart' (Prov. 3:3). And so anyone who seeks to bring forth an interpretation must get it from this heart, by prayer and supplication. It is for this reason that teachers of Torah, before they begin their expositions, first have to pour out their prayers to God, in order that the heart be aroused to pour forth words like blazing coals. Only afterwards may one begin to teach, for the rock has been opened and its waters have begun to flow.[32]

The teaching, to which (at least in later years) the public was invited, was followed by a discussion with the closest disciples, who were then encouraged to ask questions and to discuss what they had heard. When the teaching was offered on a Sabbath, it was presented at the closing meal *(se'udah shelishit)*, and the discussion would take place later in the evening, after *havdalah*.

But there were also more informal times at Bratslav, when Nahman would sit in the synagogue courtyard, or go for walks into the hills surrounding the town, and there expound his teachings to his disciples.[33] The love of the outdoors that he had developed while living in the rural setting of Usyatin stayed with Nahman in his later years. He particularly tried to persuade his disciples to follow his example and go out to pray in the fields and forests. Indeed, Nahman's ideal image of a Hasidic community, with which he opens his tale *The Master of Prayer*, depicts a ragged band of disciples living in the woods and sustained by the fruits of nature. This description shows Nahman's dissatisfaction with life in the town and the house of study, and reflects a deep longing in him for another type of community, one he was never to realize, but which remained the object of his dreams:

> Once there was a master of prayer, who spent all his time in prayer, song, and praise to God. He lived in a place outside any town or village, but would frequently go into the nearby town. There he would go up to someone, generally choosing a poor person or one of low status, and would enter into conversation with him about the ultimate meaning of life in the world. 'There is no meaning in the world,' he would say, 'except to serve God while you are alive. Therefore you should spend all your years in prayer to Him, and in songs and praises.' He spoke at length about these matters, hoping to awaken something in the other, until finally the words would find their way into the other man's heart, and he would decide to join him. As soon as the person agreed, the master of prayer would take him to his place outside the town. In that place which he had chosen there ran a stream, and beside the stream were fruit trees, and they would eat of the fruit. As for clothing—that didn't concern them at all; you wore whatever you wanted.
>
> This was the regular way of the master of prayer: he would go into town, convince people that they should only serve God and sing to Him all their days, and when they were willing to do so, he would bring them out to his chosen place. There they spent all their time in hymns and praises, confessions and fasts, penitence and self-mortification. The master of prayer would give them some of his books, which were filled with hymns and confessions, and they would pore over them.

When Nahman advised his disciples to take young people out into the woods with them, there to teach them the ways of being alone with God, this ideal went beyond the realm of fantasy and became, in some part, a model to be followed.[34]

To this image of the ideal Hasidic community, we should add a fantastic description of the patriarch Abraham found in Nathan's writings, quoted in the name of his master. Here we have another portrayal of an ideal Hasidic master: Abraham in the tale is clearly meant to be Nahman, rejecting all of the "pagan" world around him and reviled by its leaders as a spiritual seducer of the young:

> Abraham our Father would also bring young people close to God: these are the converts he made. This was his way: when he came into a town, he would run through the streets screaming *'Oy! Oy! Gevalt! Gevalt!'* People would run after him as they run after a madman. Then he would get into lengthy arguments with them, to show them their errors. Abraham knew all the rational arguments upon which paganism was based. In this way he was able to show them how wrong they were, and to reveal to them the true and holy faith. A few of the young people were drawn to him. (He didn't bother with the elders, who were too rooted in their erring ways and thus harder to change. But young people did follow him.)
>
> Thus he went from town to town, and they went after him. The parents and wives of these young men argued with them, saying that they had turned to wicked ways and had renounced their faith. Some of the young men backed away when they heard their families' complaints, while a few stayed with Abraham and remained close to him.[35]

The extreme demands these ideal pictures made upon both Nahman and his disciples should be noted. While neither the *Master of Prayer* story nor this account of Abraham was an accurate description of life in Bratslav, these were the ideals toward which both master and disciple were to strive. Of himself, Nahman was demanding that he ever be the homeless, wandering holy man, reviled by society as he rejected many of its conventional norms. His disciples were called upon to reject wives and parents, cut themselves off from the world, and follow him into the woods and fields, where they would create an ideal brotherhood under his leadership. No wonder neither disciple nor master could live up to such a vision: the weakness of the flesh, the natural bonds that people form while living in society, including those of family, and the complex nature of the master himself all combined to ensure that this ideal *Bratslav-shel-ma'alah* community never came to be. At the same time, *the devotion to this romantic ideal meant that neither Nahman nor those around him would be permitted to rest easy with anything less.* He who had depicted himself as constantly growing was also one who was constantly dissatisfied with his present state; no matter how intense the loyalty of his followers, no matter how sublime his own inner vision, Nahman did not allow himself to remain content with what he had created.

Sometimes it was upon the inadequacy of his disciples that Nahman placed the blame for this "failure." Most of them, he once said, understood him no better than did his enemies. At times he considered them unworthy even to hear teachings as holy and awesome as his own. His goal, stated in his own words, was "to give my people a wondrous sense of awe, an awe that has never yet existed in this world!" While there were times when they did seem to understand him and share his feelings, he complained that they were not able to sustain the intensity he demanded of them, and that they would repeatedly fall back from the heights he sought and return to a less than fully serious level of living.[36]

The real problem with the disciples, however, seems to have lain in the nature of the master/disciple relationship, which stood at the very core of Nahman's approach to Hasidism. In this area Nahman differed seriously from his friend Abraham Kalisker, who had seen himself in the role of leader and teacher in a group composed of *ḥaverim*, each of whom had primary responsibility for his own spiritual life.[37] In that elite community the *ẓaddiq* himself receded somewhat into the background; the central relationship seems to have been that of the *ḥaverim* with one another. In direct contrast to this, Nahman demanded of his disciples an attitude of utter dependency; the relationship with the *ẓaddiq* was of ultimate importance, for it was *only* through that relationship that the *ḥasid* could hope for progress in his own spiritual life. Bratslav *ḥasidim* were expected to follow Nahman completely and unconditionally:

> He said: 'Whoever obeys me and fulfills all that I command him will certainly become a great *ẓaddiq*, no matter what [obstacles] may befall him.' The main thing is to cast aside one's own mind totally, and to do whatever he says.

> The foundation upon which all else depends is the binding of the self to the *ẓaddiq ha-dor*, and the acceptance of his words in every case in which he says: 'this is it' (Ex. 22:8), both great and small. One should not turn aside from his words either to the right or to the left, as our sages said: 'even if he tell you that right is left.' One should cast aside all of one's own clever thoughts, removing one's mind from the matter as though he had no intelligence at all, except for that which he receives from the *ẓaddiq*. As long as any of his own intellect remains he is not whole, and is not [truly] bound to the *ẓaddiq*. Israel, at the time when they received the Torah, were indeed very clever, as the idolatry of their day was based upon certain philosophical errors involving great intellect. And had Israel not set aside this cleverness, they would not have received the Torah at all.[38]

Nahman criticized his disciples for their expectation that he assign them spiritual tasks in line with their own understanding. The patient, he told them, does not have to understand the medicine the great doctor prescribes for him in order for the medicine to take effect.[39] Faith in the *ẓaddiq* was to be pure and simple, transcending all the objections the disciple's own intellect might raise against a master who made even the most extreme and baffling demands.

There was something childlike about the type of devotion Nahman expected of his followers. Not without cause did Nathan say of his first days in Bratslav that Nahman "took me by the hand and drew me close to him in his great compassion, raising me up 'as a nurse lifts the infant' (Num. 11:12)." Nahman at one point described himself as a mother to his disciples, nourishing them with the milk of his Torah. It is perhaps psychologically significant that later Bratslav tradition identifies Nahman with *binah,* the primal mother of the sefirotic world. The stern and somewhat frightening young man we have seen in the initiation of R. Yudil could also appear as the flowing and compassionate source of maternal nourishment—a duality well-known, of course, among Hasidic and other spiritual masters. More daring still, this image of dependency and passivity on the part of the disciples was also sometimes depicted in terms of the "holy union" of matrimony. Receiving advice from the *ẓaddiq* is like receiving his seed; the intimacy of that moment between master and disciple may only be compared to the intimacy of union between man and wife.[40]

Turning to a radically different metaphor, Nahman will claim that the task of the *ẓaddiq* is to lift the disciples out of the mud where they are wallowing; their involvement with this-worldly pursuits has covered them with filth and has made their faces lose their God-given lustre. They struggle their way out of the mud to reach the master, for only he is the one who can restore their glowing faces to them, or restore them to themselves. In this connection, the following passage is particularly striking: the *ẓaddiq* as collector of lost souls who restores to man what has been missing in his life since the moment of birth:

> Know that a person has to go to the *ẓaddiq* to seek that which he has lost. For before a person comes out into the air of the world, he is shown and taught everything he will need to achieve in this world. As he is born, however, he forgets everything, as our sages have taught. Now forgetting a thing is the equivalent of losing it . . . so a person has to go out and search for what he has lost. That which he has lost is to be found with the *ẓaddiq,* who first went out to seek his own loss, but then went on to seek out the lost qualities of others, until he had amassed the losses of everyone in the world. Therefore one must come before the sage [*ẓaddiq*], to identify one's loss and to retrieve it from him. . . .[41]

In this passage and in similar statements, it is the disciple's own self that he seeks at the hand of the *ẓaddiq*. To put it in more conventional Kabbalistic language, the *ẓaddiq* knows the upper root of each disciple's soul, and can thus help to set him on his particular course. This image of the *ẓaddiq* as the wizard of the inner world, helping men to find their individual paths, appears several times in Nahman's *Tales*. It may be traced back to the community around Isaac Luria in sixteenth-century Safed, and certainly has some relationship (as yet unexplored) to the image of the Imām in various Islamic circles. It was said of Luria that he could determine which letter of the mystical Torah lay at the root of each disciple's soul, and would at times instruct the individual disciple accordingly. The BeSHT's reputed ability to effect *tiqqun* for the souls of both the living and the dead was also based on the assumption that he knew the soul-root of each individual among them.[42]

There are other passages in Nahman's writings where the very opposite seems to be the case. Rather than searching for *his own* soul, these passages depict the disciple as being in search of his *master's* soul. Here the *ẓaddiq* becomes the end, rather than the means, of the endeavor. It is only through continued attachment to the master, and even through participation in *his* life struggles, that the disciple will reach the goal. The *ḥasid* must identify so fully with the *ẓaddiq's* soul that he, in fact, becomes a part of it, losing rather than gaining a sense of his own uniqueness in the course of his relationship with the *ẓaddiq:*

> There are various kinds of disciples. But he who is really bound to the *ẓaddiq,* as a branch is bound to the tree, will feel all the rises and falls the *ẓaddiq* undergoes, even when he is not with the *ẓaddiq*. It is proper for a disciple to feel within himself all the fluctuations of the *ẓaddiq,* since he is bound to him as the branch is to the tree. For the branches feel all the upward and downward motions that take place within the tree. That is how they come to life and grow in the summer: the tree draws its sustenance from the root, and, through certain inner channels, causes the life-force to flow upward from it. In winter, when the tree's moisture dries up and these channels are narrowed, the branches also shrink, and shed their leaves. And he [the true disciple] is bound to the *ẓaddiq* in this way, feeling all the inner ups and downs of the *ẓaddiq*. . . .[43]

The task of the disciple in this instance is not to undergo his own struggles, as the master did, but rather to attune himself so finely to the *ẓaddiq's* own alternating inner rhythms that he will at all times be aware of what is happening in the soul of his master. Rather than the master's knowing the disciple's true self, as was the case above, here it is the disciple's task to know and fully identify with the inner life of his master!

These two sides of the relationship between master and disciple are perhaps best illustrated by two versions of a rather daring interpretation Nahman offered of the verse "Face to face the Lord spoke to You" (Deut. 5:4). He interpreted "face to face" to refer to the relationship between master and disciple: the word of the Lord is with them when they are face to face with one another. The way in which they face one another is of particular interest here: the point is not that they are to encounter one another's faces, but rather that one face is to become a mirror that reflects the other. This interpretation, however, is preserved in two versions, each of which reflects one aspect of the relationship under discussion:

> People wonder why it is that one has to travel to the *ẓaddiq* to hear his words from his own mouth. Is it not possible to read books of moral preaching? . . . But there is a great difference between the reading of books and hearing the words from the *ẓaddiq* himself.
>
> One [the *ẓaddiq* or teacher] has to purify one's face, so that others will see their faces in his, as in a mirror. In this way the other will come to regret his deeds without need of preaching or moralizing, just from seeing the face itself. For in looking into that face, the other will see his own face, as in a mirror, and will see the darkness of his own countenance . . . This is the meaning of "Face to face the Lord spoke to you"—when the word of God is in you, and your speech is pure, your face will shine so brightly that the other will see his face in yours.[44]

In this version it is quite clear that the purpose of the master/disciple encounter is to bring the disciple to grips with his own personal situation; through the mirror of the master's face, he sees his own face and is forced to confront the bleakness of his own spiritual life. This version is to be contrasted, however, with the following:

> The matter of reverentially visiting [literally, 'receiving the face of'] a sage:
>
> The moon has no light of its own at all, except for that which it receives from the sun. That is to say, the moon is like a polished mirror, receiving the light of the sun and reflecting it upon the earth. But if it were coarse and dark, without a shiny surface, it could not receive the sun's light at all.
>
> The same is true of master and disciple, who are compared to sun and moon, as has been explained elsewhere. If the disciple's face shines like a polished mirror, then he can 'greet,' receiving the light of his master's face. Thus the master will be able to see himself in the face of the disciple who has received his face, just as one would when standing before a mirror . . . the disciple has taken the master's face into himself, so that the master's face is seen reflected in him. This is the meaning of *qabbalat panim*, literally "receiving the face". . . . Thus Scripture says: 'Face to face the Lord spoke to you'—when they received the Torah, Israel had a shining [mirror-like] countenance, and were thus able to receive the holy face, so that this holy face would be visible in them. . . .[45]

This dual mirror image is a subtle one. Both parties in this sacred encounter, disciple as well as master, hope to approach the other with that radiant countenance immediately recognizable as a sign of spiritual fullness. Through looking into the master's shining face, the not-yet-perfected disciple comes to see all that he lacks, without a word of reprimand having to be spoken. As the master looks into the face of the disciple, he may or may not see his own radiance reflected there, telling him how ready the disciple is to receive his light. When the disciple, like the master, has become a polished mirror *(i.e.* free both from enslavement to ego and from the struggle against it), he may return the master's light, being a moon to his master's sun.

These two usages of the mirror metaphor are not, however, simply two sides of the same mutual encounter. On closer examination it becomes clear that they represent two distinct stages along the path of spiritual development. In one stage the disciple is yet in search of self, or is yet on the path toward his own fulfillment. Here he seeks that which is lost to him, he looks into the master's eyes to find out where it is that he must go, what it is that he must do, in order to reach his end. The second stage, that in which disciple reflects back the master's light, is one where he has gone beyond that search for self. He now stands in the relationship to the master that parallels the master's relationship to God: a relationship of emptiness and potential fullness at once. Israel were not ready to receive the Torah, Nahman tells us, until they were both empty and pure enough to serve as mirrors that reflect back the light of God. In that very moment of receiving they become so filled with Torah that they may pass it down throughout all generations and teach it to all the nations. Thus it is with the disciple: in the empty radiance of his receptivity he becomes so filled with the master's presence that he too may enter into that relationship with yet another, sharing with him what he has received.

In these two stages of master/disciple relationship, we may come to see the two aspects of Hasidic teaching scholars have chosen to designate as the "existential" and "mystical" sides of the teaching. Insofar as it is the disciple's own self that he seeks at the master's hands, and insofar as it is his own lacks that he sees mirrored in the master's face, we are dealing with a relationship focused in helping man to discover his own real situation in the world and come to terms with it, in other words an "existential" master/disciple relationship. Here the ethic of personal growth is paramount and the uniqueness of each disciple must be fully recognized. When we move on into the second stage, however, it is clearly of a mystical sort of relationship that we are speaking. Here the ideal of human community would seem to be a great hall of mirrors, each of them serving as another reflector of divine light. Ego-individuality is here to be transcended, as the disciple who was formerly a self in search of a corrective mirror now seeks to become a mirror on his own.

These two types of thinking (perhaps we should prefer 'individualizing' and 'unitive' over 'existential' and 'mystical') are manifest in Nahman's thought, running side by side, in any number of areas. At times it seems, as in this case of master and disciple, that the individualizing is a stage on the way to the ultimately unitive. The man of God seeks out the individual and distinct spark of divinity in each corner of the natural world, sees each blade of grass as the wondrous and unique creation of God—but only on the way toward bringing them all together, at least in harmony, if not in union. The act of *hitbodedut*, the ultimately existential form of prayer in its emphasis on man's aloneness and despairing state, is meant as but a way toward *biṭṭul*, the utter negation of the self that one may be fully contained in God. Now master helps disciple to find his own self, but only so that the very self he finds may ultimately be transcended. At other times, as we shall see later, the two types of thinking seem more to contend with one another, especially in those areas where Nahman hesitates to espouse a fully mystical point of view.

We should also finally recall that the matter of relating to the *ẓaddiq ha-dor* as Nahman depicts him is never quite fully a relationship between self and "other." The *ẓaddiq* bears a soul that contains that of the *ḥasid* within it, but in fully realized fashion. Nothing the disciple tells him about his own inner life is news to the master; he has seen it all within himself. No wonder that such a soul may serve as a mirror to all who seek it out. And no wonder that the ultimate message of one whose soul encompasses all in a great unity will be the transcendence of separate identity and selfhood.

The dynamic of relationship between master and disciple in the determining of spiritual tasks is always quite complex. The assumption is that the master is the one who knows, long before the disciple does, what path the disciple will have to follow on his journey; yet if the master is too open in revealing this path to the disciple, the value of the journey will be greatly compromised. If the disciple does not struggle on his own in the search for truth, no matter how much the master shows him, truth will continue to elude him. The master thus has to attain to a certain degree of subtlety, revealing enough to the disciple to guide him on his way, but not so much that there is nothing left for the disciple to discover on his own.

Such is the conventional wisdom of spiritual masters. At times it does seem that Nahman was aware of this issue, and tried to avoid heavy-handedness in directing the lives of his disciples. Certainly he realized that each of them had a unique path to follow, in which the *ẓaddiq* at best could serve as guide. This awareness is probably seen most clearly in Nahman's tale of *The Portrait*, which we shall have occasion to discuss below. There the point is that each seeker must find his own image of the King, one which may be known only through the life which he alone is to live. Elsewhere, too, Nahman makes it clear that he does not want to overwhelm the disciple by doing the task for him. "I could make you all into total *ẓaddiqim!* But what would it be? Just a case of God worshipping Himself!"

Similar pronouncements were not infrequent in Bratslav. Once there was a disciple who pleaded with Nahman, against the master's own better judgment, to fill him with the fear of God.

> A great and exaggerated fear fell upon him; he began to scream out to God in strange tones which he had never used before. This lasted until the next day, and he almost went out of his mind. When he came in to our master the next day he was asked whether the fear of God had come to him, and he replied 'I no longer want it' and asked that it be taken from him.

Nathan records that the same once happened to him, when in an apparently weak moment he must have asked for more help in the task than the master deemed appropriate. Nahman's reply was curt and to the point: "If God wanted to worship Himself, He wouldn't need you!"[46]

In all such formulations, it is the individualizing side of the master/disciple relationship that obtains. "God worshipping Himself," a formulation some mystics would find attractive (disciples of the Maggid among them!), here seems to be rejected. Nahman's sense of struggle as essential to attainment rules in this case; that which he has undergone must be experienced by the disciple as well, each in his own way. And yet, side by side with all such formulations, Nahman's teachings also contain their exact opposite, here again expressed in the metaphor of the mirror:

> There is a tale told of a king who built himself a palace and hired two men to decorate it for him. He divided the palace in half, and each man was commissioned to be responsible for one half of the work, which was to be completed by a certain set time.
>
> One of the workmen struggled very hard, carefully teaching himself the art of painting and pottery-making. He made some truly wondrous designs in his half of the palace, drawing beasts and birds and all sorts of beautiful things. The other worker, however, did not take the king's decree to heart, and did not work on his section at all.
>
> As the appointed day drew near, and the first worker had completed his task so beautifully, the other man began to examine himself. 'What have I done, wasting all my time in vanities,' he asked, 'and giving no heed to the decree of the king.' He began to think about what he might do, since it was no longer possible for him to paint half the palace in the time that remained. He then hit upon the idea of covering his entire section with a coat of shiny black varnish, in which things shone as clearly as in a mirror. After doing this, he hung a curtain between the two sections of the palace.
>
> When the final day arrived, and the king came in to examine their work, he was greatly pleased with the beautiful decorations which he found in the first workman's half of the palace. The other section was covered with a curtain. When the second workman pulled the curtain aside, the sun shone in, and all the ornaments from the other side of the palace were reflected in the varnish. All that the king had seen in the first half of the palace he saw here as well. More than that, as the king had his beautiful vessels and

does not have to go far to get a more accurate picture of Nahman's inner life. Particularly in *Shivḥey ha-RaN*, where Nathan is most revealing of his master's emotions, it is made clear that neither the initiatory journey to Erez Israel nor Nahman's self-proclamation as the paradoxical *ẓaddiq ha-dor* was sufficient to quell the turbulence of his spirit:

> Even after his return from Erez Israel, having reached there all the high rungs that he did, from the day of his return until the very day of his death, he was filled with longings and yearnings for God like one who had not yet begun at all . . . His path was one of constant longing for God; he was low in his own sight, and would take pity on himself like one who had never even tasted what it meant to be a servant of God. . . . He never rested and was never still, even in his adult years, despite the awesome heights of spiritual understanding which his mind had reached. He would never be satisfied with anything he had attained. He was constantly in a state of struggle, accepting hard and bitter sufferings upon himself, sufferings which have almost no parallel in the world. He constantly prayed and begged and pleaded, with tremendous yearnings, until he reached a still higher rung. When he reached that he would be happy for a while and we were fortunate enough to hear him tell of this new stage, *etc.* Yes, then there was a bit of joy. But right after that he would begin again from the beginning, forgetting the entire past, as though he were a complete newcomer. . . . We once heard his holy mouth form the question, said with the greatest of longing: 'How can one merit to become a Jew?'
>
> Many times he said to us that he now knew absolutely nothing at all. Sometimes he swore to it, to show us that he *really* knew nothing, despite the fact that on the previous day, or even in the previous hour, he had revealed the most precious words to us.[49]

While Nathan has tried to present this material in such a way as to give the impression that the struggle was one of steady ascent to higher and higher rungs, without any "falls" or depressions, the attempt is really quite transparent. The disciple presents Nahman's sufferings as something his master took on almost voluntarily; Nahman's cries of pain, however, do not bear out that view. A man who was struggling to ascend from one high place within the upper worlds to one still more elevated does not cry out: "How does one merit to become a Jew?" On the contrary, everything in this description that is Nahman and not Nathan points to a man who is in deep difficulty, struggling spiritually to keep his very head above water, not merely reaching for higher and higher degrees of enlightenment. Of course the disciples, including Nathan, could not live with this image of their struggling master. They had a need to interpret this behavior as a sign of a struggle for the highest attainments, far beyond their own comprehension. But Nahman himself could not accept that interpretation of his struggle; when he said, "I know *nothing* now," he meant it quite literally and seriously. Why else would he have to *swear* to his disciples that what he had said of himself was the simple truth? On another occasion, when his disciples refused to believe that his "I know nothing" was serious, he said to them that his not knowing was exactly the same as their own, and should not be taken as anything more than that.[50]

At the same time, however (again the paradox emerges!), Nahman had a need, along with admitting the bitter truth, to maintain the mystery of his own person. So he added: "My teachings are completely new, but my 'I don't know' is even higher than my teachings!"[51]

The depressions that pursued him are reflected in his teachings as well as in these conversations with his disciples. Projecting from his own situation, his view of human life as a whole is often morose and bleak. He seemed to view suffering as the natural state of the human spirit, one which could be overcome only by nearly superhuman effort. The struggle against despair, so frequent a theme in his teachings, was very much his own struggle:

> The main thing is that one must struggle with all one's strength to be joyous always. It is the nature of man to be drawn into melancholy and sadness, because of the things that happen to him; every man is filled with sorrows. He spoke to us many times about the sufferings of this world, telling us how everyone in the world is full of sorrow. . . .
>
> Our master said: 'Everybody says that there is this world [*i.e.*, the world of earthly pleasures], and there is also the world to come. Now with regard to the world to come—we believe in its existence. Perhaps "this world" also exists somewhere. But [this place] where we are now appears to be hell, since everyone is so constantly filled with sorrows.' And he said: ' "This world" does not exist at all.'[52]

Such a vision of human existence is not the vision of one whose life is wholly involved with ever-rising ascents into the upper worlds. It bespeaks real and bitter personal experience, and frequent confrontation with a sense of the emptiness of one's own life. When Nahman says, "Every man is filled with sorrows," it is first about himself that he is speaking. In the Christian tradition he is to be compared to such figures as Augustine and Kierkegaard, men whose vision of the universe was filled with human suffering, and whose knowledge of such pain came to them firsthand from their confrontations with their own inner lives.

This view of Nahman as one who lived ever close to the brink of bitter depression and the state of "knowing nothing" is borne out not only by these and many other statements, but also by certain of his dreams, perhaps the most faithful mirrors of the true state of his soul. These dreams, which Nahman reported to Nathan, and which the faithful disciple dutifully recorded (generally without comment and perhaps with little understanding), are obvious enough in their general meaning to reveal a great deal about Nahman's personal condition, even without full psychoanalytic interpretation. We shall present here three of these dreams, in chronological sequence. It is our contention that these three dreams are closely related, in that the first two dreams are earlier appearances of themes which are much more fully elaborated in the third:

1. (Sometime during the year 1804, on a Friday evening)
I was living in a certain city, which in the dream appeared to be very large. A *ẓaddiq* of olden times came along, one who was considered a very great *ẓaddiq*. Everyone was going out to him, and I too went along. Then I saw that when they reached him, everyone passed him by and nobody stopped to greet him. It seemed that they were doing so intentionally. I was most astonished at their audacity, for I knew the man to be a great *ẓaddiq*. Then I asked how it was that they had the nerve not to greet such a man. I was told that he was indeed a great *ẓaddiq*, but that his body was made up of various unclean parts, despite the fact that he himself was a great man. He had taken it upon himself to redeem this body, but since 'one should not greet one's fellowman in an unclean place,' no one offered any greeting to him.[53]

2. (Before Shavu'ot, 1805)
He dreamed that the holiday of Shavu'ot had come, and that we had all gathered there as usual, but that he was unable to teach any Torah at all.[54]

3. (December, 1809)
I was sitting in my house, and no one came in to see me. Finding this surprising, I went out into the other room, but there too I found no one. I went to the main house, and then to the House of Study, but they too were empty. I decided to go outside, and there I found groups of men standing about in circles and whispering to one another. One was mocking me, another was laughing at me, and still a third was acting rudely toward me. Some of my own people were there among them, acting rudely and whispering about me. I called one of my disciples over and asked him: 'What is this?' He answered: 'How could you have done a thing like that? How could you have committed such a terrible sin?' I had no idea what all this mockery was about, so I asked that fellow to gather some of my disciples together. He walked away from me, and I did not see him again.

I decided that there was nothing to be done, so I sailed away to a far-off country. But when I arrived, I found that even there people were standing about and discussing this thing; they knew about it there, too. So I decided to go off and live in the forest. Five of our people gathered around me, and together we went off to dwell in the woods. One of the men would periodically go into town to fetch provisions for us, and on his return I would ask him: 'Has the matter quieted down yet?' But he would always answer: 'No, there is still a great commotion about it.'

While we were there, an old man came calling for me, announcing: 'I have something to say to you.' I went to talk with him, but he immediately began to berate me: 'Could you have done such a thing? How is it that you were not ashamed before your ancestors, Rabbi Nahman [of Horodenka] and the BeSHT? And have you no shame before the Torah of Moses? Or before the patriarchs? Do you think you can stay here forever? You don't have much money, you know, and you're a weak man. So what will you do? Don't think you can flee to still another country, for if they don't know who you are they won't support you, and if they do know who you are, they'll know of this thing too.' Then I said to him: 'Since I'm such an exile in this world, at least I'll have the world to come.' But he answered: 'Paradise you expect? There won't be a place in hell for you to hide, not for one who has desecrated God's name as you have!' I asked him to leave me alone, saying: 'I thought you were here to comfort me, not to increase my suffering. Go away!' And the old man left.

Since we were living there in the forest for so long, I became afraid that we would forget our learning altogether, so I asked the one who brought our provisions to obtain some holy book from the town on his next visit. But when he returned, he had no book with him. 'I couldn't dare say for whom I wanted the book,' he explained, 'and without saying for whom I wanted it, they wouldn't give it to me.' I was terribly distraught over that: here I was, a wanderer with no books, in danger of forgetting all my learning.

Meanwhile, the old man returned. This time he was carrying a book under his arm. I asked him: 'What's that you're carrying?' He told me that it was a book, and he handed it to me. I took it from him, but I didn't even know how to hold it, and when I opened it, it seemed completely strange to me, a foreign language in a foreign script. I became terribly upset, for I feared that my own companions would leave me if they found this out. The old man then began to speak to me as he had before, asking me if I was not ashamed of my sin and telling me that there would be no place in hell for one like me to hide. But this time I responded: 'If one who came from the upper world were to tell me such things—only then would I believe them!' He said: 'I am from there.' And he showed me a sign.

I then recalled the story of the BeSHT, who, when he heard he was to have no place in the world to come, said : 'I love God without the world to come!' I tossed my head back with tremendous remorse. As I did so, all those before whom the old man had said I should be ashamed, my grandfathers and the patriarchs and all the rest, came to me, reciting over me the verse: 'The fruit of the land shall be pride and splendor' (Is. 4:2). They said to me: 'On the contrary, we shall take pride in you.' They brought all my disciples and children back to me (for my children, too, had cut themselves off from me). And they continued to speak to me, reversing all that had been said. If a man who had transgressed the entire Torah eight hundred times over could toss his head back with the bitterness [of remorse] that I felt in that moment, surely he would be forgiven. . . .[55]

These dreams, particularly the third and most fully recollected one, weave together many themes that had been plaguing Nahman over the years: feelings of persecution, loneliness and isolation, states of "knowing nothing," and a sense of guilt. The last dream in particular is filled with an overwhelming sense of ancient and unspeakable guilt. It should be noted that nowhere in the dream does he confront his challengers by denying their accusations, nor does he demand any explanation of their behavior toward him. While not being able to specify the nature of his sin, he seems to accept the bitter truth of their accusations. Weiss has suggested that the old man of this dream is none other than the Shpoler Zeide, pointing the finger of accusation against Nahman once again. Whether this is true, or the dream figure is but a figment of his own inner world, is not important. In either case, Nahman is vulnerable to the accusation, and he can only relieve his situation by so total an act of remorse as would pardon the transgression of even the most wicked sinner imaginable.

It is to the first dream that we must turn for an explanation of the third. In that earlier dream, the motif was quite similar: the *ẓaddiq* is rebuffed by the community because of his impurities. Assuming, as we safely may, that the *ẓaddiq* of that dream is also a projection of Nahman himself, the nature of this impurity becomes clear. While he is indeed a true *ẓaddiq*, he nevertheless inhabits a body derived from the "unclean places." Nahman's guilt is that of the body, and particularly, as we shall see, that of sexual desire.[56]

The extent of Nahman's preoccupation with sex and its evils during his adolescent years has already been shown. This was the greatest trial of his early life. It was his goal then, we recall,[57] to destroy his own sexual urge completely. Indeed, he made this absolute conquest of sexuality into the *sine qua non* of the true *ẓaddiq's* existence:

> He was once speaking with someone about a certain well-known *ẓaddiq* . The other praised this *ẓaddiq* by saying that he had completely broken in himself the passions for food and drink. Our master asked him: 'But how does he do with regard to *this* [sexual] desire?' 'Who knows that?' was the reply. Said our master: 'But the root is really this alone. All other passions are really easily subdued. The level of a *ẓaddiq* is most basically determined by his degree of holiness in this area: whether he has been able to subdue it completely.'[58]

Read in the context of Nahman's own youthful trials, it is clear that this passage does not refer to mere *control* of the sexual passions (to which all traditional Jewish moralists would agree), or to an avoidance of *illicit* sexuality, but rather to an utter conquest and obliteration of this most basic human passion. It will be recalled that Nahman himself claimed to have reached the point where "to me men and women are the same," meaning that the sight of a woman aroused no greater desire in him than that of a man. Of his own powers as *ẓaddiq*, he had asserted, "any child brought to me before he is seven years of age will surely remain free from sin until marriage."[59] The mention of marriage as the end of the 'danger period' here makes it clear that the sin from which he protects the child is that of sexual temptation.

Again and again in Nahman's writings one finds it said that sexual desire is the most basic root of human sin, the source of all evil. All other attainments of piety seem to be naught, in comparison to this one constant preoccupation. While at times avarice and gluttony seem to share the stage with lust as the most rooted human evils, it is frequently made clear, as in the above comment on the *ẓaddiq*, that sexual lust outweighs all others.[60]

Comparing Nahman's own system of values with the great burden of guilt he seems to bear, we cannot but come to the conclusion that Nathan's statement "our master was completely stripped of all desires and evil qualities, and not a drop of them remained in him" is something of an exaggeration, though one to be expected of a worshipful disciple. We would perhaps do better to listen to Nahman himself, who understood the tremendous difficulty involved in the eradication of such desires:

> The breaking of desires . . . is like tanning a hide. Even though the leather has already been worked over, some bit of its rotten smell remains. In the same way, some people have already broken their desires, but a bit of the odor is still present in them, and their desires still pursue them a bit.
>
> At another time he had said that you have to cleanse the body of desires as you tan a hide, turning it over on both sides. The body has to be worked over so fully that it is completely free from sin, so that you can turn it over and see that it is completely clean.[61]

Is the hide ever completely tanned, or is Nahman himself within the category of those who continue to "smell" some bit of their repressed desires lurking within them? Nahman's preoccupation with the evils of sexuality, combined with his sense of personal guilt, leads us to conclude that the struggle with desire was a theme that continued to plague Nahman throughout his life. Nahman's own statements to the effect that he himself was completely free of any such desire[62] clearly belong to his moments of elation and self-aggrandizement, moments which were possible for him only when he felt that he had conquered this greatest of all evils. His constant return to states of depression and guilt bears witness to the fact that the feelings of conquest were generally short-lived.

The emphasis Nahman places upon sexual purity as the only real test of the true *ẓaddiq* is the result of his own ongoing struggle in this area. While there are deep roots in Jewish sources of the association of *ẓaddiq* with the motif of sexual purity,[63] the sources alone do not adequately account for Nahman's degree of insistence upon this matter, an insistence far beyond that of his contemporaries in the Hasidic world. True, the moralistic literature of eighteenth-century Jewry was filled with dire exhortations as to the great evils of sex, or even of wayward thoughts of lust, but we must remember that it was in *opposition* to this excessive preoccupation with sin that the BeSHT had elaborated much of what was to become Hasidism. Both the warnings against excessive concern with sin *(da'agat 'awonot)* and the very idea of the 'uplifting' of wayward thoughts are stated as early Hasidic reactions against the moroseness of these ever-threatening preachers. But for Nahman, all this did not matter. Just as his own sadness led him to challenge the Ba'al Shem's teachings on the easy accessibility of joy, so his own battles with sexual guilt caused him to return to the pre-Hasidic emphasis on purity in this area. While other third generation *ẓaddiqim* had sought to *limit* the BeSHT's more radical formulations in these matters, Nahman must here be seen as the great *protagonist* of the BeSHT, bringing back into Hasidism the heavy burden of the awareness of sin that the movement's founder had sought to lighten. True, Nahman, too, had as his *ultimate* goal the lightening of the burden of guilt, but he felt this could be achieved only through a heightened awareness of sin, followed by great acts of penitential catharsis. Sin weighed so deeply on Nahman's mind that the usual Hasidic warnings against overly morose preoccupation with one's own sins did not work for him. The institution of *tiqqun ha-kelali,* the recitation of certain Psalms as atonement for sexual sin (particularly that of onanism) that Nahman promulgated among his disciples[64] undoubtedly had its origins in Nahman's own struggles for the unburdening of his soul from the weight of sexual guilt.

We may now understand more fully the nature of Nahman's depressions, and the tortured self-image that took shape in his dreams. Out of his own struggle with his passions, he had come to determine that absolute victory over those passions was the defining characteristic of the true *ẓaddiq*. Yet here he was claiming to be the greatest of all the *ẓaddiqim,* indeed the only true *ẓaddiq ha-dor,* still secretly torn by his own inner conflicts, and feeling that his claim to leadership was, on some level, nothing but a lie. This tension must have magnified his guilt enormously. We are not suggesting, it should be understood, that Nahman really was "guilty" of any terrible misdeeds in this area. What he sought was perfection, and perfection meant the overcoming of *desire* itself. Being a young man of volatile emotions and great passion, it is neither surprising nor judgmental to say that this was an endless struggle. Nahman is the wise man of his story *The Wise Man and the Simpleton,* suffering terribly for his flaw in the engraving of a precious stone, albeit a flaw that only his own specially trained eye can discern. Such pain is only heightened by the constant praises of those insufficiently perceptive to see the "truth." We also do not mean to propose that sex alone was the subject of Nahman's ongoing sense of imperfection. If anything, the sexual area was paradigmatic for him: a *ẓaddiq* had to be master of himself before he could claim to lead others. This first meant control of the passions; one who could not master even his own lust or gluttony surely would not be fit to deal with the more refined spiritual enemies of doubt and reason. The first great battle was to be fought here; it was one which never quite reached a proper conclusion.

The proclamation of oneself as *ẓaddiq ha-dor* could be undertaken even by the strongest of men only at the risk of a terrible psychological price. Nahman, plagued by personal guilt and riddled by self-doubt, was never able to assume the mantle of leadership without overwhelming ambivalence. The conflicts that tore him were reflected in the sad countenance he often showed in public situations. On one occasion he felt it necessary to warn his disciples:

> Do not learn from me as I appear. Even though you generally see me with a sad demeanor, you should not copy this. Do you liken yourselves to me in all things, doing exactly as I do? In truth I am happy. It is only because I am clearing a path for you in the wilderness, cutting away the underbrush [that I appear this way].

Nathan felt it necessary to add:

> It is known that his family was descended from the House of David. That is why they generally go about brokenhearted and without a smile. For David composed the Psalms, which are filled with remorseful talk that comes from a broken heart; indeed all his words are broken-hearted outcries and supplications. That is why his descendants, even now, generally have a broken heart.[65]

But what now of the disciple? What was he to do? What light can he reflect, if the master's own countenance is dark and gloomy? If his task is to be a mirror to his master's life, is he then to reflect that gloom, and live out the master's constant struggle against the forces of inner darkness, making Nahman's burden his own? While calling for the disciple to be such a mirror, he then turns around and says, "Do not learn from me as I appear." Which counsel is the one to be followed? The contradictions involved in intimate discipleship with a master who himself is filled with conflict are truly enormous. It is terribly frightening to be called upon to become a "branch" of a tree which itself is locked in mortal combat with the forces of inner turmoil.

Nahman suffered from a terrible fear that both his disciples and his enemies knew, or would come to know, the true complexity of his inner situation. This is the meaning of the long dream which we have quoted: the world, including his own disciples (and perhaps his enemy, if the old man is indeed the Zeide), would come to know of his hidden sin, and desert him because of it. Burdened by the double weight of guilt and loneliness, he fears coming to that state (which he knew well in his waking life) of forgetting all his learning, of "knowing nothing at all." At that point even his most faithful followers would leave him, completing his isolation. Only an act of penitence and his faith in his ultimate vindication could save him from utter despair.

Plagued by this fear that others would come to see him as less than holy, he tried to encompass his own lack of holiness in the most audacious attempts at paradoxical self-justification, finding in his very lack of apparent holiness the truth that he was the Holy of Holies among the *ẓaddiqim:*

> Know that there is a very great *ẓaddiq* whose holiness the world cannot bear. Because of this he remains deeply hidden, not displaying any particular quality of holiness or abstinence. This is parallel to: 'All of the songs are holy, but the Song of Songs is the Holy of Holies.' The Song of Songs contains much greater holiness than any other book of the Bible.
>
> We find that King Solomon wrote three books: Proverbs, Koheleth, and the Song of Songs. Proverbs and Koheleth are filled with moral preaching and the fear of God. We find in them many words of holiness and purity, none of which are to be found in the Song of Songs. Examine the Song of Songs and you will find in it not a single word about holiness. This is because it is so very holy that not a trace of holiness may be seen in it.[66]

Here is the ultimate in paradox: holiness is vindicated, finally, only by its absence.

Insofar as his disciples and enemies were concerned, Nahman did not have much real reason for concern. The disciples went their own way, interpreting everything in a positive light. This is the picture, at least, as painted by Nathan. Who knows what better understandings of Nahman's inner life, perhaps particularly by Simeon, who had been a youthful friend as well as a disciple, were left unsaid or unprinted? As for the enemies, they have left no documentary evidence pointing to any real depth of understanding. Their accusations offer us nothing in this area. It is possible, again, that they did understand more than they said, but remained silent so as to avoid scandal or insult to the Ba'al Shem Tov's family. Such arguments from silence, however, are impossible to pursue.

It was Nahman's own mind, ever turning a critical focus inward, that was not satisfied with his many attempts at self-justification. The periodic cries of pain and suffering that continued to punctuate his conversations with his disciples bear terrifying witness to the fact that his doubts were never permanently stilled. He said that "when the suffering of his sorrows came upon him, the pain was so great he could almost bite through wood with his teeth."[67]

As though to identify clearly the nature of his pain, he said elsewhere that "all the sufferings of the world are nothing, when compared with the heavy burden of sin."[68]

Virtually the only physical description of Nahman which we possess tells us that

> even when he was just conversing with people about worldly matters, his body trembled greatly. His legs shook so badly that when he was seated at the table with other people, the whole table would shake on his account.[69]

Much as he would have liked, Nathan was not able to point to any moment in Nahman's life when the pain ended and the master came to fully accept the mantle of leadership without ambivalence. On the contrary, the tensions seemed to worsen, and even during his last months in Uman, Nahman considered abandoning the entire enterprise and going off voluntarily to live in the woods with his wife and family, far from the demands of leadership and disciples.[70] He advised his followers that even when they see themselves as the worst of sinners, they should seek out some bit of good within themselves to save them from utter despair—advice that he struggled all his life to follow.[71] At times the claims and counter-claims that welled up within him must have been nothing short of maddening. Already in his youth he had feared that madness would ensue if he did not find some respite from the torments of the flesh. Sin itself, he taught, was a form of madness, and it had to be driven out of the body by force before meaningful penitence could take place.[72] We have seen madness romanticized in Nahman's description of Abraham and heard of the fear of madness for one who "sits alone in the forest." The theme was one to which Nahman turned with some frequency. Later Bratslav literature preserves two tales, almost certainly stemming from the master himself, which speak of madness. Each of these will require some comment.

> The parable about a turkey. The king's son once went mad and decided that he was a turkey. As a turkey, he had a need to sit naked under the table and gobble up crumbs of bread and bones. The doctors all despaired of helping him, and the king was greatly troubled. Then a wise man came and announced that he would take it upon himself to heal the prince. He stripped naked and sat under the table alongside the king's son, pecking with him at the crumbs and bones. The prince asked him: "Who are you and what are you doing here?" He replied: "What are you doing here?" "I," said the king's son, "am a turkey." "And I," said the sage, "am a turkey too." So the two of them sat there together for some time, until they got used to one another. Then, at the wise man's signal, a shirt was thrown to them. "Do

> you think," said the turkey-sage to the prince, "that a turkey cannot wear a shirt? You can wear a shirt and still be a turkey!" After a time he signaled again, and they were given trousers. He said the same again: "Do you think that with pants on you can't be a turkey?" Thus they both put on pants and all the rest of their clothing. He signaled again, and regular human food was thrown to them from the table, and he said: "You think that if you eat good food you're not a turkey? You can eat and still be a turkey!" And so they ate. Then the sage said: "Do you think that a turkey can only sit under the table? You can be a turkey and sit right at the table." Thus he went on with him, until he had cured him completely.

The wise man or *ẓaddiq* here has exactly the role which Nahman sought to play among his disciples: he is doctor of souls. "Dressed" in the garb of madness, this healer offers to the patient that empathy at which all others had failed; with that empathy comes healing. But the story masks as much as it reveals. What is the source of this wise man's knowledge, that which allows him to do more for the patient than had all the others? Must it not be his own experience? Must he himself not be a now-cured madman? Accepting this, we dare to go a step further: is he any more "cured" than the state to which he brings his patient? Might the wise man himself indeed be a turkey, but one who has learned to eat with knife and fork? In curing the king's son in this way has he not just found himself a compatriot in the feigning of sanity? Fear not, however. Once we have seen the king's son and wise man in this way, we begin to look around the table and see the rest of the guests with a new eye as well.

The motive of the wise man in this tale should also be of interest to us. Why has he bothered to come heal the king's son? There is no talk here of reward or of hope for gain. Again we turn to Nahman. Oppressed by guilt, driven by self-doubt, Nahman proclaims himself to be the greatest of teacher-healers. Is it in working toward the "sanity" of others that the *ẓaddiq* hopes to find some respite from his own bouts with madness?

> The parable of the produce. Once the king said to his beloved vizier: 'Since I am a star-gazer, I see that all the produce which grows this year will cause madness in anyone who eats of it. What advice do you have?' The vizier replied that enough food should be set aside so that the two of them would not have to eat of that produce. But the king answered: 'If we alone, from among the whole world, are not mad, and everyone else is, we are the ones who will be considered madmen. We too must eat of that produce. But let us place signs on our foreheads, so that we shall at least know that we are mad. If I look at your forehead or you look at mine we shall see the signs—and know that we are madmen.[73]

This parable is perhaps even more frightening. Here we are in a world gone mad, a place where only master and disciple (or God and the *ẓaddiq?)* can choose to preserve some modicum of sanity. Realizing the folly of such a choice, they join with the madmen (at the king's table?), having only their self-awareness to separate them from the rest. Yes, the *ẓaddiq*-soul does eat the maddening food of this world; he must, after all, share in our humanity. At the same time, he strives to maintain his awareness of a prior state, the time before the maddening crop was harvested. That awareness is the only link any of us in the kingdom has with that earlier time, with that which once dared to call itself "sanity." We cannot but wonder, however, whether king and vizier do not turn out to be all the madder for having to bear that extra burden of complexity in their psyches, and whether those of us who have cut our ties with that past do not have a better chance of achieving a new wholeness on this other side of the great divide.

Wholeness was not to be Nahman's strength. The broken heart was as central to his own experience of life as it was to the teachings he offered to his disciples. Cycles of guilt, recrimination, and ecstatic release, moments of elation and true elevation of the spirit alternating with attacks of the most severe depression and self-castigation—these seem to have characterized Nahman's inner state throughout the years of his tragically shortened life. Never was his triumph complete; never did the burden of guilt ever finally release its hold on him. While he was able to prescribe the recitation of a mere ten Psalms to unburden the souls of others, inner peace for his own spirit could not be bought at so meager a price. In the course of one of his many attempts to demonstrate that sex lies at the root of all the torments of the mind, Nahman quotes "medical scholars" as saying that castration is a cure for madness. Could the *ẓaddiq* have had his own struggles with "madness" in mind when he picked up this curious bit of information?[74]

NOTES

1. On Zlotopolye, *cf. Ḥayyey* 4:2. It is interesting to note that Nahman's later travels, which included annual visits to his earlier home in Medvedevka *(Ḥayyey* 4:25) apparently never included any return visit to Zlotopolye. The move to Bratslav is discussed in *ibid.* 13, 19.

2. *Ibid.* 12; *Ḥayyey II* 3:99. It is for this reason that the name of the town is always written as ברסלב by Hasidic authors, rather than the phonetically more correct בראצלאוו or ברצלב.

3. *Zohar* 1:77b–78a.

4. See the author's article to which reference has been made in chapter three, n.66. This sense of the *ẓaddiq* as the new center of the world is further confirmed thus in the later Bratslav tradition:

> He [Nahman of Tulchin, Nathan's successor] told his son Yizhak not to settle permanently in the Land of Israel before he was sixty years old. (It was understood from his words that even though dwelling in the Land is considered a great virtue . . . our master has said that there is nothing greater than his Rosh Hashanah. It is also known that *all the greatness of 'Ereẓ Israel comes from him . . .). Kokhvey 'Or,* p. 68 (emphasis mine).

Presence at Nahman's grave in Uman was required of later Bratslav *ḥasidim;* an annual journey from Erez Israel would in those days have been impossible.

5. *Liqquṭim* 44 and see Genesis Rabbah 1:7 and RaSHI to Gen.1:1; Giṭṭin 8a; Nazir 54b–55a; Berakhot 6b. There then follows the passage on Abraham quoted immediately above.

6. This sense of the transformation of foreign territory into holy soil is also reflected in *Liqquṭim* 76. To inject a note of realism into this discussion, it should be remembered that Bratslav, like many other Ukrainian towns of its size, had a predominantly Jewish population. As late as 1897 (after a marked increase in the number of non-Jews in the towns during the nineteenth century) the population of Bratslav was 43 percent Jewish. *Encyclopedia Judaica,* s.v. Bratslav.

7. *Ḥayyey II* 4:1. *Cf.* also *Ḥayyey* 1:4: 4:13: *Yemey MaHaRNaT* p.13. The emphasis on song and dance in this period is reflected in *Liqquṭim* 3, taught shortly before Rosh Hashanah of 1802.

8. *Liqquṭim II* 63. On Nahman's love for nature see also *Ḥayyey* 2:13.

9. This conference of *ẓaddiqim* and other communal leaders has been described in the memoirs of Abraham Baer Gottlober, reprinted as *Zikhronot u-Masa'ot,* p.173. The thorough mixture of fact and fancy, often vindictive, in this work, means that as a historical source it is to be used with great caution. According to Dubnov, the economic restrictions of this constitution, by ending the "arenda" system, would have taken away the livelihoods of fully half the Jewish population in certain parts of Russia. *History of the Jews in Russia and Poland,* v.1, p.343. In fact many of the constitution's provisions were not carried out; the expulsion of the Jews from the villages did not finally happen until 1824–27. On the particular Hasidic fear of Jewish children's learning the Russian language, see *Ḥayyey II* 7:12.

10. *Yemey MaHaRNaT* p.13. Also concerned with *gezerat ha-punktin* are *Liqquṭim* 5 and 10. Nahman's involvement with this matter is further seen in *Ḥayyey* 1:1 and *Ḥayyey II* 2:37.

11. *Degel Maḥaneh Ephraim,* Yitro. Nahman makes mention of this parable in *Ḥayyey* 6:7.

12. Typical of the Hasidic attitude is the story told of the Maggid's disciple Zusya of Anipol, who was reputed to have undergone terrible privations in the course of his life. When asked about the problem of the righteous' sufferings, he replied, "I don't understand why you ask me this question. Ask it of someone who has known such evil. As for me, this does not apply, for nothing ill has ever happened to me." *Buẓina Qadisha,* Jerusalem, 1957, 1b. In vain would one search the writings of the BeSHT's disciples for a serious encounter with the problem of evil. On the BeSHT's own attitude toward the sufferings of the righteous, see *Toledot Ya'aqov Yosef* 15a.

13. *Liqquṭim II* 23.

14. *Liqquṭim* 56.

15. This estimate has been made by J. Weiss in *Encyclopedia Judaica, s.v.* Nahman of Bratslav. See his *Meḥqarim,* p.222, n.19.

16. *Ḥayyey* 2:19.

17. *'Avaneha Barzel,* pp. 13, 16*f.*

18. In *Liqquṭim* 112 Nahman says that by your struggle to come out of your own personal darkness you help others to do the same. The teaching in *Liqquṭim II* 48 is almost a direct paraphrase of *Shivḥey ha-RaN* 5 and 12–15, except that in the *Liq-*

quṭim this description of Nahman's early life has been rewritten as prescriptive counsel for the disciples. Or may it be assumed that Nathan, in composing his biography, *re*constituted as biography that which his master had offered as teaching? Nathan makes clear the didactic purpose of recording Nahman's biography in his introduction to *Shivḥey ha-RaN*.

19. *Liqquṭim II* 25. The basic sources on *hitbodedut* in Nahman's writings are that teaching, *Liqquṭim II* 101; *Siḥot* 227–234; *Ḥayyey II* 10.

20. *Siḥot* 229, quoting *Mishneh Torah, Tefillah*, beginning.

21. *Liqquṭim II* 100.

22. *Liqquṭim II* 96, 99; *Ḥayyey II* 10:2, 4; *Siḥot* 234.

23. Early sources on the disciples around Nahman are collected in *Ḥayyey II* 3 and are also found scattered through Nathan's writings, particularly in *Yemey MaHaRNaT*. Later traditions—often clearly legendary—are to be found in the *'Anshey MoHaRaN* section of *Kokhvey 'Or* and in *Ṭovot Zikhronot*. There seems to have been a falling-out between Nahman and Simeon after their return from Erez Israel. Only three years later, in Bratslav, were relations between them restored. *Siḥot* 173. On the *minyan* in Nemirov *see Ḥayyey II* 3:91. For the home towns of most of Nahman's followers *see 'Avaneha Barzel* p.28*f*. and Weiss, *Meḥqarim*, p.38*f*, n.6–9.

24. There is a great deal of material available for a study of Nathan. *Cf*. Weiss *Meḥqarim* p.66*ff*., the starting point for all further work. In addition to his autobiographical memoir *Yemey MaHaRNaT*, from which we have here quoted frequently, there is a published collection of his correspondence (*'Alim li-Terufah*, Berdichev, 1896 and augmented edition 1930. See also the further letters of Nathan in N.Z. Koenig's *'Emunat 'Oman*.). Such later Bratslav collections as *Kokhvey 'Or* and especially *'Avaneha Barzel* are also filled with material on the life of Nathan and his role in the Bratslav community. *Yemey ha-Tela'ot* is a special work covering the persecutions he and the other followers suffered at the hands of Moses Sevi of Savran in the 1830s. On Nathan's psychological affinities to Nahman and on his fears of death in particular see *'Avaneha Barzel*, pp.3 and 6. The basic versions of what is called *hitqarevut MaHaRNaT*, the tale of how Nathan first became Nahman's follower, are found in *Yemey MaHaRNaT* p.12ff; *Kokhvey 'Or*, p.9*ff*; *'Avaneha Barzel* p.3*ff*. The last-mentioned of these is the most elaborate. The quip on the knish is found in *'Avaneha Barzel* p.5.

25. Piekarz, *op. cit.*, p. 12 and especially pp. 203*ff*. Weiss in *Encyclopedia Judaica*, *s.v.* Nahman of Bratslav. That the conflict came to the fore immediately after Nahman's death is seen by the account of a controversy over his burial site, recorded in *Sippurim Nifla'im* p. 7*ff*. For a later Bratslav reference to this struggle, *cf*. *Naḥaley 'Emunah*, Beney Beraq, 1967, letter #10, by Abraham Hazạn. The particularly heavy-handed censorship evident in that letter shows that Nathan's conflict with the others is still well-known and considered a highly sensitive matter within the circles of Bratslav *ḥasidim*. It is interesting to note here that later Bratslav tradition emphasizes that Nahman *must* be studied as mediated through the filter of Nathan's understanding; the light of Nahman himself is too bright for our eyes. It thus becomes more important to study the works of Nathan than those of Nahman himself! *Cf*. *Kokhvey 'Or*, introduction. If the later Bratslav tradition is to be believed, Dov of Cheryn, the founder of the Dashev group, himself admitted that

Nathan had understood the master better than he and his friends. *Kokhvey 'Or*, pp. 25*f*.

26. *Ḥayyey* 4:12.

27. But could Nahman's words of praise concerning Nathan to Yizhak of Tirhavitse (*Ḥayyey II* 3:98) have been in response to some ill feeling?

28. The three annual visits to Nahman are mentioned in *Sippurim Nifla'im* p.168. *Cf.* also the full treatment by Weiss in *Meḥqarim* p.9, n.9 and p.221, n.19. Nahman was sometimes annoyed when his disciples appeared on his doorstep outside these regularly appointed seasons. *Cf. Ḥayyey* 1:6. His own regular rounds included visits to Tirhavitse, Medvedevka, Cheryn, and Kreminchug; see *Ḥayyey* 4:13 and 7:1. On the meaning he found in these travels, see *Liqquṭim II* 38. *Shabbat Shirah* is the Sabbath when Exodus 15, the Song of Moses, is read in the weekly Pentateuchal cycle; it generally occurs in January. *Shabbat Naḥamu* is the Sabbath following the fast of Tish'ah be-'Av, in mid-summer.

29. The following chart, listing Nahman's teachings offered on the three appointed dates for assembly over a period of ten years, will show how important these assemblies were. Many of Nahman's longer and more important teachings are found here; the numbers refer to the chapters in *Liqquṭim*.

YEAR	ROSH HASHANAH	HANUKKAH	SHAVU'OT
5561 (1800/01)	78		4?
5562			4?
5563	5	7	11
5564	13	14	19
5565	20	54	56
5566	58–59	17	29
5567	60	30	67
5568	61		
5569	II:1	II:2	II:4
5570	II:5	II:7	
5571	II:8	(Nahman died during Sukkot of 5571)	

30. *Ḥayyey* 1:15.

31. In *Liqquṭim II* 118, Nahman speaks against those who do not prepare their Torah before teaching. In *Liqquṭim II* 79 we have a series of brief notes for a teaching that was never written out. These notes seem to be the sort from which Nahman would speak. The train of associations is listed, while the specific connections were not spelled out. Not all other *ẓaddiqim* agreed with Nahman as to the preparation of teachings. The ideal in the Maggid's school seems to have been one of pure spontaneity, which would preclude such preparations. *Cf.* Weiss' article "Via Passiva in Early Hasidism," *JJS* 11 (1960) 137*ff*. and especially the description of the Maggid's sermon in Solomon Maimon's *Autobiography*, p.54.

32. *Liqquṭim* 20:2. This teaching will be discussed at length in the following chapter. On Nahman's style of teaching *cf.* also *Ḥayyey* 1:15. On "words as hot as burning coals" in some other holy-man traditions *cf.* Eliade, *Rites and Symbols of Initiation*, p.85*f*.

33. *Ḥayyey* 1:2, 50.

34. *Ḥayyey II* 1:1; 11:96. See also Piekarz, *op, cit.*, p.149.

35. *Ḥayyey II* 5:4. See *Gen. Rabbah* 39:14.

36. Quotation from *Ḥayyey II* 3:56; *cf.* also *ibid.* 83; 4:51; 11:72; *'Avaneha Barzel* p.25. In *Liqquṭim* 163 Nahman makes the revealing statement that he feels more fulfilled among dangerous enemies than he does among small-minded people, from whom his soul can obtain no nourishment. This seems to be a reference to his disciples.

37. This is the tenor that emerges from Kalisker's letters, published in editions of his *Ḥesed le-Avraham,* Chernowitz, 1851. *Cf.* also J. Weiss' article "R. Abraham Kalisker's Concept of Communion," *JJS* 6 (1955) 87*ff.*

38. *Ḥayyey II* 3:80; *Liqquṭim* 123 and see *Sifre,* shofetim 154.

39. *Liqquṭim* 164.

40. *Yemey MaHaRNaT* p.12; *Kokhvey Or* p.103ff; *Liqquṭim* 7:3. On the *ẓaddiq* as mother *cf. Liqquṭim* 4:8. Piekarz, *op. cit.* pp.77 and 138*f.*

41. *Ḥayyey II* 3:55, 70; *Liqquṭim* 188, and *cf.* also *Siḥot* 180.

42. On Luria *cf.* Jacob Ẓemah, *Naggid u-Meẓawweh* p.80, and on the Ba'al Shem Tov *cf. Shivḥey ha-BeSHT* p.64*f.*

43. *Liqquṭim* 66:1 (early 1807). A similar point is made in *Liqquṭim* 176.

44. *Liqquṭim* 19:1, 9 (Shavu'ot, 1804). The motif of *ẓaddiq* as mirror is also found in the writings of the Maggid of Miedzyrzec. *Cf. Maggid Devaraw le-Ya'aqov,* ed. R. Schatz, p.275 and the treatment by Scholem, *Von der mystischen Gestalt der Gottheit,* p.129.

45. *Liqquṭim* 153; *cf.* Rosh Hashanah 16b ("A man must greet his master's 'face' on a festival."); *Liqquṭim* 6:5; *Liqquṭim II* 91. For the ensuing discussion *cf.* also *Degel Maḥaneh Ephraim, naso,* 191b, where Nahman's uncle quotes a passage from the *Zohar* to the effect that the *ẓaddiq's* face is a revealed form of the face of God; the author takes the priestly blessing ("May God cause His face to shine upon you") to mean that the *ẓaddiq* receives the divine face.

46. *Ḥayyey II* 3:90

47. *Ḥayyey* 3:18. Parentheses in original.

48. *Ḥayyey* 1:8, 10. *Cf.* also the introduction to that work.

49. *Shivḥey II* 33. The passage from *Liqquṭey Halakhot, 'Oraḥ Ḥayyim, tefillin* 5, cited by Piekarz *(op. cit.* p.42) is largely a repetition of this text.

50. *Ḥayyey* 1:24. A later Bratslav source *(Sippurim Nifla'im,* p. 167) records that on a certain Rosh Hashanah Nahman did not feel up to dealing with his disciples, who had come to be with him. He said to them: "Why do you come to me? What do you want of me? If you hadn't come, I would simply be asleep, and only the blast of the *shofar* would wake me up." It should be noted that daytime sleep on Rosh Hashanah is proscribed by well-known custom; the only reason for Nahman's desecration of this holiday, which he held so dear, seems to be that he was so overwhelmingly depressed on that occasion that in fact he could do nothing but sleep.

51. *Shivḥey II* 33; *Ḥayyey* 2:8.

52. *Liqquṭim II* 24, 119.

53. *Ḥayyey* 3:7. The rabbinic passage is from *Shabbat* 10a-b and *Lev. Rabbah* 9:9. The "unclean place" to which the Talmud refers is the lavatory.

54. *Ḥayyey* 1:24.

55. *Ḥayyey* 3:11. Weiss has dealt with this dream in *Meḥqarim* p.42*ff.*

56. In Nahman's tale of *The Rabbi and His Son,* the forces of evil lead the rabbi to prevent his son from visiting the great *ẓaddiq,* and thus bring about the son's

death. They do this by spreading abroad a rumor that the *ẓaddiq* is a sinner; the term used to describe the *ẓaddiq* is *'over 'averah* (Yiddish: *getun an aveyre).* Weiss has already suggested in *Tarbiẓ* 27 (1958) 237 that the meaning of *'averah* here is sexual sin. This story was told in the summer of 1807, some two-and-a-half years before the final dream. As will be further clarified below, we are not claiming that the Zeide or any other enemy actually accused Nahman of sexual misconduct, but rather that such an accusation did occupy a prominent place in Nahman's own imagination.

57. *Cf.* Chapter One. In *Liqquṭim* 39 Nahman says that the only pure sex act is one devoid of all desire, one done as though under compulsion. See also Nathan's introduction to the *Tiqqun ha-Kelali* on Nahman's wish to force a change in nature.

58. *Ḥayyey II* 11:149. *Cf.* also *Liqquṭim II* 72.

59. *Ḥayyey II* 11:71.

60. For a few of many sources on sexual lust as the root of all evil, *cf. Liqquṭim* 36:2; *Siḥot* 115; *Liqquṭey 'Eẓot*, s.v. *berit; Sefer ha-Middot*, s.v. *ni'uf.* The three great evils of lust, avarice and gluttony are listed together in *Liqquṭim II* 1. Of course this emphasis upon sexual desire as the most basic of all sins is not new in Nahman; it is well known throughout the whole history of Kabbalistic ethics. For the *Zohar's* attitude on this matter, *cf. Zohar* 2:263b–264a and many parallel passages. It may be said of earlier Rabbinic Judaism as well that sexuality was viewed as the root of evil: the Rabbinic term *yeẓer ha-ra'* ("evil inclination") has a specifically sexual connotation. What is surprising here is not Nahman's *belief* that sexuality lies behind the will to evil, but rather the tremendous emphasis he places upon it, the degree of constant repetition, and the extremes to which he carries this concern. The origin of sexual sin, he says, is in the mind. Extensive sexual activity, by releasing fluids the body (particularly the brain) needs, will have a debilitating effect upon one's mental life. *Cf. Liqquṭim* 43 and *Liqquṭim II* 5:5. He sometimes went so far as to say that

> Eating at least adds to a man's strength and vigor. But this desire does just the opposite: it is most damaging to one's vigor, and weakens the person terribly. Surely it has no value other than the propagation of the species. *Liqquṭim II* 107.

There is a particular relationship in Nahman's writings between the purity of speech and sexual purity, based upon an older Kabbalistic association between the sexual *(berit ha-ma'or, i.e.,* circumcision) and verbal *(berit ha-lashon, i.e.,* the acceptance of Torah at Sinai) covenants between God and Israel. (These terms originate in *Sefer Yeẓirah* 1:2; their relationship is spelled out in Isaiah Horowitz's *Sheney Luḥot ha-Berit, Sha'ar ha-'Otiyot*, s.v. *shetiqah,* ed. Jerusalem, 1959, 72a.) This association has many ramifications in Nahman's thought. By *speaking* to people and making them hear his message, he also affects their reproductive organs, helping them to conceive *(Liqquṭim* 60:8). A person whose sexual life is not pure will also be unable to pray, since holiness in sexual matters and the holy speech of prayer are interdependent. This theme, in rather varied garb, is stated quite frequently *(Liqquṭim* 2, 46, 50; *Liqquṭim II* 83). Poetry also is subject to this connection; the German word *Poesie* is related, in a play on words by Nahman, to *pfeh! sie!* (disgust with women), meaning that only he who had overcome sexual desire could be a true poet. This remark was made to the *maskilim* of Uman whom he befriended in his last year *(Ḥayyey,* Uman 31–32; discussed by Piekarz, *op. cit.*, pp.42*ff.*). *Cf.* also *Liqquṭim* 19, the central theme of which is the holiness of speech, and which contains several references to the relationship between sexuality and language.

61. *Ḥayyey II* 1:5.

62. *Siḥot* 171.

63. It is interesting to note that of all the Biblical heroes, many of whom are designated by the term *ẓaddiq* in the early rabbinic sources, it is only Joseph that the later (chiefly Kabbalistic) tradition regularly calls by this title. In his resistance to the seductive advances of Potiphar's wife, Joseph becomes the great symbol of sexual purity. See *Yebamot* 98a; Scholem, *Von der mystischen Gestalt der Gottheit*, p.83*ff*; sources quoted in the article mentioned in n.4 above. On Joseph as a figure in Nahman's imagination and in Bratslav see Piekarz, *op. cit.*, p.125.

64. The text of these ten Psalms along with various introductions and meditations has been published very frequently by the Bratslav *ḥasidim* as *Tiqqun ha-Kelali*. Recently Rabbi Gedaliah Fleer, leader of a small Bratslav group in New York, has published this work in English as *Rabbi Nahman's Foundation*. The use of this *Tiqqun* is still very widespread among the *ḥasidim;* along with *hitbodedut* it comprises the regular form of religious practice unique to the Bratslav sect.

65. *Ḥayyey II* 1:6–7.

66. *Liqquṭim* 243 and see Mishnah Yadayim 3:5. See also *Ḥayyey* 1:40. While the context there shows that Nahman was not speaking directly of himself, the inference was probably quite clear. In another paradoxical formulation, found in *Liqquṭim* 275 and *Siḥot* 134, he speaks of himself as being dead within life, undoubtedly a comment on the intensity of his own suffering. But because he is already like a dead man, he can effect those *tiqqunim* at which other *ẓaddiqim* can work only in the upper worlds after their own deaths. Thus being dead, in effect, makes him more fully alive!

67. *Shivḥey* 24. That his sufferings are not those of the body alone is seen from the censored reference in *Yemey MaHaRNaT*, p. 21:

> He said that he bore great suffering, both outer and inner . . . for he had great bodily pain and suffering from his terrible disease, and also inside etc. [!]

68. *Liqquṭim II* 7:3. *Cf.* also *Liqquṭim* 112, on the terrible and oppressive *darkness* of the burden caused by sin. Note also *Siḥot* 16:

> It is possible to cry out a very great scream in a still small voice that no human being can hear.

Compare this with *Ḥayyey II* 2:1:

> 'When do I practice *hitbodedut (i.e.,* 'When am I alone with God?')?' When everyone was standing around him and he was seated in their midst—that was his *hitbodedut*.

The picture emerges of Nahman, seated among his adulating disciples, and silently screaming out to God from a state of utter loneliness.

69. *Ḥayyey II*, 2:3, It is noteworthy that Nahman never served as prayer leader in Bratslav. He did not even lead the singing at his own Sabbath table. The recitation of *Kiddush* and the teaching at the table were themselves a great struggle for him. *Siḥot* 210.

70. *Ḥayyey* 8:12, 29; *Ḥayyey II* 2:19.

71. *Liqquṭim* 282.

72. *Liqquṭim* 1.

73. *Sippurim Nifla'im* p.26. Elie Wiesel is the master teller of these two tales. Cf. his *Souls on Fire,* p.169*ff.* The tale of the turkey seems to be a radical response to a parable in the *Toledot* (see Dresner, *The Zaddik,* pp.179f, 290f.) where the *ẓaddiq* is said to have to put on the garments of this world in order to descend to its level and deal with it. Nahman's response to the BeSHT and the *Toledot:* the world the *ẓaddiq* enters is a madhouse, and in order really to do his task there he will have not to dress up but to strip naked! With regard to the tale of the produce, Zalman Schachter has called to my attention a most interesting parallel tale told among the Sufis, and recorded by Idres Shah *(Tales of the Dervishes* p.21). This tale tells of a day when the waters changed and all who drank them went mad. The one person who had a supply of old water eventually abandoned it when, alone in his sanity, he felt the loneliness of being considered a madman; as he started to drink of the new source, he was hailed by all those around him as a madman miraculously healed!

74. *Liqquṭim* 36:6. Nahman was also a contemporary of the earliest Skoptsy, a Russian sect that practiced castration in order to rid man of the evils wrought by sexual desire. It is not known whether Ukrainian Jews were acquainted with this sect, which was centered well to the east of the Jewish areas of population.

5

Messianic Strivings

The *ẓaddiq*, as he appears in the literature of early Hasidism, is a leader with many faces. We have seen that in Bratslav he takes on the quality of *axis mundi*, being possessed of the soul that lies at the center of his entire generation. He is also portrayed, in Bratslav and elsewhere, as parent, teacher, spiritual guide, intercessor in prayer, healer, and protector from sin. Hasidic masters and communities varied insofar as they chose to emphasize one aspect of *ẓaddiqut* above another, though this emphasis seldom resulted in the total exclusion of other elements. Thus in *ḤaBaD* circles the emphasis was upon the *ẓaddiq* as guide, while in Lezajsk (and later Galician dynasties) the *ẓaddiq's* intercessory function in prayer was more important, and in Przysucha (including later Polish Hasidism) it was the aspect of *ẓaddiq* as teacher that gained prominence.

All of these images of the *ẓaddiq* are present in Bratslav. We have already had occasion to refer to a number of them, and the particular ways in which they functioned in the context of Nahman's unique relationship with his disciples. But when we turn to a closer examination of the *ẓaddiq*-idea as presented in Nahman's teachings, it becomes clear that there is a most serious difference in emphasis between Nahman and all other Hasidic teachers: in Bratslav alone is the *ẓaddiq* portrayed most prominently as *redeemer*, and particularly as redeemer from the burden of sin.

The idea that a *ẓaddiq* may be of help to his disciples in atoning for their sins is not completely new with Nahman; it is part of the intercessory function of the *ẓaddiq* in other schools as well. We have seen how the Ba'al Shem Tov was wont to engage in *tiqqun neshamot*, restoring the souls of those who had already died, and were too weighed down by sin to enter paradise. The very term *"pidyon"* ("redemption"), applied to the gift the *ḥasid* brought when seeking his master's blessing, bespeaks something of the *ẓaddiq's* function as redeemer of souls. But only in Bratslav does this aspect of the *ẓaddiq's* role outstrip all others; only here does the effecting of *tiqqun* come to be depicted as his central task.[1]

> I heard that when he was in Lipovits he said to his disciples: 'In what way can you repent? Would all of your combined strength and all your days suffice to repair even a small bit of the damage you have done? But I do penance for you, and God gives me the power to repair all that you have damaged (so long as you desist from conscious sin).'[2]

In the light of our preceding chapter, it is not difficult to understand how this shift in emphasis came about. Nahman, so constantly aware of his own sinfulness and distance from God, has constructed a Hasidism built upon an awareness of sin. Gone are the Ba'al Shem Tov's warnings against excessive brooding; the movement's early optimism about the nature of man has here been cast aside. Bratslav writings, indeed a faithful mirror to Nahman's own countenance, depict human life as a morass of suffering and guilt.[3] The devastating effects of sin are everywhere; the powers of *siṭra aḥra* and its representatives within the soul form an active and dangerous foe. In the context of this new emphasis on human sinfulness and its destructive effects, the image of *ẓaddiq* as teacher or spiritual guide will not suffice: in order to be of real help to his disciples, the *ẓaddiq must* be able to do battle for them, rescuing them from forces of darkness that threaten to overwhelm them.

We have noted that this rediscovery of the omnipresence of sin in certain ways places Nahman beyond the bounds of what is usually considered 'Hasidic' thought, and brings him closer to the Kabbalistic *mussar* writers of earlier generations. The emphasis upon sin (particularly sexual sin) as the working of the evil forces, and man's great need to overcome its power through acts of penitence and through mystical meditations, was a central theme for these authors, particularly for those who wrote in the Lurianic tradition. This was the purpose of the many *tiqquney teshuvah,* penitential guides, published by Kabbalistic authors both before and after the Sabbatian period. Certain of these liturgical *tiqqunim* continued to be printed in late Kabbalistic or even Hasidic prayerbooks, and exercised considerable influence, despite the BeSHT's alleged disdain for their ascetic worldview. Nahman's own *tiqqun ha-kelali* clearly belongs to the genre of this non-Hasidic literature of penitential prescriptions. In promulgating this litany of penitence for sexual misdeed, and in the great promises he made as to its effectiveness,[4] Nahman is revealing himself as *ẓaddiq*-redeemer, as one who can save his followers from the harm wrought by their sins.

In the wake of this emphasis upon *tiqqun,* it should come as no surprise to us that the Hasidic ideal of *devequt* ("attachment" to God) receives little attention in Nahman's writings. As Scholem has pointed out, the ideal of *devequt* served in Hasidism to supplant that of *tiqqun,* which was the central goal of Lurianic Kabbalah. Following the Sabbatian and Frankist debacles, the circle around the Ba'al Shem Tov and especially the Maggid chose a path of inner illumination, one which would effect the individual transformation of the worshiper without raising the dangerous spectre of messianism implicit in the striving for *tiqqun*. As preached by the Kabbalists, *tiqqun* was a process of restoring wholeness to a world still suffering the effects of the primal cataclysm; this restoration would culminate in the advent of messiah, symbolizing the completion of man's theurgic task. *Devequt*, on the other hand, implied no such restoration, but was merely the ascent of the soul, through devout prayer and contemplation, to a state of union or near-union with the divine.[5]

The promulgation of *devequt* as the Hasidic ideal must, however, be seen not merely as an escape from messianic tension. It is a natural outgrowth of the Ba'al Shem Tov's new emphasis upon the presence and ready accessibility of the divine in the world. Early Hasidic doctrine came quite close to the borderline of pantheism, or at least 'panentheism'. The constant repetition of such formulae as "the whole earth is filled with his glory" and "there is no place devoid of Him" points to a religious world view that could readily allow for 'attachment' to the Creator as its ideal. For the early Hasidic authors, the seeming absence of God is but illusion, rather readily to be overcome through the techniques of contemplative prayer. There is no real and unbridgeable gulf between man and God. While sin still was described as a barrier keeping man from God, it was felt, particularly in the school of the Maggid, that contemplation could break through that barrier.

This could not be the case for Nahman, for whom the sense of distance from God was a real, and crucial, experience. Where sin remains a serious burden and God is far from man, *devequt* is not an accessible ideal. Until the soul is cleansed, man remains a prisoner of his own inner darkness. It is clear that in this context the first task of man must be that of *tiqqun*, and that the *ẓaddiq* must be one who can help in that effort. But this *tiqqun* by its very nature was the repair of the cosmos as well as the repair of the individual soul. For Nahman, as for any Kabbalist, the greatest danger of sin was not that harm which it did to the soul, but rather the damage it wrought in the upper worlds. Sin has a cosmic effect: the unification of the *Sefirot*, or the restoration of wholeness to *Adam Qadmon*, is retarded only by the corrosive action of human sin. The forces of evil, which work to bring about disharmony above, have been cut off from their original wellsprings in the divine world; only through man's transgressions, depicted by the Kabbalah as filled with demonic potency, do they receive the nourishment needed to sustain their work.

Here we have traced a full circle: Hasidism rejected the *tiqqun* ideal in part to escape the dangerous messianic tension. Nahman, because of his personal world view, in turn rejected *devequt* as a goal and returned to the earlier emphasis. This emphasis, however, brought him right back to the place early Hasidism had sought to avoid: a religious life clearly eschatological in its central thrust. If Nahman is the redeemer from sin, and the real import of any individual's sin is that which it contributes to the state of universal alienation, then the salvation of each sinner will of necessity bring the world another step closer to the ultimate *tiqqun,* which is the advent of messiah. By reemphasizing the reality of sin and the need for redemption—an emphasis that grew out of his own, inner life—Naḥman was also opening the doorway to a fully active and resurgent messianism, the likes of which had not previously been known within the Hasidic camp.

The place of messianism in the early years of the Hasidic movement has been much debated by modern scholars. While some historians (particularly B.Z. Dinur, and to a lesser extent I. Tishby) have claimed that Hasidism began with a clearly messianic goal in mind, and only later, perhaps as a result of failure, turned to the goal of personal redemption through *devequt,* others (G. Scholem and R. Schatz) have seen the 'neutralization' of messianic tension as a basic characteristic of the movement as a whole.[6] In either case, however, the discussion revolves primarily around the period of the Ba'al Shem Tov. Even Dinur, the most extreme among those who attribute a messianic character to the movement, agrees that by the end of the BeSHT's lifetime (1760) there had been a turn away from messianic urgency. In the writings of the Maggid and his school, which Schatz has studied, the emphasis on *devequt* as the central value and a turn away from talk of messianic redemption is quite pronounced. Of course there is a continued belief in messiah, as well as an echoing of such pious phrases as "may he come speedily in our days." But *activity* directed toward bringing the final redemption, serious predictions of his imminent arrival, or even extensive theoretical preoccupation with the nature of messianic redemption, are absent[7]—absent, that is, except in Bratslav.

Any discussion of messianism as presented in the Bratslav sources is greatly complicated by the fact that here, more than in any other area, the hand of the inner censor has been particularly heavy. For reasons that will presently become clear, the relationship of Nahman to the final redemption and the rather open messianic agitation that dominated his career between 1804 and 1806 were considered too controversial to be discussed outside the community or to be allowed to appear in print. Thus it happened that the one document written by Nahman purporting to deal most specifically with this matter, called *Megillat Setarim* by the later sources, has never been published, and exists to this day as a manuscript shared only within the most intimate circles of Bratslav *ḥasidim.*[8] It is also quite likely that those of Nahman's works which were burned, on his orders, both within his lifetime and immediately following his death, may well have had to do with this most sensitive area. Nonetheless, as we shall show, enough material is available within the printed Bratslav corpus to give one a rather clear picture of Nahman's messianic strivings, as well as an indication of what it was that Nahman and others felt might best be left unsaid, or at least unprinted.

We will recall that as *ẓaddiq ha-dor* Nahman claimed to be the bearer of the soul that had belonged to Moses in the generation of the Exodus. This same soul, according to Nahman's writings and based on accepted Kabbalistic tradition, will belong to messiah in the last generation. While a parallel between the first and final redeemers of Jewish history had been drawn in most ancient times, it was only the Kabbalistic belief in metempsychosis that made possible a declaration that Moses and messiah were in fact one and the same.[9] This soul, which had also been that of Simeon ben Yohai, Isaac Luria, and the BeSHT, lends to its bearers a particular responsibility in the work of redemption. Both Rabbi Simeon and Luria were identified, in traditions known to Nahman, as redeemer-like figures. A still greater urgency about this redemptive task is felt in Bratslav through Nahman's claim that he is more than the *ẓaddiq ha-dor* of his *own* generation: he is in fact the last in this chain of *ẓaddiqey ha-dor,* the final bearer of the great messianic soul who will appear in the world before the advent of messiah himself. His life and teachings are, in a sense, the last opportunity the world will have to effect the great *tiqqun* before the coming of the final judgment. When Nahman said, "My fire will burn until messiah comes," he expected that the redeemer's arrival was imminent, and that he himself was the final preparer of the way. There was a point at which he felt he knew the exact day of messiah's intended arrival, and that day was designated as being "within a few years." It was only due to certain events that transpired in and around Bratslav during Nahman's lifetime, as we shall see, that the final redemption was to be delayed.[10]

It should be noted that the traditional "signs" of the final days, if pursued with a searching eye, were readily to be found in the opening years of the nineteenth century. We have seen that the oppression of the Jews (as perceived by *ḥasidim)* was on the increase in Russia under Alexander I. The growth of heresy, another sure sign of messiah's imminent arrival, was beginning to be felt even in the Ukraine, as the influence of the Berlin *Haskalah* started to move eastward. Perhaps most significantly, the astounding and unprecedented successes of Napoleon's army, which Nahman had encountered first-hand in his flight from Acre in 1799, led many to believe that Gog and Magog (perhaps France and Russia) were about to destroy one another, and that messiah would rise from the ashes of their final battle. We know that Nahman followed the news of his day with great interest; when disciples came to visit, he would frequently ask them for reports on what was happening in the outside world. The reports he received regarding persecutions, heresies, and the Napoleonic advances all fed his belief that redemption was in fact at hand.[11]

It has long been known and generally accepted that Nahman and the group around him were involved in renewed messianic speculations. The frequent and secretive references to the final redemption in Bratslav literature as well as the highly-charged, mysterious mood of penitence and excitement at once leave no doubt that deep stirrings of redemption-longing were aroused here. It was Hillel Zeitlin who first remarked that although it seems at first glance that the figure of the *ẓaddiq* dominates all of Bratslav thinking, it is possible to see a thinly-veiled reference to messiah behind each mention of *ẓaddiq*. What has not been heretofore clarified was the precise nature and full extent of Nahman's involvement with millennarian activities. What sort of claim was it that Nahman made? Was he merely the final preparer of the way, as the exoteric Bratslav tradition might have it, or did he claim something more? Was there a belief or hope in Bratslav that Nahman might himself be messiah, and how much was he himself responsible for such belief? There is no question that during the years 1804 to 1806 there was a tremendous upsurge of eager anticipation of the End in Bratslav; earlier scholars have documented the events of that period quite fully.[12] But was it out of the air that Nahman turned to messianism in the middle of his career? True, he was heartened or even elated by such personal happenings as the marriages of his daughters and especially by the birth of his first son, Shlomo Ephraim, in the spring of 1805. But what have these to do with messianism? And can these events alone explain so daring a turn in the man's career? Or are the roots of this messianism in fact to be traced earlier, and did something happen that made the "fullness of time" seem closer as those crucial years approached?

The fact is that throughout a great many of Nahman's early teachings, if they are read closely, a messianic strain can be detected. We shall turn our attention here first to those teachings, and only afterwards to the dramatic events that characterized the messianic climax of Nahman's years at Bratslav.

The second teaching in *Liqquṭey MoHaRaN*, though it is not dated by Nathan, clearly belongs to Nahman's early days, and probably to Zlotopolye.[13] It begins with the words, "Messiah's chief weapon will be that of prayer." The power of true prayer, Nahman explains, comes to man through the Kabbalistic figure of Joseph, the ninth *sefirah*. Because Joseph is a symbol of sexual purity for Kabbalists, this power of prayer can only be attained by those who have followed Joseph's example, and have been careful about matters of sexual purity in their own lives. The prayer such people fashion will ultimately become the messiah's weapon, a spiritual "sword" with which he will vanquish his enemies. The use of this sword, however, is not restricted to the messianic future; it can also be employed by the righteous who live in pre-messianic times: "he who attains this sword must know how to do battle with it. He must turn neither to the right nor the left, but must strike his mark without fail." In fact, as we shall see, it is Nahman himself who has access to the messianic sword.

The teaching then goes on to speak of *mishpaṭ*, here defined as the proper balance of the sefirotic world. *Mishpaṭ* depends upon Jacob, the central pillar of the *sefirot*, and the progenitor of Joseph. Although he is a younger son, Joseph was given the rights of primogeniture over Reuben, who had defiled his father's bed by seducing his concubine (Gen. 35:22). By means of prayer, which is directed toward the sefirotic Jacob, the righteous can help to maintain the precarious balance of the upper worlds. These prayers are directed through the *ẓaddiq ha-dor*, who has the power to unite them and bring out their efficacy. As Moses, he assembles all the prayers of Israel, and out of them he builds the tabernacle *(mishkan)*, here taken as a symbol of the reconstituted *shekhinah*.

While the train of associations here is somewhat fragmentary and confusing, as is true with the written versions of many of Nahman's teachings, it is clear that underlying this whole series of associations is the figure of *Messiah ben Joseph*, even though he is not mentioned directly in the text. This figure of the messianic warrior, who is to precede Messiah ben David, is the link between the motifs of Joseph and *ẓaddiq*, on the one hand, and the messiah and his spiritual "weapon" on the other.[14] Of Messiah ben Joseph we will have more to say below. Also evident in the background of this teaching is a sefirotic model of the redemptive process: both *ẓaddiq* and Joseph are symbols of the ninth *sefirah;* it is through their efforts that the tenth *sefirah*, the *Shekhinah* (also associated with David and the advent of Messiah ben David) shall be restored to her original place. The sword of Messiah ben Joseph prepares the way for Messiah ben David. The understated phallic associations in this chain of thought are also highly interesting for the psychology of messianism.

We have already had occasion to discuss the elation Nahman felt upon his move to Bratslav, and his description of that place as a sort of new Jerusalem. The wording of that description, speaking as it does of the *tiqqun* involved in returning the lands of the nations to the bounds of the sacred, itself has a strong messianic flavor. The growing messianism of that period (late 1802) is even more directly found in a teaching offered on Hanukkah, in which Nahman ingeniously distorts a Talmudic reference to *orzila bar yoma* (lit.: "a one-day-old gazelle") to refer to "the desecrated light which is about to emerge any day." With regard to this light, the glory of the *shekhinah*, Nahman says:

> It will be revealed only through messiah, of whom it has been said: 'When will he come? Today! "Today if you will harken to His voice" (ps. 95:7).' Every day the glory is ready to emerge from its debasement.[15]

Later that same winter, in the early months of 1803, Nahman again spoke of messianic redemption, making it quite clear once again that such redemption would come about through the actions of the *ẓaddiq*. Israel is in exile only because of its lack of faith. Faith is best realized in prayer, which attests to man's belief in the ability of God to intervene in the natural order. Belief in the supernatural, however, is directly associated with the Land of Israel, that place which, even in pre-messianic times, is under the direct guidance of God himself and is not ruled by nature. Thus it is that through prayer, which bears witness to their faith, Israel can overcome the heretics' denial of the supernatural, and bring about the redemption, the return to Erez Israel. "When this [denial of the supernatural] ends, and there is an abundance of faith in the world, messiah will come. Redemption depends primarily upon this."[16] Faith is restored, Nahman goes on to say, and prayer is made possible, only through the advice of the *ẓaddiq*. Receiving counsel from the *ẓaddiq* is an act entailing the actual flow of his mind into yours, purifying you of heretical thoughts, just as the revelation at Sinai purified Israel from the taint of original sin! It is this purification, initiated by the *ẓaddiq*, that will enable Israel's prayers to hasten the messiah's arrival.

It was at the wedding of his daughter Sarah, held in the spring of 1803, that Nahman first made explicit reference to a relationship between messiah and his own family. We will recall that Nahman, in addition to claiming possession of the messianic soul, was in fact the product of a union between two families that claimed descent from the House of David. Given this confluence of messianic symbols, it is no wonder that he first expressed a hope, later to turn to certainty, that the redeemer would emerge from among his own offspring:

> In the year 1803, he married off his daughter Sarah in the holy community of Medvedevka, to his son-in-law Isaac, the son of the wealthy Leib Dubrovner. . . . The wedding took place on the New Moon of Nissan, which that year fell on a Thursday. After the ceremony, which took place in the evening, they spoke of messiah, *etc.* (and our master hinted that it would be fitting that he come from this union, etc.).[17]

A few weeks later, in a teaching offered on Shavu'ot (May, 1803), he again referred to exile and the coming return to Erez Israel. He reminded his disciples that it was because of sin, particularly the sins of pride and self-glorification, that Israel was in exile from its homeland. It is not the power of the nations that keeps us from our land, he said, but it is rather our own sinfulness that lends power to those who would oppress us.[18]

But the most striking among these early messianic teachings was one offered in midsummer of 1803. The text preserved in this case is quite brief, and is surely a fragment of a much longer teaching. Like many of Nahman's early teachings, this fragment takes the form of an intricate commentary on one of the more fantastic *Aggadic* passages of the Talmud. The Talmudic text, stated in the name of R. Yohanan, reads:

> Once we were traveling in a ship, and we saw a fish raise its head out of the water. Its eyes were like two moons, and water poured forth from its two nostrils, as [much water as is contained in] the two rivers of Syria.

The great fish, in Nahman's interpretation, turns out to be the *ẓaddiq,* who sometimes has to leave contemplation and study (raising his head out of water) in order to deal with the two great enemies of Israel, Esau and Ishmael, who threaten to darken the *ẓaddiq's* eyes and destroy his vision. These enemies will ultimately be defeated by the two messiahs, who are the streams of water issuing from the fish's nostrils (read: from the *ẓaddiq's* seed).[19]

This text has, however, been censored, presumably on Nahman's own orders (it was published within his lifetime). We are made aware of this by a most significant passage in *Ḥayyey MoHaRaN,* from which it is possible to recover at least the sense of the passage that has been eliminated:

> He presented that teaching at the morning meal. His eyes had the appearance of two moons as he said that there are seventy nations, divided between the domains of Esau and Ishmael [traditional designations for Christendom and Islam]. Each of these domains is composed of thirty-five kingdoms, and they will be conquered in the future by the two messiahs, Messiah ben Joseph and Messiah ben David. *And there is one ẓaddiq in whom these two messiahs are combined.* He said several other things there, *more than have been printed.* At that point the table broke, because so many people were pressing around him. He became harsh and said, 'Are there gentiles sitting around my table? Are these then messianic times, that gentiles should approach the *ẓaddiqim* as in "all the nations shall flow unto him" (Is. 2:2).[20]

The meaning of this dramatic moment seems quite clear. Whenever Nahman used a phrase like "there is one *ẓaddiq,*" his disciples knew well that the reference was to none other than himself. Here he was revealing to them his belief that his own soul included elements of both messianic figures. This much is stated openly by Nathan. What is it then that has been deleted from the text, and to which Nathan can only refer in such an oblique manner? What was it that caused so much excitement among those assembled that they crowded around him until they broke the table? It is not at all impossible that the deleted passage here contained the revelation that Nahman himself is Messiah ben Joseph, the messianic warrior whose battles are to precede the final redemption. Nahman saw himself as a precursor of Messiah ben David, and as one who bore the messianic soul. While the time for Messiah ben David's arrival had not quite been reached, it may well be that on this occasion Nahman did announce himself as Messiah ben Joseph, a role not at all unsuited to his self-image as the suffering *ẓaddiq* whose pains contain within them the hope for redemption.

The weapons in this messiah's battle, as we have seen, are weapons of prayer. Who is the great prayer-warrior, constantly struggling in prayer to break through to God, if not Nahman himself? What real, inner meaning does Nahman attribute to the battles and torments that fill his life, if not the sense that they are mythic encounters with the forces of evil, aimed at the liberation of both self and others from their clutches, and serving to prepare the path for the final redemption? Here, as in Sabbatianism, the ancient figure of the warrior-messiah has been transformed. No longer is he, as in the early apocalyptic literature in which he played so great a role, a warrior in the literal sense of the word. In the spirit of mysticism, the scene of his battle has shifted from the material world to the world of inner spiritual striving. As Sabbatai Sevi had done in his time, Nahman seeks to find in his inner struggles and in the rapid variations of his own moods a spiritual battleground in which the cosmic forces of evil encounter the forces of redemption and engage in their final battle. In the case of both of these would-be redeemers, it is the climate of mysticism, with its emphasis on the inner religious life of man as the true scene of divine activity, that allows of forging a mystical messianism focused upon their own struggles with the personal forces of darkness.[21]

Leaving aside for just a moment the further documentation of Nahman's messianic claim, we should here mention that there is a most significant precedent for the claim to being Messiah ben Joseph, a precedent of which Nahman surely knew and one he would have taken most seriously. We refer to the well-known claims of the Safed Kabbalists that both Isaac Luria and Hayyim Vital were incarnations of Messiah ben Joseph, but that the sins of their unworthy generations had caused them to pass away without effecting the great and final *tiqqun*. Whether Luria actually made the claim of messiahship for himself is somewhat doubtful; it is abundantly clear, however, that Vital and others did make it for him.[22] In the case of Vital, he seems to have had no hesitation in claiming this mantle for himself; his *Sefer ha-Ḥezyonot* is filled with dreams, predictions by others, and outright statements of his claim.

More interesting than the personal claims made for these two masters, however, are a number of conclusions about the relationship between the *ẓaddiq* and the two messiahs proceeding from the circles of Safed Kabbalah. According to Naftali Bachrach, author of *'Emeq ha-Melekh*, for example, the year 1575 (associated with the claims of Luria and Vital) indeed was the start of the messianic period. Because the Jews of that year were not deserving of redemption, however, God sends the soul of Messiah ben Joseph back into the world in every generation, in the form of a single *ẓaddiq*, and "if his generation is worthy, he will redeem Israel." In other words, *any ẓaddiq ha-dor* may in fact reveal himself to be messiah; there is no difference between the 'bearer of the messianic soul' and messiah himself except the quality of the generation in which he lives! The *ẓaddiq ha-dor* is indeed messiah, and if his generation is deserving, he may reveal himself as such. Sources emanating from Safed further portray the messiah, in a description intended to fit the figures of Luria and Vital, as

> 'a man of pain and one who has known illness' (Is. 53:5). I have received from my master [Vital] this interpretation of the verse: the redeemer of Israel will be distinguishable by two signs, pain and illness. 'A man of pain' means that he should be one who suffers always, and he should also be one 'who has known illness' constantly in his life.

It would be hard to imagine a description more like those of Nahman, which we quoted in the preceding chapter! While it is somewhat unlikely that Nahman had read the rather obscure work in which this passage is found, the ongoing tradition of the suffering attributed to messiah, stretching through the history of Judaism from Deutero-Isaiah down to Sabbatai Sevi, surely had a great effect upon him. The image of the suffering messiah, based on the verses in Isaiah, is found in Nahman's writings, an image that seems remarkably like the descriptions of Nahman himself.[23]

The specific claim that Nahman is Messiah ben Joseph has not generally been noted by scholars who have studied the literature of Bratslav. For this reason, the evidence for such a reading of the sources should be presented in full. Of course we could hardly expect either Nahman or Nathan to have the audacity of Hayyim Vital in this matter; the leaders of Hasidism, still aware of the calamities associated with messianic claims, would hardly have tolerated such openness. The fact that the point is made, albeit esoterically, in the sources, is in itself surprising in this climate.

The documentation for the belief that Nahman saw himself as Messiah ben Joseph is as follows:

1. The associations of messiah, Joseph, *ẓaddiq*, and sexual purity in *Liqquṭim* 2, as described above. Though the figure of Messiah ben Joseph stands in the background of this teaching, the evidence here in itself is not conclusive.

2. *Liqquṭim* 16, also quoted above, speaks of the two messiahs contained in the single *ẓaddiq*. The fact that Nathan, in commenting on this teaching, quotes Nahman as referring to a certain *ẓaddiq* whose spirit comprises both messianic figures, rather clearly associates Nahman with Messiah ben Joseph as well as Messiah ben David. The fact that we are told that this teaching has been censored, and that it aroused great agitation when it was revealed, tends to increase our suspicions.

3. It will be recalled that Nahman announced upon entering Zlotopolye that he had come there to perform a *tiqqun* for the sin of Jeroboam ben Nebat. Jeroboam's sin was that of idolatry, and we were hard-pressed to

understand why Nahman found that particular sin so rampant in Zlotopolye, or why he used that rather obscure reference, rather than referring to idolatry in a more direct and simple way. The figure of Jeroboam also appears elsewhere in Nahman's writings, as a symbol of the great unbeliever.[24] Why should Jeroboam, who is not a particularly significant figure in later Jewish mythology, have such importance for Nahman? The answer to this puzzle lies in a Kabbalistic association of Jeroboam with the Josephite Messiah, an association fairly widespread in the Kabbalistic literature of the seventeenth and eighteenth centuries. This association figures prominently in the closing chapter of *Megalleh 'Amuqot* by Nathan Shapira of Cracow,[25] where it is stated specifically that the sin of Jeroboam can be repaired by none other than Messiah ben Joseph, who will emerge from among his descendants. Because Jeroboam, the first ruler of the Northern Kingdom, was the leader of the tribe of Joseph, only the messiah whose roots are in that patrimony can set aright that wrong. We have had occasion elsewhere to show that Nahman had read the *Megalleh 'Amuqot*, and that this work is one of the major sources for the idea of *ẓaddiq ha-dor*. In describing his mission in Zlotopolye as that of providing a *tiqqun* for the sin of Jeroboam, Nahman was making a direct, if esoteric, reference to a messianic claim.

4. The following passage, based on that same chapter in *Megalleh 'Amuqot*, is found in one of the later collections of Bratslav literature:

> All of the elect ones in recent generations, including Luria, the BeSHT, and Nahman, come from the 'side' of Messiah ben Joseph. The very need for this messiah stems from the deaths of the *ẓaddiqim*. The *ẓaddiqim* are greater in their deaths than in their lives; even in the Exodus from Egypt, Moses had to take the bones of Joseph with him, and was thus bound to him.[26]

The obscure reference to the deaths of the *ẓaddiqim* here seems to point to the very idea we quoted from the *'Emeq ha-Melekh:* it is only because the previous *ẓaddiqey ha-dor* died without completing their task of redemption that Messiah ben Joseph has yet to come. Had the time been right, any of those listed could have revealed himself as the redeemer. The last line of this passage is of great interest. The Biblical Joseph was a prior, perhaps the first, incarnation of Messiah ben Joseph. Moses, who prefigures Messiah ben David, has to take Joseph's bones with him in order to bring about the redemption. The relationship of Joseph to Moses is thus a prototype of the relationship between the two messiahs; Ben David's coming requires the deaths of Nahman and the others, all of whom here are seen to be participants in the Josephite Messiah's soul. This text was of course written after Nahman's death, and seeks to account for the delay in Ben David's arrival.

5. A later passage in that same volume makes the point completely explicit and leaves no further need for interpretation. That passage com-

ments first on Nahman's statement concerning the "certain *ẓaddiq*" who contained both messiahs:

> It appears clearly from his holy words [preserved] orally that these words referred to our master himself. Even though the soul of ben David was also in him, *he was primarily from the side of Messiah ben Joseph.* Even though the ARI and various other singular figures in their generations were derived from Messiah ben Joseph, in him [Nahman alone] were fulfilled Scripture's words: 'Many daughters have done valiantly, but you have risen above them all' (Prov.31:)

Immediately following this unequivocal explanation is a further comment on the matter of Moses and the bones of Joseph:

> It may be further understood by bringing together certain words of Rabbi Nathan that like the changes mentioned above . . . [the difference between the redemptions from Egypt, Babylonia, and that of the future] so too is there a change in Israel's relationship to the bones of Joseph. In the first redemption this relation was marked by the taking of his bones. But now in each generation thousands of Jewish souls may merit to be bound to him by worshiping at that place where his bones are buried. This is what our master promised us is his great promise to all who would come to his holy grave. This too is an essential part of the 'beginning of redemption.'[27]

These passages are both so clear as to need little comment. To the later Bratslav community, at least by the latter part of the nineteenth century, it was completely accepted that Nahman had been Messiah ben Joseph. Others before him may have possessed that soul, but he had "risen above them all"; worshiping at his grave was worshiping at the burial-place of Joseph, and would surely help to bring about the final redemption. This belief of the later community was based on its understanding of Nahman's own teachings, and we have not the slightest reason to believe in this case that their reading was inaccurate.

6. Although Nahman's *Megillat Setarim* remains inaccessible to the scholarly world, its existence in manuscript form was disclosed by Nathan Zevi Koenig, a leading Bratslav *ḥasid*, as recently as 1969. Respecting the traditional ban, which forbids the publishing of the text itself, he does quote a highly revealing statement by Abraham Hazan, the son of one of Nathan's leading disciples and himself leader of the Jerusalem *ḥasidim* at the turn of this century. In conjunction with *Megillat Setarim*, Koenig quotes Abraham Hazan as saying:

> The matter of Messiah ben Joseph. He [Nahman?] said that certain things will have to happen to Messiah ben David, and he will have need of the merits of those *ẓaddiqim* who have died before him. And Messiah ben Joseph will also die beforehand. And our master said *etc.* that he was completely pure in guarding the covenant, until he was able to reach the highest rungs and see how far this damage reaches. He wanted to negate this com-

pletely, but one cannot change nature *etc.* The aspect of Joseph, guarding the covenant, *etc.* And messiah *etc.* and will reveal the truth in the world. Amen, speedily in our days.[28]

Though the censor, author of those omnipresent 'et ceteras,' has obliterated a good bit of this passage, its meaning remains quite clear, particularly in the light of *Liqquṭim* 2 and certain other passages we have seen. Messiah ben Joseph is associated with the Biblical Joseph, the symbol of sexual purity. Nahman, in his struggles to completely obliterate his own sex drives, is identified with Joseph the *Ẓaddiq*. The fact that Nahman equals Joseph equals Messiah ben Joseph cannot now be made public; when Messiah *ben David* comes, however, he "will reveal the truth in the world," the truth that Nahman was Messiah ben Joseph.[29]

7. The climax of the messianic activity that gripped Bratslav took place, as we shall see, during the years 5565 and 5566 A.M. (1804–06). Toward the end of 5566, this period of messianic agitation came to a rather abrupt end. While there were certain events in Nahman's personal life that may account both for the upsurge and the waning of the eschatological fever, the passing of that year itself may be of great significance. The year (5)566 is nothing other than the numerical equivalent of the Hebrew words Messiah ben Joseph! While this equivalence is not mentioned anywhere in the published Bratslav sources, it is more than likely that it was central to the esoteric teachings distributed during that year, and afterwards burned. It seems inconceivable that Nahman, who is so concerned with the motif of Messiah ben Joseph, and whose works are so filled with numerological calculations, should not have noticed this fact.[30]

Some of the evidence presented here is admittedly circumstantial. Perhaps only Nahman's stated intention to rectify the sin of Jeroboam[31] may be most strictly called an unqualified statement on his own part of messianic intent. But together with this single statement, the various bits of circumstantial evidence, including the clearly expressed later beliefs of his followers, combine to point in this direction. Why all the censorship around this matter, both on the part of Nathan and of Nahman himself, if not to hide some "dangerous" claim lying at the heart of the matter? The assertion that Nahman is *ẓaddiq ha-dor*, said openly countless times in his own writings, could hardly be the source for such agitated concern. Was it mere coincidence that Nahman had his disciples disseminate secret teachings in the midst of great messianic fervor in the year that added up to "Messiah ben Joseph" and that his messianism sputtered to a close as that year ended? The picture that emerges from these sources is one of a growing messianic self-consciousness in Nahman, beginning with the move to Zlotopolye and climaxing in 1806, the year in which Nahman hoped his role as the Josephite Messiah would come to be known to the world. Throughout the period when he was publicly proclaiming himself to be *ẓaddiq ha-dor*, Nahman was entertaining the hidden hope that his generation would be found worthy, and that he would be *the ẓaddiq ha-dor* to bring about the End.

One might at this point ask what difference it makes whether or not Nahman thought of himself as Messiah ben Joseph. Is it not quite clear that he had openly claimed that role in fact, if not in title? The last of the great redeemers, he who makes the final preparations for the advent of Messiah ben David, is in fact Messiah ben Joseph, whether he chooses to claim that title or not. But to ask this question is to miss the point. Within the symbolic universe Nahman inhabited, a claim to the *title* of Messiah ben Joseph was vastly more radical than any assertion that one prepares the way for messiah's coming. The most exaggerated claims for the centrality of the *ẓaddiq* were quite acceptable within the particular orthodoxy characteristic of Hasidism; while *mitnaggedim* might scoff, *ḥasidim* would have little difficulty in appreciating a *ẓaddiq's* claim that he could redeem the souls of his disciples. A claim of messiahship, on the other hand, even that of ben Joseph, was an entirely different matter. Had this claim become public knowledge, Nahman's name would have become anathema to *ḥasid* (outside his own community of followers) and *mitnagged* alike. The painful memories of Sabbatianism and Frankism were by no means dead in early nineteenth-century Poland; to evoke the symbol of messiah on one's own behalf would have been unthinkable blasphemy to most of the Hasidic masters. No wonder that Nahman took care in his early years to keep all the handwritten copies of his teachings safe from the probing eyes of any outsider. Even when he did print the teachings, he was careful to delete some of the most sensitive passages. A learned and perceptive reader might easily have seen between the lines, and brought untold wrath down upon the heads of Nahman and his disciples.

The preeminence of the talk about Messiah ben Joseph in Nahman and in the later Bratslav sources surely does not exclude an aspect of Nahman which is also related to the final redeemer, the messiah of the House of David. He spoke, we will recall, of a *ẓaddiq* who included within him elements of *both* messianic figures; it was from the Davidic line that both of Nahman's parents' families claimed descent, a claim which surely had some influence on his own messianic dreams. By pointing to himself as Messiah ben Joseph, Nahman did not mean to exclude himself from a role in the final act of the redemptive drama as well. True, that messiah must die before the son of David may arrive. But now there enters into the Bratslav tradition a new element, one not ordinarily associated with the Josephite messiah tradition: the hope of his *return* from death. The writings of both Nathan and the later Bratslav leaders point to this anticipated return any number of times. Particularly in their interpretations of the master's highly esoteric *Tales*, as Piekarz has shown, do these hints show through. At times the relationship of this return from death to the final redemption is perhaps peripheral: Nahman has to come back to tell a tale he never got a chance to tell in his lifetime, or the like. Such a prediction in itself is not totally strange in a world where metempsychosis is the norm. But in other places, both in Nathan's *Liqquṭey Halakhot* and in the writings of his successors, there is no indication of the slightest doubt that it is to claim the final redeemer's mantle that Nahman is to return to earth.[32]

Given the alleged Davidic descent of his family, as well as his claim to possess the soul Messiah ben David would bear in the future, we might ask why Nahman seemed to prefer the Messiah ben Joseph title for himself, at least in his present incarnation. We understand why later disciples would ascribe that role to him; he had indeed died in the course of the redemptive struggle, exactly as that figure was supposed to do. But why should Nahman himself have gone that way? In the heat of his messianic fervor he might have claimed, as had the Sabbatians, that the Josephite messiah had already died unnoticed some time earlier, and that therefore the road was already prepared for the Great Event itself.

Even at his most grandiloquent, in the moment when he dared to put forth his messianic fantasies, Nahman remained his own torn, ambivalent self. As we have said, the associations of Messiah ben Joseph with suffering and martyrdom undoubtedly seemed appropriate to him. But more than that, one discovers by a close reading that the legacy of Messiah ben Joseph's soul, unlike that of David, is a morally ambiguous one. The soul of the Davidic messiah, according to Lurianic sources, came through Moses and David; its first appearance in the world had been in Adam's son, Abel. It had then been the soul of those *ẓaddiqim* whom we have had occasion to mention elsewhere. There is no "blemish" to be found in this record. But Messiah ben Joseph's soul had formerly been that of *Cain,* the original sinner and object of divine curse. True, it had then been incarnate in Joseph the *ẓaddiq*—but it had also been the soul of none other than Jeroboam, the first Josephite king, one whom God had hoped to make into that messiah, but who had turned out to be a sinner and idolator of the worst sort. Messiah ben Joseph comes to atone for Jeroboam's sins not only because he is a descendant of that king, but because he has *been* Jeroboam himself. Jeroboam, described elsewhere by Nahman himself both as idolator and as the father of all heretics or doubters, and now returned in the person of redeemer, is precisely the kind of figure with whom Nahman can identify. Here his own doubts and burdens of guilt are explained, while at the same time his vindication is clearly to be seen. He who had depicted himself as both the great tree and the one who was rotting in hell now makes the final claim for himself as suffering redeemer. What more appropriate rubric for such a claim on Nahman's part than that of this messiah, Joseph the righteous and

Jeroboam the sinner all in one? How perceptive, perhaps beyond its own ability to articulate, was the later Bratslav tradition that said "he was primarily from the side of Messiah ben Joseph"![33]

Further examination of most of Nahman's teachings from the years 1803 and 1804 would show that they are filled with semi-veiled references to his emerging messianic mission. But it was only on Rosh Hashanah of 5565 (September, 1804) that these emerging lines were drawn together into what must be seen as one of Nahman's most significant teachings, in which he presents a clearly drawn step-by-step *plan* of action to bring about the final redemption. It is hard to think of any other instance in all of later Jewish literature (before Zionism) of such a clear blueprint for the bringing on of the millennium as there is in the twentieth teaching of *Liqquṭey MoHaRaN*. While the battle is to be fought strictly within the realm of the spirit, as before, the political implications of Nahman's scheme are now quite clear: he is calling for nothing less than the liberation of the Jewish people through the (forced?) cooperation of its Russian oppressors and the return of Israel to the Holy Land. Because this teaching is so revolutionary in its implications and has not generally been recognized as such, we shall focus a good deal of attention on it. Later tradition records that Nathan felt "thunder and lightning in his mind" as Nahman spoke this teaching, a clear indication that the disciple recognized it as a unique event.[34]

Uniquely among Nahman's teachings, *Liqquṭim* 20 is offered as a commentary on a dream or a vision he had. Both dream and teaching are expressed in terms of a highly complex personal symbolism, a symbolism for which the reader is asked to have an extra measure of patience, as we seek to expound it. We begin with the text of the dream/vision:

> This is what he told in early summer of 1804. He said:
>
> I shall tell you what I saw, and you tell it to your children. There was a man lying on the ground, and about him people sat around in a circle. Outside that circle was another circle, then another, and yet several more. Some other people were standing about, in no particular order, outside the outermost circle.
>
> The one seated (he was leaning on his side) in the center was moving his lips, and all those in the circles moved their lips after him. Then I saw that he was gone, and everyone's lips had stopped moving. I asked what had happened, and they told me that he had grown cold and died. When he had stopped speaking, they all stopped.
>
> Then they al' began to run, and I ran after them. I saw two very beautiful palaces, and in them stood two officials. Everybody ran up to these two and began to argue with them, saying: 'Why do you lead us astray?' They wanted to kill them, and the two officials fled outside. I saw them and they seemed good to me, so I ran after them.

In the distance I saw a beautiful tent. Someone from there shouted to the officials: 'Go back! Collect all the merits which you have and take them to the candle which is suspended there: in that way you will accomplish all that you need to do.' They went back and took their merits—there were bundles of merits—and ran to the candle. I ran after them and I saw a burning candle suspended in the air. The officials came and threw their merits onto the candle. Sparks came out of the candle and entered their mouths.

Then the candle turned into a river, and they all drank of its waters. Beings were created inside them; as they opened their mouths to speak, these beings—which I saw as they ran back and forth, were neither man nor beast—came out of them.

They then decided to go back to their place. But they said: 'How shall we be able to go back?' One of them answered: 'Let us send someone to him who stands there with the sword that reaches from heaven to earth.' They said: 'Whom shall we send?' And they decided to send those newly-created beings. I ran after them, and I saw the frightening one who reached from earth to heaven, as did his sword. The sword had several blades; one was for death, one for poverty, another for illness, and still others for other forms of punishment. They began to plead: 'It is so long that we have suffered from you. Now help us, and bring us back to our place.' (He said: 'I cannot help you.') They pleaded: 'Give us the blade of death and we shall kill them.' But he was not willing. They then asked for some other blade, but he was not willing to give them any. They went back.

Meanwhile, a command was issued to execute the officials, and they were decapitated.

Then the whole thing began again: there was someone lying on the ground, people about him in circles, running to the officials, and all the rest. But this time I saw that the officials did not throw their merits into the candle. They rather took their merits with them, walked up to the candle, and began to plead before it in broken-hearted supplication. As sparks from the candle entered their mouths, they once again began to plead. The candle became a river, the creatures emerged, and so forth.

They said to me: 'These will live. The former ones were condemned to death because they threw their merits into the candle, and did not supplicate, as these did.'

I did not understand the meaning of this thing. They said to me: 'Go into that room and you will be told the meaning.' As I entered the room, I saw an old man, and I asked him about it. He took his beard in his hand and said: 'This is my beard, and that is the meaning of the thing.' I said to him: 'I still don't understand.' He told me to go into another room, and there I would find the meaning. As I entered that room I saw that it was of endless length and endless breadth, and completely filled with writings. Any place I opened any one of them, I found another comment on the meaning of this thing.

[Nathan adds:]
I heard all of this directly from his holy mouth. He said that all of his teachings contain hidden references to this event, and that his teaching in *Liqquṭim* 20, which begins: 'Nine *tiqqunim*' is wholly a commentary on this.[35]

Before we turn to that teaching, where much of this fantastic web of symbols is explicated, we may point out a few of the more obvious associations. The figure at the center, given Nahman's association of *ẓaddiq* and center, is most probably the *ẓaddiq* himself. "A beautiful tent," from which a voice emerges, would seem to be the Tent of Meeting; the strange beings which "ran back and forth" seem to be somehow linked with the beasts of the *Merkavah*. The tall, frightening figure with the many-sided sword is surely some kind of demonic character, based upon the figures of the Cherubim with their flaming swords who block off the way to Eden after Adam is expelled. All such identifications, however, are tentative and inconclusive, until we have a better idea of the meaning of this vision as a whole. For a further understanding of the vision, we turn to the teaching Nahman himself has characterized as a commentary on it:

NINE PRECIOUS *TIQQUNIM* HAVE BEEN GIVEN TO THE BEARD . . .[36]

Know that there is a soul in the world through which all interpretations of the Torah are revealed. That soul is burdened with suffering, subsisting on bread and salt, and drinking measured bits of water, for such is the way of Torah. All interpreters of Torah receive [their words] from this soul. All the words of this soul are as hot as burning coals, for it is impossible to draw forth words of Torah except from one whose words are like burning coals, as Scripture says: 'Are not my words like fire?' (Jer. 23:29). And when this soul falls from that rung, and its words become cold, it dies. When it dies, the interpretations that had come through it also disappear. Then all the interpreters are unable to find any meaning in the Torah, and this gives rise to the controversies that come about between the *ẓaddiqim*. Controversy exists in the world primarily because of a lack of proper interpretation of the Torah, as such an interpretation would have provided an answer to silence all the controversies and objections.

This is the meaning of 'the Wilderness of Ẓin' (Num. 20:1), referring to the words which have grown cold [*Ẓin* equals *ẓanan*, 'to grow cold']. That is where Miriam died, for Miriam represents that soul which has suffered the bitterness [Miriam equals *merirut*, 'bitterness'] of slavery for the sake of Torah. Only then did 'the people quarrel with Moses' (*ibid.*, vs. 2–3), as this [death] gave rise to controversy. Interpreters of the Torah are called teachers *[morim]* because they receive from that soul which is called Miriam. . . .

We may interrupt Nahman's discourse at this point, to note a number of associations in the vision that are now better understood. The person at the center is indeed the *ẓaddiq ha-dor*, the channel through which all his contemporaries receive their Torah. They are able to move their lips only when he does, as their interpretive powers flow only from him. That figure's "growing cold" probably refers to Nahman's own periodic states of "knowing nothing," when the flow of his Torah ceases; these periods are a kind of "death" within life. Nahman's soul is here identified with Miriam, for whose sake, according to the rabbis,[37] a miraculously portable well accompanied Israel through their wanderings in the desert. There is an unspoken play on words here, involving the rabbinic statement, "When Miriam died, the well disappeared." The Hebrew word for well *(be'er)* can also have the meaning of 'interpretation'; the phrase would then come to mean, "When the soul that suffers bitterness dies, interpretations cease." The *ẓaddiq* is the wellspring of interpretation.

Nahman continues:

> He who wants to interpret the Torah has to begin by drawing unto himself words as hot as burning coals. Speech comes out of the upper heart, which Scripture calls 'rock of my heart' (Ps. 73:26). The interpreter [first] has to pour out his words to God in prayer, seeking to arouse His mercies, so that the heart will open. Speech then flows from the heart, and interpretation of the Torah flows from that speech. This heart is called 'rock' *[sela']*, and speech comes from it, as has been said: 'a word for a *sela'*[38]. . . As the heart's compassion is aroused it gives forth blazing words, as Scripture says: 'My heart blazes within me; the fire of my words burns on my tongue' (Ps. 39:3). On this heart are inscribed all the interpretations of the Torah, as in: 'Write them upon the tablet of your heart' (Prov. 3:3). And so anyone who seeks to bring forth an interpretation must get it from this heart, by prayer and supplication. It is for this reason that teachers of Torah, before they begin their expositions, first have to pour out their prayers to God, in order that the heart be aroused to pour forth words like blazing coals. Only afterwards may they begin to teach, for the rock has been opened and its waters have begun to flow.
>
> But there is a difference between those interpretations which a man comes upon when he is alone and those which he explicates in public. For when one preaches publicly, he first binds his soul to those of his audience, and then pours out his prayer to God. And surely 'the great God will not reject this prayer' (Job 36:5). The prayer of a lone individual may, however, be rejected. This is the meaning of 'Speak to the rock before their eyes' (Num. 20:8). Your prayer must take place when the people are already assembled, as it says [earlier]: 'Assemble the people' *(ibid.)*.

The identity of the two officials in Nahman's vision is now clear to us: they are Moses and Aaron, and the entire passage is revealed as a commentary on Numbers 20, the story of the Waters of Meribah. The two officials' act of throwing their merits into the candle is the sin of Moses and Aaron in striking the rock, for which they, like the officials in the dream, must die. Because of their sin, they also fail to lead those about them to "go back to their place," a reference to the fact that Moses and Aaron, because of this sin, were not able to lead Israel into the Promised Land. We shall have more to say below of this symbolic view of Moses and Aaron at Meribah. While the appearance in the vision of "that frightening one who reaches from earth to heaven" and his sword had led us to believe that the theme was the return to Eden, it is now clear that the two great motifs of redemption, the return to Eden and the restoration of Israel to the Holy Land, have come together through the various symbols here, a confluence which is in no way surprising. The teaching continues:

> This is the difference between learning from a book and hearing the teaching personally from a sage. He who hears from the sage directly binds his soul to that of the sage in this prior prayer . . . and the wickedness which lies inside each of those people who hears the teaching is vanquished by the goodness which dwells within the sage. As their wickedness is vanquished, so are those enemies, the *qelipot*, which surround the upper heart. Thus Scripture refers to the heart by saying: 'I have placed Jerusalem in the midst of the nations' (Ezek. 5:5), and she is the heart, as in 'Speak unto the heart of Jerusalem' (Is. 40:2).
>
> This is the staff, of which God said to Moses, 'Take your staff and assemble the people' (Num. 20:8). The staff is the authority and power which the *ẓaddiq* has created by his worship, through which the enemies, both above and below, are vanquished. . . .

The *ẓaddiq* who prays before he begins to teach (the figure at the center of the circle in the vision) has a threefold purpose in mind. He seeks to join his prayer to that of the community, ensuring that God will not reject his plea. He also hopes to uplift his hearers by his words, and vanquish the evil that lies within them. But this act of conquering evil has yet another meaning, which brings it close to the area of sympathetic magic: the *ẓaddiq* is the heart of the lower world; as he vanquishes the evil in those who surround him, he also vanquishes the evil forces that surround the upper heart, his counterpart in the world above. This was also the task of Moses and Aaron in assembling the people, a task in which they did not succeed.

> When he prays before teaching, he has to pray in supplication, begging of God that He give him a free-will gift, and not making the matter dependent upon his own merits. Even though the 'staff of power' (Ps. 110:2) that comes from his own devotion has been aroused, this staff does not exist to be used pridefully, but only to vanquish evil from those who are assembled. . . .
>
> This was the mistake of Moses . . . he used his staff not for the community, but used it in his prayer . . . he 'lifted up' his prayer [showing pride before

> God], and did not bind himself with the community. 'He struck the rock twice with his staff' (Num. 20:11) . . . he struck the upper heart, as one taking something by the force of his own power . . . and [therefore] he died before his time. . . .

The authority of Moses, here fully identified with that of the *ẓaddiq*, is to be used to rectify the sins of those around him. When turning to God, however, the only proper attitude is that of Nahman, that of supplication with a broken heart. In terms of the vision, Nahman now knows the mistake of the officials. *The vision repeats itself, meaning that the opportunity of Moses is given to each later bearer of the Mosaic soul. Now Nahman can correct Moses' error, supplicating the candle (equals "rock" equals "upper heart") rather than forcing it,* and thus bringing about the desired result. This result, while not stated in the vision, is clear in the teaching, which notes that the account of the Waters of Meribah is immediately followed in the Biblical text by: "Moses sent messengers [*mal'akhim* also can mean 'angels'] from Kadesh [lit.: "from the holy"] to the king of Edom, [saying]: Thus says your brother Israel: You know of all the suffering which we have undergone . . . We called out to the Lord and He heard our voice and sent an angel, bringing us out of Egypt . . . Let us pass through your land . . ." (Num. 20:14–17). Edom, the conventional symbol for Christendom, is the force standing in the way of Israel's return to the Holy Land. The teaching goes on to make this clear:

> By virtue of the Torah which one draws forth, one merits the land of Israel, as Scripture says: 'He gave them the inheritance of the nations' (Ps. 105:44). But the land of Israel is one of those things that is attained only through suffering. These sufferings stem chiefly from those obstacles caused by the wicked, who speak ill of the Land. First one has to vanquish these wicked ones, punishing them by the sword, and only then can one get to the Land of Israel.
>
> But the power to punish these wicked ones can only be obtained from the hands of Edom, for this is his power, as is written: 'You shall live by your sword' (Gen. 27:40), and he derives his power from the planet Mars.[39]
>
> Know, however, that through the spiritual powers generated by the letters of the Torah which one has brought forth, powers which are themselves angels, one can obtain from Edom the power to put the wicked to the sword. . . .
>
> But sometimes the situation is reversed. Sometimes there is so little holiness to be found that these angels created by the words of Torah are weak, and can only humble or frighten the wicked, but not destroy them. And sometimes even humbling them is beyond the angels' power. There is so little holiness that they have the strength only to arouse the power of the nations against those who speak ill of the Land [but not to take that power themselves]. This is the situation in our present exile, where we ourselves do not

have the power to punish the wicked except through [Edom's] laws . . . receiving from them the power to pursue the wicked. . . .

This is the meaning of NINE PRECIOUS *TIQQUNIM* HAVE BEEN GIVEN TO THE ELDER. To the elder who sits and teaches, these nine qualities have been given:

1. 'Take the staff.'
2. 'Assemble the people' to vanquish their wickedness.
3. 'Speak to the rock' in supplication.
4. Do this 'before their eyes' and be joined to them.
5. Draw forth words of fire.
6. Draw forth Torah.
7. The creating of angels.
8. Receiving the power from Edom to overcome our enemies.
9. Going to the Land of Israel.

These are the nine *tiqqunim* which have been given to the elder who teaches.

In the last part of this teaching, not reproduced here, all the strands of associations in the teaching are woven together to form a verse-by-verse commentary on Moses' request of the King of Edom. The picture presented here is now quite complete. Nahman has presented himself as the new Moses, marshaling the spiritual forces that are at the *ẓaddiq's* command, to bring about the redemption. The true focus of his entire career is here laid out before us. The gathering together of his band of followers, his teachings, and his heartfelt prayers are all part of a larger plan, one that will allow Israel to pass through the Kingdom of Edom (read: Russia) to return to the Holy Land. As Israel does not have the power in the exile to take command of Edom by force, Nahman seems to have in mind an attempt to persuade the Russian government to allow the rabbis and *ẓaddiqim* to share in its powers. They are to be won over by the strength of Israel's exemplary piety, which will motivate them to allow the pious to punish the "wicked" (probably the *maskilim*)[40], thus vanquishing the spiritual foe and allowing for the return to Ereẓ Israel. It is perhaps fortunate that Nahman's plan was never put to the test; the Western-looking government of Alexander I would hardly have chosen to share its powers with the leaders of Hasidism, which was viewed as the great reactionary obstacle to the improvement of the Jews' position. Politically Nahman remained utterly naïve. He lived wholly within his own mythic universe, and saw the drama of redemption as one to be played out in the world of spiritual struggle between the classic warring forces of good and evil, Israel and the nations. Even though the specific events, both political and personal, of his own lifetime may have contributed to his messianic consciousness, the real plane of action for him was still the timeless world of mythical and spiritual confrontation.

We are now able to trace certain stages within the development of Nahman's strivings for redemption. While there was not yet any messianic intent involved in his 1798 journey to Erez Israel, it was shortly after his return from that journey that this new sense of his own role began to develop. Undoubtedly it was in part the inspiration of the journey that began to move him in this direction. When he moved to Zlotopolye in the summer of 1800, he already had begun to think of himself as Messiah ben Joseph. Publicly proclaiming himself as *ẓaddiq ha-dor,* he knew within himself (as witnessed by his comments on seeking a *tiqqun* for the sin of Jeroboam) that the *ẓaddiq ha-dor* could in fact be messiah if his generation would allow it. He was at this point afraid to reveal his sense of messianic mission, even to his own disciples, except in veiled terms. Having seen the tremendous storm caused by his challenge to the Zeide even without the issue of a messianic claim, he undoubtedly thought it better to keep this belief completely quiet. In Zlotopolye the public emphasis was upon the single true *ẓaddiq* as the center of all things, absolving the sins of his disciples as they came to confess before him, and building the image of the *ẓaddiq's* soul as that of Moses and messiah.

On his arrival in Bratslav, as we have seen, he became fascinated with *place,* and it was the image of uplifting the gentiles' lands to the spiritual level of Erez Israel that took primacy in his consciousness. This fascination with Bratslav, we should add, by no means indicates an abandonment of his messianic strivings. Some two years later, however, Nahman's messianic dreams had gone beyond the conversion of Bratslav into a new spiritual center. As his messianic pronouncements became more frequent and open, it became clear to him that only a return to the *real* Land of Israel could satisfy his mission. This is proclaimed in the teaching we have just expounded, which dates from exactly two years after his arrival in Bratslav. As though to dispel any doubts as to what was meant by this teaching, Nathan records:

> After he presented the teaching on the *Nine Tiqqunim* . . . during the discussion I asked him: 'What do you mean when you refer to Erez Israel as the great climax of victory in the battle?' He was harsh with me and said: 'I really mean the Land of Israel, with those very buildings and houses!'[41]

While the geographical focus of Nahman's attention shifted between 1802 and 1804 from Bratslav to the Land of Israel, another *galut*-centered motif in Nahman's struggle for *tiqqun* did not change. Throughout Nahman's teachings, beginning in 1803, we find a strong current of interest in the *conversion* of gentiles to Judaism as a necessary prerequisite for the advent of messiah. While this idea in itself is not unusual, the emphasis placed here on the desirability of such conversions is completely unique within Hasidism. Rabbinic Judaism had always contained a certain degree of ambivalence toward converts. While the rabbis' suspiciousness of converts' motives and sincerity had caused them to say, "Proselytes are as bad to Israel as a sore on the skin," they had also formulated the belief that "Israel went into exile only so that they should gain converts." Generally speaking, Jews in Eastern Europe who were confronted by a potential convert were more frightened by the prospects of their neighbors' wrath than they were joyous that a new soul had discovered the truth of Judaism. Such conversions, which did occasionally take place in early nineteenth-century Russia, especially from within the ranks of the Subbotnik sectarians, aroused little elation in the Jewish community. This was not at all the case with Nahman: he was filled with joy when he heard reports of such conversions, and he saw these proselytes as individual precursors of the entire world's imminent conversion to Judaism.[42] His desire for *tiqqun* had to extend beyond the bounds of Israel; the coming redemption was to be that of all mankind, not that of Israel alone. The fact that almost all of Nahman's later tales are set outside the bounds of any particularly Jewish context may be seen as a continuation of this universal concern. In fact the central motif of several key tales is the salvation of a wicked or foolish kingdom through the *ẓaddiq*-redeemer, a motif more easily applicable to the conversion of gentile kingdoms than to wayward Jews.

Having presented a picture of the development of Nahman's messianic consciousness until the year 1804, we are now prepared to outline the events of the following two years, which represent the height of messianic activity in Bratslav. The teaching of the *Nine Tiqqunim,* with its plan of bringing the redemption, was the opening event in what may only be described as a period of intense millennarian fever, which was to climax in the dramatic happenings of summer, 1806. The significant events of that period are divisible into two groups, each of which should be described as a separate aspect of messianic activity: the sphere of penitential activity within the Bratslav community, and the publication of Nahman's teachings for a wider audience.

It was in the fall of 1804 that Nahman first asked his disciples to begin reciting the *tiqqun ḥaẓot* ("midnight vigil") prayers on a regular basis. This rite, first instituted by the medieval Kabbalists, had been widely disseminated with the spread of Lurianic Kabbalah in the sixteenth century. Among *ḥasidim* it had fallen into neglect, along with the general abandonment of Lurianic *kawwanot* in the liturgy among the *ḥasidim.* A dramatic rite of participation in the exile of the *shekhinah,* it is also to be seen as a theurgic activity aimed at restoring the *shekhinah* to its place and bringing an end to the exile. It should be remembered that Nahman had already described his own mission as that of *tiqqun ha-shekhinah;* his demand now that this rite be reinstituted among his *ḥasidim* indicates a move from theoretical discussion of this task to its real implementation in the sphere of ritual action.[43]

It was some half a year later that Nahman began promulgating the rite of *tiqqun ha-kelali,* which we have already had occasion to mention. As atonement for their sexual misdeeds, his disciples were instructed to recite ten psalms, paralleling the ten terms for praise commonly employed in the Psalter. Apparently convinced that this area of human sinfulness was a major factor in delaying the general redemption, he sought to neutralize its ill effects by the formulation of a relatively manageable rite of atonement. While reflecting Nahman's own concern about the evils of sexual sin, the *tiqqun ha-kelali* may also be seen as his attempt to free his disciples of the guilt he himself knew so well, lest it keep them (as it sometimes did him) from doing the work of redemption.[44]

In the fall of 1805, just as the year 5566 (equals Messiah ben Joseph) began, Nahman went still further in the matter of personal *tiqqunim.* Turning now to a more individualized approach to the matter of penitence, he assigned each of his close followers a certain regimen of private fasts during the new year, an act far less radical than, but somehow reminiscent of, the promulgation of a new sacred calendar in the days of Sabbatai Sevi. The setting in which this new discipline was proclaimed has been preserved for us by Nathan:

> In the year 5566 [1805/06], between Rosh Hashanah and Yom Kippur, our master one day emerged from the ritual bath and announced that it had been revealed to him from heaven how our people were to conduct themselves with regard to fasting, all the days of our lives. [He was told] how many times each of us should fast in the course of a year, as well as how and when we were to observe these fasts. After the holidays, each one of us went in to him individually, and he gave us a slip of paper telling us when we were to fast. He had a list in front of him, written in his own holy hand, which we were not permitted to see. When I went in to receive my own list of fasts, I saw him sitting at the table with that paper, but I don't know what was written on it. He sat there for a long while, poring over his list, and it took him considerable effort before he could tell me on which days I was to fast. When he did reveal them to me, he had me copy them down, and warned me to take special care not to forget them, and not to lose my paper on which they were recorded. . . . We understood from his words that these fasts were very great and precious practices; happy are we who merited to receive them![45]

This three-stage succession of new devotional practices (*tiqqun ḥaẓot, tiqqun ha-kelali,* and private fast days), all instituted within the course of a single year, shows a remarkably intense climate of preparation for the messianic event. As Scholem has indicated with regard to Sabbatianism, an upsurge of penitential rites was one way in which Jews indicated their belief that redemption was at hand.[46] As was the case in much of early Sabbatianism, there was nothing in these rites themselves that was contrary to the law, or even in conflict with the norms of accepted pietistic behavior. At the same time, one cannot but wonder whether this rapid succession of new penitential practices, if indeed they were known of beyond the immediate Bratslav community, did not arouse some suspicion. Might this have been the time at which the Zeide's and Barukh's personal enmities toward Nahman grew into an attitude of suspicion on the part of the Hasidic camp as a whole? It seems likely that Nathan's need to deny certain unstated things of which Nahman was accused, things "which never entered his mind," stems from this period, and from a, perhaps vague, awareness on the part of outsiders that the excitement brewing in Bratslav had a familiarly dangerous edge to it.[47]

Interwoven with these acts of purification was the greatly heightened activity of Nahman and his disciples in collecting, editing, and disseminating Nahman's teachings. The teachings, which had been kept secret until this point, were recorded only in various notes written as each teaching had been presented. Now Nathan was to edit these notes, some in the master's hand and some in his own, into a single volume. This was completed, with great effort, shortly before Shavu'ot of 1805. The manuscript volume was given to a binder in Bratslav, but Nahman took great care that Nathan or another member of the inner circle constantly keep watch over the binder, lest he should show the teachings to anyone from outside the immediate community.

At the same time, Nathan was also instructed to prepare an abbreviated version of the teachings, more appropriate for popular use among householders, which was to present in distilled form the practical implications of each teaching, eliminating the abstruse and complicated literary references. This volume was to serve as a practical daily guide to life for the *ḥasidim*, pointing out the ways in which Nahman's thought might be crystallized into a workable set of spiritual disciplines. Nathan published this volume in Mogilev in 1811, under the title *Qiẓẓur Liqquṭey MoHaRaN*.[48]

While the wheels of this messianic activity had already been set in motion toward the end of 1804, further impetus was surely given the program by the birth of Nahman's first son, Shlomo Ephraim, just as Nahman was entering his own thirty-third year in the spring of 1805. This child was seen as the fulfillment of all his fondest hopes; no longer was it a grandchild, the son of one of his daughters, who was to be the last redeemer, but rather Nahman's own male heir.[49] It is not coincidental that the promulgation of the *tiqqun ha-kelali* was announced only weeks after this child's birth; the presence of the newborn redeemer on the scene greatly added to the urgency of preparing the way. Shortly after Passover in 1805, Nahman made another of his mysterious journeys, this time to Shargorod (a place where he had no known disciples). While we do not know what transpired on this journey—Nathan tells us only that it was "a great and exalted wonder"[50]—it certainly had to do with this mission of redemption. Shargorod, like Kamenets-Podolsk, had once been a center of Sabbatian activity, and it is possible that this journey, like his 1798 visit to Kamenets, was meant to expunge some remnant of the Sabbatian heresy before the effecting of the final redemption.

In any case, this visit to Shargorod somehow involved a great risk. Nahman felt that some terrible danger lay in the stirring of messianic longings, a danger which could bring to himself and others bodily harm, as well as spiritual harm that might damage the cause itself. After spending about two weeks in Shargorod

> he left there suddenly, fleeing as one would flee a fire. Afterwards there were indeed some terrible conflagrations there. But he said: 'If the people of Shargorod had only known how much good I did them, *etc.* Nonetheless, all this is better than blight, God forbid.' It was understood from his words that by his visit there he had saved them from a blight.[51]

This passage, like so many others here, must also be read through the censor's "*etc.*". Perhaps Nahman had seen that the sparks of Sabbatian impurity had condemned Shargorod to undergo some terrible fate in the coming judgment, and he had sought to effect a *tiqqun* that would avoid this fate. His success, however, was only partial, as it seems from this passage that he admits responsibility for the fires that took place after his departure.

The fears that accompanied Nahman's messianic activities were also evidenced closer to home. In that same spring of 1805, one of his granddaughters became seriously ill. Nahman seems to have felt that he was responsible for her illness, though even this could not ultimately deter him from his task:

> He spoke to me at that time of the great and endless sufferings that he was undergoing. The focus of this suffering was his granddaughter, who was very ill with measles or the pox. He said that he felt each of the child's cries in his own heart, and wished that he suffered the disease in her place. He said that these are the incomprehensible ways of God. For there are, he said, ways of God that cannot be understood. He was referring to the fact that one righteous man may prosper, while another suffers, *etc.* . . . He then told of that which is found in *Shivḥey ha-ARI:* once Hayyim Vital was most insistent that Luria [the ARI] reveal a certain secret to him, and the ARI refused, on account of the danger. Vital, however, was adamant, until his master finally had to reveal that thing. The ARI himself had said, after all, that he had come into the world only to effect the *tiqqun* of that single soul, the soul of Vital. But as soon as the ARI revealed that secret, his own son became ill and died. How is it possible to understand this? He did have to reveal that secret, after all, and yet he was punished nevertheless. These are the incomprehensible ways of God.[52]

Spoken in the spring of 1805, this reference to Luria and Vital must have meant a great deal to Nahman. Here he was, about to do much more than Luria had, by publishing his teachings and making many of his secrets available to anyone. And here was his grandchild, already ill, as though to show him that punishment lay not far off. He was undoubtedly familiar with the legend of Joseph Della Reina, as well as various other accounts of the dangers that lie in store for those who try to hasten the end before its proper time. The fact that his activities continued, despite the frightening portents of the fire in Shargorod and the illness of his grandchild, shows how thoroughly convinced he was of the authenticity of his mission—at least in those moments when doubt did not cause him to falter.

It was in the early summer of 1806 that Nahman finally deemed the world ready to have a taste of his teachings. He had an extra manuscript copy made of the *Liqquṭim*, and also entrusted some fragments of his more intimate teachings, which were later burned, to two of his most trusted disciples, Yudel and Shmu'el Isaac. The two of them were to go from town to town through the Ukrainian countryside, teaching bits of the esoteric (and probably messianic) doctrine, and leaving behind them in each town a few pages of the soon-to-be-printed *Liqquṭim*. This mission, little discussed by Nathan, is assigned great significance in later Bratslav writings. Abraham Hazan tells us explicitly that the purpose of the mission was "to hasten our redemption." He also informs us that Nahman tried to enlist the support of his friend and patron Levi Yizhak in this effort. The two messengers were to stop in Berdichev and ask that *ẓaddiq* for financial help in their journey. Nahman instructed them to ask for this money as funds for "dowering a bride." As Piekarz has rightly pointed out, this, too, is a code-name for the restoration of the *shekhinah*, the "bride" of God.[53]

The messengers had apparently departed shortly before Shavu'ot of 1806, the occasion that marked the great climax of Nahman's messianic activity. On that holiday he for the first time appeared among his disciples clad in an all-white garment, a symbol of purification that could hardly be ignored. While the custom of dressing in white had been known in some prior Kabbalistic and Hasidic circles, it had not been followed by Nahman before that time, and the teaching he presented on that day made its meaning quite clear. The teaching is filled with imagery of red and white, based on the verse "If your sins be red as scarlet, they shall become white as snow" (Is. 1:18). He also made extensive references to redemption through the *ẓaddiq*, here personified by Simeon ben Yohai, and to sexual purification. The white garments Nahman wore on that day served as his announcement that the *tiqqun*, if not yet completed, had reached a significant new stage, one which now allowed for the symbolic proclamation that redemption was at hand.[54]

We may now do well to view this entire sequence of messianic events in consecutive order, which should more clearly show how they built to the single climax of this event:

September 17, 1804 (Rosh Hashanah)	The teaching of *Liqquṭim* 20, containing the plan for redemption.
Fall, 1804	Institution of *tiqqun ḥaẓot*.
Winter, 1804/05	Writing of *Qiẓẓur Liqquṭey MoHaRaN*.
Winter/spring, 1805	Editing of *Liqquṭey MoHaRaN*.
March, 1805	Birth of Shlomo Ephraim.
April/May, 1805	Journey to Shargorod.
April/May, 1805	Binding of *Liqquṭim* manuscript.
May, 1805	Institution of *tiqqun ha-kelali*.
October, 1805	Assigning of personal fast days.
May, 1806	Mission of Yudel and Shmu'el Isaac.
May 23, 1806 (Shavu'ot)	Wearing of white garments.

One further event must now be added to this list, one that marked the abrupt end of Nahman's active messianic strivings, in his own view the single most tragic event by far of his whole tragedy-filled life. Within a few weeks after that Shavu'ot at which he came out in white garments, Nahman's only son and the focus of his hopes, Shlomo Ephraim, lay dead of an unknown illness. All of Nahman's worst fears had been realized; in an attempt to bring about the end, he had managed to destroy (so he thought) the one on whom all his hopes were pinned. There was to be no immediate redemption after all; the feverish activity of master and disciples had come to nothing. This, the greatest disappointment of Nahman's life, though somewhat veiled in the sources, does come through in certain places:

> We heard from him [in August, 1806] the whole order of messiah's arrival. He said that he [messiah] had been ready to arrive within just a few more years, and he himself had known the precise year, month, and day on which he was expected. But now he certainly would not come at that time. We understood that this delay had taken place because his son Shlomo Ephraim had died. He had also told me the same thing previously, shortly after the child's death. . . .[55]

The messianic hopes of Nahman continued to flicker for a brief while. In August of 1806, during the week of Tish'a be-Av, he revealed some portion of his hidden *Megillat Setarim* to a few disciples, and spoke again of the coming of messiah. But, as can be seen from the preceding passage which describes that event, it was already clear that messiah's coming was to be delayed and was no longer the object of direct agitation. The mission of his two disciples had failed for lack of support among their hearers, many of whom were undoubtedly *ḥasidim* of Nahman's detractors.[56] The private fast days were abolished in 1808; the *tiqqun ha-kelali* survived (as it does to this day) as a matter of personal purification among the Bratslav *ḥasidim*, but its original context was forgotten. Of the practice of *tiqqun ḥaẓot* and the wearing of white garments we hear no more from the sources; these were undoubtedly quickly abandoned. Nahman did go ahead with the publication of his exoteric teachings, still believing that their dissemination had some relationship to the ultimate redemption, but that redemption was now seen as somewhere in the distant, and unknown, future.

On Yom Kippur of 1806, just after the intended year of redemption had drawn to a close, Nahman apparently made a last, desperate attempt to force the hand of heaven and bring about the redemption.

> On that Yom Kippur there was a fire here in Bratslav, during the Kol Nidre service. As the *ḥazzan* began the hymns which follow the evening service . . . we all scattered to save his house and his property, and the service was interrupted. Only after the fire was ended that night did about ten of us, including our master, gather together to complete the hymns. At the conclusion of Yom Kippur our master said that on this Yom Kippur he had wanted to effect something with God, *etc.*, and he had various claims concerning this matter . . . but the fire had confounded the thing. After his return from Lemberg [two years later] he spoke of this event, and it was understood from his words that since he had sought to do this thing on that Yom Kippur, there were great accusations against him on high, and the illness and sufferings which he still bore were due to this. And he added: 'Even though my intent was for the sake of heaven, nevertheless,' *etc.*[57]

Never again would Nahman seek to bring about the end by theurgic activity.

Nahman was deeply aware of the tragic character of his brief messianic career. He had faced a terrible test, and had suffered its consequences. He was now about to turn inward, seeking in the world of fantasy and imagination the redemption history had failed to provide. This was the origin of Nahman's *Sippurey Ma'asiyot*, the first of which was told in the midst of that tragic summer.[58] The pent-up dreams of redemption, which had first been expressed in this abortive attempt to proclaim the end, were now to find their expression in the beautiful and poignant tales Nahman was to weave during the four years of life yet remaining to him. Out of the tragedy of this summer was to emerge the new vehicle of creativity that would remain with Nahman until the end.

It was shortly after his son's death, in speaking with his disciples Nathan and Naftali, that Nahman offered one of the most profoundly personal teachings of his lifetime, one that deals with the relationship between suffering and creativity. The opening paragraphs of that teaching are particularly significant, offering Nahman's lyrical summation of his own career. Unable to force the hand of heaven and announce himself as messiah in his lifetime, he now offers himself as a sacrifice, hoping to effect by dying what he could not within life. The longing he had already expressed as a child to die a martyr's death had now catapulted into making him *the* martyr, the Ephraimite messiah who by his death alone can allow the final work of redemption to proceed.

> Know that there is a field, and in that field grow the most beautiful trees and grasses. The great beauty and grandeur of this field cannot be described; happy is the eye that has seen it.
>
> These trees and grasses are holy souls that are growing there. And there are also a certain number of naked souls which wander about outside the field, waiting and longing for redemption, so that they can return to their place. Sometimes even a great soul, upon whom other souls depend, wanders outside the field, and has great difficulty in returning. All of them are longing for the master of the field, who can concern himself with their redemption. Some souls require someone's death in order that they be redeemed, while others can be helped by acts of worship.
>
> And he who wants to gird his loins, to enter the field as its master, has to be a very strong, brave, and wise man; a very great *ẓaddiq*. One has to be a person of the highest type in order to do this; sometimes the task can only be completed by one's own death. Even this [offering of one's life] requires a very great person; there are some great ones whose deaths would not even be sufficient. Only the very greatest of men could possibly accomplish the task within his own lifetime. How much suffering and hardship pass over him! But through his own greatness he transcends it all, tending to the field and its needs. When he does succeed in bringing those souls in from the outside, it is good to pray, for then prayer too is in its proper place.
>
> This master of the field takes care of all the trees, watering them and seeing that they grow, and doing whatever else needs to be done in that field. He also must keep the trees far enough apart from one another, so that one does not crowd the other out. Sometimes you have to show great distance to one who has become too close, so that one does not deny the other.
>
> And know that these souls bear fruit when they do the will of heaven. Then the eyes of the master light up, so that he can see where he needs to see. This is the meaning of 'the field of seers' (Num. 23:14). But when they do not do the will of heaven, God forbid, his eyes grow dark, and this is the meaning of 'the field of tears,' for it is weeping that ruins one's vision. . . .[59]

Longing as ever for the ultimate transcendence of his own suffering, and here even willing to give his life for the sake of that transcendence, the master finds his noblest vision clouded by his tears.

NOTES

1. Among early Hasidic writers, it was particularly Jacob Joseph of Polonnoye who emphasized the role of the preacher or Hasidic leader (the term *ẓaddiq* does not yet appear in that sense in his works) in *uplifting* those around him and binding them to God. In Jacob Joseph's view the preacher stands as an intermediary between God and the community. While maintaining his own close bond with God, he was to simultaneously bind himself to his congregation, thus creating through his own person a link between the upper and lower worlds. The influence of the *Toledot* in this area is to be felt in Nahman's thinking, but the difference between them is crucial. The *Toledot's* preacher, in sharing his own illumination with those around him, does effect a *tiqqun* in a very general sort of way, a *tiqqun* brought about by his sharing of his own *devequt*. The individual soul of each of his hearers and the particular 'damage' it has suffered are not much taken into account. Nahman's sort of *tiqqun* is much closer to that promulgated by the original Lurianic sources: a *repair* of the particular damage sustained by a given soul, through the *ẓaddiq* who both knows that soul and has the occult power to designate effective *tiqqunim*.

2. *Ḥayyey II* 2:64.

3. *Cf.* especially such later Bratslav collections as *Meshivat Nefesh, Hishtapkhut ha-Nefesh*, etc. Most of these, including *'Ot Berit*, dealing wholly with sexual sin and atonement for it, are completely composed of selections from the writings of Nahman and Nathan. In all of these, of course, the goal is to lift the reader from sorrow and lighten his burdens, but the "realistic" descriptions of "every man's" life which they contain are most interesting.

4. *Liqquṭim* 205. The *tiqqun ha-kelali* was first published in 1821 by Nathan's son Shakhna. See *Neweh Ẓaddiqim*, p.57, which lists no fewer than fifty-four editions of the *tiqqun*, making it by far the most frequently printed work in all of Bratslav literature.

5. See Scholem, *Messianic Idea*, pp. 203*ff*. Both *devequt* and *tiqqun* are found as ideals in the Kabbalistic traditions of Safed. While *tiqqun* appears to play little role in such non-Lurianic works as De Vidas' *Reshit Ḥokhmah* or Azikri's *Sefer Ḥaredim*, in such Lurianic writings as Vital's *Sha'arey Qedushah* it is hard to separate the two goals from one another. The devotee does seek an experience that may be considered one of personal illumination, but in attaining this higher state of consciousness he is also helping to bring about *tiqqun*. On the relationship between *devequt* and *tiqqun* among the mystics of Safed, *cf.* Werblowsky's *Joseph Karo, Lawyer and Mystic*, p.52*ff*. Scholem's claim (*Major Trends*, pp. 123, 278) that Jewish mystics seldom speak in terms of actual union with the divine is much less applicable to Hasidism than it is to earlier Kabbalah. Such formulations as "one should lose oneself completely in prayer" or "prayer is an act of coupling with the *Shekhinah*," rare in the earlier literature, are commonplaces in the prayer literature of Hasidism. See Green and Holtz, *Your Word Is Fire*, where a number of such texts are translated. I. Tishby has also raised some questions on this thesis with regard to earlier Kabbalah; *cf. Mishnat ha-Zohar*, v.2, p. 287*ff*.

6. The major sources for this debate are Scholem, *Major Trends*, p.325*ff*., *Messianic Idea*, p.203*ff*.; *Dinur*, *Be-Mifneh ha-Dorot*, p.170*ff*.; Tishby in *Zion* 32 (1967) 1*ff*.; Schatz, *Ha-Ḥasidut ke-Mistiqah*, p.168*ff*.

7. There was an upsurge in messianic feeling in the wake of Napoleon's victories, particularly around the years 1812–1814. While this is hardly seen in the theoretical literature of Hasidism, a number of the tales told of Jacob Isaac of Lublin, the Yehudi of Prsyzucha, and Menahem Mendel of Rymanow do reflect a high degree of messianic expectation. See for example *'Ohaley ha-Rabbi mi-Lublin,* pt. 3, p. 1. There does not seem to be any direct connection, however, between Nahman's messianism and that of these other figures, who were centered in Poland and Galicia, and whose messianic activities took place primarily after Nahman's death.

8. Weiss had guessed at the survival of this manuscript in his article on *Megillat Setarim* in *Qiryat Sefer* 44 (1969) 279ff. [equals *Meḥqarim* p.189*ff.*]. As Chone Shmeruk noted on p. 443 of that same volume, N.Z. Koenig's recently published *Neweh Ẓaddiqim* had indeed made mention of *Megillat Setarim* as an extant work (p. 77*ff.*).

9. *Contra* Scholem in *Alexander Marx Jubilee Volume,* Hebrew Section p.461, this idea is not an original contribution of the Sabbatians. It is found quite explicitly in the Lurianic literature: *Sha'ar ha-Gilgulim,* chapter 12, ed. Przemysl 30, and *Sefer ha-Liqquṭim,* wa-etḥanan, ed. Jerusalem 105c. *Cf.* also the remarks by Tishby, *Netivey 'Emunah u-Minut,* p.176*ff.* Nahman, too, sometimes identifies the future redeemer as Moses: *cf. Liqquṭim* 7:2.

10. On R. Simeon as a redeemer-figure see Genesis Rabbah 35:2 and *Zohar* 2:9a and frequently. On Luria, see below. For another Hasidic view on this see Israel of Ruzhin in *'Eser 'Orot,* p.24. On *ẓaddiq ha-dor* as redeemer in Sabbatian sources see Scholem in *'Aley 'Ayin,* p.175. The Bratslav sources quoted here are *Ḥayyey II* 2:66 and *Yemey MaHaRNaT,* p.22.

11. *Ḥayyey* 2:2; *Ḥayyey II* 2:3. For the traditional messianic signs see *Sanhedrin* 97–98.

12. Piekarz, p.56*ff.*, Weiss in *Qiryat Sefer* 44 (1969) 279*ff.*, and Zeitlin in *'Al Gevul Sheney 'Olamot,* p.327.

13. *Liqquṭey MoHaRaN* is arranged in roughly chronological order, with some major exceptions. The third teaching of the book was said on his entry into Bratslav; the first two teachings are undated and presumably earlier. In any case, this teaching cannot be any later than 1803, when Nahman completed the cycle of teachings surrounding the Rabbah bar Hanna legends, of which this is a part. On the setting of this teaching see also *Ṭovot Zikhronot* 2. It is based on a passage in *Tiqquney Zohar* 21, ed. Margaliot 44b.

14. The association of the Biblical and Kabbalistic Joseph with the figure of Messiah ben Joseph is also found in Lurianic sources. *Cf. Sha'ar ha-Gilgulim* chapter 13 and especially Nathan Spira's notes *ad loc.* where the matter is discussed at length and with full awareness of the sexual side of this association. It is thence carried over into the writings of Nathan of Gaza and other Sabbatians *(cf.* Ya'el Nadav in *Sefer Shazar,* p.320*ff.)* and also into the writings of Moses Hayyim Luzzatto, as quoted by Tishby, *op. cit.*, p.178. There are a number of ways in which the messianism of Luzzatto parallels that of Nahman; a comparative study of these two figures might prove most rewarding. It would seem doubtful, however, that Nahman was directly influenced by Luzzatto's Kabbalistic writings, the most significant of which had not yet been printed in his day.

15. *Liqquṭim* 14:5, based on *Baba Batra* 73b and *Sanhedrin* 98a.

16. *Liqquṭim* 7:1.

17. *Ḥayyey* 4:13; *Yemey MaHaRNaT* p.31; *Ḥayyey II* 2:34. Later editions of *Ḥayyey* based on that of Frampol, 1913, give the date for the wedding as 5502, an obvious misprint, since Nathan speaks of his presence there; *cf. Yemey MaHaRNaT*, p.13.

18. *Liqquṭim* 11, end.

19. *Liqquṭim* 16, based on *Baba Batra* 74a.

20. *Ḥayyey* 1:6; emphases mine. This passage is repeated, with no significant addition, in *Parpera'ot le-Ḥokhmah*, a commentary on the *Liqquṭim* by Nahman of Cheryn, 15a. From there it is quoted by Weiss, *op. cit.*, p.279. The reference to the two messiahs, in the same phrase used by Nahman, is found in *Sha'ar ha-Gilgulim* chapter 13, a chapter which seems to exercise a major influence here.

21. Sources dealing with Messiah ben Joseph may be found in the collection *Midreshey Ge'ulah*, edited by Y. Ibn-Shmu'el (Kaufmann), as well as in Ginzberg, *Legends of the Jews*, index, *s.v.* Messiah of Joseph.

The serious differences between Sabbatianism and Nahman's messianic longings should not be minimized. In Nahman's case the concept seems to have been largely of his own making; his Nathan did not have nearly so central a role in forging the image of messiah as did the Sabbatian prophet Nathan of Gaza. Sabbatai Sevi was seen as Messiah *ben David*, a more radical claim than that which we are attributing to Nahman. Most significantly, there did not develop in Bratslav a myth of the messiah who transgresses the law in order to bring about the redemption. Nahman's movement thus remained within the pale of Jewish orthodoxy, and did not create around its central figure a mythology of demonic fascination.

22. D. Tamar, "Ha-ARI weha-RaḤaV ke-Mashi'aḥ ben Yosef," in *Sefunot* 7 (1963) 167*ff.*, has collected the relevant sources. On this particular matter, *cf.* p.170.

23. *Cf.* *'Emeq ha-Melekh* 33b as quoted by Tamar, *op. cit.* For the penetration of this sort of thinking into the consciousness of Jews who stood far from Kabbalah or Hasidism *cf.* the note by Aryeh Lieb Lipkin in H. Medini's *Sedey Ḥemed*, v.1, p.193. The same notion of a messianic figure in each generation is found in Nahman's writings in *Liqquṭim* 79 and *Ḥayyey* 1:36. The description quoted is from Hayyim ha-Kohen's *Torat Ḥakham*, also cited by Tamar, p.171. For Weiss on Nahman as a type of the suffering messiah *cf. Studies in Mysticism*, pp.106*f.*, 111.

24. *Liqquṭim II* 32, 80; *Ḥayyey*, addenda.

25. *Megalleh 'Amuqot*, *'ofan* 252, Lemberg, 1858, 50a, and not in *'ofan* 150, as stated by Tishby, *loc. cit.* A comparison of *Liqquṭim* 16, the text which speaks of the *ẓaddiq* who contains both messiahs, with the opening lines of this same chapter in *Megalleh 'Amuqot*, which tells us that Moses contained both messiahs, leaves no doubt that Nahman knew this chapter and was influenced by it.

26. *Sippurim Nifla'im*, p.109.

27. *Ibid.*, p.123*f.* Emphasis mine.

28. *Neweh Ẓaddiqim*, p.79.

29. *Cf.* also *Ḥayyey* 3:10; *Ḥayyey II* 2:3; *Yemey MaHaRNaT*, p.32.

30. It is noteworthy that Yizhak Eisik Safrin of Komarno, a later Hasidic master with messianic dreams, bases his own claim to be Messiah ben Joseph on the fact that he was born in precisely this year—5566—numerically equivalent to that figure. See his mystical diary *Megillat Setarim* (composed in 1845) 2a.

31. I am not at all convinced by Joseph Weiss' suggestion that the figure of Jeroboam in Nahman's writings is a cipher for Jacob Frank. Weiss says this *(Meḥqarim, 25ff., 245ff.)* without any evidence at all other than his own rather romantic reading of Nahman as one who was ever attracted and fascinated by any and all sorts of heretical literature and desires. It is at this point that the careful scholar in Weiss was overtaken, perhaps by his own projections onto the figure of Nahman. The identification of holy books and heretical books that he attributes to Nahman (p.245*ff.)* is the result of a similar wishful reading on his part.

32. See *Siḥot* 198, the first introduction to the *Sippurey Ma'asiyot*, and the various sources quoted and discussed by Piekarz, p.140*ff*. To these may be added the *Shir Yedidut*, a poem in Nahman's honor written by Yehiel Mendel, a nineteenth-century *ḥasid*, and first published in Jerusalem, 1907. The first verse of the poem contains the line, "Your soul and your name were among the seven things that preceded Creation," an obvious reference to the rabbinic tradition *(Pesaḥim* 54a) to the effect that the name of messiah was one of the seven pre-existents. On the matter of Nahman's identity as Messiah ben Joseph or ben David, we should also bear in mind Scholem's observation *(Sabbatai Ṣevi*, p.55) that "not all writers were careful to distinguish" between the two, and that we should therefore not apply the distinctions over-rigorously. On both the matter of Nahman's predicted return from death and the meaning of the obvious parallels here to Sabbatian doctrine, see Piekarz' very important note in Weiss' *Meḥqarim*, p.233. I tend to agree with Piekarz rather than Weiss that in several cases what we see is a structural parallel between Sabbatian and Bratslav thinking, rather than any direct historical borrowings.

33. The association of Jeroboam and Messiah ben Joseph has a long and complex history in Kabbalistic literature. In the Zohar *(Zohar Ḥadash, Balaq* 56a) it is stated that this messiah will arise from the *seed* of Jeroboam, through his son Abijah, who died in his youth (I Kings 14:17). According to the Talmud *(Mo'ed Qatan* 28b), Abijah was a righteous child, who disobeyed his father's wicked commands. The *Zoḥar Ḥadash (loc. cit.)* claims that a child fathered by Abijah was born on the day that Abijah died, and that this child, who was raised in the wilderness, shielded from his grandfather's sins, is the progenitor of the Josephite messiah. Ginzberg *(Legends of the Jews*, v. 6, p. 308) knows of no pre-*Zohar* source for this notion. Thus far the idea is in no way surprising. Just as Messiah ben David comes from the Davidic royal house, it is entirely appropriate that the Josephite messiah stem from the royal family of the Northern Kingdom. Nothing is said in the *Zohar* literature of this messiah's repairing the damage wrought by Jeroboam.

It is in the Kabbalistic writings of the sixteenth century that this formerly obscure idea gained prominence and was dramatically altered. It is Vital, in *Sefer ha-Gilgulim*, chapter 67, who says that "the soul which departed from Jeroboam before he sinned is to be reincarnated in the future as Messiah ben Joseph." In *Sha'ar ha-Gilgulim* chapter 13 the soul of that messiah is associated both with Cain and with Jeroboam without that reservation as to its undefiled state. Messiah ben Joseph as Jeroboam reincarnate is a new idea here, one which goes far beyond the rather unspectacular claim of the *Zohar*, and one which indeed would open the door to speculations of the Sabbatian type.

Following Vital, the Italian Kabbalist Menahem 'Azariah of Fano (1584–1620) took the idea still further, claiming that God had originally planned to make the Judaean king Rehoboam the messiah, and Jeroboam his second-in-command. *Cf.* his *'Asarah Ma'amarot, 'em kol ḥay* 10 (ed. Cracow, 1556?, 77b–c) and the other sources cited by Tishby, *op. cit.*, p. 320, n. 108. From Vital, the idea is also taken up by Nathan Shapira, whose *Megalleh 'Amuqot* was first published in his home city of Cracow, 1637, and who is, in part, Nahman's source for this idea. At the very same time Nathan Shapira's book was being printed, however, the matter of Jeroboam and Messiah ben Joseph was also being debated in Amsterdam by the rabbi and Kabbalist Isaac Aboab and his opponents. Like Shapira, Aboab claimed that the soul of Jeroboam would be reincarnate in every generation, and would eventually be that of Messiah ben Joseph. *Cf.* the text of Aboab's *Nishmat Ḥayyim*, published by A. Altmann in *PAAJR* 40 (1972) 65*f.* Aboab cites the *Tiqquney Zohar* as a source for this idea, but Altmann notes (n. 49) that he was not able to find such a passage in the *Tiqqunim* or anywhere else in the *Zohar* literature, except for the single source we have mentioned above. Altmann does note, however, that yet another Kabbalist of the same generation, Abraham Azulai of Hebron (1570–1643) mentions the identification of Jeroboam and Messiah ben Joseph in his *Zoharey Ḥamah* to *Zohar* 2:120a. That text is paraphrased by Altmann from a reference in Reuben Margaliot's *Sha'arey Zohar* 50a–b, but it seems that the text there does clearly describe the two as identical. A less definitive statement to the same effect is found in Azulai's *'Or ha-Ḥamah ad loc.* (ed. Jerusalem, 1879, 102d), in a passage attributed to Cordovero: "He [Messiah ben Joseph] is condemned to die in return for *[temurah le-]* the sin of Jeroboam, for idolatry is punishable by death." It would appear that this idea took hold in sixteenth-century Safed, and became the common property of the disciples of both Luria and Cordovero. The emphasis on *tiqqun* in the thought of Luria and Vital combined with the thought that one or the other of these masters himself was Messiah ben Joseph to ensure the popularity of this idea. From these sources the idea was taken over by the Sabbatians, for whom the idea of a messiah who had been tainted with sin in a previous incarnation was most exciting. It was from these Sabbatian sources that the idea came down to Moses Hayyim Luzzatto, who made much of it in his esoteric writings. See Tishby, *op. cit.*, p.178*ff.* There is no reason to think, however, that Nahman's statement of this claim has Sabbatian sources; he learned it directly from the works of Vital and Nathan Shapira.

34. Nathan's reaction to this teaching is recorded in *'Avaneha Barzel*, p.45. Zeitlin, *op. cit.*, p.337, does quote a bit of it, but with little explanation and seemingly without recognizing its unique character. For other teachings of messianic import See *Liqqutim* 13 and 14, dating respectively from Rosh Hashanah and Hanukkah of 1803.

35. *Ḥayyey* 3:3.

36. *Zohar* 2:177b, *Sifra di-Ẓeni'uta*. The word *diqna* as used by Nahman will mean "elder" *(zaqen)* rather than the usual "beard" *(zaqan)*; this play on words undoubtedly accounts for the last episode in the vision, where the elder makes reference to his beard. If Nahman is sticking closely to the text of the *Zohar*, that elder is God Himself, and the encounter with Him seems to mean: "Either you will understand all this through direct and immediate confrontation with Me, or you will have to seek its meaning in endless books."

37. *Ta'anit* 9a; *Mekilta, wa-yasa'* 5 (ed. Horovitz, p.173). For a Hasidic parallel on

the *zaddiq* as well or fountain *cf. Qedushat Levi, Yitro,* 134a.

38. *Megillah* 18a. In the Talmudic context *sela'* refers to a small coin; Nahman is interpreting it to mean "rock."

39. *Edom* and *Ma'adim* (Mars) are etymologically related; both are derived from the stem *'dm* ("red"). The warlike quality of Mars is here attributed to Edom, also based on Gen. 27:40. On the Land of Israel coming through suffering see Berakhot 5a.

40. The text sounds as though there were some specific incident in its background. Perhaps he was trying to justify the calling in of Russian authorities against the *maskilim,* though I have found no evidence of such a particular incident in this time and place. For a similar statement of the need for supernatural intervention with the nations in order that they act on Israel's behalf, *cf.* the *hope* expressed by Levi Yizhak in *Qedushat Levi, Purim,* 364a.

41. *Ḥayyey* 1:15.

42. The major source for Nahman's attitude toward proselytes is *Liqquṭim* 17:5–6. *Cf.* also 48, 59, 62, 215. This interest is still evidenced in his last teaching, *Liqquṭim II* 8:3–4, despite the decline of messianic urgency by that time. Zeitlin *(op. cit.,* p.353*ff.)* has recognized the importance of this theme in Nahman's thought and its uniqueness in his time. On the Talmudic views of proselytes see *Yebamot* 47b and *Pesaḥim* 87b. Nahman echoes the latter view in *Liqquṭim* 17:6. On the Judaizing tendencies of the Subbotniks see *Encyclopedia Judaica, s.v.* Judaizers; S. Bolshakoff, *Russian Nonconformity,* p.107*ff.*

43. *Yemey MaHaRNaT,* p.14. *Tiqqun ḥazot* is not generally printed in Hasidic editions of the liturgy. On the Hasidic abandonment of Lurianic *kawwanot cf.* Weiss in *JJS* 9 (1958) 163*ff.* In this matter Nahman did follow the example of his Hasidic predecessors. See *Siḥot* 185.

44. *Yemey MaHaRNaT,* p.17f; *Liqquṭim* 205; *Ḥayyey* 7: 17.

45. *Ḥayyey II* 11:45.

46. *Messianic Idea,* p.99*f.*

47. See Nathan's introduction to the *Sippurey Ma'asiyot.*

48. *Yemey MaHaRNaT,* p.15*ff.*

49. *Ḥayyey* 1:28. *Cf.* Weiss in *Tarbiz* 44 (1969) 285, n.15.

50. *Yemey MaHaRNaT,* p.15.

51. *Ḥayyey* 4:18.

52. *Yemey MaHaRNaT,* p.19. See also *Siḥot* 189. The tale of Luria's son is found in *Shivḥey ha-ARI,* p.22.

53. *Ḥayyey* 7:8–11; *Kokhvey 'Or,* p.52; *Neweh Zaddiqim,* p.80; Piekarz, p.67.

54. *Liqquṭim* 29; *Ḥayyey* 1:20.

The wearing of white garments on the Sabbath is mentioned in the Brody community's ban against the *ḥasidim. See* Dubnov, *Toledot ha-Ḥasidut,* p.121. It is possible that this custom was eliminated in response to the opposition it aroused. Y. Eliach, in *PAAJR* 36 (1968), has pointed to the parallel between the Hasidic and Russian sectarian customs in the wearing of white garments. There is no need, however, to assume non-Jewish influence in this matter. White garments for the Sabbath are already prescribed in the *Ḥemdat Yamim,* pt. 1, ch. 3 (Constantinople, 1738, 27b), where Luria and Vital are quoted as authorities for the custom. *Cf. Shivḥey ha-ARI,* p.6.

55. *Yemey MaHaRNaT,* p.22, added by a later editor. On the death of Shlomo

Ephraim *cf.* also *Ḥayyey* 6:1; 7:12; Piekarz, p.78*f.*; Weiss, *op. cit.*, pp.282 and 288.

56. *Kokhvey 'Or*, p.52. The summer of 1806 was also a particularly rough period in Nahman's relations with the Zeide, who sought to denounce him to Levi Yizhak at that time. See above, chapter three, and especially Piekarz, *op. cit.*, pp. 68*ff.*, where the matter is discussed in great detail. Later Bratslav tradition says quite openly that Nahman came very close to bringing messiah during that summer, had not Satan, personified in the Zeide, intervened. See *Be'ur ha-Liqquṭim*, p. 80, n. 6.

57. *Ḥayyey* 6:1. See also *Yemey MaHaRNaT*, p.24.

58. *Ḥayyey* 1:59; 6:1. Piekarz, whose entire chapter on the events of 1804–06 is offered as an attempt to explain the origin of the *Sippurey Ma'asiyot*, in the end does not clearly state what connection he finds between Nahman's messianic attempt, which he describes in great and accurate detail, and the *Tales*. One gets the impression that he sees the tales as a direct continuation of that effort. If so, the thesis I am proposing here is contrary to his; I see Nahman's telling of tales as a result of the *failure* of that attempt, and a need to seek a new outlet for his longings. This matter is further discussed in the following chapter.

59. *Liqquṭim* 65:1–2. *Cf.* the discussion in Weiss, *Meḥqarim*, p.176. On the setting of this teaching, *see 'Avaneha Barzel*, p.30. The reference to the "field of tears" is from *Mo'ed Qatan* 5b; the *ẓaddiq* as gardener may derive from *Zohar* 2:166b.

6

Nahman's Final Years

The feverish pitch of activity that characterized Nahman and those around him during the years 1805 and 1806 abated considerably as it became clear to them that the attempt to bring redemption had been a failure. We are told that "many" of the disciples were overcome by obstacles, undoubtedly their own doubts as well as the taunts of others, and left Nahman in the year 1806/07. While the more intimate circle remained mostly intact and maintained its unswerving loyalty to the master, even the members of this group had to find some means of explanation for his inability to bring about the great event. In large part they attributed this failure to the workings of evil forces, personified by those "false" *ẓaddiqim* who continued to denounce Nahman and to persecute his followers. As we have seen during the summer of 1806 the Shpoler Zeide sought to openly denounce Nahman before Levi Yizhak of Berdichev, and Nahman's bitterest period of persecution was around this same time. It was during the winter of 1806/07 that Nahman confided in Nathan

> with regard to an event that had recently happened to him, in which a wicked and worthless man had made up some lie concerning him, something which was really senseless. He had suffered greatly on account of this.[1]

In 1806 Nahman's messianic claim was no longer the well-guarded secret it had been a few years earlier. The two Bratslav emissaries who had gone from town to town during the early summer of that year, teaching passages from Nahman's secret writings, had surely at least broadly hinted that the redemption was at hand and that their master was to be its bearer. While we have denied the allegation that Nahman's detractors accused him of Sabbatianism, it seems too striking to be coincidental that the persecution of Bratslav was at its height in the period during and immediately after this outbreak of messianic fever. Some outside of the immediate circle did know of Nahman's great expectations for the year 1805/06, and the general derision with which Bratslav was met in broader Hasidic circles may well stem from this period.

The conduct of the Bratslav disciples in the period following the tragic summer of 1806 falls into a well-known pattern ensuing upon the failure of a would-be messianic movement. It should come as no surprise to us that a good number of the "fringe" followers abandoned Nahman at that point in his career. As the promised redemption fails to materialize, those whose commitment to the belief had been marginal tend to fall away, even joining the ranks of the opposition. The most committed, however, are not deterred by the seeming failure, and their faith is even more confirmed as they become the butt of persecution. Such was the case in the history of the Sabbatian movement, and it has also been documented in a recent study of a mid-twentieth-century chiliastic cult in the United States.[2] Persecution and derision in fact provide the ideal climate for the continued growth of such beliefs in the hearts of those who have the strength to remain faithful to the last. What greater proof of our rectitude than the fact that the wicked are so persistent in seeking to destroy us because of it? What further vindication of our claim is needed than the great inner strength we feel in holding fast to it? It was in this period (and later, during the persecutions of Nathan's day) that the sharply sectarian consciousness characterizing Bratslav undoubtedly first arose, a consciousness that divided the world clearly between members of the community and outsiders, and gave rise to the practice of referring to members of other Hasidic groups, insofar as they opposed Nahman, as *mitnaggedim*.

So much for the reaction of the disciples. Those who could hung fast to every word their master spoke, as they had before, always seeking some new bit of confirmation that the greatest of all the *ẓaddiqim*, despite all the setbacks, was still continuing in his redemptive work.

But what of Nahman himself? Here we have a problem of a rather different order. The disciples may indeed remain faithful, looking to the master to quell their doubts. But the would-be messiah himself has no one to whom he can turn for words of consolation. He is the one who has let the others down, and cannot but see the failure of his mission at least in part as a sign of his own inadequacies. In Nahman's case, this awareness of personal failure was infinitely compounded by his sense of guilt over the death of his son, the fire in Bratslav on Yom Kippur of 1806, and (in the spring of 1807) the death of his wife. All of these were somehow attributable to his own sins, and most particularly to the great *hubris* of a false messianic claim.

All indications are that Nahman was a broken man in the winter of 1806/07. The teaching he delivered on that Hanukkah is a comment on the prophet Elisha's words to his master Elijah, just as Elijah was preparing for his death:

> 'May your spirit be upon me twofold' (II Kings 2:9) . . . Know that sometimes the disciple may be greater than the master, possessing twice the powers that his master had. Nonetheless, all of it is through the power of his master.[3]

Nahman goes on to speak of the *ẓaddiq's* death and the transfer of his charismatic powers to his disciple in the moment when his spirit leaves him. This is the first of many teachings in which Nahman makes the death of the *ẓaddiq* a central motif. After mid-1807, when Nahman became seriously ill, this concern is understandable. But at this point Nahman was not yet ill, and he had no reason to believe, at age thirty-four, that death was close at hand. Yet he seemed to feel somehow that his career was at an end, and that his greatness would henceforth best be known through the presence of his spirit in the lives of his disciples. When he undertook his journey to Navritch in the early spring of 1807, a journey we shall presently discuss in some detail, he planned to leave Bratslav and the world of his disciples behind him forever. Whatever ambivalence he had felt in earlier years with regard to his right to the mantle of the *ẓaddiq* was now heightened to the point where he was ready to entirely abandon the enterprise of communal leadership.

The greatest change in Nahman's conduct during these years, however, was his turn to the telling of stories. As we have noted, the first of the fantastic tales that make up his *Sippurey Ma'asiyot* was told during that crucial summer of 1806. Between that time and the spring of 1810, some six months before his death, all of those thirteen 'canonical' tales were told.

It is not our intention at this point to offer a full analysis of the tales themselves. Excursus II (herein, below) is wholly devoted to that purpose, and even there only a beginning has been undertaken. Here we only wish to add a few words concerning the meaning these tales may have had for Nahman at this point in his life, as he faced the collapse of his messianic attempt.

The *Tales* clearly indicate that Nahman had not fully abandoned his dreams of redemption. It was the approach, but not the essential message, that was to change. The central motif underlying all the tales is that of *tiqqun,* the restoration of the cosmos to its proper order. Motifs such as those of the captive princess whose liberation is delayed by the sleeping courtier, the rabbi's son who longs to reach the great *ẓaddiq,* the true prince who must repair the broken throne in order to regain his kingdom, and the master of prayer who struggles to reestablish the kingly order that has been disturbed by a great wind—all of these are thinly veiled references to the mystic's dream of restoring harmony to the distraught cosmos, the central redemptive goal of the Kabbalah since the sixteenth century. *Having failed to bring about the redemption by means of direct agita-*

tion, Nahman now expresses his longings through the medium of these fantastically elaborated stories.

If the message was the same, the nature of the activity by which Nahman thought he was to have a role in the drama of redemption had changed drastically. We hear of no more public pronouncements, no more disseminations of secret teachings, no appearances in white garments or suggestive calls to repentance. Instead of all these activities, aimed at hastening the end through *revealing* (albeit in somewhat furtive form) its approach, the movement after summer of 1806 is all in the direction of *hiding*. Controversial passages are to be censored, secret works are to be burned, and the master's teachings that have most directly to do with the matter of redemption are to be continued, but now "hidden" in the form of stories, as though to keep out those who have no business with them.

This at least is the interpretation of Nahman's storytelling that emerges from a teaching he offered just in this period when the first of the *Sippurey Ma'asiyot* was told, on Rosh Hashanah of 1806.[4] This teaching is certainly deserving of our careful attention in any attempt to understand what it meant to Nahman to turn to the telling of tales. He speaks there of the story as a way *to reveal his teachings while yet keeping them in hidden form;* the tale is a 'garbing' of words of Torah. Nahman offers three reasons for the necessity of hiding his teachings:

1. Since the teaching seeks to awaken the spiritual sleeper, or to enlighten the eyes of those who have been spiritually blind, its meaning must become clear only gradually. When the blind man has been healed, he notes, he is at first blindfolded, so that his newly-found sight will not be destroyed by an excess of light.

2. The evil forces that seek to hold back the redemptive power contained in words of Torah will not be attracted to a seemingly harmless story.

3. If the evil forces should take note of the story, they will be tricked by its intricacies, and will remain unaware of the message lying hidden within it.

This threefold (or perhaps really twofold) explanation is itself in need of further interpretation, however. Nahman still believes in the imminent redemption, but he now realizes that one must take certain precautions in proclaiming that truth. True, the year of the original prediction has passed, but that does not form an essential obstacle. We know from other messianic movements that the failure of redemption to materialize within the predicted period does not necessarily spell the end of all hope; dates are changed and calculations adjusted in order to make it possible for the faithful to persist in their belief. The once disappointed messianist, however, will seek to disguise his teachings, in order to avoid the taunts and persecutions of those who do not believe, but also to silence the doubts that have arisen in his own mind and in the hearts of the faithful. This garbing of the teaching in fantastic tales allows master and disciple to feel that some deep change has taken place, that the process has *advanced* to some new level of *inwardness*, while in fact the message of redemption remains essentially the same. As history fails us, we raise our sights to the realm of myth. Once again, the developments within Sabbatianism provide an excellent example.

Nahman asks himself why the redemption failed to come about in 5566 (1805/06). His answers, based on a long tradition of messianic failures, are twofold: the people were not ready, and the evil forces had done their part. In response to these "obstacles" Nahman had now to come up with a new means of giving vent to the deep longings for redemption, one that would serve to arouse souls without rushing them beyond their capabilities into tragedy, one that thus would not awaken those forces that ever seek to delay messiah's steps.

For the present, a denial of messiah's near approach was needed, and was fully consonant with his motive in telling the tales, that of hiding the messianic message. Deeply scarred by the events of that year, Nahman was not ready to be rushed again. In contrast to his own actions only four years earlier, Nahman now voiced his strong opposition to the renewed messianic expectations in the Hasidic community for the year 5570 (1809/10).

> On the evening following the Sabbath of Penitence in 5570 [September 16, 1809], they spoke of messiah. It was well-known that the arrival of messiah during that year had been predicted. He did not agree with this view. He said that before messiah comes there will be more than one who cries aloud over the loss of faith. There will be many *ẓaddiqim* who cry aloud concerning this until they are hoarse, but it will be of no avail . . . Surely there will be no community like ours in those times, a group of people who truly desire to hear the word of God. There will still be a few good people in that generation, but they will be scattered.
>
> He further said: 'Write this down in a book, so that it will be remembered in days to come that there already was one who knew it all beforehand. This will strengthen their faith in God and in His true *ẓaddiqim*.'[5]

The complexity of Nahman's ambivalences, however, cannot be overestimated. While he had openly denounced these new messianic predictions, he may have entertained some secret hope that they would be fulfilled. The final and most elaborate tale in his collection, that of the *Seven Beggars*, was completed only a few days before Passover of 1810, exactly the time when messiah would have been most expected to arrive. The tale of the seventh beggar, however, was left untold, as that final tale could not be revealed until messianic times. Could it be that Nahman allowed himself to dream that messiah would appear in the following week and complete his story?

Fantasies and ongoing dreams did not fully succeed, however, in masking the deep sense of disappointment that marred Nahman's final years. He was able at times to speak quite realistically about his own failure to bring about the redemption. He sought some measure of comfort, sometimes in his disciples and sometimes in his own bit of spiritual attainment, but his disappointment was obvious nonetheless.

> I heard that he said: 'I have so great an understanding of God that I could bring messiah! But I put it all aside and betook myself to you, in order to return you to the good. This is greater than anything; "blessed is the man who holds the sinner's hand." ' He then reproved our people sharply, saying: 'How much I have struggled for you! How many times has my throat gone sore and my mouth gone dry from speaking at such great length to each and every one of you? And now; what have I accomplished? Even though you are good people, this is not how I wanted it to be. How shall I come before the throne of glory? I comfort myself only when I think of those few people whom I already have in the World to Come.'[6]

In the closing discourse of the first volume of his teaching, delivered in the fall of 1807, Nahman urged his disciples to look always for some bit of good in themselves, with which they could sustain themselves in periods of self-doubt. Even one who considers himself to be on the very lowest rung, he taught, must surely have done some bit of good in his lifetime; only by seeking out that bit of good, in oneself as in others, and by nurturing it and allowing it to grow, could one hope to maintain life.

Here, too, he was clearly talking first and foremost to himself.

Such are the general outlines of Nahman's life in his last four years: his wanderings, his illness, and the telling of tales. Three journeys were undertaken in the course of those four years, each with a unique character and purpose. It is to the first of those journeys, that to Navritch[7] in the spring of 1807, that we now turn our attention for a more complete account.

We have already mentioned that Nahman's teaching on Hanukkah of that winter, referring to Elijah and Elisha, may be read as proclaiming the end of his public career. Frankly frightened by what he had been through, he felt that he had paid a terrible price for the sins involved in his attempt at leadership, and he now wanted no more part of it. Nahman knew well that

> it is terribly dangerous to be a public figure and to lead a community. This is not to speak of one who is unfit for that role, wearing a mantle which does not belong to him. But even the leaders of the generation, true servants of

> God as they may be, place themselves in a frighteningly dangerous position by leading the public. An ordinary person is very far from committing murder, even if he is not generally a person of character; most people have no particular lust for murder. Even should one have such a desire (God protect us!), one has few opportunities to act upon it, and there are many obstacles in the way. And even if one should transgress this prohibition, it is not a very frequent occurrence; few murderers commit more than one murder in their lifetime.
>
> But in leading the community, and in revealing *novellae* in the Torah, one may truly transgress the prohibitions against theft, adultery, and murder—constantly, in every moment.[8]

How much more so for Nahman, ever troubled by his own burden of secret desires and wayward thoughts. Nahman's sense of his own sinfulness must now have been redoubled, his fears that he was inadequate to the role of *ẓaddiq* and less than worthy to lead his disciples now complicated by the burden of having issued what amounted to nothing less than a false messianic claim.

The feeling of guilt for the sins of his career at this point in Nahman's life is perhaps best seen in connection with his behavior as his daughter Sarah was about to give birth to a child. These events took place, we should remember, only about eight months after the death of his beloved Shlomo Ephraim, and perhaps but a month or two after the death of another infant son.[9]

> His grandson Israel, the son of his daughter, the righteous Sarah, was born during that winter while [Nahman] was in Kreminchug, as he was every year, following his *Shabbat Shirah* visit to Cheryn . . . Before the child was born, he spent several weeks in Kreminchug with his daughter, waiting for her to give birth. Throughout the period before that birth he did not smile at all; he was angry when two cooked foods were placed before him at a meal. His only concern through that entire period was that his daughter, may she live, survive the delivery unharmed. He remained prepossessed with worry until the night when she delivered the child. After the birth, he was immediately filled with joy; he ordered that candles be lit and that a festive beverage called 'punch' be prepared. He was indeed very happy.
>
> On the eighth day, he circumcised his infant grandson, as is proper, and he was extremely joyous all that day following the circumcision. He took special pleasure when he heard people remark that the newborn's name was Israel ben Sarah, the same as the name of the BeSHT.
>
> But afterwards, on the third day following the circumcision, his daughter took ill. He became terribly distraught, and fled quickly from Kreminchug.[10]

Nahman was obviously worried that some harm might come to his daughter or her child; this was the reason for his lengthy stay in Kreminchug. But his flight from that city, when Sarah did take ill, is hardly the reaction one would expect from a concerned father! This strange reaction shows that he feared it was his own presence in Kreminchug that had placed her in danger, a sign that the necessary atonement for his sins was not yet completed, and that he could still do great harm to himself and to those nearest to him.

It was just shortly before this event—and probably for the same reason—that a group of disciples who came to visit Nahman had been greeted with "Why do you come to me? I hate you!"[11] If the master was to have to suffer punishment for his sins, better at least that those around him be protected by keeping a certain distance.

It was right after his return from Kreminchug that Nahman set out on another journey, called "his journey to Navritch" and treated with great awe by Nathan and the later Bratslav tradition. This is one of Nahman's "mysterious" journeys, the true meaning of which, we are told, can never be fathomed.[12] Indeed, of all Nahman's many forays around the Ukrainian countryside this is perhaps the most difficult to explain. His visit to Kamenets was preparatory to his journey to the Holy Land; his brief stay in Shargorod had something to do with the messianic outburst. But what to say of this journey? If we are right in identifying "Navritch" with Ovruch in Polesia, why did Nahman want to go there? Here there were neither disciples nor great secrets, neither living souls to be encountered nor a mysterious Frankist past to exercise its fascination.

The fact is that the "journey to Navritch" was not intended as such at all. Navritch was but a stop on what was planned as a longer trip. Having a distant relative by marriage in that place, he stopped there for a brief visit, and it was there that circumstances forced him to turn back, thus by accident giving this event the name of the journey to that place. But what then was the goal of this journey? If a town in relatively distant Polesia to the north was but a midway stop, where was it that Nahman was headed? The nature of this journey is clarified in a unique and poignant document, a letter Nahman wrote to his disciples at home during the course of his travels, sent to Bratslav from Zaslav somewhat later that spring and preserved by Nathan in his memoirs:

> An exact copy of a letter written in our late master's own hand, which he wrote to our community while he was dwelling in Zaslav in the year 1807.

> I wish to inform all of our people that I have wearied of living in Bratslav,[13] due to the many troubles and misadventures which have befallen me. *I shall henceforth be a wanderer from tent to tent, settling nowhere permanently but only sojourning.* I now plead with you that all the work I have done for you, taking my own life in my hands for the sake of your souls, not have been done in vain. The Lord is righteous, and I have done evil. My own deeds have brought about my sufferings and the deaths of my precious children;

> these are also the source of the controversy and the accusations. At the same time, I well understand that it is the work I have done in rescuing you from the very jaws of the wicked Samael which has caused him to beam his eyes and gnash his teeth at me.
>
> Therefore, my beloved brothers and companions, be strong in your fear of God, each according to his own powers and in his own way, so that my struggle not have been in vain. Keep the Torah of Moses, the servant of the Lord, as I have taught you. Know that even though I am far from you now, this distance is only a separation of our bodies, for in our souls we remain close. My beloved brothers and friends, I beg of you that my pleas stay with you day and night.
>
> I inform you that I am now dwelling in Zaslav, and I expect to be here, God willing, for about three months. These are the words of your beloved, who writes with tears because of the great joy that is in my heart, since God has given me the iron strength to bear wanderings and sufferings like these.
>
> Nahman, the son of Simhah, may God preserve him. I inform you that I am, praise God, completely healthy, without recourse to any physical medicines. Nahman, as above.[14]

This document is of interest to us for a number of reasons. It shows the complexity of Nahman's thinking about his own sinfulness: he is responsible for all of his misfortunes, but he still knows that he was led into sin by the evil forces, who feared the redemptive power of the good works he was performing. The letter also gives us a touching glimpse into the affectionate style of communication that existed between master and disciples, an affection that manages to come through even despite the rather formal style of old Hebrew letter-writing. Most interesting of all, however, is the rather startling announcement that Nahman has no intention of returning to Bratslav. The "journey to Navritch" is not intended as a mere visit to Navritch or anywhere else, but rather as the beginning of an endless pilgrimage, a life of wandering upon which Nahman has embarked for the atonement of his sins.

This tradition of voluntary exile, known in Hasidic parlance as *oprikhtn golus,* has a long tradition in the history of Jewish pietism. Wandering and exile as atonement for sin, stretching back in the tradition's memory as far as the punishment of Cain and encompassing the fate of Israel as a whole since the great destruction, was also in various periods taken as an option by individuals who felt the burden of their sins was more than they could bear. This sense of wandering as personal penance also combined, especially after Lurianic times, with a sense of participation in the sufferings of the *shekhinah;* pious persons, even without a terrible burden of personal guilt, might thus take it upon themselves to wander for a while. Such, for example, was the case of the two brother Elimelekh and Zusya, disciples of the Maggid, who were reputed to have spent years in such wanderings. In the likes of these the tradition of voluntary exile drew near to that of the wandering seeker, a type well-known, by the way, in the Orthodox Christian piety of Eastern Europe.[15]

A strange sort of optimism marked Nahman's departure on this new venture; it, too, is a part of his new, hidden path in working toward redemption. Nathan records several statements his master made as he was about to set out on this journey, all of which seem to indicate that this grave step was taken with a certain trembling sense of pious joy. It is also obvious from these statements that he did not inform his disciples of the intended extent of the journey as he set out; only when they received the above-quoted letter did they realize that he had no intention of coming back to them.

> I have heard in his name: As he departed for Navritch and other communities, he spoke of this journey, which no one understood at all. On his travels he remained hidden from the public, and he accepted no money along the way. He said then [as he was leaving]:
>
> ' "My hands are dirtied with blood and female issue in order to purify a woman for her husband." ' It was somehow hinted that this was the meaning of his journey.
>
> Before the journey he said: 'I am like a young child who does not want to go to school. When he gets into the schoolroom, however, he is able to learn. If people only knew why I am going on this journey, they would kiss my footsteps! With every step that I take, I shall be turning the world's balance toward the side of merit.'
>
> He said: 'My place is only the Land of Israel. Wherever I journey, I am journeying only to the Land of Israel. For now I am in Bratslav' and so forth.
>
> Before he departed on the above-mentioned journey, he clapped his hands together and said: 'Today begins something new. This is like one who plays music while people are dancing. Those who do not understand, and who do not hear the music, wonder why others run after this person and dance about so. Thus people wonder why you all run after me. When I return from my travels, I shall be able to play and you will be able to dance![16]

Taken as a whole, this rather amazing series of statements teaches us a great deal about Nahman's feelings as he undertook this latest journey. Most revealing is the first and seemingly strangest of these statements, one which turns out to be an elliptical reference to a most interesting passage in the Talmud:

> 'Guard my soul, O Lord, for I am a pious one' (Ps.86:2) . . . Thus said David to the Holy One, blessed be He: 'Lord of the World! Am I not pious? All the

> other kings of east and west are sitting about in groups, basking in their glory, while my hands are dirtied with blood and female issue in order to purify a woman for her husband!'[17]

The Talmudic David is here, as elsewhere (though nowhere more graphically!) seen as a halakhic authority, examining the menstrual blood and issue of a woman to determine whether she is ritually pure and may thus be approached by her husband. Nahman reads the Talmudic passage in a mystical-symbolic way: David (or Nahman as the new David) has had to defile himself in course of working at the redemption of the *shekhinah* and restoring her to her divine Husband. There was still "dirty work" to be done as part of the redemptive task, he was telling his disciples, and he was setting off to do it.

A similar motif attaches to the image of the reluctant schoolchild. The task may seem unpleasant to him, but if he really knew what this "learning" was all about he would look forward to it with joy, as would all those about him. He will be able to make such music through the powers he will acquire on this journey that even those who have been previously deaf to the spirit will now be able to dance.

The brief reference to Erez Israel here is also fascinating. We seem to see, though in very abbreviated form, yet another stage in Nahman's continuing fascination with the Holy Land and its place in his scheme of things. The journey to Erez Israel was the great rite of passage; only after it could he live as one who is considered a *ẓaddiq*. That *ẓaddiq* had the power, however, to evoke the Land of Israel in his own place; thus is Bratslav described as a new Zion, and Nahman as Abraham who has found the center. Two years later, in the midst of his messianic activity, it was to the *real* Erez Israel that his thoughts were once again directed, and for which he would accept no substitute (" . . . those very buildings and houses"). Now, it would seem, in a sort of wistful way he proclaims that all his journeys are in fact the great pilgrimage; even by heading northward (perhaps toward Byelorussia or Lithuania, where he indeed would have been an unknown) he is in fact going to the Land of Israel.

In fact, the great journey was of short duration. From Navritch, where he spent the Purim festival, Nahman returned as far as Ostrog, and after a short stay there he went off to Zaslav, the town where his wife's family resided, and hardly a place where he could preserve his anonymity. The events of this period are presented with some confusion in the sources, but their proper sequence seems to be as follows. While he was in Navritch, he became concerned with the health of his wife, who had remained at home in Bratslav. Sosia, who had borne Nahman at least seven children, but of whom we hear nothing from the time of their marriage until now, was desperately ill with tuberculosis. He sent word to her that she should meet him in Ostrog, where he wanted her to be treated by the well-known Dr. Gordia. This doctor, unlike the many of his profession who were among the first to turn toward Haskalah, was an old man who had a particular reputation for piety. He had once served as physician to the Maggid of Miedzyrzec, and legend had it that he had turned to the Maggid for spiritual healing as he had healed the Maggid's physical ills.[18] Sosia did join her husband in Ostrog,[19] but there she announced that she preferred to be treated by the doctors in her own home town, Zaslav. Nahman and Sosia together reached Zaslav a few days before Passover. We have no record of what medical treatment Nahman's wife received in Zaslav, nor is the name of any well-known doctor of the period associated with that town. It seems likely that Sosia, realizing that death was near, simply sought to be with her own family. They lived together for two months in Zaslav, and were followed there by a number of Nahman's disciples. Sosia's end came in June of 1807, on the eve of the festival of Shavu'ot.

In vain would we look through Nahman's teachings of that summer to find out what meaning his wife's death had for him. He seems once again to have blamed his own sins for the calamity, but beyond that he says very little. The teaching of that Shavu'ot[20] contains many references to symbols of the feminine, showing that his wife was probably on his mind, but there is no explicit reference to his feelings about her. The two tales that belong to that summer, *The Spider and the Fly* and *The Rabbi and His Son,* are also devoid of any reference to his recent loss. Nahman's religious life was lived in the exclusively male universe of the Hasidic court, in which the death of a wife, in stark contrast to the death of his infant son, was not an object of public discussion. If Nahman was deeply grieved, his grief was a private matter. In fact it was only a few weeks after the thirty-day mourning period had ended that he announced the arrangement of a second marriage, to the daughter of a wealthy community leader in Brody named Ezekiel Trachtenberg.[21] The wedding took place in mid-Elul, three months after Sosia's death.

It was apparently only after Sosia's death that Nahman decided that he would return to Bratslav. In a letter written to his brother Yehiel shortly before she died, he said: "I intend to stay here in the holy community of Zaslav for about three months, and then I will know where to turn." In fact he remained in Zaslav for only a few weeks after Shavu'ot. He traveled briefly to Radwil and Brody, making the arrangements for his forthcoming marriage, and then he returned home. He was back in Bratslav in time to make his usual round of visits to the *ḥasidim* during that summer, spending the Sabbath following Tish'a be-'Av in Cheryn, as was his custom.[22]

Here we are confronted with a major change of plans, one accepted without comment in the sources, but which calls out for some attempt at explanation. Here was Nahman about to set off as a permanent wanderer, cutting all ties with his *ḥasidim* and more or less abandoning his family as well. His wife's illness called him back from his wanderings, as is understandable. But upon her death he did just the opposite of what we might expect. Now that he was free of marital obligation and his ties to the settled life were thus loosened, one might expect that with a certain sense of relief he would immediately set out again on his mysterious journey. Instead, he rushed to remarry as soon as possible, and returned to the life in Bratslav that he had so recently decided to abandon!

Several possible explanations offer themselves. It may be that Nahman (who had already temporarily abandoned wife and children when he went to Erez Israel) was the type of husband who, while having little conscious desire to be with his wife on a daily basis, nevertheless relied deeply upon her support, and now felt himself rootless without her. The fact that he had a wife at home may have meant that wander as he might, there would always be a place to which he could return should the need arise. It may also be that Sosia functioned like many another Hasidic *rebbetsin* (though we have no reports to this effect in her case) and handled the financial and householder side of her husband's life. With a wife still at home in Bratslav, the *ḥasidim* could be counted on to maintain their *rebbe's* household, and some portion of those funds could also be used to sustain the wanderer himself. Without Sosia, Nahman would be left without the living link between himself and his supporters.

At the same time, there is another sort of explanation that might help us make sense of this sudden change of plans. It was in the summer of 1807 that the first signs of Nahman's tuberculosis appeared. Having just witnessed Sosia's death from that same illness, Nahman harbored no illusions about his own chances; already in that summer he announced that his own death was not far off.[23] The romance of a wanderer's life might do for a healthy man; once he was ill, however, Nahman may have realized that he would need the care only a devoted mate could offer. Nahman reportedly never entered into conjugal relations with his second wife,[24] thus fulfilling the ascetic side of the life of wandering that he had planned. He did allow himself to return to the comfort of home, however, and his wife provided support to him throughout the three trying years of his illness.

From the summer of 1807 until his death, Nahman was constantly fighting an uphill battle against tuberculosis. The sheer physical struggle for survival necessarily became a major preoccupation of his life, and it is no wonder that his teachings in this final period are filled with references to the disease that was consuming him. Nahman's naturally curious mind led him to learn all that he could about tuberculosis; the lungs, the heart, and the bloodstream are very frequently used as metaphors in Nahman's later teachings.[25] The spiritual struggles of his early life now came to be joined by great physical hardships, hardships which almost seemed appropriate to him as they were used as comments on his spiritual situation.

In Nahman's frequent and varied treatments of the themes of illness and healing, we see another aspect of the historical situation we will note when discussing his complex attitudes toward the problems of faith and doubt: Nahman is a *ẓaddiq* who stands at the edge of the modern world, anxious to taste of its fruits, yet fearful lest it lead him astray and burdened with guilt by any deviation in his behavior from the path of his revered ancestors.

The older generation of Hasidic masters, among whom Nahman was raised, had maintained a longstanding attitude of suspicion toward the practice of medicine, an attitude traced back, at least in legend, to the Ba'al Shem Tov himself.[26] Hasidism in the early nineteenth century continued to live in the pre-modern world, in which folk medicine was the province of the *ẓaddiq*. Prayer, herbal recipes, and magical amulets were all joined in the *ẓaddiq's* approach toward the healing of the sick. The very figure of the Hasidic master stands in opposition to that of the modern doctor, with his attempt to treat illness on a purely physical basis. Only in our own day is medicine changing in this regard. Illness was viewed by Hasidism as an outward sign of some inner spiritual disturbance; the *ẓaddiq* as healer was committed to a holistic view of the human being, which could not allow for the separate treatment of his spiritual and corporeal woes. From this point of view, the doctor could not but be viewed as a new type of sorcerer,[27] one who effects cures in a purely mechanistic way, without having the moral or religious stature to be a true healer. This view was supported by the fact that Jewish physicians, given their secular medical education, were often among the first in their communities to accept and lend prestige to the ideas and life-style of the Haskalah.

In the face of all this, the fact remains that Nahman did consult with doctors, first for his dying wife in 1807, and then, later in that same year, for the treatment of his own illness. His journey to Lemberg (Lvov), undertaken in the fall of 1807, was primarily for the purpose of visiting physicians in that city. This stands out in the sources, despite Nathan's protestations to the contrary.[28]

We find in Nahman's writings a strange mixture of attitudes toward healing. In this mixture three strands may be delineated:

1. Belief in the folk-medicine practices of earlier Hasidism.
2. A belief that healing depends completely upon *faith* and prayer, denying the value of both traditional and modern prescriptions for bodily healing.
3. Attempts to justify his own recourse to the "dangerous" world of modern medicine.

At times we may tend to forget, in the midst of considering Nahman's own complex and ambivalent attitudes toward wonder-working *ẓaddiqim*, how much he remained a part of the previous Hasidic world. His condemnations of the Zeide and other figures of popular piety notwithstanding, one finds much in Nahman's own writings that clearly identifies him as belonging to their universe of discourse. For the sake of a more well-rounded picture of Nahman, perhaps it would serve us well to quote some of the more traditional formulae of healing to be found in his own popular writings:

> The feather of a wild bird is a protection against lung disease, and strengthens one's life-breath.
>
> Rainwater is a cure for impotence.
>
> If one becomes suddenly mute, a kosher slaughterer's knife should be passed over his lips.
>
> Looking at an *etrog* is a cure for eyestrain.
>
> A woman who bleeds frequently but has no regular menstrual period may be cured by wine into which the true *ẓaddiq* has peered, even though other wine will be harmful to her.[29]

We have no reason to believe that Nahman disbelieved these charms and cures, which were an important part of his particular inheritance through the family of the BeSHT. He is not, however, creative in this area, and one might say that the remains of such folk belief are vestigial in him, especially since they are recorded side by side with such statements as:

> A person is best off when he relies upon nothing but God Himself. He who does not rely upon God has to pursue a complicated course of action. When a person is in need of healing, for example, he has to seek after many different sorts of herbs. Sometimes the particular herb which he needs is not to be found in our country, and those which are found here are of no use for his illness. But God is good for all that ails man; He is able to cure any disease, and He is always to be found . . .[30]

Such an attitude reflects a certain disapproval of both modern medicine and traditional herbal prescriptions for healing. While the potential efficacy of medicines is not denied here, the route of medicinal healing is depicted as more complex and less effective than the simple path of faith, which is available to every person without the benefit of any "professional" intermediary. It is thus no surprise to us when we learn that the chapter on medical advice in Nahman's *Sefer ha-Middot* was originally of much greater length, "and there was no disease in the world for which some healing was not listed there. But afterwards, he refused to recopy this list and he burned it."[31]

In a number of other teachings, Nahman clarifies his position on this matter, claiming that illness is a result of sin, and particularly of insufficiency in faith. It is thus only through prayer and the restoration of faith that a true cure can be attained. There are many passages in Nahman's teachings that reflect this attitude, particularly in those writings stemming from the period of his own illness. In some of them, *doktorei* is proclaimed to be the very antithesis of faith, an "enemy," which is defeated by the example of the pious and their trust in God.

> When prayer is redeemed, all *doktorei* falls by the way, as there is no need for medicine.
>
> All medicines are compounded of herbs, and each herb receives its power from a particular star or constellation. Thus our rabbis have said: 'There is not a single blade of grass which does not have a star or constellation that strikes it and says to it: "Grow!" ' Now every one of these stars and constellations in turn receives its power from some force higher than itself, and that force is sustained by something still higher; all of them are ultimately sustained by the highest angels . . . These angels, however, also receive their power from that which is above them; 'Height above height' (Eccles. 5:7). Finally, all of them are derived from the root of all, the word of God, as Scripture says: 'By the word of God were the heavens created, and all their hosts by the breath of His mouth' (Ps. 33:6).
>
> For this reason, a person who is able to pray is no longer in need of medicines. For prayer *is* the word of God, which is the root of all . . .
>
> This is the meaning of 'When you serve the Lord your God, He will bless your bread and water; I shall remove illness from your midst' (Ex. 23:25). 'When you serve'—the service meant here is prayer. Then He will bless your bread and water, to remove disease. That is to say: He will send you your healing through bread and water. Since everything is blessed through the one root, which is the word of God or prayer, bread and water should potentially have the same healing powers as do medicinal herbs. The distinctions between the various powers, those which designate that this plant should have these medicinal powers, while another plant will have different effects, exist only below. In the upper root, the word of God, all is one, and there is no distinction between bread, water, and herbs. Thus when one takes hold of this root in prayer he is able to draw those healing powers into his bread and water.[32]

We now understand the difficulty Nahman must have had in justifying his turn to the practitioners of medicine as his own disease began to frighten him. Why should the true *ẓaddiq*, the great master of prayer, waste his efforts (at best!) on journeys to such doctors who know nothing of the 'root,' but simply prescribe their rather chancey herbal compounds? Were Nahman fully convinced of the position he so beautifully expounds here, he could hardly have undertaken his visit to the physicians of Lemberg.

The truth seems to be that Nahman's journey to Lemberg represented a certain failure of nerve. His illness was the result of his own sins, and his prayers had done nothing to save his wife from her fate. Again, but now in a newly desperate way, God seemed to be far from him and was ignoring his pleas for help. Seeing the progressive deterioration of his physical condition, he allowed himself to follow the "modernist" tendency within his own conflicted soul, and went (much to the chagrin of Nathan and certain other disciples) to see a doctor.

There are two undated passages within Nahman's later writings in which he seeks to legitimize the work of doctors in healing the sick; it seems likely that these belong to the period of his Lemberg journey. One of them follows the general outline of the teaching we have just quoted, but then moves in a very different direction. There he reiterates his belief that illness is always the result of some divine decree, and states that the physician's power to heal depends upon whether the heavenly decree has been rescinded. While the decree is in force, there is indeed some particular herbal formula that would cure the ailment, but doctors are seldom sufficiently wise to detect it. When a *pidyon*, or gift, is given to the *ẓaddiq*, however, and the *ẓaddiq* prays for healing, the heavenly decree can itself be rescinded. If the doctor catches the right moment and acts before a new decree has been issued against his patient, *any* of his herbs will have the same healing power. Here, however, Nahman does not go as far as to say that the same healing could as well be achieved by means of bread and water. Some degree of legitimacy is thus left to the physician's practice, though it is reduced to a fairly mechanistic level. *Ẓaddiq* and doctor work together in healing, but it is the prayers of the *ẓaddiq* that account for the greater part of the physician's success.

In the other passage, Nahman once again seeks some integration of medical practice with his own religious value system. In seeking to explain how it is that prescribed medicines are somehow effective after all, he says:

> When a person pays no heed to the ultimate meaning of life, why should he live at all? When the soul, ever longing to do the will of its Creator, sees that the person is not doing God's bidding, it develops a longing to return to its source. It begins to pull itself away from that body which it inhabits. This is the source of illness; a person is weakened as his soul begins to draw away from him. . . .
>
> The reason why people's health is restored through medicines is as follows: The soul now sees that this person is able to control his passions after all,

forcibly doing that which is against his usual habits. He who has been accustomed to eating bread and various other kinds of foods now forces himself to consume bitter drugs and potions for the sake of his health. When the soul sees that he can control his passions for any purpose, it returns to him in the hope that he will also conquer his desires for the sake of the true and ultimate purpose, the fulfillment of his Creator's will.[33]

It was shortly after the festival of Sukkot in 1807—less than half a year after his return from his aborted Navritch journey—that Nahman set out to visit the doctors of Lemberg. As the capital of Austro-Hungarian Galicia, that city was the nearest outpost of Western culture and medicine to Nahman's home in the much more backward Russian Ukraine. Nahman's oldest friend Simeon, who had been with him in Erez Israel, accompanied him on this journey as well. It may have been that Simeon was less outspoken in his opposition to *doktorei* than Nathan or some of the others, and so was chosen to accompany his master.[34]

Nahman stayed in Lemberg through that winter, placing himself under the doctors' care. For a time, the cures they offered seemed to have some effect. While he was in Lemberg, the doctors were able to ensure that he got the nearly total bedrest required for tuberculosis patients. Nahman, however, (or perhaps Nathan) was not inclined to ascribe the improvement in his condition to the physicians alone:

There was a long period during which he lay on one side, and could not turn over to lie on the other. Then God performed awesome and wondrous miracles for him, and he began to feel a bit better. One night he suddenly was able to turn over onto his other side, and he lay that way.

He said that his healing had not come about through the doctor, but rather someone had come to him during the night and had said: 'It is the King's decree that you should lie on your right side!' He then turned over and lay on his right side. . . . The one who came to him that night was Rabbi Aaron of Titov, the grandson of the BeSHT. Our master said that now R. Aaron was a true and deeply beloved friend of his.[35]

We are given only the vaguest hint as to what transpired in Nahman's inner life during the approximately eight months he spent in Lemberg. We have neither teachings nor stories dating from this period. It seems reasonable to assume that the disease, and the rest cure as well, wearied him greatly, and that his creative life was more or less at a standstill for a while.[36] There is one strange passage in the account of his Lemberg visit, however, which leads us to believe that this period in a relatively Westernized environment affected him in some ways other than purely medical ones. Nahman tells us that while he was in Lemberg

I also received medicine and drank quinine. There, in China [*khine* equals quinine equals China], they are complete heretics, claiming that there is 'neither judgment nor judge.' Various other drugs came from other places, each bearing its own brand of heresy. When all these things entered my body, something happened to me.[37]

Nathan, realizing the ambiguity of this last phrase, hastens to add: "It was necessary that this drug enter his body, in order to defeat that particular heresy. And so it was with the other drugs as well." For Nathan it is obvious that his master, seated in the demon's lair of a Lemberg doctor's office, is fighting heresy with every bit of medicine that he imbibes. Nahman's own statement, however—and here we see a good example of how faithfully Nathan reported his master's words, even when he must have wished he could emend them—gives no such indication. On the contrary, he seems to be implying that he was somehow *infected* as he consumed those heresy-bearing drugs.

Later Bratslav tradition, based upon this remark of Nathan's, views Nahman's stay in Lemberg as a preliminary engagement in the great "battle" he was later to fight in Uman against the encroachments of Haskalah. This is the way in which Nahman of Cheryn, perhaps through oral traditions, interprets Nathan's references to the "mysterious" quality of the master's sojourn in the Galician capital: "it is known . . . that in Lemberg our master concerned himself with the defeat of heresy and disbelief, which he prophetically foresaw was about to overwhelm Israel.[38]

We may assume, both from Nahman's words and from this later reference, that Lemberg was a point of some significant contact between Nahman and the world of Haskalah. Unfortunately, we are given no further details, and we can only look for the effects of Lemberg upon those things he wrote or said after his return from there. Nahman's dreams may be particularly revealing in this regard. The long dream quoted earlier was reported to Nathan several months after his return from Lemberg. There, it will be recalled, he saw himself deserted by all, off in the woods, and unable even to read a book. Could that dream somehow be a reflection of the Lemberg period, when he undoubtedly had little, if any, energy to devote to study, and when he found himself in a distant and hostile place, cut off from his disciples? Another dream, also recorded in the year following Lemberg, sounds as if it might be a further reflection of this period:

There was a community of Jews that had a very great leader. A decree was issued saying that all the Jews were to be killed. In order to stave off the decree, the leader decided that he would have to convert and become a Gentile. He called in a barber, who shaved off his beard and *pe'ot*.

Afterwards it turned out that the whole thing was a lie; there had been no such decree after all. How embarrassed that leader was! He could not show

> his cleanshaven face to people at all. He wanted to run away and hide—but how could he even go out the door to hire a wagon? His disgrace would have been more awful than can be imagined. He was thus forced to dwell with a non-Jew for a while, until his beard could grow back.[39]

Could it be that Nahman, seeing his own life as vital to his community and to the world, viewed his Lemberg journey as an act in which he abandoned his faith for the sake of survival? Did he in fact have to make some compromises with the life-style appropriate to a *ẓaddiq* while he was in the hands of the doctors, or perhaps in a sanitorium, there? If so, one could well imagine that he felt a sense of shame about it all once his stay there had ended.

There was indeed some degree of spiritual "danger" present in Lemberg at the time. As a province of the Austrian realm, Galicia was exposed to Haskalah ideas and ways of life decades earlier than Nahman's Russian homeland. Here German-language schools for Jewish children had already been in existence for some twenty years, and in language, dress, and outlook a good many young Jews were beginning to imitate the style of the Austrian capital. The educational and religious reform programs of Herz Homberg, while looked upon with justified suspicions by the Galician Jewish masses and their rabbis, had found much favor in Vienna's court circles, and had achieved some measure of success. While it happened that the first decade of the nineteenth century was a period of reaction in the touch-and-go process of emancipation in the Austrian Empire, it would have been difficult for a man of Nahman's perceptiveness and curiosity to spend eight months in the Galician capital and not deeply feel the winds of change. Certainly the class to which Nahman's doctors, and perhaps many of their patients, belonged, represented a somewhat Westernized element.[40]

Whatever of Nahman's energies were not consumed by the rest-cure he devoted to a new and to him now all-important project: preparations for the publication of his book. The teachings of *Liqquṭey MoHaRaN*, which Nathan now had in a bound manuscript copy, were finally to be made available to the world. Nahman took that copy with him on the journey to Lemberg, and around January of 1808 he was in touch with a number of the leading rabbis and *ẓaddiqim* in Poland and Galicia, seeking their approbation for publication of his teachings. He did receive five such *haskamot*, though as it turned out they were omitted from the original edition and were only printed later.[41]

It seems somewhat strange that Nahman should choose this time in his life to be concerned with the publication of his teachings. In the face of the tragedies of 1806, as we have shown, it was toward hiding, rather than revealing, that Nahman had moved. True, it was not his esoteric teachings he was now offering for publication, but the teachings did include those of the *Liqquṭim* that we have seen to be filled with only half-hidden references to the coming redemption. This surprising move seems best explained by Nahman's sense of impending death. The end he had feared so greatly since childhood was now coming upon him more quickly than he had expected and was giving him a sense that his time had run out. Under other circumstances, Nahman indeed might have chosen to wait until controversy quieted down before making such a move, but now he may have felt that he had no choice. The world was going to be leaderless after his death, and in terrible need of his teachings. What if they should be lost or distorted? Best to be sure, as a final act in the face of death, that he would make those teachings he wanted preserved available in a form that would render them accessible to future generations.

It may also be, as Weiss has suggested, that the trip to Lemberg provided an opportunity Nahman did not want to miss. The publishing-house in Bratslav (which Nathan was to establish later) did not yet exist, and the controversy surrounding Nahman would have made it difficult to publish the work nearer to home. Surely it is interesting that all of the *haskamot* he received were from far away; two of the five writers (Jacob Isaac the "Seer" of Lublin and Abraham Hayyim of Zloczow) say that they have never even met the author. Particularly conspicuous by his absence is Levi Yizhak of Berdichev. If this is the case, however—that Nahman felt he could publish *only* in far-away Lemberg—it is difficult to explain why the book in fact finally was published, and without apparent difficulty, in the closer Volhynian town of Ostrog.

Nahman at first hoped that Nathan would follow him to Lemberg, there to work with him on the final editing. When this proved impossible—the objections of Nathan's family this time could not be overcome—the manuscript was sent back to Bratslav for his editorial polishing. It was then handed over to a certain Jacob of Medvedevka, possibly an old-time *ḥasid* of Nahman's who was acquainted with the brother-in-law of the Ostrog printer, and he took care of the actual negotiations. The book was printed in a thousand copies, a fairly small run even for that time, but on fine paper and in attractive form, much to Nahman's pleasure.

Shortly after Nahman began preparing his exoteric writings for publication, he became particularly concerned with that more secret document, parts of which he had had his disciples teach publicly in various towns during that fateful summer of 1806. As the seriousness of his illness became more obvious to him, he had sought various means to deal with his situation. The most extreme of these was a decision to burn the latter book, on which he now came to place the blame for all of his recent sufferings.

> In Lemberg, between Purim and Passover of 5568 (1808), he went into his private room and wept a great deal. With tears running down his cheeks, he called to R. Simeon, and, sighing, he said: 'There is no one to consult.' He

then told him about a book which he had in his house, which had brought about the deaths of his wife and his children. He had also risked his own life for this book, and now he did not know what to do. He saw that he would have to die there in Lemberg, but if the book were burned he would live. He was in grave doubt, not knowing what was the proper course of action. It pained him to burn this holy and awesome book, for which he had already risked so much. Indeed, the true holiness of this book is beyond all description. Had it remained in the world, everyone would have seen the greatness of our master, face to face.

Nathan had begun recopying this work for Nahman some two years earlier, and had completed that task just before his master's departure for Lemberg. He was the only one other than Nahman who had ever seen the document in its entirety. Nahman's sense of the need to destroy the book may serve to confirm our suspicions that this document was quite explicit concerning his messianic claims, and perhaps also about the significance of the year 1806. The burning of the book was yet another repudiation of this aspect of his career, a repudiation that he hoped, even at this late date, would serve to prolong his life.

R. Simeon responded: 'Surely if there is any reason to think that your life depends on this, it is better that the book be burned and that you remain alive.' Our master explained that it would at least give him some more time; if the book were burned, his life would be lengthened at least a bit. But then he went on: 'You don't understand how great is the sanctity of this book, over which I lost my first wife and my children! How much have I suffered for this!' He broke down and wept again.

It was finally agreed that the book should be burned, and Simeon set off for Bratslav to do as he was reluctantly bidden.[42]

It was in the summer of 1808 that Nahman finally ended his sojourn in Lemberg and returned home to Bratslav. It seems that after a brief period of recovery during his early days in Lemberg, he had a relapse of the illness during that spring. It was at this point that he became sufficiently desperate to order the burning of his precious writings. Eventually the doctors gave up on him, telling him there was nothing more they could do for him and that he had but a short time to live. They advised him to restrict his diet, to get plenty of rest, and to take special care not to overexert himself on the homeward journey.

Nahman promptly ignored all the advice of his physicians. He rushed home as quickly as possible, and refused to allow himself any extra measure of rest. In his generally weakened condition, of course, he could no longer do all the things he had previously managed. He no longer wrote down his own teachings at all, but rather turned that enterprise entirely over to Nathan. But he felt himself too much needed by his community to do any less than the maximum permitted by his strength.[43]

He now spoke with new vehemence against all contact with doctors, apparently feeling he had been let down by them, and that their knowledge was of no use after all.

> With regard to doctors and medicine: He spoke to us at great length about these matters, taking special pains to denigrate both physicians and their cures. He warned that whoever wants to protect his life and the lives of his family should avoid them completely. . . . This is true even where there are the very greatest doctors; one should not trust them with one's life, for they themselves are more closely allied with death. . . .
>
> He told us that when he was in Lemberg, a place of many great doctors, a certain prominent doctor had himself warned him to stay away from all practitioners of medicine. He said that medical research had now gone so far that they now knew nothing at all; they had seen that it was impossible to arrive at the truth with regard to medical matters.
>
> There are also great controversies among them concerning the proper methods of healing. In the city of Lemberg, there are two groups of doctors, between whom a great controversy exists about the treatment of a certain dread disease. One group says that any strong or spicy foods are dangerous to anyone suffering with this ailment, and that they should restrict their diet accordingly. The other group says just the opposite: that strong foods are good for this disease, but that sweet and lightly-flavored foods should be avoided. Each group brings forth strong proofs to defend its point of view, and claims that anyone who follows the contrary opinion is truly poisoning himself . . . Each of these groups contains very clever and well-known doctors, and nevertheless they cannot reach the proper conclusion. . . .
>
> Let not a man who has a sick person in his house say: 'On whom can I rely? I have to try some natural remedy, rather than just give up on him without making an attempt.' This in truth is a foolish opinion, since the doctors are closer to death than they are to life. In the end you will have to rely on God alone; better to trust only in Him from the very beginning, and not entrust the patient to the care of doctors, who are usually nothing but emissaries of the angel of death. Think of yourself as one who lives in a desert or a forest, where indeed you have no one but God in whom to place your trust. You are in the same situation, even though you live in a place where there are doctors, since they themselves are in such a state of confusion. . . .
>
> Once he said jokingly that the angel of death, who has rounds to make throughout the world, is too busy to kill everyone himself. He therefore appoints messengers called 'doctors' in various places, to take care of some of the killing for him. . . .[44]

Nahman lived for just over two years after his return from Lemberg. We do not know whether he would have lived any longer had he shown greater respect for the medical profession and followed more closely the advice of his physicians. The rate of cure for tuberculosis was not high before very recent times; perhaps Nahman was not wrong in his estimate of the science of medicine as it was practiced in his day.

Coupled with the increased denunciations of *doktorei* that followed Nahman's return from Lemberg, we also find a renewed emphasis upon *faith* and *joy* in his teachings. He now seems to have recovered for a while from the bleak depressions of his Navritch period, and he was ready once again to provide real leadership to his people. Since faith and prayer were now recognized as the only legitimate weapons in his battle against the disease that was destroying him, he took to these weapons with new vigor, finding in them the strength that the dying sometimes discover on the far side of desperation. He seems to have come to terms with the likelihood of his impending death and to have decided that in the short time remaining for him there was still a great deal to be done. He particularly sought to show by his own conduct that one should never give in to utter despair, and that even one whose time was short could live a life of pious joy. There is a special poignancy to the passage that follows, when one realizes that it was spoken by a man whose doctors had just told him that his end was near:

> The reason why people remain far from God is that their minds are not settled. They do nothing to help themselves in this regard. The main thing is to get it clear in one's mind that there is no ultimate meaning to our passions and to those things that bind us to this world. [When a person realizes that this is true of] all such passions, both bodily desires and those external to the body, such as personal glory, then he will surely return to God.
>
> But know that depression keeps one from guiding the mind in the directions that one wills, and makes it difficult to come to any inner resolution. Only by means of joy can a person lead his mind where he wants, and thus settle his mind. Joy represents the world of freedom, as in 'For in joy will you go forth' (Is. 55:12). It is by means of joy that a person becomes free and goes forth from exile. When the mind is linked to joy, it is taken out of bondage, and that mind becomes free. Then that liberated mind can be guided by the will. . . .
>
> This is the meaning of the Talmudic phrase 'His mind was humored.' When one brings joy into the mind, the mind is liberated and may thus become settled. And this humoring of the mind also brings about great unifications above.[45]

Translated into a comment on Nahman's personal situation, this teaching is an announcement that he is not going to let his illness get the best of him. The threat of depression is a real one, perhaps now more than ever before. He seeks to escape it by reasserting his own ability to maintain willful control over his own mind. He contrasts himself with those who "do nothing to help themselves," who do not work to fight off the depression that engulfs them in times of adversity. The very fact of such adversity, he says, may become an occasion for the renewal of one's religious life. While he sees his illness as a force that "persecutes" or pursues him, he seeks in that feeling of persecution a new closeness to God:

> 'Many fight against me on high' (Ps. 56:3). A person has enemies above, in heaven. Thus the rabbis say: 'Just as there are enemies below, so are there enemies above.' When a person has enemies who persecute him, he flees ever closer to God. *The more a person is pursued, the closer he is to God,* since God is everywhere. 'If I rise up to heaven, there You are; I go down into Sheol, You are there' (Ps. 139:8). *Wherever a person flees, he is fleeing to God.* This is the meaning of 'Pharaoh drew near' (Ex. 14:10)—he drew Israel nearer to their Father in heaven. As he pursued them, they came closer to God.[46]

No longer physically able, after the summer of 1808, to make his usual rounds of visits to his *ḥasidim* in various towns and villages, Nahman nevertheless did resume his regular schedule of public discourses in Bratslav and encouraged his disciples to visit him somewhat more frequently than they had before. We thus have teachings, including some of Nahman's longest and most profound discourses, delivered on Rosh Hashanah, Hanukkah, and Shavu'ot, as well as on various lesser occasions, during the last two years of his life.[47]

The period between Nahman's return from Lemberg and his departure for Uman in the spring of 1810 was a period of unusual creativity, even for him. All of the longer tales in *Sippurey Ma'asiyot* stem from these days, as well as a number of important teachings published in the second section of the *Liqquṭim.* Considering the physically weakened condition in which Nahman found himself, this burst of creative energy is astounding.

Whatever changes took place in the content or style of Nahman's teachings in these last two years were subtle and have not yet been studied systematically. Of course there is a lessening of the messianic tension now, as well as a continued harping on the ill effects of sexual and other sins. His ongoing ambivalence concerning his role as *ẓaddiq ha-dor* continues, perhaps even worsening to some degree. On Rosh Hashanah following his return from Lemberg, he spoke of the need to bind oneself to *all* the leaders of the generation, since each of them stands at the head of a particular group of the souls of Israel. A little over a year later, after offering what is perhaps his most elaborate description of the *ẓaddiq ha-dor* concept, he must have shocked his hearers when he said:

> When Israel have no leader or guardian of this sort, the whole world is truly confused and in disarray. Then whoever wants to 'take the name' is able to do so, *as is the case now,* due to our many sins.[48]

What does Nahman mean by describing his own day as a time without true leadership? It is certainly clear from various other teachings that he has not completely abandoned his self-designation as *ẓaddiq ha-dor*.[49] But with the waning of his physical strength and the sense of his approaching end, he is forced to face the fact that he is not the one to whom all Israel will turn, at least not within his lifetime. Perhaps he somehow has begun to see that his old image of Bratslav as the center of the world is more pitiable than serious. His ambivalence toward his own position as *ẓaddiq*, even for his own community, has now grown to monstrous dimensions. We have seen from his dream that the thought of abandonment by his disciples was one that frightened him terribly. Yet at other times we see that he felt so closed in by the press of admirers around him that he had to seek some way to free himself from them. On Hanukkah of 1808 Nahman described this feeling in an almost overly appropriate metaphor:

> When a person is overcome by troubles, God forbid, they take their greatest toll upon the heart. The heart knows and feels the affliction; 'The heart knows the soul's bitterness' (Prov. 14:10). 'The heart understands' and thus it feels the trouble most acutely.
>
> But in a time of trouble, all the blood is joined together and rushes up into the heart. Just as when there is a problem, God forbid, in some place, everyone goes in to the wise man to seek counsel, so does the blood flow into the heart to take counsel with it in times of affliction. Then the blood overflows in the heart, and the heart is in very grave trouble indeed. Not only is it concerned about the original infliction, which it had felt most keenly, but now it is drowning in the blood that keeps on rushing into it.
>
> This is why the heart pounds so violently when a person is in trouble. It wants to shake itself loose from the blood, and to keep it flowing outward. . . .[50]

We can imagine the scene in Bratslav on both Rosh Hashanah and Hanukkah of that year. These were the times of great assembly, and a particularly large group of the faithful had come there drawn from towns and villages throughout the region. Ostensibly, they had come to hear the master's teaching, which they had sorely missed during the previous year, while he was away in Lemberg. The real concern in everyone's mind, however, was for Nahman's health. *Ḥasidim* who have been isolated for months from news of their *rebbe* rush about to inquire as to the latest turns in his illness, hoping to hear of some slight sign of improvement. The town is undoubtedly rife with rumors: the master almost died in Lemberg, the doctors nearly murdered him, and so forth. As each of the visiting disciples comes in to receive his private blessing, Nahman is able to read the worry in their faces. Rather than relieving him of his own worries about his illness (which he, the heart, surely feels more than anyone else!), they are in fact increasing his burdens. In the teaching he lets them know, in no uncertain terms, that oversolicitousness is oppressive, rather than comforting, to him.

At the same time, his continuing need for his disciples and his demand for their unswerving, or even increased, loyalty was not abated. On that same Hanukkah he said to them:

> You are not yet considered my people. A time is yet to come when the whole world will turn against me and denounce me. Only those who are strong enough to stay with me then will truly be considered my people.[51]

Here we begin to get a more accurate picture of Nahman's ambivalence toward his role. Nahman himself was about to die, but the troubles of the world, and especially the trials of the pious, were far from over. We have already seen that in denouncing the proclamation of 1809/10 as a messianic year Nahman had indicated that there would yet be a much greater loss of faith in the world before the redemption would arrive. He still felt himself to be, so long as he would live, the true *ẓaddiq ha-dor*. He had to recognize, however, that Israel was once again *about to* be bereft of leadership, in a time when its needs for a true leader would be most desperate. This view of the fast-approaching future is clearly central to his stories, even though he places them within a literary framework of events that took place long ago.

In Lemberg Nahman had seen enough of the incipient modern world to understand that great changes were about to take place, changes over which he could have no control. As he had come into his first contact with more-or-less Westernized Jews, so he had undoubtedly heard a good deal about courtly life in Vienna and the other capitals of Europe. He surely knew of the recently-established Napoleonic Grand Duchy of Warsaw, ruled by someone who had not the slightest relationship to the old royal families of Poland. It is no accident that Nahman's tales are filled with motifs of kings and princes who rule without legitimacy and who doubt the true kingship of God, or rule in opposition to the will of heaven. While these kings and princes may on one level be seen as depictions of the false *ẓaddiqim* who surround him, and they also allegorically represent the rule of demonic forces over the universe, they are at the same time reflections of the collapse of the old order of royal legitimacy in Europe, a collapse that was shockingly evident in the first decade of the nineteenth century.[52]

Coupled with this theme of illegitimate kingship, one also finds a sense of universal cataclysm pervading Nahman's stories. Some horrendous natural event, such as a great storm at sea, has wrenched all things out of their proper order. The weathering of this storm, and an awareness of the proper state of affairs resulting from it, are essential steps toward the redemption that stands as the final goal in Nahman's tales. Nahman's tale of *The Burgher and the Pauper*, told in the spring of 1809, is filled with such images. A burgher and a poor man live together in a certain city; the burgher has a son and the pauper has a lovely daughter. Because various noble suitors are interested in his daughter's hand, the pauper is elevated to a position of nobility in the land—a position hardly befitting his humble origins, which now places the daughter far beyond the reach of the burgher's son, who was her original intended. As the nobles cannot agree upon the choice of a new monarch (a situation well-known in the old Polish kingdom), the pauper actually becomes king of the country. Much to everyone's chagrin, however, his daughter remains loyal to the burgher's son, and refuses the hand of any other suitor. Her young man has meanwhile been shipwrecked and cast upon a desert shore; there he lives a hermit-like life of isolation, finally abandoning all hope of winning his beloved. Only after a highly contrived series of events in which the now deposed pauper-king and his beautiful daughter (who had meanwhile been captured by a pirate) are both shipwrecked and washed up on that same seacoast, can the conflict of the story be resolved with the marriage of the pair and their inheritance of the kingdom. The twin motifs of royal illegitimacy and chaos that fill this story are at some level a highly fictionalized representation of Europe in Napoleonic times, combined with a fairy-tale happy ending, which was, of course, not a part of the political reality.

In the tale of *The Master of Prayer*, which dates from early 1810, the motif of an order destroyed by cataclysm is made still more important. The hero of that tale, whom we have seen as Nahman's idealized *ẓaddiq*-type, is revealed to be a member of an ancient group of courtiers who had once loyally served the king. That king had an only daughter, who in turn was the mother of a beautiful wonder-child. The courtiers each possessed some particular skill employed in the king's service: one had wisdom, another had great strength, and so forth. It was the king himself, however, who had shown to each a secret place to go to improve his special powers.

> There was once a time [says the master of prayer] when each of us had gone to his own special place. The warrior, the orator, and all the rest of the king's men—each had gone to renew his particular strength.
>
> At that time a great windstorm swept over the world. The entire earth was confounded; dry land was transformed into sea and sea into land, deserts came to be where there had been towns, and new towns sprang up in areas where there had been only desert. The whole world was turned upside down by that wind.
>
> When the wind came into the king's palace, it did no damage at all. As it whipped through the palace, however, it grabbed up the beautiful child and carried him away, all in an instant. The king's daughter ran off in pursuit of

> her child. Soon she was followed by her mother, the queen, and then by the king himself. Thus all of them were scattered, and nobody knows their place.
>
> None of us was there when this happened, as we had each gone off to renew our strength. When we did return to the palace, we found no one there . . . Since then we have all been scattered, and none of us can now get back to that place where he needs to go to renew his strength. Since the wind came and turned the entire world around, changing land into sea and sea into land, the old paths which led us to those places are no longer of any use. We are now in need of new paths, because all the places have been altered. Meanwhile, we cannot renew our former strength. We do however retain an imprint of those former times—and that in itself is very great.[53]

In searching for the symbolic keys necessary for an understanding of such a tale, it is possible to lose sight of the contemporary relevance these images must have had. Indeed, the symbols are entirely appropriate to the Kabbalist's view of the universe. God, the King, dwells at the beginning with His daughter, the *shekhinah,* and the wonder-child she has produced: the soul of the messiah, or perhaps the soul of Israel as a whole. The winds of evil pass over that primal world, destroying its simple harmony and sending the messianic or Israelite soul into exile. The *shekhinah* follows her child into wandering, and even the King Himself participates in their exile. The courtiers of the kingdom are clearly the *ẓaddiqim,* who have formerly served the King, each in his unique way, by means of well-trodden paths, but now find themselves unable to continue in their former ways, and seek new paths to His service.

It is particularly the courtiers who make us realize that what we have here in part is a tale of Europe in the Napoleonic era. The old order (be it that of *ancien régime* France or pre-partition Poland) has been swept away by the great winds of change. The Napoleonic wind was bringing with it changes in the religious order as well: Nahman saw the advent of chaos in the incipient Haskalah, which was now beginning to penetrate the borders of the Hasidic "empire." How was a *ẓaddiq* to act in times like these? Nahman had already noted early in his career that the enthusiasm of the Ba'al Shem Tov's day was now difficult to muster. In his own struggles he could see clearly that faith was no longer to be taken for granted, as it had been in the past.

Here Nahman's tale diverges seriously from Lurianic myth, and becomes an attempt to explain his own times. For Luria, the great cataclysm was an event that had taken place *before* the Creation. The very existence of man was part of God's attempt at *tiqqun,* at restoring what had been rent asunder in the *primordial* period of chaos. For Nahman, the cataclysm is an event that has taken place *within* history, even within very recent history. There was a period, according to Nahman, when the *ẓaddiqim* were indeed able to serve the King by following in the paths He had shown them. Here he could hardly be referring to the pre-mundane existence of the *ẓaddiq's* soul; he is rather talking about the old order, the time before the recent storm, when everything was in its proper place. Now the great storm has come upon us, and it is because of this calamity that "we are now in need of new paths, because all the places have been altered." No wonder Nahman can at once see himself as a true *ẓaddiq* and bemoan a world bereft of leadership! There are indeed *ẓaddiqim* in the world, but he begins to perceive that their power is being taken from them. The *ẓaddiqim* knew the *old* paths to God, in which each of them was a master in his own particular way. But now those paths have become obstructed, and there is no one who can point out the new ways that will be needed in the future. It is here that Nahman most clearly reveals himself as a figure at the very border of the modern consciousness.

In this area there has been a shift of focus in Nahman's interests since his return from Lemberg. Nahman is no longer primarily concerned with fighting 'false' *ẓaddiqim* or shallow popular Hasidism. The enemy of the true *ẓaddiq* has now been redefined as the *maskil*, the Western enlightener whose ideas and life patterns threaten the very fabric of traditional religious life. The *ẓaddiq*, as the survivor of the great cataclysm, must combat him with all his strength. While one could hardly expect so radical a formulation as that of this tale to appear in his more explicit teachings, there, too, we see a subtle change, and a greater awareness of the new world about him. It is in this vein that Nahman spoke in his discourse of Shavu'ot in 1809:

> Not everyone hears the clarion call of the festival. There are certain wicked beasts, who trample and gore their prey: these beasts are the natural scientists, who show through their distorted 'wisdom' that everything occurs by natural causes, as though there were, God forbid, no divine will.
>
> Even the awesome miracles which the Lord has performed for us are interpreted by them as though they were natural events. These scientists are like wicked beasts, trampling and goring many of our people, those who follow in their way and who think, as they do, that all occurs by reason of natural law.
>
> When these forces are powerful, their roar drowns out the call of the festival, which is calling forth the will of God. Then the festive joy ceases, God forbid, for real joy comes about only through the revelation of His will. . . .
>
> The defeat of these wicked beasts, the scientists, comes about only through the great sage of holiness. He is capable of binding all desires to their root in the divine will, as Moses did in the hour of his death . . . All the desires in the world have to be tied to that single root; only in this way can the sage overcome the claims of those scientists, who say that there is no divine will at all. [54]

Changes in a thinker like Nahman are neither sudden nor ever quite complete. When one deals with a thinker who allows his thought to flow in associative patterns, one can hardly expect that an oft-repeated theme will disappear completely. Nahman knew of *maskilim* before 1808, and even in his later teachings he continues to blame their proliferation on the false leaders among the *ẓaddiqim*. But never before had he been so outspoken or so obviously worried as he criticized the Haskalah. One cannot help but wonder whether conversations with the Lemberg doctors, or with some internalized representation of them, do not form the background for the new emphasis in this teaching. The doctors must have had little tolerance for their patient's mystical biology, or for his belief that his brief periods of recovery were due to supernatural intervention. They must have sought to explain his malady to him in naturalistic terms, which left no room for his own conviction that his suffering was in accord with the will of heaven. His own sometime temptation to listen to them, in his more rational moments, is the final proof of how dangerous these ideas can be:

> There are times when this 'forehead of the snake' actually takes power. A single individual, who derives his knowledge from that place, the source of all natural science, can indeed demonstrate that all things come about through natural means. And then this 'forehead of the snake,' the root of natural science, can even enter into the sage of holiness. It carries him from thought to thought, bringing him into the most subtle investigations. There even he might seek to cast some aspersions upon the will, even denying, God forbid, that there is any divine will at all.[55]

Nahman here confesses that he, too, has been attracted to the intellectual "temptations" of Haskalah, which is the current weapon employed by the demonic snake to turn men aside from the path of righteousness. The task of the *ẓaddiq* is to fight off such temptations—but not by means of intellectual struggle alone. His weapon in the battle with the naturalists is significantly that of desire. He must call forth the *longings* for God, the desire for a restored wholeness, in himself and in those around him, in order to reassert the will of God as the activating force in the universe. Soon we shall meet the prince in Nahman's opening of *The Seven Beggars,* who is held back from utter denial of God not by any reservation of thought, but rather by a deep inner longing for some truth beyond what reason is able to grant him. This truth may be that of the imaginative rather than that of the rational faculty, called forth by elaborate fantasy rather than by discursive reasoning. But no matter, it is a truth that appeals to the deepest instincts of the human being, and as such it will save him from the demonic rationalist's denial of the Holy.

There is a direct line leading Nahman from Lemberg to Uman. In that latter city, to which he moved some five months before his death, he was engaged in frequent and often polemical encounter with the local *maskil-*

im. The battle lines of that struggle, however, had already begun to take shape in Nahman's mind upon his return from Lemberg. Once he knew, through his visit there, how serious the erosion was, and how high were his stakes in this battle against the new heresy, the unchallenging atmosphere of innocent and backward Bratslav was too confining for him. Only in Uman could he find enemies worthy of his efforts. The dying *ẓaddiq*, still committed to his proposition that growth could take place only where there was challenge, was prepared to engage himself in yet another great battle.

Nahman's move to Uman[56] was not the result of a sudden or impulsive decision. Long before the spring of 1810 he had felt a peculiar relationship to that city. The Bratslav sources that describe the special place Uman had captured in Nahman's imagination show a twofold reason for this fascination, and point to two reasons for his choice of Uman as his last home and final resting place.

Some forty years before Nahman went to Uman, that city had been the site of a major Ukrainian uprising in which many thousands of Jews had been martyred. The old cemetery of Uman contained the mass grave of the Jews who had fallen victim to this uprising, the Gonta massacre of 1768. Nahman, whose concern with the redemption of the dead was increasing in his later years, decided upon Uman as a home in order to work with the poor souls of those martyred Jews—and in order to be buried among them when his own time came to die. Already in 1802, according to Nathan, he had passed through Uman on his way from Zlotopolye to Bratslav, and had remarked that this would be a good place to be buried. On the way from Bratslav to Uman in 1810, Nahman reminded Nathan of a tale told of the BeSHT, in which the great master had been called upon to repair the souls of the unredeemed dead in a certain town. The BeSHT had nearly paid with his life for his willingness to take part in this task; Nahman seems to be telling Nathan that his own final task, that for which he will die, is to be the redemption of the sainted dead in Uman.

During his months in Uman, Nahman spoke with some frequency of his work with the dead of that city. On one occasion in particular, as he moved into the last of the three homes he was to occupy in Uman, one that commanded a particularly good view of the cemetery, he said:

> You have no idea how great is the holiness of this cemetery; it is indeed most precious and holy.

And Nathan adds in his narration:

> On many occasions he spoke with various people in praise of the Uman cemetery, where tens of thousands of martyrs are buried . . . Several times he said, both to me and to others, that he would like to be buried there. . . .

> There are innumerable things to tell of his time in Uman . . . there he especially concerned himself with the redemption of souls, as he had indicated to us when he went there. Before his death he reminded me of that incident, saying: 'Do you remember that tale [of the BeSHT] which I told you?'

As his own end drew near, Nahman already saw himself more closely bound to the dead than to the living. In having a constant view of the cemetery and in concerning himself with the redemption of its martyrs, he was preparing for the still-greater task of redeeming dead souls in which he was to engage after his own demise.[57]

The other reason for Nahman's choice of Uman concerns the redemption of the living, rather than the dead, of that city. Uman was well-known as an early center of Haskalah; it was one of the first Ukrainian cities east of the Russian Austrian border to contain a group, albeit a small one, of 'enlightened' Jews.[58] On Nahman's brief visit to Uman in 1802, he had already encountered these *maskilim* and had established some significant contact with them. A late Bratslav source gives us a colorful, if apocryphal, account of that initial meeting between Nahman and the *maskilim:*

> When our master traveled from Zlotopolye to Bratslav, he spent a Sabbath in Uman. There were at that time three great heretics in Uman. One was called Haykel, and the others were his two sons-in-law, Hirsch Baer, the greatest heretic of his time, truly the 'forehead of the snake,' and a doctor named Landau, who was not quite as bad as his brother-in-law,[59] They were prominent people, and were influential in government circles; they even possessed a golden sword which had been given to them by the Czar. They had achieved this because their wisdom was known throughout Russia, and indeed all over the world.
>
> Whenever a well-known *ẓaddiq* came to Uman, it was their practice to go and mock him, or to talk with him if they found him to be an intelligent person. The *ẓaddiq* of Berdichev had once wanted to become rabbi of Uman, but they had not permitted it. The same had been true in the case of the rabbi of Shepetovka.
>
> When our master spent the Sabbath there, Haykel said to the others: 'I will go test him out while you two take a nap. If I find that he is someone worth talking to, I'll send for you to come.' Haykel came to the house where our master was staying, and our master asked him what it was that he wanted. Haykel replied: 'I have heard that a great man has come to town, and I want to greet him.' 'There is a great man staying across the road from me,' said the master, (for a certain general was staying in the house opposite our master's lodging). 'Why do you not go to greet him?' This retort was like a slap in the face to Haykel, and he remained silent. When he went home he reported: 'Even though I spoke to him just a bit, and he did insult me somewhat, I see that there is someone here worth talking to. Sleep a while, and we'll go to him during the meal.'

> They returned as our master was teaching Torah at the table. When they came in, he stopped for a moment and cleverly turned his teaching toward a difficult mathematical calculation. When they heard it, they said to one another: 'He's not doing this for his *ḥasidim*, but for us!' They delved deeply into this mathematical problem, but could not solve it. They said to him: 'Since you raised this problem, you offer a solution.' He gave them a most satisfactory answer, and they considered him to be a very wise man. They asked him to remain in Uman, and he asked them for a copy of the book *Yeyn Levanon*.
>
> He then traveled on to Bratslav, where he remained for eight years.[60]

Despite the likely embellishments in this tale, the point of it remains quite clear: Nahman was acquainted with the *maskilim* of Uman long before he settled in that city, and his choice of Uman as a dwelling-place was somehow related to their presence there. Since Nahman's contact with the *maskilim* was later to become so controversial, it is hard to imagine that latter-day Bratslav tradition would *invent* a tale increasing the importance of these enlighteners in its revered master's life.

The two reasons for Nahman's final journey in fact have a good deal in common, and both of them make good sense. By the spring of 1810, Nahman's tubercular condition was very critical; he must have realized that he had but a few months to live. He saw the unfulfilled dreams of a lifetime closing in on him, and was forced to realize that he would accomplish little more before his death. Given his exaggerated sense of self-importance, he must have felt his life to have been a terrible failure. The world had not recognized him as the true *ẓaddiq*, and redemption seemed no closer now than when he had started out. He longed now for some final act of spiritual greatness; if his life had accomplished little, at least his death would have some great spiritual meaning. He wanted to die as a martyr in the cause of redemption, not merely as the victim of an uncontrollable disease. Perhaps he still even wanted to vindicate his role as Messiah ben Joseph, who has to die in battle before the world can be redeemed. Both of these explanations of his turn to Uman would fit such a strategy. The struggle with the living *maskilim*, as well as the struggle to uplift the souls of the dead, could be seen as the final great engagement in Nahman's lifelong struggle to effect the spiritual uplifting of those around him, and in that process to redeem his own burdened soul as well.[61]

Early in May of 1810 Nahman set out from Bratslav on the way to his new home. Some time earlier, his *ḥasid* Meir of Teplyk had been in touch with the heirs of the late Nahman Nathan Rapoport, and had arranged that a place be found for Nahman within the house of that well-known *maskil*. Before Meir was able to report back, however, a great fire devastated much of Bratslav and destroyed Nahman's home. This seemed to him a sign that the move to Uman could be put off no longer. Three days after the fire, he set out on his final journey. On the road he and Nathan ran into Meir, who was coming to tell his master that all had been arranged for him in Uman. Nahman was much excited about the fact that he would have an opportunity to live in and 'purify' the home of a heretic, and while on the road he made half-mysterious and half-joking remarks to Nathan concerning their right to 'inherit' the home of one who had been their joint namesake. He raised his hand as though holding out a cup for *Kiddush*, and said, "This *Kiddush* ("sancitification") will be recited in a home where the name of God has never before been mentioned!"[62]

Life in the Rapoport household seemed a great challenge to Nahman, a spiritual adventure fraught with terrible dangers. He had now entered the very heart of the enemy camp,

> the far edge of Israel, the place where the boundary of Israel ceases.

Thus he would have to be on the alert at every moment:

> We have to take great care not to stumble, God forbid . . . They will surely not be able to persuade us to abandon our holiness, since we are strong in that. Intellectually, they will not be capable of confounding us with their nonsense . . . But with regard to external matters, such as food, we must take particular care. For this we will need divine protection, and we should pray to God that he guard us in these matters.[63]

Nahman's disciples were not particularly happy about their master's new choice of residence, or about his generally open attitude toward the *maskilim* of Uman. How could the greatest of the *ẓaddiqim* live in a place where even the *kashrut* of the food was under suspicion? Nahman's claim that the late Rapoport himself had come to him during his prayers and had asked for redemption did not alleviate their worries about their master's fate at the hands of the living. Some opponents of Nahman went so far as to cast aspersions on his choice of Uman altogether, claiming that he had sought some personal gain in leaving Bratslav for this larger and more prestigious city. Nahman seems to have been angered by such criticism; in response he quoted the question of the prophet Hosea (7:13): "Shall I redeem them, since they have spoken lies about me?"[64]

Among his own disciples, it was particularly Yekutiel of Tirhavits and Naftali of Nemirov who dared question their master. The former was brushed aside with clever answers. When he asked why Nahman had come first to the house of a heretic, he was reminded that the Creation of the world had also been preceded by a period of chaos. When he went on to ask why Nahman drew such wicked people close to him, the master replied, "Since the *ẓaddiqim* won't come near to me, I have to draw these others near. Perhaps out of them I'll make truly good people." Naftali received a still more harsh answer. When he asked, "What are these people to you?" he was told: "And what are you [disciples] to me? You are nothing more than feathers on my coat. If I were to give one good blow, you'd all fly away."[65] Some of the lesser disciples indeed did "fly away" during Nahman's final months; the rumors concerning their master's conduct in Uman must have been more than they could bear. When a certain member of the circle in Nemirov failed to show up in Uman for Rosh Hashanah of 1810, Nahman did not make any effort to contain his anger.[66]

Controversy and denunciation had never been very effective means of getting Nahman to change his plans, however. Having decided that the saving of the *maskilim* was a part of his task in Uman, he was not to be deterred by the questions of the opponents or even of troubled followers. In earlier years he himself had warned of the great dangers that lie in wait for those who associate too readily with the wicked, even in the process of trying to save their souls. Now he was ready to cast such cautions aside and throw himself headlong into the battle. He no longer sought any new followers from among the pious folk of Uman;[67] among the living of that city his attentions were focused upon the 'heretics' alone. He took great pride in every bit of contact that he had with the enlighteners, sure that even the slightest sign of respect they might show him was a foretaste of their impending repentance.

> He said that the bit of self-humiliation or respect that these great sinners display when they come in to see the true *ẓaddiq* itself brings about some great *tiqqun*. They are so very wicked that even the slightest degree of submission before the true *ẓaddiq* has a great effect.
>
> Israel recite every day: 'The Lord is great above all gods' (Ps. 95:3) and this causes no great commotion. But when Jethro came and said: 'Now I know that the Lord is great' (Ex. 18:11), then the name of God was glorified and sanctified both above and below. Because he had come from such a great distance, indeed from the very depths of the *qelipot*, and humbled himself before the holy—it was because of this that God's name was glorified so greatly.[68]

He claimed that when the *maskilim* came into his presence they were filled with regret for the sinful lives they had led. Even though their souls were derived from the "side of evil," the true *ẓaddiq* was able to bring out some sparks of holiness within them.

Nathan tells us rather little of what actually transpired in the frequent conversations his master held with members of the Rapoport and Hurwitz households. It is clear that there were serious religious debates, in which Nahman did try to bring the *maskilim* to the point of repentance. To this end he undoubtedly combined intellectual argument with strong emotional appeal, knowing as he did that neither of these methods alone could convince opponents such as these of the truth of his faith.

From a defense found in one of Nahman's own teachings, however, it also becomes clear that not all of his contacts with the *maskilim* were of a polemical nature. He did allow himself to discuss worldly matters with them, and he was more than happy to use them as a source of information concerning the outside world, particularly the current state of the Napoleonic wars. At the same time, he felt a need to justify such conversations in terms of his higher purpose:

> This is why the *ẓaddiqim* carry on conversation with indecent people or even with gentiles [with whom they normally have no contact].
>
> When the *ẓaddiq* speaks with the wicked, and he uplifts his mind to bind himself to God, he also uplifts their minds along with his own, and he thus brings them close to God. The true *ẓaddiq* contracts his intellect, speaking to them with great cleverness and artfulness, binding all his words to God and thus bringing them [inadvertently] to repent. . . .
>
> In conversing with the wicked, the true *ẓaddiqim* sometimes discuss battles or various other worldly matters with them, cloaking the great light of Torah within their words . . . Were the *ẓaddiq* to speak directly of Torah to these wicked ones, his hearer might only become still greater a sinner than before; he could indeed be made totally wicked. [Of Torah's ways it is said:] 'The righteous shall walk in them, but sinners will stumble over them' (Hos. 14:10). 'If a person merits, the Torah is an elixir of life for him; if he does not merit, it is poison.' Therefore, were the *ẓaddiq* to reveal the Torah as it is, the sinner would move still further away from it, the Torah itself serving as a poison to him. Because he is far from Torah, it must be given him in guarded form, through these various permutations.[69]

The same justification that was used for the telling of tales is now employed to justify "profane" conversation with the sinners. Unlike storytelling, however, conversation is a mutual act, in which the *ẓaddiq* must receive as well as give. While Nahman in this passage seems aware of the *ẓaddiq's* role in "hiding" the Torah as he cleverly presents it to the other under the guise of ordinary conversation, he does not seem bothered here about the effects of these contacts upon the *ẓaddiq* himself, or about the dangers of hearing the wicked opinions of those who deny the Torah.

Nahman's allowing himself to establish a relationship with the *maskilim* that apparently went beyond the bounds of polemic is confirmed by later sources in the camps of both Bratslav Hasidism and Haskalah. Indeed, had the relationship consisted purely of disputation, it is doubtful that it would have raised such controversy among Nahman's own disciples. Nathan's need to minimize the import of this relationship and the constant censoring of references to the *maskilim* of Uman in his and his followers' writings only make sense if there indeed was some embarrassment concerning the master's behavior. Given the Bratslav tradition of censorship, it is rather surprising that we find a long and elaborate account of the contact between Nahman and the maskilim in the source we have already quoted on the pre-1810 contacts with Uman. While we should not take this account completely at face value, it does contain certain important elements relevant to our present discussion:

> Once they were playing chess at our master's house. As happens in the midst of a game, they forgot to pay great respect to the master, and became comfortable with him. R. Nathan and R. Naftali entered during the game, with their usual fear and dread. When they saw the scene that greeted them, they were greatly disturbed. Our master said to them [to the *maskilim*], 'You are not of my army.' He then told the tale of a certain king who once took his closest friend to a special room, and played chess with him. They too forgot that they were king and subject, and played as two ordinary people. Sometimes the king won a game, and sometimes his friend won, and so forth, until some of the awe was forgotten. But then it happened that certain princes of the realm needed to see the king; they walked into the room where the chess game was going on, bearing their usual trepidation in coming before the king. The friend, seeing this, began to recall that he was playing with the king, and intentionally played less well, in order that the king might win. The king realized what was happening, and said to the friend, 'This is no concern of yours. With them I rule nations; with you I play chess!' Our master pointed with his hands to R. Nathan and R. Naftali, saying: 'With them I rule nations; with you I play chess.'[70]

While the details of this encounter may be fictionalized, it is again impossible to imagine that later Bratslav tradition would invent the notion that Nahman played chess with 'the forehead of the snake' and allowed the other to consider it a simple game of chess. A hagiographic tradition would hardly invent an action it then would have to take special pains to justify.

This sense of Nahman's non-argumentative contact with the maskilim is confirmed also by a relatively early account from Haskalah circles. Published in a Russian-Jewish periodical in 1862, only a year after the death of Hirsch-Baer Hurwitz, it tells the following story:

> . . .The said Rabbi Nahman was a grandson of Israel Ba'al Shem Tov. He was a man of parts, but strongly inclined to mysticism. He is said to have been a friend of Hirsch Baer Hurwitz (of Uman), later famous as a professor of Oriental languages at Cambridge University. Hurwitz would read and explain to Rabbi Nahman the German classics, to which he listened very attentively. If an idea appealed to him, he would incorporate it in his own works, ascribing it to a Hasidic master. Once Hurwitz read to him the passage in Schiller's drama *Kabale und Liebe*, in which the father, reproaching

> his daughter for thinking of her beloved even in church, receives the following retort: 'Should not the Almighty be delighted over the fact that my joy in the best of His creatures leads me to forget the Creator Himself?' The rabbi was deeply impressed by this reflection, and shortly thereafter it appeared in his own works, not in the mouth of Louise, of course, but in the mouth of a Hasidic master.[71]

Here, too, the details are unreliable, and the *maskil* describing the scene is undoubtedly taking furtive pleasure in the thought that Nahman's tales, well-known by the middle of the nineteenth century, are nothing more than reworked borrowings of 'enlightened' literary motifs. The tales, of course, were all completed *before* Nahman came to Uman. Once again, however, we see described here a non-polemical friendship between *ẓaddiq* and *maskil*, one that could hardly be a pure invention of later times.

Nahman's months in Uman were in fact a period of terrible consternation for him. Whatever peace he had made with himself concerning his approaching death after his return from Lemberg now seems to have fallen apart as he entered this new and frightening world. Not since the burning of his book, two full years earlier, was Nahman in so troubled a state as that which we witness in his early weeks in Uman. All the trials of his later years now seemed to close in about him: physical illness, public controversy, inner doubts, and temptations toward heresy all converged to heighten his final torments. This turmoil is reflected in a number of Nahman's own statements, faithfully recorded and dated by Nathan, ranging from late spring through mid-summer of 1810.

Only a few weeks after his arrival in Uman, Nahman sought to shed the mantle of leadership altogether, and expressed regret that he had ever allowed himself to become a public figure. He had taken a bold step in seeking out the "wicked" of Uman, and now, in the privacy of a conversation with his disciple, expresses grave doubts over whether that step was a proper one:

> On Monday, the twenty-fourth of Iyyar [May 28, 1810], in Uman, he said in a conversation with me that in these times he had a strong desire to get people away from him. He would like to find a place where he could live by himself, without the burden of being constantly surrounded by people. He said that had he never begun to conduct himself as a *mefursam*, he might have attained something. I answered him: 'Did not Moses also concern himself with leading the people and bringing them to God?' He responded: 'But Moses too did wrong in this; *he was punished for having attempted to bring in the mixed multitude.*'

> He said that the greatest service of God is in those areas which are left up to personal choice, in which there is no *miẓwah* involved. . . . It is up to man whether or not to do these things; he is not told to do them at all, and the

> decision is completely his own. This is like the extra day [of preparation for Sinai] which Moses added of his own accord. This aspect is present in every act of serving God; something is always left up to man, concerning which there is neither commandment or prohibition. Moses added that day without being commanded to do so. This is the highest form of service, as one is always in doubt as to whether it is the will of God or not, since nothing is commanded with regard to it.
>
> He said that there is no suffering in the world, and surely no difficulty in the religious life, compared to this question of the will of God. All of the sufferings in the world—and he knew more of them than he chose to mention—he would gladly take upon himself, if he only knew with certainty that they were the will of God. . . .

This general reflection on the ambiguities of the religious life was then focused directly upon the question that was of present concern to him:

> He said: 'Have we not already spoken of this—the time and effort that it takes to help even a *ẓaddiq* who is yet alive in matters of God's service . . . When you want to help him or uplift him to his proper rung, it is more difficult than helping even thousands of [deceased] wicked ones to repair their souls. It is terribly difficult to work with one who still has choice, to tear him away from his own choosing and to guide him to the path of truth. Even the worst of sinners, once he is dead, will do as you want and will follow any command . . . Conversely, even a *ẓaddiq* who is still alive in the body has a will, and it is thus terribly hard to turn him toward the truth. . . .
>
> 'Surely the time spent . . . with one who has free will is particularly precious, but it takes so very much time to work with him. This is the doubt: in the time spent with a single willful person, whom it is so hard to help, one could uplift many thousands of the dead.'
>
> He was in grave doubt about this matter, and could not decide upon the proper course.[72]

Here the two motives for Nahman's choice of Uman compete with one another. Were he to concentrate on the dead alone, he would surely suffer no controversy; this was a proper and noncontroversial activity for a *ẓaddiq*, especially one who was facing his own death. But the attraction to the living, and particularly to the tough-willed opposition he encountered in the *maskilim*, was too much for Nahman the battler for souls to resist. Struggling with the living undoubtedly also confirmed his own sense of life, a confirmation he sorely needed as he saw his own life-force quickly slipping away from him.

Some two weeks later, he shocked his disciples by refusing to offer a teaching to them as they gathered in Uman for the festival of Shavu'ot. Shavu'ot had always been one of the three great assembly times in

Bratslav; his disciples naturally were especially interested in hearing what their master would have to say on this particular occasion. This indeed would seem to have been a great opportunity for Nahman: a month after his controversial move to Uman, his disciples were gathered together on the festival of revelation. What better time to speak of the *ẓaddiq's* mission in revealing Torah to the unbelievers, to invoke the image of Jethro, whose conversion was a necessary prelude to the events at Sinai, or to offer some other justification for his controversial conduct. Instead, he brushed the gathered throngs aside, telling them that they were not sufficiently wicked (in contrast to the *maskilim!)* to evoke words of teaching from the *ẓaddiq:*

> On Shavu'ot of 5570 [June 9–10, 1810] he was in Uman; he had arrived there a short time previously. He did not teach Torah on that holiday, saying to us in a joking manner: 'You are not sinful enough for me to teach you.' He then went on to say that certain teachings were brought about only because of sinners, like the story of the golden calf. That entire section of the Torah was created by their sins. Thus the Rabbis also said: 'Had Israel not sinned, they would have been given only the Torah and the Book of Joshua.' The remainder of the Bible was written only as reproof for the sins of Israel. . . .[73]

Here Nahman is feeling the sting of accusations made against him by his own disciples. His 'joke' in fact contains tremendous bitterness, as though to say: "You speak against me for teaching Torah to the wicked? Very well; I'll show you that they, and not you, are the *only* ones deserving of my teaching."

Despite this sharp retort on the matter of teaching, he did give in to the pressures of his assembled disciples on another matter. On the day after Shavu'ot, he moved out of the house of Nahman Nathan Rapoport, and took up lodging with a certain Joseph Samuel, a pious Jew of Uman and a more fitting host for a *ẓaddiq*. The accommodations in this place were not particularly to his liking, but the apartment he did want (also owned by a *maskil)* was not yet available, and he felt that he could stay with the Rapoports no longer. Once at Joseph Samuel's house, he did make an attempt to offer some teaching, but he interrupted himself and refused to complete his talk. He had given in on one crucial issue, but he was still too agitated and too ambivalent about his disciples to be willing to teach them as he had in the past.[74]

A little more than a month after this episode, we once again hear of Nahman's being torn by ambivalences and regretting the course of his entire adult life.

> On Sabbath eve, the twelfth of Tammuz [July 13] he spoke at the table about matters concerning himself. He expressed amazement that he kept on doing strange things which people could not understand, always wandering from place to place. What had he lacked in Medvedevka? He should

> have remained there always, where he had such peace and quiet. But he had not been satisfied with that quiet life, and had uprooted himself from there to settle in Zlotopolye. There he suffered terribly from the great controversy, so he left that town and moved to Bratslav. Now, this summer, he had gone from Bratslav to Uman. Here he should have chosen some fitting person to live with, and instead he had set himself up in that place, etc. He wondered at himself, and at all the strange things he had done.[75]

Nathan, ever the faithful disciple ready to justify his master's actions, had a ready reply:

> I said to him: 'But why did Moses choose one of Jethro's daughters for a wife?' (My intent was simply to say that this is God's way: the unification of opposites. Moses had to be joined to Jethro . . . In the same way, he had to be joined to people like these . . .)

Nahman was not prepared at this point to accept any facile justification. He related to Nathan's answer as though it were yet another challenge. His response again bears witness to the great anguish of his situation:

> He then said to those who were assembled around the table: 'Did you hear the great question he has asked?' He then said: 'You are not worthy to bear witness,' but we failed to understand this matter of witnessing. . . .
>
> On Sabbath morning he spoke further of this matter, saying to me: 'Do you have an answer [to your own question]?' I explained to him that I felt no problem with regard to Moses. He said: 'In that case, you are merely answering one question by raising another!' He said that I had guessed what was on his mind. He had been dealing with this question for some time, and had been praying that an answer be given him. 'Now,' he said, referring to me, 'he has raised the question. But you all know nothing of this. I have thought about this matter for so long, and have offered so many prayers concerning this—not only within my regular thrice-daily prayers, but with various additional prayers of my own—for I sought an answer from heaven to this problem. I wanted to be answered by a voice from heaven.' He said, however, that he would refuse any human answer to this problem. Afterwards he had lessened his demands of heaven, seeking to be answered by some messenger, or at least by means of beasts or birds. Any answer that was not from man would be acceptable—but he had not yet received it.
>
> He said: 'You are really very small people, and I have no one with whom I can talk.'

We now begin to understand the psychological complexity of Nahman's months in Uman. He realized that the final crucial decision of his life, that of whether or not to continue in his association with the *maskilim,* was his alone to make. At the same time, he felt himself utterly torn by that decision, and was looking desperately for some divine guidance in the matter. The answers of Nathan and the other disciples were in no way acceptable to him; he was aware of their strong prejudice against the enlighteners, and thus could not take them seriously. In the course of this conflict he was also forced to realize that his disciples were rather small-minded people, and that he could carry on an intelligent conversation more readily with his opponents than with his own followers. It must have pained the disciples terribly to hear such sharp words of criticism come out of their master's mouth, but Nahman must have been equally pained to realize that the disciples over whom he had labored so hard were not people with whom he now felt he could communicate. Nahman saw himself trapped in an impossible situation, caught between pious detractors, uninteresting disciples, and the frightening enlighteners.

Seeing no way out of this dilemma, he turned in despair to Naftali and said: "Who knows what we have done here in Uman that we are forced to remain here so long? It seems as though we cannot leave this place. We are captives here, and they won't let us go."[76] Since the move to Uman had been Nahman's own choice, one about which Naftali himself had raised objections, this statement can only be read as a sign of terrible frustration as the tension of those final months continued to erode whatever confidence was still left in him.

In the midst of this heightening spiral of consternation in that summer of 1810, there is one event that stands out both as climax and as resolution of Nahman's inner conflict. On *Shabbat Naḥamu,* in mid-August of that summer, Nahman offered one of the most memorable of all his teachings. In better years, that Sabbath had been one of the occasions on which he would travel from Bratslav to visit with his *ḥasidim* in the surrounding communities. Now a large group of them gathered once again in Uman, hoping still to hear some words from their master, whose health was known to be failing quickly. The events of this Sabbath are of particular significance for an understanding of Nahman's final days, and have been recorded and discussed by Nathan in several places.[77] Nahman had just moved to yet another home, this the one having the window that looked out over the Uman cemetery. Though its owner, referred to by Nathan only as the Lukaczer (designating the man's town of origin) was also a *maskil,* he was away in St. Petersburg, and it was the less-tainted members of his family who had let the house to Nahman. There a large crowd had gathered for the Friday evening meal.

> On the Sabbath eve, he came from his room to the main house, where the people had assembled. He was so very, very weak that he hardly had the strength to speak. He immediately recited *Kiddush* over the wine, and then sat down at the table. He did not return to his room after *Kiddush,* as was his usual custom when there were large gatherings. He sat there, in all his weakness, and feebly he began to talk a bit. He said:

'Why do you come to me? I don't know anything at all now. When I teach Torah, there is some reason to travel in order to be with me. But why have you come now? I don't know anything now; I'm just a simple person.' He kept on in this manner, repeating two or three times that he was just a simple person who knew nothing at all. He then said that he lived now only by virtue of his one time journey to Erez Israel. From this he went on to explain the whole awesome matter of how he sustained himself, in time of 'simplicity,' by his journey to Erez Israel.

He spoke of the fact that everyone at some point in his life is in this state of knowing nothing, and of how the true *ẓaddiq*, by entering this state of emptiness in his own life, binds himself to those others and helps in their redemption. Here he managed most successfully to apply the Hasidic doctrine of the *ẓaddiq's* descent to his own frequent vacillations of mood, and he realized, quite spontaneously, that the state of depression in which he had been so deeply engulfed during those months in Uman did indeed have some greater meaning. This teaching is most particularly characteristic of the 'personal' quality we have found time and time again in Nahman's discourses: while the first person is never used, there is not the slightest doubt that he is speaking of his own experience; further, while the theme of his words is that of the *ẓaddiq's* power to redeem *others*, the desired result of the teaching is really first the justification of his own life and the rescue of his own spirit from the pit of despair. Toward the end of the teaching he said:

The *ẓaddiq* therefore must go down and fall into this state of simplicity, and become a truly simple man for some time. In this way he brings life to all the simple ones, whoever they may be . . . All of the simple ones get their life through him, each in accord with how near he is to holiness, and to the *ẓaddiq*. . . .

The main thing is this: It is forbidden to despair! Even a simple man who cannot study at all, or one who finds himself in a place where he is unable to study, or the like, should in his very simplicity be strong in worship and in the fear of God. Even at that very moment he is receiving life-giving sustenance from the Torah, through the great simple one, the great *ẓaddiq*, who has himself undergone that simplicity and therefore can sustain them all.

Even he who stands on the very bottom rung, God forbid, or in the very depths of hell, may God protect us, should nevertheless not despair. He should fulfill the Scripture: 'Out of the belly of the deep I cried' (Jonah 2:3), and be as strong as he can. Even he will be able to return and receive the Torah's sustenance, by means of the *ẓaddiq*. The main thing is to strengthen yourself in whatever way you can, no matter how far you have fallen. If you hold on even just the slightest bit, there is yet hope that you will return to God.

In the course of that teaching, Nahman had managed to transform his own mood. Gone was the oppressive confusion that had tortured him for those months in Uman. Gone were the doubts about his own fallen state, and the torments of his attraction to the sinners. In this moment he was able to affirm once again that his life did have meaning after all, and that his own, inner suffering had existed for a redemptive purpose. In the very midst of his despair he had somehow found strength, and had come through in triumph, both for his people and for himself.

> After the teaching he became very joyous, and told the people to begin singing *'Azamer bi-Shevaḥin* immediately, before the [ritual] washing [of hands preceding the meal]. He had been so weak of late that they had hardly sung at all, but now he was so elated that he ordered them to sing. He himself sang along with them. Afterwards he spoke with us, very happily, and with an awesome and wondrous grace. He sat through the meal with great joy, talking with us and strengthening us greatly . . . Then he shouted from the very depths of his heart:
>
> *'Gevalt! Do not despair!'* He went on in these words: *'There is no such thing as despair at all!'*[78]
>
> He drew forth these words slowly and deliberately, saying: 'There is no despair.' He said the words with such strength and wondrous depth that he taught everyone, for all generations, that he should never despair, no matter what it is that he has to endure.[79]

The message of that *Shabbat Naḥamu* was indeed the final legacy left by Nahman to his people. He died two months later, without again having fallen into the abyss of despair. The example of his life, at least equally with the content of his tales and teachings, was to serve as a prime source of truth and strength for the community he left behind, a community which survives down to our own day. It is no accident that the Bratslavers were to become the "dead *ḥasidim*," alone in the Hasidic world not appointing anyone after Nahman to be his successor as *rebbe*. The relationship he had with his disciples, unique in both quality and intensity, did not allow him in any way to be "replaced." Those who remained faithful to the Bratslav community—and other latter-day penitents who were to choose to enter into relationship with the master—had to pay the price of not having a living *rebbe* to follow, but gained in exchange the example of a man who had suffered all the torments of hell in his lifetime, but had refused to give in to ultimate despair.

Emmanuel Ringelbaum's diary of life in the Warsaw ghetto contains the following brief notice, in the entry for February 19, 1941:

> In the prayer-house of the *ḥasidim* from Bratslav on Nowolipie Street there is a large sign: 'Jews, Never Despair!' The *ḥasidim* dance there with the same religious fervor as they did before the war.

NOTES

1. *Yemey MaHaRNaT*, pp. 28, 37: *Ḥayyey* 6:1.

2. See Leon Festinger et al, *When Prophecy Fails*, especially the methodological introduction (where Sabbatianism is discussed briefly) and the chapter entitled "Reactions to Disconfirmation", pp.193*ff*. Other studies of millennarian hopes and their disconfirmation, including the extensive work done on Melanesian Cargo Cults, are relevant here, if used with appropriate caution.

3. *Liqquṭim* 66: *Ḥayyey* 6:1; 7:3.

4. *Liqquṭim* 60:6. On the tales see also Excursus II, below. Most of these tales are dated in *Ḥayyey* 1:59 and 2. Nahman's other tales, including some in *Ḥayyey* 3 and others printed still later, are usually undated. Since it was in the summer of 1806 that Nahman said: "I shall now begin to tell stories" (*Ḥayyey* 6:1) we may assume that he saw some significant distinction between whatever parables etc. he had used before then and the tales that emerged afterward.

5. *Siḥot* 126. See also *Siḥot* 32 and *Ḥayyey II* 11:81. The messianic expectation for 1810 was based upon the fact that the Hebrew cipher for that year is תק"ע which, read as a word, means "sound a horn," evoking the associations of "Sound the great *shofar* for our freedom" in the daily liturgy. See the reference to this hope in R. Mahler, *A History of Modern Jewry*, p.365.

6. *Ḥayyey II* 2:17, 26. See *Zohar* 2:128b.

7. I have not succeeded in finding a Navritch anywhere on the map of the Ukraine or Southern Russia. From the location it seems most likely that the reference is to Ovruch, a large town in Polesia or Northern Ukraine. There was a considerable Hasidic presence there under the leadership of Abraham Dov Baer, a disciple of Menahem Nahum of Chernobyl. I have retained the name Navritch, traditional in the Bratslav sources, because this identification is not certain.

8. *Liqquṭim II* 18.

9. Nahman had a second son, Jacob, who was born in the fall of 1806 but lived no longer than a few months. See Ḥayyey 1:59 (end); *Yemey MaHaRNaT*, p.27; *Kokhvey 'Or*, p.65; *'Avaneha Barzel*, p.32. From the lack of renewed hopes attached to this second son and from the general silence surrounding him one gets the impression that he may have been somehow physically defective from birth.

10. *Ḥayyey* 6:1; *Yemey MaHaRNaT*, p.31. Two cooked foods are a traditional standard for a luxurious meal. The custom of lighting candles at the birth of a child goes back to the Talmud; *cf.* Sanhedrin 32b.

11. *'Avaneha Barzel*, p.33.

12. On Navritch see *Ḥayyey* 6 and the parallel account in *Yemey MaHaRNaT*. *Cf.* also *Ḥayyey* 5:15; 7:9. The account of the Navritch journey was given Nathan by Shemu'el of Teplyk, who accompanied Nahman on his way. See *Sippurim Nifla'im*, p.150*f*.

13. Heb.: *qaẓti bi-yeshivat Braslav*. One might also translate: "I have made an end of dwelling in Bratslav."

14. *Ḥayyey* 6, end.

15. As it comes down to Hasidism this tradition of voluntary exile is a most complex phenomenon, combining early practices of Ashkenazic pietism with elements from the Zohar, Safed, and an original tone perhaps related to the Russian Christian environment. The association between voluntary exile and the

punishment of Cain is made in *Sefer Ḥasidim*, ed. Wistinezki-Friemann p.71, pars.175-176. *Cf.* also *Roqeaḥ* par.23. In both of these sources it is particularly as atonement for *murder* that wandering is prescribed. I am grateful to Professor Ivan Marcus for his help with these references. In the *Zohar* literature, particularly its later portions, it is *ẓaddiq* rather than sinner who is the wanderer, identifying with the exile of Israel. See for example *Tiqqunim*, introduction, ed. Margaliot 1b, and the parallels cited there. For Rabbi Simeon as an exile see *Zohar* 2:159a (R.M.). While basing itself on older traditions *(e.g. Berakhot* 58b) this is an area of Kabbalistic piety Baer has shown to have been influenced by the model of the wandering Franciscans in thirteenth-century Spain. *Cf.* his study in *Zion* 5 (1939) 1–44 and his *History of the Jews in Christian Spain*, v.1, p.243*ff*. It was in Safed that this model of the *ẓaddiq's* wandering to participate in the exile of the *shekhinah* (now commonly spoken of this way for the first time) was converted into actual practice. See Werblowsky's *Joseph Karo*, p.51 and index, *s.v.* exile, and also the very lovely portrayal of this motif in Abraham Azulai's *Ḥesed le-Avraham* 4:28, where he also connects it to the notion of *'ibbur* as the continued "wanderings" of *ẓaddiqim* after death. For a Hasidic view of the importance of such exile *cf.* the passage quoted in *'Eser Orot*, p.14.

16. *Ḥayyey* 6:4-7. The introductory qualifying phrase indicates that Nathan was not present when these words were spoken. Nathan's own family situation forced him to live in Mogilev, at some distance from Bratslav, for much of 1807–08. See *Yemey MaHaRNaT*, pp. 24 and 32*f*.

17. *Berakhot* 4a.

18. A brief account of Dr. Gordia is found in M. Biber, *Mazkeret li-Gedoley Ostrog*, pp. 246*f*. His tombstone, which was still standing at the beginning of the twentieth century and was seen by Biber, makes mention of his ministry to the Maggid. See also Weiss, *Meḥqarim*, p.252, n.2.

19. Much confusion as to the events of this period is caused by a letter purportedly written by Nahman from Ostrog to the community leaders in Bratslav, asking them to send some money with Sosia as she set out on her journey. The letter makes no mention of Sosia's illness, but mentions that Nahman himself has been seriously ill, something of which we do not know from any other source. If Nahman's own tubercular condition, which Nathan dates from the summer of 1807, in fact did show up as early as Purim, it may have been his own ill health, rather than that of his wife, that so abruptly ended this journey. This letter was first published in the Warsaw, 1930, edition of Nathan's *'Alim li-Terufah* and has been reprinted in subsequent editions of that work as well as in Zeitlin's biography, pp. 203*f*. It now appears, however, to be a later forgery, and its "new" information is nothing but misleading. The letter seems inauthentic for the following reasons. In the course of it, Nahman asks the community leaders to convey regards to his own *ḥasidim*. He refers to these as *yedidi morenu ha-rav rabbi Natan wekhol anshey shelomenu*. While extended honorifics were commonplace in communications even between friends, this form of address from master to disciple seems a bit out of place. More significantly, it clearly depicts Nathan as head of the Bratslav community during Nahman's absence. Nothing in Nathan's own writings gives any indication that this was the situation. A later Bratslav *ḥasid*, of course, would naturally assume that this was the case. In point of fact, Nathan was not in Bratslav at all while Nahman was on this journey. His own autobiography tells us clearly that he was

living in Mogilev at the time (*cf.* n. 16, above), and only after Purim of 1807 did he return to his home in Nemirov. With Nahman away, there would have been no reason for him to go to Bratslav.

The forgery is to be explained as follows: Nathan makes reference (*Ḥayyey*, 6 end) to a *missing* letter, written by Nahman from Zaslav, in which he mentions his own illness and asks the *ḥasidim* to pray for him. The letter in *'Alim li-Terufah* was probably a later attempt to "supply" this missing letter, but composed by one who was somewhat confused about the chronology of events. He thus combines Sosia's journey, undertaken before Passover, with Nahman's illness, which first became obvious some months later. The editor of the volume, realizing that this letter could not possibly have been written from Zaslav, where Nahman went only after his wife joined him, tried to rectify the matter by entitling the letter "A letter which our master wrote from Ostrog."

20. *Liqquṭim* 67.

21. In a letter written to his prospective father-in-law on the last day of *'Av* [September 3] in 1807, Nahman complains that the wedding has already been delayed too long, and insists that it take place within two weeks! This letter is also published at the front of *'Alim li-Terufah. Cf.* also *Yemey MaHaRNaT*, p. 40 and *Ḥayyey II* 11:143.

22. *Ḥayyey* 6:12 and end.

23. *Ḥayyey* 6:9-12; *Yemey MaHaRNaT*, p.41; Weiss, *Meḥqarim*, p.175.

24. After his death she is reported to have said, in the words of the *Shir ha-Kavod:* "I have seen your image and called you by name, but I have known you not." *Sippurim Nifla'im*, p.8.

25. For a few examples of this concern *cf. Liqquṭim* 225, 267: *Liqquṭim II* 2, 4:12, 6, 7:12, 8:12.

26. *Shivḥey ha-BeSHT*, pp.67*ff*, 71. Opposition to medicine has a long history in Jewish pietistic circles. See the sources quoted by H.J. Zimmels in *Magicians, Theologians, and Doctors*, p.6. For an example of an anti-medical polemic fully as vituperative as Nahman at his height *cf.* the opening stanzas of Moses Zacuto's *Tofet 'Arukh*, written in seventeenth-century Italy.

27. In Nahman's tale of *The Prince Who Was Made of Jewels (Sippurey Ma'asiyot*, p.38*ff*.) sorcerers and physicians are consulted together.

28. In *Ḥayyey* 2:9 Nathan (or perhaps Nahman of Cheryn) offers a lengthy defense of Nahman's Lemberg journey, in which he denies that its main purpose was that of consultation with doctors:

> With regard to the fact that our master himself journeyed to Lemberg and had to do with medicines there—this contains some great and hidden secrets. His intention in going there was not to seek medicinal healing, but rather some other matter which was known to him [alone]. Just as all his other journeys were filled with the most elevated wonders, like the visits to Kamenets, Navritch, and Shargorod, as we have told elsewhere, so was this journey also for some secret purpose. . . . Once he got there, he was forced by divine command to take medicines for some reason that only he knew. . . .

29. *Sefer ha-Middot, segullah* 1, 3, 7, *refu'ah* 4; *Liqquṭey 'Eẓot, refu'ah* 2. *Cf.* also *Liqquṭim* 164, 231.

30. *Liqquṭey 'Eẓot, refu'ah* 5, and the longer version in *Liqquṭim II* 5:1.

31. *Ḥayyey* 1:15. This attitude is an application to the realm of healing of the

same principle reflected in the Hasidic rejection of Lurianic prayer—*kawwanot*. The point in both cases is that simple faith in the omnipresence of God is more effective than any of the more complex alternatives, including those considered sacred. See further *Liqquṭey 'Eẓot, refu'ah* 10; *Liqquṭim II* 8:6.

32. *Liqquṭim II* 1:9. *Cf. Gen. Rabbah* 10:6 and *Baba Qama* 92b. This teaching is dated Rosh Hashanah 1808. A briefer and necessarily earlier version is found in *Liqquṭim* 231. This interpretation of Ex. 23:25 is much older than Nahman. *Cf.* the commentaries of Ibn Ezra and Bahya *ad loc.* Nahman's formulation of course places much greater emphasis on the supernaturalist implications of this interpretation.

It is interesting to note that his Rosh Hashanah teaching of the following year *(Liqquṭim II* 5:1) opens with a similar treatment of medicinal herbs, but places the emphasis upon *faith* rather than prayer as the true source of healing.

33. *Liqquṭim* 168; *Liqquṭim II* 3.

34. *Ḥayyey* 1:33; 7:1–3. For the tale of an "old style" *ẓaddiq* going to seek cures in Lemberg see *Zikhron Tov*, p.11, re: R. Mordecai of Neskhiz. Zeitlin *(op. cit.*, p.205) goes so far as to say that only Nathan was opposed to *doktorei* and that Nahman did not share this view. Nahman's attitude was in fact ambivalent, though Nathan remained an implacable foe of doctors to the end. In his account of his master's death Nathan broadly hints that those disciples who, against his (Nathan's) will, insisted on calling in the doctors, bore some burden of responsibility.

35. It was undoubtedly to the rest-cure that Nahman referred when he said on his departure from Lemberg that he felt like Honi Ha-Me'agel, who according to Talmudic legend slept for seventy years. See *Ta'anit* 23a. R. Aaron, the son of the BeSHT's son Herschel, and thus a first cousin of Nahman's mother, was still alive at the time. He died in 1828. From here it appears that R. Aaron had been less than friendly to Nahman in earlier times. Certain of Nahman's first disciples, who came to him in Medvedevka, had formerly been disciples of R. Aaron. A certain rivalry thus existed between them, and it is likely that R. Aaron supported his cousin Barukh in the opposition to Nahman. *Ḥayyey*, 7:2.

36. This is confirmed by the alleged eyewitness report of Nahman in Lemberg found in *'Avaneha Barzel*, p.59. The report is attributed to the son of the Lemberg rabbi, himself later rabbi of Jassy, Romania. He recalled of Nahman's visit in Lemberg: "He did not say Torah, nor did he speak at all, due to his lung ailment. All his communication was by motions and signals." He adds, however, that the silent Nahman did manage to tell some stories, and that his tales of Erez Israel in particular were most popular. The authenticity of this account is deserving of further investigation.

37. *Ḥayyey* 7:14.

38. *Papera'ot le-Ḥokhmah* to *Liqquṭim* 282.

39. *Ḥayyey* 3:6.

40. Mahler, *op. cit.*, pp.314*ff*. On Lemberg in particular see J. Caro, *Geschichte der Juden in Lemberg* and S. Buber, *'Anshey Shem.*

The first major literary figure of the Galician Haskalah, Mendel Lefin (1749–1826), was also already active in the first years of the nineteenth century. Though he lived most of his life in other Galician communities, his *Ḥeshbon ha-Nefesh*, a translation of Benjamin Franklin's *Autobiography*, augmented by several original chapters on moral philosophy and psychology, was published in Lemberg in 1808, just a few months after Nahman left that city. It thus happens that these two works, representing what seem to be entirely different eras in Jewish intellectual history, were published in the same year, and in places very near to one another.

41. *Ḥayyey* 7:17 and *Yemey MaHaRNat*, p.47*ff*. On the printing of this book *cf.* in great detail Weiss, *Meḥqarim*, p.251*ff*. I agree with Piekarz that Weiss's identification of the "R.D." who helped in the publication as Hirsch Baer (equals Dov) Hurwitz is entirely out of place. The entire latter section of that article is unnecessarily speculative and mystifying.

42. *Ḥayyey* 7:3–8; *Yemey MaHaRNaT*, p.43. On the *Sefer ha-Nisraf cf. Neweh Ẓaddiqim*, p.80*ff*. and Weiss, *Meḥqarim*, p.215*ff*. The justification for the burning of holy books found in *Liqquṭim II* 32 is somehow related to this incident.

43. *Ḥayyey* 1:20; 4:16; 7:14–17; *Yemey MaHaRNaT*, p.47*ff*. Nahman's weakened condition also meant that such strenuous activities as long periods of singing at the Sabbath table were abandoned. *Liqquṭim II* 104.

44. *Siḥot* 50. *See* also *Siḥot* 219 and *Liqquṭim II* 1:11. In *'Avaneha Barzel*, p.43, doctors are paralleled to false *ẓaddiqim:* one kills the body and the other the soul. The doctor is depicted as an emissary of the angel of death also in the passage by Moses Zacuto to which we have referred above in n.26.

45. *Liqquṭim II* 10. See *Shabbat 77b*. The teachings numbered 10–17 in *Liqquṭim II* were all presented in the summer of 1808, following Nahman's return from Lemberg. See *Ḥayyey* 1:50 and 59.

46. *Liqquṭim II* 13–14. Emphases mine. *Cf. Sanhedrin* 44b. Nahman is here following *Exodus Rabbah* 21:5 in noting that the verb *hiqriv* in the phrase "Pharaoh drew near" is in the *hif'il* conjugation, which should make it a transitive verb.

47. The following is a chronological list of Nahman's teachings and stories ascribed by Nathan to the period between his master's return from Lemberg and his death in 1810.

Summer, 1808	*Liqquṭim II* 10–17
Rosh Hashanah, 1808	*Liqquṭim II* 1
Hanukkah, 1808	*Liqquṭim II* 2
Parashat Yitro, 1809	*Liqquṭim II* 32
Before Purim, 1809	*The Wise Man and the Simpleton*
After Purim, 1809	*The Burgher and the Pauper*
Shavu'ot 1809	*Liqquṭim II* 4; *Siḥot* 5
After Shavu'ot, 1809	*Siḥot* 7
Summer, 1809	*Siḥot* 24
Rosh Hashanah, 1809	*Liqquṭim II* 5
Before Sukkot, 1809	*Liqquṭim II* 66
Parashat Bereshit, 1809	*Liqquṭim II* 67
Parashat Noaḥ, 1809	*The Two Sons*
Before Hanukkah, 1809	*Liqquṭim II* 68
Hanukkah, 1809	*Liqquṭim II* 7; *Siḥot* 40
After Hanukkah, 1809/10	*Siḥot* 32.
Winter, 1809/10	*Siḥot* 60
Shabbat Shirah, 1810	*Liqquṭim II* 71
Parashat Yitro, 1810	*Liqquṭim II* 72

Parashat Wa-Era', 1810	*The Master of Prayer*
Parashat Shemini, 1810	*The Seven Beggars*
Shabbat Nahamu, 1810	*Liqquṭim II* 78
Rosh Hashanah, 1810	*Liqquṭim II* 8

48. *Liqquṭim II* 72, emphasis mine. *Cf.* also *Liqquṭim II* 1:3. The phrase "due to our many sins" is a standard formula and should here not be taken too seriously.

49. *Liqquṭim II* 7:6; 78; 117.

50. *Liqquṭim II* 2:2.

51. *Ḥayyey* 4:22.

52. The motif of royal legitimacy is central to *The Burgher and the Pauper, The Two Sons,* and *The Master of Prayer,* and it appears incidentally in several other of the tales as well.

53. *Sippurey Ma'asiyot,* p.115*f.*

54. *Liqquṭim II* 4:6–7. *Cf.* on Moses' death *Zohar* 2:88b.

55. *Liqquṭim II* 4:7–8; 63. *Meẓaḥ ha-naḥash* is a term used several times by Nahman for heretics, based on the imagery of the *Zohar (e.g.* 3:129a), where it would refer to the highest of the demonic archons.

56. Two important studies have been written concerning the final months of Nahman's life. Hayyim Lieberman's "Reb Nahman Bratslaver un di Umaner Maskilim," *Yivo Bleter* 29 (1947), establishes the identity of the *maskilim* mentioned in the Bratslav sources, and gives an accurate and detailed account of the relationship between the *ẓaddiq* and the enlighteners. Quotations from Lieberman here refer to the English translation of that article, which appeared in the *Yivo Annual of Jewish Social Science* 6 (1951) 287*ff.* Mendel Piekarz has also carefully studied this period in his work, p.21*ff.* Piekarz' greatest contribution here is the chronological ordering of events and statements of this period, allowing for the first coherent picture of these final months of Nahman's life. In the present section of this work I am greatly indebted to both of these treatments.

57. For Nahman on the martyrs of Uman *cf. Ḥayyey* 8:6–8, 33; *Yemey MaHaRNaT,* p.68. Uman was the largest city close to Bratslav. The Czarist census of 1897 listed nearly 18,000 Jews in Uman, compared to 3,290 in Bratslav. See EJ, *s.v. Uman.* Sources on the pogroms of 1768 have been collected by Jonas Gurland in *Le-Qorot ha-Gezerot 'al Yisra'el,* v.3. Nathan reports in *Ḥayyey* 5:17 that Nahman had been in Uman as early as 1799, on his return journey from the Holy Land, and had undergone some great trial there. The details of that account are censored with the usual *"etc."* On the redemption of the dead in Uman see also *Ḥayyey II* 11:150. Nahman lived in three homes during his few months in Uman. From the time he entered the town until just after Shavu'ot, he stayed in the home of Nahman Nathan Rapoport. From the day after Shavu'ot until the week of Tish'a be-'Av, he was in the home of one Joseph Samuel. From that time until his death, he rented a house owned by one designated only as "the Lukaczer." For details, see *Ḥayyey,* 8:, *passim,* and *Yemey MaHaRNaT,* pp. 69*ff.*

58. There were two significant families within the small group of *maskilim* in Uman: those of Haykl Hurwitz and Nahman Nathan Rapoport. Haykl Hurwitz (1749–1822), a wealthy lumber merchant, was one of the earliest Russian Jews to be attracted to Haskalah. Although he was by no means an anti-religious extremist in his views, he came to be known as *"Haykl Aprikoros"* in Uman. He translated

Johann Heinrich Campe's *Entdeckung von Amerika* into Yiddish, which he published as *Ẓofnat Pa'aneaḥ*, Berdichev, 1817. See Gottlober, *Ha-Boqer Or* 1 (1876) 361*ff.*; Piekarz, *op. cit.*, p. 28. Haykl's son, Hirsch Baer Hurwitz (1785–1861) had a particularly interesting career. A banker in Uman, he was well-known as a linguist. Of the Uman enlighteners' circle, it was he who became closest to Nahman. After he was forced to declare bankruptcy in 1822, he left Uman for England, where he took the name of Hermann Bernard. There he embarked upon a scholarly career, eventually becoming professor of Oriental languages at Cambridge. His commentary on Job appeared in London, 1864. It is thought that he became a convert to Christianity. See Lieberman, *op. cit.*, p. 296, as well as the letter by Jacob Eichenbaum, a Haskalah writer in Odessa, to Hirsch Baer, published in Odessa, 1867. Hirsch Baer was a son-in-law of Nahman Nathan Rapoport, another wealthy Jew of Uman, who also supported Haskalah. Rapoport died in 1809. See *Yemey MaHaRNaT*, p. 62 and *Sippurim Nifla'im*, p. 12. His other son-in-law, who was very close to Hirsch Baer, was Moses Landau, a grandson of the famous Ezekiel Landau, rabbi of Prague and author of the Responsa Collection *Noda' bi-Yehudah*. See Lieberman in *Biẓaron* 45 (1963) 52*ff.*

59. This is a mistake: Hirsch Baer was the son of Haykl, and both he and Landau were sons-in-law of Rapoport, as we have said in the preceding note.

60. *Sippurim Nifla'im*, p.3*f.* Lieberman notes (*op. cit.*, p.293) that it seems highly unlikely for Levi Yizhak to have sought to leave the much larger and more prestigious city of Berdichev for Uman. The rabbi of Shepetovka is apparently the same Jacob Samson whom Nahman met on his journey to Erez Israel. *Yeyn Levanon* is a commentary on Avot by the early enlightener N.H. Wessely, and it is most interesting that even the Bratslav source recalls that Nahman sought to obtain a copy of it.

61. This of course would be the fulfillment of those dreams and fantasies of martyrdom he had known since childhood. See above, Chapter One, and Weiss, *Meḥqarim*, p.176*ff.*

62. *Ḥayyey* 8:1,2,8,11; *Yemey MaHaRNaT*, p.65; Piekarz, p.27*ff.*

63. *Ḥayyey* 8:11.

64. *Ḥayyey* 8:16, 19; *Ḥayyey II* 5:5

65. *Ḥayyey* 8:24.

66. *Ḥayyey II* 6:4.

67. *Liqquṭim* 59:1, 6; *Siḥot* 80–81; *Ḥayyey* 8:27.

68. *Ḥayyey* 8:9. Based on *Zohar* 2:67b.

69. *Liqquṭim II* 91; See *Yoma* 72b. *Cf.* further *Ḥayyey* 8:12, 14, 15.

70. *Sippurim Nifla'im*, p.6*f.*

71. *Ṣion* 2 (1862) 479*f.* Quoted in Lieberman, *op. cit.* p.296. I have used his translation.

72. *Ḥayyey* 8:12–13. Emphasis mine. On Moses and the extra day *cf.* the sources in Heschel, *Torah min ha-Shamayim*, v.2, p.128*f.* As we shall see below, the idea that those forms of service concerning which there is room for doubt are the highest forms of religious expression fits in perfectly with Nahman's entire search for affirmation of faith from within doubt itself. His claim that the greatest service of God takes place in those areas where "there is no *miẓwah* involved" flies in the face of the Rabbinic dictum: "Greater is the one who is commanded and performs than the one who performs without command." *Qiddushin* 31a; *Baba Qama* 38a.

73. *Ḥayyey* 8:18. *Cf. Nedarim* 22b.
74. *Ḥayyey* 8:28, 33. Piekarz, p.41, interprets this event differently, but offers no explanation for Nahman's failure to complete the teaching.
75. *Ḥayyey* 8:20.
76. *Ḥayyey* 8:29.
77. *Ḥayyey* 1:49; 8:31–32; *Siḥot* 153; *Yemey MaHaRNaT*, p.69*ff.*; *Liqquṭim II* 78.
78. *Siḥot* 153.
79. *Liqquṭim II* 78, in a parenthetical remark by Nathan.

Appendix
The Death of Rabbi Nahman

Nathan's autobiography, *Yemey MaHaRNaT*, contains the following account of his master's last days.*

It was on the third day of Seliḥot that I arrived at Uman, planning to be there for Rosh Hashanah. I stayed there, however, until he departed from us in peace, and I merited to be present at the hour of his holy and awesome death.

The first day of Rosh Hashanah that year occurred on the Sabbath; on that day he became considerably weaker and began to cough up a great deal of blood. He was quite frightened at this, especially when he saw how much blood he was losing through his cough.

It had always been his way to say words of Torah at the close of the first day of Rosh Hashanah. A great crowd had gathered in the large house which had been designated for that purpose, and the room where he was to speak was already packed with people. Evening began to fall as we waited for him to appear, but he was near death and did not have the strength to enter the room. While we were standing there a message came that he had called for me. I left the crowd and went to the place where he was staying.

I found him seated on the edge of his bed, with a brass bowl beside him; the bowl was fast filling up with blood. As soon as he saw me enter, he cried out to me: "What shall I do about my teaching?" My first reaction was that there was nothing to be done; surely he could not go teach in that condition. But he persisted, saying how sorry he felt for the people who had gone through such great difficulties in order to hear him. [How could he refuse them?] All summer long he had been looking forward to this

Yemey MaHaRNat, p. 71*ff*. This translation, by the present writer, has appeared in *Conservative Judaism* 28 (1973) 82*ff*.

Rosh Hashanah, when he would say Torah in Uman. Then I understood how deeply he longed to teach. I began to say to him: "When you returned from your journey to Lemberg you were also very weak, and there seemed to be no natural way that you would have the strength to teach. Yet on that occasion God was with you and you managed to speak at great length." I kept saying things of this sort for a while, until he finally responded, "I'm willing to give my life for it." . . . And it really was at the risk of his life that he would go to teach; he seemed about to die at any moment.

He asked me to set up his chair near the doorway to the room where he would speak, so that if he became faint we would be able to get him out of there quickly. . . . I told him that it was no small task to move his chair from the front of the room to the doorway, since the room was so completely packed with people. But he was insistent, and said that he would not enter the room unless we moved his chair. I went into the room and created a great commotion by scattering people about, until we were able to bring his chair over to the entrance-way.

He came into the room and sat down on his chair, and we all stood around him. The room was really so terribly filled with people that it was hard to be there at all. People were almost standing on top of one another; the crowding and noise were so awful that some people became faint and had to be taken out. . . . But he sat there in the midst of the crowd, waited a while before he spoke, as was his custom, and then began to speak. . . . His voice was so much lower than usual that it seemed impossible that he could go on for long. But the God of mercy had compassion upon us and upon all Israel and upon all the generations to come, and he was able to continue, as though by the most wondrous miracle. . . . When he finished, he had us sing a *niggun*, as we always did on such occasions, and he went back to his room.

All that second night of Rosh Hashanah he was terribly weak, and his condition seemed to be growing still more dangerous. They sent for the doctor, but could not get him to come. Afterwards he said that he was very fortunate that the doctor had not been able to make it, and he said [repeating his oft-stated advice] that whoever wanted to take care of his life should never let a doctor get near him. He asked that even if he himself should call out for the doctor in his illness, they should not let the doctor in to him. Though I was not present when he said those words, I would never have let a doctor treat him. Nevertheless, on the Eve of Sukkot my objections were overruled, and the doctor was called. Who knows if that visit of the doctor did not help to bring about his death?

On the second day of Rosh Hashanah, he did not come in to pray with us or to join us in the meal, as was his custom on that holiday. He stayed in his own adjoining room and there he prayed alone. And though he was weak beyond description in those days following Rosh Hashanah, he managed to speak to each of the people who had come to be with him, giving to each of them according to his needs. As people came to take leave of him after the holiday, he spoke to each at length. It was because of this show of strength that people did not realize he was so near death; otherwise they never would have left him. Even his own daughters and his son-in-law went home after the holiday, never imagining that he was to die so soon. Had we really paid attention to what was happening, we would have realized that he lived each moment only by miracle.

He himself said to us countless times and in numerous ways that he was about to die. But we, sinful creatures that we are, could not believe that God would take this pure light from us at such a time. We lost so much by not accepting that his death was near. How much more would we have wanted to hear from him, had we only known! We can only give thanks to God, who in His mercy allowed us to hear sufficient teachings from our master to nourish all the future generations . . . until the end of time. . . .

On the eve of Yom Kippur, we went in to him, and he blessed each one of us, as was his custom. His appearance, however, was somehow frightening, so that an awesome sense of shame overtook us all. How hard it is to describe his face as it was at that moment of receiving his blessing, for he had a holy and awesome glow about him. Truly blessed are we, who were able to receive that final blessing from him before he died.

On Yom Kippur day, he again did not join us in prayer as he used to, but again stayed in his room alone. When the day was about to draw to a close, and the time for the *Ne'ilah* prayer arrived, we could not decide among ourselves who should lead the service. It was agreed that Reb Naftali and I should ask him to appoint a prayer-leader for us . . . The two of us walked into his room, filled with trembling. (It was always that way when we sought to approach him; we would be overcome by a sense of embarrassment. . . . How much more so at this hour of *Ne'ilah,* and so close to the hour of his death.) We stood shaking at his doorstep. He turned to us briefly and asked, "Why have you come?" And we hesitatingly blurted out, "Who should lead *Ne'ilah?*" At that, he waved us away with his hand, as though to say: "I have no concern for that now. Do what you want."

When we returned to his room after the fast was over, we found him very weak, and of sad demeanor. The next morning, however, his mood was improved, and he spoke joyfully with people. . . . It was on that day that he had to change his dwelling, returning to the house where he had lived before Rosh Hashanah. . . . As we began to move his possessions into the new apartment and to arrange things in their proper order, he became especially concerned about where we should place his bed. Wherever we tried somehow did not seem right to him. Finally I tried moving a chest of drawers, and placed the bed where the chest had stood. This seemed right to him. . . . Only afterwards, when he died on that bed in that place, did I understand that the precise place where he was to die had been designated years before, and was somehow known to him.

From the day he entered this house, he ceased to smile. . . . On Thursday of that week, the day before the Eve of Sukkot, I went to him late in the afternoon. My friend Naftali and some others were there with him; he was very weak and had taken a turn for the worse. . . . From that moment we never left his side. That night I slept in his room and he dictated his will to me. Three hundred red rubles were to go to his daughter Ḥayyah, his wife was to be given the value of her *Ketubah, etc.*, and he said, *etc.** Then he asked me, "Is there anything else to be said?" But I answered, "Even this was not necessary. You are going to live to see your daughter married!" (For I did not want to let myself believe that he was really speaking of his death .) He said to me, "With God, all things are possible," for he never liked to argue about anything, and then he added, "These three years since I took ill, I've been living on miracles. . . . " Then he added: "You too should have said something, but you are very small people." I answered, "Then we are all the more to be pitied. You have to live longer." I didn't want to ask him for any further testament, but only wanted him to live. . . .

On Friday morning, he asked us to find him a chair that would give him good support, so that he could sit up in it [despite his weakness]. With God's help we found such a chair and he took to sitting in it. This was truly a miracle. From that Friday morning until after the Sabbath, frail as he was, he remained seated upright in his chair. . . . While he sat there on Friday morning, we brought him his *tallit* and *tefillin*. But while dressed in the garments of prayer, he began to vomit. He asked me to hold onto his head—and he nearly died there, right in my hands. Only by God's grace did he return to himself and was he able to go on with his prayer. From that time, he remained seated in the chair, as we stood before him for the next day and a half, watching the life ebb out of him. . . .

On Saturday evening, the second day of Sukkot, he asked that we lay him down on his bed. He was terribly tired then, and said that he had gotten tired out by sitting so long on the chair. Then he turned to us and said, "Do you remember the story . . . I told you when we first came to this place?" A shudder passed through me. I remembered that story very well. The Ba'al Shem Tov had come to a certain place, and had seen many great souls there which turned to him for redemption. And he had known that the only way he could redeem them was by his own death.

*Nahman's words have here been censored.

I stood there trembling as he added, "They've had their eye on me for so long already, beckoning me to this place. What can I tell you? Thousands of them, tens of thousands . . ." He turned his face toward the wall and spread out his hands, as though to say, "I give my life; I am ready to accept all for Him, bless His name. . . ."

On that Monday evening, the eve of the last day of his life, his disciples Reb Naftali and Reb Simeon stood before him (for we were sleeping in shifts, so that he was never left alone). . . . and he again spoke of the souls that longed to be redeemed, and how many there were in this place. Naftali answered him, saying, "But didn't you tell us in the teaching "Boaz said to Ruth"* that the truly great *zaddiq* could do it all within his lifetime?" He replied, "But then I only revealed a part of the thing to you; really one has to die to do this." He then recalled something and took the key to the chest and handed it to them. "As soon as I am dead," he told them, "while my body is still lying here on the floor, you are to take all the writings you find in the chest and burn them. And be sure to fulfill my request."

The two disciples were overcome by a combination of terror and sadness, realizing that he was so directly preparing for his death. One of them whispered something about it to the other, but the master overheard. "Why are you whispering?" he said. "You can speak of my death to my face. I'm not afraid of it." And then he added, "Or perhaps you are talking about yourselves. What do you have to worry about? I am going before you. And surely if the souls of those who have never known me are calling out to me to redeem them, you [who have been my disciples] have no need to worry. With those others there might be some difficulty—but with me walking before you, you have no need to fear at all." And he went on speaking about those souls and about his death. . . .

When I awoke . . . Naftali whispered to me a bit of what had happened—that he had already given them the key and told them to burn his writings. I stood there, shaking with disbelief. But then I pulled myself together, convincing myself that this was just his way. He might be preparing for death, but surely God wouldn't take him. We could not get it into our minds that God would take this great light, etc., before all those who needed him had gotten a chance to enjoy his wondrous and awesome light.

We poor sinners lost so much because of thoughts like these! If only we could have simply believed that he was going to die, as he said to us so many times, both directly and indirectly, we could have heard so much more from him in that hour. He was waiting for us to ask him that he tell us more. But we were not willing to hear anything that might concern

**Cf.* above, p.213.

what we were to do after his death; our only hope was that he get well again. And since we didn't ask, he told us nothing more . . .

I suggested to Naftali that he get some sleep, for he had not been to sleep at all. But Naftali would not let himself leave the room . . . The love he felt for our master's face as it shone at that holy moment would not let him leave. Finally sleep overcame him, and both he and Simeon fell asleep there in the room. The servant and his wife were also asleep; only I remained to serve and guard our master. I stood there before him, I alone, from shortly after midnight until we saw the light of dawn. But I heard nothing from him in all those hours—all because I did not want to accept that he was dying, and I asked him nothing. . . . He looked into me with his awesome eyes, and every look contained countless words. Now I understand so much about the looks he gave me that night, and whenever I pass through times of suffering and God saves me through His wonders, I understand that it was all there in his eyes, in the intensity with which he stared at me, for hours at a time, during that final night. . . .

He then asked me to take him back to his bed. . . . When I lifted him up and put him down on the bed, he said to me: "Slowly, slowly. . . ." And then he added, "I'm getting heavy now, so you have to be careful." (For the dying do get heavier as the life-force passes out of them.) Again he was telling me how close he was to death, and again I refused to listen. He lay there on the bed and stared at me for a long time. . . . I said to him, "Master, take a little something to sustain yourself." He asked for a bit of tea with an egg yolk in it, which was supposed to reduce his cough. I gave him a bit of water and he washed his hands before drinking the tea which I had prepared. He found it too hot, however, and he was very careful not to drink hot things, lest they bring up the blood again. For the blood had indeed stopped coming several days before his death. I poured the tea from one glass into another to cool it, but he still found it too hot. This went on three or four times, until finally he took it, recited the blessing, and drank. I stood there with him until the dawn, feeling somehow happy that I had had the chance to serve him in this way. Usually he wanted only the household servants to wait on his personal needs; it was a rare gift that I had been able to serve him all these hours. Of course I did not know that on this very day the Lord would take our master. Rather at that point I really thought that he would live.

When dawn broke and the others were awakened. . . . I left to go to the *miqveh* before my prayers on that fourth day of Sukkot. Upon my return I found him sitting up on the bed, wrapped in his *ṭallit* and saying his prayers. He then took the *lulav* and *etrog* in his hands and with the prayerbook of the ARI ZaL resting on his knees, he recited the *Hallel*. When he came to *Hosha'not* he raised his voice a bit, so that his prayers could be heard throughout the house. Happy are the eyes that saw him, happy are the ears that heard his prayers, on that last day of his holy life. . . .

[A short while later], he was seated on his chair, but life was quickly passing out of him. People were standing over him with various kinds of fragrant spices, to restore his soul. God had also caused a certain man from Tirhavits to be there on that day and he was attending to him above all the others. (Here, too, there is a tale to tell, for our master had already promised this man that he would be present on the day of his death.) When I saw the scene, I told them to put him to bed immediately, but our master himself waved me aside. Only a bit later, when I saw that sitting up was totally impossible for him, did I repeat my words. This time he was silent and did not resist. The man from Tirhavits took him in his arms and laid him on the bed. As he put him down, I took his holy hand in mine, first as in a greeting, but then in embrace, as a sign of the bond between us.

He lay on his bed, dressed in a fine silken garment, which he had asked Reb Simeon to put around him. He asked that his sleeves be buttoned, and when a bit of his shirtsleeve still showed out from under his coat, he motioned that it be set right. He then asked that we wash off his beard, for there was a bit of blood stuck to it. He lay there in great freedom.

He took a bit of wax between his fingers, and began to roll it, absorbed in thought. . . . He often did this toward the end of his days, rolling wax between his fingers as he thought. Even in this last hour of his life, his mind occupied with some unknown thought, he lay there skillfully and gracefully rolling the wax between his fingers. . . .

It took about three hours from the time he was laid down on the bed. . . . The house was filled with people who had come to honor him. When they saw that the end was near, they began to recite the *ma'avar yaboq*, the verses one recites at the death of a *ẓaddiq*. It then seemed that he was already dead, and the people began to weep. I cried out, "Master! Master! To whom do you leave us?" He heard our voice and awoke, turning his face to us as though to say: "God forbid! I'm not leaving you!" But just a bit after that, he died and was gathered unto his people, in holiness and purity, with no confusion of mind and without the slightest gesture, with an acceptance that was awesome and wondrous. All those who stood about him, the leaders of the burial society among them, said that they had seen many who had passed on in pure and conscious ways but they had never seen a death like this.

Now all this is told only according to our understanding. As to the true meaning of his death—there are no words to describe it, for it surpasses all understanding. Only those who know a bit of his greatness, who have read his holy books or have heard his stories, will begin to realize that his death was completely unique. There was never any like it, nor will there ever be. How shall we speak? What shall we say? What shall I say to the Lord, who gave me the gift of being there as his holy soul passed out of him? Had I only come into the world for the sake of this moment, it would have been sufficient.

A Brief Chronology of Nahman's Life

1772 (April 4)	Birth at Medzhibozh
1786?	Marriage to Sosia; move to Usyatin
1790	Move to Medvedevka; beginning of public career
1798–99	Journey to Erez Israel
1800 (August)	Move to Zlotopolye; conflict with Zeide
1802 (Summer)	Move to Bratslav
1805–06	Height of messianic activity
1805 (March)	Birth of Shlomo Ephraim
1806 (June)	Death of Shlomo Ephraim
1807 (early spring)	Journey to Navritch
1807 (May-June)	Onset of disease
1807–08	Sojourn in Lemberg
1810 (May)	Move to Uman
1810 (October 15)	Death

Excursus I
Faith, Doubt, and Reason

In telling the tale of Nahman's life, we have been blessed by the fact that the sources for such a biography are extraordinarily rich and abundant. The detail is so surprisingly comprehensive, and Nahman's reflections on himself and the meaning of his life so constant, that it becomes hard to imagine *any* work based on these sources not turning out to be somehow biographical. In turning away from biography, therefore, in an attempt at more systematic treatment of certain themes in Nahman's teachings, we find ourselves facing serious limitations. The sort of material—dreams, tales, parables, and the like—that is a blessing for the biographer is just as likely to lend difficulty to the task of the intellectual historian. Before embarking on this chapter, one which seeks to lay bare in Nahman's thought certain inner structures that he himself clearly would not have expressed as we do, it is in order that we share certain reservations about the task. Two points in particular come to mind.

Nahman is the very antithesis of a systematic author. He has left us no tract in which he undertakes a step-by-step consideration of the major problems of Jewish theology. While his teachings reflect penetrating insight in the realm of religious thought and a deep awareness of the issues confronting the Jewish believer, he made no attempt to construct a fully elaborated theological synthesis. On the contrary, he shared with most of his predecessors and contemporaries within Hasidism a devotion to the age-old methods of Jewish homiletics: novel interpretations of Scripture, associative thought patterns, and a particular penchant for seeking mystical significance in letters and numbers. Nahman even outstrips most other Hasidic thinkers in his ingenious twists of Biblical language and in the strikingly original patterns in which he weaves together the strands of Rabbinic and Kabbalistic exegesis that form the fabric of his teachings. He defines the process of interpretation as consisting of an ongoing chain of mental associations; it is by "likening one thing to another" that one comes to reveal new levels of meaning within the Torah. The most common technical term found in Nahman's writings is *beḥinah*, and its many uses are often a key to fathoming his associative processes. At times *beḥinah* in Nahman's writings should be translated as 'aspect'; in other places it reflects analogy or comparison; still elsewhere it will denote some other form of relationship between two terms or ideas. When Nahman says, "X is the *beḥinah* of Y," as he does countless times on nearly every page of the *Liqquṭey MoHaRaN*, he is creating some sort of loosely defined relationship between the two, which will then generally be demonstrated by reference to a Biblical or Kabbalistic association. At one point Nahman said of his work, "My Torah is entirely *beḥinot!*" which is to say that this complicated and largely undefined network of associations is the basis of his method.[1]

Opening the volume of Nahman's teachings almost at random, we see this method in a brief passage in which the term *beḥinah* will be left untranslated. For the moment, our interest is not in the specific content of the passage, but rather in the associative patterns it reflects:

> It is impossible to draw forth complete providence until one has destroyed one's lust for money. This avarice is broken by the giving of alms, for the *Zohar* says: 'A spirit comes down to cool the heat of the heart. When the spirit arrives, it is greeted by the heart with the joy of the music of the Levites.' 'Spirit' is the *beḥinah* of almsgiving, the 'spirit' of generosity, through which one cools down the heat of avarice. This is the *beḥinah* of: 'He will hold back the spirit of the wealthy' (Ps. 76:13): the spirit will hold back one's desire for wealth. The music of the Levites is the *beḥinah* of the honest business dealings of one who is content with his lot, and is not rushing to seek his fortune, as Scripture says; 'Raise up song and take the drum' (Ps. 81:2).[2] The joy to which the *Zohar* refers is that of the one who is content with his lot. This is 'Incense brings joy to the heart' (Prov. 27:9), and this is the *beḥinah* of 'They [the Levites] place incense in Your nostrils' (Deut. 33:11), for through the *beḥinah* of incense one may negate the *beḥinah* of 'By the sweat of your brow shall you eat bread' (Gen. 3:19).[3] This is the *beḥinah* in which messiah is revealed, when the lust for money will be overthrown, as Scripture says: 'On that day will every man cast aside his idols of gold and silver' (Is. 2:20), and this is the *beḥinah* of 'The breath of our nostrils, the messiah of the Lord' (Iam. 4:20.)[4]

By a highly complex web of association, here formed largely through a series of analogous terms found in totally unrelated passages in the Bible and the *Zohar*, Nahman has sought to demonstrate that providence, which will be fully revealed only in messianic times, can make its appearance only when man has overcome his reliance upon the false gods of money—an idea not unfamiliar to preachers throughout the world. The rules by which this extended chain of associations is to operate are also not original with Nahman: his *beḥinot* are not unlike the rather loose analogies that characterize Rabbinic Aggadah or the sermons of his Hasidic contemporaries. But in the extent to which he carries this process, Nahman seems to express a desire to extend the method to its breaking point. Almost any association is now possible. He frequently gives one the impression of a creative artist straining against the limitations of his medium, and seeking to extend its borders so that he will have room in which to create. In a statement rather surprising for a Hasidic master, he advocates complete freedom in the realm of interpretation, as long as the law remains unaffected:

> He said that whoever wants to offer new interpretations of the Torah is permitted to do so. He may interpret however he desires, offering all that his mind has grasped, as long as he does not derive any new laws from his homilies or esoteric interpretations.
>
> [Nathan adds:] It is understood from his words that even in the *kawwanot* of Luria or the ways of Kabbalah one may interpret insofar as one's mind reaches, so long as no law is changed, God forbid![5]

His early attraction to the most fantastic legendary passages in the Talmud and his later turn to storytelling as a means of instruction bear further witness to his struggle with the somewhat confining medium of traditional homiletics. When he does work within the homiletical framework, the medium is used with a degree of elasticity that almost lends an air of stream-of-consciousness writing to his teachings, except that each link in the ever-flowing chain of associations is forged by some technical analogy, rather than by purely personal predilection. When Nahman says, "My Torah is entirely *beḥinot*," he causes the would-be systematizer to pause: is there any way to interrupt a free-flowing chain of associations without utterly distorting their meaning?

A second factor lending difficulty to a systematic treatment of Nahman's thought is the highly personal character of much that he says. We have already seen that his constant mentions of "a certain *ẓaddiq" or "the true ẓaddiq*" are thinly-veiled references to himself; the same is true of countless other seemingly impersonal references that fill his teachings. Any comparison of Nahman's own teachings with Nathan's biographies of his master willl make this clear. When Nahman says that "every man is filled with suffering," Nathan reminds us that Nahman himself knew pain greater than that of any other man. When Nahman speaks of the great distance from God that the man of faith may feel at certain times, we cannot but recall those passages in Nathan's biographies which speak of Nahman's own awareness of the gulf between himself and God. While Nahman never speaks in the first person in the *Liqquṭim* themselves, it is quite clear that a great many passages in them cannot be understood except as oblique references to his own spiritual situation. In this way he is unique among Hasidic authors. The homilies of most Hasidic masters are largely impersonal in character; indeed, there is sometimes little in either style or content to distinguish the teachings of one *ẓaddiq* from those of another. Nahman's teachings, on the other hand, are always recognizable by their highly personal mythology as well as by their unique extensions of associative thought.

It would be valuable, in both of these areas, to contrast Nahman's literary output with that of Shne'ur Zalman of Liadi, Nahman's elder contemporary and the other great theologian of Hasidism at the turn of the nineteenth century. Shne'ur Zalman, author of the *Tanya,* numerous homiletical writings, and his own guide to Jewish ritual practice *(Shulḥan 'Arukh shel ha-Rav),* is as close to being a systematic thinker as one finds within Hasidism. Posessed of a clear and methodical mind, he sets out his doctrine in carefully constructed categories, making extensive use of those categories of thought established by previous tradition, both philosophical and Kabbalistic. In the first part of the *Tanya,* which is a treatise on the psychology of religious devotion, he carefully delineates the functions of each part of the soul and its relationship to both heart and mind. Having these relationships clearly defined, he then embarks upon a discussion of various states of worship, carrying out a systematic program for the inculcation of proper religious attitudes in the heart of his reader. While frequent use is made of Biblical and rabbinic quotations, these are employed to provide justification for a largely self-standing edifice, rather than forming the links in a chain of seemingly erratic associations. In Shne'ur Zalman's homilies, largely collected in the two volumes entitled *Torah 'Or* and *Liqquṭey Torah,* the reader is confronted with a highly elaborate and abstract series of mystical essays, treating with great dexterity all the major themes of Lurianic Kabbalah, and reinterpreting them in accord with what is clearly a unique and well-developed mystical theology of Judaism.[6] But nowhere in all this vast edifice does the author himself appear; a biographer of Shne'ur Zalman might find little need to fathom the depths of his theological writings, and a student of his thought could manage with but a cursory knowledge of the facts of his life. The classics of *ḤaBaD* literature were written with a great sense of personal detachment, while Nahman's teachings, to say nothing of his tales, were composed from a standpoint of total personal involvement. This contrast in style is rooted in the respective religious positions of the two authors: detachment from personal and individual ego-identity is central to Shne'ur Zalman's understanding of the religious task, a position which stands in direct contrast to Nahman's highly personalistic and 'existential' approach to religion. Although their terminology roots both Nahman and Shne'ur Zalman to the world of Lurianic Kabbalah, in fact the temperament of the founder of *ḤaBaD* perhaps better reflects the cool and methodical style of a Kabbalist like Cordovero, while Nahman's mind is more attuned to the deeply personal and mythic content, as well as the highly novel exegetical style, displayed by the authors of the *Zohar* and the *Tiqqunim*, of which he was particularly fond. Nahman's way of thought was one of flash insights and startling intuitions; he had little use for what could be constructed by means of discursive reasoning. He recognized the difference between discursive and intuitive thinking, and openly expressed his preference for the latter.[7]

In light of these stylistic considerations, it is clear that any attempt to treat themes in Nahman's writings systematically must be approached with the greatest trepidation. If intuitive flashes based upon a particular series of scriptural associations lie at the base of each teaching, is one justified in using one of those teachings to explain another, in which the threads that compose the fabric of thought are in fact quite different? And if the image of Nahman's own self indeed looms so large behind the teachings, do not changes in the complexities of that self-image have to be considered in the study of each teaching? It is precisely on these points that M. Piekarz has criticized the researches of Joseph Weiss, claiming that the systematic manner in which Weiss has organized Nahman's teachings does violence to their individual character and their biographical setting. Undoubtedly there is some degree of validity to this criticism. If, however, one were to carry the dictum of Piekarz to its logical conclusion, Nahman will have been made to fall silent. Such an approach can produce *only* biography; its danger lies in the reduction of a person's most serious thoughts to mere reflections of so particular a setting in time and space that they can be of no more than historical interest. If Nahman is to be taken seriously as a thinker, one must at some point bracket the biographical circumstances and especially the infinitely complex psychological motivations underlying his thought in order to ask, "What does Nahman have to say?" There are, moreover, certain central themes that confront the reader repeatedly in Nahman's writings, and thus demand such general treatment. While these themes do take on a special importance for Nahman because of his personal situation, and are obviously rooted in biography, the solutions he proposes to the problems raised are properly a part of the history of Jewish theology, and it is as such that they should be treated. No problem more clearly illustrates this than that of Nahman's struggle with faith and doubt, to which we shall now turn our attention.

A casual reader of Nahman's writings might see in them a defense of simple faith in God over against any sort of philosophical speculation or inquiry. One finds that Nahman constantly warns his disciples to avoid such inquiry. Any contact with the writings of philosophers, including the Jewish philosophers of the Middle Ages, was considered particularly dangerous; Maimonides' *Guide* was a forbidden book in Bratslav, as were those works of medieval Biblical exegesis that contained reference to philosophical ideas.[8] In this way Nahman might be viewed as a typical if extreme representative of Ukrainian Hasidism, as distinct from the more 'intellectual' manifestations in Byelorussian *ḤaBaD* or in the Prsyzucha-Kotzk school in Poland. Indeed, this is the way in which Simon Dubnov, and to some extent even the much more perceptive Hillel Zeitlin, understood Nahman. There are many statements to be found in Bratslav writings that do lend credence to such a view, as does the conduct of many latter-day *ḥasidim* in the movement. Nahman spoke very frequently of the need for simplicity *(peshiṭut* or *temimut)* in faith. His tale of *The Wise Man and the Simpleton* is entirely based upon the theme of simplicity and its rewards. The faith that Nahman demanded was "like that of women and common folk . . . without any cleverness or inquiry at all." A Jew should follow the dictates of his religion simply on the basis of the authority inherent in revealed scripture, and should not seek to fathom the reasons for the commandments.[9] There is much here that seems to echo the religious position of such a figure as Abraham Kalisker, who, it will be recalled, denounced the publication of the *Tanya* lest it confound the faith of ordinary Jews.

But such a view of Nahman's teachings on faith and simplicity vastly underestimates the complexity of Nahman's mind and ignores what is in fact a radical and highly sophisticated critique of religious philosophy. In order to appreciate the seriousness of this critique and what it meant for Nahman, we must first recall that the questions of faith and doubt were highly personal ones for him, emerging from the most profound depths of his own inner conflict. It will come as no surprise to the reader of this biography to learn that these questions were very frequently on his mind. We have seen that both in adolescence and adulthood he was plagued by a sense of the distance between himself and God. Despite repeated and constant efforts at prayer, he still felt

> that he wasn't being noticed or heard at all. On the contrary, it seemed to him that he was being pushed away from the service of God in all kinds of ways, as though he were utterly unwanted. Days and years passed, but still he was far from Him. . . .

The emptiness of those long stretches when he could not feel God's presence was a reality Nahman could not deny. At such times he had no direct personal knowledge of a Creator; he lived in an existential universe in which God as an experienced reality did not exist. This seemingly Godless universe, which stood in grave contradiction to all his theological commitments, receives a striking portrayal in the tale of *The Wise Man and the Simpleton*. The two heroes of the story each receive identical messages from the king. While the supposed simpleton responds quickly, and thus receives his due reward, the 'wise' man

> said to the sage who had brought his letter: 'Wait here tonight and let us discuss this matter' . . . The wise man, with his philosophic mind, set to thinking about it and said: 'Why should the king be sending for an unimportant fellow like me? Who am I that the king, out of all his vast kingdom, should send for me? Compared to the king I am a nobody; how can it possibly make sense that the king should send someone after a person as small as I am? If I were to say that it is because of my wisdom—certainly the king has his own sages, and he himself is also a very wise man. So what is this matter of the king's sending for me?' He became very much confounded by it until finally he said: 'It is now very clear in my mind that there is no king in the world at all. The world is full of fools who think there is a king. How is it possible that they should all have subjected themselves to one man, thinking that he is the king, when in reality there is no king at all?'
>
> The messenger answered him: 'But I brought you a message from the king!' The wise man asked: 'Did you receive that message from the king's own hand?' The messenger was obliged to admit that he had not, but rather that someone else had given him the message in the king's name. The wise man continued: 'See how right I am—there is no king at all!' He said to the messenger: 'You have lived all your life in the capital. Tell me, have you ever seen the king?' The messenger replied that he had not. (This is indeed the case. Not everyone merits to see the king, who reveals himself only on very rare occasions.) And the wise man responded: 'Now see how perfectly clearly my position has been proven; there is no king at all, for even you have not seen him' . . . so the two of them decided that the king did not exist . . . They went into the market and there they came upon a soldier. 'Whom do you serve?' they asked him. 'The king,' he replied. 'Have you ever seen this king?' 'No.' 'What a fool,' they thought . . .[10]

The wise man, the messenger, and the simple believer who appear in this story are all aspects of Nahman's own tortured and conflicted mind. Here we see the starting point of Nahman's theological speculations: *the experience of the absence of God, or man's inability to experience God directly, must be taken seriously.* Man lives in a world where God cannot be 'seen'; given this reality, doubt is an inevitable part of the life of every religious human being, and the denial of God's very existence is something at which the faithful cannot afford to scoff. Nahman interprets the rabbinic dictum: "Know what to answer the heretic" to refer to the heretic within one's own heart; he warns that the Evil One exists in the form of a philosopher, challenging faith and denying God, inside the heart of every would-be believer.[11]

As much as a person may seek the nearness of God, the rationalist sceptic who dwells within him will allow him no peace. In another of Nahman's tales, the conflicting claims of wise man and simpleton are presented more directly for what they are: the two sides of a struggle going on within the heart of a single individual.

> The prince was a wise man, and he had a great love for wisdom. He surrounded himself with sages, and whoever brought a wise word to him was highly rewarded. . . . The sages of that country, however, became heretics because of their 'wisdom,' and the prince too was drawn into heresy. . . . Because there was some good in this prince—he was, after all, a well-born and noble person—sometimes he would ask himself: 'Where am I in the world? What am I doing?' At such times he would utter a great sigh, and would moan over what had become of his life. But as soon as he began to reason again, the 'wisdom' of heresy would be strengthened within him. This happened to him many times. When he asked where he was in the world he would sigh and moan, but when he went back to reason he was again a heretic.[12]

The deep and intuitive longings for God within the human soul are contradicted by the testimony of reason, which continually returns to remind us that we live in a world where, apparently, "there is no king at all."

This is the situation in which man finds himself: his need to find meaning in his own life (for this is the true thrust of the prince's questions) brings forth in him a longing for faith in God; this longing, however, is contradicted by the testimony of his own experience, that of a universe from which God is absent. Reason confirms the testimony of experience, making faith in God impossible. If faith is to survive, therefore, it must offer some explanation for the basic existential fact of the seeming absence of God from the world. What Nahman seeks to do in this matter is ultimately to stand the challenge on its head, claiming that *only* in the seeming absence of God from the world can one truly find Him, and that true faith can come to be only where God is not readily to be found. But in order to understand how Nahman arrives at this highly paradoxical resolution of faith and doubt, we shall have to examine a number of his teachings that deal with these issues.

We begin with the notion of *maqqifin,* perhaps the single most complicated idea in all of Nahman's writings. In Nahman's usage, which is quite original, the term *maqqif* refers to a question or a challenge to faith which the mind cannot resolve; the challenge 'surrounds' the mind, and cannot be integrated into the individual's own pattern of religious understanding. As a person sets out on his search for God, he is confronted by a seemingly endless series of such *maqqifin;* as each doubt or challenge that stands before him is resolved, another comes to take its place. The path to knowledge of God is one of spiraling ascent, each step of the way marked by successively more difficult challenges to faith.[13]

At any given point where the seeker stands in his religious life, his mind is filled with some particular content of understanding: he conceives of God in some specific way. This conception is the *penimi,* that which is "within" the mind at that moment. This *penimi,* however, is inevitably attached to a *maqqif,* a conception beyond the mind's present grasp, one which at the same time both challenges the *penimi* and offers a conception on a higher level. Man's task is to seek out this *maqqif,* to bring it into his mind as a new *penimi,* and thus to seek a still-higher challenge and resolution. This is the theoretical expression of Nahman's call for constant growth.

As long as the mind remains satisfied with its conceptions, such movement is impossible. The mind must first be emptied of its current contents in order for the required growth to take place. Nahman recommends two methods for this initial step in the search for new *maqqifin.* One way of emptying the mind is through teaching others who stand on a lower level of understanding. What is a *penimi* for you is still a *maqqif* for the one you teach. As you pass the contents of your mind on to him, your own mind is emptied, and thus becomes ready to meet the challenge from beyond.

> As one man speaks to another, giving him [greater] awareness and fear of heaven, or as one raises up disciples, the "surrounding lights" *('orot ha-maqqifin)* are integrated. He is now able to understand that which had previously been incomprehensible to him. That which a man grasps with his mind is called *penimi,* as it has entered into his intellect. But that which has not been able to enter his mind, *i.e.,* that which he cannot [yet] understand, is a *maqqif,* standing outside [lit.: 'surrounding'] his mind. . . . When he speaks to others, putting his [present level of] awareness into them, his mind is emptied of its previous intellectual content, and then the *maqqif* is able to enter. . . . He can then understand this *maqqif,* which had previously been beyond him.[14]

The second method of emptying the mind, predictably enough for Nahman, is one of prayer. At times the mind is so sated with its content that it is not aware of the necessarily transitory value of any particular rung of religious understanding. This time of self-satisfaction is in fact a most dangerous one, as it most readily leads man down the path toward the greatest enemy of the true seeker, self-delusion.

> The most important thing is not to fool yourself, thinking that you have already arrived at an adequate understanding. For one who thinks this will remain there, God forbid.[15]

At such times the seeker must call out to God, hoping that his heart-rending cries will pierce the walls confining his mind, and will enable him to reach through to the next appropriate *maqqif.*

> There are times when the *moḥin* and the flow of divinity are hidden, in a state of 'gestation' *('ibbur).* At such times of hiding, outcry is helpful. This hiding or gestation is 'You weaken the rock of birth-giving' (Deut. 32:18) or 'There is no strength to give birth' (Is. 37:3), like a woman who is too weak to

deliver her child. When she goes into labor, she cries out seventy times . . . and then she gives birth . . . The cry which a person lets out while praying or studying, when the *moḥin* are hidden in a state of gestation, is the cry of a woman in childbirth. God, who knows the hidden ways of the *moḥin* and how they came to be hidden, hears our cries. This cry takes the place of the *Shekhinah's* outcry; it is as though She were crying out, and She gives birth to the *moḥin.*[16]

The "birth" of such new *moḥin,* or their coming out of hiding, now means that man is aware of the inadequacy of his former rung of understanding. The new *maqqif* challenges the old resolution, showing him that in fact his former way of knowing is no knowledge at all. This is the meaning of Nahman's frequent statement, "The end of knowledge is [the realization] that we do not know."[17] The path toward understanding is one of constant negation, in which each particular rung of attainment exists only so that it can be transcended by a new challenge, keeping man in a constant tension of 'knowledge' and 'ignorance,' but an 'ignorance' which is higher than any particular level of knowledge.

The statement 'The end of knowledge is that we do not know' refers also to each individual [rung of] knowledge. Even when one reaches the ultimate *[takhlit]* in a particular [rung of] knowing, which is [the realization that] 'we do not know,' this is not the end, but only the end of this particular knowledge. With regard to the knowledge above this one, [the seeker] has not yet begun. And so higher and higher; one *never* knows anything at all, and one never reaches the end, for there is [always] a higher knowledge, in which one has not yet begun.

With regard to 'the end of knowledge is that we do not know,' he said on several occasions that this end exists with regard to each [level of] knowledge. Therefore, even though we reach this goal of 'not knowing,' this is not the final goal, but one which refers only to that level. We then have to struggle onward to reach a still higher level of . . . not knowing—and thus forever.[18]

The method Nahman has proposed here is one of dialectical negation, in which each new synthesis exists only to bring on a still-greater challenge. In proposing this dialectical model for the constant growth of religious understanding, Nahman is making use of deep-rooted traditions within Kabbalism, but is applying them in an entirely new way.

The dialectical mode of thinking has taken a central role in each successive stage of Kabbalistic thought, though in a number of widely varied forms. In the Kabbalah of the thirteenth century, it is by means of a process of synthetic dialectic that the *sefirot* are said to unfold within God. The arrangement of these manifestations of divine life in the pattern of successive triads points to this mode of understanding. Particularly in the emergence of the second triad, that of *ḥesed, din,* and *tif'eret,* is the pattern of thesis, antithesis, and synthesis most clearly evident. *Ḥesed,* divine Love or Grace, and *din,* divine Rigor, stand in antithetical tension with regard to one another; only as they are synthesized in *tif'eret* (sometimes called *raḥamin,* divine "Compassion") can the process of God's self-revelation go foward.

In the Lurianic Kabbalah of the sixteenth century, a new element of negation is brought into the mystic's dialectical thought pattern. The idea that the very process of divine self-revelation in the *sefirot* is preceded by an act of *ẓimẓum,* of God's withdrawal into the recesses of His hidden self, is a dramatic turn in the history of Kabbalism. Each successive stage of self-revelation and of Creation must, of necessity, according to the Lurianists, be preceded by another act of withdrawal. Here the dialectic is no longer one of opposing *aspects* of the emerging divine *persona,* but one that strikes at the very root of the process by which God allows for any existence outside that of His utterly hidden and unknowable self. The dialectical relationship between emergence and withdrawal, and between the "space" that has been filled by God and that from which His presence has been removed, now becomes a central focus of the mystic's speculations.

The theoreticians of the Sabbatian movement in the seventeenth century again wrought great changes in the history of Kabbalistic dialectics. Here the locus of dialectic movement was for the first time removed from the rarified air of theosophical speculation and applied as a standard of behavior in the realm of man's religious life. The Sabbatian dialectic, applied first and foremost to the messiah himself, but later adopted by others as well, involved man's relationship to the process of the world's redemption from the forces of evil, a process now said to be in its final and crucial stage. In order to redeem from evil, Sabbatianism required a descent into the very depths of that evil; only by means of such descent could one serve the purpose of greater ascent, raising up the *shekhinah* from demonic captivity as one rose from the depths. Man is to act out the dialectical relationship between good and evil in his own life. Hasidism retained this sense of "descent for the sake of ascent," and the phrase *yeridah ẓorekh 'aliyah* is often found in Hasidic literature, though purified of its overtones of intentional sin.

Nahman's originality lies in his application of the dialectical principle to the intellectual life and to matters of challenge and doubt. Following the general Hasidic tendency toward the application of the terms of Kabbalistic metaphysics to categories of the devotee's inner life, Nahman has depicted the spiritual growth of the seeker as an ongoing chain made up of challenges, resolutions, and higher challenges. The dialectic is proposed as the only true way of apprehending a reality that is itself dialectical in its inner structure. At the root of this dialectic of religious growth is a sense of fascination with challenge, and a belief that there is value in a life of constant confrontation.

While one might expect that the achievement of a certain integration and sense of wholeness would be a goal of the religious life, here the very opposite turns out to be the case: He who is undisturbed is in a fallen state; man has to cry out to God in order that his faith be challenged! But what is the great challenge to faith if not the absence of God from the realm of human experience? Man lives in a world from which God seems to be absented, and he is now permitted to accept no explanation that might offer him comfort, assuring him that the divine Presence is with him after all. All such resolutions exist for Nahman only in order to be negated. Where the divine Presence is apparent, there is no challenge. Thus he who ultimately seeks the presence of God on its highest and most authentic level must do so by following a unique form of *via negativa*, paradoxically pushing himself toward those inner places where God is not to be found, or at least where His presence is not readily perceived. Faith must be nurtured by constant growth, growth can take place only in the face of challenge, and challenge can exist only in confrontation with the seeming absence of God.

But the paradox does not end here. One might think that there is something optimistic about this seemingly progressivist vision; the spiraling ascent, despite all its challenges, does in fact bring one closer to the knowledge of God. This, however, does not always appear to be the case. The higher a man ascends, the more difficult the challenges become, and the harder it is to find sufficient strength to deal with them. While it is not clear in Nahman's writings whether the *content* of the *maqqifin* changes as one ascends to the higher rungs, or whether one continues to confront the same issues on level after level, it is apparent that at least in the final stages of the ascent one comes face to face with certain problems on a level where they cannot be resolved at all. The sufferings of the righteous, the problem of free will and divine foreknowledge, and the relationship between providence and nature are given as examples of such ultimate *maqqifin*.[19] The difficulties inherent in these final challenges to faith cannot be met by the human mind; they thus remain eternal barriers to man's this-worldly search for true knowledge of God, barriers which even the true *ẓaddiq* himself confronts only with the greatest difficulty. What, then, one may ask, is the purpose of the ascent? If the ongoing search for God cannot bring one close to Him, but only leads to a meeting with irresolvable contradictions, would man not be better off remaining in the state of untainted innocence in which he began his search?

The answer to this question lies in Nahman's belief that there is a philosopher in every heart. The fact is, he would claim, that faith nowhere exists in a pure unchallenged state; even the seemingly simplest of believers are faced with questions they cannot answer:

> Even though it seems that ordinary folk are far from philosophy and do not ask any such questions at all, in truth they are all involved in philosophical inquiry, and each of them has questions. Even children are confounded by philosophical questions.[20]

Man must meet the challenge because he is not free to desist from it. It is of the very nature of the human mind to raise questions; even where we are not aware of them, their presence will sooner or later make itself felt.

This answer, however, is too pat; in fact Nahman is far from consistent on this point. Does he want his disciples to raise questions and seek out challenge, or does he seek for them a life of simple and unquestioning faith? The fact is that one finds in his writings two notions of faith: the simple and the dialectical. His frequent exhortations to the life of simple and unquestioning faith, which have been mentioned above, seem to lie in direct contrast to the spiral of constant growth through challenge which he has now been shown to advocate. The latter path was undoubtedly intended for an elite, comprised of the *ẓaddiq* himself and his immediate disciples. For others, simplicity would indeed suffice. At times one gets the impression that this hierarchy is reversed, and that Nahman envies the ability of the simple folk to maintain their stance of naïveté in the face of questions that would allow him no rest in his dialectical search. Were he able to achieve their simplicity, it seems that he would gladly abandon the dialectic!

It should be made clear that the process of dialectical ascent in Nahman's thought is not based upon the providing of rational answers to the questions that confront the mind. He rather seeks a faith nurtured by questioning, which grows in the face of challenge. What we really see in this process is an ever-expanding notion of faith itself, a faith growing in paradoxical complexity as it seeks to incorporate those very challenges that had sought to destroy it. *A religious life that thrives on challenge does not want to provide 'answers' to the eternal questions, but seeks rather to raise the level of struggle to an ever-higher pitch.* Nahman was highly suspicious of any attempt to answer the questions that stand in the way of faith:

> Of all the places where our master speaks of philosophical questions, nowhere does he seek to answer them. His wondrous and awesome teachings rather reveal to the mind the origin of these questions, which makes it impossible to answer them in any way . . . He who wants to see the truth must know within himself that it is impossible to resolve these questions with any [use of] intellect, even by following the ways of the true Kabbalists; *one must rely on faith alone.*[21]

The last line of this passage is highly significant: in it Nahman reveals that it is not only philosophy he rejects, but even Kabbalah, insofar as it has been "corrupted" by discursive reasoning. The passage from which we have quoted actually begins with a denunciation of this sort of Kabbalah, and only from there launches upon a more typical tirade against philosophy. Nahman was speaking of the rabbinic dictum: "Both these and those are the words of the living God," employed by the Talmud in those cases where no decision is made between the conflicting claims of two legal authorities. Of this Nahman said:

> It is impossible to understand this at all . . . Even though the books of Kabbalah do contain answers to this question and others like it, wanting to say that the sage who holds the stricter opinion comes from the side of *gevurah,* while his more lenient opponent derives from *ḥesed,* and therefore 'both these and those are the words of the living God' . . . all such answers are nothing to anyone who has even a bit of understanding.
>
> He said it in these words: 'Let someone give *me* an answer!' Let someone gird up his loins and [dare to] pronounce an answer to this question to my face. For really there is no answer at all. One says the thing is ritually fit and may be eaten, while the other says just the opposite and forbids eating it. How could the intellect possibly comprehend that both are true, if one says the opposite of the other? He meant to say that all these answers are of no account—to say nothing of those answers found in books of philosphy, which are surely of no value . . . For this reason our master forbade us to study even the works of acceptable philosophers: they raise difficult and lengthy questions as to the ways of God, but when it comes to answering the questions, their answers are weak and can easily be refuted. Therefore he who looks into them and seeks to answer their questions by means of his intellect can fall into great heresy, when he sees that his answer is nothing and that the question remains. It is thus forbidden to look into [such books] at all, and one must rely on faith alone . . . Even some of the answers that are to be found in the works of true Kabbalists, great *ẓaddiqim* who understood these matters and were possessed of the holy spirit [are of no account], since the question cannot be answered . . .[22]

Here Nahman has revealed himself as a deep and thoroughgoing anti-rationalist. The fact that Kabbalist along with philosopher receives such harsh treatment here shows that Nahman is opposed to *any* attempt to resolve the questions that confront religious man, no matter if the resolutions be of the most pious and even inspired sort. While elsewhere he does show clear preference for Kabbalah over philosophy,[23] and he frequently quotes from the Kabbalistic classics, his critique here encompasses all attempts, including those of mystics, to provide answers that would satisfy the mind. *Maqqifin* must be encountered by faith alone.

The reader of Nahman who has some familiarity with the classics of Jewish theology, both rational and mystical, will immediately be struck by the central role *faith* plays in the religious life of Bratslav. It is to the nature of faith in Nahman's writings and its unique place in the history of

Judaism that we must now turn our attention.

Nahman was by no means the first figure in Jewish history who may be called an anti-rationalist. Beginning with the opposition to Maimonides in the thirteenth century, an articulate strain of thought opposed to reason as a means of ascertaining religious truth made itself heard in Jewish circles. Such figures as Jacob ben Sheshet in mid-thirteenth century Spain, Shem Tov ben Shem Tov (*ca.* 1380–1441) and Meir Ibn Gabbai in early sixteenth-century Turkey were among the leading classical spokesmen for this point of view. Under the twin impact of the Kabbalistic revival and the counter-Reformation, Jewish opposition to rationalism reached major proportions in the sixteenth and seventeenth centuries. If we want to go back still further, it is possible to characterize the thought of Judah Halevi as anti-rational to a certain degree, though mildly so compared to these later figures.[24] But in none of these thinkers does the opposition between faith and reason take on the character it does in Nahman; none of them, indeed, defines faith as Nahman does.

Faith (*'emunah*), as seen in the medieval Jewish mind, is not self-justifying; it is the human response to the truth of revelation. The real opposition in the medieval sources is not one of faith and reason as modes of apperception, but rather one of reason and revelation as sources of religious knowledge. For Halevi, faith is based upon the authenticity of Israel's historic claim to revelation at Sinai, passed on to us by an unbroken and reliable chain of tradition. Without the assurance of that historic truth, 'faith' in his terms would be unfounded. In later anti-rationalism, largely dominated by Kabbalists, it is again an argument from alleged *tradition* that seems to prevail. Donning the mantle of tradition-rooted rabbinic orthodoxy, the Kabbalists claim that their understandings of religion go back to the most ancient sages, even to Moses himself, while asserting that the views of the philosophers are either the creations of their own minds or, still worse, are adopted from the notions of non-Jewish thinkers, and are thus *ipso facto* unworthy by comparison. The Kabbalists may bemoan the fact that the philosopher is not an initiate in his esoteric universe, a universe called "the secret of faith" (*raza di-mehemnuta*) by the *Zohar*; it is only his lack of exposure to Kabbalistic lore that has caused the poor philosopher to be led astray.[25] In all of these cases "faith" refers primarily to an unswerving loyalty to the claims of tradition over any rational arguments to the contrary. The word *'emunah*, in fact, is not used nearly so much in such theological discussions as *'emet*, truth. When it is used, particularly as a verb (*le-ha'amin*), it clearly has the sense of "belief" or lending credence to particular truth-claims.[26] *Biṭṭahon*, perhaps more properly "faith" in the sense of deep and inward trust, plays a large part in *devotional* literature but would almost never be evoked in the debate between reason and revelation.

All of this is quite different from what Nahman has in mind when he speaks of faith. Here it is precisely the devotional stance upon which his thoughts are based. Though he uses *'emunah* more frequently than *biṭṭahon*, it is the faith of the Psalmist that he bears as a model. No argumentation would matter here, for it is the heart, not the mind, that needs to be convinced. Kabbalists themselves would frequently use discursive language to argue the truth of their position; this exercise on their part is one Nahman sees as entirely vain. Nahman's frequent talk of the efficacy of faith and faith alone has little to do with the *content*, but rather more to do with the *stance* of that faith. Faith for him is an act of *defiance;* not merely a passive matter of giving assent to the truth of tradition or Scripture, it is rather the highly active means man uses to fight off those challenges and inner demons that seek constantly to overpower him. Itself rooted in the heart or soul rather than the mind, Nahman's faith has the character of a deep and ultimately unshakable personal religious *intuition*. It is manifest in the inexplicable longing of the prince in the *Seven Beggars* to find some greater meaning in his life; reason cannot apprehend it, nor can the man of faith ever fully communicate its power to one who does not have it. Faith, says Nahman,

> is both hidden and revealed. It is hidden, because if you ask a man of faith to provide some reason for it, he certainly will not be able to give you any; faith only applies to those matters where there are no reasons.[27] But it is also revealed, because to the man of faith himself it is all quite clear, as though he were seeing the object of his faith with his very eyes—since his faith is so whole.

> 'For I know that the Lord is great; He is our Lord above any god' (Ps. 135:5). Said King David: 'For *I* know,' emphasizing the 'I'. The greatness of God is something that no one can communicate to his fellowman, or even to himself from one day to the next. That which is brilliantly clear to him on one day is something that he cannot communicate to himself on the day that follows. That is why he said: 'For *I* know'—because this cannot be told at all.[28]

One would be hard-pressed to find anywhere in religious literature so clear a statement of the 'existential' nature of faith. The beginning point of the life of faith is the discovery of its presence, albeit hidden and inarticulate, within one's own soul. This native root of faith, discovered in pure subjectivity and yet existing in every human being, produces vague and undefined longings, symptomatic of the great longing of all souls to return to their root in God. These longings themselves are crucial to the path; the growth and cultivation of faith depends upon man's willingness to follow those original impulses it provides, and not to deny them because they are contravened by reason.

The motif of unfulfilled longings is a thread that runs through almost all of Nahman's tales: a maiden longs for her true spouse, a prince for his kingdom, a disciple for his true master. In the *Liqquṭim* and particularly in the shorter *Siḥot,* such terms for longing as *ga'agu'im, kissufim,* and *hishtoqequt* are found with unparalleled frequency. The most authentic manifestation of faith is in man's longings for God. This was true of Nahman's own life, as described in Nathan's biographies; it was also the core of the religious life he sought to impart to his disciples. Drawing upon the rich Gnostic imagery of exile and longing for return that so deeply colors much of Kabbalistic literature, Nahman conceived a universe filled with longing, a world in which man's desire to return to God was but a part of a hidden yearning that was greater than himself. The most poignant portrayal of this longing, undoubtedly one of the poetic gems of Jewish literature, is Nahman's parable of the heart and the spring, an episode within his tale of the *Seven Beggars:*

> There is a mountain, and on that mountain there stands a rock. A spring gushes forth from that rock.
>
> Now everything has a heart, and the world as a whole has a heart. The heart of the world is a complete form, with face, hands, and feet. But even the toenail on that heart of the world is more heart-like than any other heart.
>
> The mountain and the spring stand at one end of the world, and the heart is at the other. The heart stands facing the spring, yearning and longing to draw near to it.
>
> It is filled with a wild yearning, and constantly cries out in its longing to approach the spring. The spring, too, longs for the heart.
>
> The heart suffers from two weaknesses: the sun pursues it terribly, and burns it because it wants to approach the spring—and its second weakness is that of longing and constant outcry to draw near to the spring. The heart ever stands facing the spring, and cries out in pain because of its great yearning.
>
> When the heart needs to rest a bit, or to catch its breath, a great bird comes over it, and spreads forth its wings to shield the heart from the sun. But even at its times of rest, the heart looks out toward the spring in longing.
>
> Now if the heart is filled with so great a desire to draw near to the spring, why does it not simply do so? But as soon as it begins to move toward the mountain, the mountaintop where the spring stands disappears from view. And the life of the heart flows from the spring; if it were to allow the spring to vanish from its sight, it would die. . . .
>
> If that heart were to die, God forbid, the entire world would be destroyed. The heart is the life of all things; how could the world exist without a heart? For this reason the heart can never approach the spring, but ever stands opposite it and looks at it in longing.

The symbol of the heart of the world is a complicated one; it may be said at once to represent the *shekhinah, the true ẓaddiq* (who is the heart of his generation), and the soul of every individual who longs for God.[29] No matter which of these levels of meaning is emphasized, however, the passage reveals the emotional content of faith as Nahman sees it. An overwhelming sense of wounded passion, expressed in undying yearnings for an intimacy that cannot come to be, lies at the core of his religious life. Here Nahman again reminds us of his Western contemporaries, the Romantic poets; love's desires overflow in him as in them, but the object of those longings will ever elude him.

In this vision of the heart of the world we see the emotional side of Nahman's penchant for paradoxical thinking. The path of simple faith seems so clear: if your heart yearns for God as does this heart for the spring, what keeps you from Him? The call of simple love-faith tells you to draw ever nearer to the beloved. But what to do when it is impossible to draw near?—impossible here because the slightest approach on the heart's part would cause the spring to disappear from view and bring the heart to death. It is distance itself that causes man to long for God, and the vision that sustains him is itself born of that longing. Were he to come closer, those longings might be lessened, and the vision of faith thus be destroyed. The core of religion is faith, faith is manifest in longings, and longings can exist only over a distance—the greater the distance, in fact, the greater the longings. Thus while the heart's desire for nearness to God appears to reflect the simplest of emotions, it is in fact enmeshed in the greatest paradox.

The relationship between simple and dialectical faith has here reached a point of crisis. Simple faith cries out for the presence of God, while dialectical faith, realizing the complexity of the human situation and ever struggling to press on through the path of *maqqifin*, must perforce cry out for His *absence*. Ultimately, of course, this latter path is also one that seeks the nearness of God, but it may do so only through ever seeking to confront His distance. The distinction between these two types of faith, as well as the ultimate dialectical resolution of that distinction, is clarified in the following passage. This teaching deals with the role of the *zaddiq* in helping each of his disciples to attain the *maqqifin* appropriate to him, by raising the proper questions to challenge his faith, while avoiding those challenges too difficult for the particular disciple to handle:

> There are those who dwell above and those who dwell below: an upper world and a lower world, heaven and earth. The *ẓaddiq* has to show those who dwell above that they have no knowledge of God at all. This is the understanding called "What?" 'What have you seen? What have you examined?' This is the aspect of 'Where is the place of His glory?' But to those who dwell below, he has to demonstrate the contrary, that 'the whole earth is filled with His glory' (Is. 6:3). For there are those who dwell in the dust, on

> the lowest of rungs, and they think themselves to be far from God. The *ẓaddiq* has to arouse them, fulfilling: 'Awake and sing, you who dwell in the dust' (Is. 26:19), showing them that God is with them, that they are really near to Him, for 'the whole earth is filled with His glory'. . . This is the meaning of: 'Be deliberate in judgment'. . . the wise man has to be deliberate, knowing how to speak with each individual. When he comes before those who dwell above, he must . . . [ask them]: 'What have you seen,' etc. To those who dwell below, however, he must reveal the thought that the whole world is filled with His glory. This is judgment or justice, as Scripture says: 'The Lord judges, lowering one and raising up another' (Ps. 75:8). Those who are high have to be lowered, by being shown that they know nothing of God, while the lower ones, those who dwell in the dust, need be raised up and awakened, so that they do not despair—for the whole earth is filled with His glory.[30]

Those who 'dwell above' in this passage are the more intimate disciples of the *ẓaddiq*, those who have chosen the path of dialectical faith through the search for ever-higher *maqqifin*. In the course of the dialectical process, those who are closest to God come to realize how little they know, while those who are 'below' gain greater faith in their own perceptions. Nahman strikingly illustrates this further by reference to Moses who, though he had seen God "face to face," nevertheless said, "Man cannot see Me and live" (Ex. 33:11, 20), while Isaiah, who saw God only "through a glass darkly" was able to claim, "I saw the Lord" (Is. 6:1).[31] Whenever such seekers reach a new plateau of integration, the task of the *ẓaddiq* is to remind them that they still know nothing, and that they must continue their search as though from the beginning. "The end of knowledge is that we do not know." The *ẓaddiq* accomplishes this goal by constantly raising questions that challenge their faith, showing them that they still need to ask, "Where is the place of His glory?" Those who 'dwell below' in this context are more simple and perhaps depressed people who have come to Nahman seeking advice, feeling somehow far from God. Their path is that of simple faith, one of direct longings for the God who is hidden from them. To these the *ẓaddiq* must display a model of positive faith, assuring them that they have not been abandoned, and that in truth God is near to them.

From the terms Nahman employs in this discussion, one might think that what we have here is a somewhat obvious treatment of the age-old dichotomy between the transcendence and immanence of God, a dichotomy classically expressed in Judaism by the very phrases of the *Qedushah*-liturgy upon which Nahman has built this teaching. Those who 'dwell above' and think they have achieved real closeness to God should be taught divine transcendence, while their more simple compatriots, who are in danger of despair at their low state, should be strengthened by assurances of God's immanence. Were this the case, there would be nothing particularly original or startling in Nahman's formulation.[32] But Nahman does not allow us to interpret him in this way. In the continuation of this passage, where he points out the necessary interpenetration of simple and dialectical faith, it is clear that those who 'dwell above' are to go beyond what is usually meant by a sense of divine transcendence. Awareness of God's transcendence is generally accompanied in religious literature by an increased sense of awe; here the transcendence the seeker is to experience is so total that it *destroys* his fear of heaven. The transcendence the *zaddiq* shows him is in fact equal to the absence of God:

> These two worlds, the upper and the lower, have to be comingled. The "son" [*i.e.*, he who dwells above] must be combined with the "disciple" [he who dwells below], in order that he have a sense of awe. For the "son" who is on the level of 'What have you seen?' *will not have awe at all, because he does not see God's glory at all.* [Since the *zaddiq* has shown him that he knows nothing.] Therefore the "son" must come to include the aspect of "disciple," which will lend to him a bit of the disciple's understanding that 'the whole earth is filled with His Glory,' in order that he might have some awe. And the disciple, who well understands that 'the whole earth is filled with His glory' might pass out of existence [being so totally overwhelmed by the Presence]; he therefore needs to be shown something of the son's level, the aspect of "What?", so that he not be destroyed.[33]

The relationship between these two types of faith has now shown itself to be hopelessly complex. He who thought he knew God must be shown that he knows nothing; on the other hand, were he really to become fully convinced that he knows nothing of God at all, he would lose his awe, and simply become a denier of religion. He is being sent on a path of constant negation, one that comes dangerously close to the ultimate negation, which means the abandonment of the search. In the very heights of his ever-denying ascent, therefore, he must maintain some element of the simple man's faith, which will give him the impetus to continue in his struggle. The simple man, on the other hand, who had thought that God was far from him, must be shown His presence. But lest this new awareness of God prove destructive of his mental life, he, too, must be granted a touch of the denial that has now become the property of the other. The dialectical intertwining of these two positions is so complex that at times Nahman abandons the distinction altogether, claiming that the highest degree of ascent in the world of *maqqifin* is nothing other than simplicity itself, and that it is the simplest faith that leads to the greatest knowledge:

> One really has to cast aside one's mind, throwing off all cleverness, and serve God in simplicity. A person's deeds must be greater than his wisdom; it is the deed that matters, not the interpretation. You have to set aside all cleverness to serve God simply, not only the foolish 'wisdom' of ordinary

people, but even the real wisdom of great minds has to be cast aside for the sake of this simplicity. One may even have to do things that seem like madness for the sake of serving God . . . for one has to roll in all sorts of mud and filth in order to serve Him and to fulfill His commandments. . . .

When one's love for God is so great that he is able to set aside his mind and roll in mud and filth to serve Him, all in order to do that which pleases God, he also has done some good for his own *moḥin*. For [through such service] he may merit to understand even that which is beyond his own *moḥin*, that which Moses himself did not grasp within his lifetime: the problem of why the righteous suffer and the wicked prosper . . . this appears to be a perversion of justice, God forbid, and even Moses was not able to fathom it while he was alive. When the mind is present, and has not been set aside, the person may be compared to Moses in his lifetime. But the setting aside of one's mind, as in sleep, is parallel to the death of Moses . . . By loving God so much that you cast yourself into the mud for Him, worshipping Him with the love of an ordinary servant, you may grasp that which Moses in his lifetime, and the mind when it is operating, cannot understand: the problem of theodicy.[34]

Here the dialectic seems to have turned in on itself. Dialectical faith, by which man sought to reach out for that which was beyond his grasp, now reveals itself to be nothing other than simple faith, the unquestioning obedience of the humble servant. It is this faith, *one which is dependent for its very existence upon the suspension of intellect*, that is now the means to the highest goal. After all the tortuousness of this process, Nahman once again advocates simplicity itself, and his final position is indeed not unlike that of Zusya of Anipol' or Abraham Kalisker, who also advocated simple faith as the only true way to God. Indeed, the one who rolls in the mud as a test of his faith sounds very much like the sort of "holy fool" with whom Zusya is often identified. The *Simpleton* of Nahman's tale has here had his position articulated in terms he himself could never comprehend, but which were the only way in which Nahman—the tortuously complicated one, who at the end of his life saw himself as "the great simple one"—could return to the very simplicity that had been so abused by the popular Hasidism out of which he emerged. In Neskhiz, one of the dynasties most nearly typifing the simple Hasidism of the Ukraine, the following tale was told by R. Yizhak:

Two great *ẓaddiqim* were once sitting together and someone came before them with a petition for a woman having difficulty in childbirth. Each of them sought to defer to the other in this matter, until finally the elder of the two stretched out his handkerchief like a curtain, looked at it, and said: 'Mazal Tov! The woman has given birth.' And thus it was. The other asked him what it was that he had seen in the handkerchief. He replied: *'I did that so that those who were watching us should have simple faith.* Had I said it in some

> other way, they all would have wondered: "How does the *ẓaddiq* know?" And they would ask questions about it. But now they understand nothing of it at all. *And this is the root of faith: that the faithful one realize that he has no understanding at all* and [there is no place for] philosophizing or investigation.[35]

The *polemical* nature of Nahman's faith-idea has caused him to come full circle, back to this idealization of simplicity. Reason, to Nahman, is the great enemy of religious faith. It is only by fighting the claims of reason, and ultimately by transcending the rational mind itself, that true faith can come to be. God is completely beyond the ken of any intellectuality, even such wisdom as is properly permitted within the bounds of Torah. The greatest faith has no basis in intellect, and cannot be proven in any way. Nahman says:

> Faith is called 'light', as Scripture says: 'Your faithfulness in the night' (Ps. 92:3). Faith which is based upon the wisdom of Torah, through which man comes to an understanding of God and thus to faith in Him, is of some good. But true faith is belief in God without any sign, proof, or reason. This is the complete faith, which is alluded to as light in the passage 'Your faithfulness in the night.'[36]

Here again we have simplicity and dialectic at once. True faith can flourish only in the absence of the powers of intellect, in the absence of the very proofs that might buttress it; only in the darkness of 'night,' shielded from the false light of intellectuality, can faith take its stand. Only a fully *uncritical* attitude can embrace this faith. Better to believe in foolishness and superstitions along with faith, says Nahman, than to apply one's critical faculty in such a way that faith itself might be destroyed. Faith in God requires a complete suspension of belief in the order of nature; God rules as an absolute monarch, changing nature and suspending its rules in response to the longings and prayers of His faithful. The restrictions of rational thought have no place in such a universe. To claim that God is limited by the law of logic is no less a restriction of His infinite freedom than any other restraint:

> He mentioned that it says in their [the philosophers'] books: 'Is it possible that a triangle be a rectangle?' Our master said: I believe that God can make a rectangular triangle. For the ways of God are hidden from us; He is omnipotent, and no deed is beyond Him. But such inquiries are completely forbidden; one should rather seek wholeness of faith . . .[37]

Here Nahman has shown himself to be the most radical and consistent of the latter-day Jewish detractors of medieval rationalism. Faith is to exist even in the face of logical absurdity; indeed it is only where reason scoffs that faith is truly able to take its stand. The tradition of Tertullian has here found its Jewish parallel. Reason is the very antithesis of faith and of the revealed truth that is the object of faith. Israel were able to receive the Torah at Sinai only because they had abandoned their reason altogether. Had they held on to their rationality at all, they, like the scoffers of Nahman's own day, would have been unable to approach the truth.

> As long as a person holds on to any bit of his own reason, he is not whole [in his faith], and he cannot be bound to the *ẓaddiq*. Israel, at the time when the Torah was given, possessed great wisdom, for the idolatry of their day was based upon profound though erring philosophy, as is known. Had they not been able to cast aside all their cleverness, they would not have been able to accept the Torah. They would have found a way to deny everything, and none of Moses' awesome miracles, performed before their very eyes, would have helped. In our day, too, there are such heretics, who deny everything through the foolishness of their mistaken 'wisdom.' Only because Israel, the holy people, saw the truth, and cast aside all their wisdom to believe in God and His servant Moses, were they able to receive the Torah.[38]

The faith described in these passages requires an act of transcendence; in order to reach revelation's truth, one has to overcome the constricting and denying influence of the mind. The mind has the power to make a mockery of anything, even of Sinai itself. Confronted with such a power, miracles, whether on the part of Moses or of today's *ẓaddiq*, are of no avail. The Biblical terms for 'miracle,' *ot* or *mofet*, are also used in Hebrew philosophical literature to mean 'proof.' Both supernatural and logical demonstration are inadequate in matters of divine truth; both can be controverted by the critical attitude of the rational mind. Any faith resting upon such demonstrations is necessarily of a lower order than that which is based upon pure acceptance, 'faithfulness in the night.' Where there *is* evidence, *be it of a miraculous or a logical sort*, there is no room for such pure faith to exist.

There is yet another reason the existence of such proofs is inimical to the purity of faith. The faith that is to be a personal beacon in the darkness must be freely *chosen* by the individual if it is to have the strength needed to sustain him. Where there is no freely-willed choice, there can be no service of God. If faith were to be forced upon the believer by incontrovertible evidence, he could not be said to have chosen it freely. Only by facing the absence of God, and the lack of evidence for His existence, does man gain the freedom to choose the way of faith. Man is confronted with the soul and its longings on one side, and the mind and its scoffings on the other; his task is to choose between them. The choice for the soul involves the inevitable rejection of mind; faith and reason remain in conflict, a conflict which is nowhere to be resolved before the end of time.[39]

While it would seem that this absolute rejection of reason as a means to knowing God obviates the need for any more particular critique of philosophy, Nahman does not rest here. In direct contrast to his constant warnings to others against the study of philosophical works stands his vision of the task of the true *ẓaddiq* himself. The *ẓaddiq* must look into these works, in order to understand the source of their errors and to redeem those who have fallen into their error.[40] Ordinary *ḥasidim* might be saved for faith by mere exhortations against philosophy, but in order to reach those who have already been "entrapped," the *ẓaddiq* must descend into their world and show them the root of their errors. While the *ẓaddiq* faces great dangers in choosing such a path and exposing himself to philosphy's wiles, the strength of his faith will protect from the seductive arguments he finds in the world of reason.

Before we examine the major critique of philosophy Nahman proposes a result of this "descent," we must first say a few words about the mythic meaning of Nahman's turn to the study of rational philosophy, and its specific context within the history of Hasidic thought. We have already mentioned the idea of "descent for the sake of ascent" in Hasidism and the roots of that idea in Sabbatian theology. In Sabbatianism this idea was evolved, as Scholem has demonstrated, in response to the particular personality of Sabbatai Sevi, serving to explain both his moments of deep depression and his infractions of the Law in times of personal "illumination." After Sabbatai's apostasy, and even more after his death, the gap between the promised redemption and the actual situation of Israel in the world became intolerably wide. The notion of the messiah's descent into the realm of evil was stretched to bridge this gap, and within the more radical Sabbatian circles it evolved into a doctrine of intentional sin, by which the devoted sought to follow the example of their master. Early Hasidism, particularly as reflected in the works of Jacob Joseph of Polonnoye, accepted this idea, while "purifying" it of its antinomian character. In descending into the world of evil, the *ẓaddiq* may have a thought of sin or may undergo a particular temptation, but it is in his *resisting* of that temptation, while seeing its source in the divine, that he uplifts the fallen worlds. *Now Nahman takes that same notion and turns its focus toward the great temptation of his own day: the temptation of the rationalist denial of God.* As a young man living in the first decades of Haskalah, Nahman was quite aware of the intellectual currents affecting his contemporaries. It was no longer the *religious* antinomianism of Sabbatianism or Frankism that poses the great threat to faith in his day, but rather the rational and secularizing intellectualism proceeding eastward from Berlin. While this clearly non-mythical challenge was at times portrayed by Nahman in the mythic imagery appropriate to a Hasidic master (Haskalah as the primordial snake, *etc.)*, he was quite aware that the particular *qelipot* confronting his generation were different from those that had challenged his ancestors. The current enemy was *doubt*, born of a rationalism that raised questions against God; only by descending into the world of rationalist scepticism and raising such questions himself could the *ẓaddiq* show the inadequacies of that path.

He who seeks to appear as redeemer to such a generation must be redeemer not only from temptation and sin, but also from doubt and from the encroaching depression and insecurity caused by man's feeling of the absence of God. To effect such a redemption, both for himself and his people, Nahman would have to confront head-on doubts he himself knew so well. The uplifting and transforming of doubt now becomes Nahman's version of the BeSHT's attempts to uplift sinful and wayward thoughts. The experience of distance between himself and God characteristic of certain stages in his own religious life created in him, at times, doubt that could not be stilled. In attempting to "uplift" doubt and to include it within a notion of expanded faith, Nahman is in fact uplifting his own experiences of God's absence, and seeking in them both a paradoxical vindication of his own faith and a path for others to follow.

Nahman's "descent" into the world of philosophy (or his struggle with his own doubts) resulted in several rather interesting explanations of the theological errors brought about by rational inquiry. Just as he felt that the philosophers' method was one totally inappropriate to the discernment of religious truth, so he believed that the perception of reality characterizing philosophy[41] was mistaken at its root. Nahman is rather clearly a novice when he steps onto the unfamiliar ground of philosophical argumentation. Living completely within the mythic world of Rabbinic and Kabbalistic thought, he refuses to recognize that the philosophers he attacks do not share his assumptions. Thus, for example, he seeks with great subtlety to refute the Aristotelian belief in the eternity of matter on the basis of the rabbinic claim that the souls of Israel existed before the world came into being![42] Totally lacking in critical consciousness or historical perspective, he can use rabbinic or Kabbalistic notions to criticize the views of thinkers who never heard of them or certainly have no responsibility to think in accord with them. In Hasidism, a movement that accepted the entirety of the earlier tradition as a single and (so they thought) harmonious body, such ahistorical attempts are not surprising.

A more serious anti-philosophical critique of Nahman's, and one that does have roots in the earlier mystical tradition, is his rejection of the traditional three-tiered universe of the medieval Jewish cosmology (the intellects, the spheres, and the lower world) as being entirely too static to represent a true portrait of reality:

> Their books contain questions as to the order of Creation: How is it that a star merited to be a star, or that a constellation deserved to become a constellation? What was the sin of the lower creatures, animals and all the rest, that consigned them to their lowly state? Why not just the opposite? Why is a head a head and a foot a foot? Why not just the opposite? These and similar questions are discussed at length in their books.

> This entire pursuit, however, is a vain one. One should not ask such questions of God, who is righteous and upright. For in truth the entire universe is a spinning top, which is called a *dreidel.* Everything moves in a circle: angels change into men and men into angels; the head becomes a foot, and the foot a head. All things in the world are part of this circular motion, reborn and transformed into one another. That which was above is lowered and that which was below is raised up. For in their root all of them are one.
>
> There are separate intellects, which are angels, completely separated from matter; there are spheres, which are composed of the most refined matter, and there is a lower world, which is fully corporeal. Even though each of these is surely derived from some particular place, in their root they are all one. Therefore the universe is a spinning top, on which everything turns and is transformed. Right now one thing may be highest, and it is considered a head, while that which is at the bottom is called a foot. But when they spin around again, the head will become a foot and the foot a head, men will become angels, and angels will be men. We find in the words of our sages that angels were cast forth from heaven down to the lower world until they even had human desires, *etc.* We also find angels, on a number of occasions, clothed in material garb, as is explained in various places. We also find the opposite: that a man may become an angel. Everything in the world is a *dreidel,* moving in a circle, for in truth they are all one in their root.[43]

The meaning of this piece and its intent as a critique of medieval philosophy are self-explanatory. We might only add that it is a critique entirely consonant not only with examples of Nahman's thought elsewhere but with his intellectual temperament as a whole. The thinker whose "teachings are all *beḥinot,*" for whom the free flow of the associative process is the essential way of creating Torah, now rejects also any attempt at rigidity in cosmological thinking. The universe is one of flow and transformation; *any* categories—here philosophical, elsewhere Kabbalistic—tending to freeze reality into rigid patterns must be rejected.

Nahman's most sustained and penetrating critique of philosophy, however, is one that seeks to explain it through the language of Lurianic Kabbalah, and particularly through the dialectic of that Kabbalah mentioned earlier. Philosophy fails because it is discursive rather than dialectical in its method. The dialectical approach Nahman proposed for the ongoing apprehension of *maqqifin* is more than a mere psychological tool. The dialectic reflects the inner nature of reality; the universe itself is born of paradox, and thus only a thought-method able to comprehend such paradox may give one an accurate picture of the world. The persistent questions facing the dialectician are part of an ontological reality greater than the thinker's mind. In raising these questions and trying to deal with them by discursive reasoning, however, philosophers lose themselves in an eternal web of paradox from which they do not know how to free themselves. It is in this way that they are led to the denial of God, a state which for Nahman seems tantamount to madness.

These conclusions are most sharply drawn in the sixty-fourth teaching in *Liqquṭey MoHaRaN*, undated in the sources, but probably presented in 1805 or 1806. Perhaps the most important single statement of Nahman's thoughts on the themes of faith, doubt, and reason, it brings together and builds upon several of the ideas we have already mentioned. A detailed exposition of this teaching will thus serve to clarify a number of points:

> It was out of compassion that God, blessed be He, created the world. He sought to reveal His compassion; if the world had not been created, to whom could he reveal it? For this reason He brought forth the entire Creation, from the very beginning of emanation down to the [lowest] central point in the corporeal world.
>
> When He set about creating the world, however, there was no place in which to create it, for all was *'Eyn Sof*. He therefore withdrew His light to the sides, and through this withdrawal *(ẓimẓum)* a void was formed. Inside this void, all the 'days' and 'measures' came to be; they are the creation of the world.
>
> Now this void was essential for the Creation, for without it there would have been no room for the world to exist. At the same time, God's withdrawal in forming the void remains incomprehensible until the end of time. Two contradictory things must be said of it: the void comes about through *ẓimẓum*, the withdrawal of God. There is, as it were, no God there, for if divinity were present in it, it would not be a void, all would be *'Eyn Sof*, and there would be no room for Creation. Yet in a deeper sense, surely there is divinity there nevertheless, for nothing exists without His life-flow. For this reason it will be possible to understand the void only in the Future.[44]

What we have here is on the face of it a rather simple repetition of the *ẓimẓum* myth, one of the basic themes of Lurianic Kabbalah. Since Kabbalists believe that the primordial *'Eyn Sof* aspect of the divine was always all-pervasive, and that even nothingness did not exist outside it, the first act of Creation had to be one of withdrawal, the evacuation of a certain place in which the non-God could come to exist. It was already recognized by Luria's disciples that the myth of *ẓimẓum* served to account for the origin of evil in the world; the evil forces have their origin in the void, in that place from which the goodness of God has been withdrawn. I. Tishby has shown that this is in fact the real meaning of *ẓimẓum;* the withdrawal of God from that primal 'space' is at the same time a purging from *'Eyn Sof* of the roots of evil, which had already existed within it.[45]

Nahman, however, does not concern himself directly with the demonic properties of the void. His concern rather focuses around the idea that there is some place from which God is absent. This will allow him to account for the great errors of the philosophers, and to encompass their doubts (which are also his own) within the Kabbalistic metaphysic: doubt concerning God's existence arises from an encounter with the void, from which God has chosen to absent Himself.

The great and inexplicable paradox Nahman finds in this assertion (that the void, created by God, must *ipso facto* contain something of His divinity) was already noted by Luria himself. It was partly in response to this difficulty that he and his followers promulgated the notion of *reshimu,* a certain vague film of divine light that never fully departs from the void. Because of this *reshimu,* one may indeed say that God is absent, allowing the void to exist as such, while He remains present there in some hidden way. It is significant that Nahman never mentions the idea of *reshimu,* a notion which he surely knew but chose to ignore. *Reshimu* allows for a resolution of the tension; it is essential for Nahman's purposes that the conflict be presented in its full extremity, to reflect the paradoxical nature of the very first act of Creation.

Nahman continues:

> Know that there are two types of heresy. There is one heresy which is derived from 'extraneous' wisdom. Of this heresy it is said: 'Know what to answer the heretic.'[46] [The claims of] this heresy may be answered, for they come from 'extraneous' wisdom, brought about by the breaking of the vessels. Because the light was too bright, the vessels were broken, and it was thus that the *qelipot* came into being, as is known. This extraneous wisdom was derived from there, from the breaking of the vessels, the leftover waste-matter of the holy. Just as a human being produces certain bodily wastes, such as nails, hair, sweat, and the like, so does the holy have its own wastes, and extraneous wisdom, including magic, is derived from them. For this reason, he who falls into this sort of heresy, even though he should have fled it, may find a way to be saved from there. God can be found there, if one looks for Him and seeks Him out. Since all this is derived from the broken vessels, which were intermingled with sparks of holiness and fallen [divine] letters, one can find divinity and 'mind' there, to resolve the questions that result from this sort of heresy. . . . Therefore it is said: 'Know what to answer the heretic.'

Here Nahman has made reference to the second major Lurianic myth, that of the broken vessels. As the light of divinity (which had reentered the world after *ẓimẓum,* beginning the second stage in the Creation process) flowed downward from the uppermost *sefirot* into the lower ones, its power was too intense for the lower vessels to bear. These Sefirotic vessels, meant to contain the light and thus to allow for an orderly process of graduated emanation, were broken, and the shards, commingled with certain sparks of divinity, were scattered through the universe. The shards of the broken vessels became the *qelipot,* the demonic forces that hide the bits of divinity lying beneath them.

Here, too, it has been shown that the underlying meaning of the myth is one of the self-distancing of the divine from evil. The purified light of God, which entered the void after *ẓimẓum,* had to be protected from the roots of evil awaiting it there. The cataclysm of the breaking of the vessels, while it brought evil into the lower world, at the same time allowed for the existence of a divine good untainted by evil.

In Nahman's reading of the Lurianic myth, evil consists of the denial of God. When man comes face to face with the world of the *qelipot,* he may indeed be led into such denial. In a world where the demonic seems to rule, there is no place for God. Nonetheless, because the demonic is possessed of certain sparks of light, man can ultimately come to find God within it. The absence of God from the seemingly demonic world may be painful, but it is not absolute. Such heresies may therefore be resolved. "Resolution," we will recall from our discussion of *maqqifin,* is equivalent to the finding of God within the denial, by means of an expanded sense of faith. The resolution is not so simple, however, when it comes to the second sort of heresy:

> There is a second type of heresy, made up of wisdom, which is really no wisdom at all. Because these things are deep and incomprehensible, they have an appearance of wisdom. For example, if a person offers a wrong interpretation in the study of the Talmud or its commentaries, and he is not sufficiently learned to resolve the difficulties that proceed from this misunderstanding, it seems to him that his opinion is a most profound one, even though it is all based upon a wrong interpretation. Philosophers encounter similar perplexities and objections, even though in truth there is no wisdom at all in their claims, and their objections are in fact quite groundless. Because it is beyond the power of the human mind to resolve such difficulties, however, they appear to be most profound.
>
> In truth it is impossible to resolve these difficulties, for the objections raised by this sort of heresy come from the void, and in that void there is, as it were, no God. For that reason, questions which come from the void cannot be answered; God cannot be found there. If one were to find God there, the void would not exist, and all would be *'Eyn Sof!* Of this heresy it is said: 'All who go there do not return' (Prov. 2:19). There is no answer to this heresy; it comes from the void, from which God, as it were, has withdrawn Himself.

In the Lurianic notion of the void, Nahman found an answer to the most pressing theological problem of his life; the seeming absence of God from the world. As we have already seen, he was too personally familiar with the experience of God's absence merely to wave the problem aside. Much of human experience, Nahman realized, in fact lends credence to the philosophical denial of religion. Here Nahman admits that this denial corresponds to a certain true perception of reality: the confrontation with the void. The reason such philosophical speculations are forbidden is that their erroneous conclusions are irrefutable. When philosophers confront the void and deny God they are in fact right in a certain way: they have arrived at that place where there is, in fact, no God. Within the universe of philosophical discourse there is no way out of this frightening conclusion.

> But Israel, by means of faith, transcend all 'wisdom,' even such heresy as is derived from the void. They believe in God without any intellectual inquiry, by the wholeness of their faith. [They affirm that] God both fills and surrounds all the worlds.[47] He is, as it were, inside all the worlds, and yet He surrounds them. But there must remain some space between His immanence and His transcendence, for if not all would be one [and the world could not exist]. Thus the void from which God has withdrawn, and inside which He created the universe, surrounds the entire world, and God is also without, surrounding the void itself. . . .

This paragraph, in spelling out more clearly some of Nahman's previously drawn conclusions, now makes clear to us why Creation had to be preceded by *ẓimẓum:* the void is necessary for the world's existence. If there were no void, all would be swallowed up in God, and there would be only *'Eyn Sof,* but no world. Thus we are brought face to face with the most basic paradox of existence: *the world can survive only because of the absence of God.* God's removal of Himself from the void is the gift that allows for the existence of the non-God.

This notion, while it is presented here in its most radical form, is not completely alien to previous Kabbalistic and Hasidic speculations. In more traditional Kabbalistic language, it is the balancing of the opposed Sefirotic forces of *ḥesed* and *din* that allows the world to be. *Din* unchecked by *ḥesed* would show itself as ultimately demonic, and thus destructive of the world. But *ḥesed,* containing a limitless abundance of God's love, could also prove destructive to the otherness of the one who sought to receive it, were it not held back by the restraining forces of *din.* It is the divine self-restraint as much as the divine openness that allows for *relationship* between God and the world. The intent of this Kabbalistic notion, however, is quite different from Nahman's. The Kabbalists sought to place a check upon their own tendencies toward mystical pantheism; the power of *din* allows for a certain *distance* between man and God, across which the bridge of theistic relationship can be built. In choosing to speak of *ẓimẓum* and the void rather than of *ḥesed* and *din,* Nahman has very much radicalized this idea: rather than relationship thriving on a certain degree of distance between God and man, here we have the very existence of man dependent upon God's *totally* absenting Himself from a certain level of reality.

This is made more clear as Nahman continues, offering paradoxical faith as the only means to transcending this absence of God:

> By means of faith, however, faith that God both fills and surrounds all the worlds, [one comes to realize that] the void itself was created by His wisdom. In a deeper sense, therefore, His divinity is there, even though it is impossible to understand this or to find Him there. Thus Israel transcends all the intellectual challenges and heresies that come from the void—by knowing that they cannot be answered. For if one were to find an answer to them, one would be finding God in them; there would thus be no void, and the world could not exist.
>
> In that deeper sense there indeed is an answer to them, for God surely is there. But by philosophical thinking one sinks there, for God cannot be found in the void. One must only have faith that God surrounds the void as well, and that His divinity is there. For this reason, Israel are called *'Ivrim,* [lit.: "those who cross over"] because in their faith they transcend all intellectuality, even those false wisdoms of this second sort of heresy that originates in the void. God is called "The God of the *'Ivrim'* (Ex. 3:18) . . . for His divinity is also present on the far side of the void . . . Israel, who are called *'Ivrim,* through their faith in the Lord, God of the *'Ivrim,* transcend all intellectual thought, even this second sort of heresy.
>
> One must take great care to flee such heresies, not daring to look into their words at all, lest he sink there, for this is the place of which it is said: 'All who go there do not return.'

Once again the opposition of faith and intellectual pursuit has been sharply drawn, and faith has been defined as an act of transcendence, having the strength to overcome all the mind's objections and to assert the presence of God even in those places where He admittedly *cannot* be found. We now understand the truly paradoxical nature of this faith: it can assert its true power *only* where God's presence is not apparent. When read as an ontological statement, this teaching demonstrates that the absence of God is necessary for the world's existence. But when read as a statement of devotional experience, it comes to show once again, as did the tale of the heart of the world, that faith, which for Nahman is the only basis of true religion, thrives on the absence of God and gains in strength where He is most hidden. We now understand why Nahman's path is one constantly seeking to draw forth new *maqqifin,* ever reaching out to the areas that challenge it. Only in seeking out those places from which God is apparently absent can one gain the strength in faith ever needed to assert His presence.

In this teaching, however, Nahman seems quite reserved about the matter of seeking out *maqqifin.* Particularly when it comes to the void, which is the great *maqqif,* surrounding the entire universe, the reader is specifically warned to stay away, least he sink in the eternal mire of unanswerable questions. But if man's path requires him constantly to seek out those places from which God is absent, why should he be warned to stay away from the questions that proceed from the void? Nahman's warning may only be understood if we recall that each man should confront only those *maqqifin* appropriate to his particular stage of development. If he goes beyond what he can handle, he is in danger of getting lost.[48] The cycles of *maqqifin* are, as we have seen, described in hierarchical patterns; in order to have room in my mind to integrate a new *maqqif,* I may pass my present state of resolution on to one who stands below me. Thus the entire process of ascent to ever-new *maqqifin* is a collective enterprise, one in which all are bound together by a hierarchical arrangement of minds.[49] At the top of this hierarchy stands the *ẓaddiq ha-dor;* only he has the strength to stare into the void and to confront its eternal questions. Thus philosophy, proscribed for all others, becomes an obligation for the *ẓaddiq*. He alone can understand that neither language nor rational thought is appropriate to the void, and that he may approach it only by the power of his awesome silence:

> But know that if there is a very great *ẓaddiq,* one who has the quality of Moses, he really has to look into these words of heresy, even though it is impossible to resolve them. By means of his very inquiry into these matters, he raises up those souls who have fallen and sunk into that heresy.
>
> The perplexities and questions of this heresy derive from the void. They have about them a quality of silence, because no intellect or language can resolve them. Creation came about through the word, as Scripture says: 'By the word of God were the heavens created, and all their hosts by the breath of His mouth' (Ps. 33:6). In language there is intellect . . . language defines all things. [God] has bounded His wisdom in letters, making one combination of letters the definition of this thing and using other letters to designate something else. But in the void which surrounds all the worlds and is completely empty, there is no language, nor is there even pre-verbal intellect. Therefore the questions which arise there are silent.
>
> We find that when Moses asked about the death of Rabbi Akiba, saying: 'Is this Torah and is this its reward?' he was told: 'Silence! Thus it is in the highest thought.'[50] You must be silent and not demand an answer to this question, for thus it is in the highest thought, that which is beyond language . . . there are no words to resolve it. The same is true of all these questions which come from the void, where there exists neither mind nor language. As they are silent, so must one confront them by silent faith alone. For this reason, only the *ẓaddiq* who is like Moses may enter into the maze of heresies; Moses was a silent one, whom Scripture describes as 'hesitant of speech' (Ex. 4:10). This refers to that silence which is beyond

> speech. Only the *ẓaddiq* who is silent, like Moses, may enter into these mazes of silence. And he has to do so, in order to save those who have fallen there.

This beautifully-drawn description of the need to transcend words and enter into the realm of silence is Nahman's ultimate statement of his own faith. Face to face with the absence of God on the most absolute level, daring to enter the void itself, he holds fast to a faith that can be communicated to no one, because it reaches beyond all speech. This faith cannot do away with the paradoxical nature of reality; the void remains a void, a place where God indeed cannot be found. But in personal existential terms, the nature of that void has been transformed, as the silent power of the *ẓaddiq* confronts it and goes beyond. Nahman once gave dramatic expression to this existential stance when he said:

> I *am* a "know what to answer the heretic."[51]

His words could do nothing to proclaim God in the void where man lives, but his own life bore silent testimony to His presence.

All that we have seen of Nahman's thought until this point shows him to be a prime example of what is called the 'existential' tendency in religious thought. This viewpoint, which is to be distinguished from both the rationalist and mystical tendencies in Western religion, takes as its departure point the concrete situation of the lone individual who seeks a path to God. For the religious existentialist, logical proofs for God's existence and concern are immaterial, insofar as they are not verified by the testimony of his own life experience. Similarly, the claim of the mystic to have overcome the distinction between self and other in proclaiming man's true oneness with God seems vacuous to the one who experiences his own life as that of a solitary individual, not knowing within himself the divine immanence the mystic asserts. Religious existentialism tends to eschew the grand metaphysical systems of both rational and mystical theology, on the grounds that they do not leave room for those concerns and life-experiences of that individual whom the existentialist considers to be the core of significant reality.[52]

On the face of it, Nahman does seem to fit into this pattern of religious thought. We have already seen the sharpness with which he rejects rational defenses of religion, as well as his avoidance of those concepts and thought patterns that comprise Kabbalah as a theosophical system. The definition of faith emerging from his teaching on the void seems to be one that perforce must reject mysticism as the basis of religion. If faith can come to be only where God is absent, the mystic's constant assertion of God's immanence would in fact stand in the way of such faith. The entire edifice of Nahman's thought, as we have traced it this far, is built upon the foundation of his inability to experience the divine presence directly in his life, an inability hardly recognized by the mystic. At the same time, however, there is a clearly mystical side to Nahman, which comes out in any number of his teachings and stories. As a product of Hasidism, which at its theoretical core is a mystical movement, Nahman did not totally break with the spiritual world in which he was nurtured. It would be unfair to the complexities of Nahman's position on any number of issues to label him simply as a non-mystical 'existentialist' thinker, who represents the antithesis of the emphasis elsewhere on contemplative mysticism.[53] It is to this mystical side of Nahman we must now turn our attention, seeking also to account for the presence of his existentialist position on matters of faith and doubt *within* the context of his own mysticism.

We have seen that faith and longing are the very core of Nahman's religious life; the soul's innermost longings for God are the starting point of man's struggle. But what is the source of these all-pervasive longings? A closer examination of Nahman's thoughts on this question reveals to us that they are in fact the classic longings of the mystic: man's soul, which was originally one with God, is filled with desire to be reunited with its source. According to the *Zohar,* the human soul is born of the union between the masculine and feminine potencies within God and is primarily rooted in the *shekhinah,* the feminine tenth *sefirah.* The *shekhinah* herself, however, lives in a state of longing, seeking ever to reestablish her unity with God above. Man's soul merely reflects the longings of its source. In Nahman's words:

> There is a root of faith; faith itself has a life-source and a root. For there is a World of Faith from which all faith is drawn. This World of Faith itself has faith in God. This root is the innermost part of faith, which is the innermost soul, for soul and faith are one category *(beḥinah).*[54]

We see here that the existential and the mystical in Nahman are inseparable. Faith, seemingly the most 'existential' of all categories, turns out to be identical with the soul and with the *shekhinah.* The longing for return to the source, well known to many Kabbalists and going back to both Gnostic and Neoplatonic sources, gives birth to the existential situation in which man finds himself. Were it not for his soul's origins in the upper world, man would feel no dissatisfaction with his material existence; were he not of "noble birth," the prince in Nahman's *Seven Beggars* would not feel the inner disquiet that leads him to his repeated sighs of longing. No notion is more characteristic of what is generally considered 'mysticism' in the Western tradition than that of the soul's rootedness in God and its longing to return to its source.

As we closely examine certain passages dealing with the very heart of Nahman's 'existential' teachings, the constant struggle to search out and integrate *maqqifin*, we find that the end of that process is in fact mystical, in the most proper sense of that term. In his teaching concerning the void, Nahman gives the impression that the goal of the *maqqifin*-process is reached only by the silent and paradoxical assertion of the *ẓaddiq*. At the very end of that teaching, however, in a passage we have not quoted, Nahman offers a hint that the entire process is illusory. Elsewhere the idea becomes more clear, adding a final stage to the ongoing struggle for higher *maqqifin*, one that culminates in a state which is nothing less than man's final inclusion within *'Eyn Sof* and an ultimate identification with the mind of God. Here is an assertion of mystical union the daring of which could hardly be duplicated in pre-Hasidic Kabbalah. Two sets of symbols are employed to this end in the teaching we are about to quote: instead of the terms *maqqif* and *penimi*, Nahman here refers to challenging thoughts as 'prayer' (one must still pray for their integration) and as 'let us hear' (Ex. 24:7); thoughts the mind already encompasses are 'Torah' (the known) and 'we shall do,' reflecting the classic expression of Israel's readiness to fulfill God's commands:

> One must ever go from rung to rung, higher and higher, until one reaches the first point of Creation, the beginning of divine emanation *[Keter]*. There too one finds 'hearing' and 'doing.' The 'hearing' which is found there is the true Torah of God. On all other levels and in all other worlds, the term 'Torah of God' is used only in a relative way: because it is hidden from him [who stands on that lower rung] it is called the Torah of God. When he reaches that Torah's rung, it becomes his own Torah. But the 'hearing' which is at the very beginning of emanation is the true Torah of God. There is nothing higher than it, except for the Torah of God Himself.[55]
>
> When one finally is included within *'eyn sof*, his Torah is the Torah of God Himself, and his prayer is the Prayer of God Himself. There is a Torah of God, to which our sages have referred as follows: 'I was first to fulfill it'; 'The Holy one, blessed be He, clothes the naked, visits the sick, etc.'; 'How do we know that the Holy One, blessed be He, puts on *tefillin?'* There is also a prayer of God, of which the sages say: 'How do we know that the Holy One, blessed be He, prays? From the verse: "I shall grant them joy in My house of prayer" (Is. 56:7)."
>
> We thus find that there exist a Torah of God and a prayer of God. When a person merits to be included within *'eyn sof*, his Torah and prayers are those of God Himself.[56]

Torah and prayer exist on every level of spiritual ascent. The Torah one acquires at any given point (i.e., the *maqqifin* one has integrated) becomes one's *own* Torah. The prayer of that level is the outcry described earlier, the longing to bring forth *maqqifin* of a still-higher world. This two-stage process goes on continually, even as one reaches the stage of *keter*, where one's own Torah and the 'true' Torah of God are to be identified. The 'prayer' that continues to exist at that level is the longing to overcome any bit of separation that might yet exist between God and the self, to be a part of *'eyn sof,* fully identified with the undifferentiated oneness of God. "Meriting to be included within *'eyn sof'*" is indeed a far cry from silent assertions of faith at the edge of the void. Here Nahman is imbued with the truly mystical spirit of the Kabbalah, including its tradition of speculations on the 'true' Torah as it exists in the supramundane World. His dialectical principle of ascent is now transformed; true, one may encounter stages on the way where there seems to be no God, but ultimate mystical verification is to be found at the greatest heights, and mystical identification with God now shows itself to be the final goal of man's journey.

As though the slightest doubt were left as to Nahman's intentions in this passage, or perhaps to make it accessible to those who could not follow all its complexities, the later Bratslav tradition contains an added line, probably omitted from the original printed version for reasons of caution: "I heard from R. Nathan that when our master said teaching #22 concerning the Torah of God and the prayer of God he said that you have to reach such a state of self-negation that you come to God's Torah and prayer and are able to say: *'May it be my will.'* "[57] Nowhere in Jewish mystical literature does the cry of Hallaj have so clear an echo!

Elsewhere Nahman will choose other paths to express a mystical awareness contradicting the 'existential' image we have drawn of him. While *sekhel* and *ḥokhmot* may be villains in Nahman's world, he is not afraid to use the word *da'at* to refer to the knowledge of God in a postiive way. In several passages he speaks of the way to God as a path of mystical knowing, a knowing that (following the extended meaning of the Hebrew *YD'*) is itself a path leading to *unio mystica.*[58] In a passage typical of this tendency Nahman writes:

> Eternal life belongs only to God, who lives forever. But he who is included in his root, in God, also has eternal life. Since he is included in the one and is one with God, he lives eternally just as God does . . . The basis of this inclusion within God is knowing *[da'at]* Him, as the sage said: 'If I knew Him, I would be Him.' The core of man is his mind; where a man's mind is, there is the whole man. He who knows, and attains to a divine understanding, is really there [in God]. The greater his knowing, the more he is included in his root in God.[59]

Again we hear Nahman speaking rather freely about the 'inclusion' of man within God, a conception at the very core of mystical religion. Nahman nowhere tells us exactly what he means by *da'at;* the general use of this term in Hasidism indicates, however, a sense of religious awareness and an openness to God's presence, rather than any particular form of esoteric knowledge.

The mystical consciousness found with some frequency in Nahman's writings is again most clearly evidenced in the following passage, which may only be described as an extended mystical meditation. Here Nahman seeks to demonstrate that both time and space, the generally accepted bounds of man's existential universe, are in fact the products of illusion. The fully realized man, portrayed here in the figure of messiah, will totally identify with the mind of God and, like Him, be liberated from all spatial and temporal limitations:

> God, praised be He, is above time. In truth this matter is wondrous and hidden, and it cannot be grasped by the human mind.
>
> Know, however, that time is rooted in the fact that we do not understand, in the smallness of our minds. The larger the mind becomes, the smaller and closer to negation is time. In a dream, when the rational mind *[sekhel]* is absent, and man has only the imagination, one may traverse as much as seventy years within a mere quarter hour. It seems to the dreamer that all this time is really passing, within [what is to the mind] a very brief period. Afterwards, when he awakens, he sees that just a short time has passed, and that all those 'years' transpired within it. This is because his rational mind returned to him as he awoke, and to that mind the dream's seventy years were but a quarter hour. Seventy 'real' years are seventy years as measured by our rational faculty.
>
> But in truth, to a mind which is higher than ours, that which our mind has taken to be seventy years might also turn out to be a quarter hour or less. Just as in a dream one may experience seventy years only to find out, upon waking, that just a quarter hour has passed, so are our seventy years to the mind above us. We cannot comprehend this: were one to say to a dreamer that all the time which is passing is in fact but a quarter hour, he would not believe it. Indeed, according to the imagination which is active in the dream, these are real years which are passing; we are in the same position with regard to that mind which is higher than our own.
>
> And thus higher and higher: in a mind yet higher than that one which is just above ours, its time too will seem to be nearly nothing. And so higher and higher, until one reaches a state of mind so high that all of time is not noticed by it at all. All of time has been absolutely negated in that mind, because of its great elevation. Just as our seventy dream-years turned out to be but a quarter hour, there exists mind above mind,until time is negated.
>
> Therefore messiah, who has gone through all that he has, since the beginning of the world, suffering all that he has suffered, at the very end will be addressed by God: 'You, My son, this day I give birth to you (Ps. 2:7).' This seems very strange, but may be understood by reference to the elevated mental state which messiah will have attained at that time. Because his mind will be so very greatly expanded, all of time since the Creation will be

> completely negated, and he will really be like a newborn. His mind will have transcended all of time, so that God may say: 'This day I give birth to you.' Really 'this day'—for all that has passed will be as nothing.
>
> We see the same with regard to space. A strong man may travel a great distance in a short amount of time. For weak persons, however, this is considered to be a much greater distance, and they must go a long time until they reach its end. Here, too, one may go higher and higher: the greater the strength, the shorter the distance, until one reaches so high that space has been completely negated. But our mind cannot comprehend this. . . . [60]

In truly mystical fashion, the most basic categories of our ordinary perceptions are here called into question. The reality of any fixed point in time or space, so basic to the existential consciousness, is now seen to be not qualitatively different from the imagined reality of our dreams. Consciousness is depicted as an ever-ascending continuum; any cut-off point at which man determines his 'reality' is as arbitrary as any other. The purpose of this meditation, as that of much of mystical literature, is to allow man to see beyond the artificial limits of his own ordinary consciousness, and to enable him to realize that he lives as a prisoner of self-created illusion, an illusion cloaked in the highly deceptive garb of 'rationality.' The mystic seeks to liberate man by showing him a way to higher perception, through a limitless expansion of human consciousness, until that consciousness is one with the infinite mind of God.

In the face of these mystical passages and others like them, how are we to understand the emphasis found in so much of Nahman's writing on the absence of God and the constant struggle for Faith? If man's mind is capable of ascending from rung to rung until it reaches God, and if the limitations of ordinary consciousness are to be transcended, why can Nahman not more easily assert that the absence of God is itself illusion, and that, by simply ascending to a higher mode of thought, His presence can be known? This sense that the distance between man and God is mere illusion is well-known in the teachings of the BeSHT, and is particularly the core of Shne'ur Zalman's mystical theology. Why should Nahman often appear to reject this path, if his conclusions here seem to be the same? What is the meaning of his great existential *Angst*, if its roots are to be located in the world of illusion?

No single answer to this question, perhaps the key question for an understanding of Nahman's thought, is possible. It may be argued that the very attempt to seek an answer is to force a consistency and systematization alien to the material. In suggesting the three possible answers to this problem we shall presently propose, we should make it clear that while we seek to address an incongruity we find in Nahman's work itself, it is one we express in terms far different from his own. Nahman surely felt no problem or tension between 'mystical' and 'existential' sides of his teaching, nor did he consciously seek to combine the two in any startling way. At the same time, far more than any other figure among the mystical teachers of Hasidism, he chose to dwell on the distance between man and God, the pained longings of the human heart, and the reality of a seemingly Godless universe. It is entirely likely that this uniqueness was perceptible to those around him, disciples and enemies alike, far as they were from our contemporary categorizations of religious thought.

Knowing what we do of Nahman's highly volatile and erratic personality, we might first suggest that the two modes of thinking are simply products of different moods. In times of elation, when God was present to him, he was able to speak of transcending time and space or of absorption within *'eyn sof*. It was in times when God seemed far away and he felt himself alone and abandoned that the path of outcry and longing, mitigated sometimes by paradoxical assertion, seemed the only real alternative. A consistent mystical theology is perhaps more than we have a right to expect from a personality such as Nahman's; there is a confident trust about the mystic life which Nahman knows too sporadically and too much in the painful breach simply to preach it without reservation. The fact that moments of true mystic elation do come through in Nahman's work is itself sufficient, it might be argued, and any more than that would have betrayed the faithfulness with which Nahman described his own encounter with life.

There is no good way to verify such an assertion. The two approaches we have outlined appear scattered through Nahman's works. The fact that they sometimes appear even within a single teaching would seem to give the lie to this as a total explanation. But such a reading should still not be dismissed out of hand. The point that Nahman knew the absence of God too well and too frequently to ignore it is essential to any understanding of him.

Another way of reading this problem is somewhat less psychological, and borders on an assertion that Nahman knew quite well what it was that he was mixing. We must recall that Nahman always saw himself as a spiritual guide and teacher, rather than as an abstract thinker. Each of the teachings in the *Liqquṭim* is just that: an oral teaching offered before a particular group or in particular circumstances. As a teacher, Nahman had to be aware of the *process* of growth which he sought in his disciples, not only in its end result. The *stages* of increasing awareness are important to him; pushing the disciple into a level of awareness he was not yet ready to handle would do him harm rather than good.

The mystic may be aware that the only ultimate truth in the universe is the oneness of God. But if that mystic is also a teacher, he recalls that most people do not live with such awareness, and that to bring them to that ultimate point is a long and difficult process. It is Nahman the teacher or guide who is all 'existentialist'—the only beginning-point on the road is where the real human being stands, in the fullest confrontation with the misery and loneliness of his life. *Hitbodedut* as described by Nahman is an attempt to do just that: to heighten man's awareness of his aloneness in an attempt to overcome it. We have seen elsewhere that the same is true in stages of the master/disciple relationship as Nahman portrays it: though ultimately ego-individuality is to be overcome in the context of that relationship, the disciple had best begin it by seeking out his own self. We have seen that Nahman will speak of the uniqueness and beauty of each soul, tree, melody, or blade of grass—but only ultimately to proclaim their oneness. This same Nahman will seek out the presence of God by asserting his absence. There is a consistent pattern here of holding out mystical assertions for the very end of the road; Nahman the guide seems to believe that *only by a catharsis of individuality may one finally transcend the self; there is a dramatic tension in the search for the One, which must be held taut until the very last moment*.

There is, however, yet a third way of approaching the relationship between mystical and existential motifs in Nahman, one that will require some more extended discussion. The fact is that underlying certain of Nahman's teachings one may find a great ambivalence toward the ultimate mystical discovery of God. This ambivalence, not unique to Nahman but rather common to many writers within early Hasidism, has its roots in the necessarily imperfect grafting of a mystical theology onto the roots of a clearly non-mystical rabbinic religion, a religion Hasidism is ever at pains to defend.

Let us first reexamine Nahman's teaching concerning the void. We recall that God cannot, indeed *must* not, be found within the void separating His transcendent self from the world. Were one to find Him there, the void would cease to exist, and there could be no world, but only endless God. Why, however, should this be such a distressing prospect? Is not the very goal of all mystical religion to be found in the return of all things to their undifferentiated oneness in God? Should not the discovery of God within the void be *sought*, rather than avoided? This indeed is the position taken by Shne'ur Zalman, who declares *ẓimẓum* to be a beneficent illusion granted to man in order that he may continue to live in this world, but not as a reflection of ultimate reality.[61] In taking *ẓimẓum* so seriously, Nahman has avoided the final mystical assertion that God *is* to be found everywhere after all. All he offers is the silent and paradoxical assertion of the *ẓaddiq* that God is present, even though He cannot be found. And that assertion would hardly seem sufficient to quell the doubts of the wise man who asked: "Have you ever *seen* the King?" Nahman draws the existential assertion of faith to its final paradoxical limits, but he refuses (at least for the while!) to release the tension he has created by announcing that God is to be found in the void after all, and that the void itself is mere illusion.[62]

The meaning of this hesitation will be clarified for us as we examine another of Nahman's teachings, which deals with the motif of God's presence in the world, though in somewhat different terms. The departure point of this teaching is the Rabbinic assertion that the world was created through ten divine utterances. While the words "let there be" are to be found only nine times in the first chapter of Genesis, the rabbis claim that "In the beginning" is also an utterance of God. Kabbalistic tradition associated the ten utterances with the ten *sefirot,* matching the first pre-verbal utterance with *keter,* the first step in the emanation of the *sefirotic* world.[63] Nahman, continuing in this tradition, notes that the glory of God, which fills the universe, flows into the world through these ten *sefirotic* 'utterances.' While each of the nine lower *sefirot,* however, is articulated in some particular way, thus having its flow carefully directed, the flow of *keter* itself remains unbounded. Since the bounds set about all the lower *sefirot* keep their flow safe from evil or impurity, the sustenance needed for the impure to exist may derive only from the very highest source. Paradoxically, therefore, the highest and most recondite aspect of God's glory is to be found in the most unexpected places:

> . . .'The whole earth is filled with His glory' (Is. 6:3): even sin and things of evil, where His glory is not [apparently] present. The verse: 'I shall give My glory to no other' (Is. 42:8) indicates that the glory is bounded, in order that it not flow there. Even though 'the whole earth is filled with His glory,' there is a limit placed upon that glory so that it does not flow into those [evil] places . . . But know that they too receive their life from God; even places of filth and temples of idolatry require divine sustenance . . . This is the meaning of: 'if someone asks you, "Where is your God?" say to him: "In the great city of Rome." '[64] . . . .Know that these receive their life from the hidden utterance of 'In the beginning,' which contains within it all the other utterances, and which sustains them all. [The places of evil] could not receive their life through the revealed utterances, because of 'I shall give My glory to no other,' but it is only through this completely hidden utterance that they may be sustained. *It is impossible to understand this matter, and it is forbidden to contemplate it at all.*[65]

The dangers of contemplating this startling assertion were clear to Nahman; they also serve to explain his hesitancy about proclaiming the accessibility of God within the void. He stands here at the edge of an assertion that the *highest* form of divine presence is to be found in places where one would least expect it. The divinity present in Judaism, as the product of revelation, emerges through the nine lower *sefirot* or utterances. The realm of evil, however, is nurtured by *keter* itself, and thus contains the highest manifestation of the divine. If the very highest form of divinity is most directly to be found in sin and idolatry, the most natural conclusion of his path would be a choice for intentional sin, seeking, as did the Sabbatians, the greatest divine light within the greatest debasement. No wonder that he forbade speculation on this theme!

Applying the same logic to Nahman's teaching on the void, we understand why one is not permitted to seek God there, and why Nahman will not allow himself the authentically mystical assertion that the void is but illusion. Were he to allow this, the great task of religion would no longer be the transcendence of the void through faith, but rather a descent into the void itself, in order to seek God there. But in plummeting oneself into the void's depths to seek God's presence, one would have to set aside all the carefully drawn categories and distinctions lying at the core of conventional religion. Surely distinctions between 'holy' and 'profane' or between 'permitted' and 'forbidden' make no sense as one enters that void where language itself is said to have no place. If man were permitted to enter into the void in his search for God, all the trappings of traditional religion could not be seen but as obstacles to be overcome in the final assertion of God's paradoxical presence. Only the silent *ẓaddiq*, stripped of all such verbal 'garb,' may enter there. *In facing the assertion that God in some sense is to be found within the void, Nahman stands at the brink of religion's mystical self-transcendence, which viewed differently, is also its self-destruction.* No wonder he equivocates in the face of such a prospect.

This ambivalence in the face of the ultimate mystical assertion that there is no gulf between man and God, and that everything, including sin, is an embodiment of God's glory, is not unique to Nahman. It is found throughout the literature of early Hasidism, and may in fact be considered a basic characteristic of Hasidic thought. Students of Hasidism[66] have depicted the movement as one radical and conservative at once; while the most seemingly 'heretical' thoughts may be expressed in theory, no less typical of Hasidism (including Bratslav) is an ultimate commitment to the demands of *halakah*, even in their most stringent form. One may indeed say that it is this very conservatism that allows Hasidic thinkers the "luxury" of radical speculations; it was their strong roots in the world of normative Judaism that protected them from falling into a repetition of the Sabbatian cataclysm. But what to do when those radical speculations threatened to destroy the conservative hold of *halakah* itself? Here one could only retreat and, at the very edge of transcendence and chaos, offer some justification that would allow one to continue on the safe, well-trodden path.

We have already on several occasions mentioned the Baʿal Shem Tov's emphasis on the omnipresence of God, and his practice of uplifting 'evil' thoughts in order to purify them and return them to their root in the divine. Contained within this idea, which is itself a neutralized remnant of Hasidism's Sabbatian origins, are the seeds of heretical transgression. If one's own evil thoughts may be shown to be divine in origin, why not apply the same logic to an "uplifting" of evil deeds? Certainly ordinary acts, those neither commanded nor specifically forbidden, are taken by the BeSHT and his disciples to be a proper arena for the service of God. Such a figure as Menaḥem Naḥum of Chernobyl, whose writings closely reflect the teachings of the BeSHT, places particular emphasis upon the need to serve God through ordinary acts like eating and drinking, and apparently ranks such acts of devotion on the same level with the performance of the *miẓwot* themselves.[67] But if *any* human act may become an avenue of service, what role remains for the particular *miẓwot?* And if the elevation of both neutral deeds and wayward thoughts become ways to God, what justification remains for a refusal to serve God through the 'purification' of acts of sin as well?

A similar crisis of conflict between mystical and normative values affects certain disciples of the Maggid, though in slightly different form. In the school of Miedzyrzec, *devequt* is promulgated as the central goal of religious life. If this is the value *par excellence,* however, all devotional activities, including the *miẓwot* themselves, must be examined from this vantage point: do they lead one to a state of *devequt?* Given the radically spiritualistic and even quietistic tendencies of certain Miedzyrzec disciples, we are again faced with a crisis. *Devequt* requires an utter transcendence of the material world; he who is bound to corporeal existence cannot attach himself to God. But the *miẓwot* themselves require activity of the body, and even consciousness of one's physical activities. Those very deeds that are supposed to bring one near to God in fact stand in the way of the transcendence required to reach Him! In order to fully realize his spiritual nature, man should have to transcend the *miẓwot* themselves; in order to reach God, one should first have to destroy the earth-bound "shackles" of religion. Clearly such a position is untenable to anyone within Hasidism; at this point such radical thinkers as Menahem Mendel of Vitebsk or Hayyim Haikl of Amdura step in to offer one or another rationalization for maintaining the normative religious life. At times the rationale is theological: God *wants* man to be His this-worldly servant; the physical dimensions of man and his corporeal ways of service distinguish him from the angels, and allow him to redeem the material universe. Elsewhere a psychological justification is offered: man *needs* the *miẓwot* in their corporeal form in order to contain his overflowing spirit. This movement toward the brink of heresy and the conservative return from it are most clearly evidenced in *ḤaBaD,* where the most radically spiritualist and nearly pantheistic doctrine in all of Judaism ends up, in reaction against itself, claiming that the physical performance of the *miẓwah* is the most essential ingredient of its spirituality.[68]

In order to maintain its commitment to an essentially non-mystical Rabbinic religion, Hasidism of necessity equivocates when it comes face to face with the revolutionary implications of its own mystical speculations.

Nahman was well aware of this entire series of questions and the resulting need for caution in formulating a mystical theology. In his own moments of exultation, the *miẓwot* of Rabbinic Judaism became an issue to him. We will recall that on his return journey from Erez Israel, at the height of his dangerous sea voyage, he concluded that he had reached a level where he should ever be able to fulfill the commandments spiritually, even if (sold into captivity) he should be forced to trangress them in their physical sense. This moment of realization exercised great influence upon his later thinking, as is evidenced in a most interesting teaching promulgated some eleven years later, only two months before his death. In this teaching,[69] he speaks most poignantly of those times when the true *ẓaddiq* is unable to find his place in the Torah and feels cut off from study or intellectual creativity as a path to God. At such times, the *ẓaddiq* becomes a simple man *(prostak)*, similar to those who have never studied Torah at all, and he is forced to seek another way:

> Know that the root of life is in the Torah, as Scripture says: 'It is your life and the length of your days.' (Deut. 30:20). When one cuts himself off from Torah, it is as though he were cut off from life itself. It seems strange, therefore, that a person should cut himself off from Torah even for a moment. But in truth it is impossible to remain attached to the Torah day and night, without a moment's interruption . . . there are times when one must leave the Torah, either to conduct some affairs of business or to care for one's bodily needs, so that one cannot remain involved in Torah and intellectual pursuit in an uninterrupted manner . . . But in that moment when he is separated from Torah, the scholar or person of understanding becomes a simple man *(prostak)*. Still it seems difficult that a person should cut himself off from Torah even for a moment, since the Torah is life. Who would want to cut himself off from life, even for a moment . . .
>
> Know, however, that in those times when he is a simple man, the true *ẓaddiq* is sustained by the way of his journey to Erez Israel . . .
>
> All simple folk, including both the scholar who has interrupted his studies . . . and others, are sustained in their times of simplicity by the world as it existed before the Torah was received—each according to his own portion in that Torah. Before the receiving of the Torah, the world was sustained by God's love *(ḥesed)* alone; there was not yet any Torah or any deed or *miẓwah* to sustain the world. The world's existence was rooted in love alone. The *ẓaddiq*, in his times of simplicity and separation from the Torah, receives his life from this quality . . . he who has no merits receives from there. . . .
>
> At that time [before Sinai] there was no Torah; people concerned themselves only with the settling of the world and *derekh 'ereẓ* [lit.: "the way of the land"]. This is what the sages meant by "Great is *derekh 'ereẓ*, for it preceded the Torah by twenty-six generations." The world then existed by virtue of love alone.

In fact, the Torah, which is eternal, existed even before it was given, though in hidden and recondite form. Since the entire Torah is contained within the ten commandments, and the ten commandments were hidden within the ten utterances of Creation, the entire Torah was hidden within the process of settling the world. Torah is hidden in every word and every deed—even the cutting down of trees and the like, since all was created through the ten utterances. . . . The *ẓaddiq*, when he is cut off from Torah and is a simple man, receives his life from this aspect of pre-Sinaitic existence. This is the meaning of 'the way to 'Ereẓ Israel' which has been mentioned above . . .[70]

"The way to the Land of Israel," identified with *derekh 'ereẓ*, is now depicted as a way of reaching God when the medium of Torah is closed to man. It was indeed on his journey to the Land of Israel that Nahman first concluded that he could observe the *miẓwot* in a purely spiritual form. This path takes him back to that time before Sinai when there were no specific obligatory *miẓwot*, and when the patriarchs served God through everyday human activities.[71] In times of simplicity, which are here depicted as moments of "fall," the *ẓaddiq* has access to this channel. But since Nahman often stated that simplicity was the highest service, and that his own "I don't know" was higher than any of his teachings, it is not difficult to imagine that this type of religious life would in fact become the ideal, rather than an alternative for moments of emptiness.

Nahman understood the dangers of such an attitude. In his moment of realization on the sea, he had concluded that

He would be able to serve God even when, God forbid, he would be unable to perform the *miẓwot*. He understood the service of the patriarchs, before the Torah was given, who fulfilled all the *miẓwot*, though not in their ordinary sense.[72].

At the same time, Nahman saw himself as a defender of the faith, particularly against the encroachments of Haskalah. This role called for a staunch and unswerving loyalty to the *miẓwot*, not to be weakened by a commitment to 'higher' spirituality. Seeing the dangers inherent in the mystical proclamation that God is present in all things, Nahman chose to emphasize the existential, with its sense of eternal longing and its realization of the distance between God and man. *It is where God is not directly present that man seeks out those means, provided by traditional religion, to evoke His presence.* This is stated explicitly by Nahman in the following passage, which follows upon a discussion of the need to serve God through material things:

But nevertheless, if He were to cause His love to flow upon us, we would have no need of all this. How did God create the world, bringing it into existence out of not-being, when there was not yet present any lower creature to arouse Him? He created everything out of love, without any arousal from below, as Scripture says: 'The world was built by love' (Ps. 89:3). Since

He was able to create such worlds by love alone, without any arousal, He could certainly sustain those worlds in the same way, *and we would not have to perform any works at all . . . it is only because this love has been withheld and does not flow down upon us that we have to do those things which arouse Him from below.*[73]

Now it is clear why *ẓimẓum* has to be real for Nahman, and why it is forbidden to seek God in the void: only in a world from which God is in some degree absent does the life of religion continue to make sense.

Such a conclusion was, of course, particularly well suited to Nahman's own frame of mind. He certainly saw in this need for distance from God a vindication of his own states of alienation and doubt. Though perhaps he was personally nourished by memories of his own mystical moments, he would not allow such moments to become the basis of his faith. The greatness of God, it will be recalled, "is something that no one can communicate to his fellowman, or even to himself from one day to the next." A religious life based upon the testimony of other moments would be no more valid than one based upon any other sort of "proof" of God's presence. The moment of doubt or of God's absence had to be confronted on its own terms, without the comforting thought that it was but a passing phase. Only by seeking faith *within* doubt, and by the paradoxical assertion that in God's very absence is He to be known, may the doubter be transformed once again into a seeker after Him, and the need for religion be maintained.

In the end, the paradox of Nahman's thought may be applied to his life as well. His greatest success in expanding the horizons of faith lay in his struggle with his own doubts. In this he became, despite all his attachments to the world of the past, a *ẓaddiq* for modern man. In his willingness to live at the edge of the void, a void that was to become apparent to so many in the generations following his death, Nahman did indeed earn his title as the *ẓaddiq ha-dor* of times to come, the *ẓaddiq* who could continue to show how to struggle for faith in times when the absence of God would seem to be most complete.

NOTES

1. *Liqquṭim II* 105; *Ḥayyey II* 4:11.

2. The Hebrew idiom for business dealings, *massa' u-mattan,* is reflected in the verbs of this verse, here translated 'raise up' and 'take.' The quote above is from *Zohar* 3:224a.

3. The Hebrew term for 'nostrils' in Deut.33:11 *('af)* is used also for 'brow' in Gen. 3:19.

4. *Liqquṭim* 13:1.

5. *Siḥot* 167. For a surprising precedent in medieval Kabbalistic literature, see Recanati, *Ta'amey ha-Miẓwot,* introduction, 3a. My thanks to Mr. Morris Faierstein for this reference. Nahman's Uncle Ephraim had similarly liberal thoughts con-

cerning freedom to reinterpret the tradition. See *Degel, bereshit* 6a and *pequdey* 147b. On Nahman's unwillingness to be limited by the lines of conventional thinking, in this case including those of Kabbalah, see *Ḥayyey II* 2:27.

6. A full bibliography of *ḤaBaD* literature by A. M. Haberman is found in *'Aley 'Ayin*, p.273*ff*. For an outline of Shne'ur Zalman's thought see M. Teitelbaum, *Ha-Rav mi-Liadi u-Mifleget ḤaBaD*. A brief but very clear summary of *ḤaBaD* doctrine is presented by Louis Jacobs in *Seeker of Unity*. See also the many books and pamphlets published by Kehot, the *ḤaBaD* publishing house in New York.

7. *Liqquṭim* 21:1. See Weiss in *'Aley 'Ayin*, p. 253*ff*.

8. In addition to the *Guide*, the following works are expressly forbidden: the philosophical *Sha'ar ha-Yiḥud* in Baḥya Ibn Paquda's *Ḥovot ha-Levavot;* Maimonides' *Be'ur Millot ha-Higayon;* Joseph Albo's *'Iqqarim* (this despite the work's general reputation for orthodoxy); Isaac Arama's *'Aqedat Yizḥaq*, because of the quotations from philosophical literature found in it; the Bible commentary of Ibn Ezra, and especially the super-commentary *Margaliot Ṭovah;* and the Biblical commentary of Gersonides. *Cf. Ḥayyey II*, 7: 1 and 4. This list was probably compiled by Nathan and his disciples. According to *ibid*. 3, it is possible to tell by looking at a man's face whether he has ever studied the *Guide*. Further sources for Nahman's denunciation of philosophy are to be found in *Liqquṭim* 21, 62, 64; *Liqquṭim II* 44; *Siḥot* 5, 32–38; 216–226. *Cf*. Piekarz, p. 21. A number of these sources will be discussed below. In a line quoted by Horodezky allegedly from an unpublished Bratslav source (the uncensored version of *Ḥayyey?*) given him by a *ḥasid*, Nahman goes so far as to say: "There are certain philosophers generally considered great, particularly Maimonides, but in the future it will be known that he was a heretic and an unbeliever . . ." Horodezky, *Ha-Ḥasidut weha-Ḥasidim*, v.3, p.40. Of course there have been readers of Maimonides, in both the thirteenth and the twentieth centuries, who concur in this view. On attitudes toward Maimonides and the *Guide* elsewhere in Hasidism *cf*. J. Dienstag, "*Ha-Moreh Nevukhim we-Sefer ha-Mada' be-Sifrut ha-Ḥasidut*."

9. *Siḥot* 33; *Ḥayyey II* 7:5.

10. *Sippurey Ma'asiyot*, p. 58*f*. The motif of the messages sent by a distant king is probably taken by Nahman from Judah Halevi's *Kuzari* 1:19*ff*., where the rabbi compares revelation to a message from the King of India. In Halevi's work, however, the tokens of the message's authenticity are accepted by the king; Halevi does not know the tortured complexity of Nahman's struggle over faith.

11. *Liqquṭim* 62:2; *Siḥot* 32, 40. In some cases, according to Nahman, a person's tendency toward philosophy may be explained by his parents' having conceived him in sin. Such persons must work doubly hard to overcome the doubts that plague them.

12. *Sippurey Ma'asiyot*, p.139*f*. *Cf*. Weiss, *op. cit*., p.250. The word *khokhmes* in Yiddish (equals Heb. *ḥokhmot)* has a cynical edge to it, which is often intended in Nahman's writings and remains quite untranslatable. One might do best to think of the 'wisdom' attributed to a 'wise guy.'

13. *Liqquṭim II* 7:6 and *Parpera'ot le-Ḥokhmah ad loc*. and *II* 7:2; *Siḥot* 3. Other major sources for Nahman on *maqqifin* are *Liqquṭim* 21 and 63. The term is adapted from its frequent usage in Lurianic literature, where its meaning is quite different. The followers of Luria use the terms *'or maqqif* or *'orot maqqifin* with reference to the *sefirotic* world, not to the human mind. As the light of *'eyn sof* reentered the void

following *ẓimẓum*, it formed ten concentric circles, which were to become the ten *sefirot*. The light that entered each of these circles formed the *'or penimi* ("inner light") of that particular *sefirah*, while the light in the circle outside it was an *'or maqqif* ("surrounding light") to that *sefirah*. *Cf. 'Eẓ Ḥayyim, sha'ar ha-kelalim*, beginning, and Immanuel Hai Ricci's *Mishnat Ḥasidim, beri'at Adam Qadmon* 1:1. As the progressive revelation of the *sefirot* indicates a growing 'distance' from *'eyn sof*, the *maqqifin* of any given *sefirah* are the lights too intense for that *sefirah* to contain within itself. In transferring the use of the terms *maqqif* and *penimi* from the *sefirotic* realm to the realm of human mental processes, Nahman is following a generally familiar pattern within Hasidism. A passage strikingly reminiscent of Nahman here is found in *Qedushat Levi, shemot*, 92*f*. There Levi Yizhak is building upon teachings attributed to the BeSHT and Yehiel Mikhel of Zloczow. The progression of dialectical thinking from the BeSHT to Nahman may be traced by close comparative study of such passages. Interestingly, the term *maqqif* does not appear here at all. Another example of such thinking is found in *Qedushat Levi, wa-era'*, 97a.

14. *Liqquṭim II* 7:6.

15. *Liqquṭim* 245.

16. *Liqquṭim* 21:7. Deut. 32:18 is more conventionally translated: "You were unmindful of the Rock who begot you." See also *Zohar* 3:249b. The term *moḥin* is Nahman's inclusive term for both *maqqifin* and *penimiyim;* they are the "levels of awareness" the seeker is to integrate. Here, too, a Lurianic term has been reapplied. In Lurianic texts (e.g. *'Eẓ Ḥayyim* 5:6:22, 67a; and *Siddur Qol Ya'aqov* 18a–b) the term is applied to the inner powers of each *sefirotic* configuration *(parẓuf)*, which may then exist in a "greater" or "lesser" state, *e.g., moḥin de-gadlut de-ze'ir*. In earlier Hasidism, the term is used to refer in a general way to the worshiper's mental powers or strength of concentration. *Cf.* for example the quotation from the Ba'al Shem Tov in *Toledot Ya'aqov Yosef* 83a. The term *'ibbur* as used by Nahman here is another example of transference of Lurianic terminology from the theosophical to the mental sphere. It is based upon the notion of the 'gestation' of the upper lights within the womb of *Malkhut*. *Cf. Mishnat Ḥasidim, 'ibbur ze'ir we-nuqveyh*, 13 a–b. It has nothing directly to do with the idea of *'ibbur ha-neshamot*, a part of the Kabbalistic doctrine of metempsychosis.

17. This phrase becomes a sort of watchword in Bratslav and is frequently quoted in the later sources. For its use by Nahman and Nathan *cf. Ḥayyey II* 2:42 and *Shivḥey II* 35. I have not found this formula in the Hebrew philosophical literature of the Middle Ages and suspect that it is of late, but pre-Hasidic, origin. The BeSHT already seems to be commenting on it in a passage quoted in the opening lines of the introduction to *Ben Porat Yosef*. Similar formulations are found elsewhere in Hasidic sources, e.g. *Me'or 'Eynayim*, p.140. The phrase is reminiscent of the idea of *Docta Ignorantia* in the thought of Nicholas of Cusa, though I know of no historical link.

18. *Siḥot* 3: *Shivḥey II* 35.

19. *Liqquṭim* 21:4; 64:4. *Cf.* Weiss, *op. cit.*, p.256.

20. *Siḥot* 32.

21. *Ḥayyey* 1:24. Emphasis mine.

22. *Loc. cit.* Here the personal emphasis is found in the word order of the Yiddish original: *"Mir loz emetser zogn a terets."*

The reference to "books of Kabbalah" is to the *Sheney Luḥot ha-Berit* by Isaiah Horowitz, 26a. Scholem quotes an earlier part of this same passage in *Messianic Idea*, pp. 302*f.*, but deletes the *SheLaH's* comments to the effect that the House of Hillel was rooted in *ḥesed* and the House of Shammai in *gevurah*. It is for this reason, according to Horowitz, that *halakah* generally prefers the Hillelite rulings.

23. *Ḥayyey II* 7:2. See Weiss, *op. cit.*, p.276*f.*

24. For Ben Sheshet's anti-rationalist polemics see his *Meshiv Devarim Nekhoḥim*. This work is primarily a refutation of the *Ma'amar Yiqqawu ha-Mayim* of Samuel Ibn Tibbon. It is discussed by Vajda in the more general context of the thirteenth-century tension between philosophy and Kabbalah in his *Recherches sur la Philosophie et la Kabbale dans la Pensee Juive du Moyen Age*. Shem Tov's major work is *Sefer 'Emunot*, in which an outline of his own Kabbalistic system is preceded by a sharp attack on philosophy, particularly as seen in the *Guide*. *Cf.* particularly Section II, 11b–16a. Ibn Gabbai was a major synthesizer of the Kabbalistic tradition. His *'Avodat ha-Qodesh* was a sort of *summa kabbalistica* for the generation just before Luria and Cordovero. The third part of that work is devoted to a critique of philosophy; Ibn Gabbai was intimately familiar with the *Guide* and was well-read in both the philosophical and anti-philosophical literature of the preceding centuries. His work exercised a wide influence in later Ashkenazic circles in part through the extensive quotes from it in Isaiah Horowitz' *Sheney Luhot ha-Berit*. On Kabbalism and anti-rationalism in Italy *cf.* I. Barzilay, *Between Reason and Faith*, p.63*ff.* At least in the case of the Kabbalists and those directly influenced by them I cannot accept Barzilay's conclusion in the introduction to his book that it was primarily for Jewish national reasons that philosophy was rejected. True, the Kabbalists were generally less universalistic, perhaps even xenophobic in comparison with the relative universalism of certain medieval rationalists, but this was a by-product rather than a central motivating force in their struggle against philosophy.

25. *Sefer 'Emunot* 2:1, 12b; *'Avodat ha-Qodesh* 3:15–21.

26. The one exception to this statement is the place of 'faith' in the Sabbatian theology of Nathan of Gaza and his followers.

See particularly Nathan's letter to Raphael Joseph, published in Scholem's *Sabbatai Ṣevi*, pp. 270*ff.*, and Scholem's comments on it, pp. 282*ff.* For Nathan of Gaza, faith was primarily directed toward the messiah and his saving power. He goes so far as to indicate that this faith alone is the true criterion for redemption. As Scholem has pointed out, it is here that Sabbatianism veers closest to a theological outlook generally associated with Christianity rather than Judaism.

There are certain clear parallels between Nahman's notion and that of the Sabbatians. We will recall (*cf.* above, Chapter Three) that the *ẓaddiq*, like God Himself, is the object of paradoxical faith. Nahman's assertion that faith cannot be dependent upon miracles, which will be detailed below, is also presaged by the Sabbatians (*cf.* Scholem, *op. cit.*, pp. 210*f.*), though that idea has roots, as Scholem shows *ad loc.*, in orthodox Jewish theology. On the other hand, the quality of longing and yearning that turns out to be the content of Nahman's faith, which lends it its particularly 'existential' coloring (see below), is unknown to the Sabbatian sources.

27. Here it would seem that Nahman is using, but intentionally inverting, a philosophical notion. Maimonides states (*Guide* 2:25) that one may accede to the claims of prophecy in areas where no rational demonstration to the contrary is

possible. Nahman agrees with this, but uses it to claim that any rational demonstration in the area of religion necessarily eclipses the legitimate role of faith, and therefore should be eschewed.

28. *Liqquṭim* 62:5; *Siḥot* 1.

29. *Cf. Liqquṭim* 20:1–2; *Liqquṭim* II 2:2.

30. *Liqquṭim II* 7:7–8. Cf. Avot 1:1 and Zohar 1:1b.

31. This distinction probably comes to Nahman via RaSHI's understanding of Moses' unique prophecy in his comment to Yebamot 49b. A. Altmann, in a yet unpublished paper, has traced this idea to early Geonic sources.

32. Nathan does interpret this passage as referring to transcendence and immanence. *Cf.* his *Liqquṭey Halakhot, talmud Torah* 2. This interpretation, which ignores the crucial passage in Nahman, is typical of Nathan's frequent attempts to mitigate the most radical tensions in his master's thought.

33. *Liqquṭim II* 7:9. Emphasis mine.

34. *Liqquṭim II* 5:15. *Cf. Avot* 1:17 and 3:9, *Berakhot* 7a, *Menaḥot* 29b. According to the rabbis *(Berakhot* 57b) sleep is one-sixtieth part of death. Nahman plays on a dual meaning of *histalequt: histalequt ha-moḥin* is the setting aside of one's intellect; *histalequt Mosheh* is the *death* of Moses.

Cf. also *Liqquṭim* 55:3, where Nahman notes that the *ẓaddiq* is given the *perspective* to see the justice of God, despite the fact that the wicked seemingly triumph in this world. I do not agree with Weiss *(op. cit.,* pp. 283*f.)* that the passage here quoted suggests madness as a way out of the paradoxical human situation. The servant here described is a 'holy fool' in his search for the most humbling and even degrading forms of worship, but not quite a madman.

35. *Zikhron Ṭov,* p.8 #6.

36. *Siḥot* 106.

37. *Yemey ha-Tela'ot* p.61 (190). Quoted by Weiss, *op. cit.,* p.248. "Their books" here may be a garbled reference to Maimonides' *Guide* 3:15. For a mystic who expresses the very opposite point of view on this matter *cf.* Ezra of Gerona on the Song of Songs 3:9, quoted by Altmann in *JJS* 7 (1956) 203*f. Cf.* also *Siḥot* 101, 103.

38. *Liqquṭim* 123.

39. In the Eschaton, the need for freedom of choice will no longer exist; man will thus be able to know God more fully and directly than he can in this world. *Liqquṭim* 21:4, 9. In *Liqquṭim* 51 Nahman makes it clear that the final mystical goal of life is a state where man is beyond choice, as choice exists only as a result of the duality of good and evil, a duality that will be obliterated as man returns to the pre-mundane state of monistic bliss.

40. *Ḥayyey II* 7:6; *Liqquṭim* 64:3. *Cf.* also Nathan's *Liqquṭey Halakhot, shabbat* 6:8 and Piekarz, p.54*f.*

41. "Philosophy" throughout Nahman's works refers to medieval Aristotelianism as he encountered it in the *Guide*. Nahman does not seem sufficiently familiar with the *content* of Haskalah literature to realize that the philosophical assumptions of the eighteenth-century enlightenment are far from those of the medieval sage.

42. *Liqquṭim* 52.

43. *Siḥot* 40. For earlier roots of this idea *cf.* Werblowsky, *Joseph Karo,* p.248*ff.* and Scholem, *Pirqey Yesod,* p.336*f.*

44. See above n.39. At the end of time, according to well-known rabbinic tradition, Elijah will answer all those questions men were unable to resolve through the course of history. "Days" and "measures" *(yamim u-middot)* above are classical designations for the *sefirot*, but here one could also translate them "time" and "space." The phrase "in a deeper sense" translates *be-emet le-amito*.

45. *Cf.* Tishby, *Torat ha-Ra' weha-Qelipah be-Qabbalat ha-ARI*, p.52*ff*. Discussion of the Lurianic myth may also be found in *Major Trends*, seventh lecture, and Scholem's "Schöpfung aus nichts und Selbstverschränkung Gottes."

46. *Avot* 2:14.

47. The terms *sovev kol 'almin* and *memale' kol 'almin* are first found in *Zohar* 3:225a (R.M.). They are common later as designations for transcendence and immanence, and play an especially great role in *ḤaBaD* writings.

48. *Liqquṭim* 21:5,9.

49. *Liqquṭim* 25:3; *Liqquṭim II* 7:6–8.

50. Menaḥot 29b. Nahman's intentionally over-literal reading of the text, often employed by him as a homiletic device, understands the phrase *kakh 'alah be-maḥashavah* as "Thus it is in the highest thought" rather than the idiomatic "Thus have I decided." A likely source for such a reading is Cordovero's *Pardes Rimmonim* 24:11, v.2, 51a. On Moses' silence see the magnificent passage in *Zohar* 2:25b.

51. *Ḥayyey II* 7:13. See also the answer given by Nahman of Tulchin when asked about the truth of miracles: *"A moifes bin ikh!" Kokhvey 'Or*, intro.

52. For definitions of religious existentialism *cf.* J. Hutchinson, *Faith, Reason, and Existence*, p.31, *passim*.

53. The distinction between the 'mystical' and 'existential' forms of piety within Hasidism was first proposed by J. Weiss in his pioneering article "Contemplative Mysticism and 'Faith' in Hasidic Piety," *JJS* 4 (1952) 19*ff*. Weiss there uses Dov Baer of Miedzyrzec and Shne'ur Zalman as paradigms of the contemplative type, while Nahman is proposed as the example *par excellence* of faith-centered 'existential' Hasidism. While Weiss admits (p. 21) that these are not "pure types," he does consider Nahman to be an "extreme case" (p.20) of the existential trend. Both here and in his above-quoted article in *'Aley 'Ayin*, Weiss tends to ignore the clearly mystical side of Nahman's thought. This section of our present chapter should serve to correct the rather one-sided impression given by Weiss, and to explain why Nahman chooses to highlight the existential dimension of religion despite his own attraction to mysticism.

54. *Liqquṭim* 173.

'Emunah is a common Kabbalistic term for the *shekhinah*. The union of *'emet* and *'emunah* ("truth" and "faith") is a symbolic expression for the coupling of *tif'eret* and *malkhut*. *See* the sources quoted by Cordovero in *Pardes Rimonim* 23:1, s.v. *'emunah* and *'emet.*, v.2, 6a–b.

See also *Liqquṭim* 152, which speaks of the *ẓaddiq's* soul in similar terms and see above, Chapter One, n.97. Here, too, we seem close to a deification of faith itself. For a further example of this tendency *cf.* Nathan on the Tales as quoted by Piekarz, p.135*f*. This point is worthy of further study.

55. The Hebrew terms are *torat ha-shem be-emet* and *torat ha-shem mamash*, the latter being of a higher and ultimately mysterious character. The relativization of the "lower" Torah in the face of God's own Torah is a well-known Kabbalistic

motif, which also played a role in Sabbatianism. See Scholem, *On the Kabbalah and Its Symbolism*, p.83*ff*. This passage also echoes the rabbinic reading of Psalm 1:2. *Cf*. RaSHI *ad loc*. and *Qiddushin* 32b.

56. *Liqquṭim* 22:10. *See Berakhot* 6a, 7a; *Soṭah* 14a; *Yer. Bikkurim* 3:3.

57. *'Avaneha Barzel*, p.44.

58. On *da'at* in Nahman's thought *cf. Liqquṭim* 4:4, 53, 58:5, 255; *Liqquṭim II* 1:5.

59. *Liqquṭim* 21:11.

The saying of the sage is well-known in Hebrew writings of the later Middle Ages. It first appears, already as a quotation from "one of the sages" in the sermons of the fourteenth-century Talmudist and opponent of philosophy, Nissim ben Reuben Gerondi. This and other sources are mentioned by David Kaufmann, *Geschichte der Attributenlehre*, p. 326, n. 190. "Where the mind is, there is the whole man" is a well-known saying of the BeSHT. *Cf. Toledot, shelaḥ*, 129b and *Sefer Ba'al Shem Ṭov, Noaḥ*, n.31.

60. *Liqquṭim II* 61. On the pre-existent messiah *cf. Sanhedrin* 98b.

61. Shne'ur Zalman's concept of *ẓimẓum* is discussed in Teitelbaum, *op. cit.*, v.2 p.43*ff*. and Jacobs, *op. cit.*, p.55*ff*.

62. From the concluding paragraph of *Liqquṭim* 64, not translated here, one might draw the conclusion that Nahman, too, denies the ultimate reality of *ẓimẓum*. There Nahman dismisses the first sort of heresy, that which is derived from the *qelipot*, as a sort of divine prank (based on RaSHI to Ex. 10:2). He hints that in the future man will also become aware of the illusory nature of the second sort of heresy, as he will see that God exists in the void itself.

63. *Avot* 5:1; *Megillah* 21b; *Bahir* 141 (96) and the sources quoted by Margaliot *ad loc*.

64. *Yer. Ta'anit* 1:1 (64a). In the original this sentence is an addendum to the teaching.

65. *Liqquṭim II* 12. Emphasis mine. An earlier and less radical treatment of this theme is found in *Liqquṭim* 56:3–4. The motif is developed by Nathan in *Liqquṭey Halakhot, Shabbat* 3:17, 23, and *dagim* 2:2. Nahman of Cheryn, in his commentary *Parpera'ot le-Ḥokhmah ad loc.*, considerably mitigates the radicalism of Nahman's statement by interpreting the "hidden utterance" to refer to the aspect of *Keter* within *Malkut*. If "temples of idolatry," also associated with Rome, refers to Christian churches, the statement is even more shocking in its near-Frankist implications.

66. Scholem, *On the Kabbalah and Its Symbolism*, p.25*ff*.; *Major Trends*, p.338*ff*. This is taken up as a major theme in Schatz, *Ha-Ḥasidut ke-Misṭiqah*.

67. *Ibid.*, p.56

68. *Cf. ibid.*, p.75*f*. and "Anti-Spiritualism ba-Ḥasidut," *Molad* 171–2 (1963) 513*ff*.

69. *Liqquṭim II* 78. This is the same teaching with which chapter six is concluded.

70. *Cf. Zohar* 1:92a; *Lev. Rabbah* 9:3. There is a play here between *derekh 'ereẓ* and *derekh 'Ereẓ Yisra'el*.

71. *Cf.* the Hasidic parallels in Schatz, *Ha-Ḥasidut ke-Misṭiqah*, p.57*ff*.

72. *Shivḥey II* 22.

73. *Liqquṭim II* 4:3. Emphasis mine.

Excursus II
The Tales

We have had occasion many times, while telling the story of Nahman's life, to make reference to his *Tales,* which of course constitute an important and highly interesting portion of his creative work. For a long time it was primarily for the *Tales* that Nahman's name was known outside Hasidic and scholarly circles, this in no small part due to the influence of Martin Buber's translation. The time has now come for us to speak of them more fully, a task to be approached with considerable trepidation. Since the early years of this century, historians and literary critics have again and again pored over the often obscure texts of Nahman's *Sippurey Ma'asiyot,* each offering some nuance of interpretation. Some have been interested in the tales from the standpoint of language, viewing them as rare documents of early nineteenth-century Yiddish prose, and raising various complex linguistic problems. Others have seen them from a literary point of view, particularly as an object for the study of folklore motifs and their influence on literary works; much fruitful work in this area remains to be done. Those closest to the Bratslav traditions of reading the *Tales* have been interested in their symbolic meaning in the realm of mystical theology, while some of the more recent scholarship on them has tended toward a psychological reading, using these stories as a set of mirrors through which to see into the labyrinth of Nahman's soul. Of these many scholars some have claimed that the stories are to be read didactically, more or less as parabolic presentations of Kabbalistic ideas. Others have assured us that such a didactic approach is bankrupt when it comes up against works of fiction, and that the tales must be seen as literary creations in the fullest sense, products of the same inner drives that lead any writer of fiction to create. In the telling of tales, it is claimed, Nahman finally achieves liberation from the constraints of the literary conventions to which he had formerly been bound, and is able to express the deepest yearnings of his soul most freely. Recently an attempt has been made to apply a detailed structural analysis to one of Nahman's tales, an approach that may prove profitable for future readings. Finally, there are even some serious historians who have claimed that nothing that makes any sense at all may be derived from the tales, since they are nothing more than the deranged ravings of Nahman in the throes of his final illness.[1]

Before we, too, enter into the fray and offer some suggestions of our own as to how the stories might best be read, a few words of bibliography are in order. The tales attributed to Nahman fall into two categories: the thirteen stories published by Nathan in 1815 under the title *Sippurey Ma'asiyot*, and a number of other tales and parables, some of which were published by Nahman of Cheryn in the 1870s, some more of which were included in *Sippurey Ma'asiyot Ḥadashim* (1909) and still others of which appear scattered through the later collections of Bratslav materials. The thirteen 'canonical' tales were originally printed in both Hebrew and Yiddish, a practice followed by the *ḥasidim* in most later editions of that work. These tales vary in length from a page or two to the *Seven Beggars*, which runs twenty-five pages in a frequently reprinted edition. The non-canonical tales are generally short, were printed only in Hebrew, and were not the object of commentary and veneration as were the tales of the earlier collection.[2] Most scholarship concerning Nahman's tales, including the present chapter, focuses on the original thirteen tales. All of these, as we have noted earlier, were told between the summer of 1806 and the spring of 1810, a period of great trials in Nahman's life. This was also a period, incidentally, when Nahman was quite productive in terms of his homiletic output; there was not a turn *from* teaching to storytelling in Nahman's career, but rather a discovery, in his last four years, of an *additional* means of communication.[3]

The telling of the tales in itself was of course nothing new in the Hasidic world. From the times of the Ba'al Shem Tov and down to our own day, Hasidism has been distinguished by its rich traditions of storytelling. Tales of the *ẓaddiqim*, passed on from one *ḥasid* to another, or, in later generations, told by latter-day masters about the saints of old, lay at the very core of Hasidism as a popular movement. Undoubtedly they functioned both as edification and entertainment for a class and time when neither of these was readily accessible through other channels. Though collected and recorded in writing only rather late in the development of the movement, the tales in oral form had tremendous influence in the spread of Hasidism, an influence probably no less great than that of the published teachings and homilies of the early masters.[4]

Nevertheless, Nahman's tales did constitute a major innovation. In the early days of Hasidism, tales were told *about* the masters rather than *by* them. Nahman is the author, not the subject—at least not ostensibly—of the tales he tells. The vast majority of Hasidic stories concerned the lives of the *zaddiqim;* Nahman's tales dealt rather with such figures as bewitched princesses, kings, and heroes, wood-spirits and wizards, mysterious beggars, and the like. In most of his tales it seems unlikely that the characters are Jews: at least the issue never comes up, a matter that, of itself, sharply distinguishes Nahman's tales from others current among the *ḥasidim.* Nahman freely admitted adapting stories from non-Jewish sources; some entire tales and various motifs in others are traceable to collections of Slavic folk-tales.[5] While there are traditions—difficult to document—to the effect that the Ba'al Shem Tov himself was a teller of fantastic yarns and used the tale as a major teaching device, we have nothing attributed to the founder of Hasidism that begins to equal Nahman's creations for mythic quality or complexity of literary allusion. These *Sippurey Ma'asiyot* are clearly distinguishable from the entire corpus of Hasidic hagiographic legends, *märchen,* and parables. Nothing else is quite like them, and thus they are deserving of analysis in their own right.

Previous references to Nahman's *Tales* in this volume have largely been within the context of an examination of Nahman's life and thought; such extraneous use of the *Tales* as sources for understanding their author is a relatively simple matter. In pursuing an approach to the *Tales* in themselves, however, we are immediately confronted with a whole host of issues we were previously able to put aside. We seek to understand Nahman's stories, which are highly complex works of symbolic fiction. How will we go about such an undertaking, and what claims will we make for the interpretations we offer? Not believing that we (or any other latter-day interpreter of literature) have such occult powers as to penetrate Nahman's mind and discover a tale's "true" meaning, but at the same time not being of sufficient modesty to admit that our reading of a tale is nothing more than our own, we seek here to strike a middle course between 'objectivism' and 'subjectivism' in our critical viewpoint. We do not know what was in Nahman's mind as he told the *Tales.* While it might be possible to make such a claim concerning the sort of discursive writing that appears in his homilies, surely in the case of complex symbolic fiction such an attempt would be folly. Nahman's mind will always remain beyond our grasp; in this claim the *ḥasidim* are correct. At the same time, it should be clear that this is a *biographer's* interpretation. What we seek here is a reading of the tales consonant with the figure of Nahman as we have portrayed him. Such a reading takes upon itself the burdens of avoiding anachronisms, steering clear of obvious projections, and generally setting the tales in a context appropriate to their author's life and thought. We are, of course, greatly aided in this by the large body of non-fiction Nahman composed, particularly the *Liqquṭim,* in which meanings are considerably less obscure. While we do not claim for the *Tales* the same didactic function as that the homilies served, it makes sense to assume that similar ideas and motifs would appear in both *genres.* A biographer's reading should pay particular attention to what is known of the circumstances and date of a particular tale, coördinating these with other events in the author's life at the time, seeing the tales in terms of the intellectual and religious concerns he is likely to have garbed in such form, and having in mind whatever is known to him of the author's psychological states, insofar as they might have bearing on his literary works. Such is the intended contribution of this reading: to restore discussion of the tales to the context of Nahman's life and person, a context from which they have often been removed. All of our work up to this point may serve as an extended prolegomenon to this task.

It was in the context of Nahman's longings for redemption that we originally discussed his turn to storytelling. It is to those longings and to the trauma of that summer of 1806 which we shall now return. The close relationship in Nahman's mind between the various events of that summer should be recalled: the passing of the year that numerologically hinted at Messiah ben Joseph, the death of his infant son, the failure of his secret writings to make any impression outside the very limited circles of his own faithful—all of these added up to the failure of his more-or-less open messianic agitation. Late in that summer, just before the turn of the year, the first tale was told. The messianic attempt had failed, Nahman tells us in a teaching, because the people were not ready. The dream of redemption has not left Nahman—far from it!—but now it is clear that the light of that coming redemption will have to be given to the people more gradually, through the complex veils of stories. The tales thus represent both an innovation and a continuity in Nahman's pursuit of his constant goal: the spiritual preparation of his followers and hearers for the advent of messiah.

The problem with this explanation is that it does not show us *how* Nahman now seeks to effect the redemption. True, the evil forces will be fooled by the clever garbing of his teachings, and the hearer will not be so startled as to be blinded by Nahman's great light. But if we are at this point still dealing with what may be termed active messianism, we must still ask *how*, through the tales, Nahman hopes to bring about the end.

In answering this question, we must remember that Nahman stands within the tradition of Lurianic Kabbalah, which is a tradition of *mystical* messianism. For the Kabbalist, true activism in bringing about the desired end takes place within the human mind. It is the contemplative act, with its theurgic ramifications, that restores wholeness to the cosmos. Contemplation may of course take place within the framework of prescribed ritual practice, and is thus related to deed. But it is nevertheless the proper meditation, not the deed alone, that carries theurgic power. The movement toward redemption begins within the human mind; only in its final stages is it transposed to the external realm.

Once again we examine Nahman's situation: he is trying to explain to himself the failure of his messianic attempt. He discovers that man was not ready to receive redemption. But this lack of readiness is a matter of the soul: man's longings are not yet deep enough, his awareness of the true spiritual exile is not sharp enough to call forth those redemptive energies that lie buried deep within the self. The stuggle for redemption, Nahman realizes, must first take place within the souls of those who hear him. Only when their spirits are sufficiently aroused will they be ready for redemption in the external world. The inner life, always the true focus of Nahman's concerns, is now to be addressed in a new way; this address is to be of such power that it will awaken the hearer's soul to the true possibilities of new and redemptive life hidden within it. When the redeemer finally does come, man will be prepared for his arrival.

Tales of the *ẓaddiqim*, says Nahman, purify the mind. He also says: "Know that tales of the *ẓaddiqim* are a very great thing. Through these tales *the heart is aroused and enraptured with the most powerful longing for God.*"[6]

The clearest evidence for this understanding of the tales is seen in a curious about-face in Nahman's later teachings on the issue of the *imagination* and its role in the religious life. In several of Nahman's earlier teachings the term *medammeh* (an ellipse of the phrase *koaḥ ha-medammeh*, the "imaginative faculty") has a decidely negative connotation. An overly-developed imagination retards the growth of the intellect *(sekhel)*, which is the faculty on which man needs to concentrate his attention. Faith may, of course, reach higher than intellect, but in the early Nahman there is no identification or link between faith and imagination. The *medammeh* is rather the "shell" or "husk," which surrounds the true fruit of intellect lying within it; one must break through this outer husk in order to get to the fruit itself. Here it would seem that no distinction exists in Nahman's mind between "imagination" and "illusion," *medammeh* being used to convey both of these meanings at once. If allowed to run freely, Nahman says, the *medammeh* would naturally lead one to thoughts of evil; it is nurtured by base talk, and is the aspect of the human mind that links man to the animal kingdom. Most interestingly, in the early Nahman the *medammeh* is the great enemy of true prophecy, a force that must be overcome if there is to be prophetic inspiration.[7]

A total reversal of this attitude toward the *medammeh* is found in a teaching Nahman offered on Rosh Hashanah of 1809. A play on words possible in Hebrew allows Nahman to interpret "Let us make man in our likeness" *(ki-demutenu)* (Gen. 1:26) as "Let us make man endowed with an imagination"! In direct contrast to earlier views, which saw man's *medammeh* as binding him to the animal world, here the imaginative faculty (when its purity is maintained) is explicitly related to the divine or angelic side of man's nature.[8]

Finally, in a teaching presented just a few weeks before his death,

Nahman speaks in positive terms of the relationship of prophecy, faith, and imagination. Man's *medammeh*, which has been defiled by sin, can only be redeemed through the spirit of prophecy, here identified with the charismatic gifts of the *ẓaddiq:*

> As prophecy spreads forth, the imaginative faculty is purified and restored. This is the meaning of 'I am imagined by the prophets' (Hosea 12:11). The imagination can only be restored by the prophets. When this takes place, true and holy faith can also be restored, and false beliefs are rejected. Faith is chiefly reliant upon the imaginative faculty; when the mind fully understands something, the term 'faith' is not applicable to it. Faith exists only where intellect ceases; only there does man need faith. But when something is not apprehended by the mind, only the imaginative faculty remains, and it is there that faith is required. Thus it is that the *medammeh* is the main locus of faith. The imagination is restored by prophecy, and this leads to the restoration of proper faith.[9]

The *ẓaddiq's* task is to provide his *ḥasid* with a purified imagination. What more appropriate self-definition for Nahman the story-teller than this? If it is the fantasies of men's minds that lead them into sin, let the *ẓaddiq* provide for them a richer and more intricate life of fantasy than they could ever dream up for themselves, so long as it leads them, through its symbolic content, back to the holy. Rather than simply denouncing the evil imaginings of men's hearts, *Nahman has decided to fight fantasy with fantasy*. The 'prophetic' powers of the *ẓaddiq* can lend to his disciples a new and purified imagination; through this new imagination their faith will be restored and they will then be prepared to share in their master's dreams of redemption.

Of the many struggles of Nahman's life, none may be said to have been more all-pervasive than the struggle over issues of fantasy and reality. From childhood on, it was evil thoughts and temptations—products of the imagination—that kept him far from God. His image of himself as the greatest of all the *ẓaddiqim*, as the center of his generation, was a fantasy he was at pains to declare true. He was a person who remembered dreams, sometimes in great detail, and was pursued by them. In earlier years, it was the *battle* against fantasy that occupied a great part of his energies; in this we have seen how different he was from the Ba'al Shem Tov, who taught that one should uplift evil thoughts rather than vainly seeking to fight them off. In his later years Nahman seems finally to be coming to terms with his great-grandfather's wisdom, though giving it a new twist. Not an acceptance and uplifting of negative fantasy, but rather the attempt to provide a new life of holy fantasy as an alternative to the old marks Nahman's attempt in the tales. He has come to realize that *sekhel* will never be strong enough to fight off the deep and all-pervasive powers of *medammeh*, but that within the realm of the imagination itself there remains more room for movement than he had previously recognized.

In his earlier days Nahman had felt that what man needed was liberation *from* fantasy; only by freeing himself from the personal desires that torment him could man become sufficiently pure to stand before God. In the tales, and in the theoretical position hinted at in his last public discourse, Nahman began to propose a liberation *within* fantasy: the imagination itself had to be purified so that it could become a vehicle that would lead man back to God. Here Nahman has much in common with his English contemporary, William Blake, who, as a mystic living at the edge of the industrial revolution, sought to restore to his readers the life of dream and fantasy of which he felt they were being robbed with the onset of modernity.

Nahman and Blake may be said to represent, respectively, the final and most elaborate constructions of the fantastic imaginations of medieval Jewry and Christendom, brought forth for a last stand on the very eve of the modern era. The western tradition, about to go through a prolonged bout of subjection to the religions of scientism and materialism, was to have a long wait before its worlds of sacred fantasy could again be so fully appreciated.

Nahman's tales partake of the world of fantasy and yet go beyond it. Other Hasidic tales may in a certain way be described as "fantastic," insofar as the miracles attributed to their saintly heroes are utterly beyond belief to one who stands outside their orb of faith. Some tales go even further, being populated by such fantasy creatures as the werewolf, the *golem,* or the supernatural sorcerer; here even the Hasidic hearer was perhaps not expected to be entirely credulous. Even such tales, however, are not fantasies in their entirety. Nahman's tales go beyond both of these. Here there is no pretense that the events narrated actually ever took place. Nowhere is the name of any historic personage, place, or time, tied into the tale. There is not the slightest attempt at realism in character, plot, or narrative sequence. The *Tales* are fantastic in that their entire world, at least on the face of things, makes no pretense of being anything other than the spinning forth of their teller's imagination, using whatever elements of the folk and Kabbalistic traditions he may have absorbed. And yet the stories are hardly simply entertainments: they have about them an air of utter seriousness, and a sense that they contain a truth in them somehow other and higher than the truth of history. In this they go beyond the folktale of which they make such thorough use; the combination of folk-motif and intentional symbolism here lends to the tales a quality only to be described as *mythic.* As Nahman allowed his imagination free reign in the search for a life of sacred fantasy he, remarkably, seems to have stumbled into the very particular state of consciousness that allows for a relatively rare event in the life of the mind: the creation of myth.

In using the term "myth" to describe Nahman's tales, we may do well to keep the following three elements of definition in mind: 1) The *Tales* take place in a dimension of reality other than our own. At the same time, this reality claims to have a higher status or represent a deeper truth than that world which is the object of our everyday experience. 2) They have about them an archaic tone that lends them a certain simple dignity, allowing them to transcend the poverty of language and style in which they were recorded. 3) As distant as their characters and events may seem to us, the tales are meant to evoke in the reader a sense that it is his own inner life, a secret truth buried in the depths of *his* soul, that is being spoken of here. In short, *a myth is a tale that bespeaks an inner truth portrayed as an ancient truth.* But before going any further with such definitions it is best that we allow Nahman the storyteller or mythmaker to speak for himself, and that we continue our discussion in the context of interpretation. The first of the *Seven Beggars* begins his tale thus:

> I am a very old man, and at the same time entirely youthful. I haven't even begun to live, and yet I'm very old. It's not just I alone who say this—I have the agreement of the great eagle on it. And now I shall tell you a tale:
>
> Once there were people in a fleet of ships on the sea. A storm wind came and broke up the ships, but the people were saved and gathered together at a certain tower. They went up into the tower and there they discovered all sorts of food, drink and clothing; they found there all they needed and all the good and pleasurable things in the world.
>
> They then said that each of them should tell an old story, the story which represented the earliest thing that he could remember, from that very point where his memory began. There were both old and young people there, and they gave to the eldest among them the honor of beginning. He said: 'What can I tell you? I remember when they cut the apple from the branch.' No one quite understood what he meant by that, but the wise men agreed that this was indeed a very ancient memory. The second elder, who was just a bit younger than the first, was then given the honor. 'Is that an old tale?' he said. 'I remember that one too, but I also remember when the candle was yet burning.' They agreed that this memory was older than the first, but were puzzled to find that it was the younger man who had the older memory. They then called upon the third, who was still younger. 'I remember,' he said, 'when the fruit first began to be formed.' They agreed that this was a still older memory. The fourth, who was yet younger, said 'I remember when they carried the seed to plant the fruit.' The fifth claimed that he remembered the sages who contemplated the seed. The sixth remembered the taste of the fruit before it entered the fruit. The seventh remembered the aroma before it entered the fruit, and the eighth recalled its appearance in

> that same way. And I (said the blind beggar who was telling all this) was yet a child, but I was there too. I said to them: 'I remember all these events. But I also remember nothing *(Ikh gedenk gor nisht)*.' And they answered: 'This is indeed an older memory than all.'

The beggar goes on to explain this cryptic contest in terms of pre-natal memories: each successive speaker recalls an earlier event in his infancy or pre-natal existence. The one who remembered the appearance of the fruit was recalling his soul before it was called upon to come down into the world at all.[10] As the child opens his mouth, however, the nature of these "pre-natal" memories shifts. His memory of "nothing" has lifted the tale to a mythical plane; suddenly we realize that it is not only our individual lives being capsulized here, but the existence of the world as a whole. It is neither his prior incarnation nor some ancient event of sacred history the young-old one recalls; it is the "nothing" that precedes all of existence. The jump here is what is significant for the evocation of myth: *now "my" pre-existence reveals itself simultaneously to be that of the universe.*

Of course such a term as "myth" for these stories seems to us a contemporary critical designation, and perhaps one inappropriate to the tales' original context. We often hesitate, in any case, to apply that term to conscious literary creations of the post-medieval West. How striking, then, to find that it is Nahman himself who designates his *Sippurey Ma'asiyot* as mythic tales, and that the term "myth" is virtually a direct and simplifying translation of what Nahman says about them in his own teachings. It will be worth giving attention once again to an abstruse bit of homiletics in order to see how there emerges in Nahman a notion of reality strikingly parallel to what the contemporary historian of religion designates as *myth*. In a teaching to which we have already referred as central to an understanding of the tales, Nahman returns to the metaphor of the face, which we have previously seen him use in so intricate a way with regard to the master-disciple relationship. The Torah has seventy "faces" according to the Rabbis; every human face, adds Nahman, has some relationship to these faces or ways of interpretation. One who is out of touch with his own roots in God has, as it were, lost his face, and needs to have it restored to him:

> When you have to show a person his face, to wake him up from his sleep, that 'face' has to be garbed in tales *[lit.:* accounts of deeds—*sippurey ma'asiyot]*. The Torah has seventy faces; these are the seventy years [of the human lifespan], and each is different from all the others . . . this is the meaning of 'Lord, give life to Your deed in the midst of years' (Habbakuk 3:2). Rashi interprets 'give life' as 'awaken.' 'Your deed' refers to tales or accounts of deeds; 'the midst of years' refers to the deeds and their seventy faces or the seventy years. You wake a person up by means of tales, tales which [take place] in the midst of years, representing one or another of the

> seventy faces. But some have fallen so low that they cannot be aroused in any way [or by any face]; these can only be awakened by tales of 'days of yore' *(shanim qadmoniyot)*, from which all seventy faces and years derive their sustenance.[11]

Nahman seems to be repeating counsel often given to preachers: in order to 'reach' people and restore them to the proper path, you have to tell stories. Sooner or later the hearer will recognize himself in one or another of the preacher's tales. The tales you tell, Nahman says, should be accounts of actual events, things which happened within the "seventy years." This designation, referring ostensibly to the lifespan of an individual, also has a hidden meaning, however. Seventy years, like seven days, is a way of referring to the seven lower *sefirot*, each of which contains ten aspects. The seventy 'faces' are now the seventy masks of God as well, for it is through the seven lower *sefirot* that the divine takes on specific content and becomes the object of knowledge. The God of seventy years has some relation to the world of time and space; the God beyond these seventy is seemingly one of utter abstraction, nothing other than the primal process itself. But now Nahman makes an important switch: some people, he says, are so deeply asleep that they cannot be awakened through any of the seventy faces; these people may be approached only by tales that themselves come from the realm beyond. But how is that realm, representing the hidden godhead, which is prior to space and time themselves, translated into *stories?* Such stories must be of a uniquely mysterious quality, representing *a narrative account of that which is itself beyond the very notion of event.* The God beyond the seventy manifestations cannot be known or described, indeed can hardly be reached at all—yet Nahman claims both the need and the ability to turn it into story. Again we see Nahman the master of paradox at work. To reach into those depths and give them expression in words, and in fiction rather than in metaphysical abstractions at that—such a task seems to beyond the range of human capability. Surely it involves a stretching of the mind and of narrative language beyond where they ordinarily reach. And that is precisely what Nahman sought—a way to achieve the impossible task of giving verbal expression to the impenetrable depths. So he tells *sippurey ma'asiyot mi-shanim qadmoniyot:* of the innermost hidden rungs of divinity he fashions a prose narrative. Nahman has discovered a way to express in language what we call *myth,* the narrative account of a transcendent and primal reality. If Nahman's stories seem to speak of a different dimension in time and space, it is because they come from a realm that *precedes* both the spatial and temporal orders as we know them.

Our definition of myth has told us, however, that the depths bespoken by such narrative are the truth of the soul as well as the truth of the universe. The particular stance of Hasidism within the Kabbalistic tradition is one much concerned with mystical psychology, one which seeks frequently to read the old metaphysical language in terms of a journey within the self. Thus it is that Nahman's attempts to lend expression to the impenetrable depths must be seen in personal and psychological, as well as cosmic, terms. The "primal years" from which these stories come do indeed represent the most archaic memories, hidden fears, and unspoken fantasies of the self, as well as those of the universe.

As such, it is no wonder that the tales are highly revealing in a psychological sense and may be used by the biographer in this way. It is hard to disagree with Weiss when he claims that there is hardly a word in the tales not to be read as yet another version of Nahman's constant commentary on his life and his unique mission.[12] Even a cursory reading of certain of the tales makes it quite clear that this is the case. In them Nahman is sharing the deepest longings, fantasies—and sometimes doubts and fears—of his own soul. His conflict over the issues of faith and doubt is the central theme of *The Wise Man and the Simpleton*. His torment over the question of the legitimacy of his leadership is writ large in such tales as *The Burgher and the Pauper* and *The Two Sons*. Behind the mask of the tales he at times seeks to share his inner conflicts to a degree of frankness he would not have dared attempt in more direct forms of speech. The tales may indeed be viewed as a way Nahman found to share his most intimate self with others, perhaps confident that only the rarely perceptive hearer would perceive the suffering *ẓaddiq* behind the thick veil, suspecting the while that even such a hearer would so venerate him (the more so for this feat!) as not to pay overly much attention to the darker sides of self woven into the fabric of the tales.[13]

At the same time, Nahman's own conception of the tale goes far beyond that of self-revelation. He sees himself, we will recall, as *ẓaddiq ha-dor;* as such he has unique access to the upper lights and the secrets of the Torah, all of which flow into his generation through him alone. When such a figure reveals his most intimate self, it is hardly *just* an individual soul that is being bared. How is the hidden light ever revealed to mankind, indeed, except through the prism of the *ẓaddiq's* soul? *And this is precisely the point where the revelation is a mythic one: at the meeting-place between the truth of the soul and the truth of the cosmos.*

In the face of this self-understanding of Nahman's, certain of the discussions among critics as to whether the tales are to be read "didactically" or not seem rather beside the point. Of course their purpose is not to teach Kabbalistic ideas or symbols as such, nor are they intended as anything so simple as moral preachments. If one speaks of teaching on another level, however, a level on which it is a part of the ever-continuing process of revelation, clearly there is an element of such teaching in these tales. Nahman uses his Kabbalistic symbols, Biblical images, broken folktale plots, and all the rest as vehicles for a revelation of the mysterious inner self that is at once the self of the universe and the innermost personal self of that figure who stands at its center and embodies its mysteries within him: the *ẓaddiq* of the generation. As we have seen in so many areas, for Nahman the most essential teaching, even the most redemptive teaching, is the communication of his own self. Surely Biblical and Kabbalistic symbolism could do much to restore the imagination, and thus they are amply present in the tales. But this imaginative life will only be a *true* one insofar as it corresponds to the fantasy-life of the true *ẓaddiq*, the one who contains within his own mysterious person the secrets of the universe. An intimacy of inwardness, a sharing of dreams, between master and disciples must be created before the latter are ready for redemption. What better way to create such intimacy than by the telling of tales that will "draw the heart like water," bringing the hearer ever closer to his master's own mental orbit, the state that will most prepare him for the redemption that is soon to come.

The redemption-myth of these tales is a personal one, in that it makes a claim for the author/hero who constantly appears in them. Nahman as messiah, proto-messiah, messianic herald, what-have-you, fills the tales. Certain of the interpretations of the tales within Bratslav tradition itself—particularly those of Nathan and of Abraham Hazan—share this reading quite openly, as scholars have shown.[14]. That the redeemer figure, the prince, the messenger, the wise man, and so forth, represent Nahman is a level of the stories' meaning that we should not seek to deny. At the same time, we would do well to remember that myth by its very nature is never univalent. That which seeks to express in narrative form the life of a world beyond any ordinary sequence of time and space cannot do so unambiguously; when it loses a certain mysterious ambiguity it ceases to be myth. Those same Bratslav commentaries on the tales that find the character of Nahman veiled in them also rightly insist upon the legitimacy of multi-leveled readings of these texts.[15] One reading of a particular tale may serve to convince the reader that the hero of the plot is Nahman and none other, while a second reading may just as thoroughly persuade him that there stands before him the tale of Israel and its mission in the world, a tale of the *ẓaddiq*, or of Moses, of messiah, or the tale of every human soul in its journey through life. None of these may be eliminated as alien to Nahman's concerns or to his possible intentions in the telling of the tale. Let the interpreter, in his zeal to find the 'right' meaning, take care that he not rob the tale of its richness of ambiguity. The fact is that the mythic hero around whom these stories are written is all of these at once; any attempt to label him, whether as Nahman, Israel, Moses, messiah, or Everyman is an unnecessary limitation of one's reading. That Nahman, Moses, and messiah are somehow one in our storyteller's literary imagination has already been amply documented in this study: the soul borne by the *ẓaddiq ha-dor* is shared by all three. But that soul functions as redeemer only in that it is *also* the soul of all Israel or all mankind, the all-inclusive soul *(neshamah kelalit)* of its generation. This requires some further explanation, including perhaps a few more general remarks on myths of the redeemer.

By its very nature, myth is a concretization of abstract truth or notion in narrative form. As such, it characteristically takes the form of a *particularizing* tale, locating the general notion it wishes to convey in the life of some individual figure who best exemplifies it. In doing so, the myth does not make a claim only about that individual but rather concerning the human situation as reflected in (in the frequent language of myth: "as originated by") that individual. One who reads the Biblical story of Adam and Eve only as a tale of some ancient couple has turned the myth into legend and thereby missed the point. It is a tale of Man and Woman, of God and disobedience, concretized in those two human beings. Though entirely specific in its narrative form, the mythic intent is universal, hoping to tell us something of significance about all that first pair's descendents. The same is true—though not so readily recognizably so—in myths of the redeemer. That ancient (or future) savior, no less than any of the other classic figures who people mankind's myths, is representative of humanity as a whole and expresses its collective longings for redemption, particularized in mythic form. The specific redeemer figure of the myth does not here make his appearance chiefly to present a claim for himself. He serves rather as the embodiment of human (or Jewish or Christian or Gnostic) dreams of redemption. In the case of Christianity one may say that its *mythic* truth was perhaps best realized by the Gnostic who sought to be "no longer a Christian but a Christ," a truth periodically rediscovered by the mystics of the church in their most liberated moments. There is a level on which one must say that to seek redemption "in him alone" is to miss (or intentionally reject, viz. the orthodox church in seeking to reread myth as history) the point of the myth; if the redeemer is indeed Everyman, it is to the redeemer within the self that the myth calls one to turn. Yes, a specific claim for Nahman *is* being made in these tales, just as a claim clearly is made in Christianity for Jesus of Nazareth as *the* Christ. It may be argued that the redeemer even in the Gnostic sources is specifically other; it is from the beyond that he comes to redeem you. But all of these claims, insofar as they exist on the plane of myth rather than history, are at the same time symbolic claims and therefore universal ones. Remember: if Nahman bears the overarching soul that contains your soul within it, or of which your soul is but a specification, the relationship you have with him is not quite that of self and other. To say that "he" is redeemer hardly means that "you" are not. There is ultimately no conflict between the Nahman-centered reading of these tales and the most universal reading: as Nahman is seeker, messenger, lost prince wandering in the woods, and redeemer or repairer of the cosmos, so is all Israel (of which he stands at the center), so are all humans, and so is the one who hears the tale.[16]

So far our general guidelines for a reading of Nahman's tales.[17] The approach is an eclectic one, but one which should yield a rich and authentic reading. Its essential components boil down to the following: 1) thorough biographical familiarity; 2) a comprehension of the goals and values Nahman articulated in his writing and teaching outside the tales, particularly around the theme of redemption; 3) an attempt to see how Nahman viewed his role as storyteller and a translation of some of his terms of self-understanding *(medammeh, shanim qadmoniyot)* into our contemporary idiom (fantasy, myth); 4) a rejection of any unilinear interpretation of the tales in favor of an openness to multiple suggestions: 5) a specific understanding of the nature of redeemer-myths which *of necessity* calls for a simultaneously multileveled reading of these texts. Using the tools of understanding here suggested, we shall now turn to an examination of three tales in the *Sippurey Ma'asiyot*. We have intentionally not chosen the tales that have been most worked over by interpreters (e.g. *The Lost Princess, The Wise Man and the Simpleton)*. These tales are also among the more obvious, at least in their initial layer of meaning. We choose from the collection one long tale, *The King and the Emperor*, one short tale, *The Portrait*, and one episode from the tale of the *Seven Beggars: A Little That Contains a Lot*. In the first case we shall have to content ourselves with a plot summary to precede our discussion; in the case of the two shorter pieces, the tale will be translated in full.

There follows a summary of *The King and the Emperor*, the second tale in Nahman's *Sippurey Ma'asiyot:*

> There were once a king and an emperor, both of whom were childless. Each sought various remedies for his condition, but to no avail. It once happened, while each of them was out in search of healing, that the two of them met at an inn. Discovering their shared plight, they agreed that should one's wife give birth to a son and the other's to a daughter, the two children would marry. After a time, the emperor's wife did indeed give birth to a daughter and the king's wife to a son. But time passed and the pact was forgotten.
>
> As the two children grew up, it happened that they were sent to the same school. There they met, fell in love, and were secretly married, in token of which the king's son gave the emperor's daughter a ring. Both of the young people were then called home. Though she said nothing of her secret marriage, the princess refused all suitors who came to seek her hand. The prince, back at his father's palace, fell ill with longing, and no one knew how to heal him. Finally the servant who had been with him at school revealed the secret. Hearing of this marriage, the king recalled his old pact with the emperor, and sent his son to claim his beloved and bride by right.

The emperor, however, sought to test the young man by placing him in a room with a mass of state papers, to see whether he would be a fit ruler. Looking up from the papers, to which he was in any case too lovesick to give much attention, he spotted his wife through a mirror. On seeing her he fell into a faint. She roused him and the two of them fled away on a ship across the seas.

After traveling for some time, they went ashore and lay down to rest. As she went to sleep, the princess gave her ring to her mate for safekeeping. When he saw that she was about to awaken, he put the ring on the ground beside her. They got up and went back to the boat, but once there realized that she had left the ring behind. The prince went out to look for it, but could not find the spot where they had been. He wandered further and further until he became utterly lost. Finally seeing a town before him, he went there and hired himself out as a servant. What else was there for him to do? The princess, while looking for her beloved, also got lost. Eventually she sat down by the shore of the sea, hoping to stop passing boats in search of news of him. Meanwhile she ate the fruit of trees that grew by the seashore, and for protection she climbed up in a tree at night.

Now there was a certain wealthy merchant who had grown old and whose son wanted to seek his fortune on his own. He persuaded his father to give him a ship loaded with merchandise, and he would set sail in search of markets. Having succeeded in his mission, he was on his way home when his ship sailed by the clump of trees where the princess lay. First attracted to the trees as a resting place, he then saw a person at the top of a tree. Discovering a young woman, he sought to coax her down into his ship. She agreed on the condition that he not touch her until they reached his home and were properly married. Finding her to be a woman of breeding—she played music and spoke several languages—he rejoiced at the prospect of marriage, and they sailed toward his home. As they approached the port she convinced him that a proper lady of her status should receive an appropriate welcome from his family and that the sailors who had brought them home should also be allowed to participate in the festivities. Thus it was that the young merchant went ashore in search of his family, the sailors became drunk on the fine old wine that was on board and also went ashore in their drunken stupor, and the princess was left alone on the ship. She cut the ship loose from its mooring and sailed away. When the merchant's father and his entourage arrived and saw the ship was gone they were greatly angered; they banished the young merchant and forced him to become a wanderer.

A certain king was building himself a palace by the shore of the sea. As the princess sailed by he saw her and was attracted. Once again she persuaded the suitor not to touch her until marriage; this time she even decided it was appropriate that she continue to dwell upon her ship in his harbor. As he set to work building a special palace in her honor, she asked that eleven ladies-in-waiting be provided her. Eleven daughters of eleven noblemen were brought to her, and the king in his enthusiasm ordered that a special palace be commissioned for each of them. One day she had her ladies on board ship where they were singing and playing for her. She offered them some of her special wine and when they were asleep, she once again cut loose from shore and sailed off, taking the eleven young women with her. When their fathers found out what had happened, they banished the king; he too became a wanderer.

When the ladies awoke, she convinced them that they were all victims of an unfortunate accident, but that they now had no choice but to remain together. Sailing onward they came across an island in the sea. The island turned out to be inhabited by twelve pirates, who at first threatened to kill the women and plunder their ship. The princess suggested to them that this was foolish; they could marry the twelve of them and have themselves fine, cultured wives, as well as all the bounty. On the night of the first of the twelve intended wedding feasts, she entertained the pirates with her fine old wine, and when they were fast asleep, each of the women chopped off the head of her intended. They then raided the pirates' store, traded their former cargo for gold and jewels, and set sail once again. At this point they decided they no longer wanted to dress as women, so they made themselves men's garments—in the German fashion—and set out in disguise.

There was an old king who had married off his son and had just given him his kingdom. Thinking that his new queen should get used to the sea travel, lest they ever have to flee that way, the two of them, along with a large party of courtiers, went out for a sail. During their voyage the king, in a playful mood, climbed up to the top of the mast. At that moment the princess and her ladies approached. Seeing a man atop the mast in a nearby ship, she showed the ladies a trick and burned him from a distance with a reflecting glass. The young king fell into the sea and drowned. His party, at their wits' end from grief, saw the other ship approaching. Having no idea that their troubles came from there, they hailed it down in hope of finding a doctor. Though she denied that she was indeed a physician, the princess impressed them greatly by showing them that it was their king's brain that had been burned. They respected her greatly, and, thinking that she was a man, eventually suggested that she marry the now-widowed queen. After some time and another bout of wine, this marriage took place, and the disguised princess was pronounced king of the land.

Her first command was that a large wedding feast be prepared, and that every wayfarer and stranger in the land be forced to attend. She then ordered that fountains be erected outside each town and that her picture be placed over each fountain. Guards were to be stationed nearby and anyone who looked too long or hard at the picture was to be brought immediately before the king. Thus the three wanderers were brought before her; her original spouse, the merchant's son, and the [first] young king. To the king she returned the eleven noblemen's daughters, thus enabling him to regain his kingdom. To the merchant's son she gave the ship laden with the pi-

> rates' treasure, allowing him to return in triumph to his father. And she and the king's son—her true bridegroom—returned to their home. Blessed is the Lord forever. Amen. Amen.

Such is a summary of the tale as Nahman told it, or at least as recorded by his faithful disciple. It must be admitted that the plot, suffering terribly from overcomplexity, has a certain comic-opera quality about it. In order to show how far the temper of Bratslav is from such a reading of it, perhaps we should begin with a few lines from the brief commentary (one long paragraph) by Nahman of Cheryn:

> The secret of this tale has not yet been interpreted. What may we say of it, especially we who know nothing of hidden things? . . . The precise hidden secret which lies in each and every word and detail of this tale—and of all the tales—is indeed 'deep, deep; who can find it?' (Eccles. 7:24)[18]

Despite the disclaimer of access to secrets, the third generation Bratslav leader does give us some very helpful hints. The story is about the "holy supernal union," he tells us, which was planned from the beginning, but was then lost and forgotten by both sides. He also tells us that the ring and the wine are well-known symbols, and hints that they will provide some further key to the story's meaning.

One of the interesting things about this tale is that it is one of the few in which it cannot be claimed that Nahman is the chief character. This seems rather clearly to be a tale of the wandering *shekhinah;* it provides a complement to his earlier tale of *The Lost Princess.* In that tale the princess played a completely passive role; the adventure was that of the king's assistant—Nahman, Israel, everyman, what-have-you—seeking to liberate her. Here Nahman shows us the other side of the coin: just as his hero wanders the face of the earth in search of the *shekhinah,* so, too, does the exiled *shekhinah* herself wander in search of her beloved. She has but one purpose as she goes through the world, a purpose she strives to fulfill with a singlemindedness that may include some cruelty. All she desires is to be reunited with her original intended; the affections of all other suitors are only to be used as steppingstones along the way.

Nahman's willingness to show this harsh side of the *shekhinah* may at first seem strange; our associations with that figure are usually those of a passionate longing for the God above her and bountiful motherliness toward the world below. But a certain quality of fierceness, even bordering on the demonic, is not absent from the portrait of the *shekhinah* in the *Zohar.*[19] The figure of the demonic or devouring mother-goddess, well-known in Indian tradition, is occasionally to be found in Kabbalistic literature. It is no surprise that the fantasy life of Nahman, whose problems in relationship to women were central in his mind, would find room for this aspect of the feminine.

If one pole of the story is clear, the other retains the ambiguity that we claim is essential to the mythic tale. An interpreter following the methodological principles enunciated by recent scholarship on the tales (Weiss, Piekarz, Dan) would run it through as follows: the true mate of the princess is the soul of the messiah. This soul, which was created before the world came into being, is also the soul of Nahman in this generation, as it has been the soul of Moses and other *ẓaddiqey ha-dor*. The episode of losing the ring represents Eden, from which both man (Adam/Messiah) and the *shekhinah* went forth as wanderers. The other suitors represent false, would-be messiahs; perhaps the figures of Jesus, Muhammad, and Sabbatai Sevi could be listed as the three who attempt to gain her hand. She, however, has merely used them along the way, and now, in Nahman/messiah, is reunited with her true beloved.

There is no essential flaw in such an interpretation; we do not claim that it is "wrong" in any particular way. At the same time we resist the designation of such a reading as "right," as *the* meaning that truly lay in Nahman's mind, conscious or unconscious, as he spun forth this tale. There are certainly other readings highly plausible as such tales go. Let us agree for a moment that the hero is that wandering soul of the messiah, with whom the *shekhinah* is to be reunited at the end of time. Remember that the tale was told sometime between the summer of 1806 and the fall of 1807, the same fall Nahman set off on the journey to Navritch, seeking to flee his disciples altogether. Suppose he has discovered in the failure of his messianic attempt that he is not the one he thought he was, and that redemption has once again slipped away. The tale would then place Nahman as one of the unsuccessful suitors, each of whom thought for a while that redemption lay within his hands, only to discover that the *shekhinah* had tricked him, perhaps in order to use him as a pawn, in some inexplicable way, along her journey. This reading would fit the details of the *particular* time in Nahman's life far better than the first reading, which relates to a much more *general* idea of Nahman's view of self throughout his lifetime. The *shekhinah*, manifest in such a tale, indeed *is* dangerous; Nahman has just been badly burned in pursuit of her.

But there is no need for us to remain wedded to the notion of the messianic soul as hero of this tale. Perhaps the hero is Israel, the *shekhinah's* true mate. Promised to one another before they were born (Israel arose in God's mind before creation); the school where they learned together represents the Torah; the place of their meeting is Sinai, and the field where they lie down is the land of Israel. The ring is the covenant of marriage between them; its loss, then, symbolizes the destruction of the Temple, beginning the period of mutual exile and wandering. The other suitors represent the other nations who seek the *shekhinah's* hand: she may give power to one, dominion to another for a while, but only as a ruse toward establishing the true messianic kingdom of Israel. The redemption motif in the tale remains, but a personal claim for Nahman is no longer found in it.

From the national we may also go to the universal level. The hero is the true soul of everyman, the object of the *shekhinah's* longings. Alienated from man by the fact of his birth into the earthly body, she wanders through the cosmos in search of him. Angels offer her "wealth" and "beauty"; demons threaten to kill her—but it is man alone whom she truly seeks. In a well-known parable attributed to the BeSHT, the king's true son is the one who may pass through chambers of glittering but illusory silver and gold, knowing that it is the king alone he is to seek. Now the *shekhinah* is shown to pass that same test, in converse fashion. She, too, will reject all that glitters as she remains faithful to the search for her true beloved, the king's son who has become a servant, the soul of man fallen into its lowly corporeal state.

The tale makes sense on all three levels: personal, national and universal. For the Kabbalist, whose universe is often laid out visually in a series of concentric circles, this is no surprise. As to which of the personal readings is more accurate—Nahman as true beloved or Nahman as rejected suitor—the author has succeeded in preserving his most private thoughts.

Perhaps one more pattern of interpretation should here be briefly mentioned. The psychologist, and particularly the Jungian, would have us internalize our reading of such a tale. The entire tale takes place within the self; the hero and the *shekhinah* are the inner male/female polarities. Thus Nahman's first two tales must be read as a pair: inner male and female ever in search of one another for completion of the self. This longing for inner wholeness, a theme so utterly familiar to the reader of Nahman, is of course projected by religion into the scenes of history and cosmos, and is discussed in the language of an externalized redemption. But the primary adventure, the object of such a tale, is the longing for fulfillment within the self.[20]

We need have no objection to such a reading, which may be applied with considerable ease to most or all of Nahman's tales, so long as its claim also is not an exclusive one. Surely it was the inner self that was the focus of all Nahman's most intimate concerns, and he would gladly admit that these tales came to him from deep within. It is precisely this sort of material the depth-psychologist seeks out, and we should not be surprised to find that its tools will lend further insight into the meaning of these tales.

The Portrait*

There was once a king who had a wise counselor. One day the king approached him and said: 'There is a certain king who seals his documents

*Translated by Elliot Ginsburg

with the words: "A great and awesome man, a man of truth and humility." I know that this king is in fact a great man. For his kingdom is surrounded by a sea and a fleet of ships with cannons roams this sea, keeping people from drawing near. And at at the edge of this sea there is a swampy bog and men stand in danger of drowning there. This swamp encircles the kingdom and the only way to walk through the mire is on a narrow path, wide enough for only one person. Here, too, cannons are stationed. When one comes to do battle, cannons are poised to shoot. And so, one cannot draw near the king. [All this I do know] Yet, I don't know why this king signs his documents "A man of truth and humility." This remains a mystery to me. I want you, counselor, to bring me a portrait of this king.'

Now the counselor's king had the portraits of all other kings, but no king had a portrait of this great and humble king, for he is hidden from men. He sits behind a curtain and is far from the people of his land.

The wise man went to that land. He thought: 'I really must discover the nature of this land. What better way to find out than through the pranks and humor of the land?' To really know the heart of something, one must be able to mock that thing, to make fun of it. Of course, there are several types of mockery and jest [for humor may be used in many ways]. One sort is when one wholly intends to hurt his friend through his words. When the friend lifts his eyes and looks back, the prankster says: 'Oh, I was only joking.' As it says, 'Like a madman who casts firebrands, arrows and death, so is the person who deceives his friend and says: "Am I not in sport?" ' (Proverbs 26:11) [Then there is another sort of jest:] We all know that one may joke good-naturedly, with the best of intentions, and still one's friend may be wounded by these joking words. And there are still other sorts of humor and jest . . .

Now there is a country that contains within it all countries. And in that country there is a city that contains all the cities of that country that contains all countries. And in that city there is a house that contains all houses of that city that contains all the cities of that country that contains all countries. And in that house is a man who bears within him all of this. There is one there who is laughing; he clowns and pulls all the pranks of that land.

The wise man gathered together a great sum of money and went to that house. And there he saw that they were acting out all sorts of pranks and jokes. From the pranks he understood that the country was shot through with lies. Through coming to know the humor of the land, he saw how they cheated and shortchanged men in business; he saw the 'justice' of the magistrate court, whose judges were full of lies and took bribes. He went to a higher court. And there too, all was lies. Through the joking and jesting, they showed all these things. So the wise man understood from this that the entire land was fraught with lies and deception, stripped of all truth.

> The wise man left the house and did business in the land. He let himself be cheated, and he sought justice before the judges. And they were filled with lies. If on one day someone gave them a bribe, by the next day they wouldn't even recognize him. So the wise man proceeded to a higher court. And there too, all was lies. He went to the Senate and the men there were full of lies and bribes.
>
> Finally, the wise man came to king himself. He asked the king: 'Over whom are you king? For this land is shot through with lies; not a shred of truth can be found.' And he began to tell of the lies of the kingdom. When the king heard his words he pressed his ear to the curtain that concealed him and listened intently. For he was astonished that there was a man in his kingdom who could recognize the lies. Now the royal officers who heard the man's words were enraged. But the wise man went on, enumerating the lies of the land. He added: 'One might think that the king, too, would be like his people; that he too would love falsehood. But now I see that you are a man of truth. And precisely because of this you are far from them. For you cannot bear the lies of the kingdom.'
>
> The wise man began to praise the king exceedingly. And the king was very humble. For his greatness and his humility were one. Such is the way of a humble man. The more he is praised and magnified, the smaller and more humble he becomes. And as the wise man offered more praise, exalting and magnifying the king, the king grew smaller and more humble till he became nothing at all. And at that moment the king could not withhold himself any longer, and he tore open the curtain to see this wise man, as though to say: who is this person who knows and understands all this?
>
> The face of the king was revealed, and the wise man saw him. He made a portrait and brought it to the king.

The story confronts us as a series of puzzles. Who is this king who collects portraits of all the kings in the world, but is missing just this one? Who is the wise man sent to obtain it, and what is the true nature of his mission? And who is the jokester at the center of the world who helps the wise man on his way? How does the hero get through the barriers of sea and swamp and suddenly arrive in the market-place of that kingdom? What are the lies, the officials, and most puzzling of all, who is the king at the end of the tale and what does the wise man see when the curtain is cast aside?

The tale is almost too brief and somehow fragmented. The ending is abrupt, though (unlike several others in the collection) the story does not seem to be incomplete. Even before it is understood, however, this tale has about it a promise of profundity somehow greater than that of *The King and the Emperor*. The unusually defined mission, the strange encounter with the laughing man at the center, and the unique confrontation with the hidden king at the end are all calculated to increase the hearer's sense of mystery and anxiety, fairly forcing him to deep reflection on the meaning of the tale. The light and somewhat entertaining quality we encountered in the former tale is here no longer to be found; all one can do upon hearing this tale is confront one's astonishment and begin to seek out its meaning.

In contrast also to the great complexity of the previous story, here we have before us a plot containing a mere four characters: the original king, the wise man, the figure at the center, and the king of the kingdom of lies. Our familiarity with the Midrashic/Kabbalistic legacy upon which Nahman drew immediately makes us seek to identify the king as God: this is one of the most common stock images of that tradition. As soon as we try to make such a move, however, we are forced to ask ourselves: "Which king?" Is God the portrait-collector who sends the hero on his way, or is God the one he discovers at the end of the tale? Since he is to bring the portrait of the latter back to the former, it hardly seems likely that they are one and the same—or does it?

Further details woven into the story seem to make it fairly clear that the king who is discovered behind the curtain must surely be identified as God. He signs his name, we are told, in ways that clearly echo classic Jewish descriptions of God. He dwells behind a curtain so as to hide from the lies constantly uttered in his name: a rather striking rendition of the classic Jewish theodicy, *hester panim,* the hiding of God's face. God is hidden because He can't stand men's lies; a sharp remark, which anticipates the bitter wit of Rabbi Mendel of Kotzk.

The confrontation with God, the culmination of the hero's search, is a particularly fascinating one. Reaching Him, at the far end of the kingdom of lies, one reaches only that curtain behind which He is said to dwell. It is then that prayer begins—and what a strange half-parody and half-defense of traditional Jewish liturgy, with its highly repetitive words of praise, has Nahman given us! Such prayer's goal is nothing less than forcing God out of hiding. Rather than doing so by supplication, here prayer so embarrasses His humble Self as to force Him to cast aside the curtain! What Nahman further seems to have in mind here is again the notion of *ẓimẓum:* revelation requires an act of divine self-contraction, as the fullness of the presence cannot be known to man. He dramatically adds that this self-limitation verges on threatening God's very existence, and it is only at the edge of self-annihilation that He reveals Himself to the seeker. This is another aspect of that same highly radical version of *ẓimẓum* we encountered in the preceding chapter.

Accepting this identification of the king behind the curtain as God, we see the kingdom of lies as the world, or at least the world of human affairs. The wise man, of course, is our well-known hero, who again may be seen as concretely as "Nahman" or as abstractly as "the seeker." It has been suggested that the sea and the dangerous narrow path through the swamp surrounding the kingdom represent the womb and the birth-canal; the seeker's soul is *born* into the kingdom of lies. He is able to best it, however, because he turns to the one at the center who knows to make light of it and not to take its folly seriously. This wizard-figure appears in several of Nahman's tales: in *The Two Sons* he lives in the forest, in a house suspended in the air; in the *Seven Beggars* he is represented by each of the six deformed narrators; here he lives at the center of the world and laughs at all its lies. He is a prototype of the *ẓaddiq*, of whom Nahman has told us elsewhere that he can help find what you have lost and can laugh at the entire world.[21]

So far the tale fits together rather nicely, and does not badly as an allegorical folk-tale plot of the wise man in search of the hidden king, helped by a wizard along the way. This works until we try to deal with our fourth character, the king with whom the story opens. This figure, too, as it turns out, can be none but God. Who else would Nahman dare to designate as the king who sends the seeker's soul on its journey into the world? But with this designation, the story again becomes entirely perplexing. Since Nahman's monotheism can safely be presumed, how can the two kings both be God? What does it mean to say that the Lord is lacking His own portrait? And—when the curtain is finally lifted at life's end—could it be that nothing has been accomplished, that the seeker sees before him the very one who sent him? Is life then not some terrible trick, a game played out by a God who wants nothing but endless praises?

In order to understand what Nahman is doing here, a few reminders on Kabbalistic theology are important. Kabbalism represents a highly anthropocentric world view, in which the participation of man in the redemptive process is viewed as essential. This is a part of the divine self-limitation central to the Kabbalists' view of Creation; the keys to the universe are given over to man. Man's redemptive task may be described as the restoration of the *shekhinah*, the uplifting of the divine sparks, or the defeat of the forces of evil, but it always has to do with a reestablishment of the primal harmony, which has been disturbed. The pre-Hasidic Kabbalist generally placed his emphasis on the collective character of this redemption-work; while the origin of each soul was recognized, the point was that all of Israel had to work together and cumulatively through history in order to effect the redemption. In Hasidism, however, much more emphasis was placed upon the particular task of the individual: because your soul comes from such-and-such a root, and complicated by the fact that your soul has had a particular set of experiences in its prior incarnations, there are bits of divinity in the world that can be uplifted by you and you alone. These sparks, which God in His providence has caused to come your way through people, objects, and places you encounter (for without this providential help the task would be impossibly difficult!) have been waiting through time for you, their redeemer, to arrive.

The making of the king's portrait is yet another way of speaking about this work of redemption, one especially appropriate to Nahman, who is so occupied with images of the face. The portrait-gallery is full except for the portrait you and only you can contribute. The seeker goes through life, stumbling about in the world of lies, until he finally returns to that world from which he was sent, bearing with him a new portrait of the king, one that could be painted only at the end of that lifetime. The new portrait of God bears upon it the totality of insight, suffering, and joy the soul has undergone on its journey; it is by no means inconceivable that Nahman had yet another of his many mirrors in mind at the end of the tale, and that the hero, casting aside the curtain, takes his own self-portrait back with him as a new likeness of the king.[22]

Given this explanation of the tale, we may perhaps go a bit further in our investigation of Nahman's reappearing hero. Here it seems to make most sense to view the hero as everyman rather than as Nahman alone. While it would be hypothetically possible to say that only *ẓaddiqim* paint the portraits that fill the king's gallery, there seems to be no good reason to limit the tale in this way. But if the point of the tale is that each person has his own portrait to paint (or his own tale to tell), might that not tell us something about how the central character is to be seen in the other tales as well? Nahman is the author of the tales, and is one who believes completely in the thoroughly personal character of religious teaching. These are *his* tales; of course he is to emerge as the central character in them. That is not to say that these are the only tales worth telling, or that the hearer might not find in them inspiration to spin forth *his own* world of sacred fantasy, one in which he, rather than Nahman, would clearly be the central figure. One side of Nahman believed that all the disciple needed to do was imitate or mirror the life of the *ẓaddiq*, but there also continued to exist in him an awareness of the level on which each person would have to undertake the search on his own.

Our third extract is an episode from the *Seven Beggars*, the longest and most ambitious of Nahman's tales. Before offering this text for comment, a few words should be said about the story as a whole and its complicated literary framework. What we have in the *Seven Beggars* is a series of tales (there are six; the seventh was never told) told by a series of seemingly deformed beggars who are performing at a wedding feast. These tales are set in a dual framework, however, neither part of which is completed at the end of the story.[23]

The tale begins with a narrative about a certain prince who suffered from depressions and loss of faith. We have quoted a portion of this narrative elsewhere (p.292), and the reader is here encouraged to look at it again. That story breaks off suddenly, and there begins a tale of two children wandering in the woods, joining up with a band of beggars, and getting married. At the wedding-feast, which was made from the beggars' share of the king's birthday banquet, each beggar offered his own seeming deformity as a gift. The last beggar, who was lame, does not appear; it has been suggested that this beggar represented Nahman—"I may seem lame to you but I am a true dancer"—or perhaps Nahman as messiah, and thus is saved up for the end of time. Apparently, what was supposed to happen at the end of the tale was that the beggar couple, now blessed with all seven gifts of inner powers, would turn to the prince and be able to offer him some form of healing. Thus this story, too, is one of *tiqqun;* every episode in it, as well as the frame-story as a whole, may be seen as one aspect or another of the longing for redemption.

Kabbalistic symbols are used here as in the rest of Nahman's tales, but by the end of his career as storyteller it becomes clear that he is employing them only in a rather general and suggestive way: The young pair might perhaps represent male and female in God, or God and Israel, but in that case at least the male child should be one of the seven beggars rather than one who receives from them. The seven beggars might in a general way represent the seven lower *sefirot* or the "seven shepherds" of Kabbalistic lore (the three patriarchs, Moses, Aaron, Joseph, and David), but no rigid linking of each beggar to one of these figures can be found without doing violence to the whole.

In this case it seems that an inward reading of this story might be most suggestive. The prince who appears at the outset is obviously Nahman; no more poignant self-description can be found anywhere in his writings. (Of course this prince, afflicted by depression and constantly wavering between faith and doubt, can also be seen as Israel in the generation of the *ḥaskalah* or humanity as a whole.) In introspection he discovers the "two children in the woods," the eternal pair, inner male and female, the self and the object of the self's presumed desires, standing on the verge of nuptial union. Nahman has here described the place within man that responds to the *hieros gamos* motif in myth and fantasy, the moment of union between the eternal pair. The union here cannot be completed, however, for the two find that they are still filled with longings reaching beyond themselves. They thus turn to seven inner wizards, each of whom reaches into the depths of the soul and brings to expression another aspect of these primal longings. The tone is set by the first beggar, the one who knows the nothing that precedes all memory, and the others, each with his tale of the great contest, follow in his wake.

The fifth beggar:

> On the fifth day of the wedding-feast they were still rejoicing, and they remembered the hunchbacked beggar. They longed for him and thought: 'If

only we could bring him here! If he were only here our joy would really be great!' At that he came along and said: 'Here I am: I've come to your wedding.' He fell upon them in embrace and kissed them, saying: 'Previously, I gave you the blessing that you be like me. Now I give it to you as a wedding gift. I am not hunchbacked at all. In fact, I have such shoulders that they are called "a little that contains a lot." And others who know agree with me on that.'

'There once took place a conversation in which people were boasting about this thing; each one who was there said that he was the most "little that contains a lot." Now one of the people who made such a claim was just laughed at; all the others seemed to have pretty reasonable things to say. But my "little that contains a lot" was more so than anybody else's.'

'One of them said that his own mind was "a little that contains a lot." He was able to carry around in his mind some ten thousand people, along with all their needs, all their actions, and every move they made. All of this he carried in his head, and so he thought he must be the "little that contains a lot." But everyone laughed at him, saying that those people were nothing and in fact he was nothing as well.'

'Another person spoke up and said: I've seen a little that contains a lot! I once saw a mountain piled up high with garbage and fesces. I couldn't imagine where all that junk came from until a man who was sitting next to the mountain said: "That's all from me." That man sat there all the time and threw all his garbage, all the leftovers from his food and drink on the pile. He also defecated there, until finally all his refuse grew mountain-high. Now this man must have been "a little that contains a lot," because look how much junk came out of him! (This is the same "little that contains a lot" as that of the one who carried all those people in his mind.)

'Another claimed that this quality belonged to him. It seems that he owned a very fruitful tract of land in the country. If you added up all the fruit that this land brought forth, the fruit would take up more space than the land itself. This land, therefore, must be "a little that contains a lot" since it brought forth more fruit than it itself could contain. People liked what he said, for this indeed did seem to be a case of a little containing a lot.

'Another said that he owned an orchard of fruit trees. Since it was such a lovely place, many people, even some nobles, would go to take walks there. Especially in the summer a great number of people found their way to his orchard. Now really there was no way that all those people could have been contained in that orchard at once, so this too was a case of "a little that contained a lot." And this answer also seemed to make sense.

'Another said that his own speech was "a little that contained a lot." He was the private secretary of a great king. "A great many people came to him: one came with praises of the king, another came along with some request or other, and the like. Surely the king couldn't be expected to hear them all out. I have the ability to reduce all their talk to just a very few words; I say those few words to the king, and all of their words, whether praises, petitions, or anything else, are contained within mine. So my speech is 'a little that contains a lot' ".

'Someone else there answered that in his case it was his silence that contained a lot. There were people who hurled accusations against him and gossiped about him in terribly malicious ways. But as much as they did this, he remained silent, answering all their claims against him by silence alone. So his silence was "a little that contains a lot."

'There was yet another who claimed to be "a little that contains a lot." There was a certain poor blind man one who was very tall. This fellow who was making the claim was a really small person, and he would lead the blind man around. Since he was so small but led such a big person, one who could slip and fall if he weren't there to guide him, it was he, so he said, who was "a little that contained a lot."

'Now I (said the hunchback who was telling this tale) was there too. I told them that the truth was that each of them was "a little that contained a lot," since I knew what each of them really had in mind. "This last fellow," I said, "the one who prides himself on leading around that tall blind man, is really the greatest of you all. And yet I am still much higher than any of you. The one who leads the blind man around—he means to say that he leads the moon. The moon is blind and has no light of its own. This man, even though he's so small, leads the moon around and keeps the world going, for the world is in need of the moon. He is truly "a little that contains a lot." But my "little that contains a lot," I told them, was way above any of theirs. And here's the proof:

'A group of people was once trying to figure out the following problem: Since every animal has its own shade, and a particular shady place where it wants to rest, and since every single bird has a special branch on which it seeks to light, they wanted to know whether a tree could be found under which all the animals could agree to seek shade and on the branches of which all the birds of heaven could dwell together. They discovered that there was such a tree and they wanted to go to it. You can't imagine how great the joy would be at such a tree: a place where all the birds and beasts could live together and not a single one be harmed. All the animals would somehow get along and play together; that would certainly be one joyous place!

'When they tried to find out which way they had to go to get to that tree, however, an argument broke out among them. One said you had to go east to get there, another said it was to the west. One said one way and the other just the opposite, until no one could decide among them. Then a certain wise man came along and said: "Why are you so concerned with *how* to get to the tree? First you should find out who the people are who can go there." Not everyone was able to go to that tree; only those who shared the tree's special qualities could get there. That tree had three roots: faith, awe, and humility; truth was the trunk of the tree. The branches went forth from these, and no one who did not possess these qualities could get there. Now the members of this group were very close to one another, and they were not satisfied to be separated, with some going to the tree and others being left behind. But not all of them were found worthy; only a few of them contained the qualities of the tree. They therefore all decided to stay where they were and wait until those who had not been found fit had sufficiently worked on themselves so that they, too, could approach the tree. This they did, and through hard work they all attained to the needed qualities. Now they found that they were all of one mind, and they decided on a single path as the way to the tree.

'They walked along that path for a certain distance until they were able to see the tree from far off. When they looked further they saw that this tree did not exist in space at all. The tree took no space. But since it was not in space, how could one ever approach it?

'I too (the hunchback, that is) was there among them. I said to them: "I can bring you to the tree. This tree does not occupy space at all; it is higher than any space. Even 'a little that contains a lot' is still spatial, for even though the small space contains more than it should, there is a certain space involved. But my (that is, the hunchback's) 'little that contains a lot' reaches to the very edge of space, beyond which there is no space at all." (For this hunchback was a kind of intermediary between space and that which is beyond space altogether. His was the highest aspect of "a little that contains a lot," really the end of space, beyond which the word "space" does not exist, for it is really transcendent. That was why he could carry them into that which was above space. Understand this.)

'I took them and carried them there to the tree. So you see that I have agreement on this, that mine is the highest rung of "a little that contains a lot." (That was why he appeared hunchbacked—because he carried so many upon him, being "a little that contained a lot.") Now I give this to you as a wedding present—that you be like me.'

And there was very great joy and gladness there.

The phrase 'a little that contains a lot' is taken from an ancient *midrash*,[24] where it is used as an explanation of such Biblical feats as the gathering of the waters on the second day of Creation, Moses' handful of ash bringing the whole plague of boils (Ex. 9:8), and the assembly of all Israel in the tabernacle and at the rock Moses struck. In each of these places there is a problem of a small space containing more than seems possible, and in each case the rabbis conclude that there took place another instance of the miracle whereby 'a little contained a lot.'

Nahman begins his account by one of his nastiest barbs against popular Hasidism. The first contestant is a *rebbe*, one who prides himself on being able to carry about the concerns and needs of so many disciples in his mind. Nahman reprimands the *rebbe* for boasting of mere quantity: carrying around so many worthless followers in your head is no better than sitting next to your own great heap of garbage. Quantity of *ḥasidim*, Nahman was at pains to say, proves nothing but quantity itself.

The next four contestants (here, too, there are seven) are a bit more difficult to identify specifically, and perhaps should not be labeled at all. The secretary of the king sounds either like the author of the prayer-book or the *rebbe's* assistant who writes out petitions for prayer. It is also within the realm of possibility that all seven are *rebbes* of various types. The seventh contestant, the one who leads the blind man, is a kind of hidden *ẓaddiq* figure. He has appeared previously in the third day's tale as the true man of grace, giving a day to the world's heart when it is about to run out of time. In both cases he quietly and humbly does that task which allows the world to go on living.

The hunchback in this tale presents, like all the other wizards, an aspect of Nahman's own self. Here he is Nahman's ideal of the *ẓaddiq*, as opposed to the false *ẓaddiq* who appeared as the first contestant. Rather than boasting about all the people he can carry around in his mind, this *ẓaddiq* works only with those who have already prepared themselves by hard work to come along most of the way. Bratslav remains an elite path; not all are ready for the *ẓaddiq* to help them in that final step. He is not interested in vast numbers; his 'little that contains a lot' has rather to do with the *quality* of what he can do for his disciples: he can help them to transcend space, if they are ready to do so.

We have already seen Nahman attest to his belief that both time and space are the result of illusion and can thus be transcended altogether. In the tales he seeks to *do* what he speaks of theoretically in the *Liqquṭim*. The illusion of space in particular is one constantly troubling to Nahman's religious consciousness. He feels *far* from God; he is at pains to *cross over* the great void; heart and spring are filled with longing because they are *distant* from one another, forced by the tyranny of space to remain at opposite ends of the universe. The *ẓaddiq* who can truly redeem must be able to point up the illusory character of space, and thus enable his followers to transcend it.

The *ẓaddiq's* ability to 'leap out' of space is probably related to old traditions of *qefiẓat ha-derekh*,[25] immediate transportation from one place to another by supernatural means, an ability widely held by *ḥasidim* to belong to their masters. Such traditions, however, are not truly transcendent of space, as the hunchback points out. As much as space has been reduced by such feats, it has not been obliterated altogether. Here as elsewhere Nahman seeks a spiritualizing transformation of a popular or magical *ẓaddiq* attribution; his *qefiẓat ha-derekh* will not be some mere 'rapid transit' trick, but a way to transcendence. The leap out of space will bring man back to the Tree of Life, the ultimate symbol of utopian redemption. At the same time, that tree is represented in this world by the Torah, "a tree of life to them that grasp her" (Prov.3:18). In Moses' day the Torah was kept in the tabernacle's ark, of which the Talmud already said that it existed in a miraculous manner, not being of any measure at all in the realm of space.[26] The *ẓaddiq,* Moses and messiah of his generation, is one who can bring man to the Torah, help him to overcome his feeling of distance from God, and restore him to the tree of life.

The motif of spiritual quest is not a common one in the literature of Judaism. The idea that human life is a constant search for a hidden God would have struck most pre-modern Jewish authors as a rather strange one. God has already spoken, already revealed Himself and issued His command. Your task is to do His will, to live in the light of a revelation that has already taken place, and at which your soul was present. The Jew, who has already stood at the foot of Sinai, does not usually see himself as pilgrim.

If there is any single feature about Nahman's tales, and indeed about Nahman's life as well, that makes them unique in the history of Judaism, it is just this: their essential motif is one of quest. Nahman, both as teller and as hero of these tales, is Nahman the seeker. He has already told us, outside the tales, of his refusal ever to stand on any one rung, of his call for constant growth, of his need to open himself up to ever-new and more demanding challenges to his faith. The tales now affirm this endless quest, as we see their central figure searching for the *shekhinah,* wandering through the woods or sailing the seas, stumbling through the kingdom of lies, or sailing through the air to reach the tree of life. The sojourns of Nahman's heroes are more than the wandering of the Jew in exile. Here even more than in Lurianic Kabbalah, the bleakness of exile has been uplifted and transformed into the exhilarating adventure of quest.

What is this quest that so fills Nahman's life, finding such poignant portrayal finally in the *Tales?* We may call it a search for God by one who felt himself alone, a search for wholeness by one who experienced himself as shattered or fragmented, a search for language and self-expression by one who felt himself unwillingly locked into an inner silence. Each of these is a partial way of approaching that which is essentially unapproachable, the quest that, like the *shekhinah,* is filled with all meanings because it can be limited to no one specific meaning. Nahman was one who defined his life as that of a seeker; for such people it is usually only in irreducible sacred symbols or in the ultimate profundities of silence that the object of their search can be defined. To ask the seeker: "What is it that you are looking for?" is already to misperceive totally the nature of the search.

We have seen the beginnings of Nahman's search in an early awareness of solitude. He said of himself, we will recall, that he was most alone with God when in the midst of people, and that he was capable of crying out in such a way that those around him could hear nothing at all.

> Know that it is possible to let out a very great scream in a still small voice, in such a way that no one will hear. No sound actually comes out—the scream takes place within the silence. Everyone is capable of such a cry. You just imagine the scream in your mind and let its sound penetrate your brain.[27]

Nahman's *Tales* are such a cry. The cry has now been redeemed from silence and brought into the world of skillful articulation. Nahman the silent screamer also referred to himself as Nahman the dancer, a dancer capable of such delicate motion that no one seeing him would know that he had moved at all. Here in the *Tales* he has found a medium of verbal expression that allows him to speak while maintaining his silence, allows him a form of verbal articulation parallel to that description of the dance. That which he sought at times in dance and in music he now found in the word, which was really his best medium of expression all along. He has spoken the deepest longings of his soul and yet at the same time has maintained his silence. His mystery remains uncompromised; he need fear none of the degradation of having given away his heart's secrets too cheaply.

To whom is the cry of the tales uttered? To God, before whom Nahman says you should pour out your broken heart in prayer each day? To the disciples, who are still, in this most intimate form of speech, meant to revere more than they are to understand? To himself? To whom, indeed, is our tale to be told? Or is Nahman's cry simply like that of the Heart of the World, a scream meant to go from one end of the earth to the other, capable of bearing all interpretations, limited by none?

NOTES

1. The most complete bibliography of criticism on the tales is found in Y. Elstein's doctoral dissertation *Structuralism in Literary Criticism: A Method and Application in Two Representative Hasidic Tales*, UCLA, 1974. The work, which is available through University Microfilms of Ann Arbor, also contains an excellent summary of the critical literature. The linguistic problems surrounding the tales have chiefly to do with the question of whether the Hebrew or Yiddish printed text represents the original written version. (It is agreed that the tales were *told* in Yiddish.) S. Z. Setzer advocated a Hebrew original for the written tales *(cf.* the introduction to his edition of the *Sippurey Ma'asiyot)* while S. Niger *(Bleter Geshikhte fun der Yidisher Literatur*, p. 109*ff.)* defended the originality of the Yiddish version. More recently the position of Setzer has been buttressed by the very important study in Piekarz, *op. cit.*, p.151*ff.*, though A. M. Haberman *(Moznayim* 35 (1972) 270*ff.)* has raised some further questions in this regard, and the matter is not regarded as finally settled. The most important recent studies of the tales are several essays in Pie-

karz' volume, a chapter in Joseph Dan's *Ha-Sippur ha-Ḥasidi*, published in popular format but containing serious and original readings, and the above-mentioned work by Elstein, which includes a structural analysis of *The Lost Princess*. While Joseph Weiss did not devote any single essay to the *Tales* as such, they are often referred to in his studies of Bratslav, and the above-mentioned works are all dependent on him in any number of ways. A most perceptive essay, often ignored by scholars, is that by I. Rabinowitz in his collection of critical essays *Shorashim u-Megamot*, p.163*ff*. Among recent non-academic works interpreting the *Tales*, mention should be made of several most perceptive essays by Adin Steinsaltz, formerly available in stencil and now beginning to appear in English in the journal *Shefa*. Steinsaltz has a profound knowledge of Hasidic thought and his readings of the tales, while not generally taking historical circumstance into account and making no mention of critical studies, are still worthy of serious attention. Another attempt in this vein is that of Yehudit Kook, *Rabbi Nahman mi-Braslav: 'Iyyunim be-Sippuraw*, written chiefly for inspirational purposes. For details on further studies, see the bibliography by Elstein. On the question of didactic versus artistic readings, the battle-lines are drawn between Horodezky and Buber, both in favor of various sorts of "messages" to be derived from the tales, and Dan, who debunks this approach altogether. The idea that the tales are products of Nahman's tubercular fever originated with S.M. Dubnov, who completely failed to understand them in any other way.

2. To this day a passage from one of the tales is read and commented upon each week during the *se'udah shelishit* at the Bratslav Yeshivah in Jerusalem. There is a kind of hushed reverence about this moment that utterly convinces the properly attuned participant that he is in the presence of the sacred word. The most important printed Bratslav commentaries on the tales are those by Nathan (scattered through his *Liqquṭey Halakhot*, but collected in the back of editions of the *Sippurim* since the edition of Lvov, 1902), *Rimzey Ma'asiyot* by Nahman of Cheryn, also published along with standard editions of the tales, and the collected comments of Abraham Hazan, published as *Ḥokhmah u-Tevunah*. Further discussions of the tales within Bratslav sources may be traced through the references in N. Z. Koenig's *Pittuḥey Ḥotam*, p.107*ff*. For the non-canonical tales, attention should be paid to *Sippurim Nifla'im* (published together with *Kokhvey 'Or)* and *Sippurim Ḥadashim*.

3. Buber's German translation first appeared in 1906 and was reprinted several times thereafter. This rendition took great liberties with the original text, a matter for which Buber later expressed regret. The Buber version (which included only six of the tales) was rendered into English by Maurice Friedman, first published in 1956. An earlier and somewhat less distorting English translation had been done by the novelist Meyer Levin, published in 1932 under the title *The Golden Mountain* and later reprinted as *Classic Hasidic Tales*. These are now superseded by the new English translation by Arnold Band, published by the Paulist Press in 1978. This translation remains extremely close to the Hebrew and Yiddish and does much to reproduce the oral quality of the tales. Band's introduction and notes appeared too late for consideration in this study.

4. I thus partially side with Buber in this aspect of his well-known debate with Gershom Scholem over the importance of the tales in Hasidism. True, the homiletic classics of the movement appeared much earlier in printed form. Given that

fact, however, it is shocking how little these books are quoted by other Hasidic authors in the heyday of the movement. The *Toledot* was already published in 1780: why is it that this work is never quoted by the many Hasidic authors—including Nahman, Levi Yizhak, and others—who published around the turn of the nineteenth century? An argument to the effect that direct quotation from recent works was contrary to Hasidic style will be difficult to defend: surely no such hesitation was evinced with regard to so "new" a work as Hayyim Ibn ʿAttar's *'Or ha-Ḥayyim.* Of course the fact that a work is not quoted directly does not mean it had no influence—but neither does the fact of its publication in itself indicate the contrary. The oral traditions of Hasidism were very strong, and tales were widely told and retold long before they were set down in writing. Dan's comments *(op. cit.,* p.195*ff.)* on the unsavory character and sloppy methods of the original compilers of the tales in writing points to the sad decay of the oral tradition in later years, but does not impugn its original vitality or importance.

5. In his introduction to the *Tales* Nathan freely admits that his master adapted plots from the stock of folk-tales that were to be heard in his area. Nahman found that in each case the tales needed editing; the bits of truth to be found in them were garbled beyond recognition and had to be 'restored' to their proper form and order by his retelling. In effect Nahman is making the same claim here for non-Jewish folk-tales that had long been made in Hasidism for melodies, aphorisms, home remedies, and so forth, which the masters were often willing to adapt from the surrounding culture and rededicate for sacred purposes. Nathan then adds in his introduction that the tales included in this collection of the *Sippurey Maʿasiyot* are chiefly original, containing but a few re-worked from such folk sources. A Polish parallel to *The Lost Princess* was discovered and announced by S. Petrushka some years ago *(Ketuvim,* Tel Aviv weekly, 2 (1928) 42. See also the further sources quoted in Piekarz, p.152, n.4. Some elements of Nahman's *The Two Sons* are surely rooted in a version of *The Soldier and the King* to be found in A. Afanas'ev's collection of *Russian Fairy Tales,* p.563*ff.* Further work on Nahman's sources must be undertaken by one who knows Ukrainian as well as Russian and has access to the specific folk legacy of the territory where Nahman lived.

6. *Liqquṭim* 234, 248.

7. The major sources for Nahman's early treatment of the *medammeh* are *Liqquṭim* 25 and 54. With regard to prophecy, Nahman in *Liqquṭim* 54:6 sees less role for the *koaḥ ha-medammeh* than does Maimonides! In the *Guide* 2:36–37 it is explained that the imagination has a significant role in prophecy: in order for prophecy to occur, the Active Intellect must flow into the would-be prophet's imaginative faculty as well as into his rational mind. Both these aspects must be prepared sufficiently before one may receive prophetic inspiration. On earlier notions of the imaginative faculty and particularly its relationship to prophecy *cf.* the treatment in Altmann and Stern's *Isaac Israeli,* p.140*ff,* and Leo Strauss' *Philosophie und Gesetz,* p.184*f.*

8. *Liqquṭim II* 5:9.

9. *Liqquṭim II* 8:7, and the ensuing discussion of the *ẓaddiq's* charismatic gifts in 8:8.

10. This is one of several examples of an explanation of a Tale's symbol within the tale itself. Whether this is Nahman speaking or Nathan the interpreter whose explanatory note has slipped into the text itself must be determined separately in

each instance; here there is reason to think that the explanation is an original part of the tale.

11. *Liqquṭim* 60:6.

12. Weiss, *Meḥqarim*, p.152.

13. Nathan's various reports of the occasions on which particular tales were told (collected in *Ḥayyey* 2 but also scattered through *Siḥot* and *Yemey MaHaRNaT)* consistently indicate that the tales were more-or-less spontaneous oral creations. We have no evidence of written drafts or notes preceding the oral event, as we do for a number of Nahman's teachings. If he did mentally lay out the plots in advance, he at least tried to cover this planning by starting a tale at a point where it seemed appropriate to the course of conversation, as though he were spinning it forth on the spot. Nathan describes the spontaneous character of the *Tales*, as though they emerged in the context of ordinary conversation. "That reminds me of a story . . ." frequently seems to be the way one of Nahman's tales began:

> He asked us to tell him the news, just as he so frequently was wont to do. Naftali then told him about the war with France, which was going on at that time. In that conversation we expressed our astonishment at how quickly he [Napoleon] had risen to prominence. There he was, just a simple servant, and now he was emperor. We spoke with him about this, and then he said: 'Who knows what soul he has? Perhaps it was a changeling, for it sometimes happens that in the halls of transformation souls are exchanged, *etc.*' Then he began to tell us how this had once happened already, for there was a queen who gave birth . . . (*Ḥayyey* 2:2).

There followed the tale of *The Two Sons*. Once again, preceding the tale of *The Master of Prayer:*

> After he spoke with the local *ḥazzan* R. Joseph, we and the *ḥazzan* remained standing before him. The *ḥazzan's* cloak was torn, and (our master) turned to him and said: 'You are a *ba'al tefillah*, a master of that prayer through which all blessings flow. Why then should you not have [at least a proper] *kaftan?*' And then he began to tell it in this way: 'This already happened once, that there was a master of prayer . . .' And then he told the whole story. But as he began it we did not know that he had embarked on telling one of his *Tales;* we at first thought he was just telling about some thing that had happened . . . (*ibid*.3).

14. Piekarz, p.132*ff*. is especially enlightening in this regard.

15. The most complete example may be found in Nathan's comments on the sixth tale of the *Seven Beggars (Sippurey Ma'asiyot* p.240*ff*.*)*, where he successively suggests individual (the soul versus the evil urge), historical/national (Israel versus Pharoah at the sea), and theosophical *(shekhinah* versus *sitra aḥra)* readings for the same tale. None of these is meant to contradict the others; the same truth reveals itself throughout the universe and is manifest above and below, in the whole and in the part.

16. The Gnostic quotation is from the *Gospel of Phillip*, included in *The Nag Hammadi Library*, p.140. My thanks to Dr. Elaine Pagels for this reference. I am not impressed with Bousset's comment on the "right" reading of Gnostic myth, invoked by Weiss *(Meḥqarim*, p.152) in defense of his position. The Gnostic myth is not about *either* the human soul *or* the redeemer: it tells of the former by means of the latter. The fact that later Christianity did not read the tale this way is of course decisive historically but does not change the inner logic of the myth itself.

17. This brief essay by no means claims to be an exhaustive treatment of the *Tales*, which are deserving of a full volume of critical study on their own. The Hebrew reader is encouraged to pursue further reading—particularly in the works by Piekarz and Dan—for much more detailed critical discussion.

18. *Sippurey Ma'asiyot* p.252.

19. *Cf.* Tishby, *Mishnat ha-Zohar* I, 223*f.*; Scholem, *Von der mystischen Gestalt der Gottḥeit*, p.184*ff.* The *Shekhinah* also at times takes on a masculine appearance: perhaps hence the princess' disguise in Western-style male clothes. On the demonic female in general *cf.* the expansive treatment in Erich Neumann's *The Great Mother* and Wolfgang Lederer's *The Fear of Woman*.

20. Dr. James Kirsch, a Jungian psychologist in Los Angeles, has studied and lectured on Nahman from this point of view and has written a very suggestive piece entitled "The Individuation of Rabbi Nahman."

21. *Liqquṭim* 188; *Siḥot* 180; *Ḥayyey II* 2:19.

22. There seems to be a reflection here of the old medieval Kabbalistic understanding of revelation as confrontation with the self, or at least the self as represented on a higher level. See Scholem, first in *MGWJ* 74 (1930) 28*ff.*, and expanded most fully in *Pirqey Yesod*, p.358*ff.*

23. This analysis of the framework of *The Seven Beggars* is largely dependent on the work of Dan, *op. cit.*, p.144*ff.*, though the reading I suggest based on this is my own.

24. *Genesis Rabbah* 5:7 and parallels.

25. The belief in supernatural means of immediate transportation from place to place was known in Talmudic times and rather taken for granted; See 'Eruvin 43a and Yebamot 116a. It is also discussed in R. Hai Gaon's epistle concerning mystical and magical phenomena, *'Oẓar ha-Ge'onim, Ḥagigah*, p.16. I know of no attempt to study the history of this motif.

26. *Megillah* 10b.

27. *Siḥot* 16.

Note on Transliteration and Orthography

The following schema has been used for transliteration in this study:

HEBREW

א	ʼ
בּ	b
ב	v
ג	g
ד	d
ה	h
ו	w
ז	z
ח	ḥ
ט	ṭ
י	y
כּ	k
כ	kh
ל	l
מ	m
נ	n
ס	s
ע	ʻ
פּ	p
פ	f
צ	ẓ
ק	q
ר	r
שׁ	sh
שׂ	s
ת	t

YIDDISH

a	א
o	אָ
b	בּ
g	ג
d	ד
h	ה
u	ו
v	וו
z	ז
kh	ח
t	ט
y	י
ey	יי
ay	ײַ
kh	כ
l	ל
m	מ
n	נ
s	ס
e	ע
p	פּ
f	פֿ
ts	צ
k	ק
r	ר
sh	שׁ
t	תּ
s	ת

Certain Hebrew proper nouns frequently used in English are spelled in accord with common English usage, e.g., Kabbalah, Hasidism. Diacritical marks have been omitted from names set in roman type. The *Columbia-Lippincott Gazetteer* and the *Encyclopedia Judaica* were consulted for orthography of East European place names. Where neither of these sources was helpful, names were transcribed from the Yiddish.

Abbreviations Used in Notes

Degel	*Degel Maḥaneh Ephraim* by Moses Hayyim Ephraim of Sudilkov.
EJ	*Encyclopedia Judaica.*
Ḥayyey: Ḥayyey II	*Ḥayyey MoHaRaN* by Nathan of Nemirov. (Part II subtitled *Shivḥey MoHaRaN)*
HUCA	*Hebrew Union College Annual.*
JAAR	*Journal of the American Academy of Religion.*
JJS	*Journal of Jewish Studies.*
Liqquṭim: Liqquṭim II	*Liqquṭey MoHaRaN.*
PAAJR	*Proceedings, American Academy of Jewish Research.*
Piekarz	*Ḥasidut Braslav* by Mendel Piekarz.
Scholem, *Major Trends*	*Major Trends in Jewish Mysticism.*
Scholem, *Messianic Idea*	*The Messianic Idea in Judaism and Other Essays.*
Shivḥey; Shivḥey II	*Shivḥey ha-RaN* by Nathan of Nemirov.
Siḥot	*Siḥot ha-RaN.*
Studies in Mysticism	*Studies in Mysticism and Religion Presented to Gershom G. Scholem.*
Weiss, *Meḥqarim*	*Meḥqarim be-Ḥasidut Braslav* by Joseph Weiss.

The chapters of Nathan's biography of Nahman, *Ḥayyey MoHaRaN,* are traditionally designated by title and are not numbered in the editions. For the sake of convenience, I have here supplied numerical designations to those chapters as follow. *Ḥayyey* in these notes refers to *Ḥayyey MoHaRaN*, part one; *Ḥayyey II* refers to *Ḥayyey MoHaRaN*, part two, also called *Shivḥey MoHaRaN* (but not to be confused with *Shivḥey ha-RaN,* an earlier work by Nathan. See bibliography.).

Ḥayyey,	*siḥot ha-shayakhim la-torot*	*Ḥayyey: 1*
Ḥayyey,	*siḥot ha-shayakhim le-sippurey ma'asiyot*	*Ḥayyey:2*

Ḥayyey,	*sippurim ḥadashim*	*Ḥayyey: 3*
Ḥayyey,	*meqom yeshivato u-nesi'otaw*	*Ḥayyey: 4*
Ḥayyey,	*nesi'ato le-'ereẓ yisra'el*	*Ḥayyey: 5*
Ḥayyey,	*nesi'ato le-Navritch*	*Ḥayyey: 6*
Ḥayyey,	*nesi'ato le-Lemberg*	*Ḥayyey: 7*
Ḥayyey,	*nesi'ato we-yeshivato be-Uman*	*Ḥayyey: 8*
Ḥayyey II,	*yegi'ato we-ṭirhato be-'avodato*	*Ḥayyey II: 1*
Ḥayyey II,	*gedulat hassagato*	*Ḥayyey II: 2*
Ḥayyey II,	*ma'alat ha-mitqarevim 'elaw*	*Ḥayyey II: 3*
Ḥayyey II,	*ma'alat torato u-sefaraw ha-qedoshim*	*Ḥayyey II: 4*
Ḥayyey II,	*'inyan ha-maḥloqet she-'alaw*	*Ḥayyey II: 5*
Ḥayyey II,	*godel yiqrat rosh ha-shanah shelo*	*Ḥayyey II: 6*
Ḥayyey II,	*le-hitraḥeq me-ḥaqirot*	*Ḥayyey II: 7*
Ḥayyey II,	*divrey ẓaḥot shelo*	*Ḥayyey II: 8*
Ḥayyey II,	*shelo' li-deḥoq ha-sha'ah*	*Ḥayyey II: 9*
Ḥayyey II,	*ma'alat ha-hitbodedut*	*Ḥayyey II: 10*
Ḥayyey II,	*'avodat ha-shem*	*Ḥayyey II: 11*

Glossary

aggadah (adj. aggadic). Narrative (as distinguished from legal) passages in early rabbinic literature. Includes exegesis, legend, lore; collected in Talmud and Midrashic literature.

ʿaliyah (lit.: ascent). Migration of Jews to the Holy Land; pilgrimage.

baʿal tefillah. Leader of prayers.

binah (lit.: understanding). The third of the ten *sefirot.* Often described in images of the maternal.

biṭṭaḥon. Trust; confident devotion.

biṭṭul. Negation; usually refers to negation or transcendence of self.

daʿat (lit.: knowledge). Religious awareness; intimate knowing of a sacred truth. In some systems (where *keter* is not counted), the third of the ten *sefirot,* the synthesis of *ḥokhmah* and *binah.*

devequt. Adhesion or attachment to God, the goal of Jewish mystical piety.

din (lit.: judgment). The fifth of the ten *sefirot,* representing divine judgment; the left hand of God and the divine source of the demonic.

dreidel. A top, played with by children at Hanukkah.

'Ereẓ Yisra'el. The Land of Israel.

'etrog. citron; a fruit used in the ritual celebration of *sukkot.*

'eyn sof. The endless; a designation for the hidden godhead beyond the *sefirot* and the ultimate source of all being.

gadlut (lit.: bigness). A state of higher consciousness achieved in mystical prayer.

galut. Exile; diaspora. *Ḥasidim* also speak of *galut ha-daʿat,* the 'exiled' or unredeemed state of awareness; *galut ha-dibbur,* the broken condition of human language, etc.

gemaṭria. Numerology; tallying the numerical equivalents of Hebrew letters and words to provide another level of interpretation. Very common among Kabbalists and Hasidic masters.

gevurah (lit.: power). An alternative name for *din,* the fifth *sefirah.*

golem. A man-made creature, animated by magical use of a divine name.

ḥakham. Sage; a Sephardic rabbi.

halakah. The path; legal traditions of Judaism. The legal portions of rabbinic writings.

ḥalluqah. Charitable contributions for Jews in the Holy Land.

hamtaqat ha-dinim. The 'sweetening' or transformation of negative forces; the averting of harsh divine judgment.

hanhagot (lit.: practices). A list of personal devotional practices by a Hasidic master, often published along with their homiletic works.

Haskalah. The movement of Western enlightenment among the Jews.

haskamah (pl. haskamot). Letter of rabbinic approbation, recommending the publication of a book and offering protection against unauthorized reprints.

hassagah. Attainment, particularly in the realm of understanding.

havdalah. Separation ceremony marking the conclusion of the Sabbath.

ḥaver (pl. *ḥaverim).* Friend; companion; peer.

ḥazzan. Cantor; leader of prayers.

ḥerem (pl. *ḥaramim).* Ban; writ of excommunication.

ḥesed (lit.: love, grace). The fourth of the ten *sefirot;* the right hand or love of God.

ḥiddush (pl. *ḥiddushim). Novella;* a new insight or a novel interpretation of some facet of the Torah.

hitbodedut. Aloneness with God; lone meditation.

hitlahavut. Ecstasy; enthusiasm.

ḥokhmah (lit.: wisdom). The second of the ten *sefirot;* the primal wisdom of God, the first point of being and the hiddenmost source of Torah.

——— (pl. *ḥokhmot).* Wisdom, cleverness. Often used ironically.

hosh'anot. Hymns chanted during processions around the synagogue on the *sukkot* festival.

kaftan. Robe; long coat.

kashrut. (adj. *kasher, kosher).* The system of Jewish food restrictions.

kawwanah. Inner direction; inwardness in prayer or religious acts.

kawwanot. Kabbalistic designations of proper meditational accompaniments to liturgy and ritual.

keter (lit.: crown). The first of the ten *sefirot;* the primal will of God.

kohen. Priest; descendent of the family of Aaron.

levush. Garment; often used metaphorically.

lulav. Palm-branch; used along with *'etrog* in *sukkot* ritual.

maggid. Preacher.

maḥashavah zarah. Extraneous or distracting thought that keeps one from prayer or meditation.

maḥloqet. Controversy.

mal'akh. Angel; divine messenger.

malkhut (lit.; kingdom). The tenth *sefirah,* representing the feminine and receptive element within God. Identical with *shekhinah,* in Hasidism the immanent aspect of divinity.

maqqif. That which surrounds; a thought not yet incorporated into the mind, thus 'surrounding' it in challenge.

maskil. An advocate of *Haskalah;* enlightener.

medammeh. The imaginative faculty.

mefursam (lit.: famous one). A *ẓaddiq* who has become a public figure.

meni'ah. Obstacle; that which keeps one from fulfilling his spiritual obligations.
merkavah (lit.: chariot). The throne of God; the tradition and literature of speculation surrounding the throne-vision of Ezekiel.
midrash (adj.: midrashic) Homiletical interpretation of Scripture; the literature of that interpretation among the early rabbis.
minyan. Quorum for prayer, comprising ten adult male Jews.
miqweh. Ritual bath. Used by Hasidic men daily as purification preparatory to prayer.
mishkan. Dwelling-place; the tabernacle erected by Moses in the wilderness.
mitnagged (pl. mitnaggedim). Opponent of Hasidism. Used in Bratslav also to designate Hasidic enemies of Nahman or of Bratslav Hasidism.
miẓwah (pl. miẓwot). Commandment; one of the six hundred thirteen precepts of the Torah. By extension: good deed.
miẓwot ha-teluyot ba-areẓ. Those of the commandments which are incumbent only upon one dwelling in (or eating the produce of) the Holy Land.
mussar. Ethics; chastisement. Designates books and traditions of moral and ascetic theology.
niggun. Melody.
nistar. A hidden *ẓaddiq.*
pe'ot. Sidecurls, following Hasidic custom of leaving these uncut.
peshiṭut. Simplicity; wholeness.
pidyon (li.: redemption). Gift given to *ẓaddiq* accompanying a request for his blessing.
prostak (Yiddish). A simple person.
qatnut (lit.: smallness). An ordinary state of mind; unexpanded consciousness. See *gadlut.*
qelipah (lit.: shell) (pl. *qelipot).* A negative or demonic force; that which hides the divine light.
qibbuẓ ha-qadosh. The holy assemblage. The community of Bratslav *ḥasidim,* particularly those gathered for prayers at Nahman's grave.
rav. Rabbi; ordained legal authority of a community.
rebbe. Hasidic master. Often, but not necessarily, a formally ordained rabbi.
reshimu. Residue; the remaining presence of God in the void after *ẓimẓum* has taken place. Compared to the remaining film after a vessel has been completely emptied of oil.
sefirah (pl. *sefirot).* One of the ten emanations from *'eyn sof* which together comprise the divine world of Kabbalistic speculation; an aspect of the deity.
sekhel. The rational faculty.
se'udah shelishit. The third and concluding meal of the Sabbath. Often a setting for Hasidic teaching or the telling of tales.
shekhinah. The indwelling presence of God. See *malkhut.*
shofar. Ram's horn, sounded in the New Year liturgy.
siddur. Prayerbook.
simḥah. Joy.
siṭra aḥra (lit.: other side). The demonic universe; the forces of evil.
sukkot. Autumn festival, characterized by dwelling in booths and ritual waving of *lulav* and *etrog.*

ṭallit. Prayer shawl.
tefillin. Phylacteries.
teshuvah. Penitence; return to God.
tif'eret (lit.: glory). Sixth of the ten *sefirot;* center of the lower sefirotic world. The male principle within God that unites with *malkhut.*
tiqqun. Repair or restoration; the setting right of the cosmos by means of devotion or Kabbalistic meditations. Also the 'repair' of sin-burdened souls; a liturgy for this purpose.
yesod (lit.: foundation). The ninth of the ten *sefirot,* gathering all the upper forces together for the flow into *malkhut.*
yeẓer ha-ra'. The evil inclination.
yiḥud (pl. yiḥudim). Unification; a Kabbalistic meditation built around the unification of various names of God.
ẓaddiq (pl. *ẓaddiqim).* Righteous one; holy man.
———. Master of a Hasidic community. Identical with *rebbe.*
zaqen. Elder.
zeide (Yiddish). Grandfather, elder.
ẓimẓum. The withdrawal of God from primal 'space' which preceded the emanation of the *sefirot;* the repetition of that withdrawal and concentration of divinity.
———. The reduction in intensity, intellectual difficulty, etc. of some particular content, so that one of lesser capacities will be capable of receiving it.

Bibliography

Introductory Note

The following is a list of works to which reference has been made in the notes to this volume. It is in no way intended as a comprehensive bibliographic guide to the literature of Bratslav. Two such bibliographies already exist and are mentioned in note two to the introduction to this volume.

Standard reference works have been omitted from this list, as have the basic classics of pre-Hasidic Jewish literature: Bible, Talmud, Midrashim, the works of Maimonides, Zohar, *etc*. These works have all been cited in accord with accepted practice and standard editions. Editions cited in the bibliography are those actually used in the preparation of this volume, not first or necessarily superior editions. In the case of Hasidic works of which rare editions were consulted, I have tried to offer in the notes some indication that would allow the reader to find the passage in another edition as well.

This list is divided into two sections:

I. Works by Hasidic and other premodern or traditional Jewish authors.

II. Secondary and modern works, including modern translations and adaptations of Hasidic works.

I

Aaron of Karlin	*Bet Aharon.*	Brody, 1875.
Abraham ben Dov Baer of Miedzyrzec	*Ḥesed le-Avraham.*	Chernovtsy, 1851.
Alter of Teplyk, ed.	*Hishtapkhut ha-Nefesh.*	Jerusalem, 1905.
___	*Meshivat Nefesh.*	Lemberg, 1902.
___	*Mey ha-Naḥal.*	Beney Beraq, 1965.
(anonymous)	*Buẓina Qadisha.*	Jerusalem, 1957.
___	*Galey Razaya.*	Mogilev, 1812.
___	*Ḥemdat Yamim.*	Istanbul, 1738.
___	*'Ot Berit.*	Warsaw, 1927.
___	*Qaneh (Peli'ah).*	Korets, 1784.

—	*Qehal Ḥasidim.*	Tel Aviv, 1959.
—	*Qine'at ha-Shem Ẓeva'ot.*	Jerusalem, 1965.
—	*Rishpey 'Esh ha-Shalem.*	Bilgoray, 1932.
—	*Siftey Ẓaddiqim.*	Warsaw, 1909.
—	*Ṭaharat ha-Qodesh.*	Bjelozerka, 1796.
Azikri, Eleazar	*Sefer Ḥaredim.*	Venice, 1601.
Azulai, Abraham	*Ḥesed le-Avraham.*	Lemberg, 1863.
—	*'Or ha-Ḥamah.*	Jerusalem, 1876.
Bachrach, Naftali	*'Emeq ha-Melekh.*	Amsterdam, 1648.
Barukh of Medzhibozh	*Buẓina di-Nehora.*	Lemberg, 1880.
Ben Sheshet, Jacob	*Meshiv Devarim Nekhoḥim.*	Jerusalem, 1968.
Berger, Israel	*Zekhut Yisra'el.* (Includes *'Eser 'Orot*, etc.)	Israel, 1973.
Bodek, Menahem Mendel	*Seder ha-Dorot he-Ḥadash.*	Lemberg, 1865.
Cohen, Baruch David	*Birkat ha-'Areẓ.*	Jerusalem, 1904.
Cordovero, Moses	*Gerushin.*	Venice, 1600.
—	*Pardes Rimmonim.*	Munkacz, 1906.
De Vidas, Elijah	*Reshit Ḥokhmah.*	Venice, 1579.
Dov Baer ben Samuel	*Shivḥey ha-BeSHT.*	Berlin, 1922. (ed. S. A. Horodezky)
Dov Baer of Miedzyrzec	*'Or Torah.*	Jerusalem, 1968.
—	*Torat ha-Maggid.*	Jerusalem, 1969.
Elimelekh of Lezajsk	*No'am 'Elimelekh.*	Jerusalem, 1960.
Ephraim of Pshedborz	*'Oneg Shabbat.*	New York, 1965.
Epstein, Kalonymos Kalman	*Ma'or wa-Shemesh.*	New York, 1958.
Frumkin, Michael Levi	*'Adat Ẓaddiqim.*	Jerusalem, 1959.
—	*Shivḥey ha-Rav.*	Jerusalem, n.d.
Hayyim ben Abraham ha-Kohen	*Torat Ḥakham.*	Venice, 1654.
Hazan, Abraham	*'Avaneha Barzel.*	Jerusalem, 1961.
—	*Be'ur ha-Liqquṭim.*	Jerusalem, 1935.
—	*Kokhvey 'Or.*	Jerusalem, 1961.
—	*Yemey ha-Tela'ot.*	Jerusalem, 1968.
Heilman, Hayyim Meir	*Bet Rabbi.*	Berdichev, 1900.
Heller, Meshullam Phoebus	*Liqquṭim Yeqarim.*	New York, 1963.
Horowitz, Isaiah	*Sheney Luḥot ha-Berit.*	Fürth, 1764.
Horowitz, Pinhas Elijah	*Sefer ha-Berit.*	Brünn, 1797.
Horowitz, Sabbatai Sheftel	*Shefa' Ṭal.*	Bjelozerka, 1807.
Horowitz, Samuel, ed.	*Ḥokhmah u-Tevunah.*	Beney Beraq, 1962.
—	*Sippurim Nifla'im.*	Jerusalem, 1961.
Ibn Gabbai, Meir	*'Avodat ha-Qodesh.*	Lemberg, 1857.
Isaiah of Dinovits, ed.	*Ẓawa'at RIVaSH.*	Cracow, 1896.
Jacob Joseph of Polonnoye	*Ben Porat Yosef.*	Korets, 1781.
—	*Toledot Ya'aqov Yosef.*	Korets, 1780.
Jacob Koppel of Miedzyrzec	*Siddur Qol Ya'aqov.*	Lemberg, 1859.

Koenig, Nathan Zevi	*'Emunat 'Oman.*	Beney Beraq, 1966.
___	*Naḥaley 'Emunah.*	Beney Beraq, 1967.
___	*Neweh Ẓaddiqim.*	Beney Beraq, 1969.
___	*Pittuḥey Ḥotam.*	Beney Beraq, 1968.
Landau, Isaac	*Zikhron Ṭov.*	Piotrkow, 1892.
Levi Yizhak of Berdichev	*Qedushat Levi.*	Jerusalem, 1958.
Margulies, Asher	*Seder Tefillah mi-kol ha-Shanah 'im Kawwanat ha-ARI.*	Lemberg, 1788.
Margulies, Meir	*Sod Yakhin u-Vo'az.*	Ostrog, 1794.
Medini, Hayyim Hezekiah	*Sedey Ḥemed.*	New York, 1967.
Meinstril, Shelomo Shelumiel	*Shivḥey ha-ARI.*	Bardejov, 1929.
Menahem Azariah of Fano	*'Asarah Ma'amarot.*	Cracow, 1656.
Menahem Mendel of Vitebsk	*Peri ha-'Areẓ.*	Jerusalem, 1965.
Menahem Mendel of Chernobyl	*Me'or 'Eynayim.*	Jerusalem, 1966.
Michaelsohn, Abraham Hayyim	*'Ohel 'Elimelekh.*	Przemysl, 1915.
Moses Hayyim Ephraim of Sudilkov	*Degel Maḥaneh 'Efrayim.*	Jerusalem, 1963.
Nahman ben Simhah of Bratslav	*Liqquṭey MoHaRaN.*	Jerusalem, 1969.
___	*Sefer ha-Middot.*	Beney Beraq, 1966.
___	*Siḥot ha-RaN.*	Jerusalem, 1961.
___	*Sippurey Ma'asiyot.*	New York, 1949.
___	*Sippurey Ma'asiyot Ḥadashim.*	Warsaw, 1912.
___	*Tiqqun ha-Kelali.*	Warsaw, 1898.
Nahman of Cheryn	*Derekh Ḥasidim.*	Lemberg, 1876.
___	*Parpera'ot le-Ḥokhmah.*	New York, 1955.
___	*Zimrat ha-'Areẓ.*	Lemberg, 1876.
Nathan (Sternharz) of Nemirov	*'Alim li-Terufah.*	Jerusalem, 1968.
___	*Ḥayyey MoHaRaN.*	New York, 1965.
___	*Liqquṭey 'Ezot.*	Jerusalem, 1956.
___	*Liqquṭey Halakhot.*	Jerusalem, 1950–63.
___	*Liqquṭey Tefillot.*	Bratslav, 1824–27.
___	*Qiẓẓur Liqquṭey MoHaRaN.*	n.p. (Bratslav?), n.d.
___	*Shivḥey ha-RaN.*	Jerusalem, 1961.
___	*Yemey MaHaRNaT.*	Beney Beraq, 1956.
Perlov, Shalom	*Divrey Shalom.*	Vilna, 1882.
Pinhas of Korets	*Midrash Pinḥas.*	Jerusalem, n.d.
Recanati, Menahem	*Ṭa'amey ha-Miẓwot.*	Basel, 1581.
Ricci, Immanuel Hai	*Mishnat Ḥasidim.*	Amsterdam, 1727.
Sabbatai of Raszkow	*Seder Tefillah mi-kol ha-Shanah 'im Kawwanat ha-ARI.*	Korets, 1794.
Safrin, Yizhak Eisik	*Megillat Setarim.*	Jerusalem, 1944.

Shapira, Nathan	*Megalleh ʿAmuqot.*	Lemberg, 1858.
Shem Tov ben Shem Tov	*Sefer 'Emunot.*	Westmead, 1969.
Shne'ur Zalman ben Barukh of Liadi	*Liqquṭey 'Amarim (Tanya).*	New York, 1969.
—	*Liqquṭey Torah.*	New York, 1965.
—	*Seder Tefillot . . . ʿim Perush . . .*	New York, 1965.
—	*Torah 'Or.*	New York, 1954.
Silberman, Yizhak Eisik, ed.	*Naḥal Noveʿa.*	Jerusalem, 1961.
Simhah ben Joshua of Zalozhtsy	*'Ahavat Ẓiyyon.*	Grodno, 1790.
Sternharz (Kokhav-Lev), Abraham	*Ṭovot Zikhronot.*	Jerusalem, 1951.
Vital, Hayyim	*ʿEẓ Ḥayyim.*	Jerusalem, 1866.
—	*Gilgulim.*	Vilna, 1886.
— (ascribed)	*Peri ʿEẓ Ḥayyim.*	Korets, 1782.
—	*Shaʿar ha-Gilgulim.*	Przemysl, 1875.
—	*Shaʿar ha-Pesuqim.*	Jerusalem, 1868.
—	*Shaʿar Ruaḥ ha-Qodesh.*	Jerusalem, 1868.
—	*Shaʿarey ha-Qedushah.*	Amsterdam, 1715.
Walden, Aaron	*Shem ha-Gedolim he-Ḥadash.*	Warsaw, 1879.
Walden, Moses	*'Ohel ha-Rabbi.*	Piotrkow, 1913.
Wessely, Naftali Herz	*Yeyn Levanon.*	Berlin, 1775.
Wodnik, Simeon Mendel, ed.	*Sefer Baʿal Shem Tov.*	Szinérváraljan, 1943– Landsberg, 1948.
Yehiel of Pisa	*Minḥat Qena'ot.*	Berlin, 1898.
Yehiel Mendel of Safed	*Shir Yedidut.*	Jerusalem, 1907.
Zacuto, Moses	*Tofet ʿArukh.*	Metz, 1777.
Ze'ev Wolf of Zhitomir	*'Or ha-Me'ir.*	New York, 1954.
Zemah, Jacob	*Naggid u-Meẓawweh.*	Jerusalem, 1965.
—	*Zohar ha-Raqiʿa.*	Korets, 1785.
Zevi Hirsch of Zidachov	*ʿAṭeret Ẓevi.*	Lemberg, 1875.

II

Afanas'ev, Aleksander. *Russian Fairy Tales.* New York, 1945.

Albert, Ada Rapoport. "Confession in the Circle of Rabbi Nahman of Bratslav." *Bulletin of the Institute of Jewish Studies* (London) 1 (1973) 65*ff.*

—. "Sheney Meqorot le-Te'ur Nesiʿato shel R. Nahman mi-Braslav le-Erez Yisra'el." *Qiryat Sefer* 46 (1971) 147*ff.*

Alfasi, Yizhak. *Ha-Ḥozeh mi-Lublin.* Jerusalem.

—. *Sefer ha-ADMORim.* Tel Aviv, 1961.

Altmann, Alexander. "Eternality of Punishment: A Theological Controversy Within the Amsterdam Rabbinate in the Thirties of the Seventeenth Century." *PAAJR* 40 (1972) 1*ff.*

___. "Gnostic Themes in Rabbinic Cosmology." *Essays in Honor of the Very Reverend Dr. J. H. Hertz*. London, 1942.

___. "A Note on the Rabbinic Doctrine of Creation." *JJS* 7 (1956) 195*ff*.

___. *Studies in Religious Philosophy and Mysticism*. Ithaca, 1969.

(anonymous). *The Way of a Pilgrim*. Translated from the Russian by R. M. French. New York, 1965.

Baer, Yitzhak. "Ha-Reqa' ha-Histori shel ha-Ra'aya Mehemna." *Zion* 5 (1939) 1*ff*.

___. *A History of the Jews in Christian Spain*. Philadelphia, 1961.

Balaban, Meir. *Toledot ha-Tenu'ah ha-Frankit*. Tel Aviv, 1934.

Barzilay, Isaac. *Between Faith and Reason: Anti-Rationalism in Italian-Jewish Thought 1250–1650*. Hague, 1967.

Becker, Jacob. *R. Nahman mi-Bratslav: Meḥqar Psikhoanaliti*. Jerusalem, 1928.

Ben-Shlomo, Joseph. *Torat ha-Elohut shel Rabbi Moshe Cordovero*. Jerusalem, 1965.

Benayahu, Meir. *"Ha-Ḥevrah ha-Qedoshah shel Rabbi Yehudah Ḥasid." Shne'ur Zalman Shazar Jubilee Volume*. Jerusalem, 1960.

Biber, Mendel. *Mazkeret li-Gedoley Ostrog*. Berdichev, 1907.

Bolshakoff, Serge. *Russian Non-Conformity*. Philadelphia, 1950.

Brown, Norman O. *Love's Body*. New York, 1966.

Buber, Martin. *Die Geschichten des Rabbi Nachman*. Frankfurt, 1906.

___. *The Origin and Meaning of Hasidism*. New York, 1960.

Buber, Salomon. *Anshey Shem*. Lemberg, 1895.

Büchler, Adolf. *Types of Palestinean Jewish Piety*. London, 1922.

Caro, Jecheskiel. *Geschichte der Juden in Lemberg*. Cracow, 1894.

Carter, Francis W. *Dubrovnik (Ragusa): A Classic City-State*. London, 1972.

Copelston, Frederick. *A History of Philosophy*. New York, 1962.

Corbin, Henry. "La Face de l'Imam et la Face de Dieu." *Eranos Jahrbuch* 36 (1967).

Dan, Yosef. *Ha-Novellah ha-Ḥasidit*. Jerusalem, 1966.

___. *Ha-Sippur ha-Ḥasidi*. Jerusalem, 1975.

Dienstag, J. "Ha-Moreh Nevukhim we-Sefer ha-Mada' be-Sifrut ha-Ḥasidut." *The Abraham Weiss Jubilee Volume*. New York, 1964.

Dinur, Benzion. *Be-Mifneh ha-Dorot*.Jerusalem, 1955.

Dov Baer ben Samuel. *In Praise of the Baal Shem Tov*. Translated by Dan Ben Amos and Jerome R. Mintz. Bloomington, 1970.

Dresner, Samuel. *The Zaddik*. London, 1960.

Dubnov, Simon M. *History of the Jews in Russia and Poland*. Philadelphia, 1916.

___. *Toledot ha-Ḥasidut*. Tel Aviv, 1960.

Eisenstein, Judah David. *'Oẓar Masa'ot*. Tel Aviv, 1969.

Eliach, Yaffa. "The Russian Dissenting Sects and Their Influence on Israel Ba'al Shem Tov." *PAAJR* 36 (1968).

Eliade, Mircea. *Rites and Symbols of Initiation*. New York, 1958.

___: *The Myth of the Eternal Return*. Princeton, 1971

Elstein, Yoav. *Structuralism in Literary Criticism: A Method and Application in Two Representative Hasidic Tales*. Doctoral Dissertation (Unpublished), UCLA, 1974.

Erikson, Erik. *Young Man Luther*. New York, 1958

Festinger, Leon, et al. *When Prophecy Fails*. New York, 1956.

Fleer, Gedaliah. *Rabbi Nachman's Foundation* (Translation of *Tiqqun ha-Kelali)*. New York, 1977.

___. *Rabbi Nachman's Fire*. New York, 1972.

Gihon, M. "Napoloeon's Siege of Accho." *Western Galilee and the Coast of Galilee*. Jerusalem, 1965.
Ginzberg, Louis. *Legends of the Jews*. Philadelphia, 1913.
Gottlober, Abraham Baer. *Zikhronot u-Masa'ot. Jerusalem, 1976.*
Green, Arthur. "The *Ẓaddiq* as *Axis Mundi* in Later Judaism." *JAAR* 45 (1977) 3.
— and Holtz, Barry W. *Your Word Is Fire: The Hasidic Masters on Contemplative Prayer*. New York, 1977.
Gurland, Jonas. *Le-Qorot ha-Gezerot 'al Yisra'el*. Przemysl, 1887–Odessa, 1892.
Guttmann, Julius. *Philosophies of Judaism*. New York, 1964.
Guttmann, Matthias. *Rabbi Pinhas mi-Korets*. Tel Aviv, 1950.
—. *Tif'eret Bet Levi*. Jassy, 1909.
—. *Torat Rabbenu Pinhas mi-Korets*. Bilgoray, 1931.
Haberman, A. M. "Sha'arey ḤaBaD." *'Aley 'Ayin: Sefer ha-Yovel le-R. Salman Schocken*. Jerusalem, 1948–52.
—. "Sippurey Ma'asiyot shel R. Nahman mi-Braslav." *Moznayim* 35 (1972) 270*ff*.
Halpern, Israel. *Ha-'Aliyot ha-Rishonot shel ha-Ḥasidim le-Ereẓ Yisra'el*. Jerusalem, 1947.
—. *Yehudim we-Yahadut be-Mizraḥ Eropah*. Jerusalem, 1968.
Heinemann, Isaac. *Darkhey ha-'Aggadah*. Jerusalem, 1950.
Heschel, Abraham Joshua. "Le-Toledot Rabbi Pinhas mi-Korets." *'Aley 'Ayin*. Jerusalem, 1948–52.
—. "R. Gershon Kitover." *HUCA* 23 (1950/51).
—. *Kozk: In Gerangel far Emesdikeyt*. Tel Aviv, 1973.
—. "R. Nahman mi-Kosov Ḥavero shel ha-BeSHT." *H. A. Wolfson Jubilee Volume*. Jerusalem, 1965.
—. *Torah min ha-Shamayim*. London, 1962-65.
—. "Umbakante Dokumentn tsu der Geshikhte fun Khsides." *YIVO* Bleter 36 (1954).
Horodezky, Samuel Abba. *Ha-Ḥasidut weha-Ḥasidim*. Tel Aviv, 1953.
—. *'Oley Ẓiyyon*. Tel Aviv, 1947.
—. *Rabbi Nahman mi-Bratslav*. Berlin, 1923.
Hundert, Gershon. *Toward a Biography of R. Abraham Kalisker*. Master's Thesis (Unpublished), Ohio State University, 1971.
Hutchinson, John. *Faith, Reason, and Existence*. New York, 1956.
Ibn-Shmu'el, Yehudah, ed. *Midreshey Ge'ulah*. Tel Aviv, 1954.
Jacobs, Louis. *Hasidic Prayer*. London, 1972.
—. *Seeker of Unity*. New York, 1966.
Jonas, Hans. *The Gnostic Religion*. Boston, 1958.
Kadushin, Max. *Organic Thinking*. New York, 1938.
Kaplan, Aryeh. *Rabbi Nachman's Wisdom*. New York,
Katz, Jacob. *Tradition and Crisis*. New York, 1971.
Kook, Yehudit. *Rabbi Nahman mi-Braslav: 'Iyyunim be-Sippuraw*. Jerusalem, 1973.
Laing, Ronald David. *The Politics of Experience*. New York, 1967.
Langer, M. D. Georg (Jiri). *Die Erotik der Kabbala*. Prague, 1923.
Lederer, Wolfgang. *The Fear of Woman*. New York, 1968.
Levin, Meyer. *The Golden Mountain*. New York, 1932.
Lieberman, Hayyim (Khaim). "Le-Toledot ha-Defus ha-'Ivri be-Slavuta." *Qiryat Sefer* 27 (1958).

——. "Reb Nakhman Bratslaver un di Umaner Maskilim." *YIVO Bleter* 29 (1947). English Translation in *YIVO Annual of Jewish Social Science* 6 (1951).

Lifton, Robert, ed. *Explorations in Psychohistory*. New York, 1974.

Litinsky, Menahem Nahum. *Qorot Podolia we-Qadmoniyot ha-Yehudim Sham*. Odessa, 1895.

MacRae, Gordon W. "The Jewish Background of the Gnostic Sophia Myth." *Novum Testamentum* 12 (1970).

Mahler, Raphael. *A History of Modern Jewry*. New York, 1971.

——. *Di Yidn in Amolikn Poiln*. New York, 1946.

Maimon, Solomon. *Autobiography*. New York, 1947.

Mayer, Bonaventura. *Die Juden unserer Zeit*. Regensburg, 1842.

Miklishansky, Jacques. "Erez Yisra'el be-Mishnat MaHaRaN mi-Braslav." *Ha-Ḥasidut we-Ẓiyyon*, ed. S. Federbush. Jerusalem, 1963.

Minkin, Jacob. *The Romance of Hasidism*. New York, 1935.

Neumann, Erich. *The Great Mother*. New York, 1970.

Niger (Charney), Samuel. *Bleter Geshikhte fun der Yidisher Literatur*. New York, 1959.

Patai, Raphael. *Man and Temple*. London, 1947.

Petrushka, S. "Maqor Polani le-Sippurey Ma'asiyot shel R. Nahman mi-Braslav." *Ketuvim* (Tel Aviv) 2 (1928) 42.

Piekarz, Mendel. *Ḥasidut Braslav*. Jerusalem, 1972.

Rabinowitz, Isaiah. *Shorashim u-Megamot*. Jerusalem, 1967.

Rose, Neal. "Erez Israel in the Theology and Experience of Rabbi Nahman of Bratzlav." *Journal of Hebraic Studies 1 (1970)*.

Rosenberg, Yudl. *Tif'eret MaHaRAL*. Piotrkow, 1912.

Roszak, Theodore. *Where the Wasteland Ends*. New York, 1972.

Schatz, Rivka. "Antispiritualism be-Ḥasidut." *Molad* 171–172 (1963).

——. *Ha-Ḥasidut ke-Misṭiqah*. Jerusalem, 1968.

——. "Le-Mahuto shel ha-Ẓaddiq ba-Ḥasidut." *Molad* 144 (1960).

Scholem, Gershom. *'Eleh Shemot*. Jerusalem, 1928.

——. *Kitvey Yad be-Kabbalah*. Jerusalem, 1930.

——. *Major Trends in Jewish Mysticism*. New York, 1954.

——. *The Messianic Idea in Judaism*. New York, 1971.

——. *On the Kabbalah and Its Symbolism*. New York, 1965.

——. *Pirqey Yesod be-Torat ha-Kabbalah u-Semaleha*. Jerusalem, 1976.

——. "R. Eliyahu ha-Kohen ha-'Itamari weha-Shabta'ut." *Alexander Marx Jubilee Volume*. New York, 1950.

——. *Sabbatai Ṣevi*. Princeton, 1973.

——. "Schöpfung aus nichts und Selbstverschränkung Gottes." *Eranos Jahrbuch* 25 (1956).

——. "Ha-Tenu'ah ha-Shabta'it be-Polin." *Bet Yisra'el be-Polin*, Israel Halpern, ed. v.2. Jerusalem, 1953.

——. "Three Types of Jewish Piety." *Eranos Jahrbuch* 38 (1969).

——. *Ursprung und Anfänge der Kabbala*. Berlin, 1962.

——. *Von der mystischen Gestalt der Gottheit*. Zürich, 1962.

Shah, Idris. *Tales of the Dervishes*. New York, 1969.

Steinman, Eliezer. *Be'er ha-Ḥasidut: Kitvey Rabbi Nahman mi-Braslav*. Tel Aviv, n.d.

Strauss, Leon. *Philosophie und Gesetz*. Berlin, 1935.

Tamar, David. "Ha-ARI weha-RaḤaV ke-Mashiaḥ ben Yosef." *Sefunot* 7 (1963).
Teitelbaum, Mordecai. *Ha-Rav mi-Liadi u-Mifleget ḤaBaD.* Warsaw, 1913.
Tishby, Isaiah *Mishnat ha-Zohar*. Jerusalem, 1957-61.
——. *Netivey Emunah u-Minut*. Israel, 1964.
——. *Torat ha-Ra' weha-Qelipah be-Qabbalat ha-ARI*. Jerusalem, 1942.
Twerski, Aaron David. *Sefer ha-Yaḥas mi-Chernobyl we-Ruzhin*. Lublin, 1938.
Urbach, Ephraim. *ḤaZaL: Pirqey Emunot we-De'ot*. Jerusalem, 1969.
Vajda, Georges. *Rechereches sur la Philosophie et la Kabbale dans le Pensee Juive du Moyen Age*. Paris, 1962.
Wallis, R.T, *Neoplatonism*. London, 1972.
Weiner, Herbert. *9½ Mystics*. New York, 1969.
Weinryb, Bernard D. *The Jews of Poland*. Philadelphia, 1963.
Weiss, Joseph. "A Circle of Pneumatics in Pre-Hasidism." *JJS* 8 (1957).
——. "Contemplative Mysticism and 'Faith' in Hasidic Piety." *JJS* 4 (1952).
——. "'Iyyunim bi-Tefisato ha-'Aẓmit shel Rabbi Nahman mi-Braslav." *Tarbiz* 27 (1958).
——. "The Kavvanoth of Prayer in Early Hasidism." *JJS* 9 (1958).
——. "Megillat Setarim le-Rabbi Nahman mi-Braslav." *Qiryat Sefer* 44 (1969).
——. *"Meḥqarim be-Ḥasidut Braslav."* Jerusalem, 1974.
——. "Ha-Qushiya be-Torat Rabbi Nahman mi-Braslav." *'Aley 'Ayin. Jerusalem, 1948–52.*
——. *"R. Abraham Kalisker's Concept of Communion."* *JJS* 6 (1955).
——. "R. Nahman mi-Braslav 'al ha-Mahloqet 'alaw." *Studies in Mysticism and Religion Presented to Gershom Scholem*. Jerusalem, 1967.
——. "Reshit Ẓemiḥatah shel ha-Derekh ha-Ḥasidit." *Zion* 16 (1951).
——. "Seder Hadpasat Liqquṭey MoHaRaN (Qama), Defus Rishon." *Qiryat Sefer* 41 (1966).
——. "Talmud Torah le-Shiṭṭat R. Yisra'el BeSHT." *Essays Presented to Chief Rabbi Israel Brodie*. London, 1970.
——. "Via Passiva in Early Hasidism." *JJS* 11 (1960).
Werblowsky, R. J. Z. *Joseph Karo: Lawyer and Mystic*. Oxford, 1962.
Wiesel, Elie. *Souls on Fire*. New York, 1972.
Wilensky, Mordecai. *Ḥasidim u-Mitnaggedim*. Jerusalem, 1970.
Yaari, Avraham. *Masa'ot 'Ereẓ Yisra'el*. Tel Aviv, 1946.
——. "Shetey Mahadurot Yesod shel 'Shivḥey ha-BeSHT'." *Qiryat Sefer* 39 (1964).
——. *Sheluḥey 'Ereẓ Yisra'el*. Jerusalem, 1951.
Yaari, Yehudah, ed. *Sippurey Ma'asiyot mi-Shanim Qadmoniyot*. A new rescension of Nahman's *Tales*. Jerusalem, 1971.
Zeitlin, Hillel. *'Al Gevul Sheney 'Olamot*. Tel Aviv, 1965.
——. *Rabbi Nahman mi-Braslav: Ḥayyaw we-Torato*. Warsaw, 1910.
——. *Reb Nakhman Braslaver*. New York, 1952.
Zimmels, H. J. *Magicians, Theologians, and Doctors*. London, 1952.
Zweifel, Eliezer. *Shalom 'al Yisra'el* Zhitomir, 1870.

Index of Subjects*

Antinomianism, 78
Asceticism, 27f, 35ff, 39f

Christianity, Parallels to, 11, 118, 145, 164, 306, 349
Confession (*widui*), 45f, 60n78–n79, 145

Death, 32f, 36f, 55n32–n33, 85, 196f, 222f
Depression, 28, 61n85, 71f, 82, 164f
Descent of *Zaddiq*, 15, 67ff, 264f, 308f
Devequt, 184, 214n5, 327
Disciples, 9ff, 40–47, 51, 135–181, 255, 260f
'Distance' (*Hitrahaqut*), 27, 54n20, 290
Doubt, 290, 292, 295ff, 308f, 312, 330
Dreams, 48, 57n55, 57n57, 165ff, 198ff

Eating, 28, 39, 49, 61n92, 84
Existentialism, 317–324

Faith, 3, 11, 51, 59n76, 62n97, 129n31, 189, 244, 289f, 296–307, 315–319, 322
Fantasy, 33, 212, 226, 342ff

God, 27f, 31, 34, 36, 51, 55n31, 56n46, 62n97, 245, 290ff, 296, 304ff, 313ff, 366f

Haskalah, 239f, 250ff, 254–259, 308
Hitbodedut, 32, 62n94, 145–148, 161, 324

Imagination, 30, 341ff

Journeys (Erez Israel), 34, 56n40, 63–93, 107, 231
Journeys (Other), 42, 58n67, 208f, 226–234, 238–243
Joy, 50, 244

Loneliness, 29, 31f, 33, 162

Madness, 115, 172ff, 181n73
Maqqifim, 292ff, 296, 302ff, 313, 315f, 319f, 331n13
Medicine, 234–239, 243f
Mefursam, 41, 57n62, 226f, 259f
Messiah ben Joseph, 188, 190–198, 215n14, 217n33, 254
Messianism, 87n5, 112, 182–226, 340f
Mizwot, 74, 76ff, 90n55, 91n57, 141, 327–330
Mysticism, 139f, 317–330
Myth, 4, 33, 313, 343–350

'Nearness' (*Hitqarevut*), 28, 54n20
Nistar, 41, 57n62

Obstacles (*Meni'ot*), 68, 82f

Paradox, 14, 106ff, 116, 121f, 163, 296, 302, 315
Philosophy, 289f, 296–299, 306–312, 316, 331n8, 331n11
Prayer, 27f, 33, 39, 48ff, 54n20, 62n94, 187, 189, 236, 293, 319f
Psychological Biography, 17–20, 26–34, 103–109, 114ff, 120–123, 162–174, 259–265

Reason, 292, 297ff, 306–309, 311

*My thanks to Mr. Morris Faierstein for the preparation of these indices.

Index of Names